Bringing Business on Board: Sustainable Development and the B-School Curriculum

edited
by
Peter N. Nemetz, Ph.D.

JBA
Press

Vancouver

© JBA Press 2002
Printed in Canada

ISBN 0-9689416-0-5 (book format)
ISSN 0021-941X (journal format)

National Library of Canada Cataloguing in Publication Data

Main entry under title:
Bringing Business on Board

(Journal of business administration, ISSN 0021-941X; vols. 27-29)
ISBN 0-9689416-0-5

1. Sustainable development. 2. Business enterprises --
Environmental aspects. 3. Business education.
I. Nemetz, Peter N., 1944- II. Series.

HC79.E5B74 2002   363.7   C2001-911202-5

Distributed by
UBC Press
University of British Columbia
2029 West Mall
Vancouver BC Canada V6S 1W8
604 822 5959
604 822 6083 fax
info@ubcpress.ca
www.ubcpress.ca

To my dearest wife, Roma -

lifelong companion, partner and kindred spirit.

TABLE OF CONTENTS

PART II: DISCIPLINARY PERSPECTIVES

Finance:

Strategic Management and Organizational Behaviour:

Transportation and Logistics:

Marketing:

Accounting/MIS:

BRINGING BUSINESS ON BOARD: SUSTAINABLE DEVELOPMENT AND THE B-SCHOOL CURRICULUM

Peter N. Nemetz
Professor of Strategy and Business Economics
Faculty of Commerce and Business Administration
University of British Columbia

SCOPE AND OBJECTIVES OF THIS VOLUME

The goal of achieving sustainable development is arguably the greatest challenge mankind has ever faced, requiring a concerted joint effort among consumers, business and government. It can be argued that if sustainable development is indeed to be achieved, then the *sine qua non* is the education of the emerging business elite in the fundamental principles of sustainable development, for only with the active engagement of the business community is there any realistic hope that our economic, social, and ecological systems can achieve sustainability. This will require early exposure to the core concepts by embedding them in business school curricula. The objective of this volume, therefore, is to provide a comprehensive guide to issues of sustainable development for business school students at both the senior and MBA levels. This special issue of the *Journal of Business Administration and Policy Analysis*, an international journal anchored in the Faculty of Commerce and Business Administration at the University of British Columbia, is being produced in both journal and book format in collaboration with Canada's National Round Table on the Environment and the Economy. Contributors have been drawn from academe and the business community in North America Asia, and Europe.

This volume is structured in four parts: (1) eight overview pieces to introduce the basic concepts of sustainable development; (2) ten discipline-based chapters (including Finance, Strategic Management and Organizational Behaviour, Marketing, Accounting/Management Information Systems, Environmental Law, Urban Land Economics and Transportation) showing the relevance of sustainable development to these subject areas; (3) thirteen case studies drawing on industry experience and expertise in the area of sustainable development; and (4) four country/regional studies examining the specific issues and challenges of sustainable development facing several countries and regional blocs.

WHAT IS SUSTAINABLE DEVELOPMENT?

The term "sustainable development" emerged from the World Commission on Environment and Development established by the United Nations in 1983. Known as the Bruntland Commission, after the chair Gro Harlem Bruntland, the Prime Minister of Norway, this conference was convened to discuss the critical issues of ecological degradation and Third World development. The definition of sustainable development which emerged from the Conference was beguilingly simple: development that "meets the needs of the present without compromising the ability of future generations to meet their own needs" (WCED, 1987, p. 8).

The concept has proven to be much more intractable than first anticipated; one study by the World Bank (Pezzey, 1992) enumerated almost three dozen definitions of the term. In fact, on the face of it, the concept seems profoundly oxymoronic, as no process of continual *development* can be *sustained* in a closed system. Several attempts have been made to address this paradox: first, by focusing more on the *sustainability* of human activities rather than *sustainable development* per se; and second, by adopting a more subtle definition of development, focussing on the *quality* – as distinct from the *quantity* – of output; yet the fundamental challenge of how to both conceptualize the principle and implement it remains unresolved. One of the most common interpretations of the concept is based on the analogy of a three-legged stool: sustainable development requires the simultaneous achievement of sustainability in three disparate spheres: economic, ecological and social. In the last category, sustainable development must address both intragenerational and intergenerational equity; i.e. issues of empowerment and distributional equity not only within the human generation which currently inhabits the earth, but also generations yet to be born. Clearly, empowerment across generations is beyond realization, and intergenerational equity itself poses an extraordinary challenge given basic human values and time preference. For example, Figure 1 illustrates the value of one dollar in the future under alternative discount rate scenarios. It is an inherent human trait to value the present more than the future, if for no other reason than mortality. A system with even modest discount rates assigns any future costs and benefits (i.e. specifically those which affect future generations) past 50 or more years a minimal or essentially zero value. This problem affects the distribution of resource availability across generations and, *in extremis*, can lead to the extinction or depletion of a renewable resource base required for continued human sustenance or survival.

Figure 1:

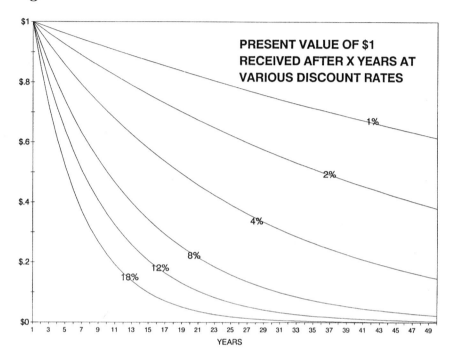

PRESENT VALUE OF $1
RECEIVED AFTER X YEARS AT
VARIOUS DISCOUNT RATES

WHY SHOULD WE BE CONCERNED WITH SUSTAINABLE DEVELOPMENT?

Several pieces of emerging evidence have led a majority of the scientific community to the conclusion that the human species and the planet we inhabit may be facing a turning point in their continuing evolution: (1) for the first time in human history, anthropogenic emissions of several gases (such as carbon dioxide, methane, suphur dioxide and nitrogen oxides) equal or exceed natural emissions (McNeill, 2000, p. 53); (2) symptoms of ecological stress have appeared at the global level, including damage to the stratospheric ozone layer and accelerating global warming with accompanying climatic changes; and (3) loss of land borne and aquatic species and consequent decrease in planetary biodiversity.

With the exception of #1, the interpretation of none of these signs or symptoms is without contention. Until recently, no scientific consensus had formed whether global climate change was indeed occurring and, if so, whether it was being significantly influenced by human activity. A major research study just published by the U.S. National Academy of Sciences (NRC, 2001) represents a crucial advance in scientific thinking on this issue and states conclusively that "Greenhouse gases are accumulating in Earth's atmosphere as a result of human activities, causing surface air temperatures and subsurface ocean temperatures to rise. . . . Global warming could well have serious adverse societal and ecological impacts by the end of this century." (See also Justus and Fletcher, 2001).

Some other symptoms of ecological distress have remained masked. A case in point is the global fisheries where well publicized declines in such important commercial catches as Atlantic cod and other species (Speer et al., 2000) have appeared to have been offset by continued increases in total global fish harvests. Only recently, with advances in fisheries theory and empirical research, has it become apparent that the fundamental threat to sustainable fisheries has been hidden by the progressive depletion of species (NRDC, 1997; see also Jackson et al., 2001) and a process of "fishing down the food chain" where fish within successively lower trophic layers are targeted for harvest. This not only threatens the survival of species within each trophic level but also robs fish within higher trophic levels of the food necessary for stock rebuilding or survival (Pauly, 1999).

Why have we been only recently alerted to these major ecological threats? Because of the arithmetic of exponential growth, only now have human population growth and economic development reached a level which poses a threat to global ecological integrity. Figures 2 and 3, which track the path of both variables over history, illustrate a fundamental difference in paradigms between the disciplines of economics and ecology – two of the three central philosophical pillars upon which the theory of sustainable development is built.

An economist would see in these figures the triumph of human ingenuity over poverty and disease, and the removal of technological constraints to the production of the basic necessities of food, clothing and shelter. In contrast, an ecologist would see a species growing exponentially without constraints in a closed system. Few such examples exist in nature. Our ecological system, based on a highly complex web of interdependencies and controls, operates to limit the unconstrained growth of any species which can threaten the integrity of their immediate environment, the survival of other species and even their very own continued existence. In those rare instances where such natural constraints have been removed – usually by the conscious or unconscious actions of mankind – the results are predictable: an initial exponential increase in population, followed inexorably by a population collapse. One sobering example of this type of phenomenon as it applies to hu-

Figure 2 - Historical Population Estimates

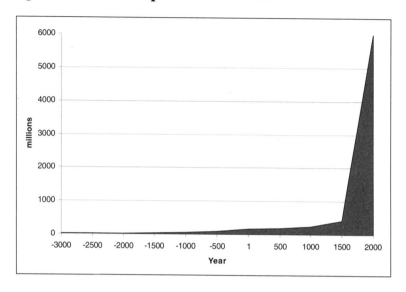

Source: U.S. Bureau of the Census

Figure 3 - Historical Total World GDP Estimates
(Billions of 1990 International Dollars - logarithmic scale)

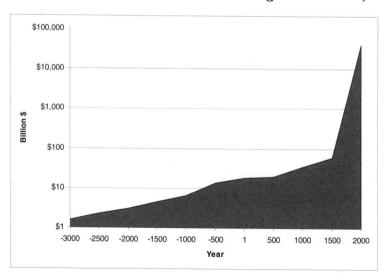

Source: Based on data generated by Professor J. Bradford DeLong, Department of Economics, U.C. Berkeley

man civilization has been demonstrated by recent research on the now disappeared population of Easter Island. [See Box 1] In fact, Easter Island is but one example of numerous civilizations throughout history which have "committed ecological suicide by destroying their own resource base" (Diamond, 1999, p. 411).

To the ecologist, the data on the growth of human population and industrial output pose the ultimate challenge – to find some level of sustainable interaction between humankind and the ecological system before natural control mechanisms such as disease and famine lead inevitably to the collapse of the environment which sustains current levels of human activity.

A cogent summary of this extraordinary challenge is provided by the prominent ecological theorist, Professor E.O. Wilson of Harvard University in his contribution to this volume entitled "Is Humanity Suicidal?" Wilson states: "The human species is, in a word, an environmental abnormality. It is possible that intelligence in the wrong kind of species was foreordained to be a fatal combination for the biosphere. Perhaps a law of evolution is that intelligence usually extinguishes itself."

It is interesting to observe that as a shift in scientific thinking has taken place, a similar change in worldview has occurred in at least one sector of the business world. One of the most conservative sectors of the business community has already concluded that global warming is indeed taking place and is actively campaigning for a concerted corporate and governmental response. Figures 4 and 5 are reproductions of graphics generated by the insurance industry to support their contention that the increase in the number and severity of certain types of natural disasters, such as floods, storms and tornadoes, is linked to human-driven climate change. (For more recent evidence, see Goldenberg et al., 2001; Wigley and Raper, 2001).

THE ROLE OF ECONOMICS

Why have economists not seen what has seemed so apparent to most ecologists? The most plausible interpretation is that much of our foundational economic theory which models human productive activity developed in an era when humanity's impact on the natural environment was orders of magnitude less than it is today. The classical model of economic exchange between households (as generators of labour and consumers of goods and services) and producers (as purchasers of labour and purveyors of products) [see Figure 6] had no need to include resources such as clean air, water or assimilative capacity because they were free and perceived to be unlimited.

BOX 1: EASTER ISLAND

When Dutch explorers first discovered Easter Island in 1722, they found only the squalid remains of a once thriving population now reduced to warfare, cannibalism and barely subsistence level food production on an island stripped of its forest cover. Juxtaposed on the collapsed civilization were 600 massive stone statues towering as high as 65 feet and weighing up to 270 tons (Diamond, 1995). The population, which had peaked at approximately 7000 almost two centuries prior to their discovery, had built an advanced society sustained by the liquidation of the stock of forest capital which blanketed the island. The trees had provided essential material for fuel, construction of housing and boats, fishing nets and the transportation of the massive stone statues from inland quarries to the shore. The inevitable loss of forest cover led to a devastating array of ecological consequences, imprisoning the inhabitants on an island without houses, canoes, proper fishing nets or fertile soil. The population collapse was inevitable.

The unsettling lesson of Easter Island is that despite the fact that the islanders could observe the exhaustion of the forest resource which was essential for their survival, they were unable to devise a social-economic-political system that allowed them to find the right balance with their environment. One suggested explanation for this suicidal behaviour was the increasingly fierce competition for the remaining dwindling resources among rival groups on the island. This bears a disturbing resemblance to modern day national behaviour toward dwindling resources such as certain fish stocks (e.g., cod and whales). The dismal history of Easter Island provides a striking example of the dependence of human societies on their environment and of the consequences of irreversibly damaging that environment. Like Easter Island, the earth has only limited resources to support human society and all its demands. Like the islanders, the human population of the earth has no practical means of escape. The economist, Kenneth Boulding, coined the phrase "Spaceship earth" in an attempt to capture the essence of this dilemma faced by mankind.

[See also: Ponting, 1991; Brander and Taylor, 1998]

Figure 4

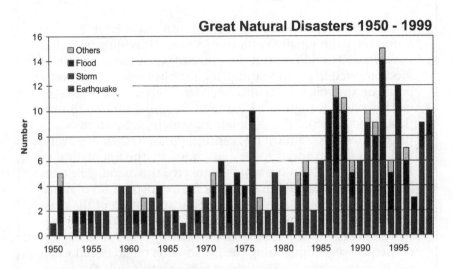

Source: Munich Reinsurance

Figure 5

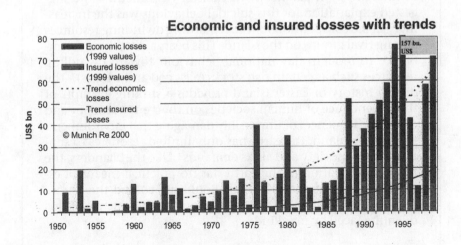

Source: Munich Reinsurance

It was only after the publication of Rachel Carson's seminal work *Silent Spring* in 1962 that the general public was first awakened to the magnitude of the potential problem of environmental degradation. To its credit, the economics profession in relatively short order proceeded to develop the new subdiscipline of environmental economics. Fundamental to this disciplinary theory is the principle that scarce resources such as environmental amenities will be overused and degraded as long as they remain outside the market system; i.e. if they are unpriced. In the language of the disciple, *externalities* have to be *internalized* and property rights assigned to common property resources in order to correct the "market failure" which can threaten the continued production of goods and services.

At one level, this new discipline has induced a remarkable transformation in government policy and corporate and individual response. New market-based initiatives have replaced many of the old economically inefficient and frequently ineffective regulatory mechanisms for the control of pollution. Yet a fundamental problem remains: while many externalities can be priced and consequently reduced or eliminated, there is no effective way to price the planet-level ecological services required for species survival.

One of the most interesting research efforts to address this problem was published in the May 15, 1997 issue of *Nature*, one of the world's most respected scientific journals (Costanza et al., 1997). Thirteen promi-

Figure 6: Classical Model of the Economy

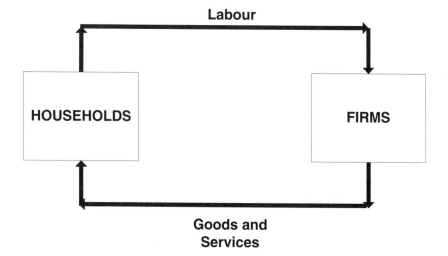

nent economists and ecologists collaborated in an attempt to establish a monetary value for the world's ecosystem services and natural capital. To quote:

> The services of ecological systems and the natural capital stocks that produce them are critical to the functioning of the Earth's life-support system. They contribute to human welfare, both directly and indirectly, and therefore represent part of the total economic value of the planet. We have estimated the current economic value of 17 ecosystem services for 16 biomes, based on published studies and a few original calculations. For the entire biosphere, the value (most of which is outside the market) is estimated to be in the range of US$16-54 trillion per year, with an average of US$33 trillion per year. Because of the nature of the uncertainties, this must be considered a minimum estimate. Global gross national product total is around US$18 trillion per year.

Table 1 enumerates the components of ecosystem value derived from this research exercise. (See also Daily, 1997) On reflection, the concept of deriving an economic value for ecosystem services seems patently absurd – for without these services, no one species, including humankind, could survive on this planet. In this respect, the value of such services is certainly infinite. Yet there is an innate human response to ignore values that are beyond the level of easy comprehension. This, then, is the real function of the analysis – to convince economists, policymakers and the lay public of the magnitude of the problem in terms which can be more readily understood and interpreted. As such, the accuracy of the estimate is immaterial; it is the fact that a dollar value has been assigned which is the ultimate value of this exercise.

If there is one major flaw of environmental economics, it is that it fails to come to grips with the complex interaction of economic and ecological systems. To address this issue, a new discipline has emerged which attempts to fuse these two paradigms. Called ecological economics, this discipline rests on a simple philosophical premise: that the economic system is embedded in the ecological system, cannot function without it, and is ultimately subject to the same laws and constraints which apply to natural systems.

Figure 7 presents a simplified representation of an integrated economic-ecological model. One of the most important components of this model is the feedback loop on anthropogenic waste products. Pollution generated by production processes and released into the environment has a negative impact on the economic system either indirectly by

Table 1: Estimated Total Value of Global Ecosystem Services

Ecosystem Service	Estimated Value (billion $)
Nutriet cycling	$17,075
Cultural	$3,015
Waste treatment	$2,277
Disturbance regulation	$1,779
Water supply	$1,692
Food production	$1,386
Gas regulation	$1,341
Water regulation	$1,115
Receation	$815
Raw materials	$721
Climate regulation	$684
Erosion control	$576
Biological control	$417
Habitat/refugia	$124
Pollination	$117
Genetic resources	$79
Soil formation	$53
TOTAL	**$33,266**

Source: Costanza et al., 1997

compromising one or more ecological services, or directly by threatening production processses or the humans which operate them.

In this volume, Costanza et al. summarize the development of the new paradigm, its basic principles and their relevance to our economic systems. To quote the authors:

The core problem addressed in ecological economics is the sustainability of interactions between economic and ecological systems. Ecological economics addresses the relationships between ecosystems and economic systems in the broadest sense. It involves issues that are fundamentally cross-scale, transcultural and transdisciplinary, and calls for innovative approaches to research, to policy and to the building of social institutions. In this sense, ecological economics tends to be characterized by a holistic "systems" approach that goes beyond the normal territorial boundaries of the academic disciplines.

Figure 7: Simplified Economic-Ecological Model

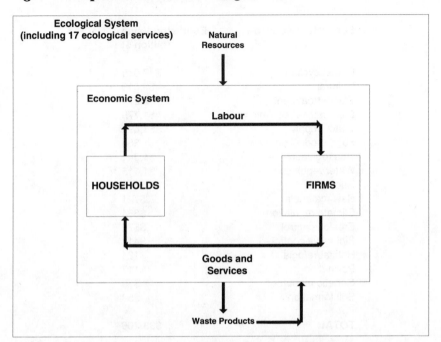

OPERATIONALIZING SUSTAINABLE DEVELOPMENT – CONCEPTS

Several common conceptual threads run throughout studies of sustainability:

(1) a critical distinction between qualitative and quantitative changes in the utilization of our technology and natural resource base (i.e. *development* versus *growth*); for example, technological advances which may permit us to raise our standard of living without increasing the throughput of resources – commonly referred to as "dematerialization." One method of determining this throughput is an index which measures the quantity of direct material inputs to produce the goods and services required by an individual;

(2) a focus on social stability, empowerment and equity with particular emphasis on reducing poverty and maintaining an adequate quality of life for all global inhabitants;

(3) borrowing from principles of business sector accounting, a direct or indirect articulation of the concept of *natural* capital — where mainte-

nance of a constant natural capital stock (including the renewable resource base and the environment) yields an indefinite stream of output or "income." One central concept is the proposition that the current generation must leave the next generation a stock of capital no less than is currently available. Implicit in this proposition is that we must, to the best of our ability, live off the "interest" on this capital stock and not draw it down. If part of this capital is consumed, it must be replaced by substitute capital. The ability to achieve this goal hinges on which of two major definitions of "sustainable development" is adopted: "weak" sustainability or "strong" sustainability.

Under the weak sustainability constant capital rule, we can consume some of our natural capital (in the form of environmental degradation, for example) as long as we offset this loss by increasing our stock of man-made capital. In contrast, under the strong sustainability constant capital rule, there is no perfect substitution among different forms of capital. Some elements of the natural capital stock (such as life-support services) cannot be replaced by man-made capital. To implement either of these concepts requires the ability to distinguish more accurately among the various forms of capital (natural, human, physical). Without more accurate measures of these forms of capital, we cannot make the right decisions;

(4) a concept known as the "precautionary principle" which states that one cannot wait for definitive scientific proof of a potential threat to the global ecosystem before acting, if that threat is both large and credible. The underlying theory is based on scientific principles, largely associated with the work of ecologists such as C.S. Holling, that suggest that by the time one recognizes or begins to feel the tangible effects of certain types of ecological threats, it may be too late to act (Holling 1973). Figure 8 presents a simplified conceptualization of the precautionary principle as applied to the issue of global warming. We are already amassing a significant body of scientific evidence to suggest what future global warming may entail – potentially profound changes in weather and climate, including a greater number and severity of super storms which concomitant economic damage and loss of life, increasing incidence and severity of droughts, a greater incidence of vector-based epidemics as the area of world favourable to disease vectors rises (for example, see Epstein et al., 1998), damage to forests and fisheries, and sea-level rises which will threaten heavily-populated low-lying areas throughout the world. Among these negative effects, two of the most daunting are the potential for significant losses to productive farmland and food production (Fischer et al., 2001) and positive feedback loops which can lead to sudden global ecological changes (see for ex-

Figure 8: The Precautionary Principle and Global Warming

	Global warming is occurring	Global warming is NOT occurring
We assume global warming is occurring and act on it	we can slow or possibly reverse the damage	Generally unproductive investment (i.e. opportunity costs greater than the benefits)
We assume global warming is NOT occuring and do nothing	we face disaster	nothing to worry about

ample, Broecker, 1987). With these potential consequences, the wisdom of considering the application of the precautionary principle becomes apparent.

One of the most critical concepts brought by ecology to the study of human activity is that of systems or holistic analysis; i.e. the effect of any action or activity cannot be viewed in isolation, but must be viewed as part of an entire system. This theory is not new to the field of economics, as general equilibrium analysis and such applications as input-output analysis incorporate the essence of this concept. It is unfortunate, therefore, that such concepts have not been applied in economics to many important issues of resource use and environmental degradation. Boxes 2-6 provide several examples drawn from the agricultural and transportation sector of how systems theory could inform public and private decision making in a manner which could advance the cause of sustainable development.

OPERATIONALIZING SUSTAINABLE DEVELOPMENT – TOOLS

The operationalization of sustainable development requires both new ways of conceptualizing the inter-relationship between human activity and the environment, and tools for incorporating these concepts into

BOX 2 – IS U.S. AGRICULTURE SUSTAINABLE?

The American agricultural system is considered the world's most efficient, providing bountiful harvests not only for it own citizens, but also for many less well endowed nations of the world. At its simplest, an efficient system minimizes inputs for a given level of output; yet, in a sense, efficiency is a function of system boundaries (Jacobs, 1993). Therein lies the paradox of American agriculture.

Figure B1 presents a simplified schematic of this sector where remarkable levels of efficiency are achieved within the bounds of a narrowly defined system. When the boundaries of this system are incrementally expanded to include uncosted spatial and temporal externalities, the purported level of efficiency – and sustainability – becomes open to question.

Figure B2 summarizes the negative effects flowing from each of the central characteristics of the U.S. agricultural system. While some of the these problems, such as aquifer depletion from excessive water use, could be remedied by simple measures such as pricing this resource at its social marginal cost, other effects are much more complex and may require more creative and decisive measures. Prominent among these problems is the serious threat to human health from the emergence of antibiotic resistant bacteria as a consequence of the widespread and indiscriminant use of pharmaceuticals in animal husbandry (OTA, 1995; Mellon et al., 2001). Such practices are significantly more difficult to address because the use of these drugs is essential to the maintenance of a complex and non-sustainable production system. One of the principal purposes of this use of pharmaceuticals is to overcome natural ecological limits to population density.

A parallel problem arises with respect to monoculture – a system of cropping which yields significant increases in production yet survives only through the massive use of pesticides and herbicides in a attempt to also circumvent natural ecological processes.

In sum, the social costs contained within the total boundary which encompasses the U.S. agricultural system and all its offsite and temporal effects are such to suggest that this model of efficiency may be fundamentally unsustainable.

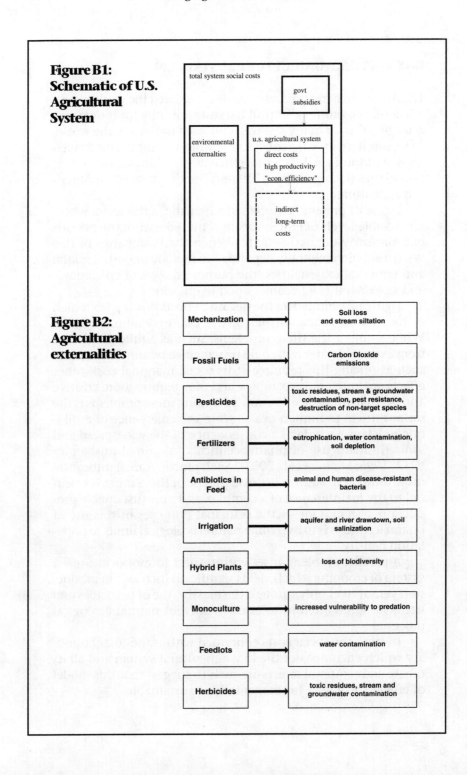

Figure B1: Schematic of U.S. Agricultural System

total system social costs

govt subsidies

environmental externalties

u.s. agricultural system

direct costs
high productivity
"econ. efficiency"

indirect
long-term
costs

Figure B2: Agricultural externalities

Mechanization	Soil loss and stream siltation
Fossil Fuels	Carbon Dioxide emissions
Pesticides	toxic residues, stream & groundwater contamination, pest resistance, destruction of non-target species
Fertilizers	eutrophication, water contamination, soil depletion
Antibiotics in Feed	animal and human disease-resistant bacteria
Irrigation	aquifer and river drawdown, soil salinization
Hybrid Plants	loss of biodiversity
Monoculture	increased vulnerability to predation
Feedlots	water contamination
Herbicides	toxic residues, stream and groundwater contamination

BOX 3 – GASOHOL

The current American administration – like its predecessor -- has renewed the government's commitment to the production and use of gasohol – a blend of 10% grain-based ethanol and 90% gasoline. The principal component of government support for ethanol production is a significant tax break which makes gasohol price competitive with regular gasoline at the pump. Several major reasons have been advanced for this de facto subsidy: (1) to reduce dependence on foreign oil supplies, (2) to reduce urban air pollution, and (3) to provide additional income to the farm sector.

To appreciate why none of these reasons is correct, one must understand the technology of ethanol production. First, grain, corn or other biomass is converted to fermentable sugar. Next, these sugars are then fermented, typically with yeast, until they reach a natural limit of 12% ethanol. Finally, the alcohol content is increased to as high as 100% through the process of distillation. The critical factor in the entire process is the quantity of energy required for distillation. When net energy analysis (IES, 1975; Winstanley et al., 1977; Gilliland, 1978) is applied to the typical American ethanol process based on corn input and fossil fuel based distillation, it becomes apparent that ethanol production has near zero or negative net energy balance (Chambers et al, 1979; Hopkinson and Day, 1980; USDA, 1988). In common parlance, this means that it takes more energy to produce this fuel that is available from the final product in the form of useful energy. Net energy confirms the suspicion that if the government was not heavily subsidizing gasohol, no one would produce or consume it.

Why does a government committed to free market principles continue to pursue a policy which appears irrational? Consider the three rationales for gasohol production. (1) *It reduces dependence on foreign oil*. Ironically, because of a potentially negative energy balance, the production of gasohol may marginally increase energy import dependence. (2) *It reduces urban air pollution*. The combustion of gasohol tends to decrease the emissions of carbon monoxide, but increase the output of hydrocarbons and production of ozone (NRC, 1999). It does, however, shift the locus of some pollution from the urban area to the areas where ethanol is produced. (3) *It produces additional farm income.* There may be a marginal increase in aggregate farm income, but there are farmers who lose as well as gain from this policy (USDA, 1988).

Several hypotheses have been advanced for government maintaining policies which are favourable to the production of gasohol. First, government may wish to appear to be tackling the problem of foreign oil dependence which now exceeds 50% of domestic consumption – a figure above that which characterized the energy crises of the 1970s. Second, the government may wish to appear to be addressing the problem of urban air pollution, although there are other more cost-effective ways of doing so. Or, finally, the government may be responding to interest group lobbying. Promoting the use of gasohol increases the income of farmers who produce the feedstock for ethanol. In addition, there has been a strong lobbying effort for many years by the agrobusiness giant, Archer Daniels Midland (ADM), which is estimated to control between 60 and 75 percent of U.S. ethanol production. ADM has made significant financial contributions to both Democratic and Republican parties over the last decade (Bovard, 1995; NYT, January 16, 1996).

Regardless of which explanation is correct, the continued production and use of ethanol in the transportation sector, with current technology, agricultural practices and feedstock, contributes nothing to sustainability and distracts government from more productive, but potentially less politically palatable, policies to create a more sustainable transportation sector.

everyday public and private sector decision making. Issues of accounting – both public and private sector – are essential to the achievement of sustainable development, for it is accounting, broadly defined, which generates measures of performance by which movement toward or away from sustainability can be gauged.

The late Robert Eisner of Northwestern University was one of the first economists to study the dysfunctional accounting practices of the U.S. and other governments. No corporation would survive if it adopted public sector accounting principles which fail to differentiate between consumption and investment. In 1991, Eisner recalculated the federal budget by changing the treatment of such important social investments as education, research & development and infrastructure. By capitalizing such expenditures rather than expensing them, Eisner demonstrated that the budget deficit in that year had been overstated by a factor of eight. (See Eisner, 1994)

A parallel effort has been underway over the last decade to broaden the definition of national accounts to include not only physical capital, but also natural and human capital. (See, for example, Ahmad et al.,1989; UN, 1993; Lutz, 1993; Serageldin and Steer, 1993; CBO, 1994; Van Dieren, 1995; Rodenburg et al., 1995; Nordhaus and Kokkelenberg, 1999). Repetto (1989) succinctly summarized the problem of dysfunctional national accounting in an early report from the World Resources Institute when he stated: "A country could exhaust its mineral resources, cut down its forests, erode its soil, pollute its aquifers, and hunt its wildlife to extinction, but measured income would not be affected as these assets disappeared."

One particularly noteworthy effort at reform began with an organization in San Francisco called Redefining Progress. They have produced a recalculated GDP called the Genuine Progress Indicator which distinguishes "bads" (i.e. expenditures related to such items as pollution, crime, accidents, etc.) from "goods." Under current national income principles, all "bads" are treated as positive contributions to GDP. Redefining Progress generated GPI per capita for the United States and compared it with the conventional measure of GDP per capita for the last half of the Twentieth Century (RP, 1999). The result, portrayed in Figure 9, suggests a startlingly different trend between the two measures. This volume contains three chapters specifically devoted to the GPI: Ronald Colman describes its general principles, Colin Dodds and Ronald Colman use this mechanism to measure the true cost of crime in Nova Scotia, and Mark Anielski has calculated a GPI time series for Alberta.

Another major initiative relating to the public sector is described by Jean-Philippe Barde of the OECD. The author describes a range of initiatives, labeled variously, green or ecological tax reform, now taking place in many European nations. The fundamental goal of such policies is to protect the environment and promote sustainability while enhancing economic efficiency.

As stated above, performance indicators are essential to the achievement of sustainable development, and several national and international studies have already been undertaken to identify a list of appropriate metrics. In this volume, William Rees describes a unique and now widely-used tool of which he was co-developer. Termed "the ecological footprint," this indicator first calculates the land area required to produce the physical stocks of capital necessary to sustain a given human population and absorb their waste discharges, and then compares this

Figure 9: U.S. GPI versus GDP per capita

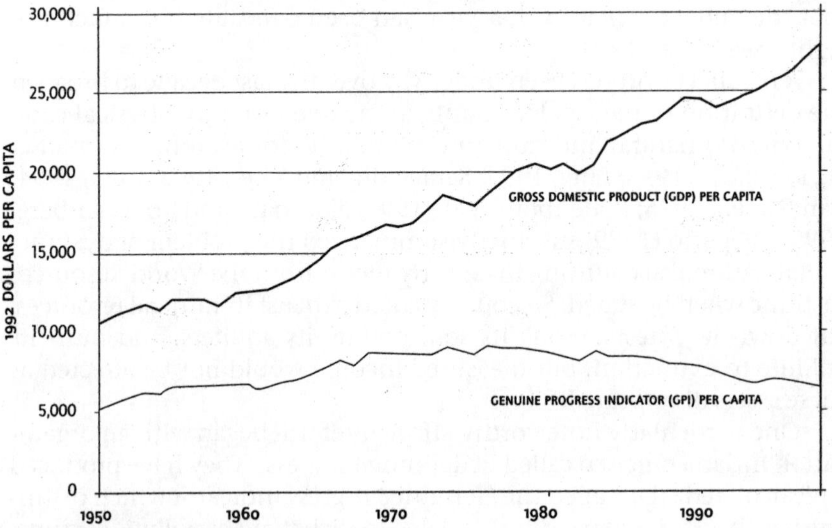

Source: Redefining Progress, 1999

value with the area which the population inhabits – whether a city, state or country.

As Table 2 demonstrates, virtually all developed nations of the world have an ecological footprint significantly larger than that contained within their physical boundaries. These appropriated resources come from other countries, are "borrowed from the past (e.g., as fossil energy) or permanently appropriated from the future (e.g., in the form of contamination, plant growth reduction through reduced UV radiation, soil degradation, etc.)" (See Wackernagel and Rees, 1996; Wackernagel et al., 1997) The implication of this concept for sustainable development at the global level is significant in light of continuing pressure for economic development, To quote the authors: "If everybody lived like today's North Americans, it would take at least two additional planet Earths to produce the resources, absorb the wastes, and otherwise maintain life-support."

Accounting concepts and practices play an equally crucial role in the corporate sector's drive for sustainability (see, for example, Rubenstein, 1994; US EPA, 1995; Bennett and James, 1998). One of the earliest and most insightful reports on this subject was produced by WRI in 1995 and authored by Ditz et al. under the title *Green Ledgers: Case Studies in Corporate Environmental Accounting*. The basic theme of this book is that

Table 2: Ecological Footprint of Nations

Country	footprint in [ha/cap]	available capacity in [ha/cap]	ecol. deficit (if negative) in [ha/cap]	Country	footprint in [ha/cap]	available capacity in [ha/cap]	ecol. deficit (if negative) in [ha/cap]
Singapore	7.2	0.1	-7.1	Denmark	5.9	5.2	-0.7
Hong Kong	6.1	0	-6.1	Philippines	1.5	0.9	-0.6
Belgium	5	1.3	-3.7	Czech Rep	4.5	4	-0.5
Netherlands	5.3	1.7	-3.6	China	1.2	0.8	-0.4
United States	10.3	6.7	-3.6	Ethiopia	0.8	0.5	-0.3
United Kingdom	5.2	1.7	-3.5	India	0.8	0.5	-0.3
Germany	5.3	1.9	-3.4	Pakistan	0.8	0.5	-0.3
Japan	4.3	0.9	-3.4	Bangladesh	0.5	0.3	-0.2
Switzerland	5	1.8	-3.2	Costa Rica	2.5	2.5	0
Israel	3.4	0.3	-3.1	France	4.1	4.2	0.1
Italy	4.2	1.3	-2.9	Norway	6.2	6.3	0.1
Korea, Rep	3.4	0.5	-2.9	Malaysia	3.3	3.7	0.4
Greece	4.1	1.5	-2.6	Ireland	5.9	6.5	0.6
Russian Fed.	6	3.7	-2.3	Argentina	3.9	4.6	0.7
Poland, Rep	4.1	2	-2.1	Chile	2.5	3.2	0.7
South Africa	3.2	1.3	-1.9	Sweden	5.9	7	1.1
Jordan	1.9	0.1	-1.8	Indonesia	1.4	2.6	1.2
Spain	3.8	2.2	-1.6	Canada	7.7	9.6	1.9
Thailand	2.8	1.2	-1.6	Colombia	2	4.1	2.1
Mexico	2.6	1.4	-1.2	Finland	6	8.6	2.6
Venezuela	3.8	2.7	-1.1	Brazil	3.1	6.7	3.6
Austria	4.1	3.1	-1	Australia	9	14	5
Egypt	1.2	0.2	-1	Peru	1.6	7.7	6.1
Hungary	3.1	2.1	-1	New Zealand	7.6	20.4	12.8
Nigeria	1.5	0.6	-0.9	Iceland	7.4	21.7	14.3
Portugal	3.8	2.9	-0.9				
Turkey	2.1	1.3	-0.8	WORLD	2.8	2.1	-0.7

Source: Wackernagel et al. (2001)

the lack of recognition of the true magnitude and location of all environmental costs in a corporation prevents it from making intelligent resource allocation decisions. Most importantly, lack of information about these costs forecloses important strategic opportunities for the firm. One major consequence of a firm's ignorance of the extent and location of environmental costs borne by the company is that "products with relatively higher environmental costs are often subsidized by those with lower ones." Products which may appear profitable may impose significant environmental costs on other parts of the business and such costs are not attributed to their original source. This introduces a major distortion in the process of profit maximization through efficient resource allocation decisions at the margin. Certain products or processes may be encouraged/discouraged on the basis of such incorrect price signals within the corporation.

Remedying this costly pathology requires a fundamental

BOX 4 – IS THE AUTOMOBILE SUSTAINABLE?

The invention of the automobile has had an extraordinary impact on the development of our modern economy and society. The motor vehicle has had a profound influence on the size and configuration of our modern cities and how we conduct our everyday lives (Freund and Martin, 1993). Despite these manifest benefits, it can be argued that the automobile is one of the largest generators of negative externalities in the world. Its effects include: (1) the emergence of vast, spread out cities with concomitant high energy costs and massive infrastructural requirements; (2) traffic congestion; (3) noise pollution; (4) injuries and fatalities. For example, in the U.S. in 1999 there were 6.3 million traffic accidents, resulting in 3.2 million injuries and 41,611 deaths (Wards, 2001a); (5) the largest single user of energy and material in our modern industrial society (see Figures B3 and B4); and (6) the creation of one of the most important contributors to environmental degradation. (See Figures B5 and B6).

Several recent studies have provided estimates of the social cost of driving – all considerably in excess of the private costs (see, for example, MacKenzie et al., 1992; Miller and Moffet, 1993; ICTA, 2000). As much as we love our automobiles, we should not delude ourselves into thinking that their continued utilization represents any contribution to sustainable development.

Figure B3: Canada's Energy Use (1993) in '000 terajoules

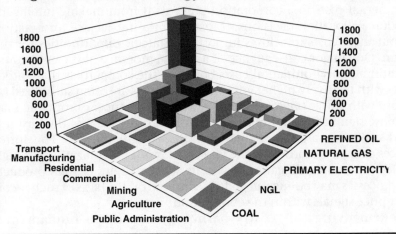

Figure B4: Automobile Consumption of Materials - U.S. 1999 (source: Wards, 2000)

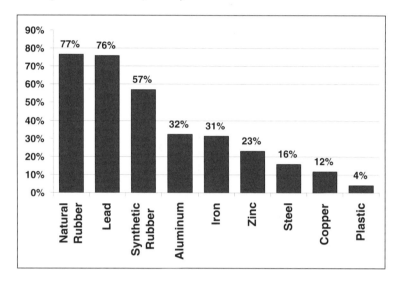

Figure B5: Canadian Air Pollution Output (1995) in '000 tons - excluding carbon dioxide

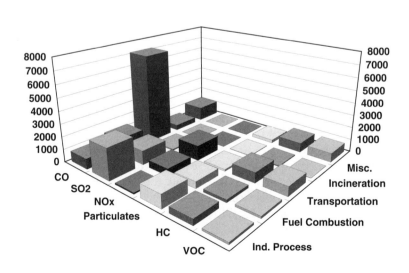

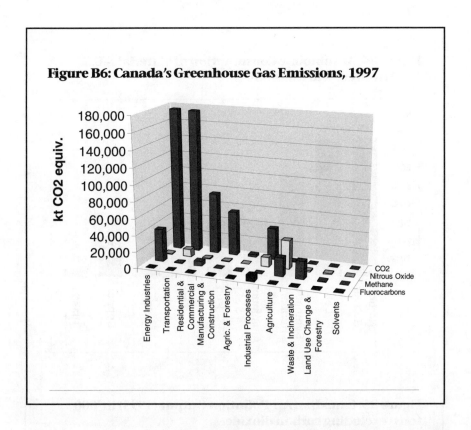

Figure B6: Canada's Greenhouse Gas Emissions, 1997

reconceptualization of the flows of goods and service through an organization and the costs associated therewith. (See, for example, NRTEE,
1999). In this volume, William Smith of Environment Canada outlines
one approach which can be undertaken to address these complex issues.

There are several models and tools available to corporations in undertaking this process of strategic change. Some of the most advanced
are found in the field of industrial ecology (Graedel and Allenby, 1995;
Ayres and Ayres, 1996) which visualizes the operation of a firm as a
living organism, absorbing and metabolizing (i.e. processing) inputs
and generating outputs, including wastes. With this theoretic as a guiding principle, it is easier to see that the generation of unnecessary wastes
is economically inefficient and ultimately represents lost profits.

One of the major tools from industrial ecology is life-cycle analysis
(and its economic counter part, life-cycle cost analysis) which produces
a comprehensive picture of the environmental impact (and cost) of a
product from "cradle to grave." Box 6 describes the application of LCA
to alternative automotive propulsion systems.

BOX 5 – IS THE PROVISION OF FREE URBAN MASS TRANSIT A SUSTAINABLE VENTURE?

Urban mass transit has traditionally been considered a money-losing venture. Efforts to manage these systems have generally been focussed on cost cutting and price increases. A few city governments (for example, Seattle, Denver and Hasselt, Belgium) have paradoxically decided to provide such transportation free of charge within parts of their urban areas, especially the Central Business District (CBD). Economic theory suggests that the provision of a good at zero price will lead to excessive and inefficient utilization. The resolution of this issue hinges on the question of system boundaries. It is clearly inefficient to provide free service if the system boundary is narrowly defined to encompass only the transportation system itself. However, if the system boundary is enlarged to include the externalities of air pollution, congestion and motor vehicle accidents, then providing free transportation in the CBD may in fact be socially efficient and the most sustainable solution.

Another promising tool to aid corporate decision making for sustainability *and* profitability is called "The Natural Step." Formulated by two Europeans, Dr. Karl-Henrik Robert and Dr. John Holmberg, this principle has been introduced into North America by Paul Hawken. As Nattrass and Altomare state in their book, *The Natural Step for Business: Wealth, Ecology and the Evolutionary Corporation* (1999), "Business is the economic engine of our Western culture, and if it could be transformed to truly serve nature as well as ourselves, it could become essential to our rescue" (p. xiv).

It was the goal of Dr. Robert to translate ecological principles into a form which could be implemented at the corporate level. As described by Nattrass and Altomare, The Natural Step includes four core processes: "Perceiving the nature of the unsustainable direction of business and society and the self-interest implicit in shifting to a sustainable direction; understanding the first-order principles for sustainability (i.e. the four System Conditions); strategic visioning through 'back-casting' from a desired sustainable future; and identifying strategic steps to move the company from its current reality toward its desired vision." The system conditions are described as follows: "In order for a society to be sustain-

BOX 6 – ARE ALTERNATIVE AUTOMOTIVE PROPULSION SYSTEMS SUSTAINABLE?

In recognition of the considerable externalities associated with the internal combustion engine which powers most motor vehicles, new government and corporate emphasis has been placed on developing alternative propulsion systems, from electric cars to automobiles powered by fuel cells. Several recent studies have applied life-cycle cost analysis to these alternatives with somewhat surprising results.

Graedel and Allenby (1995) compared life cycle energy use and greenhouse gas emissions from automotive propulsion systems based on fossil fuel electricity and conventional internal combustion. On the basis of this systems analysis of two important variables, the authors found no appreciable differences between gasoline and electricity. Figure B7 compares alternative sources for hydrogen as a power source for fuel cells in automobiles (Pembina Institute and David Suzuki Foundation, 2001). The results clearly demonstrate the value of applying systems analysis (in the form of LCCA) to the important issue of transportation. Such analysis helps to determine which alternatives are more sustainable (or less unsustainable) than others.

Figure B7: Lifecycle CO_2 Emissions over 1,000 km of travel of Alternative Sources of Hydrogen for Automobile-Powered Fuel Cells

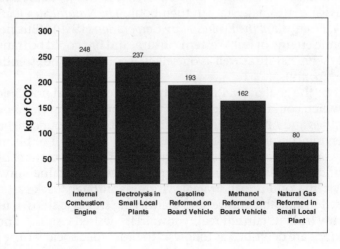

able, nature's functions and diversity are not systematically: subject to increasing concentrations of substances extracted from the Earth's crust; subject to increasing concentrations of substances produced by society; and impoverished by overharvesting or other forms of ecosystem manipulation." In addition, the conditions require that "resources are used fairly and efficiently in order to meet basic human needs worldwide."

In this volume, Nattrass and Altomare describe the experiences of IKEA, the first company to adopt The Nature Step and the competitive advantage it has generated for that firm.

SUSTAINABLE DEVELOPMENT WITHIN THE BUSINESS COMMUNITY

This volume presents several examples of corporations from a broad range of industries which have adopted creative new approaches to conducting business: Suncor, IKEA, Weyerhauser, Canfor, Shell, Cominco, Patagonia, and Interface. Prominent among these innovations are distinguishing between the physical product and the service it provides (Interface), byproduct recovery (Cominco), and integrated industrial parks (Shell, Tampico). Two seminal articles in this volume by Porter and van de Linde and Lovins et al. demonstrate that these and similar types of innovative approaches to business not only help to protect the environment, but also in many cases lead to increased corporate profitability. Central to the achievement of these changes is a fundamental reconceptualization of the nature of business itself – a re-examination of old nostrums and a willingness to adopt new and what may appear on the surface to be radical approaches.

Numerous organizations – both non-profit and business-based – have emerged to assist the corporate sector in this process of reorientation. Australia's ECOS corporation is one such entity, and this volume includes a chapter on how they motivate and facilitate change among their corporate clients. Another prominent organization is the World Business Council on Sustainable Development – a pioneering business-based group which has championed such important concepts as the "triple-bottom line." (See, for example, Schmidheiny, 1992)

How successful are such corporate initiatives? The record has been mixed, but on balance seems distinctly positive. One piece of evidence, in particular, demonstrates the value of creative thinking which incorporates sustainable development into top-level corporate strategy. The Social Investment Forum (www.socialinvest.org) lists fifty mutual funds which include environmental criteria in their choice of corporations listed. A good number of these have outperformed the market in recent years. One of the most prominent initiatives is the Dow Jones Sustainability Group of Indexes. Box 7 reproduces some descriptive material on these financial indexes. Their track record has been solid, as results have matched or outperformed the market since their inception.

Complementing these business sector initiatives have been a number of government policies which have facilitated the adjustment of corporate strategy toward more environmentally friendly processes and procedures. Prominent among these is the move towards markets in pollutant emissions, including sulphur dioxide and lead. The chapter by Brian Mclean of the US EPA in this volume describes the successful development and application of trading in SO_2 emissions in the United States. Proposals have been advanced for similar national and international markets for greenhouse gas emissions (Canada, 2000), although the economic and political issues are considerably more complex at the international level.

THE PROSPECTS

What are the prospects for achieving sustainability – economic, ecologic and social? On the face of it, the challenges some monumental and potentially insurmountable. We live in a society which celebrates and thrives on economic growth and greets with dismay any news than such growth is waning. As Ronald Colman states in his chapter on the principles of GPI:

> The costs of holding on to the illusion that "more" is "better" are frightening. Scientists recognize that the only biological organism that has unlimited growth as its dogma is the cancer cell, the apparent model for our conventional economic theory. By contrast, the natural world thrives on balance and equilibrium, and recognizes inherent limits to growth. The cancer analogy is apt, because the path of limitless growth is profoundly self-destructive. No matter how many cars we have in the driveway or how many possessions we accumulate, the environment will not tolerate the growth illusion even if we fail to see through it.

Failing a radical change in our technology of production and the value system which underlies the "growth mentality," we must conclude that few business activities can be truly "sustainable" – only less unsustainable. But even a small shift from unsustainable practices would be a step in the right direction, allowing more time to tackle this immense problem. Two papers in this volume, on Weyerhauser (and MacMillan Bloedel, its predecessor in British Columbia), illustrate both

BOX 7 - DOW JONES SUSTAINABILITY INDEXES

"CORPORATE SUSTAINABILITY CONCEPT

The concept of corporate sustainability has long been very attractive to investors because of its aim to increase long-term shareholder value. Sustainability-driven companies achieve their business goals by integrating economic, environmental and social growth opportunities into their business strategies. These sustainability companies pursue these opportunities in a pro-active, cost-effective and responsible manner today, so that they will outpace their competitors and be tomorrow's winners.

Sustainability companies not only manage the standard economic factors affecting their businesses but the environmental and social factors as well. There is mounting evidence that their financial performance is superior to that of companies that do not adequately, correctly and optimally manage these important factors.

The superior performance is directly related to a company's commitment to the five corporate sustainability principles:

• Technology: The creation, production and delivery of products and services should be based on innovative technology and organization that use financial, natural and social resources in an efficient, effective and economic manner over the long-term.

• Governance: Corporate sustainability should be based on the highest standards of corporate governance including management responsibility, organizational capability, corporate culture and stakeholder relations.

• Shareholders: The shareholders' demands should be met by sound financial returns, long-term economic growth, long-term productivity increases, sharpened global competitiveness and contributions to intellectual capital.

• Industry: Sustainability companies should lead their industry's shift towards sustainability by demonstrating their commitment and publicizing their superior performance.

• Society: Sustainability companies should encourage lasting social well being by their appropriate and timely responses to rapid social change, evolving demographics, migratory flows, shifting cultural patterns and the need for life-long learning and continuing education.

These principles are also the criteria by which sustainability companies can be identified and ranked for investment purposes. They facilitate a financial quantification of sustainability performance by focussing on a company's pursuit of sustainability opportunities -- e.g., meeting market demand for sustainable products and services -- and the reduction, ideally avoidance, of sustainability risks and costs. As a result, corporate sustainability is an investable concept. This relationship is crucial in driving interest and investments in sustainability to the mutual benefit of companies and investors. As this benefit circle strengthens, it will have a positive effect on the societies and economies of both the developed and developing world."

Source: http://indexes.dowjones.com/djsgi/index/index.html

the opportunities and challenges which face corporate innovation for sustainability in some sectors of the economy. Linda Coady, Vice President Environmental Enterprise, Weyerhauser, describes the critical challenge facing the forest giant, MacMillan Bloedel: change forest practices or risk financial disaster. The corporation undertook a series of radical steps which fundamentally transformed its strategic direction. Its successor, Weyerhauser, is now profiting from this foresight, but must overcome a series of complex economic and institutional barriers to marketing forest products from a newly created sustainably-based and multistakeholder forest entity called *Iisaak*.

It is the nature of our market system that the total output of the economy is the result of the aggregation of numerous individual corporate and individual decisions. Those corporations which have recognized and profitably implemented sustainability concepts are still among the minority. There may, in fact, be fundamental limits to how many sectors are capable of restructuring for complete or partial sustainability. One important signal in assessing the totality of our sustainability efforts can be derived from environmental trends at the national level. Here, the evidence is mixed at best. One keystone gauge of the success or lack thereof in achieving sustainability is national levels of greenhouse gas emissions. The 1997 Kyoto agreement, reaffirmed in July 2001 by 178 nations (*New York Times*, July 24, 2001), adopted as a central goal the reduction of GHG emissions from the 38 industrialized countries[1] "by at least 5 per cent below 1990 levels in the commitment period 2008 to 2012" (UN, 1998). The most recent data suggest that GHG emissions in most developed countries are in fact on the increase. Tables 3-6 illustrate the large international variance in the levels and growth of carbon dioxide emissions (US EIA, 2001). Figures 10-11 summarize historical CO_2 emission data for Canada and the United States (US EIA, 2001; ORNL, 2001). The trends in these data are not surprising considering the increasing use of energy – most notably fossil fuels — in both countries and the intimate connection between energy consumption and carbon dioxide production. Table 7 provides data on current major corporate emitters of CO_2 in Canada (Bramley, 2000).

In order to move closer to a path of sustainability, it is essential to delink energy consumption and CO_2 production from Gross Domestic Product (GDP). It was conventional wisdom prior to the oil crises of 1973 and 1979 that the delinkage of energy consumption and GDP was not possible. It has now become apparent that some countries have achieved such a delinkage with respect to energy and CO2 emissions. For example, a recent report from the U.S Department of Energy has found that the annual output of CO_2 in China has decreased in the last four years of rapid economic growth (See Figure 12) (NRDC, 2001; US DOE, 2001). Part of the explanation for this phenomenon is that China is shifting its energy base away from its extensive reliance on coal and that its rapid industrialization has entailed significant increases in the use of more efficient production technologies. Such results are encouraging, although China's rapid growth from a relatively small and inefficient industrial base is not typical of developed economies. A more salient example drawn from the ranks of the industrialized countries is that of Germany which has achieved decreases in CO_2 emissions over the last decade despite continuing economic growth (see Figure 13). Part of the reason for the delinkage of CO_2 emissions and GDP in European countries such as Germany, Denmark and The Netherlands has been the adoption of innovative ecological tax reform, as described in this volume by Jean-Philippe Barde, Head, National Policies Division, of OECD's Environment Directorate.

Several critical factors temper the optimistic conclusions that might be drawn from such recent successful examples of policy innovation and industrial restructuring which are consistent with movement toward sustainability goals. The first is contained in a recent report from the U.S. Energy Information Administration (2001) which forecasts continued increases in energy consumption and CO_2 generation until 2020 [see Table 8].

The second is the increasing attraction of the automobile to newly industrializing countries. Tables 9 and 10 shows the extent of automo-

Table 3: Total CO_2 Emissions (as C), 1999 - Selected Countries

Country	Million MT	%	Country	Million MT	%
World Total	6,143.62	100%	Brazil	88.90	1%
USA	1,519.89	25%	Poland	84.54	1%
China	668.73	11%	Iran	84.32	1%
Russia	400.09	7%	Spain	81.55	1%
Japan	306.65	5%	Saudi Arabia	73.93	1%
India	243.28	4%	Netherlands	64.35	1%
Germany	229.93	4%	Indonesia	64.34	1%
Ukraine	152.39	2%	Taiwan	63.01	1%
Canada	150.90	2%	Turkey	49.96	1%
Italy	121.28	2%	Thailand	44.57	1%
France	108.59	2%	Argentina	39.49	1%
Korea, South	107.49	2%	Venezuela	37.94	1%
Ukraine	104.30	2%	Belgium	37.90	1%
Mexico	100.56	2%	Egypt	33.49	1%
South Africa	99.45	2%	Korea, North	33.43	1%
Australia	93.90	2%	UAE	32.19	1%

Table 4: Growth of CO_2 Emissions (as C), 1990-99 - Selected Countries

Country	% change	Country	% change
World Total	5%		
Taiwan	97%	Japan	14%
Korea, South	77%	New Zealand	13%
Singapore	58%	United States	12%
India	56%	Netherlands	12%
Indonesia	55%	China	8%
Brazil	42%	Italy	8%
Argentina	39%	Sweden	7%
Spain	32%	France	6%
Australia	30%	Nigeria	6%
Norway	27%	Switzerland	0%
Saudi Arabia	26%	United Kingdom	-7%
Mexico	20%	Germany (1991-99)	-8%
Canada	18%	Finland	-10%
Austria	15%	Russia (1992-99)	-30%

Table 5: Per Capita CO_2 Emissions (as C), 1999 - Selected Countries

Country	MT/cap		MT/cap
Qatar	14.2	**World Total**	1.0
Singapore	6.4		
United States	5.6	**North America**	4.4
Australia	5.0	**Western Europe**	2.1
Canada	4.9	**E. Europe & Former U.S.S.R.**	2.0
Germany	2.8	**Middle East**	1.8
Russia	2.7	**Central and S. America**	0.6
United Kingdom	2.6	**Far East and Oceania**	0.5
Japan	2.4	**Africa**	0.3
France	1.8		
Sweden	1.8		
Switzerland	1.7		
Brazil	0.5		
China	0.5		
Indonesia	0.3		
India	0.2		
Pakistan	0.2		
Bangladesh	0.1		
Sierra Leone	0.1		

Table 6: CO_2 Emissions (as C) per '000 Dollars of GDP, 1999 Selected Countries

Country	MT/000$	Country	MT/000$
Azerbaijan	2.46	Canada	0.21
Russia	1.11	United States	0.20
Qatar	1.02	Brazil	0.15
China	0.72	United Kingdom	0.13
India	0.51	Germany	0.12
Pakistan	0.48	Japan	0.09
Indonesia	0.40	France	0.08
Singapore	0.36	Sweden	0.06
Australia	0.22	Switzerland	0.05
Bangladesh	0.22	Burkina Faso	0.03

Figure 10: Canada's Historical Emissions of CO_2 ('000 MT)

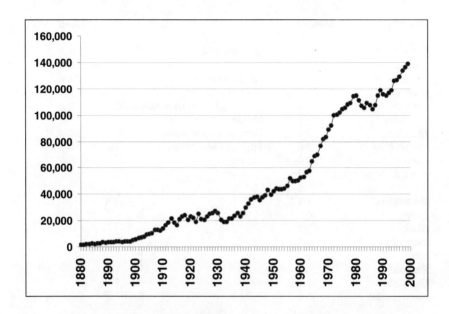

Figure 11: U.S. Historical Emissions of CO_2 ('000 MT)

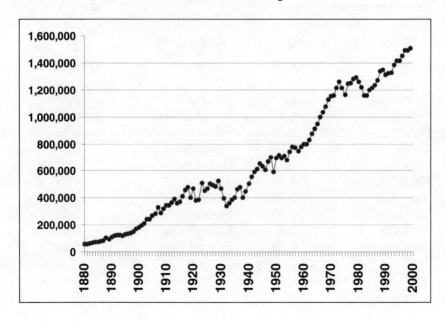

Table 7: Major GHG Producers in Canada

COMPANY	SECTOR	1990	1997	1998
		in MT CO2 equivalent		
Ontario Hydro	electricity generation	26.0	22.8	31.0
TransAlta	electricity generation	25.8	24.1	23.4
TransCanada	Pipelines; electricity generation	10.4	16.6	17.3
SaskPower	electricity generation	10.6	14.4	14.7
Imperial Oil	Oil & gas production & refining; chemicals	10.8	11.5	10.8
New Brunswick Power	electricity generation	6.3	8.6	9.7
ATCO Electric	electricity generation	7.7	10.1	9.5
Syncrude Canada	Oil & gas production	7.2	8.5	8.9
EPCOR	electricity generation	3.5	7.5	8.6
Nova Scotia Power	electricity generation	6.8	7.8	8.0
Shell Canada	Oil & gas production & refining	7.6	7.6	7.3
Petro-Canada	Oil & gas production & refining	6.9	7.3	6.9
Amoco Canada Petroluem	Oil & gas production	6.3	n.a.	6.6
Husky Oil Operations	Oil & gas production & refining	3.8	6.5	6.5
Suncor Energy	Oil & gas production & refining	5.0	5.7	6.2
DuPont Canada	Chemicals	11.2	10.4	5.4
Westcoast Energy	Pipelines; natural gas utility; electricity generation	4.1	5.4	5.2

Figure 12: China's Recent Emissions of CO_2 from Fossil Fuels

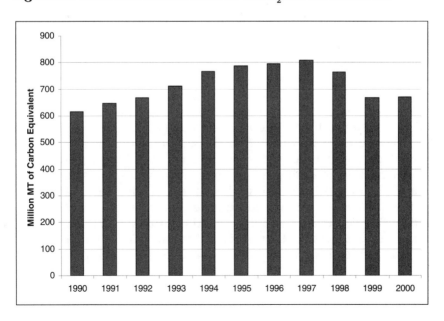

Figure 13: Germany's Recent Emissions of CO$_2$ from Fossil Fuels

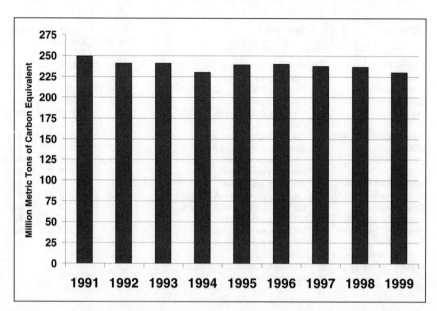

bile ownership among several countries and recent growth in car registrations (Ward's, 2000, 2001a,b). Since the transportation sector is one of the principal users of material and energy resources and generators of greenhouse gases, this shift in consumer taste and buying power will tend to be retrogressive in the quest for sustainability.

The third is the increasing pressure on agricultural lands to feed a population growing in numbers and affluence. Recent research suggests that this pressure will have major negative feedback effects on ecological systems and ultimately food production (Tilman, 2001).

The fourth issue which counsels caution in the interpretation of potential movement toward a more sustainable industrial system arises from recent pathbreaking research by the World Resources Institute on material outflows from industrial economies (WRI, 2000). In this report which focuses on five industrialized countries (Austria, Germany, Japan, The Netherlands and the U.S.), the authors conclude that while significant progress has been made in "decoupling between economic growth and resource throughput . . . on a per capita and per unit GDP basis, . . . overall resource use and waste flows in to the environment continued to grow."

Table 8: Projections of Global Energy Consumption and Carbon Dioxide Emissions

Energy Consumption in Quadrillion Btu

REGION	1990	1999	2010	2020
Industrialized	182.4	209.6	243.4	270.4
EE/FSU	76.3	50.5	60.3	72.3
Developing				
Asia	51.0	70.9	113.4	162.2
Middle East	13.1	19.3	26.9	37.2
Africa	9.3	11.8	16.1	20.8
Central & S. America	13.7	19.8	29.6	44.1
Subtotal	87.2	121.8	186.1	264.4
World	346.0	381.8	489.7	607.1

Carbon Dioxide Emssions in Million Metric Tons of Carbon Equivalent

REGION	1990	1999	2010	2020
Industrialized	2,842	3,122	3,619	4,043
EE/FSU	1,337	810	940	1,094
Developing				
Asia	1,053	1,361	2,137	3,013
Middle East	231	330	451	627
Africa	179	218	294	373
Central & S. America	178	249	394	611
Subtotal	1,641	2,158	3,276	4,624
World	5,821	6,091	7,835	9,762

Source: U.S. EIA

Table 9: Motor Vehicle Registrations - 1999

REGION	Passenger	Commercial	Total	Population (millions)	Pop/Car
Western Europe	182,397,776	25,456,628	207,854,404	390.2	2.1
Pacific	11,964,775	2,972,163	14,936,938	29.2	2.4
North America	146,011,461	92,609,997	238,621,458	405.3	2.8
Eastern Europe	21,259,292	3,556,078	24,815,370	155.6	7.3
Central & S. America	25,865,275	8,537,709	34,402,984	375.8	14.5
Middle East	13,047,916	5,855,555	18,903,471	290.0	22.2
Caribbean	1,560,800	522,795	2,083,595	36.0	23.1
Far East	81,385,752	45,534,024	126,919,776	3,251.8	40.0
Africa	8,104,743	5,156,072	13,260,815	660.6	81.5
WORLD	**491,597,790**	**190,201,021**	**681,798,811**	**5,594.6**	**11.4**

Table 10: Growth in Passenger Car Registrations - 1997-98

COUNTRY	1997	1998	Population ('000)	% increase 97-98
WORLD	**452,101,260**	**477,095,800**	**5,913,286**	**5.53**
Indonesia	409,800	491,457	209,255	19.93
Iran	572,925	684,500	66,796	19.47
China	2,493,700	2,940,243	1,266,838	17.91
Korea, South	6,694,100	7,850,926	46,480	17.28
Brazil	9,385,800	10,828,765	167,988	15.37
Thailand	1,509,900	1,712,900	60,856	13.44
Malaysia	2,102,400	2,373,200	21,830	12.88
Philippines	671,007	749,204	74,454	11.65
Argentina	3,137,500	3,468,082	36,577	10.54
Japan	45,861,700	50,353,749	126,505	9.79
India	4,446,500	4,820,000	998,056	8.40
Taiwan	4,201,000	4,536,605	22,113	7.99
Australia	7,785,800	8,400,102	18,705	7.89
United States	125,965,709	131,838,538	276,218	4.66
Canada	13,300,000	13,887,270	30,857	4.42
United Kingdom	21,881,000	22,115,000	58,744	1.07
Germany	41,371,992	41,673,781	82,178	0.73

CONCLUSION

So, what is the bottom line? Is sustainability achievable in the near to midterm future? The answer is almost certainly no, given the convergence of several critical factors. Included among these are: continued population growth, the nature of current technology, the structure of industrial production, market-driven incentives which favour current consumption over investment, and prevailing social values and attitudes. None of these, however, precludes the necessity for individuals, governments and especially corporations from modifying their behaviour in a manner which moves us off, even incrementally, our current path of non-sustainability. Failure to do so will surely foreclose ecological options, accelerate environmental degradation, and increase the probability of our being faced with a serious and potentially irreversible ecological crisis which threatens the viability of the human endeavour and the planet on which we live.

FOOTNOTE

1. The 38 industrialized nations required to reduce their greenhouse gas emissions (carbon dioxide, methane, nitrous oxide, hydrofluorocarbons, perfluorocarbons and sulphur hexafluoride) under the Kyoto Accord are: Australia, Austria, Belgium, Bulgaria, Canada, Croatia, Czech Republic, Denmark, Estonia, Finland, France, Germany, Greece, Hungary, Iceland, Ireland, Italy, Japan, Latvia, Liechtenstein, Lithuania, Luxembourg, Monaco, Netherlands, New Zealand, Norway, Poland, Portugal, Romania, Russian Federation, Slovakia, Slovenia, Spain, Sweden, Switzerland, Ukraine, the United Kingdom, and the United States (UN, 1998).

REFERENCES CITED

Ahmad, Yusuf J., Salah El Serafy and Ernst Lutz (1989) *Environmental Accounting for Sustainable Development*, UNEP-World Bank.

Ayres, Robert U. and Leslie W. Ayres (1996) *Industrial Ecology. Towards Closing the Materials Cycle*, Edward Elgar.

Bennett, Martin and Peter James (eds.) (1998) *The Green Bottom Line. Environmental Accounting for Management*, Greenleaf Publishing.

Bovard, James (1995) "Archer Daniels Midland: A Case Study in Corporate Welfare," Case Policy Analysis No. 241, Cato Institute, September 26.

Bramley, Matthew (2000) *Greenhouse Emissions from Industrial Companies in Canada: 1998*, October.

Brander, James and Scott Taylor (1998) "The Simple Economics of Easter

Island: A Ricardo-Malthus Model of Renewable Resource Use, *American Economic Review,* Volume 88 (March), pp. 119-138.

Broecker, Wallace S. (1987) "Unpleasant Surprises in the Greenhouse?" *Nature,* July 9, pp. 123-126.

Canada, Tradeable Permits Working Group (2000) *Using Tradeable Emissions Permits To Help Achieve Domestic Greenhouse Gas Objectives. Options Report,* National Climate Change Process, April.

Carson, Rachel (1962) *Silent Spring,* Houghton Mifflin.

Chambers et al. (1979) "Gasohol: Does It or Doesn't It Produce Positive Net Energy?" *Science,* November 16, pp. 789-795.

Congressional Budget Office (CBO) (1994) "Greening the National Accounts," CBP Papers, March.

Costanza, Robert et al. (1997) "The Value of the World's Ecosystem Services and Natural Capital," *Nature,* Vol. 387, 15 May, pp. 253-260.

Daily, Gretchen (ed.) (1997) *Nature's Services. Societal Dependence on Natural Ecosystems,* Island Press.

Diamond, Jared (1995) "Easter's End," *Discover,* August, pp. 62-69.

Diamond, Jared (1999) *Guns, Germs and Steel. The Fates of Human Societies,* W.W. Norton & Company.

Ditz, Daryl, Janet Ranganathan and R. Darryl Banks (1995) *Green Ledgers: Case Studies in Corporate Environmental Accounting,* World Resources Institute.

Eisner, Robert (1994) *The Misunderstood Economy. What Counts and How to Count It.* Harvard Business School Press.

Epstein, Paul R. et al. (1998) "Biological and Physical Signs of Climate Change: Focus on Mosquito-borne Diseases," *Bulletin of the American Meteorological Society,* Vol. 79, No. 3, March, pp.409-417.

Fischer, Gunther, Mahendra Shah, Harrij van Velthuizen and Freddy O. Nachtergaele (2001) *Global Agro-ecological Assessment for Agriculture in the 21st Century,* IIASA.

Freund, Peter and George Martin (1993) *The Ecology of the Automobile,* Black Rose Books.

Gilliland, Martha W. (ed.) (1978) *Energy Analysis: A New Public Policy Tool,* Westview Press.

Goldenberg, Stanley B., Christopher W. Landsea, Alberto M. Mestas-Nunez, and William M. Gray (2001) "The Recent Increase in Atlantic Hurricane Activity: Causes and Implications, *Science,* Vol. 293, July 20, pp. 474-479.

Graedel, T.E. and B.R. Allenby (1995) *Industrial Ecology,* Prentice Hall.

Holling, C.S. (1973) "Resilience and Stability of Ecological Systems," *Annual Review of Ecology and Systematics,* Volume 4, pp. 1-23.

Hopkinson, C.S. and J. W. Day Jr. (1980) "Net Energy Analysis of Alcohol Production from Sugarcane," *Science,* Vol. 207, (January 18) pp.

302-304.

Institute for Energy Studies, Stanford University (IES) and TRW Systems Group (1975) *NSF-Stanford Workshop on Net Energy Analysis*, August 25-28.

International Center for Technology Assessment (CTA) (2000) *The Real Price of Gasoline*, Report No. 3.

Kackson, Jeremy B.C. et al. (2001) "Historical Overfishing and the Recent Collapse of Coastal Ecosystems," *Science*, Vol. 293, July 27, pp. 638.

Jacobs, Michael (1993) "Symbols of Revolt: Environmental Politics and Beyond," address to The Vancouver Institute, September 25.

Justus, John R. and Susan R. Fletcher (2001) "Global Climate Change," Congressional Research Service, The Library of Congress, June 22.

Lutz, Ernst (ed.) (1993) *Toward Improved Accounting for the Environment*, UNSTAT-World Bank.

MacKenzie, James J., Roger C. Dower and Donald D.T. Chen (1992) *The Going Rate: What it Really Costs to Drive*, World Resources Institute.

Matthews, Emily et al. (2000) *The Weight of Nations. Material Outflows from Industrial Economies*, World Resources Institute.

McNeill, J.R. (2000) *Something New Under the Sun. An Environmental History of the Twentieth-Century World*, W.W. Norton & Company.

Mellon, Margaret. Charles Benbrook and Karen Lutz Benbrook (2001) *Hogging It. Estimates of Antimicrobial Abuse in Livestock*, Union of Concerned Scientists.

Miller, Peter and John Moffet (1993) *The Price of Mobility. Uncovering the Hidden Costs of Transportation*, Natural Resources Defense Council, October.

National Research Council (NRC) (1999) *Ozone-Forming Potential of Reformulated Gasoline*, Commission on Geosciences, Environment and Resources, National Academy Press.

National Research Council (NRC) (2001) "Climate Change Science. An Analysis of Some Key Questions," Committee on the Science of Climate Change, Division of Earth and Life Sciences, National Academy Press.

National Round Table on the Environment and the Economy (NRTEE) (1999) *Measuring Eco-efficiency in Business: Feasibility of a Core Set of Indicators*.

Nattrass, Brian and Mary Altomare (1999) *The Natural Step for Business. Wealth, Ecology and the Evolutionary Corporation*, New Society Publishers.

Natural Resources Defense Council (NRDC) (2001) "China is Aggressively Reducing its Carbon Dioxide Emissions," www.nrdc.org/globalwarming/achinagg.asp.

New York Times (NYT) (1996) "It's Dwayne's World – Archer Daniel's Influence is Wide as Well as Deep," January 16.

New York Times (NYT) 2001) "178 Nations reach a climate Accord: U.S. only looks on," page A1.

Nordhaus, William D. and Edward C. Kiokkelenberg (eds.) (1999) *Nature's Numbers. Expanding the National Economic Accounts to Include the Environment*, National Academy Press.

Oak Ridge National Laboratory (2000) "Global, Regional, and National CO_2 Emissions for Fossil Fuel Burning, Cement Production and Gas Flaring: 1751-1997, August. Website: http://cdiac.esd.ornl.gov/trends/emis_cont.052199.htm.

Office of Technology Assessment (OTA) (1995) *Impacts of Antibiotic-Resistant Bacteria*, Congress of the United States.

Pauly, Daniel (1999) "Global Fisheries and Marine Conservation: Is Co-existence Possible?" Address to The Vancouver Institute, November 6.

Pembina Institute and The David Suzuki Foundation (2001) *Climate-Friendly Hydrogen Fuel*.

Pezzey, John (1992) *Sustainable Development Concepts. An Economic Analysis*, World Bank, Environment Paper Number 2.

Ponting, Clive (1991) *A Green History of the World. The Environment and the Collapse of Great Civilizations*. Penguin Books.

Redefining Progress (RP) (1999) *Why Bigger Isn't Better: The Genuine Progress Indicator – 1999 Update*, November.

Repetto, Robert et al. (1989) *Wasting Assets: Natural Resources in the National Income Accounts*, World Resources Institute, June.

Rodenburg, Eric, Dan Tunstall and Frederik van Bolhuis (1995) *Environmental Indicators for Global Cooperation*, UNDP, UNEP and the World Bank, working paper number 11.

Rubenstein, Daniel Blake (1994) *Environmental Accounting for the Sustainable Corporation. Strategies and Techniques*. Quorom Books.

Schmidheiny, Stephan (1992) *Changing Course. A Global Business Perspective on Development and the Environment*, The MIT Press.

Serageldin, Ismail and Andrew Steer (eds.) (1993) *Valuing the Environment*, Proceedings of the First Annual International Conference on Environmentally Sustainable Development, The World Bank.

Speer Lisa, et al. (1997) *Hook, Line and Sinking. The Crisis in Marine Fisheries*, Natural Resources Defense Council, February.

Tilman, David et al. (2001) "Forecasting Agriculturally Driven Global Environmental Change," *Science*, Vol. 292, April 13, pp. 281-284.

U.S. Department of Agriculture (USDA) (1988) *Ethanol: Economic and Policy Tradeoffs*.

U.S. Energy Information Administration (US EIA) (2001a) *International*

Energy Outlook 2001, March.

U.S. Energy Information Administration (US EIA) (2001b) "International Energy-Related Information: Carbon Dioxide Emissions. Website: http://www.eia.gov/emeu/international/environm.html.

U.S. Environmental Protection Agency (EPA) (1995) "An Introduction to Environmental Accounting as a Business Management Tool: Key Concepts and Terms."

United Nations (UN) (1993) *Integrated Environmental and Economic Accounting.*

United Nations (UN) (1998) "Framework Convention on Climate Change, Report of the Conference of the Parties On its Third Session, Held at Kyoto from 1 to 11 December," Addendum, Part Two: Action Taken by the Conference of the Parties at its Third Session.

Van Dieren, Wouter (ed.) (1995) *Taking Nature Into Account*. A Report to the Club of Rome, Copernicus.

Wackernagel, Mathis et al. (1997) "Ecological Footprints of Nations," March 10.

Wackernagel, Mathis et al. (2001) "Ecological Footprints of Nations. How Much Nature Do They Use? How Much Nature Do They Have?" http://www.ecouncil.ac.cr/rio/focus/report/english/footprint.

Wackernagel, Mathis and William Rees (1996) *Our Ecological Footprint. Reducing Human Impact on the Earth*, New Society Publishers.

Ward's Communications (2000) *Motor Vehicle Facts & Figures, 2000.*

Ward's Communications (2001) *Motor Vehicle Facts & Figures, 2001.*

Ward's Communications (2001) *World Motor Vehicle Data, 2000 edition.*

Wigley, T.M.L. and S.C.B. Raper (2001) "Interpretation of High Projections for Global-Mean Warming," *Science*, Vol. 293, July 20, pp. 451-454.

Winstanley, Gil, Brian Emmett, Bert McInnis, Brenda Siegel and Murray Randall (1977) *Energy Requirements Associated With Selected Canadian Energy Developments*, Office of Energy Conservation, Energy, Mines and Resources Canada.

World Commission on Environment and Development (WCED) (1987) *Our Common Future*. Oxford University Press.

World Wildlife Fund WWF, UNEP, Redefining Progress, Center for Sustainability Studies (2000) *Living Planet Report 2000.*

OTHER USEFUL REFERENCES ON BUSINESS AND THE ENVIRONMENT

Aldrich, James R. (1996) *Pollution Prevention Economics: Financial Impacts on Business and Industry*, McGraw-Hill.

Arnold, Matthew B. and Robert M. Day (1998) *The next bottom line: making sustainable development tangible,* World Resources Institute.

Bansal, Pratima and Elizabeth Howard (eds.) (1997) *Business and the Natural Environment,* Butterworth Heinemann.

Buchholz, Rogene A. (1993) *Principles of Environmental Management: the Greening of Business,* Prentice-Hall.

Buchholz, Rogene A. et al. (1992) *Managing Environmental Issues: A Casebook,* Prentice-Hall.

Cairncross, Frances (1995) *Green, Inc. A Guide to Business and the Environment,* Island Press.

Cairncross, Francis (1992) *Costing the Earth: The Challenge for Governments, the Opportunities for Business,* Harvard Business School Press.

Ciambrone, David F. (1996) *Waste Minimization as a Strategic Weapon,* CRC Lewis Publishers.

Coddington, Walter (1993) *Environmental Marketing. Positive Strategies for Reaching the Green Consumer,* McGraw-Hill.

Crosbie, Liz and Ken Knight (1995) *Strategy for Sustainable Business. Environmental Opportunity and Strategic Choice,* McGraw-Hill.

Denton, D. Keith (1994) *Enviro-Management. How Smart Companies Turn Environmental Costs into Profits,* Prentice Hall.

Desimone, Livio D. and Frank Popoff (1997) *Eco-efficiency. The Business Links to Sustainable Development,* The MIT Press.

Ditz, Daryl and Janet Ranganathan (1997) *Measuring Up. Toward a Common framework for tracking environmental performance,* World Resources Institute, July.

Durnil, Gordon K. (1995) *The Making of a Conservative Environmentalist,* Indiana University Press.

Elkington, John (1998) *Cannibals with Forks. The Triple Bottom Line of 21st Century Business,* New Society Publishers.

Fischer, Kurt and Johan Schot (eds.) (1993) *Environmental Strategies for Industry,* Island Press.

Fussler, Claude and Peter James (1996) *Driving Eco-Innovation. A Breakthrough Discipline for Innovation and Sustainability,* Pitman Publishing.

Harvard Business Review (2000) *On Business and the Environment,* Harvard Business School Press.

Hawken, Paul (1993) *The Ecology of Commerce,* HarperBusiness.

Hawkin, Paul, Amory Lovins and Hunter Lovins (1999) *Natural Capitalism: Creating the Next Industrial Revolution,* Little Brown & Co.

Hillary, Ruth (ed.) (1997) *Environmental Management Systems and Cleaner Production,* John Wiley & Sons.

Hunt, David and Catherine Johnson (1995) *Environmental Management Systems. Principles and Practice,* McGraw-Hill.

Ibbotson, Brett and John-David Phyper (1996) *Environmental Manage-*

ment in Canada, McGraw-Hill Ryerson.

International Institute for Sustainable Development (IISD),Deloitte & Touche, and Business Council for Sustainable Development (n.d.) *Business Strategy for Sustainable Development. Leadership and Accountability for the '90s.*

Kinlaw, Dennis C. (1993) *Competitive and Green. Sustainable Performance in the Environmental Age*, Pfeiffer & Co.

Makower, Joel (1994) *The E-Factor. The Bottom-Line Approach to Environmentally Responsible Business*, Tilden Press.

McInerney, Francis and Sean White (1995) *The Total Quality Corporation. How 10 Major Companies Added to Profits and Cleaned up the Environment in the 1990s*, Truman Talley Books/Plume.

North, Klaus (1997) *Environmental Business Management. An Introduction.* 2nd edition, ILO.

Piasecki, Bruce W. (1995) *Corporate Environmental Strategy. The Avalanche of Change Since Bhopal*, John Wiley & Sons.

Piasecki, Bruce W., Kevin A. Fletcher and Frank J. Mendelson (1999) *Environmental Management and Business Strategy. Leadership Skills for the 21st Century*, John Wiley & Sons.

Romm, Joseph J. (1994) *Lean and Clean Management. How to Boost Profits and Productivity by Reducing Pollution*, Kodansha International.

Romm, Joseph J. (1999) *Cool Companies. How the Best Businesses Boost Profits and Productivity by Cutting Greenhouse Gas Emissions*, Island Press.

Seemer, Stephen W. (ed.) (1996) *Environmental ROI. Successful Techniques in Cost Avoidance*, John Wiley & Sons.

Sharratt, Paul (ed.) (1995) *Environmental Management Systems*, Institute of Chemical Engineers.

Shrivastava, Paul (1996) *Greening Business. Profiting the Corporation and the Environment*, Thomson Executive Press.

Smart, Bruce (1992) *Beyond Compliance: A New Industry View of the Environment*, World Resources Institute, April.

Smith, Denis (ed.) (1993) *Business and the Environment. Implications of the New Environmentalism*, Palgrave.

Von Weizsacker, Ernst, Amory B. Lovins and L. Hunter Lovins (1997) *Factor Four. Doubling Wealth, Halving Resource Use.* Earthscan.

Welford, Richard (1997) *Corporate Environmental Management 2: Culture and Organizations*, Earthscan.

ACKNOWLEDGMENT

The author would like to express his appreciation to his colleague, Dr. Les Lavkulich, Director of the Institute of Resources and Ecology at UBC for his insightful comments on an earlier draft of this paper. Any errors remain the responsibility of the author.

IS HUMANITY SUICIDAL?

Edward O. Wilson
Frank B. Baird Jr. Professor of Science, Harvard University

Imagine that on an icy moon of Jupiter — say, Ganymede — the space station of an alien civilization is concealed. For millions of years its scientists have closely watched the earth. Because their law prevents settlement on a living planet, they have tracked the surface by means of satellites equipped with sophisticated sensors, mapping the spread of large assemblages of organisms, from forests, grasslands and tundras to coral reefs and the vast planktonic meadows of the sea. They have recorded millennial cycles in the climate, interrupted by the advance and retreat of glaciers and scattershot volcanic eruptions.

The watchers have been waiting for what might be called the Moment. When it comes, occupying only a few centuries and thus a mere tick in geological time, the forests shrink back to less than half their original cover. Atmospheric carbon dioxide rises to the highest level in 100,000 years. The ozone layer of the stratosphere thins, and holes open at the poles. Plumes of nitrous oxide and other toxins rise from fires in South America and Africa, settle in the upper troposphere and drift eastward across the oceans. At night the land surface brightens with millions of pinpoints of light, which coalesce into blazing swaths across Europe, Japan and eastern North America. A semicircle of fire spreads from gas flares around the Persian Gulf.

It was all but inevitable, the watchers might tell us if we met them, that from the great diversity of large animals, one species or another would eventually gain intelligent control of Earth. That role has fallen to Homo sapiens, a primate risen in Africa from a lineage that split away from the chimpanzee line five to eight million years ago. Unlike any creature that lived before, we have become a geophysical force, swiftly changing the atmosphere and climate as well as the composition of the world's fauna and flora. Now in the midst of a population explosion, the human species has doubled to 5.5 billion during the past 50 years. It is scheduled to double again in the next 50 years. No other single species in evolutionary history has even remotely approached the sheer mass in protoplasm generated by humanity.

Darwin's dice have rolled badly for Earth. It was a misfortune for the living world in particular, many scientists believe, that a carnivorous primate and not some more benign form of animal made the breakthrough. Our species retains hereditary traits that add greatly to our destructive impact. We are tribal and aggressively territorial, intent on private space beyond minimal requirements and oriented by selfish sexual and reproductive drives. Cooperation beyond the family and tribal levels comes hard.

Worse, our liking for meat causes us to use the sun's energy at low efficiency. It is a general rule of ecology that (very roughly) only about 10 percent of the sun's energy captured by photosynthesis to produce plant tissue is converted into energy in the tissue of herbivores, the animals that eat the plants. Of that amount, 10 percent reaches the tissue of the carnivores feeding on the herbivores. Similarly, only 10 percent is transferred to carnivores that eat carnivores. And so on for another step or two. In a wetlands chain that runs from marsh grass to grasshopper to warbler to hawk, the energy captured during green production shrinks a thousandfold.

In other words, it takes a great deal of grass to support a hawk. Human beings, like hawks, are top carnivores, at the end of the food chain whenever they eat meat, two or more links removed from the plants; if chicken, for example, two links, and if tuna, four links. Even with most societies confined today to a mostly vegetarian diet, humanity is gobbling up a large part of the rest of the living world. We appropriate between 20 and 40 percent of the sun's energy that would otherwise be fixed into the tissue of natural vegetation, principally by our consumption of crops and timber, construction of buildings and roadways and the creation of wastelands. In the relentless search for more food, we have reduced animal life in lakes, rivers and now, increasingly, the open ocean. And everywhere we pollute the air and water, lower water tables and extinguish species.

The human species is, in a word, an environmental abnormality. It is possible that intelligence in the wrong kind of species was foreordained to be a fatal combination for the biosphere. Perhaps a law of evolution is that intelligence usually extinguishes itself.

This admittedly dour scenario is based on what can be termed the juggernaut theory of human nature, which holds that people are programmed by their genetic heritage to be so selfish that a sense of global responsibility will come too late. Individuals place themselves first, family second, tribe third and the rest of the world a distant fourth. Their genes also predispose them to plan ahead for one or two generations at most. They fret over the petty problems and conflicts of their daily lives and respond swiftly and often ferociously to slight challenges to their status and tribal security. But oddly, as psychologists have discovered, people also tend to underestimate both the likelihood and impact of such natural disasters as major earthquakes and great storms.

The reason for this myopic fog, evolutionary biologists contend, is that it was actually advantageous during all but the last few millennia of the two million years of existence of the genus Homo. The brain evolved into its present form during this long stretch of evolutionary time, during which people existed in small, preliterate hunter-gatherer bands. Life was precarious and short. A premium was placed on close attention to the near future and early reproduction, and little else. Disasters of a magnitude that occur only once every few centuries were forgotten or transmuted into myth. So today the mind still works comfortably backward and forward for only a few years, spanning a period not exceeding one or two generations. Those in past ages whose genes inclined them to short-term thinking lived longer and had more children than those who did not. Prophets never enjoyed a Darwinian edge.

The rules have recently changed, however. Global crises are rising within the life span of the generation now coming of age, a foreshortening that may explain why young people express more concern about the environment than do their elders. The time scale has contracted because of the exponential growth in both the human population and technologies impacting the environment. Exponential growth is basically the same as the increase of wealth by compound interest. The larger the population, the faster the growth; the faster the growth, the sooner the population becomes still larger. In Nigeria, to cite one of our more fecund nations, the population is expected to double from its 1988 level to 216 million by the year 2010. If the same rate of growth were to continue to 2110, its population would exceed that of the entire present population of the world.

With people everywhere seeking a better quality of life, the search for resources is expanding even faster than the population. The demand is being met by an increase in scientific knowledge, which doubles every 10 to 15 years. It is accelerated further by a parallel rise in environment-devouring technology. Because Earth is finite in many resources that determine the quality of life — including arable soil, nutrients, fresh water and space for natural ecosystems — doubling of consumption at constant time intervals can bring disaster with shocking suddenness. Even when a nonrenewable resource has been only half used, it is still only one interval away from the end. Ecologists like to make this point with the French riddle of the lily pond. At first there is only one lily pad in the pond, but the next day it doubles, and thereafter each of its descendants doubles. The pond completely fills with lily pads in 30 days. When is the pond exactly half full? Answer: on the 29th day.   Yet, mathematical exercises aside, who can safely measure the human capacity to overcome the perceived limits of Earth? The question of central interest is this: Are we racing to the brink of an abyss, or are we just gathering speed for a takeoff to a wonderful future? The crystal ball is clouded; the human condition baffles all the more because it is both unprecedented and bizarre, almost beyond understanding.

In the midst of uncertainty, opinions on the human prospect have tended to fall loosely into two schools. The first, exemptionalism, holds that since humankind is transcendent in intelligence and spirit, so must our species have been released from the iron laws of ecology that bind all other species. No matter how serious the problem, civilized human beings, by ingenuity, force of will and — who knows — divine dispensation, will find a solution.

Population growth? Good for the economy, claim some of the exemptionalists, and in any case a basic human right, so let it run. Land shortages? Try fusion energy to power the desalting of sea water, then reclaim the world's deserts. (The process might be assisted by towing icebergs to coastal pipelines.) Species going extinct? Not to worry. That is nature's way. Think of humankind as only the latest in a long line of exterminating agents in geological time. In any case, because our species has pulled free of old-style, mindless Nature, we have begun a different order of life. Evolution should now be allowed to proceed along this new trajectory. Finally, resources? The planet has more than enough resources to last indefinitely, if human genius is allowed to address each new problem in turn, without alarmist and unreasonable restrictions imposed on economic development. So hold the course, and touch the brakes lightly.

The opposing idea of reality is environmentalism, which sees humanity as a biological species tightly dependent on the natural world. As formidable as our intellect may be and as fierce our spirit, the argument goes, those qualities are not enough to free us from the constraints of the natural environment in which our human ancestors evolved. We cannot draw confidence from successful solutions to the smaller problems of the past. Many of Earth's vital resources are about to be exhausted, its atmospheric chemistry is deteriorating and human populations have already grown dangerously large. Natural ecosystems, the wellsprings of a healthful environment, are being irreversibly degraded.

At the heart of the environmentalist world view is the conviction that human physical and spiritual health depends on sustaining the planet in a relatively unaltered state. Earth is our home in the full, genetic sense, where humanity and its ancestors existed for all the millions of years of their evolution. Natural ecosystems — forests, coral reefs, marine blue waters — maintain the world exactly as we would wish it to be maintained. When we debase the global environment and extinguish the variety of life, we are dismantling a support system that is too complex to understand, let alone replace, in the foreseeable future. Space scientists theorize the existence of a virtually unlimited array of other planetary environments, almost all of which are uncongenial to human life. Our own Mother Earth, lately called Gaia, is a specialized conglomerate of organisms and the physical environment they create on a day-to-day basis, which can be destabilized and turned lethal by careless activity. We run the risk, conclude the environmentalists, of beaching ourselves upon alien shores like a great confused pod of pilot whales.

If I have not done so enough already by tone of voice, I will now place myself solidly in the environmentalist school, but not so radical as to wish a turning back of the clock, not given to driving spikes into Douglas firs to prevent logging and distinctly uneasy with such hybrid movements as ecofeminism, which holds that Mother Earth is a nurturing home for all life and should be revered and loved as in premodern (paleolithic and archaic) societies and that ecosystematic abuse is rooted in androcentric— that is to say, male-dominated — concepts, values and institutions. Still, however soaked in androcentric culture, I am radical enough to take seriously the question heard with increasing frequency: Is humanity suicidal? Is the drive to environmental conquest and self-propagation embedded so deeply in our genes as to be unstoppable?

My short answer — opinion if you wish — is that humanity is not suicidal, at least not in the sense just stated. We are smart enough and have time enough to avoid an environmental catastrophe of civilization-threatening dimensions. But the technical problems are sufficiently formidable to require a redirection of much of science and technology, and the ethical issues are so basic as to force are consideration of our self-image as a species.

There are reasons for optimism, reasons to believe that we have entered what might someday be generously called the Century of the Environment. The United Nations Conference on Environment and Development, held in Rio de Janeiro in June 1992, attracted more than 120 heads of government, the largest number ever assembled, and helped move environmental issues closer to the political center stage; on Nov. 18, 1992, more than 1,500 senior scientists from 69 countries issued a 'Warning to Humanity,' stating that overpopulation and environmental deterioration put the very future of life at risk. The greening of religion has become a global trend, with theologians and religious leaders addressing environmental problems as a moral issue. In May 1992, leaders of most of the major American denominations met with scientists as guests of members of the United States Senate to formulate a 'Joint Appeal by Religion and Science for the environment.' Conservation of biodiversity is increasingly seen by both national governments and major landowners as important to their country's future. Indonesia, home to a large part of the native Asian plant and animal species, has begun to shift to land-management practices that conserve and sustainably develop the remaining rain forests. Costa Rica has created a National Institute of Biodiversity. A pan-African institute for biodiversity research and management has been founded, with headquarters in Zimbabwe.

Finally, there are favorable demographic signs. The rate of population increase is declining on all continents, although it is still well above zero almost everywhere and remains especially high in sub-Saharan Africa. Despite entrenched traditions and religious beliefs, the desire to use contraceptives in family planning is spreading. Demographers estimate that if the demand were fully met, this action alone would reduce the eventual stabilized population by more than two billion.

In summary, the will is there. Yet the awful truth remains that a large part of humanity will suffer no matter what is done. The number of people living in absolute poverty has risen during the past 20 years to nearly one billion and is expected to increase another 100 million by the end of the decade. Whatever progress has been made in the developing countries, and that includes an overall improvement in the average standard of living, is threatened by a continuance of rapid population growth and the deterioration of forests and arable soil.

Our hopes must be chastened further still, and this is in my opinion the central issue, by a key and seldom-recognized distinction between the nonliving and living environments. Science and the political process can be adapted to manage the nonliving, physical environment. The human hand is now upon the physical homeostat. The ozone layer can be mostly restored to the upper atmosphere by elimination of CFC's, with these substances peaking at six times the present level and then subsiding during the next half century. Also, with procedures that will prove far more difficult and initially expensive, carbon dioxide and other greenhouse gases can be pulled back to concentrations that slow global warming.

The human hand, however, is not upon the biological homeostat. There is no way in sight to micromanage the natural ecosystems and the millions of species they contain. That feat might be accomplished by generations to come, but then it will be too late for the ecosystems — and perhaps for us. Despite the seemingly bottomless nature of creation, humankind has been chipping away at its diversity, and Earth is destined to become an impoverished planet within a century if present trends continue. Mass extinctions are being reported with increasing frequency in every part of the world. They include half the freshwater fishes of peninsular Malaysia, 10 birds native to Cebu in the Philippines, half the 41 tree snails of Oahu, 44 of the 68 shallow-water mussels of the Tennessee River shoals, as many as 90 plant species growing on the Centinela Ridge in Ecuador, and in the United States as a whole,

about 200 plant species, with another 680 species and races now classified as in danger of extinction. The main cause is the destruction of
natural habitats, especially tropical forests. Close behind, especially on
the Hawaiian archipelago and other islands, is the introduction of rats,
pigs, beard grass, lantana and other exotic organisms that outbreed and
extirpate native species.

The few thousand biologists worldwide who specialize in diversity
are aware that they can witness and report no more than a very small
percentage of the extinctions actually occurring. The reason is that they
have facilities to keep track of only a tiny fraction of the millions of
species and a sliver of the planet's surface on a yearly basis. They have
devised a rule of thumb to characterize the situation: that whenever
careful studies are made of habitats before and after disturbance,
extinctions almost always come to light. The corollary: the great majority
of extinctions are never observed. Vast numbers of species are apparently
vanishing before they can be discovered and named.

There is a way, nonetheless, to estimate the rate of loss indirectly.
Independent studies around the world and in fresh and marine waters
have revealed a robust connection between the size of a habitat and the
amount of biodiversity it contains. Even a small loss in area reduces the
number of species. The relation is such that when the area of the habitat
is cut to a tenth of its original cover, the number of species eventually
drops by roughly one-half. Tropical rain forests, thought to harbor a
majority of Earth's species (the reason conservationists get so exercised
about rain forests), are being reduced by nearly that magnitude. At the
present time they occupy about the same area as that of the 48
conterminous United States, representing a little less than half their
original, prehistoric cover; and they are shrinking each year by about 2
percent, an amount equal to the state of Florida. If the typical value
(that is, 90 percent area loss causes 50 percent eventual extinction) is
applied, the projected loss of species due to rain forest destruction worldwide is half a percent across the board for all kinds of plants, animals
and micro organisms.

When area reduction and all the other extinction agents are
considered together, it is reasonable to project a reduction by 20 percent
or more of the rain forest species by the year 2020, climbing to 50 percent or more by midcentury, if nothing is done to change current practice. Comparable erosion is likely in other environments now under
assault, including many coral reefs and Mediterranean-type heathlands
of Western Australia, South Africa and California.

The ongoing loss will not be replaced by evolution in any period of
time that has meaning for humanity. Extinction is now proceeding thousands of times faster than the production of new species. The average

life span of a species and its descendants in past geological eras varied according to group (like mollusks or echinoderms or flowering plants) from about 1 to 10 million years. During the past 500 million years, there have been five great extinction spasms comparable to the one now being inaugurated by human expansion. The latest, evidently caused by the strike of an asteroid, ended the Age of Reptiles 66 million years ago. In each case it took more than 10 million years for evolution to completely replenish the biodiversity lost. And that was in an otherwise undisturbed natural environment. Humanity is now destroying most of the habitats where evolution can occur.

The surviving biosphere remains the great unknown of Earth in many respects. On the practical side, it is hard even to imagine what other species have to offer in the way of new pharmaceuticals, crops, fibers, petroleum substitutes and other products. We have only a poor grasp of the ecosystem services by which other organisms cleanse the water, turn soil into a fertile living cover and manufacture the very air we breathe. We sense but do not fully understand what the highly diverse natural world means to our esthetic pleasure and mental well-being.

Scientists are unprepared to manage a declining biosphere. To illustrate, consider the following mission they might be given. The last remnant of a rain forest is about to be cut over. Environmentalists are stymied. The contracts have been signed, and local landowners and politicians are intransigent. In a final desperate move, a team of biologists is scrambled in an attempt to preserve the biodiversity by extraordinary means. Their assignment is the following: collect samples of all the species of organisms quickly, before the cutting starts; maintain the species in zoos, gardens and laboratory cultures or else deep-freeze samples of the tissues in liquid nitrogen, and finally, establish the procedure by which the entire community can be reassembled on empty ground at a later date, when social and economic conditions have improved.

The biologists cannot accomplish this task, not if thousands of them came with a billion-dollar budget. They cannot even imagine how to do it. In the forest patch live legions of species: perhaps 300 birds, 500 butterflies, 200 ants, 50,000 beetles, 1,000 trees, 5,000 fungi, tens of thousands of bacteria and so on down a long roster of major groups. Each species occupies a precise niche, demanding a certain place, an exact microclimate, particular nutrients and temperature and humidity cycles with specified timing to trigger phases of the life cycle. Many, perhaps most, of the species are locked in symbioses with other species; they cannot survive and reproduce unless arrayed with their partners in the correct idiosyncratic configurations.

Even if the biologists pulled off the taxonomic equivalent of the

Manhattan Project, sorting and preserving cultures of all the species, they could not then put the community back together again. It would be like unscrambling an egg with a pair of spoons. The biology of the microorganisms needed to reanimate the soil would be mostly unknown. The pollinators of most of the flowers and the correct timing of their appearance could only be guessed. The 'assembly rules,' the sequence in which species must be allowed to colonize in order to coexist indefinitely, would remain in the realm of theory.

In its neglect of the rest of life, exemptionalism fails definitively. To move ahead as though scientific and entrepreneurial genius will solve each crisis that arises implies that the declining biosphere can be similarly manipulated. But the world is too complicated to be turned into a garden. There is no biological homeostat that can be worked by humanity; to believe otherwise is to risk reducing a large part of Earth to a wasteland.

The environmentalist vision, prudential and less exuberant than exemptionalism, is closer to reality. It sees humanity entering a bottleneck unique in history, constricted by population and economic pressures. In order to pass through to the other side, within perhaps 50 to 100 years, more science and entrepreneurship will have to be devoted to stabilizing the global environment. That can be accomplished, according to expert consensus, only by halting population growth and devising a wiser use of resources than has been accomplished to date. And wise use for the living world in particular means preserving the surviving ecosystems, micromanaging them only enough to save the biodiversity they contain, until such time as they can be understood and employed in the fullest sense for human benefit.

FOR THE COMMON GOOD

Herman E. Daly
Senior Research Scholar
University of Maryland School of Public Affairs
and
John B. Cobb, Jr.
Professor of Theology and Philosophy, Claremont Graduate School

Words ought to be a little wild, for they are the assault of thoughts upon the unthinking. - John Maynard Keynes

THE WILD FACTS

In our time, it is the facts themselves that are more than a little wild and that constitute an assault on unthinking economic dogma. We need little help from wild rhetoric. The wild facts are summarized in calm words in the various State of the World reports put out by the Worldwatch Institute, and especially in the first essay of the 1987 volume by Lester Brown and Sandra Postel, entitled "Thresholds of Change." Some of the facts are:

1. There is a hole in the earth's protective shield of ozone. More ultraviolet radiation now reaches the earth and will predictably increase skin cancer, retard crop growth, and impair the human immune system. In an unprecedentedly wise response, representatives from thirty-one nations have agreed to a quantitative limit on the production of chlorofluorocarbons, the probable cause of the ozone depletion.

2. There is evidence that the CO_2-induced greenhouse effect has already caused perceptible warming of the globe. As recently as 1983, noticeable change was not expected for another 50 years. Now the warming is being connected by careful students to the 1988 drought in the Midwest.

3. Biodiversity is declining as rates of species extinction increase due to takeover of habitat, especially of the tropical rainforests, which support half the world's species on only 7% of its land area (Goodland 1987).

In addition, acid rain kills temperate zone forests and raises the acidity of lakes above the tolerance thresholds for many species. Because of industrial accidents, people in Chernobyl, Goiania (Brazil), and Bhopal are dying from air pollution, toxic waste contamination of ground water, and radiation poisoning.

All of these facts appear to us to be related in one way or another to one central underlying fact: the scale of human activity relative to the biosphere has grown too large. Over the period 1950-86, population doubled from 2.5 to 5.0 billion. Over the same time period, gross world product and fossil fuel consumption each roughly quadrupled. Further growth beyond this scale is overwhelmingly likely to increase costs more rapidly than it increases benefits, thus ushering in a new era of "uneconomic growth" that impoverishes rather than enriches. This is the fundamental wild fact that so far has not found expression in words sufficiently feral to assault successfully the civil stupor of economic discourse. Indeed, contrary to Keynes, it seems that the wildness of either words or facts is nowadays taken as clear evidence of untruth. Moral concern is "unscientific." Statement of fact is "alarmist."

In *An Inquiry into the Human Prospect* (1974) economist Robert Heilbroner reflected about the meaning of this pressure of the human economy on the biosphere. He considered especially the political traumas that will be faced when economic growth is no longer possible. In a 1980 revision of his Inquiry, he projected a continuing (but gradually slowing) growth economy until the middle of the first decade of the next century. When that ends, he sees (as in the earlier 1974 edition) the need for highly authoritarian governments to control the transition to economic decline (Heilbroner 1980, p. 167 ff.).

We appreciate Heilbroner's rare willingness as an economist to connect the growth economy and the physical limits of the ecosphere. This is at the heart of our project as well. But we believe that thought, foresight, and imagination can lead to a much less disruptive transition. Whereas Heilbroner assumes there are no realistic alternatives to capitalism and socialism (both growth economies), we do not agree. To conceive of a radically different economy forces us both to think through the discipline of economics as well as beyond it into biology, history, philosophy, physics, and theology. Part of the assault of the wild facts has been against the very disciplinary boundaries by which knowledge is organized (produced, packaged, and exchanged) in the modern university.

THE AMBIGUITY OF THE ECONOMIC ACHIEVEMENT

The wild facts of today and their conflict with standard economic theory both have a well-known history. During the past two centuries, the economy has transformed the character of the planet and especially of human life. It has done so chiefly by industrialization. Industry has vastly increased the productivity of workers, so vastly that in spite of the great population increases in industrialized nations, the goods and services available to each have increased still more. The standard of living has soared from bare subsistence to affluence for most people in the North Atlantic nations and Japan. Singapore, Hong Kong, Taiwan, and South Korea share in this prosperity. These are immense accomplishments.

During the same period, the study of the economy has matured, approaching the status of a science. Economics alone among the social studies is sometimes accorded that label by natural scientists. A Nobel prize is given in economics as in physics and biology. Other students of human society often envy and emulate the economists, much as economists emulate physicists.

Public policy has been deeply affected by the ideas and proposals of economists. Without this help the economy could not have grown to anything like the extent it has. Economists have reason to believe that if politicians and government bureaucrats would pay closer attention to their arguments, the purposes of government could be more efficiently realized. Again and again they are able to show the waste of resources that follows from regulatory measures that ignore market principles. Even Eastern European economists are now arguing for greater reliance on the market, for reasons similar to those given by their Western counterparts.

But the industrial economy has consequences for the greater economy of life. Psychologists have been disturbed by what is happening to individuals. In 1937, Karen Horney cited the pressures on Americans created by their industrial, competitive, materialistic society. She noted that three basic value conflicts had arisen: "aggressiveness grown so pronounced that it could no longer be reconciled with Christian brotherhood; desire for material goods so vigorously stimulated that it can never be satisfied, and expectations of untrammeled freedom soaring so high that they cannot be squared with the multitudes of restrictions and responsibilities that confine us all" (Henderson 1978, p. 25). Walter Weisskopf (1971) more recently has engaged in an extensive study of what the economy has done to human beings morally and existentially. He sees that it has worked against objective judgments of value and encouraged moral relativism. It has also emphasized a few aspects of human existence at the expense of others, and thus caused alienation.

Other critics have pointed out the negative social effects of economic progress. In moving words, Karl Polanyi, a great economic historian, described the social developments associated with the rise of the market as the "Satanic Mill." The opening sentence of his 1944 work states: "At the heart of the Industrial Revolution of the eighteenth century there was an almost miraculous improvement in the tools of production, which was accomplished by a catastrophic dislocation of the lives of the common people" (Polanyi [1944] 1957, p. 33). Joseph

Schumpeter was equally troubled. He saw economic thought as a part of the utilitarian philosophy that dominated the nineteenth century. "This system of ideas, developed in the eighteenth century, recognizes no other regulatory principle than that of individual egoism .... The essential fact is that, whether as cause or consequence, this philosophy expresses only too well the spirit of social irresponsibility which characterized the passion, and the secular, or rather secularized, state in the nineteenth century. And in the midst of moral confusion, economic success serves only to render still more serious the social and political situation which is the natural result of a century of economic liberalism" (Schumpeter 1975).

Recently it has been ecologists especially and those whom they have aroused who have turned on the economy as the great villain. They see that the growth of the economy has meant the exponential increase of raw material inputs from the environment and waste outputs into the environment, and they see that little attention has been paid by economists either to the exhaustion of resources or to pollution. They complain that economists have not only ignored the source of inputs and the disposition of outputs, but also that they have encouraged the maximization of both, whereas living lightly in the world requires that throughput should be kept to the minimum sufficient to meet human needs.

Most economists have ignored these criticisms. They are convinced that the great majority of people are far more interested in the economic goods whose production economists have encouraged than in any psychological or environmental losses. They suspect that those who speak of the suffering accompanying industrialization exaggerate. They show that the industrializing nations grew rapidly in wealth, a wealth in which most shared, albeit unevenly. And they are convinced that those who worry about the future of the environment underestimate the capacity of a prosperous economy to take care of that, too. Where there is "capital and ingenuity there will be technological breakthroughs. Now that the environment is a concern, inventive genius will be directed to solving these new challenges.

TOWARD A PARADIGM SHIFT IN ECONOMICS [1]

When a discipline is both this successful and this severely criticized, one may assume that its assumptions and methods apply well in some spheres and poorly in others. The key assumptions in this case have to do with Homo economicus, that is, the understanding of the nature of the human being. Economic theory builds on the propensity of individuals to act so as to optimize their own interests, a propensity clearly operative in market transactions and in many other areas of life. Economists typically identify intelligent pursuit of private gain with rationality, thus implying that other modes of behavior are not rational. These modes include other-regarding behavior an actions directed to the public good.

The assumption that rationality largely excludes other-regarding behavior has deep, although conflicting, roots in the Western theological understanding of human nature. Theologians have held that other-regarding action is an ethical ideal, but many, especially after St. Augustine, have seen self-regarding behavior as dominant in the actual "fallen" condition. This fallenness was strongly accented by the Reformers and their followers, encouraging general suspicion of claims to genuinely other-regarding action in Protestant cultures. It is not surprising that the philanthropist Robert Owen, living in such a culture, rejected Christianity for its individualism (Polanyi [1944] 1957, 128). Catholic theology followed St. Thomas in giving more credence to socially concerned, community-building aspects of human activity.

In Calvinism, the skepticism about human virtue was connected with the suspicion of earthly authority in both church and state. The relation to God was conceived as immediate and decisive. This led to a claim to personal autonomy in both secular and religious affairs and restrictions on government interference. In Roman Catholic cultures, the emphasis on community was connected with hierarchical organization in both church and society.

Modern economic theory originated and developed in the context of Calvinism. Both were bids for personal freedom against the interference of earthly authority. They based their bids on the conviction that beyond a very narrow sphere, motives of self-interest are overwhelmingly dominant. Economic theory differed from Calvinism only in celebrating as rational what Calvinists confessed as sinful.

Calvinism encourages other-regarding behavior as truly Christian even while warning against believing too readily in its reality. Catholicism encourages other-regarding behavior as a natural virtue. When Christianity was dominant, these forces checked blatantly self-seeking activity, although they certainly did not prevent it. But economists have taught us to think that checks on self-interest are both unnecessary and harmful. It is through rational behavior, which means self-interested behavior, that all benefit the most. Well-meaning attempts by government to oppose or check such behavior actually do more harm than good. As this belief displaces traditional Christian thinking, and as the market in which these principles are applied takes over a larger and larger role in society, the psychological, sociological, and ecological problems noted by critics of the economists have become more acute.

Economics contributed to freeing individuals from hierarchical authority, as well as to providing more abundant goods and services. These have been achievements of such importance that it has seemed wise to most persons of good will to treat the negative effects as secondary, as a necessary price for a crucial advance. For a long time that may have been an appropriate stance. But with each passing year, the positive accomplishments of the economy have become less evident and the destructive consequences larger. There is a growing sense that it is time for a change. The change may well take the form of a paradigm shift. The recognition of the importance of paradigm shifts in physics generated by the work of Thomas Kuhn has opened the way for thinking about paradigm shifts in the social sciences as well.

Shlomo Maital (1982) reports on a poll of professors of economics at fifty major universities. One question asked was, "is there a sense of lost moorings in economics?" Two-thirds of the respondents answered affirmatively (p. 17). Maital believes the discipline is at a crisis. "Evidence contradictory to the conventional wisdom of economics continues to accumulate." "As dissonant evidence mounts and assails cherished propositions of a discipline, virtuoso acrobatics of that discipline's believers put things right again" (p. 262). To Maital, all this is a sign that a paradigm shift is on its way.

Lester Thurow (1983) concludes Dangerous Currents on a similar note. "Economics cannot do without simplifying assumptions, but the trick is to use the right assumptions at the right time. And the judgment has to come from empirical analysis (including those employed by historians, psychologists, sociologists and political scientists) of how the world is, not of how our economics textbooks tell us it ought to be" (p. 237). Elsewhere in the book, he notes: "Psychology, sociology, and politics all have theories that might produce a set of expectations very different from those ascribed to Homo economicus. Patterns of socialization, cultural and ethnic history, political institutions, and old-fashioned human will power all affect our expectations" (p. 226). Thurow points in the direction of a new paradigm when he says: "Societies are not merely statistical aggregations of individuals engaged in voluntary exchange but something much more subtle and complicated. A group or community cannot be understood if the unit of analysis is the individual taken by himself. A society is clearly something greater than the sum of its parts" (pp. 222-223). He distinguishes, following Stephen Marlin, "private-personal preferences" from "individual-social" ones (p. 224), and chides economists for trying to work with the first alone.

Human beings are extremely complex and can be studied from many points of view. Each point of view abstracts from the concrete actuality and focuses on particular aspects of human behavior. Homo religiosus is the human being considered as religious; Homo politicus, as political; and Homo economicus, as economic. We focus on Homo economicus while trying not to forget that human beings can also be viewed, among other things, as religious and political. It undertakes to follow Thurow's injunction to avoid viewing Homo economicus in terms of private-personal preferences alone. Accordingly, instead of Homo economicus as pure individual we propose Homo economicus as person-in-community.[2] This is more consonant with the other social sciences and with the evidence that economists are themselves uncovering. It does not deny that in the market the actions of person-in-community approximate to those attributed to Homo economicus in the received theory. But normative conclusions about the goal of economic life should not be drawn from this fact alone. Polanyi notes that in capitalist society, "instead of economy being embedded in social relations, social relations are embedded in the economic system" ([1944] 1957, p.57). It is this reversal that an economics for community cannot tolerate.

We cannot claim that our model fully meets Maital's requirements for a new paradigm. He writes: "No science will agree to junk its tried and true axioms, even when they become trying and untrue, until a new and more powerful set of axioms is available" (1982, p. 262). We are not offering a new set of axioms. Indeed, we suggest that this view of economics as a system of deductions from axioms is part of the problem. But we do believe that economics can rethink its theories from the viewpoint of person-in-community and still include the truth and insight it gained when it thought in individualistic terms. It need not "junk" its axioms. Many of them can continue to function, only with more recognition of their limits. The change will involve correction and expansion, a more empirical and historical attitude, less pretense to be a "science," and the willingness to subordinate the market to purposes that it is not geared to determine.

THE NEW PARADIGM AND THE OLD OPTIONS

The first question in many people's minds when confronted with an economic proposal is how to locate it on a scale from left to right. Dudley Seers offers a diagram, which we reproduce in Figure 1, that expresses what many people have at least vaguely in mind (Seers 1983, pp. 46-48).

Leaving out the extremes of anarchism and fascism, there are important issues debated along this line. But Seers is quite correct in arguing that the larger issues are better represented when another axis is introduced. He does this in terms of nationalism and antinationalism (see Figure 2).

Seers discusses not only national economy but also the European economic community. Hence his title, "The Political Economy of Nationalism," is a bit misleading. It associates his ideas more closely with the long tradition of economic nationalism in the nineteenth century

Figure 1

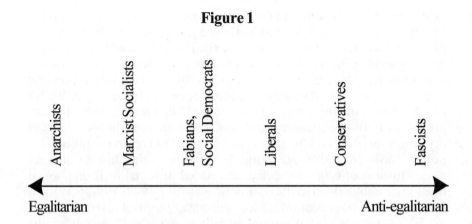

Figure 2

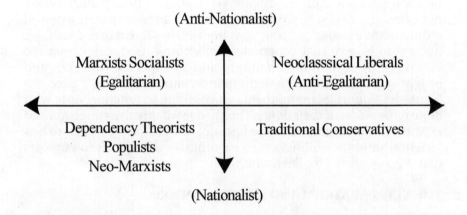

than is warranted by his fresh reading of the situation. We would like to carry his qualifications of traditional nationalism much further. Nations are only one of the levels at which community is to be prized and served. Our diagram would replace "nationalist" and "antinationalist" by such words as "communitarian" and "anticommunitarian." Nevertheless, nations are a desirable form of community and in many instances today, the only ones that have the power to assert themselves effectively against anticommunitarian forces. For practical purposes, therefore, the alternatives posed by Seers are important. With these caveats, we accept his formulation. Our attention, like his, is focused on the vertical axis.

Viewing matters in this light, Seers writes at length of the close similarities of Marxism and standard Western economics in a chapter startlingly entitled "Marxism and Other Neo-Classical Economics." Among other commonalities, both oppose nationalism in particular and, at least implicitly, attention to community in general. Because we believe that the extent to which an economy supports or destroys healthy communities is more important than where it is to be located from left to right, we, like Seers, refuse to see our proposals as somewhere on the horizontal line of his diagram.[3] The greatest obstacle to gaining a hearing for proposals like Seers' and ours is the continuing widespread assumption that all positions must be located along the line from left to right. It is an idee fixe that every economy must be socialist, capitalist, or a compromise between the two. We offer our understanding of how this situation came about and of the limited options remaining when these parameters are assumed to be exhaustive.

This whole way of thinking was brought into being by the problems and promises of the industrial age. It is for an industrial society that capitalism and socialism are supposed to be the only options, and it is their common participation in the methods and structures of industrialism that determines the extensive similarities between the two systems.[4] Some features of industrialism are necessary in any society in which manufacturing plays a large role. Other features are not. Since we intend to offer an alternative to both forms of industrialism, we need to explain how we understand its basic features.

The well-known features of industrialism include the use of new energy sources: coal first, followed by petroleum and natural gas; use of new materials: iron and steel; new inventions: the steam engine, the spinning jenny; advances in transportation and communication: the steamship, the locomotive, telegraph, and radio; new techniques: the factory system of production; and the increasing application of science to technology. Along with this in England went the enclosure of the commons that "freed" rural labor for the urban industrial factories. Later came the increasing mechanization of agriculture.

The invention of the factory system stands out in this list as the one item that was truly an economic rather than a technical invention. The factory is not a new tool but an organization of production that eliminates the periods of idleness in the use of tools, machines, and men that t are characteristic of agrarian and artisan production. In the artisan's shop the saw, chisel, file, and so forth are all idle while the hammer is being used. In the factory all tools are simultaneously in use in the hands of specialized workers; production is "in line" rather than "in series." But production in line requires a large scale of total output before it becomes feasible. The division of labor is limited by the extent of the market, as Adam Smith told us. But transportation, urbanization, and international trade provided a market of sufficient scale. In agriculture, of course, harvesting equipment must be idle during seedtime,

and planting equipment idle during harvest. Seasonality in agricultural production limits the applicability of factory organization on the
farm. We can be sure, for better or for worse, that the economic impe-
tus of modern genetic engineering will be to reduce seasonality, to design plants and animals capable of being fitted into a factory system of
production. This is already evident in "chicken farms," which are really
chicken factories.

The feature of the industrial revolution whose implications are in-
sufficiently appreciated is the shift to fossil fuel energy and mineral
materials. This is a shift from harvesting the surface of the earth to
mining the subsurface or, in Georgescu-Roegen's (1971) terms it is a
shift from dependence on energy currently coming from the sun to
stored energy on the earth. This shift is extremely significant because
these two ultimate sources of life sustenance differ in their patterns of
scarcity. Radiant energy from the sun is practically infinite in total
amount (stock), but it is strictly limited in its flow rate-that is, the
amount that arrives on earth during any period. Energy stored in fossil
fuels and minerals is strictly limited in its total amount (stock), but
relatively unlimited in its flow rate-that is, we can use it up at a rate
largely of our own choosing. We cannot use tomorrow's sunlight today, but in a sense we can use tomorrow's petroleum, coal, iron, and
helium today. The industrial revolution has shifted dependence from
the relatively abundant to the relatively scarce source of the ultimate
resource: low-entropy matter-energy.

The idea that low-entropy matter-energy is the ultimate natural resource requires some explanation. This is can a provided easily by a
short exposition of the laws of thermodynamics in terms of an apt
image borrowed from Georgescu-Roegen. Consider an hour glass. It is a
closed system in that no sand enters the glass and none leaves. The
amount of sand in the glass is constant -- no sand is created or destroyed within the hour glass. This is the analog of the first law of
thermodynamics: there is no creation or destruction of matter-energy.
Although the quantity of sand in the hour glass is constant, its qualitative distribution is constantly changing: the bottom chamber is filling
up and the top chamber becoming empty. This is the analog of the
second law, that entropy (bottom-chamber sand) always increases. Sand
in the top chamber (low entropy) is capable of doing work by falling,
like water at the top of a waterfall. Sand in the bottom chamber (high
entropy) has spent its capacity to do work. This hour glass cannot be
turned upside down: waste energy cannot be recycled, except by spending more energy to power the recycle than would be reclaimed in the
amount recycled. As explained above, we have two sources of this ultimate natural resource, the solar and the terrestrial, and our dependence
has shifted from the former toward the latter.

This shift was not consciously made, but it was certainly no accident. The newly discovered terrestrial resources had advantageous properties. Fossil fuel is a more concentrated energy source than sunlight, or even wood. Iron and steel have properties of strength and durability that, unlike wood and stone, permit construction of the machines and boilers capable of harnessing the more intense energy sources. Technology exploited these new qualities. Furthermore, the new materials and energy came from under the ground. That meant that they did not (until the advent of strip mining) compete for land surface area capable of capturing sunlight. As populations grew, the land previously devoted to growing fodder for draft animals was devoted to growing more food. The new mechanical oxen were fed with fossil fuels from underground and far away. In the enthusiasm for growth and the unlimited faith in technology, the realization that the benefits of industrialism came at a price, namely increasing dependence on the scarcer source of ultimate means, was submerged.

The industrial revolution is still being repeated in traditional societies today and is almost synonymous with "economic development." Its evolution has been toward larger scale and greater specialization, with the consequences of increasing integration and interdependence and of increasing vulnerability to systemic failure. At the same time, industrialization has given a higher standard of consumption to more people than any other mode of production, so its universal dominance is hardly surprising.

Although industrialism grew up historically under capitalist institutions, it has proven to be compatible with socialist institutions as well. The conflict between capitalism and socialism is not about the desirability or possibility of industrialism. That is taken for granted by both sides. The conflict is over which economic system can better produce a growing quantity of goods and services and equitably spread the benefits of the industrial mode of production. Whatever their ideological differences both systems are fully committed to large-scale, factory-style energy and capital-intensive, specialized production units that are hierarchically managed. They also rely heavily on nonrenewable resources and tend to exploit renewable resources and waste absorption capacities at non-sustainable rates.

Capitalism consists of private ownership of the means of production along with allocation and distribution provided by the market. Individual maximization of profit by firms and maximization of satisfaction (utility) by consumers provides the motive force, while competition, the existence of many buyers and sellers in the market, provides the famous invisible hand that leads private interest to serve the public welfare. Collective action by government is limited to (a) providing the institutional precondition of property rights enforced by law, (b) providing certain public goods or natural monopolies and prohibiting the formation of private monopolies, (c) maintaining aggregate demand at a level that gives an "acceptable" combination of inflation and unemployment; (d) providing a minimum social welfare safety net to keep people from destitution; and (e) intervening to correct "externalities" (situations in which voluntary exchange between two individuals, although mutually beneficial to them, has important effects on third parties).

Socialism is defined by government ownership of the means of production with allocation and distribution by central planning, but with some reliance on the market when central planning gets overwhelmed. Motive force comes from a combination of moral and material incentives. Reliance on the market comes in degrees, and Polish economist Jan Drewnowski (1961) has distinguished first-, second-, and third-degree market economies. In a first-degree market economy, quantities of consumer goods are fixed by planners, but households are free to purchase or not. The planned mix of goods may be rationed by queues or by prices, but the planner does not adjust quantities in accordance with this information on shortages and surpluses. In the second-degree market economy, the planner does adjust quantities of consumer goods according to observed shortages and surpluses, or according to changes in price if that is allowed. However, the planner only reallocates current resources among existing plants. No new capital investment takes place as a result of consumer demand signals. In the third-degree market economy, the pattern of new investment also responds to the pattern of consumer demand, but the overall volume of investment, the decision of how much to consume and how much to invest, is still made centrally by the planners.

When household decisions on saving versus consumption are allowed to determine the aggregate social investment, then we would have a "fourth-degree" market economy, which would require capitalist rather than socialist institutions, since households must own the means of production if they are going to invest in them as individuals. But the first-, second-, and third-degree market economies are consistent with socialist institutions. Just as in the capitalist world we have considerable variation in collective influence, extending to indicative planning and extensive social welfare sectors in such countries as France or Sweden, so in the communist countries there existed a wide range of market influence extending to the relatively decentralized economies of Hungary and Yugoslavia.

The issues raised along the spectrum of socialist and capitalist options are real. Therefore once we have made clear that these are for us secondary to the question of community, it behooves us to locate ourselves with respect to them. Our position is that centralized economic planning is inefficient, that allocations are better effected in the market than by bureaucratic planning. The role of government is to set fair conditions within which the market can operate. It is also responsible for setting the overall size (scale) of the market. The market is not the end of society and is not the right instrument through which the ends of society should be set. We favor private ownership of the means of production. We favor the widest possible participation in that ownership, including worker ownership of factories, against its concentration in a few hands.

Nevertheless, our opposition to Marxism is not automatic opposition to all policies and proposals stemming from socialist thinkers. Where those policies and proposals require centralized planning for their implementation, we remain skeptical. But we hope to be open to ideas from every source, and when the thinkers are passionately committed to justice and the relief of suffering, we intend to listen with special care. We find that today many who come from the socialist tradition have shifted attention away from centralized planning, indeed that they share our suspicion of centralization and our concern for community. Some explicitly support, as we do, decentralization of political and economic power, worker ownership of factories or participation in their management, and the subordination of the economy to social goals, democratically defined. Socialism of this sort is not what we have described above.[5] Instead it is a partner in fresh thinking about the possibilities of humane life in community.[6]

THE THIRD MODEL

This interest in a third model based on concern for human community is not new. It was vigorously pursued by the Roman Catholic Church in the nineteenth century. The Catholic critique of both capitalism and socialism is quite similar to our own. Richard E. Mulcahey summarizes this criticism:

> Individualism sees in society no real unity. What it calls "society" is a mere mechanism, the interplay of the actions of individuals seeking their own ends; or it is a mere sum of economic relations. It postulates a natural order based on unrestrained freedom, on whose unhindered effect the welfare of all depends. The national economy is viewed as a sum of isolated units, which are bound together only by mere exchange relationships .... In socialism the concept of the unity of society is distorted. The collective society which it requires presents the unity of "oneness" rather than a union of the

many. The individual is only an "associate," not an autonomous personality. [Mulcahey 1952, p. 161]

Mulcahey is describing and affirming the economic theory of
Heinrich Pesch, a Roman Catholic economist whose work both informed
and was informed by papal encyclicals. Pesch understood economics as
"the science of the economic life (the process of providing material goods)
of a people, considered as a social unit, bound together by the
politico-social community life" (Mulcahey 1952, pp. 13-14). Mulcahey
states, "Pesch's solidaristic system rejects the one-sidedness of a mere
aggregate concept of the economy and of a single economy controlled
by society, and proposes an economic order and a moral-organic unity
and community of many independent private economic units" (p. 27).
Pesch thus aims at "the full carrying out of the idea of community" (p.
161).

It would be easy to suspect that Catholic teaching is simply calling
for a return to more authoritarian and hierarchical patterns. But this is
not true. Central to Catholic teaching is the "principle of subsidiarity."
According to Pius XI, "It is an injustice, a grave evil and a disturbance of
right order for a larger and higher organization to arrogate to itself
functions which can be performed efficiently by smaller and lower bodies" (1931, p. 80). Commenting on this, Bernard W. Dempsey writes:
"Each higher society is subsidiary, that is, designed to be of help to the
lesser societies beneath it. It is not the other way around: the persons
who comprise the more fundamental societies are not means to serve
the societies. Nor are the closely knit natural communities such as the
municipality to be used as means by the larger but more remote organizations like the regional or provincial government (our 'states') or the
national state" (1958, p. 281).

These Roman Catholic doctrines are remarkably similar to those of
Thomas Jefferson, who wrote: "The article nearest to my heart is the
division of counties into wards. These will be pure and elementary re-
publics, the aim of all of which taken together composes the State, and
will make of the whole a true democracy as to the business of the wards,
which is that nearest and daily concern. The affairs of the larger sections, of counties, of States, and of the Union, not admitting personal
transactions by the people, will be delegated to agents elected by themselves, and representation will be substituted where personal action becomes impracticable" (Dumbauld 1955, pp. 97-98).

Alexis de Tocqueville also emphasized the importance of community in American life. In the explanation of why American democracy
worked, he noted, "too much importance is attributed to legislation,
too little to customs." These customs were nurtured in local communi-

ties, and it was "the influence of customs that produces the different degrees of order and prosperity which may be distinguished in the several Anglo-American democracies" (1945, p. 334).

After noting these views of Jefferson and de Tocqueville, Edward Schwarz comments: "Unfortunately most political leaders and writers today have forgotten these communitarian concerns of Jefferson, de Tocqueville and early Americans in general. The irony is that a wide range of evidence is now affirming empirically what these traditional theorists could assert only instinctively. It now appears certain that a strong, local community is essential to psychological well-being, personal growth, social order, and a sense of political efficacy. These conclusions are now emerging at the center of every social science discipline" (1982, p. 264).

Schwarz exaggerates at one point. John C. Raines is more careful: "That the social is primary in regard to the human has become by now less a claim than a taken-for-granted starting point in most American sociology and anthropology. But it is a starting point that has little penetrated American political and economic thought" (1982, p. 295).

The emphasis on community was important when Pesch was writing sixty years ago. Today it has become urgent. Amitai Etzioni devoted the first half of An Immodest Agenda to analyzing the critical situation in the United States resulting from the dissolution of community into individuals. He rightly notes that "the individual and the community make each other and require each other" (1983, p. 25). Further, he writes, "A society and its members require mutual civility for sheer survival. Unless the retreat to ego is overcome and community institutions reconstituted, the level of conflict and frustrations will rise, and the limited energy channeled to shared concerns will make for an ineffectual 'can't do' society, continued deterioration, and even, ultimately, the possibility of destruction" (p. 185). Unfortunately, when he turns to economics in the second half of the book, he seems to ignore its role in the undercutting of community through its own individualistic ideology and practice.

There is one major respect in which our approach is markedly different from that of Pesch and the papal encyclicals. Certain issues have become critical today that were little anticipated during Pesch's lifetime. Today it is important to think of the community served by the economy as enduring indefinitely through time. It is also important to see that the human communities Pesch envisioned are part of a larger community that includes the other creatures with whom human beings share the world. The industrial economy is only a part of what Wendell Berry has called the Great Economy -- the economy that sustains the total web of life and everything that depends on the land. It is the Great

Economy that is of ultimate importance.

Like Pesch, we approach economics for community from the side of the market economy, discussing the revisions required in neoclassical theory and in actual capitalist practice in order that the destruction of community be ended. Precisely for this reason, it is inevitable that our work should appear to be an attack on the current discipline. In one sense it is. We do emphatically believe that humanity is in need of an approach to its economic problems that differs markedly from that supported by most of the practitioners of the present discipline, and since we think these practitioners are sensitively and honorably expressing the implications of current theory, it is this theory we criticize. We believe the failures of the discipline of economics as now practiced have to be shown before there is much chance of reconstructing economics on a different basis.

But while we offer a severe critique of the contemporary discipline of economics our purpose is not to reject the core of its teaching. On the contrary, we are convinced of the general soundness of the account of markets and of the affirmation of their excellence for certain purposes that is at the heart of classical and neoclassical theory alike. We believe many public purposes could be better served by the application of market principles than by the patchwork of government regulations now so prevalent. Our intention is not that economic theory begin over again, but that it be reconstructed on the basis of a paradigm that both clarifies the excellence of its past work and sets it in a larger context. Newtonian science continues to play an extremely important role in the context of the Einsteinian worldview. The analysis of the market can continue to play an extremely important role within a context that sees the purpose of the economy as the service of community.

Of the authors of this work, one is an economist, one a theologian. Both of us have strong ecological concerns. We have come to our economic views through disturbance about what standard development is doing in the Third World. Both of us are Protestants. Both have been influenced by the philosophy of Alfred North Whitehead.

We recognize that much of our work falls outside the boundaries of what is regarded as the discipline of economics, but we feel that the economy, the Great Economy, is far larger than what that discipline studies. We think that our collaborative work is a type of reflection in which citizens from many backgrounds need to share. Decisions that will be made soon in this country will shape the world of our children and grandchildren, probably irreversibly. They should not be made within the restricted context that now governs the academic discipline of economics.

The great achievement of economics is to have become a "science."

That involves two major elements: it has the characteristics of an academic discipline and it has chosen the deductive model. Immersion in the science makes it very difficult to remember the degree of abstractness involved and to discount one's scientific results with that in mind.

An alternative approach to the economy, instead of shaping the study to the requirements of a science, would propose that reflection be ordered to the needs of the real world. This will not put an end to abstraction, since all thought abstracts, but it will provide a basis for selecting better abstractions and for keeping the elements abstracted from constantly in view.

New policies would follow from this different perspective. At an abstract level, the policy implications everywhere would have certain similarities, and at some points the formulations are quite general. But policies mediate between overall perspective and particular situation.

How might changes in the required direction might come about? We have seen our chief task to provide an image or vision of an economic order that, in the language of the World Council of Churches, would be just, participatory, and sustainable. We need help from many points of view in thinking through how it could be attained. Nevertheless, we do want to broach the subject and initiate some lines of discussion. We do so in two ways. First, we propose a variety of reforms toward which we can now work, and we recommend ways of raising public consciousness so as to make deeper changes possible. One of our proposals is to use a more appropriate measure of how well the national economy is doing.[7] Second, it is our judgment that without changes at a deep religious level responses to crises will be ad hoc and insufficient. Accordingly, clarification of the needed religious worldview is urgent.

We want, above all, not to disparage the lifelong efforts of many have advanced the discipline of economics and shaped policies to reflect it. We respect their integrity, their commitment to human welfare the keenness of their insights.

But at a deep level of our being we find it hard to suppress the cry of anguish, the scream of horror-the wild words required to express wild realities. We human beings are being to a dead end - all too literally. We are living by an ideology of death and accordingly we are destroy our own humanity and killing the planet. Even the one great success of the program that has governed us, the attainment of material affluence, now giving way to poverty. The United States is just now gaining a foretaste of the suffering that global economic policies, so enthusiastically embraced, have inflicted on hundreds of millions of others. If we continue on our present paths, future generations, if there are to be 'any, are condemned to misery. The fact that many people of good will do not see this dead end is undeniably true, very regrettable, and it is our main reason for our work.

Victor Furkiss describes our situation graphically: "Present-day society is locked into four positive feedback loops which need to be broken: economic growth which feeds on itself, population growth which feeds on itself, technological change which feeds on itself, and a pattern of income inequality which seems to be self sustaining and which tends to spur growth in the other three areas. Ecological humanism must create an economy in which economic and population growth is halted, technology is controlled, and gross inequalities of income are done away with" (1974, p. 235). We would add also an arms race that feeds on itself. We believe that an economics for the common good is what ecological humanism calls for, and even more what stewardship of creation calls for.

The global system will change during the next forty years because it will be physically forced to change. But if humanity waits until it is physically compelled to change, its options will be few indeed. None of them will be attractive. If it changes before it has to change, while it can still choose to change, it will not avoid suffering and crises, but it can be drawn through them by a realistic hope for a better world.

Before this generation are set two ways, the way of life and the way of death. May humanity choose life!

FOOTNOTES

1. The term "paradigm" is difficult to define, and its applicability in the social sciences has been questioned. See Richard J. Bernstein, The Restructuring of Economic and Political Theory (1976, 84-106). We believe the term can be useful in relation to economics, but admittedly we use it loosely.
2. There is nothing original about this term. According to Max L. Stackhouse (1985) the "Christian sociologists" responded to the industrial revolution in the United States "in conversation with the best social theories available to them . . . and equally fully committed to the biblical witness as the source and norm for their efforts," and "articulated a doctrine of `person in community' that attempted to establish decisive boundaries for Christian thinking about economic life" (p. 132). For current efforts in the Protestant context to find a third way, see Ulrich Duchrow, Global Economy: A Confessional Issue for the Churches? (1987, pp. 158-162): "It is false to say there are no alternatives. There are new economic approaches which make the meeting of the basic needs of concrete human beings and ecological sustainability the starting point for the economic system." Duchrow finds support for this direction in the work of institutional economists, especially Chris-

tian Leipert and R. Steppacher.
3. A similar polemic against regarding the alternatives as capitalism and socialism has been made by Benjamin R. Barber in "Against Economics: Capitalism, Socialism, but Whatever Happened to Democracy?" (1986). He calls for democratic control over the economy, which would require community control. He seems to have the national level of community in mind.
4. Others have noted that Marxism and capitalism are but two forms of a modern industrial society that is more determinative of the human and ecological conditions than is any difference between them. See Robert Nisbett, The Sociological Imagination (1966). Also Robert Heilbroner (1980) writes that both capitalist and socialist societies have organized work, life, and even thought "in ways that accommodate men to machines rather than the much more difficult alternative" (p. 94).
5. As an example of radical social thinking with congenial views, see Samuel Bowles and Herbert Gintis, Democracy and Capitalism: Property, Community, and the Contradictions of Modern Social Thought (1986). The democratic control of the economy they advocate involves decentralization rather than centralized planning. The recent work of Michael Harrington hardly focuses on socialism as we have treated it. His ideas about a shorter work week, empowering citizens, and worker participation in industrial decisions are highly congenial to us. See Michael Harrington, The Next Left (1986). He himself comments on the similarities between the programs of the sophisticated Right and Left (p. 15). Their difference, he says, is that the Right wants to move from the top down, and the Left from the bottom up. By this definition we are on the Left. This is quite different from centralized planning. But we find the Left as well as the Right to be lacking in appreciation of ecological limits to economic expansion.
6. Our hope is to move forward to a new type of economy different from either capitalism or socialism as they have been understood in the past. But for those who still find it difficult to think of an economy that does not fit on this spectrum, we suggest that they consider feudalism. Feudalism, surely, is neither capitalist nor socialist, yet it endured longer in Europe than either of these is likely to do. Feudalism is the bete noir of both, and that will help to indicate how one can be opposed to both. The feudal system was more communitarian than either socialism or capitalism in both theory and practice. It has been badly maligned since the Enlightenment by those whose interest required the extirpation of the continuing power of community in human life. Even economically the mature medieval society was far more successful and affluent, as well as more just and humane, than moderns have been willing to acknowledge. John Stuart Mill noted that the widespread

proprietorship of the late Middle Ages gave England a "yeomanry who were vaunted as the glory of England while they existed, and have been so much mourned ever since they disappeared" (1973, p. 256). It was of course the application of capitalism to agriculture that destroyed these products of feudal society. Marshall also writes favorably of features of the feudal society: "In the Middle Ages . . . the great body of the inhabitants frequently had the full rights of citizens, deciding for themselves the foreign and domestic policy of the city, and at the same time working with their hands and taking pride in their work. They organized themselves into Guilds, thus increasing their cohesion and educating themselves in self-government" (1925, p. 735). We do not recite these points in order to call for a return to feudalism. It had many faults, and in any case it is not directly applicable to an industrial society. But we do believe that surveying a wider range of economic systems can open our eyes to new possibilities. Of these, feudalism is worthy of careful consideration. The most careful comparison of English life at the end of the feudal era with modern life has been made by Peter Laslet in The World We Have Lost (1965). Those interested in a sustained argument for the superiority of the medieval system should see Hilaire Belloc (1913). Belloc contrasts the medieval system of ownership of the means of production with the capitalist and Marxist systems. In the medieval system, it is owned by the many; in capitalism, by the few; in Marxism, by the state. Leopold Kohr (1957) argues that mature medieval economies did better than ours. Nicholas Georgescu-Roegen (1950) has shown that feudalism, under conditions of overpopulation and low productivity, will allow more people to live than would capitalist institutions-in other words, in poor countries feudalism allows fewer people to starve than does capitalism. Our own hope is to recover some of the communal advantages of pre-modern society in a postmodern form, that is, without sacrificing the gains in individual freedom, human rights, and political equality achieved in the modern period (see Gould 1978, chap. 1).

7. Editor's Note: The authors have created an "Index of Sustainable Economic Welfare" which is based on the following variables: personal consumption, distributional inequality, household labor services, services from consumer durables, services from highways and streets, improvements in health & education public expenditures, expenditures on consumer durables, defensive private expenditures/health & education, cost of commuting, cost of personal pollution control, cost of auto accidents, costs of water pollution, costs of air pollution, costs of noise pollution, loss of wetlands, loss of farmland, depletion of non-renewable resources, long-term environmental damage, cost of ozone depletion, net capital growth, and change in net international position. For a full description of the construction of this index and the results

for the United States from 1950 and 1990, see the Appendix in Daly & Cobb (1994).

To quote the authors: "Despite the year to year variations in ISEW, it indicates a long-term trend from the late 1970s to the present that is indeed bleak. Economic welfare has been deteriorating for a decade largely as a result of growing income inequality, the exhaustion of rsources, the unsustainable reliance on capital from overseas to pay for domestic consumption and investment. . . . The most fundamental problem in terms of sustainable economic welfare is the decline in the quality of energy resources as measured by the ratio of energy output to energy input (p. 507)."

REFERENCES

Barber, Benjamin R. 1986. "Against Economics: Capitalism, Socialism, but Whatever Happened to Democracy?" In *Democratic Capitalism?* edited by Fred E. Bauman. Charlottesville: University of Virginia Press.

Belloc, Hilaire. 1913. *The Servile State*. London: T. N. Foulis.

Bernstein, Richard J. 1976. *The Restructuring of Economic and Political Theory*. New York: Harcourt Brace Jovanovitch.

Bowles, Samuel, and Herbert Gintis. 1986. *Democracy and Capitalism: Property, Community and the Contradictions of Modern Social Thought*. New York: Basic.

Daly, Herman E. and John B. Cobb, Jr. 1994. *For the General Good*, Beacon Press: Boston.

Drewnowski, Jan. 1961. "The Economic Theory of Socialism: A Suggestion for Reconsideration." *Journal of Political Economy* 69, no. 4.

Dumbald, Edward, ed. 1955. The Political Writings of Thomas Jefferson. Indianapolis: Bobbs Merrill.

Georgescu-Roegen, Nicholas. 1950. "Economic Theory and Agrarian Economics." *Oxford Economic Papers* 12.

Georgescu-Roegen, Nicholas. 1971. *The Entropy Law and the Economic Process*. Cambridge, Mass.: Harvard University Press.

Goodland, R. J. A. 1987. "How to Save the Jungle: Opportunities for Personal Action." November 7. Mimeograph.

Gould, Carol C. 1978. *Marx's Social Ontology: Individuality and Community in Marx's Theory of Social Reality*. Cambridge, Mass.: MIT Press.

Harrington, Michael. 1986. *The Next Left*. New York: Henry Holt.

Heilbroner, Robert. 1980. *An Inquiry into the Human Prospect: Updated and Reconsidered for the 1980's*. New York: Norton.

Henderson, Hazel. 1978. *Creating Alternative Futures*. New York: Berkley.

Kohr, Leopold. 1957. *The Breakdown of Nations*. New York: Rinehart.

Laslet, Peter. 1965. *The World We Have Lost*. New York: Scribner.

Maital, Shlomo. 1982. *Minds, Markets, and Money*. New York: Basic.

Mill, John Stuart. 1973. *Principles of Political Economy*, edited by William Ashby. Clifton, N.J.: Kelly.

Mulcahey, Richard E. 1952. *The Economics of Heinrich Pesch*. New York: Holt.

Nisbett, Robert. 1966. *The Sociological Imagination*. New York: Basic.

Polanyi, Karl. [1944] 1957. The Great Transformation. Reprint. Boston: Beacon.

Schumpeter, Joseph. 1975. "The Future of Private Enterprise in the Face of Modern Socialistic Tendencies." *History of Political Economy* 7, no. 3: 294-298.

Seers, Dudley. 1983. *The Political Economy of Nationalism*. Oxford: Oxford University Press.

Stackhouse, Max L. 1985. "Jesus and Economics." In *The Bible in American Law, Politics, and Political Rhetoric*, edited by James Turner Johner. Philadelphia: Fortress.

Thurow, Lester C. 1983. *Dangerous Currents*. New York: Random House.

Weisskopf, Walter. 1971. *Alienation and Economics*. New York: Dutton.

THE DEVELOPMENT OF AN ECOLOGICAL ECONOMICS

Robert Costanza
Professor, Center for Environmental Science and Biology, and
Director, University of Maryland
Institute for Ecological Economics

Cutler Cleveland
Director, Center for Energy and Environmental Studies
Boston University

and

Charles Perrings
Head, Department of Environmental Economics and
Environmental Management
University of York

HISTORICAL ROOTS AND MOTIVATIONS

Ecology and economics have developed as separate disciplines throughout their recent histories in the 20th century. While each has addressed the way in which living systems self-organize to enable individuals and communities to meet their goals, and while each has borrowed theoretical concepts from the other and shared patterns of thinking with other sciences, they began with different first principles, addressed separate issues, utilized different assumptions to reach answers, and supported different interests in the policy process. Bringing these domains of thought together and attempting to reintegrate the natural and social sciences has lead to what we call ecological economics. After numerous experiments with joint meetings between economists and ecologists in the 1980's (e.g. Jansson 1984), the International Society for Ecological Economics (ISEE) was formed in 1988, the journal, Ecological Economics, was initiated and published its first issue in February of 1989 (currently publishing 12 issues per year), and major international conferences have brought together ecologists, economists and a broad range of other scientists and practitioners. Several ecological economic institutes have been formed around the world, and a significant number of books have appeared with the term ecological economics in their titles (e.g. Martinez Alier 1987, Costanza 1991, Peet 1992, The Group of Green Economists 1992, Jansson et al 1994, Barbier et al. 1994, Costanza et al. 1997a, Edward-Jones et al. 2000).

As Martinez-Alier (1987) and Cleveland (1987) point out, ecological economics has historical roots as long and deep as any field in economics or the natural sciences, going back to at least the 17th century. Nevertheless, its immediate roots lie in work done in the 1960s and 1970s. Kenneth Boulding's classic "The economics of the coming spaceship Earth" (Boulding 1966) set the stage for ecological economics with its description of the transition from the "frontier economics" of the past, where growth in human welfare implied growth in material consumption, to the "spaceship economics" of the future, where growth in welfare can no longer be fueled by growth in material consumption. This fundamental difference in vision and world view was elaborated further by Daly (1968) in recasting economics as a life science - akin to biology and especially ecology, rather than a physical science like chemistry or physics. The importance of this shift in "pre-analytic vision" (Schumpeter 1950) cannot be overemphasized. It implies a fundamental change in the perception of the problems of resource allocation and how they should be addressed. More particularly, it implies that the focus of analysis should be shifted from marketed resources in the economic system to the biophysical basis of interdependent ecological and economic systems, (Clark, 1973; Martinez-Alier, 1987; Cleveland, 1987; and Christensen, 1989).

The broader focus of ecological economics is carried in a 'systems' framework. The systems approach, with its origins in non-linear mathematics, general systems theory, non-equilibrium thermodynamics, and ecosystem ecology, is a comparatively recent development that has opened up lines of inquiry that were off the agenda for earlier work in what Lotka termed biophysical economics (Clark 1976, Cleveland 1987, Martinez-Alier 1987, Christensen 1989, Clark and Munroe 1994). While bioeconomic and ecological economic models both incorporate the dynamics of the natural resources under exploitation, the former tend to take a partial rather than a general equilibrium approach (van der Ploeg et al. 1987).

The core problem addressed in ecological economics is the sustainability of interactions between economic and ecological systems. Ecological economics addresses the relationships between ecosystems and economic systems in the broadest sense (Costanza 1991). It involves issues that are fundamentally cross-scale, transcultural and transdisciplinary, and calls for innovative approaches to research, to policy and to the building of social institutions (Costanza and Daly 1987, Common and Perrings 1992, Holling 1994, Berkes and Folke 1994, d'Arge 1994, Golley 1994, Viederman 1994). In this sense, ecological economics tends to be characterized by a holistic "systems" approach that goes beyond the normal territorial boundaries of the academic disciplines.

BASIC ORGANIZING PRINCIPLES OF ECOLOGICAL ECONOMICS

Ecological economics is not a single new discipline based in shared assumptions and theory. It rather represents a commitment among natural and social scientists, and practitioners, to develop a new understanding of the way in which different living systems interact with one another, and to draw lessons from this for both analysis and policy. Ecological economics is conceptually pluralistic. This means that even while people writing in ecological economics were trained in a particular discipline (and may prefer that mode of thinking over others) they are open to and appreciative of other modes of thinking and actively seek a constructive dialogue among disciplines (Norgaard 1989). There is not one right approach or model because, like the blind men and the elephant, the subject is just too big and complex to touch it all with one limited set of perceptual or computational tools.

Within this pluralistic paradigm, traditional disciplinary perspectives are perfectly valid as part of the mix. Ecological economics therefore includes some aspects of environmental economics, traditional ecology and ecological impact studies, and several other disciplinary perspectives as components, but it also encourages completely new, hopefully more integrated, ways to think about the linkages between ecological and economic systems.

The broad spectrum of relationships between ecosystems and economic systems are the locus of many of our most pressing current problems (i.e. sustainability, acid rain, global warming, species extinction, wealth distribution) but they are not covered adequately by any existing discipline. Environmental and resource economics, as they are usually practiced, are subdisciplines of economics focused on the efficient allocation of scarce environmental resources but generally ignoring ecosystem dynamics and scale issues, and paying only scant attention to distribution issues (Cropper and Oates 1992). Ecology, as it is currently practiced, sometimes deals with human impacts on ecosystems, but the more common tendency is to stick to "natural" systems and exclude humans. Ecological economics aims to extend these modest areas of overlap. Its basic organizing principles include the idea that ecological and economic systems are complex, adaptive, living systems that need to be studied as integrated, co-evolving systems in order to be adequately understood (Holling 1986, Proops 1989, Costanza et al. 1993).

Ecological economics also focuses on a broader set of goals than the traditional disciplines. Here, again, the differences are not so much the newness of the goals, but rather the attempt to integrate them. Daly

(1992) lays out these goals in a hierarchical form as:

(1) assessing and insuring that the scale of human activities within the biosphere are ecologically sustainable;

(2) distributing resources and property rights fairly, both within the current generation of humans and between this and future generations, and also between humans and other species; and

(3) efficiently allocating resources as constrained and defined by 1 and 2 above, including both marketed and non-marketed resources, especially natural capital and ecosystem services.

That these goals are interdependent and yet need to be addressed hierarchically is elaborated by Common and Perrings (1992), who differentiate between "Solow" or economic sustainability (Solow 1974, 1986) and "Holling" or ecological sustainability (see Holling 1986) and find them to be largely disjoint. The problem of ecological sustainability needs to be solved at the level of preferences or technology, not at the level of optimal prices. Only if the preferences and production possibility sets informing economic behavior are ecologically sustainable can the corresponding set of optimal and intertemporally efficient prices be ecologically sustainable. Thus the principle of "consumer sovereignty" on which most conventional economic solutions is based, is only acceptable to the extent that consumer interests do not threaten the overall system - and through this the welfare of future generations. This implies that if one's goals include ecological sustainability then one cannot rely on consumer sovereignty, and must allow for co-evolving preferences, technology, and ecosystems. One of the basic organizing principles of ecological economics is thus a focus on this complex interrelationship between ecological sustainability (including system carrying capacity and resilience), social sustainability (including distribution of wealth and rights and coevolving preferences) and economic sustainability (including allocative efficiency).

A major implication of this is that our ability to predict the consequences of economic behavior is limited by our ability to predict the evolution of the biosphere. The complexity of the many interacting systems that make up the biosphere means that this involves a very high level of uncertainty. Indeed, uncertainty is a fundamental characteristic of all complex systems involving irreversible processes (Costanza and Cornwell 1992, Ludwig et al. 1993, Costanza 1994, Clark and Munro 1994). It follows that ecological economics is particularly concerned with problems of uncertainty. More particularly, it is concerned with the problem of assuring sustainability under uncertainty. Instead of locking ourselves into development paths that may ultimately lead to ecological collapse, we need to maintain the resilience of ecological and socioeconomic systems (Hammer et al. 1993; Holling 1994, Jansson and Jansson

1994, Perrings 1994) by conserving and investing in natural assets (Costanza and Daly 1992).

MATERIAL AND ENERGY FLOWS IN ECOLOGICAL AND ECONOMIC SYSTEMS: THEORY AND APPLICATIONS

One focus of the work on joint ecological economic systems has been material and energy flows. A dominant theme in this body of work has been the grounding of conventional economic models in the biophysical realities of the economic process. This emphasis shifts the focus from exchange to the production of wealth itself (Cleveland et al. 1984). Cleveland (1987) traces the early roots of this work dating back to the Physiocrats (Quesnay 1758, Podilinsky 1883, Soddy 1922, Lotka 1922, and Cottrell 1955). The energy and environmental events of the 1960's and 1970's pushed work in this area to new levels. Energy and material flow analysis in recent times is rooted in the work of a number of economists, ecologists, and physicists. Economists such as Boulding (1966) and Geogescu-Roegen (1971, 1973) demonstrated the environmental and economic implications of the mass and energy balance principle. Ecologists such as Lotka (1922) and Odum (Odum and Pinkerton 1955, Odum 1971) pointed out the importance of energy in the structure and evolutionary dynamics of ecological and economic systems. And physicists such as Prigogine (Nicolis and Prigogine 1977, Prigogine and Stengers 1984) worked out the far-from-equilibrium thermodynamics of living systems.

The principle of the conservation of mass and energy has formed the basis for a number of important contributions. The assumption was first made explicit in the context of a general equilibrium model by Ayres and Kneese (1969) and subsequently by Mäler (1974), but it also is a feature of the series of linear models developed after 1966 (Cumberland 1966, Victor 1972, Lipnowski 1976, Geogescu-Roegen 1977). All reflect the assumption that a closed physical system must satisfy the conservation of mass condition, and hence that economic growth necessarily increases both the extraction of environmental resources and the volume of waste deposited in the environment.

Perrings (1986, 1987) developed a variant of the Neumann-Leontief-Sraffa general equilibrium model in the context of a jointly determined economy-environment system subject to a conservation of mass constraint. The model demonstrates that the conservation of mass contradicts the free disposal, free gifts, and non-innovation assumptions of such models. An expanding economy causes continuous disequilibrating change in the environment. Since market prices in an interdependent economy-environment system often do not accurately reflect environmental change, such transformations of the environment often will go unanticipated.

Ayres (1978) describes some of the important implications of the laws of thermodynamics for the production process, including the limits they place on the substitution of human capital for natural capital and the ability of technical change to offset the depletion or degradation of natural capital. Although they may be substitutes in individual processes in the short run, natural capital and human-made capital ultimately are complements because both manufactured and human capital require materials and energy for their own production and maintenance (Costanza 1980). The interpretation of traditional production functions such as the Cobb-Douglas or constant elasticity of substitution (CES) must be modified to avoid the erroneous conclusion that "self-generating technological change" can maintain a constant output with ever-decreasing amounts of energy and materials as long as ever-increasing amounts of human capital are available.

Furthermore, there are irreducible thermodynamic minimum amounts of energy and materials required to produce a unit of output that technical change cannot alter. In sectors that are largely concerned with processing and/or fabricating materials, technical change is subject to diminishing returns as it approaches these thermodynamic minimums (Ayres 1978). Ruth (1995) uses equilibrium and non-equilibrium thermodynamics to describe the materials-energy-information relationship in the biosphere and in economic systems. In addition to illuminating the boundaries for material and energy conversions in economic systems, thermodynamic assessments of material and energy flows, particularly in the case of effluents, can provide information about depletion and degradation that are not reflected in market price.

There is also the effect of the time rate of thermodynamic processes on their efficiency, and more importantly, their power or rate of doing useful work. Odum and Pinkerton (1955) pointed out that to achieve the thermodynamic minimum energy requirements for a process implied running the process infinitely slowly. This means at a rate of production of useful work (power) of zero. Both ecological and economic systems must do useful work in order to compete and survive and Odum and Pinkerton showed that for maximum power production an efficiency significantly worse than the thermodynamic minimum was required.

These biophysical foundations have been incorporated into models of natural resource supply and of the relationship between energy use and economic performance. Cleveland and Kaufmann (1991) developed econometric models that explicitly represent and integrate the geologic, economic, and political forces that determine the supply of oil in the United States. Those models are superior in explaining the historical record than those from any single discipline. Larsson et al. (1994) also use energy and material flows to demonstrate the dependence of a renewable resource such as commercial shrimp farming on the services generated by marine and agricultural ecosystems.

One important advance generated by this work is the economic importance of energy quality, namely, that a kcal of primary electricity can produce more output than an kcal of oil, a kcal of oil can produce more output than an kcal of coal, and so on. Odum (1971) describes how energy use in ecological and economic hierarchies tends to increase the quality of energy, and that significant amounts of energy are dissipated to produce higher quality forms that perform critical control and feedback functions which enhance the survival of the system. Cleveland et al. (1984) and Kaufmann (1992) show that much of the decline in the energy/real GDP ratio in industrial nations is due to the shift from coal to petroleum and primary electricity. Their results show that autonomous energy-saving technical change has had little, if any, effect on the energy/real GDP ratio. Stern (1993) finds that accounting for fuel quality produces an unambiguous causal connection between energy use and economic growth in the United States, confirming the unique, critical role that energy plays in the production of wealth.

The analysis of energy flows has also been used to illuminate the structure of ecosystems (e.g. Odum, 1957). Hannon (1973) applied input-output analysis (originally developed to study interdependence in economies) to the analysis of energy flow in ecosystems. This approach quantifies the direct plus indirect energy that connects an ecosystem component to the remainder of the ecosystem. Hannon demonstrates this methodology using energy flow data from the classic study of the Silver Springs, Florida food web (Odum, 1957). These approaches hold the possibility of treating ecological and economic systems in the same conceptual framework - one of the primary goals of ecological economics (Hannon et al. 1986, 1991, Costanza and Hannon 1989).

ACCOUNTING FOR NATURAL CAPITAL, ECOLOGICAL LIMITS, AND SUSTAINABLE SCALE

Most current economic policies are largely based on the underlying assumption of continuing and unlimited material economic growth. Although this assumption is slowly beginning to change as the full implications of a commitment to sustainability sink in, it is still deeply imbedded in economic thinking as evidenced by the frequent equation of "sustainable development" with "sustainable growth". The growth assumption allows problems of intergenerational, intragenerational, and interspecies equity and sustainability to be ignored (or at least post-poned), since they are seen to be most easily solved by additional material growth (Arrow et al 1995). Indeed, most conventional economists define "health" in an economy as a stable and high rate of growth. Energy and resource depletion, pollution, and other limits to growth, according to this view, will be eliminated as they arise by clever development and deployment of new technology. This line of thinking often is called "technological optimism" (Costanza 1989, 2000).

An opposing line of thought (often called "technological skepticism") assumes that technology will not be able to circumvent fundamental energy, resource, or pollution constraints and that eventually material economic growth will stop. It has usually been ecologists or other life scientists (e.g. Ehrlich 1989, Daily and Ehrlich 1992 - chapter 28) that take this point of view (notable exceptions among economists are Boulding, 1966, and Daly, 1968, 1977), largely because they study natural systems that invariably do stop growing when they reach fundamental resource constraints. A healthy ecosystem is one that maintains a relatively stable level. Unlimited growth is cancerous, not healthy, under this view.

Technological optimists argue that human systems are fundamentally different from other natural systems because of human intelligence and that history has shown that resource constraints can be circumvented by new ideas (Myers and Simon 1994). Technological optimists claim that Malthus' dire predictions about population pressures have not come to pass and the "energy crisis" of the late 70's is behind us. Technological skeptics, on the other hand, argue that many natural systems also have "intelligence" in that they can evolve new behaviors and organisms (including humans themselves). Humans are therefore a part of nature not apart from it. Just because we have circumvented local and artificial resource constraints in the past does not mean we can circumvent the fundamental ones that we will eventually face. Malthus' predictions have not come to pass yet for the entire world, the skeptics would argue, but many parts of the world are in a Malthusian trap now, and other parts may well fall into it. This is particularly important because many industrial nations have increased their numbers and standard of living by importing carrying capacity and exporting ecological degradation to other regions.

The debate has gone on for several decades now. It began with Barnett and Morse's (1963) "Scarcity and growth" but really got into high gear only with the publication of "The limits to growth" by Meadows et al. (1972) and the Arab oil embargo in 1973. Several thousand studies over the last fifteen years have considered aspects of our energy and resource future, and different points of view have waxed and waned.

But the bottom line is that there is still considerable uncertainty about the impacts of energy and resource constraints. In the next 20-30 years we may begin to hit real fossil fuel supply limits. Will fusion energy or solar energy or conservation or some as yet unthought of energy source step in to save the day and keep economies growing? The technological optimists say 'yes' and the technological skeptics say 'maybe' but let's not count on it. Ultimately, no one knows.

The more specific issues of concern all revolve around the question of limits: the ability of technology to circumvent them, and the long run costs of the technological "cures." Do we adapt to limits with technologies that have potentially large but uncertain future environmental costs or do we limit population and per capita consumption to levels sustainable with technologies which are known to be more environmentally benign? Must we always increase supply or can we also reduce demand? Is there an optimal mix of the two?

If the 'limits' are not binding constraints on economic activity, then conventional economics' relegation of energy and environmental concerns to the side of the stage is probably appropriate, and detailed energy analysis are nothing more than interesting curiosities. But if the limits are binding constraints, then energy and environmental issues are pushed much more forcefully to center stage and the tracking of energy and resource flows through ecological and economic systems becomes much more useful and important.

Issues of sustainability are ultimately issues about limits. If material economic growth is sustainable indefinitely by technology then all environmental problems can (in theory at least) be fixed technologically Issues of fairness, equity, and distribution (between subgroups and generations of our species and between our species and others) are also issues of limits. We do not have to worry so much about how an expanding pie is divided, but a constant or shrinking pie presents real problems. Finally, dealing with uncertainty about limits is the fundamental issue. If we are unsure about future limits the prudent course is to assume they exist. One does not run blindly through a dark landscape that may contain crevasses. One assumes they are there and goes gingerly and with eyes wide open, at least until one can see a little better.

Vitousek et al. (1986) in an oft-cited paper estimated the percent of the earth's net primary production (NPP) which is being appropriated by humans. This was the first attempt to estimate the "scale" or relative size of human economic activity compared to the ecological life support system. They estimated that 25% of total NPP (including the oceans) and 40% of terrestrial NPP was currently being appropriated by humans. It left open the question of how much of NPP could be appropriated by humans without damaging the life support functions of the biosphere, but it is clear that 100% is not sustainable and even the 40% of terrestrial NPP currently used may not be sustainable. Daily and Ehrlich (1992) add more depth to these arguments by considering the relationships between the size and relative impact of the human population relative to the earth's carrying capacity and the implications for sustainability. Arrow et al. (1995) add a recent interdisciplinary consensus on this relationship.

A related idea is that ecosystems represent a form of capital - defined as a stock yielding a flow of services -- and that this stock of "natural capital" needs to be maintained intact independently in order to assure ecological sustainability (El Serafy 1991, Victor 1991, Costanza and Daly 1992). The question of whether natural capital needs to be maintained independently ("strong sustainability") or whether only the total of all capital stocks need to be maintained ("weak sustainability") has been the subject of some debate. It hinges on the degree to which human-made capital can substitute for natural capital, and, indeed, on how one defines capital generally (Victor 1991). In general, conventional economists have argued that there is almost perfect substitutability between natural and human-made capital (Nordhaus and Tobin 1972), while ecological economists generally argue on both theoretical (Costanza and Daly 1992) and empirical grounds (Kaufmann 1995) that the possibilities for substitution are severely limited. They therefore generally favor the strong sustainability position.

Another critical set of issues revolve around the way we define economic income, economic welfare, and total human welfare. Daly and Cobb (1989) clearly distinguish these concepts, and point out that conventional GNP is a poor measure of even economic income. Yet GNP continues to be used in most policy discussions as the measure of economic health and performance, and will continue to be until viable alternatives are available. According to Hicks (1948) economic income is defined as the quantity we can consume without damaging our future consumption possibilities. This definition of income automatically embodies the idea of sustainability. GNP is a poor measure of income on a number of grounds, including the fact that it fails to account for the depletion of natural capital (Mäler 1991) and thus is not "sustainable" income in the Hicksian sense. GNP is an even poorer measure of economic welfare, since many components of welfare are not directly related to income and consumption. The Index of Sustainable Economic Welfare (ISEW) devised by Daly and Cobb (1989) is one approach to estimating economic welfare (as distinct from income) that holds significant promise. [Editor's Note: for a brief description of this index, see footnote 7 in the chapter by Daly and Cobb in this volume.] The ISEW has been calculated for several industrialized countries and shows that in all these cases, an "economic threshold" has been passed where increasing GNP in no longer contributing to increasing welfare, and in fact in most cases is decreasing it (Max-Neef, 1995).

VALUATION OF ECOLOGICAL SERVICES

All decisions concerning the allocation of environmental resources imply the valuation of those resources. Ecological economics does not eschew valuation. It is recognized that the decisions we make, as a society, about ecosystems imply a valuation of those systems. We can choose to make these valuations explicit or not; we can undertake them using the best available ecological science and understanding or not; we can do them with an explicit acknowledgment of the huge uncertainties involved or not; but as long as we are forced to make choices about the use of resources we are valuing those resources. These values will reflect differences in the underlying world view and culture of which we are a part (e.g. Costanza 1991, Berkes and Folke 1994), just as they will reflect differences in preferences, technology, assets and income. An ecological economics approach to valuation implies an assessment of the spatial and temporal dynamics of ecosystem services, and their role in satisfying both individual and social preferences. It also implies explicit treatment of the uncertainties associated with tracking these dynamics (Costanza et al. 1993).

Ecological economics is different from environmental economics in this regard in terms of the latitude of approaches to the ecosystem valuation problem it allows. It includes more conventional willingness to pay (WTP) based approaches, but it also explores other more novel methods based on explicitly modeling the linkages between ecosystems and economic systems in the long run (Costanza and Folke 1997). Costanza et al. (1989) explore this comparison by estimating both WTP based and energy analysis based values for wetlands in coastal Louisiana, and find an interesting degree of agreement. This emphasis on the direct assessment of ecosystem functions and values, independently and prior to attempting to tie it to people's perceptions of those functions and values, is extended in de Groot (1994) and Larsson et al. (1994), who enumerate these functions and estimate them for an example in Columbia, respectively. A more recent study (Costanza et al. 1997) synthesized a range of previous studies using a variety of techniques and estimated the total global value of ecosystem services at 16-54 trillion $US/yr -- in the same order of magnitude as global GNP.

Spash and Hanley (1995) look at the issues of preference formation and limited information in estimating WTP based values for biodiver-

sity preservation. They conclude on empirical grounds that a significant portion of individuals exhibit "lexicographic" preferences - that is
they refuse to make trade-offs which require the substitution of biodiversity for other goods. This places significant constraints on the use of
stated preferences, as used in contingent valuation studies, for valuation of ecosystem services and decision making. It places more emphasis on the need to develop more direct methods to assess the value of
these resources as a supplement to conventional WTP based methods.

Bingham et al. (1995) provide a broad interdisciplinary consensus
and summary of these issues, which resulted from a US EPA funded
policy forum on ecosystem valuation. The forum emphasized the need
to develop "decisive information" relevant to management problems
and choices.

The issue of ecosystem valuation is far from solved. In fact it is
probably only in the early stages of development. Conventional WTP
based approaches have severe limitations. Key directions for the future
pointed to in Bingham et al. (1995) and Costanza et al. (1997) include
integrated ecological economic modeling, as elaborated in the next section.

INTEGRATED ECOLOGICAL ECONOMIC MODELING AND ASSESS-
MENT

The emphasis on (a) issues of scale and limits to the carrying and assimilative capacity of ecological systems, and (b) underlying dynamics of
those systems both imply the need for a new approach to the modeling
of joint systems. It is not surprising, therefore, that this is an active area
of research in ecological economics. Indeed, it is where we most expect
new advances to be made as a result of the ongoing dialogue between
economists and ecologists.

The range of issues that need to be addressed in attempting to integrate economic and ecological models was first explored by Braat and
van Lierop (1987). While the next steps are likely to be even harder, as
we shall see later, they indicate just how difficult it is to take even the
first steps in bridging the modeling gap between disciplines that have
long diverged both methodologically and conceptually. Costanza, Sklar
and White (1990), Hall and Hall (1993), Bockstael et al (1995) and Voinov
et al. (1999) illustrate some of the reasons why this is so, while developing new types of ecological economic models to overcome these difficulties. One reason for the difficulty in bridging the modeling gap is that
economics, as a discipline, has developed almost no tools or concepts to
handle spatial differentiation beyond the notions of transport cost and
international trade. The spatial analysis of human activity has been

seen as the domain of geographers, and has had remarkably little impact on the way that economists have analyzed the allocation of resources. This makes collaboration between economists and disciplines based more directly on spatial analysis very difficult. Yet, recent work in this area shows just how important an understanding of economic and ecological landscapes is to the development of integrated models. The program of research, is having to develop new concepts as well as new models to deal with this problem. Liu, Cubbage and Pulliam (1994) offer another example of the importance of landscape in identifying the economic implications of such familiar concepts as forest rotation times. Since the development of spatially explicit integrated models is one of the areas in which ecological economics is expected to develop most rapidly in the next few years, it would seem that geographers are likely to become an increasingly important part of the research agenda in ecological-economics.

A second characteristic of ecological-economic models concerns the way in which the valuation of ecological functions and processes is reflected in the model structure. The point was made in the previous section that valuation by stated preference methods (estimation of willingness to pay or accept using contingent valuation or contingent ranking) may capture the strength of people's perceptions and their level of income and endowments (their ability to pay), but it generally fails to capture the impact of a change in ecosystem functions and processes on the output of economically valued goods and services. Unless the role of non-marketed ecological functions and processes in the production of economically valued goods and services is explicitly modeled, it is hard to see how they can be properly accounted for in economic decision-making. Barbier (1994) and Ruitenbeek (1994) illustrate ways in which ecological functions and processes are embedded in decision-models, and the implications this has for valuation.

A third characteristic concerns the role of integrated modeling in strategic decision-making. One of the challenges to ecological economics has been to devise methods to address strategic 'what if' questions in a way that reflects the dynamics of the jointly determined system. This is clearly an extremely difficult task, and we indicate some of the reasons why this is so momentarily. Baker, Fennesy and Mitsch (1991) and Duchin and Lange (1994) illustrate different approaches to the task at the microeconomic and macroeconomic levels respectively. The general problem confronting anyone attempting to model long-run dynamics explicitly is that ecological economic systems are complex non-linear systems. The dynamics of economic systems are not independent of the dynamics of the ecological systems which constitute their environment, and that as economies grow relative to their environment, the dynamics of the jointly determined system can become increasingly discontinuous (Perrings 1986, Costanza et al 1993, Arrow et al. 1995). Indeed, the development of ecological economics can be thought of as part of a widespread reappraisal of such systems.

In ecology, this reappraisal has influenced recent research on scale, complexity, stability and resilience; and is beginning to influence the theoretical treatment of the coevolution of species and systems. The results that are most important to the development of ecological economics concern the link between the spatial and temporal structure of coevolutionary hierarchical systems. Landscapes are conceptualized as hierarchies, each level of which involves a specific temporal and spatial scale (Holling 1987, 1992, Costanza et al. 1993). The dynamics of each level of the structure are predictable so long as the biotic potential of the level is consistent with bounds imposed by the remaining levels in the hierarchy. Change in either the structure of environmental constraints or the biotic potential of the level may induce threshold effects that lead to complete alteration in the state of the system (O'Neill, Johnson and King, 1989).

In economics there is now considerable interest in the dynamics of complex non-linear systems (Anderson et al. 1988, Brock and Malliaris 1989, Goodwin 1990, Puu 1989, Hommes 1991, Benhabib 1992). Economists have paid less attention to spatial scale and its significance at or near system thresholds (though see Puu 1981, Rosser 1990), but there is now a growing body of literature with roots in geography which seeks to inject a spatial dimension into nonlinear economic models (see for example White, 1990). There is also an economic analog to the biologist's interest in evolution and the significance of codependence between gene landscapes. The steady accumulation of evidence that economic development is not a stationary process, that human understanding, preferences and technology all change with development and that such change is generally non-linear and discontinuous, has prompted economists to seek to endogenize technological change (Romer 1990). Although the adaptation of this work by environmental economists has been rather disappointing, the treatment of technology and consumption preferences as endogenous to the economic process is a fundamental change that brings economics much closer to ecology.

The challenge to ecological economics in the future is to develop models that capture these features well enough to incorporate at least the major risks in economic decisions that increase the level of stress on ecological systems.

SUMMARY AND CONCLUSIONS

This paper is a sample of the range of transdisciplinary thinking that can be put under the heading of ecological economics and the theories and models that have informed that work. While it is difficult to categorize ecological economics in the same way one would a normal academic discipline, some general characteristics can be enumerated.

- the core problem is the sustainability of interactions between economic and ecological systems.
- an explicit attempt is made at pluralistic dialogue and integration across disciplines, rather than territorial disciplinary differentiation.
- an emphasis is placed on integration of the three hierarchical goals of sustainable scale, fair distribution, and efficient allocation.
- there is a deep concern with the biophysical underpinnings of the functioning of jointly determined ecological and economic systems.
- there is a deep concern with the relationship between the scale of economic activity and the nature of change in ecological systems.
- since valuation based on stated willingness to pay reflects limitations in the valuer's knowledge of ecosystems functions, there is an emphasis on the development of valuation techniques that build on an understanding of the role of ecosystem functions in economic production.
- there is a broad focus on systems and systems dynamics, scale, and hierarchy and on integrated modeling of ecological economic systems.

These characteristics make ecological economics applicable to some of the major problems facing humanity today, which occur at the interfaces of human and natural systems, and especially to the problem of assuring humanity's health and survival within the biosphere into the indefinite future. It is not so much the individual core scientific questions that set ecological economics apart - since these questions are covered independently in other disciplines as well - but rather the treatment of these questions in an integrated, transdisciplinary way, which we feel is essential to their understanding and the development of effective policies. The solutions being considered in ecological economics are deserving of increasing attention.

REFERENCES

Anderson P., K. Arrow, and D. Pines 1988. *The economy as an evolving complex system*, Santa Fe Institute Studies in the Sciences of Complexity V, Redwood City CA, Addison Wesley.

Arrow, K., B. Bolin, R. Costanza, P. Dasgupta, C. Folke, C. S. Holling, B-O. Jansson, S. Levin, K-G. Mäler, C. Perrings, and D. Pimentel. 1995. Economic growth, carrying capacity, and the environment. *Science* 268:520-521.

Ayres, R. U., 1978. Application of physical principles to economics. pp. 37-71 in: R. U. Ayres. *Resources, Environment, and Economics: Applications of the Materials/Energy Balance Principle*. John Wiley and Sons, New York

Ayres, R. U. and A. V. Kneese. 1969. Production, consumption, and externalities. *The American Economic Review*. 59:282-297

Baker, K. A., M. S. Fennessy, and W. J. Mitsch. 1991. Designing wetlands for controlling mine drainage: an ecologic-economic modelling approach. *Ecological Economics*, 3:1-24.

Barbier, E. B., J. C. Burgess and C. Folke. 1994. *Paradise lost? the ecological economics of biodiversity*. Earthscan, London. 267 pp.

Barbier, E.B. 1994 Valuing environmental functions: tropical wetlands, *Land Economics* 70:155-174.

Barnett, H. J. and C. Morse. 1963. *Scarcity and growth: the economics of natural resource availability.* Johns Hopkins, Baltimore.

Benhabib J. ed. 1992. Cycles and chaos in economic equilibrium, Princeton, Princeton University Press.

Berkes, F. and C. Folke. 1994. Investing in cultural capital for sustainable use of natural capital. pp. 128-149 in: A. M. Jansson, M. Hammer, C. Folke, and R. Costanza (eds). *Investing in natural capital: the ecological economics approach to sustainability*. Island press, Washington DC. 504 pp.

Bingham, G. R. Bishop, M. Brody, D. Bromley, E. Clark, W. Cooper, R. Costanza, T. Hale, G. Hayden, S. Kellert, R. Norgaard, B. Norton, J. Payne, C. Russell, and G. Suter. 1995. Issues in ecosystem valuation: improving information for decision making *Ecological Economics* 14:73-90

Bockstael, N., R. Costanza, I. Strand, W. Boynton, K. Bell, and L. Wainger. 1995. Ecological economic modeling and valuation of ecosystems. *Ecological Economics*. 14:143-159.

Boulding, K. E. 1966. The economics of the coming spaceship Earth. pp 3-14 In: H. Jarrett (Ed.) *Environmental quality in a growing economy.* Resources for the Future/Johns Hopkins University Press, Baltimore, MD.

Braat, L. C. and W. F. J. van Lierop. 1987. Integrated economic-ecological modeling. pp. 49-68 in:. L. C. Braat and W. F. J. van Lierop (eds). *Economic-ecological modeling*. North Holland, Amsterdam.

Brock W.A. and Malliaris A.G. 1989. Differential equations, stability and chaos in dynamic economics. North Holland, Amsterdam.

Christensen, P. 1989. Historical roots for ecological economics: biophysical versus allocative approaches. *Ecological Economics* 1: 17-36.

Clark, C. W. 1973. The economics of overexploitation. *Science*, 181:630-634.

Clark, C.W. 1976. *Mathematical bioeconomics: the optimal management of renewable resources*. Wiley-Interscience, New York.

Clark, C. W. and G. R. Munro. 1994. Renewable resources as natural capital: the fishery. pp. 343-361 in: A. M. Jansson, M. Hammer, C. Folke, and R. Costanza (eds). *Investing in natural capital: the ecological economics approach to sustainability*. Island press, Washington DC. 504 pp.

Cleveland, C. J. 1987. Biophysical economics: historical perspective and current research trends. *Ecological Modeling*. 38:47-74.

Cleveland, C. J. and Kaufmann, R. K. 1991. Forecasting ultimate oil recovery and its rate of production: incorporating economic forces into the models of M. King Hubbert. *The Energy Journal,* 12:17-46.

Cleveland, C. J., R. Costanza, C. A. S. Hall, and R. Kaufmann. 1984. Energy and the United States economy: a biophysical perspective. *Science*. 225:890-897.

Common M. and Perrings C. 1992. Towards an ecological economics of sustainability. *Ecological Economics* 6:7-34.

Costanza, R. 1980. Embodied energy and economic valuation. *Science*. 210:1219-1224.

Costanza, R. 1989. What is ecological economics? *Ecological Economics* .1:1-7

Costanza, R., ed. 1991. *Ecological economics: the science and management of sustainability*. Columbia University Press, New York.

Costanza, R. 1994. Three general policies to achieve sustainability. pp. 392-407 in: A. M. Jansson, M. Hammer, C. Folke, and R. Costanza (eds). *Investing in natural capital: the ecological economics approach to sustainability*. Island press, Washington DC. 504 pp.

Costanza, R. 2000. Visions of alternative (unpredictable) futures and their use in policy analysis. *Conservation Ecology* 4(1):5. [online] URL: http://www.consecol.org/vol4/iss1/art5

Costanza, R., J. C. Cumberland, H. E. Daly, R. Goodland, and R. Norgaard. 1997a. *An Introduction to Ecological Economics*. St. Lucie Press, Boca Raton, 275 pp.

Costanza, R. R. d'Arge, R. de Groot, S. Farber, M. Grasso, B. Hannon, S.

Naeem, K. Limburg, J. Paruelo, R.V. O'Neill, R. Raskin, P. Sutton, and M. van den Belt. 1997b. The value of the world's ecosystem services and natural capital. *Nature* 387:253-260

Costanza, R., and L. Cornwell. 1992. The 4P approach to dealing with scientific uncertainty. *Environment* 34: 12-20.

Costanza, R., and H. E. Daly. 1987. Toward an ecological economics. *Ecological Modelling* 38: 1-7.

Costanza, R., and H. E. Daly. 1992. Natural capital and sustainable development. *Conservation Biology* 6: 37-46.

Costanza, R. S. C. Farber, and J. Maxwell. 1989. The valuation and management of wetland ecosystems. *Ecological Economics* 1:335-361.

Costanza, R. and C. Folke. 1997. Valuing ecosystem services with efficiency, fairness and sustainability as goals. pp: 49-70 in: G. Daily (ed.), *Nature's Services: Societal Dependence on Natural Ecosystems*. Island Press, Washington, DC, 392 pp.

Costanza, R. and B. M. Hannon. 1989 Dealing with the "mixed units" problem in ecosystem network analysis. pp. 90-115 in: F. Wulff, J. G. Field, and K. H. Mann (eds). *Network analysis of marine ecosystems: methods and applications*. Coastal and Estuarine Studies Series, Springer-Verlag, Heidleberg. 284 pp.

Costanza, R., F. H. Sklar, and M. L. White. 1990. Modeling coastal landscape dynamics. *BioScience* 40:91-107

Costanza, R., L. Wainger, C. Folke, and K-G Mäler. 1993. Modeling complex ecological economic systems: toward an evolutionary, dynamic understanding of people and nature *BioScience* 43:545-555.

Cottrell, W. F., 1955. Energy and society. McGraw-Hill, New York.

Cropper, M. L. and W. E. Oates. 1992. Environmental economics: a survey. *Journal of Economic Literature*. 30:675-740.

Cumberland, J.H. 1966. A regional inter-industry model for analysis of development objectives, *Regional Science Association Papers* 17: 65-94.

d'Arge, R. C. 1994. Sustenance and sustainability: how can we preserve and consume without major conflict. pp. 113-127 in: A. M. Jansson, M. Hammer, C. Folke, and R. Costanza (eds). *Investing in natural capital: the ecological economics approach to sustainability*. Island press, Washington DC. 504 pp.

Daily, G., and P. R. Ehrlich. 1992. Population, sustainability, and Earth's carrying capacity. *BioScience* 42:761-71.

Daly, H.E. 1968. On Economics as a Life Science, *Journal of Political Economy* 76: 392-406.

Daly, H. 1977. Steady-state economics: *The Political Economy of Bio-physical Equilibrium and Moral Growth*. W.H. Freeman and Co., San Francisco

Daly, H. E. 1992. Allocation, distribution, and scale: towards an economics that is efficient, just, and sustainable. *Ecological Economics* 6:185-193.

Daly, H. E. and J. B. Cobb. 1989. Misplaced concreteness: measuring economic success. pp. 62-84 in: H. E. Daly and J. B. Cobb. *For the common good: redirecting the economy toward community, the environment, and a sustainable future.* Beacon Press, Boston. 482 pp.

de Groot, R. S. 1994. Environmental functions and the economic value of natural ecosystems. pp. 151-168 in: A. M. Jansson, M. Hammer, C. Folke, and R. Costanza (eds). *Investing in natural capital: the ecological economics approach to sustainability.* Island press, Washington DC. 504 pp.

Duchin, F. and G-M. Lange. 1994. Strategies for environmentally sound economic development. pp. 250-265 in: A. M. Jansson, M. Hammer, C. Folke, and R. Costanza (eds). *Investing in natural capital: the ecological economics approach to sustainability.* Island Press, Washington DC. 504 pp.

Edwards-Jones, G., B. Davies, and S. Hussain. 2000. *Ecological economics: an introduction.* Blackwell. Oxford. 266 pp.

Ehrlich P.R. 1989. The limits to substitution: meta-resource depletion and a new economic-ecological paradigm, *Ecological Economics*, 1, 9-16.

El Serafy, S. 1991. The environment as capital. pp. 168-175 in: R. Costanza. *Ecological economics: The science and management of sustainability.* Columbia University Press, New York. 525 pp.

Georgescu-Roegen, N. 1971. *The entropy law and the economic process.* Harvard University Press, Cambridge, MA.

Georgescu-Roegen, N. 1973. The entropy law and the economic problem. pp. 49-60 in: H. E. Daly. *Economics, ecology, ethics: essays toward a steady-state economy.* W. H. Freeman. San Francisco. 372 pp.

Georgescu-Roegen, N. 1977. Matter matters, too pp. 293-313 in: K.D. Wilson (ed), *Prospects for growth: changing expectations for the future.* Praeger, New York.

Golley, F. B. 1994. Rebuilding a humane and ethical decision system for investing in natural capital. pp. 169-178 in: A. M. Jansson, M. Hammer, C. Folke, and R. Costanza (eds). *Investing in natural capital: the ecological economics approach to sustainability.* Island press, Washington DC. 504 pp.

Goodwin, R.M. 1990. *Chaotic economic dynamics.* Clarendon, Oxford.

Hall, C. A. S. and Hall, M. H. P. 1993. The efficiency of land and energy use in tropical economies and agriculture. *Agriculture, Ecosystems, and the Environment*, 46:1-30.

Hammer, M., AM. Jansson, and B-O. Jansson. 1993. Diversity change and sustainability: implications for fisheries. *Ambio* 22: 97-105.

Hannon, B. 1973, The structure of ecosystems, *Journal of Theoretical Biology*, 41:535-46.

Hannon, B., R. Costanza, and R. A. Herendeen. 1986. Measures of energy cost and value in ecosystems. *The Journal of Environmental Economics and Management.* 13:391-401.

Hannon, B., R. Costanza, and R. Ulanowicz. 1991. A general accounting framework for ecological systems: a functional taxonomy for connectivist ecology. *Theoretical Population Biology* 40:78-104.

Hicks, J. R. 1948. *Value and capital.* 2nd ed. Clarendon, Oxford.

Holling, C. S., 1986. The resilience of terrestrial ecosystems: local surprise and global change. pp. 292-317. In: Clark, W. C. and Munn, R. E.(Editors), *Sustainable Development of the Biosphere.* Cambridge University Press, Cambridge,

Holling, C.S. 1987. Simplifying the complex: the paradigms of ecological function and structure, *European Journal of Operational Research*, 30:139-146,

Holling, C.S. 1992. Cross-scale morphology, geometry and dynamics of ecosystems. *Ecological Monographs.* 62:447-502

Holling, C. S. 1994. New science and new investments for a sustainable biosphere. pp. 57-73 in: A. M. Jansson, M. Hammer, C. Folke, and R. Costanza (eds). *Investing in natural capital: the ecological economics approach to sustainability.* Island Press, Washington DC. 504 pp.

Hommes C. 1991. *Chaotic dynamics in economic models: some simple case studies.* Wolters-Noordhoff, Groningen.

Jansson, A. M. (ed.) 1984. *Integration of economy and ecology: an outlook for the eighties.* University of Stockholm Press, Stockholm.

Jansson, A. M., M. Hammer, C. Folke, and R. Costanza (eds). *Investing in natural capital: the ecological economics approach to sustainability.* Island Press, Washington DC. 504 pp.

Janson, A. M. and B. O. Jansson. 1994. Ecosystem properties as a basis for sustainability. pp. 74-91 in: Jansson, A. M., M. Hammer, C. Folke, and R. Costanza (eds). *Investing in natural capital: the ecological economics approach to sustainability.* Island Press, Washington DC. 504 pp.

Kaufmann, R. K. 1992. A biophysical analysis of the energy/real GDP ratio: implications for substitution and technical change. *Ecological Economics,* 6: 35-56.

Kaufmann, R. K. 1995. The economic multiplier of environmental life support: can capital substitute for a degraded environment? *Ecological Economics,* 12:67-79.

Larsson, J., C. Folke, and N. Kautsky. 1994. Ecological limitations and appropriation of ecosystem support by shrimp farming in Colombia. *Environmental Management.* 18:663-676

Lipnowski, I.F. 1976. An Input-Output Analysis of Environmental Preservation, *Journal of Environmental Economics and Management* 3: 205-214.

Liu, J. F.W. Cubbage and H.R. Pulliam. 1994. Ecological and economic effects of forest landscape structure and rotation length: simulation studies using ECOLECON. *Ecological Economics* 10:249-263

Lotka, A. J. 1922. Contribution to the energetics of evolution. *Proceedings of the National Academy of Science,* 8:147-155

Ludwig, D., R. Hilborn, and C. Walters. 1993. Uncertainty, resource exploitation, and conservation: lessons from history. *Science* 260: 17,36.

Mäler, K.-G. 1974 *Environmental economics - a theoretical inquiry.* Johns Hopkins Press, Baltimore.

Mäler, K.G. 1991. National accounts and environmental resources. *Environmental and Resource Economics,* 1:1-15.

Martinez-Alier, J. 1987. Introduction. pp. 1-19 in: J. Martinez-Alier. *Ecological economics: energy, environment, and society.* Blackwell, Cambridge, MA.

Max-Neef, M. 1995. Economic growth and quality of life: a threshold hypothesis. *Ecological Economics* 15:115-118

Meadows, D. H., D. L. Meadows, J. Randers, and W. W. Behrens. 1972. *The limits to growth.* Universe, New York.

Myers, N. and J. Simon 1994. *Scarcity or abundance: a debate on the environment.* Norton, New York. 254 pp.

Nicolis G. and Prigogine I. 1977. *Self-organisation in non-equilibrium systems.* John Wiley, New York,

Nordhaus, W. and J. Tobin. 1972. *Is growth obsolete?* National Bureau of Economic Research, Columbia University Press, New York.

Norgaard, R. B. 1989. The case for methodological pluralism. *Ecological Economics.* 1:37-57

O'Neill R.V., Johnson A.R. and King A.W. 1989. A hierarchical framework for the analysis of scale, *Landscape Ecology* 3: 193-205.

Odum, H. T. 1957. Trophic structure and productivity of Silver Springs, Florida. *Ecological Monographs,* 27, 55-112.

Odum, H. T., 1971. *Environment, power and society.* Wiley-Interscience, New York.

Odum, H. T. and R. C. Pinkerton. 1955. Time's speed regulator: the optimum efficiency for maximum power output in physical and biological systems. *American Scientist,* 43:331-343.

Peet, John. 1992. *Energy and the ecological economics of sustainability.* Island Press, Washington D. C.

Perrings, C. 1986. Conservation of mass and instability in a dynamic economy-environment system. *Journal of Environmental Economics and*

Management. 13:199-211

Perrings C. 1987. *Economy and environment: a theoretical essay on the inter-dependence of economic and environmental systems.* Cambridge University Press, Cambridge.

Perrings, C. 1994. Biotic diversity, sustainable development, and natural capital. pp. 92-112 in: A. M. Jansson, M. Hammer, C. Folke, and R. Costanza (eds). *Investing in natural capital: the ecological economics approach to sustainability.* Island Press, Washington DC. 504 pp.

Podilinsky, S. 1883. Menschliche Arbeit und Einheit der Kraft. *Die Neue Zeit,* Marc-April.

Prigogine I. and Stengers I. 1984. *Order Out of Chaos: Man's New Dialogue with Nature,* New York, Bantam Books.

Proops, J. L. R. 1989. Ecological economics: rationale and problem areas. *Ecological Economics* 1:59-76

Puu T. 1981. Structural stability in geographical space, *Environment and Planning* 13: 979-989.

Puu T. 1989. *Non-linear economic dynamics.* Springer, Berlin.

Quesnay, F., 1758. Tableau Economique. In: Kuczynski, M. and Meek, R. L. (Editor), *Quesnay's Tableau Economique.* Macmillan, London.

Romer P. 1990. Endogenous technical change, *Journal of Political Economy,* 98: S71-103.

Rosser B. 1990. *From catastrophe to chaos: a general theory of economic discontinuities.* Kluwer, Dordrecht.

Ruitenbeek, H.J. 1994. Modelling economy-ecology linkages in mangroves: economic evidence for promoting conservation in Bintuni Bay, Indonesia. *Ecological Economics.* 10:233-247.

Ruth, M. 1995. Information, order and knowledge in economic and ecological systems: implications from material and energy use. *Ecological Economics* 13:99-114.

Schumpeter, J. A. 1950. *Capitalism, socialism and democracy.* Harper & Row, New York.

Soddy, F., 1922. *Cartesian economics.* Hendersons, London.

Solow, R. M. 1974. Intergenerational equity and exhaustible resources. *Review of Economic Studies Symposium.* 29-46.

Solow, R. M. 1986. On the intertemporal allocation of natural resources. *Scandinavian Journal of Economics.* 88:141-149

Spash, C. L. and N. Hanley. 1995. Preferences, information and biodiversity preservation. *Ecological Economics* 12:191-208.

Stern, D. I. 1993. Energy use and economic growth: a multivariate approach. *Energy Economics,* 15:137-150.

The Group of Green Economists. 1992. *Ecological economics: a practical programme for global reform.* Zed Books, London. 162 pgs.

van der Ploeg S.W.F., Braat L.C. and Van Lierop W.F.J. 1987. Integration of resource economics and ecology, *Ecological Modelling* 38: 171-190.

Victor, P. 1972. *Pollution, economy and environment.* George Allen and Unwin. London.

Victor, P. 1991. Indicators of sustainable development: some lessons from capital theory. *Ecological Economics*, 4:191-213.

Viederman, S. 1994. Public policy: challenge to ecological economics. pp. 467-490 in: A. M. Jansson, M. Hammer, C. Folke, and R. Costanza (eds). *Investing in natural capital: the ecological economics approach to sustainability.* Island Press, Washington DC. 504 pp.

Vitousek, P. M., P. R. Ehrlich, A. H. Ehrlich, and P. A. Matson. 1986. Human appropriation of the products of photosynthesis. *BioScience* 36: 368-73.

Voinov. A, R. Costanza, L. Wainger, R. Boumans, F. Villa, T. Maxwell and H. Voinov. 1999. The Patuxent landscape model: Integrated ecological economic modeling of a watershed. *Environmental Modelling and Software* 14:473-491

Walker B.H. and Noy-Meir I. 1982. Aspects of the stability and resilience of savanna ecosystems, pp. 577--590 in: B.J. Huntley and B.H. Walker (eds), *Ecology of tropical savannas.* Springer. Berlin.

White R.W. 1990. Transient chaotic behaviour in a hierarchical economics system, *Environment and Planning.* 22:1309-1321.

Reprinted with permission of Edward Elgar Press from: Costanza, R., C. J. Cleveland, and C. Perrings. 1997. "Introduction to the development of ecological economics." pp: xiii-xxix in: R. Costanza, C. J. Cleveland, and C. Perrings (eds.), *The Development of Ecological Economics.* Edward Elgar, Cheltenham.

ECOLOGICAL INTEGRITY AND MATERIAL GROWTH: IRRECONCILABLE CONFLICT?

William E. Rees, Ph.D.
School of Community and Regional Planning
University of British Columbia

INTRODUCTION AND ANALYTIC FRAMEWORK

Many ecologists, and ordinary citizens who simply love nature, see the loss of biodiversity and the threat to ecosystems integrity as one of the most pressing problems confronting humankind today. Maintaining ecosystems structure and function has become part of even the mainstream sustainable development agenda. For example, the UN World Commission on Environment and Development (the Brundtland Commission), which popularized the concept of 'sustainable development', argued that we must protect 'the environment' by developing more benign technologies even as the world economy continues to expand (WCED 1987). Indeed, Brundtland suggested that conservation is compatible with an expected five- to ten-fold expansion of industrial activity by 2040.

This may be wishful thinking. I argue below that there is an unavoidable conflict between maintaining the ecological integrity necessary for sustainability and growth-oriented economic development. This conflict is rooted in the nature of human beings as ecological entities whose material demands are ultimately governed by the second law of thermodynamics. The problem goes beyond concern for the natural world – analysis shows there is virtually no possibility for an industrial society of six to ten billion people using prevailing or anticipated technologies to live sustainably on Earth. Greenhouse gas accumulation, climate change, ozone depletion, fisheries collapse, land degradation, falling water tables, deforestation, toxic contamination, endocrine (hormone) mimicry, accelerating species loss – these and related trends, both local and global, are indicators that the scale of the human enterprise already exceeds the long-term carrying capacity of the ecosphere.

Despite increasing awareness of biophysical limits, human pressure on the planet is relentlessly increasing. Global population reached six billion in July, 1999 and is growing by 80 million per year; by the end of the decade (and millennium), it will have almost doubled twice in the 20th Century. All these people, rich and poor alike, have rising material expectations sustained by an economic system that assumes that these expectations are insatiable.

Society seems paralyzed by conflicting perceptions of the problem (or perhaps simply mired in deep denial). A minority of eco-centric and community-oriented individuals and groups do see the growth ethic and rampant consumerism as the issue. They argue that beyond a certain point, there is no evident relationship between income and perceived well-being. Further growth may therefore be unnecessary – the solution lies more in changing consumer behaviour and in developing policies to ensure more equitable distribution of the world's present economic output. The majority of mainstream policy makers, however, including many humanists and techno-optimists, remains dedicated to growth and consumer ideals. They see freer markets and a new efficiency revolution as the only politically feasible solution to both global ecological decline (greater wealth can purchase a 'cleaner' environment) and to the problems caused by persistent material inequity (the richest 20 percent of income earners take home sixty times as much as the poorest 20 percent [UNDP 1994]).

Environmentalism is not Human Ecology

Whatever their proposed solutions, almost everyone in the mainstream shares the perception that this is an 'environmental crisis' rather than a human ecological crisis. The distinction is not a trivial one. The former term literally externalizes the problem, effectively blaming it on an environment gone wrong or on defective resource systems which need to be managed more effectively. This perception reduces the destruction of the ecosphere to mere mechanics, a problem readily amenable to the 'technical quick fix' approach favored by industrial society. By contrast, seeing the crisis as a human ecological problem places blame squarely where it belongs, on the nature and behaviour of people themselves. It also suggests that it is human wants that need to be better controlled. This is probably the least comfortable policy domain for the 'now generation' and other denizens of modern consumer societies to contemplate.

In this paper, I start from the premise that the current dilemma is at least partly rooted in this perceptual/psychological tension. The Cartesian dualism that underpins western techno-scientific culture has created a psychological barrier between humans and the rest of nature that keeps us from truly knowing ourselves. Indeed, it is a deep irony of the human-induced "environmental crisis" that people have a dismally ill-developed understanding of themselves as ecological beings.

My overall purpose, therefore, is to reinterpret the 'environmental crisis' as a problem of human ecological dysfunction. This requires acceptance of two material facts that are virtually ignored in conventional analysis. First, human economic activity (like the economic activity of any other real-world species) requires continuous, irreversible, energy and material transformation. These transformations are ultimately subject to constraints imposed by the second law of thermodynamics (Daly 1991a,b; Georgescu-Roegen 1971, Rees 1999). Second, from the ecological perspective, humans are a component of, and participant in, most of the world's major ecosystems. In this light, material economic activity is really the expression of human ecological relationships and the economy is seen an inextricably integrated, completely contained, and wholly dependent growing subsystem of a non-growing ecosphere (Daly 1992, Rees 1995).

As noted, this perspective contrasts sharply with the conventional economic worldview. Economists tend to see the economy as more or less independent of nature. This vision is reflected in 'the circular flow of exchange value,' the conceptual model that serves as the starting point for economic analysis. The circular flow model depicts the economic process as "a pendulum movement between production and consumption within a completely closed system" (Georgescu-Roegen 1971). Value embodied in goods and services flows from firms to households in exchange for spending by households (national product). A supposedly equal value, reincarnated in factors of production, flows back to firms from households in exchange for wages, rents, profits, etc., (national income).

The problem is that this conception does not 'locate' the economy anywhere in the biophysical world. It abstracts the economy from the 'environment' within which it is actually embedded. Because it depicts the economy as "an isolated, self-renewing system with no inlets or outlets, no possible points of contact with anything outside itself," the circular flow model is an impossible platform from which to understand the realtionship of the economy to the ecoshere (Daly 1991a, 196).

So it is that fundamental conventional models are blind to the material and energy sources, physical structures and time-dependent processes that are basic to understanding ecosystems structure and function (Christensen 1991). Worse, the implied simple, reversible, mechanistic behavior of the economy is quite inconsistent with the connectivity, irreversibility, and positive feedback dynamics of complex energy, information, and eco-systems, the systems with which the economy interacts in the real world.

Remarkably, it is this ecologically empty vision that drives the prevailing global development paradigm. Less remarkably, this vision has created the (un)sustainability conundrum.

FUNDAMENTALS OF HUMAN ECOLOGY

Far-from-Equilibrium Thermodynamics

The second law of thermodynamics is fundamental to all real processes involving energy and material transformations. Since ecosystem analysis often begins with the analysis of energy and material relationships, understanding the second law is essential to understanding both the structure of whole ecosystems and the functional 'niches' of individual species, including humans.

In its simplest form, the second law states that any isolated system[1] will always tend toward equilibrium; alternately, the 'entropy' of any isolated system always increases. This means that available energy spontaneously dissipates, concentrations disperse, gradients disappear. An isolated system thus becomes increasingly unstructured in a inexorable slide toward thermodynamic equilibrium. This is a state of maximum entropy in which "nothing happens or can happen" (Ayres 1994, 3).

Early formulations of the second law referred strictly to simple isolated systems close to equilibrium. We now recognize, however, that all systems, whether isolated or not, near equilibrium or not, are subject to the same forces of entropic decay. Thus any differentiated far-from-equilibrium system has a natural tendency to erode and unravel.

But not all of them do. For much of this century, people believed that living entities were exempt from the second law since they obviously do not spontaneously run down (they don't "tend toward equilibrium"). On the contrary, biological systems, from individual fetuses to the entire ecosphere seem to gain in mass and organizational complexity over extended periods of time – they actually increase their distance from equilibrium. It seems that for describing nature, "distance from equilibrium becomes an essential parameter…, much like temperature [is] in equilibrium thermodynamics" (Prigogine 1996, Ch. 2).

This seemingly paradoxical behavior can be reconciled with the second law in light of the hierarchical organization of thermodynamic systems in nature (Kay 1991). Biophysical systems exist in loose, nested hierarchies, each component system being contained by the next level up and itself comprising a chain of linked subsystems at lower levels.[2] Living systems are thus able to import available energy and material (essergy) from their host environments and use it to maintain their internal integrity and to grow. In short, living systems maintain or increase their own distance from equilibrium by 'feeding' on their hosts. The second law also dictates that such self-organizing systems export or 'dissipate' the resultant waste (entropy) back into their hosts.

Altogether, then, modern formulations of the second law posit that all highly-ordered systems develop and grow (increase their internal order) "at the expense of increasing disorder at higher levels in the systems hierarchy" (Schneider and Kay 1994). Because such systems continuously degrade and dissipate available energy and matter they are called dissipative structures.

Self-Production by the Ecosphere...

The highest order dissipative structure on Earth is the ecosphere itself. The ecosphere comprises all the biomes and individual ecosystems on the planet and all these ecosystems develop their internal structure and maintain themselves in a far-from-equilibrium, quasi steady-state by dissipating light from the sun (the next level up in the systems hierarchy). In effect, the ecosphere feeds on the sun. (The existence of a gradient of exogenous energy is a prerequisite for life as we know it.)

In nature, green plants are the factories. Through photosynthesis, plants use solar energy and the simplest of low-grade inorganic chemicals (mainly water, carbon dioxide and a few mineral nutrients) to assemble the high-grade fats, carbohydrates, proteins, and nucleic acids upon which most other life forms and the overall functioning of the ecosphere are dependent. Because they are essentially self-feeding and use only dispersed (high entropy) substances for their growth and maintenance, green plants are called primary producers.

By contrast, all animals, bacteria, and fungi are primary, secondary, or tertiary consumers whose growth and development is achieved through the assimilation and dissipation of organic energy/matter originally assembled by plants. Although dependent on plants, consumer organisms are actually essential to the continuing functioning of the ecosystem. Consumers degrade the complex energy-rich chemicals produced by plants, dissipating the energy and releasing simple organic and inorganic chemicals back into their host ecosystems for re-use by the producer plants. (Nature invented material recycling.)

... and Consumption by the Economy

Where do humans and their economies fit in? Both economists and ecologists would agree that human beings are consumer organisms. In fact, in today's increasingly market-based society people are as likely to be called 'consumers' as they are citizens, even when the context is a non-economic one! To economists, however, 'consumption' is simply spending on good and services, measured as part of the circular flow of money through the economy. As noted however, money measures are physically dimensionless and thus devoid of material considerations.

By contrast, in ecology, consumption implies unidirectional and irreversible energy and material throughput, the degradation of energy and matter and an increase in entropy.

Ecologists actually refer to humans as macro-consumers. In general, macro-consumers are large organisms, mainly animals, that consume (i.e. dissipate) either green plants or other animals to grow, develop, and satisfy their basic metabolic needs. Humans are particularly catholic and adaptable consumers – we have wide-ranging omnivorous tastes and if we cannot consume something directly (such as grass), we domesticate an animal that will and then eat the animal. "Indeed, if one feature sets humans apart from other animals, it is the breadth of the ecological niche we presently occupy" (Flannery 1994, 142). (This, combined with learning and cumulative technology, makes us particularly formidable competitors in the global ecological arena.)

Economists and ecologists also both see humans as producers. However, there is a fundamental difference between production by green plants and production by the economy. As noted, green plants are primary producers which assimilate simple low-grade materials, and a relatively dispersed form of energy, to produce the most complex and energy-rich molecules known to science. By contrast, human beings are strictly secondary producers. The production and maintenance of our bodies, and all the products of human factories, require enormous inputs of high-grade energy and material resources from the rest of the ecosphere. That is, all production by the human enterprise, from the increase in population to the accumulation of manufactured capital, requires the consumption and dissipation of a larger quantity of available energy and material first produced by nature.

This relationship implies, on theoretical grounds alone, that the continuous growth of the economy will ultimately generate an ecological crisis. Both the economy and the ecosphere are self-organizing far-from-equilibrium dissipative structures but, as previously noted, the former is an embedded dependent subsystem of the latter. In structural terms, therefore, the expanding human enterprise is positioned to consume the ecosphere from within (Rees 1999).

HOMO SAPIENS: THE ARCHETYPAL PATCH DISTURBANCE SPECIES

The consequences of this relationship have been felt down through the millennia. The mere existence of people – even pre-industrial hunter-gatherers – in a given habitat invariably results in significant changes in ecosystem structure and function. This is the inevitable consequence of two simple (but generally ignored) facts of human biology: first, humans are large consumer organisms with correspondingly large individual energy and material requirements; and second, we are social beings who universally live in extended groups. The invasion of any previously 'stable' ecosystem by people therefore necessarily produces changes in established energy and material pathways. There will be a reallocation of resources among species in the system to the benefit of some and the detriment of others. To this extent at least, humans invariably perturb the systems of which they are a part.

These basic facts, together with food productivity data for typical terrestrial ecosystems, would be enough for an alien ecologist to advance the following hypothesis: in most of the potential habitats on Earth, groups of human hunter-gatherers will sooner or later overwhelm their local ecosystems and be forced to ramble farther afield in search of sustenance. In fact, the productivity of most unaltered ecosystems is inadequate to support more than a few people for long in the immediate vicinity of a temporary camp. In pre-agricultural times, when a group of human foragers had hunted out and picked over a given area, they were forced to move on. This would enable the abandoned site to recover, perhaps to be revisited in a few years or decades. Thus, by moving among favored habitat sites, exploiting one, allowing others to rebound, early humans could exist in an overall dynamic equilibrium with the ecosystems that sustained them, albeit across their total home ranges. Hunting-gathering and closely-related swidden (slash-and-burn) agriculture, with their long fallow periods after episodes of intensive use, may well be the most nearly sustainable lifestyles ever adopted by humans (see Kleinman et al. 1995, 1996).

Such quasi steady-state systems, established after long periods of human habitation, would, of course, be quite different from the ecosystems that would exist in the same regions in the absence of people. Perhaps the most dramatic evidence of this is the major ecosystems alterations that occur when humans first invade and settle a new habitat or land mass. Some of these changes are permanent. The recent paleo-ecological, anthropological, and archeological literature tells a convincing story of the extinctions of large mammals and birds that accompanied first contact and settlement of their habitats by human beings (Flannery 1994, Diamond 1992, Ponting 1991, Pimm, et al. 1995, Tuxill 1998). "For every area of the world that paleontologists have studied and that humans first reached within the last fifty thousand years, human arrival approximately coincided with massive prehistoric extinctions" (Diamond 1992, 355).

The species so extirpated include not only those upon which humans preyed, but also various other predators to whom humans proved to be competitively superior. The resultant changes to ecosystem structure were considerable. In North America, South America, and Australia, about 72, 80, and 86 percent respectively of large mammal genera became extinct after human arrival (Diamond 1992, 357). Pimm et al.

(1995, 348) estimate "that with only Stone Age technology, the Polynesians exterminated >2000 bird species, some ~15 percent of the world total."

As noted, prehistoric humans eventually came to live in more or less stable dynamic equilibrium (or steady-state) within their altered ecosystems, often for thousands of years. However, in recent millennia, with improvements in tools and weapons, these long-term stable relationships have broken down. For example, human hunter-gatherers seem to have been instrumental in the eventual extinction of various large animals with which they had long coexisted in many parts of the world. These species include everything from giant deer and mammoths in Eurasia, through giant buffalo, antelopes and horses in Africa, to bears, wolves, and beavers in Britain (Diamond 1992, 356). In short, the slow spread of pre-agricultural humanity across the face of the Earth, accelerated by the diffusion of more advanced hunting technologies and the inexorable expansion of human numbers, seems, invariably, to have been accompanied by significant, permanent changes in the structure and function of ecosystems at all spatial scales. The human pressure is still rising: 11 percent of the 4400 mammal species extant today are endangered or critically endangered, and a quarter of all mammal species are on a path of decline which, if not halted, is likely to end in extinction (Tuxill 1998).

Upping the Impact Ante

The already significant impact of humans on ecosystems escalated dramatically with the shift away from the hunter-gatherer lifestyle. With the dawn of agriculture 10,000 years ago and the much larger populations it could support, people acquired the capacity permanently to alter entire landscapes. For the first time, we were not merely consuming other species; humans were now appropriating entire ecosystems and diverting much of the photosynthetic energy flow to their own use.

Increased food production enabled the establishment of permanent settlements, the division of labor, the evolution of class structure, the development of government including bureaucracies and armies, and other manifestations of civilization. Indeed, as Diamond has eloquently argued, "the adoption of food production exemplifies what is termed an autocatalytic process – one that catalyses itself in a positive feedback cycle, going faster and faster once it has started" (Diamond 1998, 110). More food calories made higher population densities possible, enabled large permanent settlements with the specialized skills and inventiveness this implies, and shortened the time-spacing between children. This, in turn, enabled the higher populations to produce still more people which increased both the demand for food and the technical and organizational capacity to produce it. Pressure on the land and ecosystems increased accordingly and, in the process, ended even the possibility of returning to hunter-gathering for the majority of people.

All this is to emphasize that humans are, by nature, a typical patch-disturbance species, a distinction we share with other large mammals ranging from beavers to elephants (see *BioScience* 1988, 8).[3] In simple terms, "large animals, due to their size, longevity, and food and habitat requirements tend to have a substantial impact on ecosystems" (Naiman 1988). Thus, a patch-disturbance species may be defined as any organism which, usually by central place foraging, degrades a small 'central place' greatly and disturbs a much larger area away from the central core to a lesser extent (definition revised from Logan 1996).

Patch Disturbance and Ecological Integrity

The fact that humans are natural patch disturbers is problematic when it comes to understanding the relationship between humankind and ecological integrity. As noted, there can be little question that the species composition and developmental trajectory of an ecosystem inhabited by even pre-agricultural humans will be different from the trajectory it would follow without them. However, the same statement could be made about many other ecosystems with reference to their respective keystone species. For example, the extirpation of large predators (jaguars, cougars, and harpy eagles) on Barro Colorado Island in Panama was followed by a ripple effect that saw major increases in the relative abundance of smaller predators and medium-sized seed-eaters which, in turn, led to the local extinction of little antbirds and several similar species, as well as to a large-scale shift in forest tree composition (Diamond 1992). Similarly, the early decline in passerine birds in eastern North American rural and forest ecosystems may be the direct result of an increase in small predators (including domestic and feral cats), but the distal cause is likely the elimination of cougars and wolves from the system. In short, the presence of any large predator may significantly affect the structure of its entire ecosystem, a fact that may not be fully appreciated until its removal appears to disrupt the established order of things.

Now, biological integrity is sometimes seen as a property of near-pristine ecosystems, i.e., ecosystems not significantly modified by human intervention. But this begs the question of why ecosystem modification by humans should be treated differently from that induced by other species like jaguars and cougars. After all, the presence of these large cats results in a different climax system from that which develops in their absence. Yet, few people would argue that Central American forests naturally populated by jaguars and cougars lack ecological integrity because of the unseen structural effects of their presence.

In fact, I would argue that there is a major difference, that the quality of human 'patch disturbance' should be distinguished from that of other species. However, the distinguishing feature is not related to the short-term structural impacts of early 'man' (which may be comparable to those of other species), but rather derives from unique qualities of the human animal.

First, humans display a uniquely broad and ever-widening food niche which extends from nearly pure carnivory to obligate herbivory. Second, we are uniquely adaptable which enables our species to exploit virtually all the ecosystems and 'environments' on Earth. Finally, with language, human knowledge and technology are cumulative. As a result, human patch disturbance, unlike that of other species, has tended over the millennia to expand in great leaps, and now threatens to diverge permanently from equilibrium with supporting ecosystems. Humanity's drift from long-term steady-state with nature has been accelerating since the Neolithic. It received a major boost with agriculture, and really broke free with the use of fossil fuels and the industrial revolution.

In summary then, I am arguing that the makings of the ecological crisis are programmed into the ecology and sociobiology of our species. We are naturally a patch disturbance species, whose capacity to disrupt the ecosphere has been greatly augmented by behavioural plasticity and cumulative learning. Moreover, because of our extraordinary energy and material demands, and the 'nesting' of the economy in within the ecosphere, the growth of human numbers and cultural artifacts (manufactured capital assets) inevitably occurs at the expense of other organisms. Indeed, since the Paleolithic era, humans have invariably expanded their presence on Earth by:

1. Displacing other species from their niches and appropriating their habitats (e.g., various ungulates in Africa; bison in North America; thousands of species from tropical forests);

2. Eliminating competition for 'our' food (e.g., seals from fisheries; wolves from wild and domestic ungulates,; insects from crops);

3. Depleting both self-producing and non-renewable 'natural capital' stocks (other species populations such as fish; whole ecosystems such as forests; ground-water; soils; petroleum and other hydrocarbons).

The thermodynamic reality is that energy/material flows appropriated from the ecosphere for humans are irreversibly unavailable for use by other species or to maintain life support functions. (A form of 'competitive exclusion' is operating here – what we get, other species don't.)

OUR ECOLOGICAL FOOTPRINT: QUANTIFYING THE MODERN HUMAN 'PATCH'

Despite – or because of – the marvels of modern technology, the industrial era has brought little change to the nature of human-ecosystems interaction except in the scale of the 'patches' we disturb, the intensity of the disturbance, and the risk to our own survival. This can be shown using ecological footprint analysis, a method I developed with my graduate students, that, in effect, estimates the area of the modern human patch (Rees 1992, 1996, 1999; Rees and Wackernagel 1994; Wackernagel et al., 1999).

Ecological footprint analysis is an adaptation of trophic analysis applied to humans and extended to include both our biological and our "industrial metabolism" (see Ayres and Simonis 1994 for an explanation of the latter concept). It recognizes that all our toys and tools, factories and infrastructure, are "the exosomatic equivalent of organs" (Sterrer 1993) and, like bodily organs, require continuous flows of energy and material from and to the ecosphere for their production, maintenance, and operation.

We start by constructing what is, in effect, an elaborate 'food-web' for a specified human population, showing its material connections to the rest of the ecosphere. This step quantifies the material and energy flows (resources) required to support that population and identifies significant sources and sinks for its wastes.

Eco-footprinting is further based on the fact that many material and energy flows can be converted into land- and water-area equivalents. These are the ecosystem areas effectively appropriated for human use to produce food, fibre,[4] and minerals, and to assimilate selected categories of waste[5]. Thus, the theoretical 'ecological footprint' of a specified population is the area of land and water ecosystems required on a continuous basis to produce the resources that the population consumes and to assimilate the waste that the population produces, wherever on Earth the relevant land and water is located. It therefore includes both the area appropriated through commodity trade and the area needed for the referent population's share of certain free land- and water-based services of nature (e.g., waste assimilation and nutrient recycling).

How Big is Our Ecological Footprint?

Since the beginning of the industrial revolution the economy has been largely propelled by the constantly expanding use of 'extrasomatic' (out-side the body) energy supplies, particularly fossil fuels. By the early 1990s, extrasomatic energy consumption totaled about 407.5 x 10^{15} Btu annu-ally by a population of about 5.5 billion people. "It is as if every [person] in the world had fifty slaves. In a technological society like the United States, every person has more than 200 such 'ghost slaves'" [at an assumed working level of consumption of 4000 Btu person^{-1} day^{-1}] (Price 1995).[6]

As might be expected, much of this extra somatic energy has been used to increase humanity's 'harvest' of photosynthetic energy as fixed in ecosystems and, indeed, of all other resources from ground water to mineral ores. In short, cheap plentiful fossil fuels enabled humans steadily to increase food production and to accelerate the exploitation of every-thing else. As a result, humans have become the dominant consumer organism in virtually all the major ecosystems types on earth. For ex-ample, we are clearly the most ecologically significant marine mammal. Fossil energy and modern technology enables the global fishing fleet to appropriate seafood for humans that represents 25-35% of net marine primary productivity from shallow coastal shelves and estuaries. This 10% of the oceans produces 96% of the catchable fish (data from Pauly and Christensen 1996). Similarly, humans are the principal consumer in most of the world's significant terrestrial habitats, diverting from grasslands and forests at least 40% of the products of photosynthesis for direct and indirect human use (Vitousek et al. 1986, Haberl 1997). This is a remarkably paradoxical situation for a species whose economic models assume its material existence is essentially disconnected form nature.

The most recent studies of high-income countries show that the average resident has an ecological footprint of five to ten hectares (Wackernagel et al. 1999) (see Figure 1). It follows that the land and water (ecosystem) area required to support a typical high-income city is two to three orders of magnitude larger than the geographic area the city physically occupies. For example, assuming Vancouverites are aver-age Canadians with an ecological footprint of about 7.7 hectares per capita, the 472,000 residents of my home city require an area of 3,634,400 ha, or 319 times the political-geographical area of their city (11,400 ha) to support their consumer lifestyles. In a particularly comprehensive analysis, Folke et al. (1997) estimate that the 29 largest cities of the Baltic basin in northern Europe appropriate for their resource consump-tion and waste assimilation an area of forest, agricultural, marine, and wetland ecosystems 565-1130 times larger than the area of the cities them-selves.

We usually think of cities as centers of economic production and

Figure 1: Per Capita Eco-Footprints of Selected Countries
(Data from Wackernagel et al., 1999)

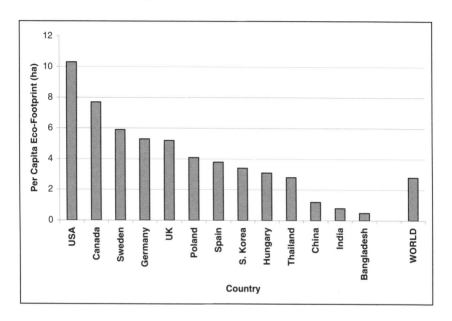

the engines of national economic growth. And indeed, cities undoubt-edly do generate the bulk of our money wealth. However, from the strictly ecological perspective, cities and urbanized regions are also intensive nodes of consumption sustained almost entirely by biophysical produc-tion and life-support processes occurring in a vastly larger area outside their political and geographic boundaries (Rees and Wackernagel 1996, Rees 1997). In effect, cities represent the highly disturbed 'central place' in the modern human patch which now extends over the entire surface of the Earth.

This is not to denigrate cities – indeed, the concentration of popu-lation and infrastructure characteristic of cities generates economies of scale and agglomeration economies (Mitlin and Satterthwaite 1994) that can significantly reduce the per capita ecological footprints of their inhabitants compared to those of people living a comparable lifestyle at lower population densities. In present circumstances, this makes cities a potential key to sustainability (Rees and Wackernagel 1996). The point here is to emphasize the inherent dependence of cities on an increas-ingly dispersed hinterland and their potential vulnerability in a world of accelerating ecological change. As incomplete consumptive systems, cities per se can have no ecological integrity. However, by redefining and restructuring the 'city-as-system', it may be possible to improve at least the ecological health of the entire urban hierarchy as the embedded consuimng urban core achieves a stable relationship with its producing regional hinterland.

Ecological Disparity and the Fair Earth-Share

Ecological footprinting reveals another insight relevant to both future human development and conservation efforts. As noted, the citizens of high income countries typically have eco-footprints of five to more than ten hectares. This compares to less than one hectare per capita for many developing countries such as India and Bangladesh (Figure 1). By extrapolation, most First World countries have an ecological footprint several times the size of their domestic territories. They are living on trade and by imposing heavily on the global commons – i.e. by 'importing' carrying capacity.

Now, prevailing international development strategies assume that we can relieve chronic poverty through sheer economic growth, thus avoiding political pressure for income redistribution. Indeed, the Brundtland Commission assumed we could safely bring eight to ten billion people up to 1980s Western European material standards by the middle of the next century (WCED 1987). The problem is, that on a finite planet, not all countries can be net importers of carrying capacity. This reality begs the following question: What would be the global ecological footprint if the entire world attained a typical western European lifestyle using prevailing (fossil fuel-based) technologies?

At a conservative five hectares per capita, the present world population of six billion people would need 30 billion hectares to supply its resources and assimilate its wastes. If the human family grows by an additional four billion by, say 2050, the human eco-footprint could reach 50 billion hectares. Unfortunately, there are only about 12 billion hectares of adequately productive land and water on earth. If the world's ecologically productive space were evenly divided among the present human population, we would get only about 1.5 ha of terrestrial and 0.5 ha of aquatic ecosystem each. In other words, the citizens of wealthy countries inadvertently already appropriate three to five times their 'fair Earthshare' (Rees 1996). To bring 10 billion people up to average European material standards with the technologies likely to be available in the next few decades would require at least three additional habitable planets. (Note that these data take no account of the needs of other species.)

Since we are unlikely to acquire several additional Earth-like planets, it seems that the world will have to deal with both socioeconomic and ecological inequity by means other than economic growth if it is serious about achieving sustainability.

DISCUSSION AND CONCLUSIONS

Many technological optimists believe that industrial 'man' is no longer bound by ecological constraints. As famed growth advocate, the late Julian Simon, recently wrote: "We have in our hands now... the technology to feed, clothe, and supply energy to an ever-growing population for the next seven billion years..." (Simon 1995). By contrast, this paper argues that humankind is as dependent on nature as ever. The principal ecological effect of technological advance has been merely to extend the scope and intensity of resource exploitation. This creates an illusion of abundance that is sutained by the liquidation of natural capital -- a process that is being intensified by globalization and growing trade.

With the expansion of the human ecological footprint, the niches of other organisms necessarily shrink. Over-harvesting, pollution, and particularly habitat destruction, are producing what some analysts are calling "the sixth extinction", the greatest extinction episode since the natural catastrophes at the end of the Paleozoic and Mesozoic eras (Wilson 1988, Pimm et al.1995). The current extirpation rate is 100-1000 times "pre-human levels" inferred from the fossil and paleontological record (Pimm et al. 1995). As humans breach the biophysical limits to growth, the loss of ecosystems integrity is measured by persistent trends, accelerating biodiversity loss, and increasing systems variability.

Ominously, evidence is gathering that humans themselves will increasingly bear the consequences of ecological degradation. In 1998, a record number of natural disasters caused massive property damage and drove more people from the land and their homes than war and civil conflict combined. According to the International Red Cross's 1999 World Disasters Report, singular events such as Hurricane Mitch and the El Niño weather phenomenon, plus declining soil fertility and deforestation, drove a record 25 million people from the countryside into crowded under-serviced shanty-towns around the developing world's fast growing cities. This is 58% of the world's total refugees. The World Disasters Report predicts that developing countries in particular will continue to be hit by super-disasters driven by human-induced atmospheric and climatic change, ecological degradation, and rising population pressures.

Sustainability's Bottom Line

At this stage in global development, there is a thermodynamically irreconcilable conflict between further expansion of the human enterprise and contemporary conservation efforts. It is becoming clear that the only thing that will ensure the long-term integrity of the ecosphere -- and thus geopolitical stability -- is an absolute reduction in the dissipative load imposed on ecosystems by people. There are two fundamental elements in the relevant equation: (1) reducing human populations everywhere, (2) cutting back on material consumption (where: impact = population x average per capita resource use).

The need for population control is self-evident to many analysts but, for religious and cultural reasons, official population programs in many countries receive little support. Even in supposedly enlightened countries like the US and Canada, discussion of population objectives is suppressed. (Anyone raising the issue is likely to be labeled racist). Much of the current sustainability debate therefore focuses on ways of lowering the energy and material intensity of the human economy. Almost never, however (and certainly not in mainstream institutions), does this discussion seriously contemplate slowing growth or reducing consumption (incomes and spending).

There is, of course, a strong argument that continued material growth – more consumption – is actually a prerequisite for sustainability, at least in the developing world. Higher incomes mean greater access to healthy food, clean water, adequate clothing, satisfactory shelter, and acceptable levels of public infrastructure (sewers, water, transportation, electricity, etc.). Given the squalid living conditions of the inhabitants of many 'third-world' cities, improving living conditions for the chronically impoverished is actually a moral imperative.

However, there is little population health or welfare argument to support further income growth in the wealthy North. In high income countries, standard indicators of population health – longevity, infant mortality, fecundity, literacy, etc. – have long-since peaked (or bottomed out) and stabilized. There is no further improvement with GDP beyond $8000 per year (World Bank 1993: Fig. 1.9).[7] It is also a truism (proved by various surveys and studies) that (more) money does not bring happiness. Indeed, we have reached the point where for many, fatter paychecks come at the expense of mental health, family, community and, of course, ecological security. Why then is the entire developed world engaged in a potentially fatal competition for the biggest GDP? Just what is the ultimate prize in the global growth sweepstakes? In the absence of any satisfactory answer to these questions, it would seem reasonable to reserve any unclaimed biophysical capacity for growth for the world's poor, particularly the two billion who live on less than two dollars a day. However, as suggested above, no political campaign has yet been fought on the best means to induce wealthy consumers to adopt materially simpler lifestyles.

On the contrary, most of our effort is being expended on ways to enable increased consumption but at lower ecological cost. In theory, this might be achieved for a time through improved resource productivity – significant gains in energy and material efficiency would allow further growth with less environmental damage (von Weizsäcker and Jesinghaus 1992, Rees 1995a,b, Roodman 1997). Even the international Business Council on Sustainable Development subscribes to the efficiency approach, recognizing that: "Industrialized world reductions in material throughput, energy use, and environmental degradation of over 90% will be required by 2040 to meet the needs of a growing world population fairly within the planet's ecological means" (BCSD 1993, 10). This ultimate objective is sometimes referred to as the 'factor-10' economy.[8]

Certainly the environmentally-decoupled economy implied by factor-10 efficiency gains is theoretically attractive and may well be the most politically palatable of solutions for today's material world. However, typical of expansionist 'solutions', it is a purely technical response to a systemic crisis. It permits continued growth while ignoring the sociocultural context and accepting unquestioned the fundamental values of consumer society.

Quite apart from the doubtful benefits of continued GDP growth in rich countries, there are several reasons why such a single-minded approach to sustainability may not succeed. Limited public understanding of the issues, irreducible scientific uncertainty, the power of vested interests, and the large potential costs associated with required structural adjustments to the economy all present barriers to the decisive political action required for the 'factor-10' scenario, particularly in North America.[9] How receptive would today's politically cynical electorate be to the massive tax reform that may be required to stimulate adequate technological efficiency gains? Yet, without public intervention to drive the efficiency revolution and to tax away the money savings, technological advance will be relatively slow and may actually work against sustainability.

Indeed, history suggests that spontaneous efficiency gains in the economy result in product diversification, increased profits (income), and lower prices, all of which lead to increased consumption and accelerated resource depletion (Rees 1995b). Economists call this the 'rebound' effect. For example, U.S. data reveal that despite the increasing fuel efficiency of automobiles in the 1980s, aggregate fuel consumption continued to increase as more cars were used more frequently for longer trips. It seems that under prevailing circumstances, growth can eventually overwhelms gains from efficiency (Brown et al. 1991). We should also remember that there are technical and economic limits to efficiency in practice – food, cars, and television sets cannot be completely dematerialized. A good cup of coffee needs some minimal number of beans.

Two recent studies led by the World Resources Institute (WRI) provide the most compelling empirical evidence yet that technology is not yet succeeding in decoupling economic growth from the environment. A 1997 report on four of the world's most technologically advanced economies (Germany, Japan, the Netherlands, and the U.S.) showed that the average citizen now requires 45-85 metric tons of natural resources (excepting air and water) annually -- including 17 to 38 metric tons of direct material inputs -- to produce his/her goods and services. The study concluded that overall, there continues to be "...a gradual rise in per capita resource use and [that] ...an absolute reduction in natural resource use, is not yet taking place" (WRI 1997).

The results of an expanded analysis (with Austria added to the 1997 list) covering the 1975-1996 period are even more discouraging. Again, industrial economies are becoming more efficient and there is a modest trend toward the decoupling of energy and material use/outflows from GDP growth. However, much of this trend is attributable to the increasing relative contribution of so-called 'knowledge-intensive' businesses to GDP, not to reduced energy and material use. Indeed:

· both gross and per capita processed output (solid, liquid and gaseous discharges) are generally increasing;

· the extraction and use of fossil energy resources dominate waste flows in all countries examined. Carbon dioxide, accounts for more than 80% by weight of material outflows from economic activity in the five study countries;

· except in Germany, carbon dioxide emissions rose in both total and per capita terms in all countries studied.

In general, this study shows that the resource savings that the study economies have realized from efficiency gains and economic restructuring have been negated by population growth, increased *per capita* consumption, and the increased output of wastes. Thus, while technological improvements and the shift to service-based industries have weakened the link between GDP growth and resource consumption, gross dematerialization is still not being realized. In particular, the data underscore that "modern industrial economies, no matter how high-tech, are carbon-based economies, and their predominant activity is burning material". The report concludes that "in the absence of further policy incentives, structural economic change and technological efficiency gains alone appear unlikely to bring about a real reduction in resource use and waste outputs" (WRI 2000).

If unaided technology cannot solve the throughput problem, perhaps it is time to get back to basics. This paper started from the premise that the so-called 'environmental crisis' is really a problem of human ecological dysfunction. This dysfunction springs from fundamental values of industrial society that have become maladaptive through excessive growth on a finite planet. It can be addressed only by adjusting these values. Indeed, it is often said that achieving sustainability will require a genuine 'paradigm shift'. This means actually letting go of many of the most cherished values, beliefs, and assumptions of industrial society. Fortunately most such values are actually social constructs, so it should be possible to reconstruct society more in harmony with the new biophysical reality.

In a politically supportive environment, we could undoubtedly create the economic incentives needed to induce required behavioural change. Similarly, we have the skills and knowledge needed to transform our sociocultural values and beliefs using all the communicative power of modern electronic media. This would likely prove to be a far more effective strategy for sustainability than mere technological extension of the status quo. "...It is also the most ethically responsible strategy in many cases, since it demands that solutions to problems be located in their source: humans, their behavior, and their institutions" (Jamieson 1996).

REFERENCES

Ayres, RU and U Simonis. 1994. *Industrial Metabolism: Restructuring for Sustainable Development*. New York: United Nations University Press.

Ayres, RU. 1994. *Information, Entropy and Progress: A New Evolutionary Paradigm*. Woodbury, NY: AIP Press.

BCSD. 1993. *Getting Eco-Efficient*. Report of the BCSD First Antwerp Eco-Efficiency Workshop, November 1993. Geneva: Business Council for Sustainable Development.

BioScience. 1988. Vol. 38, No. 11 (special issue on "How Animals Shape their Ecosystems").

Brown, L., C. Flaven, and S. Postel. 1991. *Saving the Planet: How to Shape an Environmentally Sustainable Global Economy*. Washington, DC: Worldwatch Institute.

Christensen, Paul. 1991. "Driving Forces, Increasing Returns, and Ecological Sustainability." In: Robert Costanza, ed. *Ecological Economics: The Science and Management of Sustainability*. New York: Columbia University Press.

Daly, HE. 1991a. "The circular flow of exchange value and the linear throughput of matter-energy: a case of misplaced concreteness." In: H.E. Daly. *Steady-State Economics* (2nd ed.) Washington: Island Press.

Daly, H.E. 1991b. "The concept of a steady-state economy." In: H. Daly. *Steady-State Economics* (2nd ed.) Washington: Island Press.

Daly, HE. 1992. *Steady-state economics: concepts, questions, policies.* Gaia 6:333-338.

de Bruyn, S.M. and J.B. Opschoor. 1993. "De- or re-linking economic development with the environment." (draft manuscript). The Netherlands: Department of Spatial and Environmental Economics, Free University and Tinbergen Institute.

Diamond, J. 1992. *The Third Chimpanzee.* New York: HarperCollins Publishers.

Diamond, J. 1998. *Guns, Germs and Steel: The Fates of Human Societies.* New York: W.W Norton and Company.

Duncan, RC. 1993. "The Life Expectancy of Industrial Civilization: The Decline to Global Equilibrium." *Population and Environment* 14: 325-357.

Flannery, TF 1994. *The Future Eaters: An Ecological History of the Australasian Lands and Peoples.* Chatsworth, NSW: Reed Books.

Folke, C., A. Jansson, J. Larsson, and R. Costanza. 1997. "Ecosystem Appropriation by Cities." *Ambio* 26:167-172.

Georgescu-Roegen, N. 1971. *The Entropy Law and the Economic Process.* Cambridge, MS: Harvard University Press.

Haberl, H. 1997. "Human Appropriation of Net Primary Production as An Environmental Indicator: Implications for Sustainable Development." *Ambio* 26:143-146

Jamieson, D. 1996. "Ethics and intentional climate change." *Climatic Change* 33:323-336.

Kay, J. 1991. "A nonequilibrium thermodynamic framework for discussing ecosystem integrity." *Environmental Management* 15:483-495.

Kay, J.J. H.A. Regier, M. Boyle, G. Francis. 1999. "An ecosystem approach for sustainability: Addressing the challenge of complexity." *Futures* (in press).

Kleinman, PJA, RB Bryant, and D Pimentel. 1996. "Assessing Ecological Sustainability of Slash-and-Burn Agriculture through Soil Fertility Indicators." *Agron. J.* 88: 122-127.

Kleinman, PJA, D Pimentel, and RB Bryant. 1995. "The Ecological Sustainability of Slash- and-Burn Agriculture." *Agriculture, Ecosystems, and Environment* 52: 235-249.

Logan, J. 1996. "Patch disturbance and the human niche." Manuscript at <http://csf.Colorado.EDU/authors/hanson/page78.htm >. (also, pers. comm. 1997. E-mail exchanges with the author on patch disturbance).

Mitlin, D. and D. Satterthwaite. 1994. "Cities and Sustainable Development." Background Paper prepared for "Global forum '94", Manchester, 24-28 June 1994. London: International Institute for Environment and Development.

Naiman, RJ. 1988. "Animal influences on ecosystem dynamics." *BioScience* 38:11:750-752.

Pauly, D and V Christensen. 1995. "Primary production required to sustain global fisheries." *Nature* 374:255-257.

Pimm, SL, GJ Russell, JL Gittleman, and TM Brooks. 1995. "The Future of Biodiversity." *Science* 296:347-350.

Ponting, C. 1991. *A Green History of the World*. London: Sinclair-Stevenson.

Price, D. 1995. Energy and Human Evolution. Population and Environment 16:301-317.

Prigogine, I. 1997. *The End of Certainty: Time Chaos and the New Laws of Nature*. New York: The Free Press.

Rees, W.E. 1990. "The Ecology of Sustainable Development." *The Ecologist* 20:18-23.

Rees, W.E. 1995a. "Achieving sustainability: Reform or transformation?" *Journal of Planning Literature* 9: 343-361.

Rees,W.E.1995b. "More Jobs, Less Damage: A Framework for Sustainability." *Alternatives* 21:24-30.

Rees, W.E. 1996. "Revisiting carrying capacity: Area-based indicators of sustainability." *Population and Environment* 17:195-215.

Rees, W.E. 1997. "Is 'sustainable city' an oxymoron?" *Local Environment* 2:303-310.

Rees, W.E. 1999. "Consuming the earth: The biophysics of sustainability." *Ecological Economics* 29: 23-27.

Rees, W.E. 2000a. "A human ecological assessment of economic and population health." In: L. Westra, P Crabbé, A. Holland, L. Ryczkowski (eds.) *Implementing Ecological Integrity: Restoring Regional and Global Environmental and Human Health*. (NATO Scientific Publications). Dordrecht: Kluwer Academic Publishers (In press).

Rees, W.E. 2000b. "Patch disturbance, eco-footprints, and biological integrity: Revisiting the limits to growth." In: D. Pimentel, L. Westra, and R. Noss (eds.) *Ecological Integrity: Integrating Environment, Conservation, and Health*. Washington: Island Press (in press).

Rees, W.E. , and M. Wackernagel. 1994. "Ecological footprints and appropriated carrying capacity: measuring the natural capital requirements of the human economy." In: A-M. Jansson, M. Hammer, C. Folke, and R. Costanza, (eds.) *Investing in Natural Capital: The Ecological Economics Approach to Sustainability*. Washington: Island Press.

Rees, W.E. and M. Wackernagel. 1996. "Urban ecological footprints: Why cities cannot be sustainable and why they are a key to sustainability." *Environ. Impact Assess. Rev.* 16:223-248.

Roodman, D.M. 1997. *Getting the Signals Straight: Tax Reform to Protect the Environment and the Economy*. Worldwatch Paper 134. Washington: Worldwatch Institute.

Schneider, E and J Kay. 1994. "Life as a manifestation of the second law of thermodynamics." *Mathematical and Computer Modeling* 19:6-8:25-48.

Simon, J. 1995. *The state of humanity: Steadily improving.* Cato Policy Report 17:5. Washington, DC: The Cato Institute.

Sterrer, W. 1993. "Human economics: a non-human perspective." *Ecological Economics* 7, 183-202.

Tuxill, J. 1998. *Losing Strands in the web of Life: Vertebrate Declines and the Conservation of Biological Diversity.* Worldwatch Paper 141. Washington, DC: The Worldwatch Institute.

UNDP. 1994. *Human Development Report.* Oxford and New York: Oxford University Press for United Nations Development Program.

Vitousek, P., P.R. Ehrlich, A.H. Ehrlich, and P. Matson. 1986. "Human appropriation of the products of photosynthesis." *BioScience* 36:368-374.

von Weizsäcker, E. and J. Jesinghaus 1992. *Ecological Tax Reform: A Policy Proposal for Sustainable Development.* London: Zed Books.

Wackernagel, M. and W. E. Rees. 1996. *Our Ecological Footprint: Reducing Human Impact on the Earth.* Gabriola Island, BC and Philadelphia, PA: New Society Publishers.

Wackernagel, M., L .Onisto, P. Bello, A.C. Linares, I.S.L. Falfán, J.M. Garcia, A.I.S. Guerrero, and M.G.S. Guerrero. 1999. "National natural capital accounting with the ecological footprint concept." *Ecological Economics* 29:375-390.

WCED. 1987. *Our Common Future.* Oxford and New York: Oxford University Press for the UN World Commission on Economy and Development.

Wilson, EO. 1988. "The current state of biological diversity." In: E.O. Wilson (ed.) *Biodiversity.* Washington, DC: National Academy Press.

World Bank. 1993. *World Development Report 1993: Investing in Health.* New York: Oxford University Press.

WRI. 1997. *Resource Flows: The Material Basis of Industrial Economies.* Washington, DC: World Resources Institute, (for World Resources Institute, Wuppertal Institute [Germany], Netherlands Ministry of Housing, National Institute for Environmental Studies [Japan]).

WRI. 2000. *Weight of Nations: Material Outflows from Industrial Economies.* Washington, DC: World Resources Institute.

FOOTNOTES

1. An isolated system can exchange neither energy nor matter with its environment.
2. For example, consider the following nested hierarchy of biological organization (from high to low): ecosystem, population, individual, organ-system, organ, tissue, cell, cellular micro-organelles. Kay et al. (1999) define such complex hierarchic structures as 'self-organizing holarchic open (SOHO) systems'.
3. Predictably, with the exception of a passing reference to modern humans as "primary agents of environmental change," people are not included in this special issue of the journal on 'How Animals Shape Their Ecosystems.'
4. To facilitate international comparisons, we generally use world average land productivities in eco-footprint estimates.
5. In practice, only a limited number of wastes (e.g., carbon dioxide, plant nutrients such as nitrates and phosphates) can readily be converted to land area equivalents with present knowledge. Some contaminants such as ozone-depleting chemicals or endocrine mimics cannot be included at all in eco-footprint analysis.
6. The central role of fossil energy cannot be overstated. Indeed, so dependent is industrial society on fossil energy that some authors predict the decline and collapse of civilization as stocks of cheap, accessible petroleum and natural gas are depleted in the next few decades (e.g., Price 1995, Duncan 1993).
7. Many remaining health problems stem from life-style excesses, i.e., over-consumption of food, alcohol, drugs.
8. "Factor-10" implies getting ten times today's level of utility or 'service' out of each unit of energy or material used (e.g., five times the service from half the resources).
9. Tentative first steps are, however, being taken by a handful of European countries.

ACKNOWLEDGEMENTS

This chapter is based on a paper presented to the Technical Session on *The Global Integrity Project: Understanding and Implementing Ecosystem Health* at the International Congress for Ecosystem Health, "Managing for Ecosystem Health" Sacramento, California, 15-20 August, 1999. Parts of the paper also appear in slightly different form in Rees 2000a and 2000b.

MEASURING GENUINE PROGRESS

Ronald Colman
Director, GPI Atlantic

There is a remarkable consensus that crosses all political divisions on the fundamental principles of a decent society and on the benchmarks that would signify genuine progress. We all want to live in a peaceful and safe society without crime. We all value a clean environment with healthy forests, soils, lakes and oceans. We need good health and education, strong and caring communities, and free time to relax and develop our potential. We want economic security and less poverty.

No political party officially favours greater insecurity, a degraded environment, or more stress, crime, poverty and inequality. Why then do we see policies that promote those very outcomes? Why are we unable to create the kind of society we genuinely want to inhabit in the new millennium? Why can we not order our policy priorities to accord with our shared values and human needs?

One reason is that we have all been getting the wrong message from our current measures of progress. All of us -- politicians, economists, journalists and the general public -- have been completely hooked on the illusion that equates economic growth with well being and prosperity. Indeed, there is probably no more pervasive and dangerous myth in our society than the materialist assumption that "more is better."

Look at the language we use: When our economy is growing rapidly, it is called "robust", "dynamic", and "healthy". When people spend more money, "consumer confidence" is "strong". By contrast, "weak" or "anemic" growth signals "recession" and even "depression". Increased car sales signal a "buoyant recovery. "Free" trade actually means "more" trade. The more we produce, trade and spend, the more the Gross Domestic Product (GDP) grows and, by implication, the "better off" we are.

This was not the intention of those who created the GDP. Simon Kuznets, its principal architect, warned 40 years ago:

> The welfare of a nation can scarcely be inferred from a measurement of national income....Goals for 'more' growth should specify of what and for what.

Our growth statistics were never meant to be used as a measure of progress as they are today. In fact, activities that degrade our quality of life, like crime, pollution and addictive gambling, all make the economy grow. The more fish we sell and the more trees we cut down, the more the economy grows. Working longer hours makes the economy grow. And the economy can grow even if inequality and poverty increase.

ENGINES OF GROWTH

Here in Canada we are currently enamoured with the "dynamic" American economy and its rapid growth rates. But we do not often ask, as Kuznets counsels, what is driving that growth.

One of the fastest growing sectors of the American economy is imprisonment, at an annual growth rate of 6.2% per year throughout the 1990s. One in every 150 Americans is now behind bars, the highest rate in the world along with Russia, compared to one in 900 Canadians and one in 1,600 Nova Scotians. The O.J. Simpson trial alone added $200 million to the U.S. economy, and the Oklahoma City explosion and Littleton massacre fueled the booming U.S. security industry, which now adds $40 billion a year to the economy, with most sales now going to schools. Is this our model of a "robust" and "healthy" economy?

Gambling is another rapid growth industry -- a $50 billion a year business in the U.S. Divorce adds $20 billion a year to the U.S. economy. Car crashes add another $57 billion. Prozac sales have quadrupled since 1990 to more than $4 billion -- a sign of progress? The more rapidly we deplete our natural resources and the more fossil fuels we burn, the faster the economy grows. Because we assign no value to our natural capital, we actually count its depreciation as gain, like a factory owner selling off his machinery and counting it is profit.

Overeating contributes to economic growth many times over, starting with the value of the excess food consumed and the advertising needed to sell it. Then the diet and weight-loss industries add $32 billion a year more to the U.S. economy, and obesity-related health problems another $50 billion, at the same time that 20 million people, mostly children, die every year from hunger and malnutrition in the world

Similarly, toxic pollution, sickness, stress, and war all make the economy grow. The Exxon Valdez contributed far more to the Alaska economy by spilling its oil than if it had delivered the oil safely to port because all the cleanup costs, lawsuits and media coverage added to the growth statistics. The Yugoslav war stimulated the economies of the NATO countries to the tune of $60 million a day, and our economies will benefit even more by rebuilding what we destroy.

Measuring progress by the sum total of economic activity is like a policeman adding up all the street activity he observes. The lady walking her dog, the thief stealing the car, the children playing on the corner, the thug hitting someone with a lead pipe -- all are recorded equally. Our growth statistics make no distinction between economic activity that contributes to well being and that which causes harm. Growth is simply a quantitative increase in the physical scale of the economy, and tells us nothing about our actual well being.

HAS GROWTH MADE US "BETTER OFF"?

Are we "better off" as a result of decades of continuous economic growth? Certainly many of us have bigger houses and more cars, appliances, and home entertainment equipment. Are we happier? A recent U.S. poll found that 72% of Americans had more possessions than their parents, but only 47% said they were happier than their parents.

We are also less peaceful and secure, three times more likely to be victims of crime than our parents a generation ago. We are more time stressed. Our jobs are more insecure. Our debt levels are higher. Real incomes are declining. Child poverty is increasing. The gap between rich and poor is widening. Economists predict that for the first time since the Industrial Revolution, the next generation will be worse off than the present one.

More dangerously, blind growth has undermined our natural resource wealth, produced massive pollution, destroyed plant and animal species at an unprecedented rate, and changed the climate in a way that now threatens the planet.

Ironically, while we are so busy counting everything on which we spend money, we assign no value to vital unpaid activities that really do contribute to our well being. Voluntary community service, the backbone of civil society, is not counted or valued in our measures of progress because no money is exchanged. If we did measure it, we would know that volunteer services to the elderly, sick, disabled, children and other vulnerable groups have declined throughout Canada during the 1990s at the same time that government has cut social services, leading to a cumulative 30% erosion in the social safety net.

Even though household work and raising children are more essential to basic quality of life than much of the work done in offices, factories and stores, they have no value in the GDP, while every additional lawyer, broker and advertising executive is counted as a contribution to well being. We value the booming child care industry as the fourth fastest growing industry in the country, but we do not count unpaid child care, and so we do not notice that parents are spending less time with their children than ever before -- a sign of progress?

If we did count voluntary and household work, we would know that they add $325 billion a year of valuable services to the Canadian economy. If we measured the household not just as a source of consumption, as taught in every economics textbook, but as a productive economic unit, we would also discover that total paid and unpaid work has steadily increased, leading to an overall loss of free time.

In 1900, a single-earner male breadwinner worked a 59-hour week in Canada, while a full-time female homemaker put in an average 56-hour week of household work, for a total household work week of 115 hours. Today the average Canadian dual earner couple puts in 79 hours of paid work and 56 hours of unpaid household work a week, for a total household work week of 135 hours.

All those extra paid hours fuel economic growth and are counted as progress. But the loss of precious free time is invisible and unvalued in our measures of progress. Aristotle recognized 2,400 years ago that leisure was a prerequisite for contemplation, informed discussion, participation in political life, and genuine freedom. It is also essential for relaxation and health, for spiritual practice, and for a decent quality of life. In the GDP, time is simply money, and we sacrifice it for material comfort in the name of progress.

WHAT WE COUNT IS WHAT WE VALUE

What we measure and count quite literally tell us what we "value" as a society. If we do not count our non-monetary and non-material assets, we effectively "discount" and "devalue" them. And what we don't measure and value in our central accounting mechanism will be effectively sidelined in the policy arena. If, for example, a teacher tells students that a term paper is very important but worth nothing in the final grade, the real message conveyed is that the paper has no value, and the students will devote their attention to the final exam which "counts" for something.

Similarly, we may pay pious public homage to environmental quality and to social and spiritual values. But if we count their degradation as progress in our growth measures we will continue to send misleading signals to policy makers and public alike, to blunt effective remedial action, and to distort policy priorities.

Until we explicitly value our free time, voluntary community service, parental time with children, and natural resource wealth, they will never receive adequate attention on the public policy agenda. Similarly, until we assign explicit value to equity in our growth measures, we will continue to give little policy attention to the fact that here in Nova Scotia the poorest 20% of the population has lost 29% of its real income after taxes and transfers since 1990.

The obsession with growth and its confusion with genuine development and quality of life have led us down a dangerous and self-destructive path. It is doubtful that we will leave our children a better legacy until we cut through the myth that "more" means "better," until we stop gauging our well being and prosperity by how fast the economy is growing, and until we stop misusing the GDP as a measure of progress.

Thirty years ago, just before he was assassinated, Robert Kennedy remarked:

Too much and too long, we seem to have surrendered community excellence and community values in the mere accumulation of material things....The Gross National Product includes air pollution and advertising for cigarettes, and ambulances to clear our highways of carnage. It counts special locks for our doors, and jails for the people who break them. The GNP includes the destruction of the redwoods and the death of Lake Superior. It grows with the production of napalm and missiles and nuclear warheads.

And if GNP includes all this, there is much that it does not comprehend. It does not allow for the health of our families, the quality of their education, or the joy of their play. It is indifferent to the decency of our factories and the safety of our streets alike. It does not include the beauty of our poetry or the strength of our marriages, or the intelligence of our public debate or the integrity of our public officials.

GNP measures neither our wit nor our courage, neither our wisdom nor our learning, neither our compassion nor our devotion to our country. It measures everything, in short, except that which makes life worthwhile.

A BETTER WAY TO MEASURE PROGRESS

What is urgently, indeed desperately, needed are measures of well being, prosperity and progress that explicitly value the non-material assets that are the true basis of our wealth, including the strength of our communities, our free time, the quality of our environment, the health of our natural resources, and our concern for others. The means to do so exist.

In fact, tremendous progress has been made in the last 20 years in natural resource accounting and in developing good social indicators, time use surveys, environmental quality measures and other means of assessing well being and quality of life. We are now completely capable of measuring our progress in a better way that accords with our shared values and lets us know whether we are moving towards the society we want to create.

After three California researchers developed a Genuine Progress Indicator in 1995, incorporating 26 social, economic and environmental variables, 400 leading economists, including Nobel laureates, jointly stated:

Since the GDP measures only the quantity of market activity without accounting for the social and ecological costs involved, it is both inadequate and misleading as a measure of true prosperity. Policy-makers, economists, the media, and international agencies should cease using the GDP as a measure of progress and publicly acknowledge its shortcomings. New indicators of progress are urgently needed to guide our society....The GPI is an important step in this direction.

Here in Nova Scotia, GPI Atlantic, a non-profit research group, is now developing a Genuine Progress Index that Statistics Canada has designated as a pilot project for the country. It is designed as a practical policy-relevant tool that is easy to maintain and replicate, that can accurately measure sustainable development, and that can provide much needed information to policy makers about issues that are currently hidden and even invisible in our market statistics.

The Nova Scotia GPI assigns explicit value to our natural resources, including our soils, forests, fisheries and non-renewable energy sources and assesses the sustainability of our harvesting practices, consumption habits and transportation systems. It measures and values our unpaid voluntary and household work, and it counts crime, pollution, greenhouse gas emissions, road accidents and other liabilities as economic costs not gains as at present.

The index goes up if our society is becoming more equal, if we have more free time and if our quality of life is improving. It counts our health, our educational attainment, and our economic security. It attempts, in short, to measure "that which makes life worthwhile." It is common-sense economics that corresponds with the realities of our daily lives as we actually experience them.

COSTS AND BENEFITS

Unlike the GDP, the GPI distinguishes economic activities that produce benefit from those that cause harm. For example, more crime makes the economy grow as more money is spent on prisons, burglar alarms, security guards, lawyers, police and court costs. Having a more peaceful society may actually show up as a disadvantage in the GDP and growth statistics.

By contrast, the GPI regards a peaceful and secure society as a profound social asset, with higher crime rates a sign of depreciation in the value of that asset. Unlike the GDP, lower crime rates make the GPI go up, and crime costs are subtracted rather than added in assessments of prosperity.

GPI Atlantic found that crime costs Nova Scotians $1.2 billion a year, or $3,500 per household, including $312 million in victim losses, $258 million in public spending on prisons, police and courts, and $46 million in home security expenses. Nova Scotian households pay $800 a year more in higher prices due to in-store retail theft and business crime prevention costs, and $200 more per household in higher insurance premiums due to insurance fraud.

Canadians are three times as likely to be victims of crime as their parents a generation ago. According to the GPI, this is not a sign of progress, even though our economy grows as a result. GPI Atlantic found that if crime were still at 1962 levels, Nova Scotians would be saving about $750 million a year, or $2,200 per household, money that would be available for investment in more productive and welfare-enhancing activities.

The GPI takes a similar approach to road accidents, toxic pollution and greenhouse gas emissions, which are also seen as costs rather than benefits. Like crime and resource depletion, they are areas of the economy where more growth is clearly not desirable.

By incorporating "external" costs directly into the economic accounting structure, the "full cost accounting" mechanisms in the GPI can also help policy makers to identify investments that produce lower social and environmental costs to society. Gambling, clear-cutting and other growth industries might receive less government support if social costs were counted, and sustainable practices might receive more encouragement.

For example, GPI Atlantic recently found that a 10% shift from truck to rail freight would save Nova Scotian taxpayers $11 million a year when the costs of greenhouse gas emissions, road accidents and road maintenance costs are included. Telecommuting two days per week would save $2,200 annually per employee when travel time, fuel, parking, accident, air pollution and other environmental and social costs are included.

The GPI approach contrasts sharply with conventional accounting methods which value the contribution that commuting makes to economic growth. Canadians currently spend $102 billion a year on their cars, $11 billion more on highways, $500 million on car advertisements, and billions more on hospital beds, and police, court and funeral costs for the 3,000 killed and 25,000 seriously injured car crash victims every year. All this spending currently counts as "progress" and "consumer confidence." Car-pooling may slow GDP growth. By contrast, full cost-benefit accounting methods would lend more support to taxation policies and subsidy incentives that support mass transit alternatives and other more sustainable practices.

VALUING NATURAL RESOURCES

The costs of holding on to the illusion that "more" is "better" are frightening. Scientists recognize that the only biological organism that has unlimited growth as its dogma is the cancer cell, the apparent model for our conventional economic theory. By contrast, the natural world thrives on balance and equilibrium, and recognizes inherent limits to growth. The cancer analogy is apt, because the path of limitless growth is profoundly self-destructive. No matter how many cars we have in the driveway or how many possessions we accumulate, the environment will not tolerate the growth illusion even if we fail to see through it.

Valuing both natural resources and time provides an accounting framework that recognizes inherent limits to our economic activity and values balance and equilibrium. In the Genuine Progress Index, natural resources are valued as finite capital stocks, subject to depreciation like produced capital. Genuine progress is measured by our ability to live off the income, or services, produced by our resources without depleting the capital stock that is the basis of wealth both for our children and ourselves.

The GPI acknowledges the full range of ecological and social services provided by these resources. The GPI forestry account, for example, counts not only timber production, but also the value of forests in protecting watersheds, habitat and biodiversity, guarding against soil erosion, regulating climate and sequestering carbon, and providing for recreation and spiritual enjoyment. Healthy soils and the maintenance of multi-species, multi-aged forests in turn provide multiple economic benefits by enhancing timber productivity, increasing the economic value of forest products, protecting against fire, disease and insects, and supporting the burgeoning eco-tourism industry.

The massive unemployment created by the collapse of the Atlantic ground fishery punctured the conventional illusion that jobs and environmental conservation are in conflict. We now understand that soil erosion today threatens food security for our children and that valuing and protecting our resource wealth is essential to protect the human economy.

VALUING TIME

Like natural resources, time is also finite and similarly limits economic activity. We all have 24 hours a day and a limited life span. How we pass that time, and how we balance our paid and unpaid work, our voluntary service, and our free time, is a measure of our well being, quality of life, and contribution to society. The GPI uses time use surveys to measure and value time over a full 24-hour period and to assess the balance between its alternative uses. Measuring time as time, rather than as money, also cuts through the myth of limitless growth.

According to current accounting methods, the more hours we work for pay, the more the GDP grows, and the more we "progress." In a recent interview, a Fortune 500 Chief Executive Officer stated that he works from 6 a.m. to 10 p.m. every day and has no time for anything else except sleep. By conventional standards, his $4 million annual income makes him rich. According to the GPI, where family time, voluntary service and free time are all measured and valued, the CEO may be leading an impoverished lifestyle.

Here in Nova Scotia the head of the Sobeys empire recently advised aspiring entrepreneurs to think about business "day and night -- when you are walking, driving, eating, shaving" if they want to be successful. By contrast, a more balanced relationship with time may produce a more balanced understanding of the natural world. After all, without the leisure time to enjoy a walk in the forest, it is easy to order it clear-cut.

What happens when we start valuing time? The policy implications are profound. For example, GPI Atlantic found that Nova Scotians have the highest rate of voluntary activity in the country, giving 134 million hours a year, the equivalent of 81,000 jobs, or $1.9 billion worth of services, equal to 10% of our GDP — a reservoir of generosity complete invisible in our conventional accounts. Unmeasured and unvalued, the voluntary sector has not received the support it needs to do its work well.

Longer work hours due to downsizing and declining real incomes have squeezed volunteer time, producing a steady decline of 7.2% in voluntary service hours over 10 years. For the first time, claims by the Canadian Finance Minister that volunteers could compensate for government service cuts have been disproved. Without tracking the unpaid volunteer sector, such government statements could never be tested.

Measuring unpaid household work shines the spotlight on the time stress of working parents struggling to juggle job and household responsibilities, and on the need for family-friendly work arrangements and flexible work hours. The modern work place has not yet adjusted to the reality that women have doubled their rate of participation in the paid work force. Working mothers put in an average of 11 hours a day of paid and unpaid work on weekdays, and 15 hours more of unpaid work on weekends.

Measuring housework also raises important pay equity issues. Work traditionally performed by women in the household and regarded as "free" has been devalued in the market economy, resulting in significant gender pay inequities. Though it is an important investment in our human capital, requires vital skills and continuous alertness, child care workers in Nova Scotia earn an average of only $7.58 an hour.

GPI Atlantic found that single mothers dependent on the household economy put in an average of 50 hours a week of productive household work. If it were replaced for pay in the market economy, this work would be worth $450 a week. Because it is invisible and unvalued, 70% of single mothers in Nova Scotia live below the "low-income cut-off", the major cause of child poverty in the province. From the GPI perspective, social supports for single mothers are not "welfare" any more than taxpayer subsidies for job creation in the market economy are "welfare." They are seen, instead, as essential social infrastructure for the household economy.

EQUITY AND JOB CREATION

Millions of Americans have been left behind by the growth spurt in that country. The U.S. Census Bureau reports that income inequality has risen dramatically since 1968, by 18% for all U.S. households and by over 23% for families. The richest 1% of American households now owns 40% of the national wealth, while the net worth of middle class families has fallen steadily through the 1990s due to rising indebtedness. Bill Gates alone owns more wealth than the bottom 45% of U.S. households combined. Is this progress?

In 1989 the Canadian House of Commons unanimously vowed to eliminate child poverty by the year 2000. Since 1989 child poverty has increased by 47%. In other words, there is no guarantee that the tide of economic growth lifts all boats, and the evidence indicates that the opposite is frequently the case.

For this reason the GPI explicitly values increased equity and job security as benchmarks of genuine progress. Indeed, Statistics Canada recently recognized that concern for equity is inherent in any measure of sustainable development. Once limits to growth are accepted, the issue is fair distribution rather than increased production. If everyone in the world consumed resources at the Canadian level, we would require four additional planets earth.

Within this country, Statistics Canada points to a growing polarization of hours as the main cause of increased earnings inequality. The growth of insecure, temporary and marginal employment -- the engine of employment growth in the 1990s -- means that more Canadians cannot get the hours they need to support themselves. At the same time, due to downsizing and declining real incomes, more Canadians are working longer hours. Interestingly, a recent Japanese study found that the underemployed and the overworked suffer similar stress levels and have the same risk of heart attack.

Measuring and valuing time actually changes our approach to work and job creation. In North America we are completely conditioned to believe that jobs are contingent on more growth, forgetting that the right to work and earn a decent livelihood is a fundamental human right, enshrined in Articles 23 and 25 of the Universal Declaration of

Human Rights. "If" we bring in casinos, "if" we cut a new deal with China, "if" we entice another corporation with a tax break or subsidy, it is said, "then" perhaps we can create or save jobs.

Instead, we might learn from some European countries that have created more jobs by reducing and redistributing the existing workload. The Netherlands, for example, has a 2.7% unemployment rate and also the lowest annual work hours of any industrialized country. In that country, part-time work is legally protected, with equal hourly wages and pro-rated benefits. France has introduced a 35-hour work week. Danes have 5 weeks of annual vacation.

Sweden has generous parental and educational leave provisions that create job openings for new workers. Phased retirement options gradually reduce the work hours of older workers, who can pass on their skills and expertise to younger workers taking their place. One creative experiment gave parents the option of taking the summer months off to be with their children, with guaranteed re-entry to the work force in September, thus providing much needed summer jobs for university students and cost savings to employers.

Reducing and redistributing work hours can also improve the quality of life by creating more free time. Time use surveys show that the Danes average eleven hours more free time per week than Canadians and Americans. But free time has no value in our market statistics, and its loss appears nowhere in our current measures of progress. By counting underemployment and overwork as economic costs, and giving explicit value to equity and free time, the GPI can point to a range of intelligent job creation strategies that are not dependent on more growth.

SHIFTING THE VIEW

None of this means that there should be no growth of any kind. Some types of economic growth clearly enhance well being, increase equity and protect the environment. There is vital work to be done in our society -- raising children, caring for those in need, restoring our forests, providing adequate food and shelter for all, enhancing our knowledge and understanding, and strengthening our communities.

But we will never shift our attention to the work that is needed if we fail to value our natural resources, our voluntary service and our child-rearing, and if we place no value on equity, free time, and the health of our communities. And we will never escape from the materialist illusion that has trapped us for so long, or even know whether we are really better off, if we continue to count costs like crime and pollution as benefits, and if we measure our well being according to the GDP and economic growth statistics.

We have little time left to abandon the dogma of economic growth and its bankrupt measures of well being before the environment makes the decision for us at tremendous cost. We can still choose to begin the new millennium sanely, valuing the true strengths that we have in abundance. We can begin to fashion more self-reliant and self-sufficient forms of community economic development that provide a real alternative to the globalization that puts our destiny in the hands of forces beyond our control. Knowing that more possessions are not the key to happiness and well being, we can still take back our future, and perhaps even live a little more simply.

Nova Scotia seems particularly fertile ground for this experiment, because it has been just far enough removed from the materialist mainstream to preserve its community strength, spiritual values, quality of life, and a strong tradition of generous community service more effectively than many other parts of North America. The province has also experienced first-hand the collapse of a natural resource, and it has not generally been well served by conventional economic theory, thus creating a greater openness to alternatives. Later this year, Kings County, Nova Scotia, will begin using the GPI as a measure of progress and a strategy of community development, and other counties will do so as soon as it is complete.

The cusp of the millennium is a rare moment in history when a long-term practical vision can actually overpower our habitual short-term preoccupations. The time has never been better to contemplate the legacy we are leaving our children and the society we want to inhabit in the new millennium. It is a moment that invites us to lay the foundations of a genuinely decent society for the sake of our children and all the world's inhabitants.

[Editor's Note: The GPI Atlantic web site is: www.gpiatlantic.org]

A ROAD MAP FOR NATURAL CAPITALISM

Amory B. Lovins
Research Director and CFO
Rocky Mountain Institute

L. Hunter Lovins
CEO, Rocky Mountain Institute

and

Paul Hawken
Founder of Smith & Hawken, and cofounder, Datafusion

On September 16, 1991, a small group of scientists was sealed inside Biosphere II, a glittering 3.2-acre glass and metal dome in Oracle, Arizona. Two years later, when the radical attempt to replicate the earth's main ecosystems in miniature ended, the engineered environment was dying. The gaunt researchers had survived only because fresh air had been pumped in. Despite $200 million worth of elaborate equipment, Biosphere II had failed to generate breathable air, drinkable water, and adequate food for just eight people. Yet Biosphere I, the planet we all inhabit, effortlessly performs those tasks every day for 6 billion of us.

Disturbingly, Biosphere I is now itself at risk. The earth's ability to sustain life, and therefore economic activity, is threatened by the way we extract, process, transport, and dispose of a vast flow of resources — some 220 billion tons a year, or more than 20 times the average American's body weight every day. With dangerously narrow focus, our industries look only at the exploitable resources of the earth's ecosystems — its oceans, forests, and plains — and not at the larger services that those systems provide for free. Resources and ecosystem services both come from the earth — even from the same biological systems — but they're two different things. Forests, for instance, not only produce the resource of wood fiber but also provide such ecosystem services as water storage, habitat, and regulation of the atmosphere and climate. Yet companies that earn income from harvesting the wood fiber resource often do so in ways that damage the forest's ability to carry out its other vital tasks.

Unfortunately, the cost of destroying ecosystem services becomes apparent only when the services start to break down. In China's Yangtze basin in 1998, for example, deforestation triggered flooding that killed 3,700 people, dislocated 223 million, and inundated 60 million acres of cropland. That $30-billion disaster forced a logging moratorium and a

$12 billion crash program of reforestation.

The reason companies (and governments) are so prodigal with ecosystem services is that the value of those services doesn't appear on the business balance sheet. But that's a staggering omission. The economy, after all, is embedded in the environment. Recent calculations published in the journal Nature (Costanza et al., 1997, 387:253-260) conservatively estimate the value of all the earth's ecosystem services to be at least $33 trillion a year. That's close to the gross world product, and it implies a capitalized book value on the order of half a quadrillion dollars. What's more, for most of these services, there is no known substitute at any price, and we can't live without them.

This article puts forward a new approach not only for protecting the biosphere but also for improving profits and competitiveness. Some very simple changes to the way we run our businesses, built on advanced techniques for making resources more productive, can yield startling benefits both for today's shareholders and for future generations.

This approach is called natural capitalism because it's what capitalism might become if its largest category of capital — the "natural capital" of ecosystem services — were properly valued. The journey to natural capitalism involves four major shifts in business practices, all vitally interlinked:

(1) Dramatically increase the productivity of natural resources. Reducing the wasteful and destructive flow of resources from depletion to pollution represents a major business opportunity. Through fundamental changes in both production design and technology, farsighted companies are developing ways to make natural resources — energy, minerals, water, forests — stretch 5, 10, even 100 times further than they do today. These major resource savings often yield higher profits than small resource savings do — or even saving no resources at all would — and not only pay for themselves over time but in many cases reduce initial capital investments.

(2) Shift to biologically inspired production models. Natural capitalism seeks not merely to reduce waste but to eliminate the very concept of waste. In closed-loop production systems, modeled on nature's designs, every output either is returned harmlessly to the ecosystem as a nutrient, like compost, or becomes an input for manufacturing another product. Such systems can often be designed to eliminate the use of toxic materials, which can hamper nature's ability to reprocess materials.

(3) Move to a solutions-based business model. The business model of traditional manufacturing rests on the sale of goods. In the new model, value is instead delivered as a flow of services — providing illumination, for example, rather than selling lightbulbs. This model entails a new perception of value, a move from the acquisition of goods as a measure of affluence to one where well-being is measured by the continuous satisfaction of changing expectations for quality, utility, and performance. The new relationship aligns the interests of providers and customers in ways that reward them for implementing the first two innovations of natural capitalism — resource productivity and closed-loop manufacturing.

(4) Reinvest in natural capital. Ultimately, business must restore, sustain, and expand the planet's ecosystems so that they can produce their vital services and biological resources even more abundantly. Pressures to do so are mounting as human needs expand, the costs engendered by deteriorating ecosystems rise, and the environmental awareness of consumers increases. Fortunately, these pressures all create business value.

Natural capitalism is not motivated by a current scarcity of natural resources. Indeed, although many biological resources, like fish, are becoming scarce, most mined resources, such as copper and oil, seem ever more abundant. Indices of average commodity prices are at 28-year lows, thanks partly to powerful extractive technologies, which are often subsidized and whose damage to natural capital remains unaccounted for. Yet even despite these artificially low prices, using resources manyfold more productively can now be so profitable that pioneering companies — large and small — have already embarked on the journey toward natural capitalism.[1]

Still the question arises — if large resource savings are available and profitable, why haven't they all been captured already? The answer is simple: scores of common practices in both the private and public sectors systematically reward companies for wasting natural resources and penalize them for boosting resource productivity. For example, most companies expense their consumption of raw materials through the income statement but pass resource-saving investment through the balance sheet. That distortion makes it more tax efficient to waste fuel than to invest in improving fuel efficiency. In short, even though the road seems clear, the compass that companies use to direct their journey is broken. Later we'll look in more detail at some of the obstacles to resource productivity — and some of the important business opportunities they reveal. But first, let's map the route toward natural capitalism.

DRAMATICALLY INCREASE THE PRODUCTIVITY OF NATURAL RESOURCES

In the first stage of a company's journey toward natural capitalism, it strives to wring out the waste of energy, water, materials, and other resources throughout its production systems and other operations. There are two main ways companies can do this at a profit. First, they can adopt a fresh approach to design that considers industrial systems as a whole rather than part by part. Second, companies can replace old industrial technologies with new ones, particularly with those based on natural processes and materials.

Implementing Whole-System Design. Inventor Edwin Land once remarked that "people who seem to have had a new idea have often simply stopped having an old idea." This is particularly true when designing for resource savings. The old idea is one of diminishing returns — the greater the resource saving, the higher the cost. But that old idea is giving way to the new idea that bigger savings can cost less — that saving a large fraction of resources can actually cost less than saving a small fraction of resources. This is the concept of expanding returns, and it governs much of the revolutionary thinking behind whole-system design. Lean manufacturing is an example of whole-system thinking that has helped many companies dramatically reduce such forms of waste as lead times, defect rates, and inventory. Applying whole-system thinking to the productivity of natural resources can achieve even more.

Consider Interface Corporation, a leading maker of materials for commercial interiors. In its new Shanghai carpet factory, a liquid had to be circulated through a standard pumping loop similar to those used in nearly all industries. A top European company designed the system to use pumps requiring a total of 95 horsepower. But before construction began, Interface's engineer, Jan Schilham, realized that two embarrassingly simple design changes would cut that power requirement to only 7 horsepower — a 92% reduction. His redesigned system cost less to build, involved no new technology, and worked better in all respects.

What two design changes achieved this 12-fold saving in pumping power? First, Schilham chose fatter-than-usual pipes, which create much less friction than thin pipes do and therefore need far less pumping energy. The original designer had chosen thin pipes because, according to the textbook method, the extra cost of fatter ones wouldn't be justified by the pumping energy that they would save. This standard design trade-off optimizes the pipes by themselves but "pessimizes" the larger system. Schilham optimized the whole system by counting not only the higher capital cost of the fatter pipes but also the lower capital cost of the smaller pumping equipment that would be needed. The pumps, motors, motor controls, and electrical components could all be much smaller because there'd be less friction to overcome. Capital cost would fall far more for the smaller equipment than it would rise for the fatter pipe. Choosing big pipes and small pumps — rather than small pipes and big pumps — would therefore make the whole system cost less to build, even before counting its future energy savings.

Schilham's second innovation was to reduce the friction even more by making the pipes short and straight rather than long and crooked. He did this by laying out the pipes first, then positioning the various tanks, boilers, and other equipment that they connected. Designers normally locate the production equipment in arbitrary positions and then have a pipe fitter connect everything. Awkward placement forces the pipes to make numerous bends that greatly increase friction. The pipe fitters don't mind: they're paid by the hour, they profit from the extra pipes and fittings, and they don't pay for the oversized pumps or inflated electric bills. In addition to reducing those four kinds of costs, Schilham's short, straight pipes were easier to insulate, saving an extra 70 kilowatts of heat loss and repaying the insulation's cost in three months.

This small example has big implications for two reasons. First, pumping is the largest application of motors, and motors use three-quarters of all industrial electricity. Second, the lessons are very widely relevant. Interface's pumping loop shows how simple changes in design mentality can yield huge resource savings and returns on investment. This isn't rocket science; often it's just a rediscovery of good Victorian engineering principles that have been lost because of specialization.

Whole-system thinking can help managers find small changes that lead to big savings that are cheap, free, or even better than free (because they make the whole system cheaper to build. They can do this because often the right investment in one part of the system can produce multiple benefits throughout the system. For example, companies would gain 18 distinct economic benefits — of which direct energy savings is only one — if they switched from ordinary motors to premium-efficiency motors or from ordinary lighting ballasts (the transformer-like boxes that control fluorescent lamps) to electronic ballasts that automatically dim the lamps to match available daylight. If everyone in America integrated these and other selected technologies into all existing motor and lighting systems in an optimal way, the nation's $.220-billion-a-year electric bill would be cut in half. The after-tax return on investing in these changes would in most cases exceed 100% per year.

The profits from saving electricity could be increased even further if companies also incorporated the best off-the-shelf improvements into their building structure and their office, heating, cooling, and other equipment. Overall, such changes could cut national electricity consumption by at least 75% and produce returns of around 100% a year on the investments made. More important, because workers would be more comfortable, better able to see, and less fatigued by noise, their productivity and the quality of their output would rise. Eight recent case studies of people working in well-designed, energy-efficient build-ings measured labor productivity gains of 6% to 16%. Since a typical office pays about 100 times as much for people as it does for energy, this increased productivity in people is worth about 6 to 16 times as much as eliminating the entire energy bill.

Energy-saving, productivity-enhancing improvements can often be achieved at even lower cost by piggybacking them onto the periodic renovations that all buildings and factories need. A recent proposal for reallocating the normal 20-year renovation budget for a standard 200,000-square-foot glass-clad office tower near Chicago, Illinois, shows the potential of whole-system design. The proposal suggested replacing the aging glazing system with a new kind of window that lets in nearly six times more daylight than the old sun-blocking glass units. The new windows would reduce the flow of heat and noise four times better than traditional windows do. So even though the glass costs slightly more, the overall cost of the renovation would be reduced because the windows would let in cool, glare-free daylight that, when combined with more efficient lighting and office equipment, would reduce the need for air-conditioning by 75%. Installing a fourfold more efficient, but fourfold smaller, air-conditioning system would cost $200,000 less than giving the old system its normal 20-year renovation. The $200,000 saved would, in turn, pay for the extra cost of the new windows and other improvements. This whole-system approach to renovation would not only save 75% of the building's total energy use, it would also greatly improve the building's comfort and marketability. Yet it would cost es-sentially the same as the normal renovation. There are about 100,000 twenty-year-old glass office towers in the United States that are ripe for such improvement.

Major gains in resource productivity require that the right steps be taken in the right order. Small changes made at the downstream end of a process often create far larger savings further upstream. In almost any industry that uses a pumping system, for example, saving one unit of liquid flow or friction in an exit pipe saves about ten units of fuel, cost, and pollution at the power station.

Of course, the original reduction in flow itself can bring direct ben-efits, which are often the reason changes are made in the first place. In the 1980s, while California's industry grew 30%, for example, its water use was cut by 30%, largely to avoid increased wastewater fees. But the resulting reduction in pumping energy (and the roughly tenfold larger saving in power-plant fuel and pollution) delivered bonus savings that were at the time largely unanticipated.

To see how downstream cuts in resource consumption can create huge savings upstream, consider how reducing the use of wood fiber disproportionately reduces the pressure to cut down forests. In round numbers, half of all harvested wood fiber is used for such structural products as lumber; the other half is used for paper and cardboard. In both cases, the biggest leverage comes from reducing the amount of the retail product used. If it takes, for example, three pounds of harvested trees to produce one pound of product, then saving one pound of product will save three pounds of trees — plus all the environmental damage avoided by not having to cut them down in the first place.

The easiest savings come from not using paper that's unwanted or unneeded. In an experiment at its Swiss headquarters, for example, Dow Europe cut office paper flow by about 30% in six weeks simply by discouraging unneeded information. For instance, mailing lists were eliminated and senders of memos got back receipts indicating whether each recipient had wanted the information. Taking those and other small steps, Dow was also able to increase labor productivity by a similar proportion because people could focus on what they really needed to read. Similarly, Danish hearing-aid maker Oticon saved upwards of 30% of its paper as a by-product of redesigning its business processes to produce better decisions faster. Setting the default on office printers and copiers to double-sided mode reduced AT&T's paper costs by about 15%. Recently developed copiers and printers can even strip off old toner and printer ink, permitting each sheet to be reused about ten times.

Further savings can come from using thinner but stronger and more opaque paper, and from designing packaging more thoughtfully. In a 30-month effort at reducing such waste, Johnson & Johnson saved 2,750 tons of packaging, 1,600 tons of paper, $2.8 million, and at least 330 acres of forest annually. The downstream savings in paper use are multiplied by the savings further upstream, as less need for paper products (or less need for fiber to make each product) translates into less raw paper, less raw paper means less pulp, and less pulp requires fewer trees to be harvested from the forest. Recycling paper and substituting alternative fibers such as wheat straw will save even more.

Comparable savings can be achieved for the wood fiber used in structural products. Pacific Gas and Electric, for example, sponsored an innovative design developed by Davis Energy Group that used engineered wood products to reduce the amount of wood needed in a stud wall for a typical tract house by more than 70%. These walls were stronger, cheaper, more stable, and insulated twice as well. Using them enabled the designers to eliminate heating and cooling equipment in a climate where temperatures range from freezing to 113°F. Eliminating the equipment made the whole house much less expensive both to build and to run while still maintaining high levels of comfort. Taken together, these and many other savings in the paper and construction industries could make our use of wood fiber so much more productive that, in principle, the entire world's present wood fiber needs could probably be met by an intensive tree farm about the size of Iowa.

Adopting Innovative Technologies. Implementing whole-system design goes hand in hand with introducing alternative, environmentally friendly technologies. Many of these are already available and profitable but not widely known. Some, like the "designer catalysts" that are transforming the chemical industry, are already runaway successes. Others are still making their way to market, delayed by cultural rather than by economic or technical barriers.

The automobile industry is particularly ripe for technological change. After a century of development, motorcar technology is showing signs of age. Only 1% of the energy consumed by today's cars is actually used to move the driver: only 15% to 20% of the power generated by burning gasoline reaches the wheels (the rest is lost in the engine and drivetrain) and 95 % of the resulting propulsion moves the car, not the driver. The industry's infrastructure is hugely expensive and inefficient. Its convergent products compete for narrow niches in saturated core markets at commodity-like prices. Auto making is capital-intensive, and product cycles are long. It is profitable in good years but subject to large losses in bad years. Like the typewriter industry just before the advent of personal computers, it is vulnerable to displacement by something completely different.

Enter the Hypercar. Since 1993, when Rocky Mountain Institute placed this automotive concept in the public domain, several dozen current and potential auto manufacturers have committed billions of dollars to its development and commercialization. The Hypercar integrates the best existing technologies to reduce the consumption of fuel as much as 85% and the amount of materials used up to 90% by introducing four main innovations.

First, making the vehicle out of advanced polymer composites, chiefly carbon fiber, reduces its weight by two-thirds while maintaining crashworthiness. Second, aerodynamic design and better tires reduce air resistance by as much as 70% and rolling resistance by up to 80%. Together, these innovations save about two-thirds of the fuel. Third, 30% to 50% of the remaining fuel is saved by using a "hybrid-electric" drive. In such a system, the wheels are turned by electric motors whose power is made onboard by a small engine or turbine, or even more efficiently by a fuel cell. The fuel cell generates electricity directly by chemically combining stored hydrogen with oxygen, producing pure hot water as its only by-product. Interactions between the small, clean, efficient power source and the ultralight, low-drag auto body then further reduce the weight, cost, and complexity of both. Fourth, much of the traditional hardware — from transmissions and differentials to gauges and certain parts of the suspension — can be replaced by electronics controlled with highly integrated, customizable, and upgradable software.

These technologies make it feasible to manufacture pollution-free, high-performance cars, sport utilities, pickup trucks, and vans that get 80 to 200 miles per gallon (or its energy equivalent in other fuels). These improvements will not require any compromise in quality or utility. Fuel savings will not come from making the vehicles small, sluggish, unsafe, or unaffordable, nor will they depend on government fuel taxes, mandates, or subsidies. Rather, Hypercars will succeed for the same reason that people buy compact discs instead of phonograph records: the CD is a superior product that redefines market expectations. From the manufacturers' perspective, Hypercars will cut cycle times, capital needs, body part counts, and assembly effort and space by as much as tenfold. Early adopters will have a huge competitive advantage — which is why dozens of corporations, including most automakers, are now racing to bring Hypercar-like products to market.[2]

In the long term, the Hypercar will transform industries other than automobiles. It will displace about an eighth of the steel market directly and most of the rest eventually, as carbon fiber becomes far cheaper. Hypercars and their cousins could ultimately save as much oil as OPEC now sells. Indeed, oil may well become uncompetitive as a fuel long before it becomes scarce and costly. Similar challenges face the coal and electricity industries because the development of the Hypercar is likely to accelerate greatly the commercialization of inexpensive hydrogen fuel cells. These fuel cells will help shift power production from centralized coal-fired and nuclear power stations to networks of decentralized, small-scale generators. In fact, fuel-cell-powered Hypercars could themselves be part of these networks. They'd be, in effect, 20-kilowatt power plants on wheels. Given that cars are left parked — that is, unused — more than 95 % of the time, these Hypercars could be plugged into a grid and could then sell back enough electricity to repay as much as half the predicted cost of leasing them. A national Hypercar fleet could ultimately have five to ten times the generating capacity of the national electric grid.

As radical as it sounds, the Hypercar is not an isolated case. Similar ideas are emerging in such industries as chemicals, semiconductors, general manufacturing, transportation, water and waste-water treatment, agriculture, forestry, energy, real estate, and urban design. For example, the amount of carbon dioxide released for each microchip manufactured can be reduced almost 100-fold through improvements that are now profitable or soon will be.

Some of the most striking developments come from emulating nature's techniques. In her 1997 book, *Biomimicry*, Janine Benyus points out that spiders convert digested crickets and flies into silk that's as strong as Kevlar without the need for boiling sulfuric acid and high-temperature extruders. Using no furnaces, abalone can convert seawater into an inner shell twice as tough as our best ceramics. Trees turn sunlight, water, soil, and air into cellulose, a sugar stronger than nylon but one-fourth as dense. They then bind it into wood, a natural composite with a higher bending strength than concrete, aluminum alloy, or steel. We may never become as skillful as spiders, abalone, or trees, but smart designers are already realizing that nature's environmentally benign chemistry offers attractive alternatives to industrial brute force.

Whether through better design or through new technologies, reducing waste represents a vast business opportunity. The U.S. economy is not even 10% as energy efficient as the laws of physics allow. Just the energy thrown off as waste heat by U.S. power stations equals the total energy use of Japan. Materials efficiency is even worse: only about 1% of all the materials mobilized to serve America is actually made into products and still in use six months after sale. In every sector, there are opportunities for reducing the amount of resources that go into a production process, the steps required to run that process, and the amount of pollution generated and by-products discarded at the end. These all represent avoidable costs and hence profits to be won.

REDESIGN PRODUCTION ACCORDING TO BIOLOGICAL MODELS

In the second stage on the journey to natural capitalism, companies use closed-loop manufacturing to create new products and processes that can totally prevent waste. This plus more efficient production processes could cut companies' long-term materials requirements by more than 90% in most sectors.

The central principle of closed-loop manufacturing, as architect Paul Bierman-Lytle of the engineering firm CH2M Hill puts it, is "waste equals food." Every output of manufacturing should be either composted into natural nutrients or remanufactured into technical nutrients — that is, it should be returned to the ecosystem or recycled for further production. Closed-loop production systems are designed to eliminate any materials that incur disposal costs, especially toxic ones, because the alternative — isolating them to prevent harm to natural systems — tends to be costly and risky. Indeed, meeting EPA and OSHA standards by eliminating harmful materials often makes a manufacturing process cost less than the hazardous process it replaced. Motorola, for example, formerly used chlorofluorocarbons for cleaning printed circuit boards after soldering. When CFCs were outlawed because they destroy strato-spheric ozone, Motorola at first explored such alternatives as orange-peel terpenes. But it turned out to be even cheaper — and to produce a better product — to redesign the whole soldering process so that it needed no cleaning operations or cleaning materials at all.

Closed-loop manufacturing is more than just a theory. The U.S. remanufacturing industry in 1996 reported revenues of $53 billion — more than consumer-durables manufacturing (appliances; furniture; audio, video, farm, and garden equipment). Xerox, whose bottom line has swelled by $700 million from remanufacturing, expects to save another $I billion just by remanufacturing its new, entirely reusable or recyclable line of "green" photocopiers. What's more, policy makers in some countries are already taking steps to encourage industry to think along these lines. German law, for example, makes many manufacturers responsible for their products forever, and Japan is following suit.

Combining closed-loop manufacturing with resource efficiency is especially powerful. DuPont, for example, gets much of its polyester industrial film back from customers after they use it and recycles it into new film. DuPont also makes its polyester film ever stronger and thinner so it uses less material and costs less to make. Yet because the film performs better, customers are willing to pay more for it. As DuPont chairman Jack Krol noted in 1997, "Our ability to continually improve the inherent properties [of our films] enables this process [of developing more productive materials, at lower cost, and higher profits] to go on indefinitely."

Interface is leading the way to this next frontier of industrial ecology. While its competitors are "down cycling" nylon-and-PVC-based carpet into less valuable carpet backing, Interface has invented a new floor covering material called Solenium, which can be completely remanufactured into identical new product. This fundamental innovation emerged from a clean-sheet redesign. Executives at Interface didn't ask how they could sell more carpet of the familiar kind; they asked how they could create a dream product that would best meet their customers' needs while protecting and nourishing natural capital.

Solenium lasts four times longer and uses 40% less material than ordinary carpets — an 86% reduction in materials intensity. What's more, Solenium is free of chlorine and other toxic materials, is virtually stainproof, doesn't grow mildew, can easily be cleaned with water, and offers aesthetic advantages over traditional carpets. It's so superior in every respect that Interface doesn't market it as an environmental product — just a better one.

Solenium is only one part of Interface's drive to eliminate every form of waste. Chairman Ray C. Anderson defines waste as "any measurable input that does not produce customer value," and he considers all inputs to be waste until shown otherwise. Between 1994 and 1998, this zero-waste approach led to a systematic treasure hunt that helped to keep resource inputs constant while revenues rose by $200 million. Indeed, $67 million of the revenue increase can be directly attributed to the company's 60% reduction in landfill waste.

Subsequently, president Charlie Eitel expanded the definition of waste to include all fossil fuel inputs, and now many customers are eager to buy products from the company's recently opened solar-powered carpet factory. Interface's green strategy has not only won plaudits from environmentalists, it has also proved a remarkably successful business strategy. Between 1993 and 1998, revenue has more than doubled, profits have more than tripled, and the number of employees has increased by 73%.

CHANGE THE BUSINESS MODEL

In addition to its drive to eliminate waste, Interface has made a fundamental shift in its business model — the third stage on the journey toward natural capitalism. The company has realized that clients want to walk on and look at carpets — but not necessarily to own them. Traditionally, broadloom carpets in office buildings are replaced every decade because some portions look worn out. When that happens, companies suffer the disruption of shutting down their offices and removing their furniture. Billions of pounds of carpets are removed each year and sent to landfills, where they will last up to 20,000 years. To escape this unproductive and wasteful cycle, Interface is transforming itself from a company that sells and fits carpets into one that provides floor-covering services.

Under its Evergreen Lease, Interface no longer sells carpets but rather leases a floor-covering service for a monthly fee, accepting responsibility for keeping the carpet fresh and clean. Monthly inspections detect and replace worn carpet tiles. Since at most 20% of an area typically shows at least 80% of the wear, replacing only the worn parts reduces the consumption of carpeting material by about 80%. It also minimizes the disruption that customers experience -- worn tiles are seldom found under furniture. Finally, for the customer, leasing carpets can provide a tax advantage by turning a capital expenditure into a tax-deductible expense. The result: the customer gets cheaper and better services that cost the supplier far less to produce. Indeed, the energy saved from not producing a whole new carpet is in itself enough to produce all the carpeting that the new business model requires. Taken together, the 5-fold savings in carpeting material that Interface achieves through the Evergreen Lease and the 7-fold materials savings achieved through the use of Solenium deliver a stunning 35-fold reduction in the flow of materials needed to sustain a superior floor-covering service. Remanufacturing, and even making carpet initially from renewable materials, can then reduce the extraction of virgin resources essentially to the company's goal of zero.

Interface's shift to a service-leasing business reflects a fundamental change from the basic model of most manufacturing companies, which still look on their businesses as machines for producing and selling products. The more products sold, the better — at least for the company, if not always for the customer or the earth. But any model that wastes natural resources also wastes money. Ultimately, that model will be unable to compete with a service model that emphasizes solving problems and building long-term relationships with customers rather than making and selling products. The shift to what James Womack of the Lean Enterprise Institute calls a "solutions economy" will almost always improve customer value and providers' bottom lines because it aligns both parties' interests, offering rewards for doing more and better with less.

Interface is not alone. Elevator giant Schindler, for example, prefers leasing vertical transportation services to selling elevators because leasing lets it capture the savings from its elevators' lower energy and maintenance costs. Dow Chemical and SafetyKleen prefer leasing dissolving services to selling solvents because they can reuse the same solvent scores of times, reducing costs. United Technologies' Carrier division, the world's largest manufacturer of air conditioners, is shifting its mission from selling air conditioners to leasing comfort. Making its air conditioners more durable and efficient may compromise future equipment sales, but it provides what customers want and will pay for better comfort at lower cost. But Carrier is going even further. It's starting to team up with other companies to make buildings more efficient so that they need less air-conditioning, or even none at all, to yield the same level of comfort. Carrier will get paid to provide the agreed-upon level of comfort however that's delivered. Higher profits will come from providing better solutions rather than from selling more equipment. Since comfort with little or no air-conditioning (via better building design) works better and costs less than comfort with copious air-conditioning, Carrier is smart to capture this opportunity itself before its competitors do. As they say at 3M: "We'd rather eat our own lunch, thank you."

The shift to a service business model promises benefits not just to participating businesses but to the entire economy as well. Womack points out that by helping customers reduce their need for capital goods such as carpets or elevators, and by rewarding suppliers for extending and maximizing asset values rather than for churning them, adoption of the service model will reduce the volatility in the turnover of capital goods that lies at the heart of the business cycle. That would significantly reduce the overall volatility of the world's economy. At present, the producers of capital goods face feast or famine because the buying decisions of households and corporations are extremely sensitive to fluctuating income. But in a continuous-flow-of-services economy, those swings would be greatly reduced, bringing a welcome stability to businesses. Excess capacity — another form of waste and source of risk — need no longer be retained for meeting peak demand. The result of adopting the new model would be an economy in which we grow and get richer by using less and become stronger by being leaner and more stable.

REINVEST IN NATURAL CAPITAL

The foundation of textbook capitalism is the prudent reinvestment of earnings in productive capital. Natural capitalists who have dramatically raised their resource productivity, closed their loops, and shifted to a solutions-based business model have one key task remaining. They must reinvest in restoring, sustaining, and expanding the most important form of capital — their own natural habitat and biological resource base.

This was not always so important. Until recently, business could ignore damage to the ecosystem because it didn't affect production and didn't increase costs. But that situation is changing. In 1998 alone, violent weather displaced 300 million people and caused upwards of $90 billion worth of damage, representing more weather-related destruction than was reported through the entire decade of the 1980s. The increase in damage is strongly linked to deforestation and climate change, factors that accelerate the frequency and severity of natural disasters and are the consequences of inefficient industrialization. If the flow of services from industrial systems is to be sustained or increased in the future for a growing population, the vital flow of services from living systems will have to be maintained or increased as well. Without reinvestment in natural capital, shortages of ecosystem services are likely to become the limiting factor to prosperity in the next century. When a manufacturer realizes that a supplier of key components is overextended and running behind on deliveries, it takes immediate action lest its own production lines come to a halt. The ecosystem is a supplier of key components for the life of the planet, and it is now falling behind on its orders.

Failure to protect and reinvest in natural capital can also hit a company's revenues indirectly. Many companies are discovering that public perceptions of environmental responsibility, or its lack thereof, affect sales. MacMillan Bloedel, targeted by environmental activists as an emblematic clear-cutter and chlorine user, lost 5% of its sales almost overnight when dropped as a U.K. supplier by Scott Paper and Kimberly-Clark. Numerous case studies show that companies leading the way in implementing changes that help protect the environment tend to gain disproportionate advantage, while companies perceived as irresponsible lose their franchise, their legitimacy, and their shirts. Even businesses that claim to be committed to the concept of sustainable development but whose strategy is seen as mistaken, like Monsanto, are encountering stiffening public resistance to their products. Not surprisingly, University of Oregon business professor Michael Russo, along with many other analysts, has found that a strong environmental rating is "a consistent predictor of profitability."

The pioneering corporations that have made reinvestments in natural capital are starting to see some interesting paybacks. The independent power producer AES, for example, has long pursued a policy of planting trees to offset the carbon emissions of its power plants. That ethical stance, once thought quixotic, now looks like a smart investment because a dozen brokers are now starting to create markets in carbon reduction. Similarly, certification by the Forest Stewardship Council of certain sustainably grown and harvested products has given Collins Pine the extra profit margins that enabled its U.S. manufacturing operations to survive brutal competition. Taking an even longer view, Swiss Re and other European re-insurers are seeking to cut their storm-damage losses by pressing for international public policy to protect the climate and by investing in climate-safe technologies that also promise good profits. Yet most companies still do not realize that a vibrant ecological web underpins their survival and their business success. Enriching natural capital is not just a public good — it is vital to every company's longevity.

It turns out that changing industrial processes so that they actually replenish and magnify the stock of natural capital can prove especially profitable because nature does the production; people need just step back and let life flourish. Industries that directly harvest living resources, such as forestry, farming, and fishing, offer the most suggestive examples. Here are three:

• Allan Savory of the Center for Holistic Management in Albuquerque, New Mexico, has redesigned cattle ranching to raise the carrying capacity of rangelands, which have often been degraded not by overgrazing but by undergrazing and grazing the wrong way. Savory's solution is to keep the cattle moving from place to place, grazing intensively but briefly at each site, so that they mimic the dense but constantly moving herds of native grazing animals that coevolved with grasslands. Thousands of ranchers are estimated to be applying this approach, improving both their range and their profits. This "management-intensive rotational grazing" method, long standard in New Zealand, yields such clearly superior returns that over 15% of Wisconsin's dairy farms have adopted it in the past few years.

• The California Rice Industry Association has discovered that letting nature's diversity flourish can be more profitable than forcing it to produce a single product. By flooding 150,000 to 200,000 acres of Sacramento valley rice fields — about 30% of California's rice-growing area — after harvest, farmers are able to create seasonal wetlands that support millions of wildfowl, replenish groundwater, improve fertility, and yield other valuable benefits. In addition, the farmers bale and sell the rice straw, whose high silica content — formerly an air-pollution hazard when the straw was burned — adds insect resistance and hence value as a construction material when it's resold instead.

• John Todd of Living Technologies in Burlington, Vermont, has used biological Living Machines — linked tanks of bacteria, algae, plants, and other organisms -- to turn sewage into clean water. That not only yields cleaner water at a reduced cost, with no toxicity or odor, but it also produces commercially valuable flowers and makes the plant compatible with its residential neighborhood. A similar plant at the Ethel M Chocolates factory in Las Vegas, Nevada, not only handles difficult industrial wastes effectively but is showcased in its public tours.

Although such practices are still evolving, the broad lessons they teach are clear. In almost all climates, soils, and societies, working with nature is more productive than working against it. Reinvesting in nature allows farmers, fishermen, and forest managers to match or exceed the high yields and profits sustained by traditional input-intensive, chemically driven practices. Although much of mainstream business is still headed the other way, the profitability of sustainable, nature-emulating practices is already being proven. In the future, many industries that don't now consider themselves dependent on a biological resource base will become more so as they shift their raw materials and production processes more to biological ones. There is evidence that many business leaders are starting to think this way. The consulting firm Arthur D. Little surveyed a group of North American and European business leaders and found that 83% of them already believe that they can derive "real business value [from implementing a] sustainable-development approach to strategy and operations."

A BROKEN COMPASS?

If the road ahead is this clear, why are so many companies straying or falling by the wayside? We believe the reason is that the instruments companies use to set their targets, measure their performance, and hand out rewards are faulty. In other words, the markets are full of distortions and perverse incentives. Of the more than 60 specific forms of misdirection that we have identified,[3] the most obvious involve the ways companies allocate capital and the way governments set policy and impose taxes. Merely correcting these defective practices would uncover huge opportunities for profit.

Consider how companies make purchasing decisions. Decisions to buy small items are typically based on their initial cost rather than their full lifecycle cost, a practice that can add up to major wastage. Distribution transformers that supply electricity to buildings and factories, for example, are a minor item at just $320 apiece, and most companies try to save a quick buck by buying the lowest price models. Yet nearly all the nation's electricity must flow through transformers, and using the cheaper but less efficient models wastes $1 billion a year. Such examples are legion. Equipping standard new office-lighting circuits with fatter wire that reduces electrical resistance could generate after-tax returns of 193% a year. Instead, wire as thin as the National Electrical Code permits is usually selected because it costs less up-front. But the code is meant only to prevent fires from overheated wiring, not to save money. Ironically, an electrician who chooses fatter wire — thereby reducing long-term electricity bills — doesn't get the job. After paying for the extra copper, he's no longer the low bidder.

Some companies do consider more than just the initial price in their purchasing decisions but still don't go far enough. Most of them use a crude payback estimate rather than more accurate metrics like discounted cash flow. A few years ago, the median simple payback these companies were demanding from energy efficiency was 1.9 years. That's equivalent to requiring an after-tax return of around 71% per year — about six times the marginal cost of capital.

Most companies also miss major opportunities by treating their facilities costs as an overhead to be minimized, typically by laying off engineers, rather than as profit center to be optimized — by using those engineers to save resources. Deficient measurement and accounting practices also prevent companies from allocating costs — and waste — with any accuracy. For example, only a few semiconductor plants worldwide regularly and accurately measure how much energy they're using to produce a unit of chilled water or clean air for their clean-room production facilities. That makes it hard for them to improve efficiency. In fact, in an effort to save time, semiconductor makers frequently build new plants as exact copies of previous ones — a design method nicknamed "infectious repetitis."

Many executives pay too little attention to saving resources because they are often a small percentage of total costs (energy costs run to about 2% in most industries). But those resource savings drop straight to the bottom line and so represent a far greater percentage of profits. Many executives also think they already "did" efficiency in the 1970s, when the oil shock forced them to rethink old habits. They're forgetting that with today's far better technologies, it's profitable to start all over again. Malden Mills, the Massachusetts maker of such products as Polartec, was already using "efficient" metal-halide lamps in the mid-1990s. But a recent warehouse retrofit reduced the energy used for lighting by another 93%, improved visibility, and paid for itself in 18 months.

The way people are rewarded often creates perverse incentives. Architects and engineers, for example, are traditionally compensated for what they spend, not for what they save. Even the striking economics of the retrofit design for the Chicago office tower described earlier wasn't incentive enough actually to implement it. The property was controlled by a leasing agent who earned a commission every time she leased space, so she didn't want to wait the few extra months needed to refit the building. Her decision to reject the efficiency-quadrupling renovation proved costly for both her and her client. The building was so uncomfortable and expensive to occupy that it didn't lease, so ultimately the owner had to unload it at a firesale price. Moreover, the new owner will for the next 20 years be deprived of the opportunity to save capital cost.

If corporate practices obscure the benefits of natural capitalism, government policy positively undermines it. In nearly every country on the planet, tax laws penalize what we want more of -- jobs and income -- while subsidizing what we want less of — resource depletion and pollution. In every state but Oregon, regulated utilities are rewarded for selling more energy, water, and other resources, and penalized for selling less, even if increased production would cost more than improved customer efficiency. In most of America's arid western states, use-it-or-lose-it water laws encourage inefficient water consumption. Additionally, in many towns, inefficient use of land is enforced through outdated regulations, such as guidelines for ultrawide suburban streets recommended by 1950s civil-defense planners to accommodate the heavy equipment needed to clear up rubble after a nuclear attack.

The costs of these perverse incentives are staggering: $300 billion in annual energy wasted in the United States, and $1 trillion already misallocated to unnecessary air-conditioning equipment and the power supplies to run it (about 40% of the nation's peak electric load). Across the entire economy, unneeded expenditures to subsidize, encourage, and try to remedy inefficiency and damage that should not have occurred in the first place probably account for most, if not all, of the GDP growth of the past two decades. Indeed, according to former World Bank economist Herman Daly and his colleague John Cobb (along with many other analysts), Americans are hardly better off than they were in 1980. But if the U.S. government and private industry could redirect the dollars currently earmarked for remedial costs toward reinvestment in natural and human capital, they could bring about a genuine improvement in the nation's welfare. Companies, too, are finding that wasting resources also means wasting money and people. These intertwined forms of waste have equally intertwined solutions. Firing the unproductive tons, gallons, and kilowatt-hours often makes it possible to keep the people, who will have more and better work to do.

RECOGNIZING THE SCARCITY SHIFT

In the end, the real trouble with our economic compass is that it points in exactly the wrong direction. Most businesses are behaving as if people were still scarce and nature still abundant — the conditions that helped to fuel the first Industrial Revolution. At that time, people were relatively scarce compared with the present-day population. The rapid mechanization of the textile industries caused explosive economic growth that created labor shortages in the factory and the field. The Industrial Revolution, responding to those shortages and mechanizing one industry after another, made people a hundred times more productive than they had ever been.

The logic of economizing on the scarcest resource, because it limits progress, remains correct. But the pattern of scarcity is shifting: now people aren't scarce but nature is. This shows up first in industries that depend directly on ecological health. Here, production is increasingly constrained by fish rather than by boats and nets, by forests rather than by chain saws, by fertile topsoil rather than by plows. Moreover, unlike the traditional factors of industrial production — capital and labor — the biological limiting factors cannot be substituted for one other. In the industrial system, we can easily exchange machinery for labor. But no technology or amount of money can substitute for a stable climate and a productive biosphere. Even proper pricing can't replace the priceless.

Natural capitalism addresses those problems by reintegrating ecological with economic goals. Because it is both necessary and profitable, it will subsume traditional industrialism within a new economy and a new paradigm of production, just as industrialism previously subsumed agrarianism. The companies that first make the changes we have described will have a competitive edge. Those that don't make that effort won't be a problem because ultimately they won't be around. In making that choice, as Henry Ford said, "Whether you believe you can, or whether you believe you can't, you're absolutely right."

FOOTNOTES

1. Our book, *Natural Capitalism* (Little Brown, September 1999), provides hundreds of examples of how companies of almost every type and size, often through modest shifts in business logic and practice, have dramatically improved their bottom lines.
2. Nonproprietary details are posted at http://www.hypercar.com.
3. Summarized in the report "Climate: Making Sense and Making Money" at http://www.rmi.org/catalog/climate.htm.

GRADUATE LEARNING FOR BUSINESS AND SUSTAINABILITY

David Wheeler
Chair & Director, Business Sustainability
Schulich School of Business, York University

Dezso Horvath
Dean, Schulich School of Business, York University

and

Peter Victor
Dean, Faculty of Environmental Studies
York University

The task for business schools is to engage young leaders and give them a long-term vision of success that includes social responsibility. - William Clay Ford, Chairman, Ford Motor Company, 1999

I hope that all involved in the education of today's business students will develop and implement sustainable development educational strategies. - David Blunkett, UK Secretary of State for Education and Employment, 1999

INTRODUCTION

In a survey of 481 environmental and other business people in North America and Europe, consultants Arthur D Little discovered that only 17 per cent of respondents thought their businesses were "well down the road" towards sustainable development (Arthur D Little, 2000). But 95 per cent recognized that sustainable development was important to them. When asked "where will a company have to make the most changes in order to implement a sustainable development approach throughout its organization" 53 per cent cited aligning and motivating staff. In late 1998 opinion research company Environics International conducted a survey of 1158 sustainable development experts across mainly OECD countries embracing government, the corporate sector, voluntary organizations, institutions (including academia) and consultants. Among the 114 respondents "education and training" was cited more frequently (66 per cent) than any other factor as the element of corporate social responsibility most important in their organizations (Environics International, 1999). From these statistics we may conclude that there is a significant opportunity to connect business needs to educational offerings in the fields of sustainability and corporate social responsibility. It is not the purpose of this paper to reprise the literature on the concept of sustainability as it relates to business strategy and operations. Neither is it our intent to offer detailed prescriptions for courses aimed at delivering more sustainable practices by business. However, we will describe the current policy framework for sustainability in higher education and we will review briefly the current state of the art in graduate level business and sustainability programs, with particular emphasis on North American and European experience. We will also offer some observations on what we consider to be promising trends and opportunities for the future. In order to frame our analysis, we will offer three propositions based on our understanding of the current business context for sustainability.

First, we would assert that the concept of sustainability, whilst still ambiguous in the definitional sense (Leal Filho, 2000), does offer a compelling strategic paradigm for guiding business in contributing to society's desire for balanced progress toward economic prosperity, social justice and environmental quality (Elkington, 1998). Indeed if we accept that the journey toward sustainability in the holistic sense requires exploration and innovation as much as prescription and planning, then definitional ambiguity is no bad thing. It frees the creative potential of the human mind and maximizes the potential for deeper learning, whether in the classroom or in the executive boardroom. Thus the challenge of sustainability fits well with contemporary theory on organizational development and personal learning (Morgan, 1986; Argyris, 1990; Senge 1990) as well as with the fields of chaos theory (Levy, 1994; Stacey, 1996) and systems thinking (Clayton and Radcliffe, 1996; Capra, 1996).

Second, we would assert that as an integrated part of business strategy, sustainability has the potential to help deliver superior business performance – especially in a more complex and rapidly globalizing economy. In our view, the best future business leaders will be those who can handle the multi-dimensional challenge of sustainability and the inter-related expectations of a variety of stakeholders with legitimate interests and contributions to make. These future leaders will see complex expectations as sources of learning and competitive advantage (Freeman, 1984; Porter, 1990; Wheeler and Sillanpaa, 1998; Hart, 1997) rather than as threats to be overcome. Successful, performance-oriented business people of the future will break out of the old assumptions of environmental and social pressures representing threats to profitability. Instead, they will be strong leaders, advocates of change and they will drive performance in all three dimensions of sustainability simultaneously (economic, social and environmental).

Third, we recognize that embracing sustainability in business, partly because of its all-encompassing nature, still requires significant challenges to be addressed. These challenges are reflected in our institutions of learning and in many of our current approaches to knowledge sharing and development. They include issues such as lack of time, lack of economic incentives, lack of expertise and knowledge, lack of appropriate organizational structures and unwillingness to change. So if graduate level learning offered by institutions of higher education is to play a major part in assisting business and future business leaders in making the necessary transition to more sustainable operations - as we argue it should - then those of us working in such institutions have an obligation to examine our ways of working too. If governments and communities - global and local - are prepared to grasp the challenge of sustainability (United Nations, 1992; IISD, 2000), and if growing numbers of businesses are open to the possibilities (Schmidheiny, 1992; Hawken, 1993; Hart and Milstein, 1999), then academia must be ready to learn, challenge its own assumptions and evolve too (Orr, 1994; Leal Filho, 1999).

In the rest of this paper we will explore the implications of these propositions for current and future practices associated with our institutions of learning. We will avoid terms such as 'teaching' and 'students', except where they are absolutely necessary for purposes of clarity in describing what is happening today. Instead we will refer to 'learning', 'future business people' and 'future business leaders', because this is the market we are in and because this is how the majority of people who pay fees for business education see themselves.

CURRENT POLICY FRAMEWORKS FOR SUSTAINABILITY IN HIGHER EDUCATION

The International Association of Universities (UNESCO, 2000) recognizes the familiar Brundtland definition (WCED, 1987): i.e. that development is sustainable when it "meets the needs of the present without compromising the ability of future generations to meet their own needs". Interestingly, the IAU also places emphasis on the UN concept of sustainable human development thereby recognizing the anthropocentric nature of much of the current international sustainable development agenda. This is to be expected given the nature of global economic inequality and the resulting extent of social exclusion and human deprivation today; however fervently 'deep' ecologists may wish it, the world is not quite ready for an ecocentric global order. Indeed, as we argued in our introduction the desired state is not necessarily one in which humanity or the environment is in the ascendant. Rather there is a three dimensional balance to be achieved. Happily IAU policy allows for this.

The IAU lists a number of key declarations, charters and action plans in helping frame the role of Universities in the field of sustainable development (UNESCO, 2000). They include the Stockholm Declaration (UN Conference on the Human Environment, 1972), the Talloires Declaration (Tufts University European Centre, Talloires, France, 1990), the Halifax Declaration (Halifax Conference on University Action for Sustainable Development, 1991), Agenda 21 (Chapter 36) on Promoting Education, Public Awareness and Training (UN Conference on Environment and Development, Rio de Janeiro, 1992); the Swansea Declaration (Association of Commonwealth Universities Conference, Swansea, Wales, 1993); the Copernicus Declaration (Conference of European Rectors, 1993) and the Earth Charter (2000). The IAU also encourages member universities to adopt an action plan in which they commit to principles and practices of sustainable development, including the promotion of interdisciplinary collaboration and the development of external partnerships. The IAU draft action plan includes explicit mention of the importance of environmental and ethical understanding.

The key elements of many of the charters and action plans have been described and distilled on behalf of IAU into ten key principles (Mazurkiewicz, 1998). Interestingly, four of these principles refer specifically to environmental education and six to sustainable development as a general concept without making explicit the social and economic dimensions. And here is the paradox. For while the policy agenda of most governments and international institutions (e.g., OECD, G7 and the UN) usually centres on economic development and occasionally the social justice dimension of the sustainability paradigm, many of the strongest advocates of sustainable development describe the implications more in terms of environmental policy and the need for more environmental initiatives. As we shall see, this has profound implications for the role of Universities in sustainability education as it is articulated and perceived today and more specifically what Universities will need to do to stay relevant to all actors in society (including international institutions and corporations) in the future.

Fortunately, supported by UNESCO, in the IAU there is an international body which can help co-ordinate future policy development in this area. And there are a number of other bodies, for example the Association of University Leaders for a Sustainable Future (ULSF), the Conference of European Rectors (CRE) and a wide variety of regional and national initiatives in which Universities and Colleges of Higher Education can and should play a full part. If anything this is where the more grounded and directly relevant policy developments are likely to occur, including the creation of space for a dialogue involving business and other forces in society with something to contribute.

It would be fair to say that very little of what appears in the various international declarations and action plans has specific relevance to business learning, although the general prescriptions on the need for Universities to develop policies, strategies and practices consistent with the principles of sustainability are helpful. The declarations do not tend to assert that the most urgent priority in sustainable development education is to engage the most powerful actors (including business) and harness their resources and creativity for positive ends. Nevertheless, there are frequent references to the need for external partnerships and networking. In our view, there is a lot to be said for engaging the business community every bit as much as governments, not-for-profits and the public sector. This is where many academics have been somewhat slow off the mark, often preferring analysis and critique to engagement. Happily there are a few examples of pragmatic engagement between business and academia in the context of developing public policy for sustainable development education.

One national policy initiative worthy of note was that of the US President's Council on Sustainable Development which together with Second Nature and the Secretariat of University Presidents convened 35 academics to discuss Principles of Sustainability in Higher Education (PCSD, 1995). The resulting report was noteworthy in that it took a 'business case' publication: Changing Course (Schmidheiny, 1992) as one of its primary sources and it made a quite ambitious attempt to bridge the economic, social and environmental dimensions of sustainability. The PCSD report recognized quite realistically that at the time "education and research about the interdependence of humans with the environment is not a priority in higher education" and listed a number of the key barriers to progress, including the quite fundamental observations that current education in Universities was effectively "incomplete" and that existing structures within US institutions did not help. The report recommended ten areas which University graduates should understand as part of a more rounded education - most of which were analytical in nature; i.e. how the world works. Specific recommendations were also made on University policy and strategy as well as how greater inter-disciplinary working might be encouraged.

Other practical, business-related national policy initiatives which may be cited include those of the National Round Table on the Environment and the Economy in Canada which has long sought to engage academia both with respect to internal practices and curriculum development (Burch, 1992; MacLeod and Doucet, 1995) and more recently the UK Government's initiative on multi-level education for sustainable development.

In early 1998 the UK Government established a Sustainable Development Education Panel which included 31 industrialists who all signed a declaration stating "As a company that attaches considerable importance to reducing our environmental impacts and meeting our wider obligations to society and to future generations, it is a matter of some concern to us that a majority of graduates we are likely to recruit from business schools in the UK will apparently be ill-equipped to help us deliver these aspects of our overall mission". The companies making this point included representatives from sectors as diverse as aviation, automotive, chemicals, finance, infrastructure, oil and gas, public transportation and utilities (Forum for the Future, 2000).

The provisional conclusions of the Panel were that education for sustainable development in the UK is "best integrated into specialist courses through learning activities which are firmly set in the context of the specialism". The Panel sets out five categories of learning outcomes on sustainability concepts: understanding the interdependence of major systems; understanding of the needs and rights of future generations; understanding the value of diversity; an appreciation of the need for precaution; and an awareness of the limits to growth. They also set out five areas for potential solutions: an understanding of the role of the business community in promoting sustainable development; an awareness of the wide range of sustainability solutions tools and techniques currently available; an awareness of sustainable development related legislation, policy and control mechanisms; a sense of social responsibility; and enhanced skills in the workplace; e.g., team playing and effective communication (Forum for the Future, 2000).

The international and national public policy recommendations described above have clear implications for individual academic institutions; and not all simple to translate into action. For example, the common policy consensus on the need for more inter-disciplinary collaboration poses a real challenge for existing structures and systems within higher education. How academics can transcend their normal disciplinary bases to embrace more inter-disciplinary working when their career paths and external recognition remain locked into traditional disciplines remains a thorny issue (Gladwin et al, 1995; Springett and Kearins, 2000).

CURRENT STATUS OF UNIVERSITY INITIATIVES IN LEARNING FOR BUSINESS AND SUSTAINABILITY

In 1999 the Washington-based think tank the World Resources Institute published the second of its detailed assessments of North American business school engagement with the sustainability agenda: Beyond Grey Pinstripes: Preparing MBAs for Social and Environmental Stewardship (WRI & ISIB, 1999). The WRI surveyed 313 graduate business schools accredited by the International Association for Management Education, a sample which included 40 per cent of the total of 748 US business schools. Of the 110 responses received, just over half (60 schools) reported activity on environmental and social topics; these included 43 of the top 50 schools in the US. Business schools were rated on the basis of courses available, institutional support and faculty research. On this basis they were assigned a category in both 'business and environment' and 'business and society' arenas.

'Cutting edge' programs on business and the environment in the US included Cornell University (Johnson), George Washington, Rensselaar Polytechnic Institute (Lally), Tulane University (Freeman), University of Michigan at Ann Arbor, University of North Carolina at Chapel Hill (Kenan-Flagler), University of Pennsylvania (Wharton), University of Texas at Austin and Vanderbilt University (Owen). A further eleven schools showed 'significant activities', eight showed 'moderate activities' and 22 registered some interest.

Similarly 'cutting edge' US programs on business and society were Case Western (Weatherhead), Harvard, Loyola Marymount University, Northwestern University (Kellogg), Stanford University, University of Michigan at Ann Arbor, University of Notre Dame, University of Pennsylvania (Wharton), University of Pittsburgh (Katz) and the University of Virginia (Darden). Twelve more schools were characterized as showing 'significant activities' and another twelve 'moderate activities' in business and society. A further 18 US schools showed some level of interest.

In Canada, business schools listed (but not rated) were York University (Schulich), University of Western Ontario (Ivey) and University of Manitoba. In Europe the schools listed were Manchester Business School and Huddersfield University (UK), University of Jvyaskyla (Finland), IMD (Switzerland), IIIEE at Lund University (Sweden), Tilburg University (Netherlands) and INSEAD (France). There were ten and eight schools listed in Latin America and India respectively.

Any questionnaire-based assessment of this nature is hampered by the self-selected nature of the respondents and therefore it cannot provide a wholly definitive picture. Nevertheless, the WRI survey certainly represents the best 'state of the art' review available in terms of depth and coverage for the most important providers of graduate level business education in the world. The overall level of activity in US schools is relatively high and apparently strengthening. And the fact that leading institutions like Harvard, Stanford, Wharton and Kellogg feature so prominently in terms of commitment to sustainability issues is a reassuring sign.

A rather less positive picture emerged from a recent survey of UK business schools. In a survey of 104 British schools conducted by Forum for the Future in 1998 not one could specify a learning agenda for sustainability which was relevant to all students. Forum for the Future asked survey respondents whether they were teaching any of 36 sustainability themes clustered under six broad headings: corporate responsibility, systems thinking, corporate strategy and change, management systems, tools and techniques, managing partnerships and networks and environmental legislation, policy and control. 52 per cent of the sample did not reply, and as with the WRI survey we may safely assume that those which did represented the more pro-active schools with something to talk about. The most commonly taught elements were corporate responsibility, corporate strategy and managing partnerships - although it is not clear the extent to which these areas were taught with a sustainability focus.

The survey did not explore potential linkages with finance/ accounting, human resource management and marketing and there was a strong environmental bias within the 36 criteria explored. Only four of the UK schools had some form of sustainability-related staff development program. 66 per cent of respondents said that sustainability issues represented less than 15 per cent of teaching and 10 per cent said sustainability issues did not feature at all in core learning. The four main barriers cited to expanding sustainability learning in UK business schools were (i) constraints on time, resources or curricula; (ii) lack of faculty expertise or interest; (iii) lack of student interest or ability; and (iv) perceived lack of interest or opposition by business. On the last point, it should be borne in mind that in the majority of cases British MBAs are undertaken by mid-career professionals in business rather than recent graduates.

These surveys of business school programs provide one perspective on Universities' orientation toward sustainability in business. But of course there is a lot more management learning occurring in Universities beyond the business schools. For example, a lot of environmental management courses are offered in schools specializing in ecology, environmental studies, natural resources, design, engineering and technology and the natural sciences. And a lot of education pertinent to sustainability in business occurs in schools of law, economics and the liberal arts. In 1997, The Student Conservation Association published a Guide to Graduate Environmental Programs (SCA, 1997) which included 160 in-depth profiles of available courses. Second Nature lists 79 syllabi on its website relating to business, environmental management, ethics and social performance covering a wide variety of disciplines, including law, economics, public policy, strategy, marketing and a variety of more scientifically-based subjects (Second Nature, 2000). And the North American Association for Environmental Education website lists 56 records of graduate programs in the environment held on the Rice University database. Most of these programs are environmental science or resource based and most are in the US (NAAEE, 2000).

Two other sources of useful benchmarking information in North America are written from producer and customer perspectives respectively: the Directory of Faculty Who Teach Environmental Education Courses at Colleges and Universities in the United States (Zint, 1998), and the Making a Difference College and Graduate Guide: Outstanding Colleges to Help You Make a Better World (Weinstein, 1999).

From the foregoing we may conclude that at the graduate level sustainability is firmly on the agenda of North American universities and colleges - particularly with respect to environmental management and conservation. And if one includes corporate social responsibility and ethics – it may be reasonably asserted that sustainability has penetrated relatively well into the world of leading business schools in North America and, to a certain degree, in Europe and Asia. We will turn now to some observations on current practice of direct relevance to learning for business and sustainability.

MODELS OF GRADUATE LEVEL LEARNING FOR BUSINESS AND SUSTAINABILITY

Any broad categorization is open to challenge on the grounds of over-generalization; nevertheless it may be useful here to note a few of the more common models for graduate level learning in business and sustainability in order that we may make some general observations on current trends. We believe there are three broadly recognizable models in North America and Europe and they may be described thus:

The MBA-based Model -- where specific electives and other course offerings are developed or broadened in order to allow MBAs to specialize in sustainability issues. As noted above this trend is very much in evidence in North American business schools and appears to be developing relatively well.

The Independent Masters Model -- where a masters level qualification is developed with a particular management and sustainability focus, often offered on a modular, flexible learning basis. This trend is somewhat less pronounced in North America and is more common in Europe.

The Discipline-based Model -- where Masters and Diploma level courses (e.g., in engineering, design, law and accounting) develop an overt business and sustainability dimension. These courses may be observed equally in North America and Europe and appear to be increasing steadily in number.

The MBA-based Model

The MBA-based model typically offers one or more electives as part of a suite of MBA options. Usually the courses are one semester in length, spread across 13 - 15 weeks. They range from the strategically oriented to the operationally focused. So, for example the Kenan-Flagler school at the University of North Carolina offers a one semester course in Sustainable Enterprise which embraces the concept of 'new capitalism' and covers three emerging strategic trends in business behaviour: from confrontation to collaboration, from citizenship to competitiveness, and from greening to sustainability.

The University of Oregon Department of Business Management offers a twelve part course on Greening of Strategy developed from modules designed by the WRI Management Institute for Environment and Business. The course includes 'big picture' analysis followed by sections relating to understanding and managing external influences of a regulatory and stakeholder nature and a range of more operational issues such as environmental cost accounting, auditing, design for the environment and green marketing.

The Haas School of Business of the University of California at Berkeley offers two units dealing with both strategic business issues and environmental management tools and techniques alongside offerings in corporate social responsibility. The Stern School of New York University offers a mixed strategic and operationally-based one semester course on Environmental Assessment, Management and Strategy. This includes economic and regulatory issues as well as more practically-focused elements dealing with design for the environment, handling environmental controversy and stakeholder pressure, marketing and some case studies. And Darden offers a 15 session course on straight Environmental Management alongside ethics and other socially responsible, stakeholder-based teaching.

The Schulich School of Business at York University, Toronto offers two one semester courses - one on Business Strategies for Sustainability (illustrated by eight 'live' cases), and one on Management Practices for Sustainability in Business which covers a wide range of environmental, social and economic techniques for operationalizing sustainability. A number of other courses are also offered covering the ethical, economic and legal dimensions of sustainability.

In Europe, Manchester Business School offers MBA electives in Business and the Environment and Corporate Governance and Business Ethics. INSEAD has an elective within its MBA on Management of Environmental Resources which examines the nature of the 'environmental crisis', public policy and traditional and non-traditional managerial strategies, tools and concepts. However, it appears that for some reason uptake in European business schools more generally is slow. As early as 1993 it was estimated that twelve European business schools either had or were contemplating environmental management courses (Moser and Arnold, 1993). But two years later, a study undertaken for the European Foundation for the Improvement of Living and Working Conditions (Ulhoi et al, 1996) found that of 33 leading European institutions surveyed only three offered an MBA with significant levels of environmental learning. One (in the Netherlands) offered three environmental electives, one (in the UK) offered one environmental elective and another (also in the UK) was developing an 'environmental MBA' with four electives.

The Independent Masters Model

In the same study referred to above (Ulhoi et al, 1996), twenty of the 33 institutions surveyed were offering or planned to offer more technical learning at the graduate level . These included three UK institutions offering an environmental management MSc and significant graduate level activity in the Netherlands and Denmark. At that time the European Union was also funding a European Masters in Environmental Management established as a co-operative venture between nine EU universities.

The independent, specialized Masters approach is one which seems to have been pursued particularly actively in the UK. Typically these courses include two semesters of taught courses plus a dissertation and sometimes a work placement, but there are also examples of modular offerings which may be taken over a period of time well in excess of one year. Since 1993 the University of Bradford has offered a modular MSc and Postgraduate Diploma in Business Strategy and Environmental Management. This course is based on two semesters of mostly required modules with relatively limited scope for electives (one out of six courses per semester). Similarly the University of Surrey offers a two semester modular MSc in Environmental Strategy which includes core modules and electives plus an industrial placement and a dissertation. The Surrey Masters is quite broad, including strategic issues such as 'values, ethics and sustainability' as well as the more operational techniques such as life cycle approaches, environmental risk management and environmental law.

In 1997 Edinburgh University introduced a Diploma and MSc in Environmental Sustainability - a nine or twelve month course depending on which qualification is sought. The course embraces core modules dealing with principles and management issues associated with sustainability plus a wide range of electives ranging from the quite technical (e.g., environmental impact assessment and geographical information systems) to the legal, ethical and developmental dimensions of sustainability.

In Sweden, the International Institute for Industrial Environmental Economics at Lund University (IIIEE) has a technically based MSc in Environmental Management and Policy which draws on a number of disciplines including engineering, natural sciences, business administration, economics, law and social sciences. In Finland, the University of Jyvaskyla School of Business and Economics offers an MSc in Environmental Management which embraces corporate environmental management, material fluxes and industrial ecology, recycling technology, public policy, environmental accounting, international environmental law, environmental economics and the social context of environment and business.

The Discipline-based Model

As noted above, there is a growing trend for the development of discipline-based courses relevant to business and sustainability. Not all of these operate at the graduate level, but they are worth mentioning because of the trend of innovation they illustrate. For example, Delft University of Technology has developed sustainability management learning from a technical and engineering perspective (Mulder, 1999). Following the adoption of a new strategic vision for the University in 1994 which embraced principles of sustainable development, Delft was able to introduce an 'elementary course' in Technology in Sustainable Development for all students together with an 'intertwining' of sustainability ideas into regular courses. The Delft experience has been mirrored by Georgia Tech in the US which has developed four courses on engineering and sustainability (Chameau, 1999). And the University of California at Berkeley, Carnegie Mellon and the University of Calgary have developed specific offerings in green design.

Environmental and ethical accounting has been pioneered at the University of Dundee School of Accounting and is due (2000) to develop at Glasgow University. Environmental accounting is also found at Sheffield University and the University of Texas Business School at Austin, based again on a WRI Management Institute for Environment and Business framework.

A review of experiences of integrating environmental issues in the liberal arts in fields as diverse as anthropology, geography, history and political science has been compiled by Collett and Karakashian (1996).

GRADUATE LEVEL PROGRAMS AS PART OF A CONTINUUM OF LIFE LONG LEARNING IN BUSINESS AND SUSTAINABILITY

It would be a major omission in a paper of this nature to neglect the interface between graduate level learning in our institutions of higher education and (i) the learning which precedes it; and (ii) the quite significant amount of executive level education for mid-career professionals which follows it. Both of these will of course also be affected by the enormous potential for on-demand knowledge development and dissemination afforded by the internet. Indeed, we think it is important to see university and college-based graduate level programs as only one part of an exciting continuum of opportunities to promote business and sustainability learning. Our belief is that in coming years, there should be a seamless connectivity in provision of learning opportunities which cater for the needs of:

• **new graduates of business administration** wishing to take an MBA with sustainability built in at a serious level (i.e. strategic and operational dimensions)

• **new graduates in environmental studies, social sciences, natural science and other relevant subjects** wishing to pursue a career in business

• **early-mid career professionals** wishing to add sustainability to their knowledge portfolio for career development reasons (increasingly important for ambitious individuals working for companies with a publicly stated strategic objective of sustainability)

• **public sector and not-for-profit sector professionals** wishing to understand the business perspective on sustainability so that they may better interface and partner with it

• **business leaders** wishing to develop or re-frame their corporate mission and strategy in line with principles of sustainable development

In our view the needs of future and current business people will be met most effectively if they can access learning on business and sustainability in a way which is:

• **available** - both pre-career and mid-career

• **flexible** - in terms of mode of delivery and timing

- **compelling** – a core part of business learning rather than peripheral

- **value-adding** - as an immediate learning experience and in terms of future utility (including the question of qualifications and ongoing professional development)

- **personally enriching** – connecting personal, workplace and societal values in a way which empowers and motivates the individual

Taking into account both the types of business people and future business people who may want the learning (the market) and the nature of the provision described above (the product), we can start to explore which models of learning may make most sense to promote. Whilst outside the scope of this paper we should make brief mention of pre-university and undergraduate learning, because these are part of the wider context for promoting a positive attitude to business learning for sustainability and avoiding the hardening of negative attitudes to the potential future role of business.

Pre-University Learning

Certainly we need the impacts of business in the global economy (both positive and negative) to be featured in pre-university learning. Where schools deal with issues of sustainability it would be helpful if while providing critiques of business for its current legacy, there was equal space devoted to the possibilities of business to add value economically, socially and environmentally.

Undergraduate Learning

It is becoming more commonplace for universities and colleges to offer Bachelor-level teaching in business administration. As with MBAs, these courses should reflect the strategic and operational importance of sustainability by way of introduction and preparation for Masters-level learning. Similarly, non-business degrees with direct professional relevance to business (e.g., accounting, law and marketing) should all feature a minimum level of environmental and social enrichment. Sciences and arts students should at least have access to general studies courses and grounded case studies in business and sustainability to work on where appropriate. And innovation in non-business degrees to address business and sustainability dilemmas should be strongly encouraged, if only to help students place business in a real-world context, subject to constraining forces in society and limits to growth as well as opportunities to contribute positively to global well-being and wealth creation.

Graduate Level Learning

Following pre-university and under-graduate learning experiences, we can distinguish three priorities for graduate level learning for business people and future business people which are likely to be wholly the responsibility of institutions of higher education to develop and deliver. Based on current trends these are:

- **MBAs with a serious sustainability dimension** - by which we mean that questions of environmental, social and economic relevance to business are dealt with as required minor elements within core teaching in courses on strategy, finance/accounting, marketing, human resource management, organizational behaviour, product development and distribution, law and economics. In addition, there should ideally be electives available in at least: (i) the strategic and operational dimensions of sustainability in business; and (ii) corporate social responsibility and ethics (where the dilemma and trade-off questions may be dealt with at a philosophical and practical level). Aimed at the generalist future business person, these MBAs should become increasingly the norm as businesses large and small recognize the relevance of recruiting and promoting future leaders with the skills to handle the complexity and the opportunities associated with sustainability. This should include future business leaders responsible for finance/accounting, marketing, product development, human resources, communications and community relations, supply chain management, investor relations and strategy; i.e. future CEOs, CFOs and COOs.

- **Specialist Masters level courses** dealing with the management and technical aspects of sustainability in business and in the professions. Unlike the MBAs these courses should be aimed at individuals with a potential career specialism in one or more of the three dimensions of sustainability; i.e. environmental management, stakeholder/social relations or economics. Such courses should appeal to future heads of community relations/corporate social responsibility, environmental/HSE/sustainability management, corporate affairs and social/environmental accounting and reporting.

- **Diploma level and certificated learning events** of shorter duration which will be sought increasingly by mid-career professionals wishing to remain full time in the workplace while developing their knowledge and understanding of specific elements of the sustainability and business agenda.

Increasingly, these graduate level programs will be flexible enough to embrace part-time enrolments, supplemented where appropriate by in-company learning, on-line coaching and knowledge acquisition and modular learning events over concentrated periods of time. These more flexible offerings will allow mid-career professionals and others (e.g., young entrepreneurs) to remain fully engaged with their work whilst learning and gaining meaningful qualifications.

EXECUTIVE AND POST-UNIVERSITY LEARNING

Beyond these offerings, universities and colleges have an opportunity to be part of the coming boom in post-qualification executive development for sustainability involving short events; i.e. seminars and conferences, in-company learning and development, the facilitation of multi-company learning circles, on-line learning and coaching and so on. Currently this market is dominated by commercial conference organizers, learning consultancies and professional services firms. Examples which might be cited here are the activities of the Conference Board in questions of corporate social responsibility and governance, the Natural Step and the Society for Organizational Learning in environmental sustainability issues, and the activities of the professional firms in environment and safety management and ethics training for clients. But there are signs that smaller, niche providers as well as universities and colleges (as they become more competent and flexible) will make an even more significant contribution here in years to come, carrying as they will lower overheads and more independence.

One of the most exciting recent developments in this context is an initiative of the World Business Council for Sustainable Development. WBCSD has started to build a 'virtual university' platform for on-line learning for business and sustainability which will effectively be a brokerage between higher education institutions and other providers with something to contribute and those seeking to access learning from the comfort of their own home or office. Prospective clients will be able to navigate the platform and select the most appropriate learning style and content for them from a range of management education offerings. The ultimate goal is to provide a framework for distance learning from a number of world class providers and to establish a set of standards to which all providers must conform (WBCSD, 2000). This initiative is backed by a number of partners, including Sony, ERM, Deloitte and Touche, Dow, GM, Novartis, Hoffman LaRoche, Hoechst, Zurich Insurance and Storebrand. It should achieve, in one step, a high quality, on-line sustainability and business learning brokerage. This will provide an important complement to existing more technically based on-line education and distance learning in environmental management which is available from a number of sources (NAAEE, 2000).

Another interesting development worth watching is the role of the more pro-active higher education institutions in leadership development for sustainability. Currently two higher education institutions offer in-depth, transformational seminars for business leaders – the Cambridge University (UK) 'Prince of Wales' program, and the York University (Canada) Sustainable Enterprise Academy, which is the executive development element of the Schulich School of Business Haub Program in Business and Sustainability.

Other developments of interest to universities and colleges will present themselves. For example, it is inevitable that as companies globalize so will their need for internationally consistent learning for middle managements. This will require the formation of consortia of learning institutions and novel partnerships (e.g., between commercial and non-commercial providers) to deliver the quality and agreed learning experiences for such corporations. It will also lead to the incorporation of sustainability issues into International MBAs and in-company MBAs delivered by leading business schools.

CONCLUSIONS

In Greening Campuses (1996), David Chernushenko concluded that "whereas scholarship has spent the last several centuries specializing and compartmentalizing, we are now realizing that many of our problems stem from the fracturing of our world view into separate disciplines...Any movement toward sustainability must, therefore, focus on connections, linkages, patterns and root causes". Echoing many of the conclusions of the IAU and others, he identified priorities for three key constituencies in effecting this transition:

i) those who develop educational policy and influence curriculum must recognize the need for interdisciplinary and transdisciplinary study and the integration of sustainability thinking into all programs and courses;
ii) instructors must be encouraged to and be supported in developing such curricula; and
iii) students must be introduced to sustainability concepts as they relate to their course of study and, where possible, to their post-graduation lives.

We would add two additional constituencies external to institutions of higher education which must also be part of the transition to a more holistic education for sustainability:

iv) businesses and other employers must recognize the value in recruiting graduates and developing future leaders with an all round understanding of principles of sustainability; and
v) governments, international agencies, foundations and agents of civil society must assist in developing the partnership arrangements which will permit all involved in higher education to develop and disseminate learning in sustainability in as free and open way as possible.

In addition to these strategic considerations, the importance of curriculum design assumptions within business schools and other institutions of learning should not be underestimated. Roome (1996) and Sterling (1996) identified a number of key principles to be adopted for business schools and other educational establishments if sustainability is to be effectively incorporated into university education. Apart from the need for interdisciplinary approaches which has been stressed already, Roome and Sterling refer to guiding principles such as the importance of context, systemic and holistic thinking, the notion of inclusivity and the importance of ethics.

In the introduction to this paper we identified two compelling elements of the business case for sustainability education. They were the strategic dimension and the link between sustainability and performance. But we also identified some of the challenges. They were issues of lack of time, lack of economic incentives, lack of expertise and knowledge, lack of appropriate organizational structures and unwillingness to change. These constraints apply equally to business and to our institutions of higher education. However, within a framework of collaboration and partnership between all constituencies, as outlined above, we would have some confidence that business schools and other parts of the university and college system would be able to devote the time, resources and intellectual space to cross-disciplinary working and the development of genuinely engaging and value-added learning for future business people and business leaders.

Inevitably, the question of leadership arises. Which governments will most actively support a partnership-based, inter-disciplinary approach to sustainability education for business people and future business people? Which foundations and independent agencies will show the vision required to innovate and allow the ground-breaking experiments to flourish? Which businesses, government departments and not-for-profit organizations will contribute their knowledge and resources? And which academic institutions will set the pace?

In our view, leadership must be shown at every level, and by every constituency. In universities and colleges leadership is required simultaneously at the Faculty and the institutional level. Business schools and their sister faculties (e.g., environmental studies, law, social science, engineering, science, design and the liberal arts) must demonstrate their preparedness to address the business and sustainability challenge in a creative and collaborative way. This will in turn give permission to individual academics to break down barriers and develop truly innovative programs of broad appeal to present and future business people – at graduate and post-graduate levels. We believe that a number of academic institutions are ready to show such leadership. With luck, their social partners: governments, businesses, foundations and other actors in civil society will also commit the leadership and the resources to help deliver a central element of the search for global sustainability in business.

REFERENCES

Argyris C (1990). *Overcoming Organizational Defenses.* Boston, MA: Allyn & Bacon.
Arthur D Little (2000). *Realizing the Business Value of Sustainable Development. An Arthur D Little Survey.* Cambridge: Arthur D Little.
Burch M (1992). *Education and Training for Sustainable Development. Green Guide – A User's Guide to Sustainable Development for Canadian Colleges.* Ottawa: NRTEE.
Capra F (1996). *The Web of Life: A New Synthesis of Mind and Matter.* London: HarperCollins.
Chameau J-L (1999). "Changing a mind-set, not just a problem set. Sustainable development in colleges of engineering." Paper presented to the American Society for Engineering Education Conference on Ethics in Technology and Social Responsibility. Hawaii, 1999. Reproduced in: http://www.coe.gatech.edu (accessed 5th April 2000).
Chernushenko D (1996). *Greening Campuses.* Ottawa: Association of Canadian Community Colleges.
Clayton T and Radcliffe N (1996). *Sustainability: A Systems Approach.* London: Earthscan.
Collett J and Karakashian S, eds. (1996). *Greening the college curriculum: a guide to environmental teaching in the liberal arts.* Washington: Island Press.
Cortese AD (1993). "Building the intellectual capacity for a sustainable future." *Industry and Environment.* 16(4), 6-10.
Elkington J (1998). *Cannibals with Forks.* British Columbia: New Society.
Environics International (1999). *Globescan Survey of Experts 1998. Sustainable development trends.* Toronto: Environics International.
Forum for the Future (2000). *Business Curriculum Audit.* Reproduced in http://www.he21.org.uk/business.html (accessed 5th April 2000).
Freeman, R E (1984). *Strategic Management: A Stakeholder Approach.* Basic

Books: New York.

Gladwin T, Kennelly J and Krause T-S (1995). "Shifting paradigms for sustainable development: implications for management theory and research." *Academy of Management Review* 20(4), 874-907.

Hart S L (1997). "Beyond greening. Strategies for a sustainable world." *Harvard Business Review* 75 (January-February), 66-76.

Hart S L and Milstein MB (1999). "Global sustainability and the creative destruction of industries." *Sloan Management Review* 41(1), 23-33.

Hawken P (1993). *The Ecology of Commerce. A Declaration of Sustainability*. HarperCollins: New York.

International Institute for Sustainable Development (2000). *Sustainable Development on Campus Resource Links*. Reproduced in http://iisd1.iisd.ca/educate/reslist.htm (accessed 5th April 2000).

Leal Filho W, ed (1999). *Sustainability and University Life*. Frankfurt: Verlag Peter Lang.

Leal Filho W (2000). "Dealing with misconceptions on the concept of sustainability." *International Journal of Sustainability in Higher Education* 1(1), 9-19.

Levy D (1994). "Chaos theory and strategy: theory, application, and managerial implications." *Strategic Management Journal* 15, 167-178.

MacLeod J and Doucet C, eds. (1995). *University Presidents' Workshop – Learning and Sustainability*. Ottawa: NRTEE.

Mazurkiewicz B (1998). *Report of the First Meeting. International Association of Universities Task Force: Universities as Actors in Sustainable Development*. Bangkok, 1997. Reproduced in: UNESCO (2000). http://www.unesco.org/iau (accessed 5th April, 2000).

Morgan G (1986). *Images of Organization*. Beverly Hills CA: Sage.

Moser M and Arnold M (1993). "The greening of business schools." *Industry and Environment* 16(4), 17-21.

Mulder K F (1999). *Technology in Sustainable Development: Sustainability from Burden to Challenge for Engineers*. Faculty of Technology, Policy and Management. Delft, NL: Delft University of Technology.

NAAEE – North American Association for Environmental Education (2000). http://eelink.net/highereducation-eeprogs_grad.html (accessed 5th April 2000).

Orr D W (1994). *Earth in Mind: On Education Environment and the Human Prospect*. Washington: Island Press.

Porter ME (1990). *The Competitive Advantage of Nations*. London: MacMillan.

PCSD - President's Council on Sustainable Development (1995). *The Essex Report: Workshop on the principles of sustainability in higher education*. Boston: Second Nature.

Roome N J (1996). "Business organizations." In: *Education for Sustain-*

ability (Huckle J and Sterling S, eds.), 165-171. London: Earthscan.

Schmidheiny S (1992). *Changing Course. A Global Business Perspective on Development and the Environment.* Cambridge MA: MIT Press.

Second Nature (2000). http://www.secondnature.org (accessed 5th April 2000).

Senge P (1990). *The Fifth Discipline: The Art and Practice of the Learning Organization.* New York: Doubleday.

Springett D and Kearins K (2000). "The challenge of sustainable development for business educators: idealism meets pragmatism. " *Proc ERP Environment Conference,* Leeds April 2000, 352-359.

Stacey R D (1996). *Complexity and Creativity in Organizations.* Berrett-Koehler, San Francisco.

Sterling S (1996). "Education in change." In: *Education for Sustainability* (Huckle J and Sterling S, eds.), 165-171. London: Earthscan.

SCA - Student Conservation Association (1997). *The Guide to Graduate Environmental Programs.* Washington: Island Press.

Ulhoi JP, Madsen H and Rikhardsson PM (1996). *Training in Environmental Management – Industry and Sustainability. Part 1: Corporate Environmental and Resource Management and Educational Requirements.* Dublin: European Foundation for the Improvement of Living and Working Conditions.

UNESCO (2000). http://www.unesco.org/iau (accessed 5th April, 2000).

United Nations (1994). Agenda 21. Geneva: UN.

WBCSD – World Business Council for Sustainable Development (2000). Virtual University. Reproduced in http://www.wbcsd.ch/vuniversity/index.htm (accessed 5th April 2000).

Weinstein M (1999). *Making a Difference College and Graduate Guide: Outstanding colleges to help you make a better world.* Fairfax CA: SageWorks Press.

Wheeler D and Sillanpaa M (1997). *The Stakeholder Corporation. A blueprint for maximising stakeholder value.* London: Pitman.

Wheeler D and Sillanpaa M (1998). "Including the stakeholders: The business case." *Long Range Planning* 31 (2), 201-210.

Willums J-O and World Business Council for Sustainable Development (1998). *The Sustainable Business Challenge: A briefing for tomorrow's business leaders.* Sheffield UK: Greenleaf.

World Commission on Environment and Development (1987). *Our Common Future.* Oxford: Oxford University Press.

World Resources Institute and Initiative for Social Innovation through Business (1999). Beyond Grey Pinstripes: preparing MBAs for social and environmental stewardship. Washington: WRI.

Zint M with Larson M, Rodriguez A L and Fitch A (1998). *Directory of Faculty who Teach Environmental Education Courses at Colleges and Universities in the United States.* Washington: NAAEE.

SUSTAINABILITY AND FINANCE: TEACHING THE REAL VALUE OF GOOD CORPORATE STEWARDSHIP

Maurice D. Levi

**Bank of Montréal Professor of International Finance
Faculty of Commerce and Business Administration
The University of British Columbia**

Corporations are not driven to sustainable development by an overwhelming desire to be altruistic, but rather by their fiduciary responsibility to create shareholder value. In other words, sustainable development is good business. - Brian Schofield and Blair Feltmate, Sustainable Investment Group, Toronto

INTRODUCTION

Limited liability, which has been so instrumental in spurring investment and thereby growth in living standards, is not well suited to the sustainability of those standards: the truncation of private costs of adverse outcomes of business decisions at zero places no weight on highly negative events because the financial fallout from such events is avoided. The challenge facing business instructors in finance is to instill in students the conviction that not only should they place considerable importance on extreme adverse events which threaten sustainability through depletion of "natural capital", but to teach them that it is in their best interest. Furthermore, it is in the interest of managers to factor in all consequences of their actions for sustainability, whether these consequences be large or small, likely or only remotely possible.

As we shall argue in what follows, customers, employees, shareholders and governments will reward companies that attend to sustainability issues. Managers who ignore the views of these interest groups do so at their own peril. Good sustainability practice shows up in the bottom line: in Canada, for example, an Index of Sustainable Development Companies constructed by Brian Schofield and Blair Feltmate, who are quoted at the top of this paper, outperformed the TSE100 by an average annual compound rate of 6.9 percent per annum over the period of their comparison, August 1995 to February 1999. Indeed, with an annual average return of 18.1 percent over the period, the Index of Sustainable Development Companies outperformed the Ethical Growth Fund Index, with an annual average return of 10.9 percent, and even the Desjardins Environment Fund, which returned 11.4 percent compounded over the same period.[1]

As Schofield and Feltmate (1999) argue, the superior share-price performance of companies that have applied sustainable development concepts has not solely been a consequence of their being regarded as "good corporate citizens," even though this has played a role. Rather, companies committed to sustainable development think long-term, and this pays dividends broadly through productivity gains from training and investment, from market development, from expanded financing options and so on. This "selfish" motive for sustainable development is easy to include at any stage in a finance course, and is likely to leave a lasting impression. However, it probably fits best in the discussion of managerial objectives. In this way, sustainability can be related to maximization of shareholder value.

Most business students are primed to understand the issue of short-term managerial horizons, having been exposed to the consequences of wholesale cost-cutting to meet profit objectives: human-resource and general business courses generally deal with the issue of corporate shortsightedness as it relates to human resource management. Where the finance instructor can push in new directions which support long-term objectives and sustainable development is in highlighting the many ways that far sightedness adds value. Let us see how this can be done in the three major subdivisions of modern finance courses: corporate finance, asset pricing, and international finance. (The third of these might not universally be called a finance subdivision, and indeed, this author has argued elsewhere that international finance should be integrated in the other two subdivisions.[2] However, the fact is that international finance is usually dealt with separately, often at the end of finance courses.)

In what follows we shall explain under what topic headings sustainability can enter finance courses. It will remain implicit that topic areas which are not mentioned are areas for which this author cannot think of useful ways to refer to or incorporate sustainability.

CORPORATE FINANCE

Finance courses frequently begin with a discussion of corporate governance. Central to this subject is the "agency problem", focusing on the possible scisms between the interests of the principals – those who own the company – and their agents who manage it. Some instructors go a little further than talking about the possible differences in the objectives of principals and their agents, and the possible ways of providing compatible incentives, to talk about other stakeholders with an interest in the firm's decisions. Rather than limit discussion to the traditional stakeholder groups – shareholders, workers, suppliers, customers and the government - this is an ideal place to talk about society more broadly as a stakeholder. Furthermore, it is possible at this early stage to explain that stakeholders include future generations as well as today's owners. Future generations provide shareholders for firms which take a long-term perspective, and they will also provide customers, workers and regulators.

The financial matter which relates most directly to current versus future generations is the rate of "trade-off" between the present time and the future. The rate of trade-off is the discount rate. While the discount rate plays its main role in the issue of capital budgeting which often comes late in a finance course, the earlier the matter is addressed the better. When discussing present value and future value, finance instructors can show how quickly the future disappears as an element of decisions even at modest discount rates. Taking 30 years as the length of a generation, students quickly realise that the next generation hardly counts at all. "Does this make sense?" The instructor can ask. "What would life be like if your parents' generation had placed virtually all valuation on themselves?" A lively discussion can be sustained about the case for equal treatment of all generations. "Does this mean a zero discount rate?" "Alternatively, if each generation provides an intellectual- and physical-capital inheritance for its successors, is it ethical to discount at the rate at which provision is being made to enhance the future ability to produce?" This leads naturally to the issue of reducing future generations' access to irreplaceable resources and the need to factor in the price of impaired sustainability – deleting it from the social discount rate – just as positive provision for future production through knowledge and physical capital can support a positive discount rate.

When talking about discount rates, although it is usually left to macroeconomic perspectives, finance instructors might want to link the real discount rate to real economic growth. "How can corporations collectively provide a return equal to the real discount rate if the physical capital itself does not provide a sufficient surplus to pay the providers of financial capital their required return?"

As we have mentioned, it is in the corporate finance area of capital budgeting – sometimes called project evaluation – where sustainability should take centre stage. Most instructors begin by referring to the discount rate as the "shareholders' opportunity cost of capital" for a corresponding level of risk. Instructors who teach the Net Present Value (NPV) approach, with the "tax shield" accounted for in the Weighted Average Cost of Capital, WACC, tell students that the future is discounted at the rate the shareholders could achieve on alternative opportunities with the same leverage. This immediately begs the question of whether to use the private or the social opportunity cost of capital. "How do these differ if sustainability is impaired?" Students can be told that adjustments can be made in future cash flows or in the discount rate. The greater the impairment of sustainability the higher should be the discount rate or the greater the deduction from private cash flows.

Those instructors who prefer to use Adjusted Present Value, APV, for project evaluation can begin making the case for their chosen capital budgeting approach by showing how implications of a project for economic sustainability – either good or bad – can be handled. Also known as "Valuation in Parts", and "Valuation by Components", APV allows us to consider two categories of cash flows, "real flows" associated directly with the project, - revenues and costs from sales, production, construction etc. – and "side effects" usually linked to financing – tax shields from debt, concessionary financing, remittable income from manipulating transfer prices, capital cost allowances etc.[3] APV is based on value additivity, meaning that managers can separate different aspects of a project and then add them up. A very useful way of introducing APV to students is to use a project with implications for sustainability. The two relevant aspects of the project can then be private versus public cash flows. Specifically, the usual aspects of the project, namely real flows and side effects, can be combined under the heading of "private flows" and those connected with sustainability can be considered separately as "public flows". A project which has detrimental effects on the future through environmental or social damage incremental to the private flows will be negatively impacted and may be socially unprofitable when the two main components are aggregated. On the other hand, projects with beneficial implications for sustainability, such as hydrogen fuel cells, more efficient hydrocarbon burning engines and systematic reforestation, will have their APV enhanced, perhaps enough to tip the scales towards approval of the project – assuming managers can be persuaded to give equal weight to private and public flows of projects. At the very least, use of APV in this way forces firms to keep two sets of accounts, a private account and a social account, allowing some weight to be placed on societal side affects.

The APV approach is not the only new way of evaluating projects that lends itself to social accounting, and for teaching that accounting to finance students. Another approach with an increasing number of adherents is to view capital projects as having aspects of "real options". The opportunity to go ahead with a project if it is "in the money" can be viewed as a call option on the project. While the project itself has value as under APV (or NPV) according to its cash flow and risk, ability to delay the investment decision, along with associated cash flows, also has value. Indeed, as with all options, the value depends on the time before exercise, volatility of the value of the project through time, and the risk that circumstances will change before making any investment decision.[4] Project value also depends on the opportunity to reverse a decision if conditions change unfavourably after the project has been started.

Finance instructors can explain how sustainability consequences of a project may have to be learned only by experience. This takes time and may involve a pilot project – with final decision on the main project deferred, contingent on what is learned from the pilot. Alternatively, it may require that the project commence, with the option being to reverse the decision and scrap what has been done depending on what is learned. The value of the option depends on the cost of exercise, with "irreversibility" being a negative factor weighing on the project option value. That is, if current evidence suggests that there could be irreversible damage, but this cannot be determined until much later on, irreversibility is a negative factor, just as the ability to defer starting until studies have been done is a positive factor.

Whatever approach to project evaluation an instructor teaches, it is, of course, necessary to value the cash flows after taxes or other payments to the government. Governments have been urged to consider taxes aimed at reducing or eliminating consumption of natural capital, particularly in the form of non-renewable resources. Such taxes may be paid each period as non-renewable resources are exploited, or up front according to the "precautionary polluter pays principle", the so-called 4P approach.[5] Instructors should tell students that taxes paid each period for the depletion of natural capital can be treated in the same way as corporate income tax. They might also be told how the precautionary polluter pays principle might work, and why such a system may be preferred by government. Specifically, the timing of adverse effects can exceed the lives of investment projects or even the lives of the companies which pursue them.[6] This reduces incentives to minimize possible sustainability impacts. Contributing to a Sustainability Fund could help provide insurance for firms that do not stay around to pay eventual compensation, and if claims to any surpluses remaining in the fund are held by firms, the incentive to pay attention to adverse implications for sustainability is maintained: firms that reduce their impact stand to enjoy reimbursement.

ASSET PRICING

To the extent that consequences of actions affecting sustainability affect future cash flows, they will affect the present value of the flows. This in turn will affect prices of assets generating the cash flows. Asset prices are also impaired by risks to future cash flows from possible unanticipated consequences of damage to, or improvements in, sustainability. While the links between sustainability and asset pricing are less obvious than those involving corporate finance, there is ample room to mention sustainability in discussions about asset pricing and returns. Perhaps the best connection is to explain how attention to sustainability can affect corporate income through training and employee morale, product marketing, production and financing costs and avoiding fines from environmental destruction. As has been seen from the adoption of sustainable policies by companies such as MacMillan Bloedel – now part of Weyerhauser – sales can be expanded and asset values increased: customers favour firms that focus on sustainability and punish firms that do not.

Investors, including the increasingly important component of institutional investors, can have a direct positive impact on asset prices that goes beyond sales increases due to favourable customer reaction. For example, capable young workers are attracted to firms that adopt long-term objectives: today's college graduates want to work for firms with a solid environmental record and long-term horizons. In addition, there is a market for products companies develop that help with sustainability. Such products are more likely to come from companies with long-term objectives. In addition, firms thinking about what their actions mean for the future, not only for their own cash flows, are less likely to face fines and other punishments from governments. Investors know this and will pay a premium for such firms. Alternatively, such firms are less risky, prompting a smaller discount rate. It is not difficult to include such arguments in an introductory finance course when discussing asset pricing.

As with most risks, sustainability has two elements, one part which is systematic and which is therefore not diversifiable, and the other which is unsystematic and which can be diversified. For example, to the extent that the world experiences a global energy crisis, the value of assets in general is likely to suffer. This is mainly systematic. However, by holding a portfolio which includes firms which are imperfectly correlated, some risk is avoided. This is unsystematic risk. Indeed, sustainability might cause negative correlations: while energy users suffer from a crisis, energy producers might gain. Instructors may ask why keeping some firms' in a portfolio which benefit while others lose can reduce portfolio betas. They may also ask students about the effects of pension and investment funds which operate with rules that preclude the holding of shares of firms considered as "unethical" by adopting short-sighted, careless policies. Sustainability may even be mentioned as a factor that can be priced in the Arbitrage Pricing Theory, APT.

INTERNATIONAL FINANCE

As competition takes place more and more on a global scale the need to keep costs down puts increasing pressure on companies and governments to defer or even scrap actions supporting sustainability. Indeed, standards may be forced towards the lowest common denominator through international competition. After pointing this out to students, international finance instructors could look at what might support continued pursuit of sustainability goals. Companies that have an ecological orientation have made money by selling the products that have resulted. Sales of products more generally have been supported by good citizenship and setting good environmental standards, with the value of achieving ISO 9000, 14000 and other internationally recognized environmental standards well established. Furthermore, international cooperation may eventually lead to coordinated action against those who allow cost competition to undermine their concern for sustainability. Indeed, a policy of ecological tariffs has been advocated to deal with the cost cutters who do so at the expense of future generations[7]. Countervailing duties might be applied to keep a level playing field for those who engage in environmentally–unfriendly action in the name of price competition. The revenue from such duties could be reinvested in projects which work to improve economic and ecological sustainability.

CONCLUSION

There are many areas of finance where it is difficult to deal with sustainability, and instructors should not attempt to introduce the issue where it does not belong. The usual "irrelevance theories" concerning dividend policy and capital structure might be areas where sustainability is not mentioned.[8] However, as we have argued, there are numerous important areas of finance where the instructor could help foster the interest of future managers in keeping a sustainable scale of activities relative to ecological life-support systems, in achieving a fair distribution between current and future generations, and ensuring an allocation of resources that accounts for natural capital. Rather than finding it a struggle, instructors are likely to find today's students welcoming this focus. A large number of business students are already geared towards a shift in attitude for achieving sustainable development. Many already know that sustainable development is good business. Students may well be ahead of instructors in terms of their understanding of this issue!

REFERENCES

Costanza, R., "Three General Policies to Achieve Sustainability," Center for Environmental and Estuarine Studies, University of Maryland, 1999, unpublished.

Dixit, A., and R. Pindyck, "The Options Approach to Capital Investment," *Harvard Business Review*, May-June 1995, pp. 105-115.

Giammarino M, A. Kraus and J. Zechner, "Mine Reclamation Funds," Faculty of Commerce and Business Administration, University of British Columbia, 1990.

Levi, M., "The Teaching of International Finance" in *Global Perspective: Internationalising Management Education*, Alan M. Rugman and William T. Stanbury, editors, Centre for International Business Studies, University of British Columbia, December 1992, pp. 155-166.

Levi, M., *International Finance: the Markets and Financial Management of Multinational Business*, Third Edition, McGraw-Hill, New York, 1996, Chapter 19.

Luehrman, A., "What's it Worth? A General Manager's Guide to Valuation," *Harvard Business Review*, May-June 1997, pp. 132-142.

Myers, S., "Interactions of Corporate Financing and Investment Decisions – Implication for Capital Budgeting," *Journal of Finance*, vol. 29, 1974, pp. 1-25.

Schofield, B., and B. Feltmate, 1999, Sustainable Development vs. Share Price, *Canadian Investment Review*, Summer, vol. 12, no. 2, P. 13.

ACKNOWLEDGMENTS

The author has benefitted from the comments of Wilhelm Pfähler. Responsibility for all views expressed and any errors of omission or commission is, however, solely that of the author.

1. See Brian Schofield and Blair Feltmate, "Sustainable Development vs. Share Price," *Canadian Investment Review*, Summer 1999, vol. 12, No. 2, p. 13.
2. See Maurice D. Levi, "The Teaching of International Finance." In: Alan M. Rugman and William T. Stanbury (eds.) *Global Perspective: Internationalising Management Education*, Centre for International Business Studies, University of British Columbia, December 1992, pp. 155-166.
3. For the structure of and arguments for using the APV approach see Stewart C. Myers, "Interactions of Corporate Financing and Investment Decisions – Implication for Capital Budgeting," *Journal of Finance*, March 1974, vol. 29, pp. 1-25, and Timothy A. Luehrman, "What's it Worth? A

General Manager's Guide to Valuation," *Harvard Business Review*, May-June 1997, pp. 132-142. For the application of APV in an international financial setting see Maurice D. Levi, *International Finance: the Markets and Financial Management of Multinational Business*, third edition, McGraw-Hill, New York, 1996, Chapter 19.

4. For more on this approach see Avinash K. Dixit and Robert S. Pindyck, "The Options Approach to Capital Investment," *Harvard Business Review*, May-June 1995, pp. 105-115.

5. The case for these policies is made in Robert Costanza, "Three General Policies to Achieve Sustainability," Center for Environmental and Estuarine Studies, University of Maryland, unpublished 1999.

6. See Ronald M. Giammarino, Alan Kraus and Josef Zechner, "Mine Reclamation Funds," Faculty of Commerce and Business Administration, University of British Columbia, 1990.

7. See Robert Costanza (1999).

8. Even here there are possibilities for discussion about sustainability. Students could be asked if concern for the future supports retaining earnings and whether far-sighted firms are likely to do this. Also, what does sustainability suggest for debt versus equity? Is equity a signal of long-term orientation?

A QUANTITATIVE APPROACH TO STRATEGIC ENVIRONMENTAL RISK MANAGEMENT

Robert Repetto
Yale School of Forestry and Environmental Studies
and
Duncan Austin
World Resources Institute
Washington D.C.

INTRODUCTION

The financial performance of modern business is increasingly affected by the costs and opportunities presented by environmental issues. Regulations, materials and energy prices, consumer demands, and the development of new markets may all be influenced by environmental concerns that thereby materially affect company earnings and balance sheets. Moreover, because the outcome of many environmental issues is unclear, environmental pressures create risks that companies must manage strategically. Yet, firms and analysts find it difficult to translate the potential impacts and risks of environmental issues into the financial terms required for business planning and valuation (e.g. UNEP, 1999).

This paper presents a new methodology that enables managers and analysts to evaluate impending environmental pressures in terms of their impact on shareholder value and financial risk. These capabilities are important because in many industries environmental issues can significantly affect companies' financial results (Cairncross, 1995). Unless environmental issues are handled in ways similar to those used to manage other business risks and opportunities in those companies, then environmental control will remain an internal regulatory function superimposed on the company's core business concerns rather than become part of the process of maximizing shareholder value (Smart, 1992). The need for strategic environmental management will only intensify as affluent consumers demand better environmental quality while economic growth presses increasingly on ecological constraints.

Business managers and analysts could use this approach to:
- uncover hidden liabilities or risks in potential acquisitions;
- estimate the value of investments that would reduce environmental exposures;
- measure the self-insurance value of environmental control programs;
- benchmark a company against its competitors; and
- communicate its environmental strategy to financial analysts.

To demonstrate the methodology, we have used it to evaluate the environmental risks facing leading U.S. pulp and paper companies.[1]

THE APPROACH BRIEFLY EXPLAINED

Like financial markets, the approach is forward-looking. It is based on developing scenarios for significant future environmental issues and seeing how companies are likely to be exposed and financially affected under each scenario. It uses probabilities derived from past experience and expert judgement to weight the possible scenarios and uses these weights to forecast a likely financial impact and to construct measures of financial risk.

The successive steps in the methodology are a) identifying salient future environmental issues, b) building scenarios around each, c) assigning probabilities to scenarios, d) assessing company exposures to each issue, e) estimating financial impacts contingent on scenarios, f) constructing overall measures of expected impact and risk. The methodology can be seen as iterative, since probabilities, exposures and estimated financial impacts change over time. The underlying analysis can readily be updated as new information emerges.

A. Building Environmental Scenarios for the U.S. Pulp and Paper Industry

The pulp and paper industry is an appropriate one with which to demonstrate this approach because environmental developments will significantly affect future materials and energy costs, earnings, and balance sheets. This sector depends on forest harvests and recycled paper for its raw materials; it is one of the most energy-intensive of all industries; it emits a wide range of toxic and conventional pollutants to air, water, and land; it is one of the largest contributors to the solid waste stream; it is identified in the public mind with pollution and resource degradation; it is subject to an enormous range of environmental and natural resource regulation and litigation and it must allocate significant fractions of investment and operating outlays to environmental control programs. Scenarios can help identify these potential environmental value drivers, including new regulatory initiatives, new fiscal measures enacted for environmental purposes, potential future liabilities arising from past or current activities, and demand shifts arising from changing customer preferences or mandated product standards.

In constructing scenarios, the first step is to identify environmental developments that are likely to have significant financial impacts. Significant environmental issues might emerge throughout the product life cycle. In the pulp and paper application, the industry association and its members from leading companies cooperated with WRI to identify and characterize potential future environmental pressures.[2] The EPA and other government agencies, environmental advocacy groups, and environmental scientists were also consulted, along with an extensive published literature.

The next step is to prioritize these issues according to their likely significance for future earnings and risks. Three key criteria were used to prioritize issues:

1. Magnitude of the potential impact on earnings stream: potentially "big ticket" items are obviously more critical to include in scenarios.
2. Anticipated timing of an event or issue. Other things equal, the further in the future the impact of an issue is likely to be, the less its impact on shareholder value.
3. Likelihood of an event happening. Though a nearly certain event might have significant financial implications, it may be of lesser significance in a scenario-building exercise if those implications are already reflected in company plans and financial projections.

Table 1 provides a list and brief descriptions of the most significant environmental issues selected on the basis of these criteria. Scenarios were constructed for these issues by identifying plausible outcomes and their likelihood. Outcomes were then quantified in terms that can be translated into a financial analysis: impacts on prices, costs, revenues, expenditures, investment requirements, balance sheet liabilities and the like.[3]

B. Assessing Firm-By-Firm Exposure to Priority Environmental Issues

Even among the industry's large multi-plant firms, the scenarios would have substantially different financial implications. For some firms, should a particular scenario come to pass, the financial impact would be significant; for others, the impact would be insignificant or even opposite in direction. Companies have positioned themselves differently with respect to these environmental issues mainly through decisions taken in years past for broader business reasons. Where mills and forestlands are located, what products they turn out, and what technologies are imbedded in the capital stock are historical factors that largely determine companies' exposure to impending environmental issues. Just as a company's present exposures are determined by past

Table 1: Significant Impending Environmental Pressures on Pulp & Paper Firms

Air Quality Regulations

Cluster Rule Air Quality Provisions
    MACT I, III for process emissions
    MACT II for combustion sources
	Will require maximum available control technology for air toxics from pulping and bleaching lines, boilers, recovery furnaces, kilns, etc.

Long-Range Transport of Smog Precursors	Will require mills located in 22 eastern states to reduce nitrogen oxide emissions by 50-75 percent
Ozone and PM2.5 standard	Will require substantial reductions in emissions of nitrogen and sulfur aerosols and fine particles

Water Quality Regulations

Compliance options under cluster rule	Provides longer compliance periods for mills that install technologies beyond compliance
Total Maximum Daily Loads	May require effluent reductions beyond currently permitted levels to remediate impaired waterbodies
Sediment Remediation	Could require clean-up of polluted aquatic sediments causing water pollution downstream of mills
Endangered Species Act	Could require effluent reductions to protect endangered aquatic species in specific locales

Environmental Influences on Fiber Supply

Regulations on Private Lands	Stricter state and local forest regulations may limit harvests from private timberlands
Actions under the Endangered Species Act (ESA)	A reauthorized ESA may limit harvests in specific regions, especially if extended to sub-species and vigorously enforced

decisions, a company's current environmental management decisions will determine its future exposures.

To assess exposures, firm-by-firm information was collected on the priority issues from publicly available sources, including annual reports, SEC filings; news reports; pulp and paper industry directories; and EPA public data files on facility-by-facility environmental performance.[4] Geographical Information System (GIS) techniques were used to map the location of companies' mills and timberlands onto the regions of concern under impending environmental regulations, many of which have quite specific areas of applicability. Measures of environmental performance, such as emissions rates, and information on technologies in place were also used. Aggregating mill data by company shed light on companies' potential overall liability but disaggregated facility-wise data are useful for investment planning, benchmarking, and analysis of acquisitions and divestitures

C. Analyzing Scenario-Specific Financial Impacts

To be useful, the financial implications of environmental issues must be expressed in a way that can be incorporated into the valuation frameworks currently used to assess conventional business risks and future prospects. For each company and each scenario, the financial impacts on revenues, production costs, investment spending, and the value of owned assets were estimated individually for all years of the forecast period, then reduced to discounted present values using an estimate of the firm's weighted average cost of capital. These present values were then added to obtain a net financial impact for the scenario and the company in question. In order to standardize impacts across companies, these present value dollars were then divided by the number of equity shares outstanding to create estimates of per share financial impacts and these were in turn expressed as percentages of the current share price on financial markets. Thus, each issue-specific scenario was related to each company's shareholder value.

Several qualifications to the financial projections should be stated: The information on which they are based becomes increasingly dated as time passes and must be updated.[5] For most companies, self-reported data on the composition of production costs were scanty and had to be supplemented with data from available public sources. In applications within companies, much more extensive financial and operating data could be brought to bear. Moreover, this application abstracts from ongoing cyclical movements, restructuring and consolidation trends that are important in the pulp and paper industry in order to focus on environmental issues.

EXAMPLE: Cleanup of Impaired Waterways

This section illustrates the steps in the approach through a single issue that has important implications for the industry: the cleanup of impaired waterways.

Scenarios

Section 303(d) of the Clean Water Act calls on state regulatory agencies to establish maximum pollution loading on watercourses where technology-based effluent limits are inadequate to achieve water quality goals. Currently, approximately 15,000 miles of watercourses still fail to meet such goals (e.g., fishable and swimmable) despite twenty-five years of technology-based pollution control. Environmental groups have initiated legal action against at least 29 state regulatory agencies to force them to identify impaired waterways and then to impose TMDLs (Total Maximum Daily Loads for pollutants). Many of these states, in the Southeast, the Northwest, Northeast, and Great Lakes regions are centers of industrial timberland and pulp and paper production.

Further reductions in total pollution loadings will probably be required to improve water quality on impaired waterways. The issue for the pulp and paper industry is what further reductions will be required of it. In many watersheds, non-point sources, especially farming and animal husbandry, are now responsible for the largest share of pollution loadings through run-off and erosion. Moreover, best management practices on farms and construction sites can often reduce effluent discharge at a small fraction of the incremental cost faced by industrial and municipal dischargers that have already installed secondary waste treatment systems. Nonetheless, imposing regulations on farms and other non-point sources is politically and administratively more difficult than tightening regulations on existing point sources. EPA is encouraging states to develop permit trading systems that would allow point and non-point sources to contract for effluent reductions. Therefore, two scenarios with very different cost implications for the evolution of TMDLs can be envisaged:

Scenario A: States impose additional effluent reduction requirements on municipal and industrial dischargers, largely exempting non-point sources. Mills located on sensitive waterways would be forced to adopt enhanced waste treatment systems and/or additional water recycling and spill control measures. Costs depend on individual mill characteristics.

Scenario B: States impose best management practices on farms and other non-point sources and initiate effluent trading systems that enable mills to contract with non-point sources for discharge reductions at a small fraction of their own incremental pollution abatement costs in lieu of undertaking further pollution controls in the mill.

The financial impacts of scenario A were estimated using data on individual mill characteristics and the costs of upgrading waste treatment plants. Estimated capital and operating cost changes were reduced to a single discounted present value. The financial implications of scenario B were estimated using the results of economic studies of proposed effluent trading systems affecting point and non-point sources on waterways in the Upper Midwest.

In addition, sub-scenarios were constructed which assumed that the aggregate industry costs of compliance would be partially passed forward to customers in the form of higher product prices. The extent of pass-through is determined by estimated product demand price elasticities. The probability of the industry being able to pass these costs along to consumers over the coming years depends in large part on the recovery of world demand for commodities and the absorption of excess capacity created by the Asian and Latin American economic crises. Should that happen, given the absence of excess or even normal profits in much of the U.S. industry, price adjustments to industry-wide cost pressures become likely. High and low price elasticity sub-scenarios were analyzed. In these sub-scenarios, the net financial impacts on all firms are lowered by the recovery of costs through product price increases. Companies with relatively low compliance costs benefit from increases in net operating incomes because revenues increase by larger percentages than costs do. Thus, environmental issues create winners and losers among companies, depending on their exposures and potential compliance costs.

Exposures

If actions under section 303(d) of the Clean Water Act force mills located on impaired waterways to reduce effluents or to contract with farmers and other non-point sources for effluent reductions, then some companies will be more exposed simply because more of their mills are located on impaired waterways. Some companies (A, C, E, and H) have all or nearly all of their capacity for producing paper and market pulp on impaired waterways subject to remedial actions. (See Figure 1) These companies are likely to face higher future compliance costs. At the other extreme, M has less than 20% of its capacity exposed to the rule, and L has only 40% of its capacity on impaired waterways. This environmental regulation, like others, will have markedly uneven incidence across firms in the industry.

This conclusion is reinforced by data suggesting that some companies release conventional water pollutants such as biochemical oxygen demand (BOD) and total suspended solids (TSS) at higher rates than others, measured per ton of product. (See Figure 2) Two companies (A and

Figure 1: Share of Pulp and Paper Capacity locate on 303d Waterways, by Company

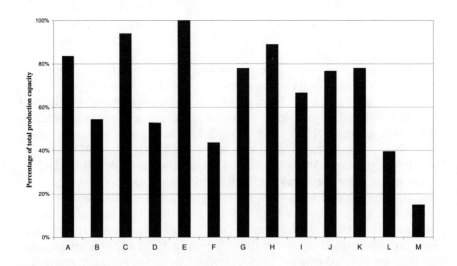

Figure 2: Discharge of Conventional Water Pollutants per Ton of Production

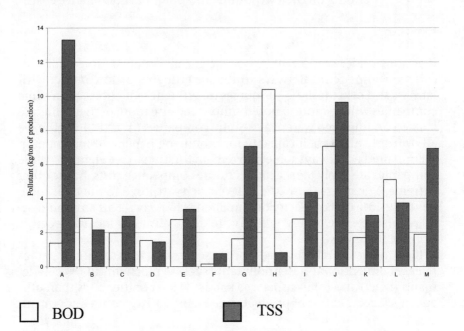

H) have most of their mill capacity located on impaired waterways and also release waterborne pollutants at above average rates, relative to production volumes[6].

Financial Impacts

The required effluent reductions for mills located on impaired waterways were assumed to be at least fifty percent, for purposes of constructing trading scenarios. The average per ton compliance costs for non-trading scenarios were estimated from the costs of upgrading effluent treatment plants from secondary to tertiary status, which would also reduce releases of trace non-conventional pollutants. Cost estimates for these upgrades took into account parameters of scale, flow rate through the treatment plant, etc., and include both incremental capital and operating costs. Average per ton compliance costs for trading scenarios were estimated from an ongoing WRI economic study of waterways in the Upper Midwest in which effluent trading systems between point sources, such as pulp and paper mills, and non-point sources, such as agricultural operations, are being designed (Faeth, forthcoming). Non-point sources have heretofore not faced regulatory abatement requirements and can reduce effluents at much lower incremental costs per ton than industrial sources can. Mills were assumed to purchase permits from non-point sources, which would be the cheaper compliance option. The resulting arrays of financial impacts for trading and non-trading scenarios, with high and low price-pass through, are illustrated below. (See Figures 3-6). In the high price pass-through scenarios, firms whose facilities are mostly or entirely located away from impaired waterways end up as net gainers from the rule, benefiting from industry-wide price increases but incurring minimal control costs.

DERIVING OVERALL FINANCIAL RESULTS

This process was repeated for all of the high-priority environmental issues in Table 1. Firms could use this approach to identify those issues that present the greatest financial risks and to plan appropriate responses. In addition, by aggregating across all issues firms can generate estimates of their overall environmental exposure. One way in which the findings for individual issues could be combined is through macro-scenarios: one might ask, for example, "What if a new Federal election led to heightened environmentalism across the board?" One would then choose among the individual issue scenarios in accordance with this overall perspective.

Another, perhaps more interesting, way is to combine the individual

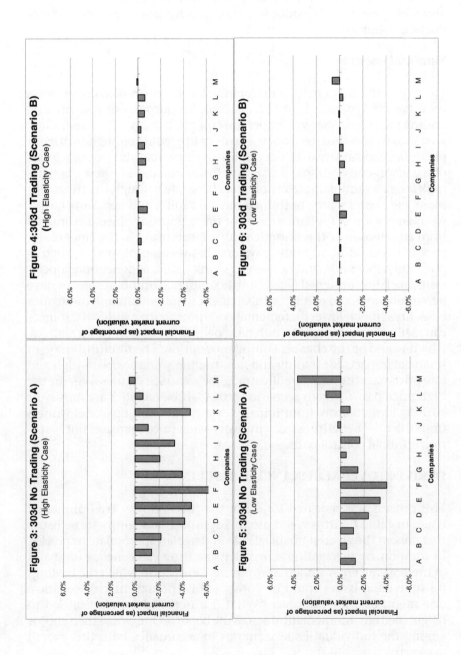

scenarios in an overall risk assessment. When industry and environmental experts participated in scenario development, they were asked to use their best judgments to assign probabilities to the occurrence of each scenario. Since many of the impending environmental issues are one-time occurrences, the use of judgmental probabilities of this type is appropriate and unavoidable. We combined these judgmental probabilities into overall consensus probabilities.

Those consensus probabilities for individual scenarios were then used to construct a likelihood distribution across all scenarios. For example, using probabilities for individual scenarios, the joint probability of all the worst-case, most costly, outcomes coming to pass was computed.[7] Then, the joint probability of all the best-case, least costly outcomes coming to pass was computed and then all the intermediate cases were filled in. When such probability distributions were constructed for each company from the information in the preceding sections of this report, substantial differences among companies became evident (see Figures 7 and 8). Even though the underlying scenario and probability assumptions are the same for all companies, the probability distributions differ substantially with respect to the range of likely outcomes (variance) and with respect to the most likely outcome (mean). Distributions also vary in their degree of imbalance toward negative or positive outcomes (skewness). These differences are entirely due to differences among companies in their exposures to the underlying environmental issues.

Such differences are made even clearer when summary statistics for all the companies in the study are arrayed together, as in the following summary chart (See Figure 9). The most likely outcome for each company is represented by a dot, indicating the expected impact on its share value of impending environmental issues. A few companies can reasonably expect an insignificantly small positive or negative effect — less than two percent one way or the other. At the other extreme, a few companies could, at this point, expect quite a significant negative impact, in the range of 10-15 percent of share value. The others face a most likely impact of 5-10 percent of current share value.

The range of potential outcomes also varies greatly from one company to another. The variance of impacts, as measure of financial risk arising from exposure to these environmental issues, is as low as 1-2 percent of share value for three companies in the group. At the other extreme, it is as high as 21% of share value for one company and 14% of share value for another. The former group is effectively hedged against environmental risk, in the sense that its future earnings will not be highly sensitive to the outcome of the issues it faces. The latter companies are greatly at risk: their earnings will depend heavily on the way these issues develop.

Figure 7: Range of Possible Financial Impacts from Environmental Issues for Company C

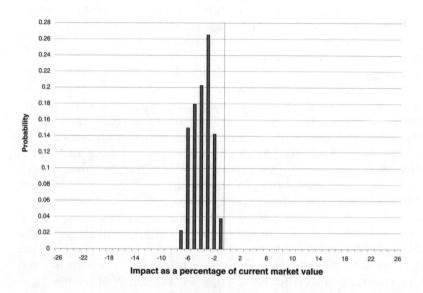

Figure 8: Range of Possible Financial Impacts from Environmental Issues for Company K

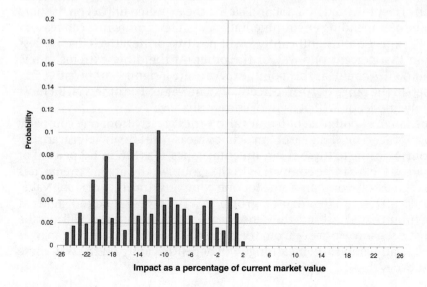

Figure 9: Possible Impact of Environmental Issues on Share Price, as a percentage of current valuation

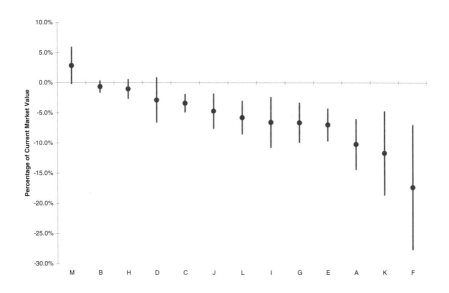

ARE THESE EXPOSURES ALREADY INCORPORATED INTO MARKET VALUATIONS?

The question immediately arises whether these differences are already factored into the market valuations of individual companies. Companies that are relatively well-positioned with respect to their environmental exposures might wish that this were recognized by financial markets. However, we found that the companies' financial reports and SEC disclosure statements disclosed little quantitative (or even qualitative) information pertinent to these issues. Companies differ in their reporting practices. Most do not report financial impacts that are still considered to be uncertain, as are all the scenarios underlying this analysis. Some companies only report on capital costs to be incurred to comply with environmental standards and regulations that have already been issued in final form and on remediation costs for which the company has already been implicated through EPA action. Even fewer companies reported potential changes in operating costs or input prices that might arise from environmental pressures. A few companies discuss a potentially important impending environmental issue such as the Endangered

Species Act in general terms without providing any quantitative estimates, or conclude that the issue is not expected to affect the company's operations significantly in the coming year but might do so in the future.

A recent study by a professor at the Yale School of Management concluded that companies can affect the way financial analysts evaluate their environmental issues "by developing a consistent internal position on how the environment adds value to their business; by linking environmental performance data to key financial valuation criteria; by collecting broader data on the financial implications of environmental risk and opportunity; by developing better techniques for quantifying and comparing the financial impacts of environmental risks and opportunities; and by placing relevant environmental financial data into the mainstream of their communications with analysts and investors." (Gentry and Fernandez, 1997). Many analysts discount or ignore the environmental reports that many companies issue because such reports often lack hard and comparable information on the financial implications of environmental exposures. The approach illustrated here can help companies make their reporting on environmental issues more influential.

OTHER POTENTIAL APPLICATIONS

Within companies, environmental managers might use an approach like this to quantify their environmental exposures in financial terms and to identify the sources of the largest expected gains or losses. This approach could help environmental managers relate their operations to other risk management operations within the company. Managers might use this approach to benchmark their companies (or facilities) against rivals. They might also use it to help identify which investments in environmental control would do most to reduce their outstanding environmental risks, allowing them to move beyond a compliance-based system toward a more forward-looking and strategic approach. Managers and CFOs might use a self-insurance model to estimate how much it would be worth annually to spend on control measures as a self-insurance quasi-premium in order to eliminate the likelihood of a loss due to environmental factors greater than a certain percentage of share value. For example, applying a typical insurance loading multiple to the expected value of losses for one company implies that it might spend up to $20 million per year over a five-year period on targeted mitigation measures as a form of self-insurance in order to ensure that its environmental exposures did not result in a loss of more than five percent of shareholder value. (See Figure 10)

Figure 10: Insuring Losses Greater Than 5% of Current Share Value - Company C

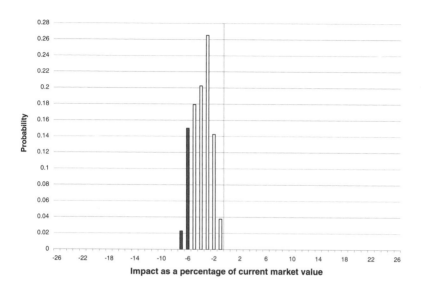

Finally, this approach lends itself readily to the estimation of the value to the company of real options with which to deal with impending environmental issues. Such real options in the pulp and paper industry might include building in the flexibility to use alternative fuels or fiber sources or to close down or divest vulnerable facilities. Once an assessment of probabilities and associated outcomes for different scenarios has been carried out, estimating the value of such options is relatively straightforward.

In all these ways, the approach presented and illustrated in this study might become a useful tool with which to relate environmental exposure and performance to investor value and risk. It answers a question that many have asked but few, if any, have been able to answer satisfactorily. This approach is sufficiently broad to be applied to other sectors in which environmental factors can be value drivers. It is sufficiently general that it can encompass not only the costs of meeting environmental standards but also the opportunities afforded by providing solutions to environmental problems.

REFERENCES

Cairncross, Frances. "Green, Inc.: A Guide to Business and the Environment," *Earthscan,* London, 1995.

Faeth, Paul, Trading as an Option: Market-Based Incentives and Water Quality, World Resources Institute, Washington D.C, forthcoming

Gentry, Bradford S. and Lisa O. Fernandez. *Valuing the Environment: How Fortune 500 CFOs and Analysts Measure Corporate Performance.* New York, New York: United Nations Development Program, Office of Development Studies, Working Paper, 1997.

Smart, Bruce. *Beyond Compliance.* Washington, DC: World Resources Institute, 1992.

UNEP. *UNEP Financial Institutions Initiative 1998 Survey.* Geneva, Switzerland: Financial Institutions Initiative Secretariat, Economics, Trade and Environment Unit, United Nations Environment Program, 1999.

FOOTNOTES

1. The companies included in this analysis are Boise Cascade, Bowater, Caraustar, Champion, Fort James, Georgia Pacific, International Paper, Mead, Potlatch, Smurfit Stone, Westvaco, Weyerhaeuser and Willamette. At the time of writing, figures for Weyerhaeuser do not reflect the recent takeover of Macmillan-Bloedel. Companies are not identified by name, nor are they ordered alphabetically in the figures that follow.

2. We gratefully acknowledge the cooperation of the American Forest & Paper Association and member companies in engaging in a scenario-building session with us. They bear no responsibility for the material presented here, however.

3. Climate issues are also potentially significant but were not analyzed because of data limitations.

4. For a full list of references, see forthcoming WRI research report.

5. The most recent information in this report dates from December 1998, when we began to write up the findings. Some data used in the analysis are considerably less recent. Consequently, readers are cautioned against relying on the results reported here as up-to-date forecasts of likely future developments. What we wish readers to take away is an understanding of the approach.

6. The EPA data underlying Figure 2 and this statement refers to 1994, the latest year available, and may be out of date.

7. In this exercise, the probabilities associated with one issue were assumed to be independent of the probabilities associated with all other issues. Alternatively, it would be feasible to develop estimates of conditional probabilities for specific issues, contingent on the outcome of other issues.

GREEN AND COMPETITIVE: ENDING THE STALEMATE

Michael E. Porter
and
Claas van der Linde
Harvard Business School

The need for regulation to protect the environment gets widespread but grudging acceptance: widespread because everyone wants a livable planet, grudging because of the lingering belief that environmental regulations erode competitiveness. The prevailing view is that there is an inherent and fixed trade-off: ecology versus the economy. On one side of the trade-off are the social benefits that arise from strict environmental standards. On the other are industry's private costs for prevention and cleanup — costs that lead to higher prices and reduced competitiveness. With the argument framed this way, progress on environmental quality has become a kind of arm-wrestling match. One side pushes for tougher standards; the other tries to roll them back. The balance of power shifts one way or the other depending on the prevailing political winds.

This static view of environmental regulation, in which everything except regulation is held constant, is incorrect. If technology, products, processes, and customer needs were all fixed, the conclusion that regulation must raise costs would be inevitable. But companies operate in the real world of dynamic competition, not in the static world of much economic theory. They are constantly finding innovative solutions to pressures of all sorts — from competitors, customers, and regulators.

Properly designed environmental standards can trigger innovations that lower the total cost of a product or improve its value. Such innovations allow companies to use a range of inputs more productively — from raw materials to energy to labor — thus offsetting the costs of improving environmental impact and ending the stalemate. Ultimately, this enhanced resource productivity makes companies more competitive, not less.

Consider how the Dutch flower industry has responded to its environmental problems. Intense cultivation of flowers in small areas was contaminating the soil and groundwater with pesticides, herbicides, and fertilizers. Facing increasingly strict regulation on the release of chemicals, the Dutch understood that the only effective way to address the problem would be to develop a closed-loop system. In advanced Dutch greenhouses, flowers now grow in water and rock wool, not in soil. This lowers the risk of infestation, reducing the need for fertilizers and pesticides, which are delivered in water that circulates and is reused. The tightly monitored closed-loop system also reduces variation in

Flowers success story - success story

growing conditions, thus improving product quality. Handling costs have gone down because the flowers are cultivated on specially designed platforms. In addressing the environmental problem, then, the Dutch have innovated in ways that have raised the productivity with which they use many of the resources involved in growing flowers. The net result is not only dramatically lower environmental impact but also lower costs, better product quality, and enhanced global competitiveness. (See the insert "Innovating to Be Competitive: The Dutch Flower Industry.")

This example illustrates why the debate about the relationship between competitiveness and the environment has been framed incorrectly. Policy makers, business leaders, and environmentalists have focused on the static cost impacts of environmental regulation and have ignored the more important offsetting productivity benefits from innovation. As a result, they have acted too often in ways that unnecessarily drive up costs and slow down progress on environmental issues. This static mind-set has thus created a self-fulfilling prophecy leading to ever more costly environmental regulation. Regulators tend to set regulations in ways that deter innovation. Companies, in turn, oppose and delay regulations instead of innovating to address them. The whole process has spawned an industry of litigators and consultants that drains resources away from real solutions.

POLLUTION = INEFFICIENCY

Are cases like the Dutch flower industry the exception rather than the rule? Is it naïve to expect that reducing pollution will often enhance competitiveness? We think not, and the reason is that pollution often is a form of economic waste. When scrap, harmful substances, or energy forms are discharged into the environment as pollution, it is a sign that resources have been used incompletely, inefficiently, or ineffectively. Moreover, companies then have to perform additional activities that add cost but create no value for customers: for example, handling, storage, and disposal of discharges.

The concept of resource productivity opens up a new way of looking at both the full systems costs and the value associated with any product. Resource inefficiencies are most obvious within a company in the form of incomplete material utilization and poor process controls, which result in unnecessary waste, defects, and stored materials. But there also are many other hidden costs buried in the life cycle of the product. Packaging discarded by distributors or customers, for example, wastes resources and adds costs. Customers bear additional costs when they use products that pollute or waste energy. Resources are lost when

Innovating to Be Competitive: The Dutch Flower Industry

The Dutch flower industry is responsible for about 65 percent of world exports of cut flowers—an astonishing figure given that the most important production inputs in the flower business would seem to be land and climate. Anyone who has been to the Netherlands knows its disadvantages on both counts. The Dutch have to reclaim land from the sea, and the weather is notoriously problematic.

How can the Dutch be the world's leaders in the flower business when they lack comparative advantage in the traditional sense? The answer, among other reasons, is that they have innovated at every step in the value chain, creating technology and highly specialized inputs that enhance resource productivity and offset the country's natural disadvantages.

In selling and distribution, for example, the Netherlands has five auction houses custom designed for the flower business. Carts of flowers are automatically towed on computer-guided paths into the auction room. The buying process occurs in a few seconds. Buyers sit in an amphitheater, and the price on the auction clock moves down until the first buyer signals electronically. That buyer's code is attached to the cart, which is routed to the company's shipping and handling area. Within a few minutes, the flowers are on a truck to regional markets or in a specialized, precooled container on their way to nearby Schiphol airport. Good airports and highway systems may be plentiful elsewhere, too. But the Netherlands' innovative, specialized infrastructure is a competitive advantage. It leads to very high productivity. It is so successful that growers from other countries actually fly flowers there to be processed, sold, and re-exported.

Paradoxically, having a shortage of general-purpose or more basic inputs can sometimes be turned into an advantage. If land were readily available and the climate more favorable, the Dutch would have competed the same way other countries did. Instead they were forced to innovate, developing a high-tech system of year-round greenhouse cultivation. The Dutch continually improve the unique, specialized technology that creates high resource productivity and underpins their competitiveness.

In contrast, an abundance of labor and natural resources or a lack of environmental pressure may lead a country's companies to spend the national resources unproductively.

Competing based on cheap inputs, which could be used with less productivity, was sufficient in a more insular, less global economy. Today, when emerging nations with even cheaper labor and raw materials are part of the global economy, the old strategy is unsustainable.

products that contain usable materials are discarded and when customers pay — directly or indirectly — for product disposal.

Environmental improvement efforts have traditionally overlooked these systems costs. Instead, they have focused on pollution control through better identification, processing, and disposal of discharges or waste — costly approaches. In recent years, more advanced companies and regulators have embraced the concept of pollution prevention, sometimes called source reduction, which uses such methods as material substitution and closed-loop processes to limit pollution before it occurs.

But, although pollution prevention is an important step in the right direction, ultimately companies must learn to frame environmental improvement in terms of resource productivity.[1] Today managers and regulators focus on the actual costs of eliminating or treating pollution. They must shift their attention to include the opportunity costs of pollution — wasted resources, wasted effort, and diminished product value to the customer. At the level of resource productivity, environmental improvement and competitiveness come together.

This new view of pollution as resource inefficiency evokes the quality revolution of the 1980s and its most powerful lessons. Today we have little trouble grasping the idea that innovation can improve quality while actually lowering cost. But as recently as fifteen years ago, managers believed there was a fixed trade-off. Improving quality was expensive because it could be achieved only through inspection and rework of the "inevitable" defects that came off the line. What lay behind the old view was the assumption that both product design and production processes were fixed. As managers have rethought the quality issue, however, they have abandoned that old mind-set. Viewing defects as a sign of inefficient product and process design — not as an inevitable by-product of manufacturing — was a breakthrough. Companies now strive to build quality into the entire process. The new mind-set unleashed the power of innovation to relax or eliminate what companies had previously accepted as fixed trade-offs.

Like defects, pollution often reveals flaws in the product design or production process. Efforts to eliminate pollution can therefore follow the same basic principles widely used in quality programs: Use inputs more efficiently, eliminate the need for hazardous, hard-to-handle materials, and eliminate unneeded activities. In a recent study of major process changes at ten manufacturers of printed circuit boards, for example, pollution-control personnel initiated thirteen of thirty-three major changes. Of the thirteen changes, twelve resulted in cost reduction, eight in quality improvements, and five in extension of production capabilities.[2] It is not surprising that total quality management (TQM) has become a source of ideas for pollution reduction that can create offsetting benefits. The Dow Chemical Company, for example, explicitly identified the link between quality improvement and environmental performance by using statistical-process control to reduce the variance in processes and to lower waste.

INNOVATION AND RESOURCE PRODUCTIVITY

To explore the central role of innovation and the connection between environmental improvement and resource productivity, we have been collaborating since 1991 with the Management Institute for Environment and Business (MEB) on a series of international case studies of industries and sectors significantly affected by environmental regulation: pulp and paper, paint and coatings, electronics manufacturing, refrigerators, dry cell batteries, and printing inks. (See Table 1) The data clearly show that the costs of addressing environmental regulations can be minimized, if not eliminated, through innovation that delivers other competitive benefits. We first observed the phenomenon in the course of our research for a study of national competitiveness, *The Competitive Advantage of Nations* (The Free Press, 1990).

Consider the chemical sector, where many believe that the ecology-economy trade-off is particularly steep. A study of activities to prevent waste generation at twenty-nine chemical plants found innovation offsets that enhanced resource productivity. Of 18 of of these waste prevention activities, only one resulted in a net cost increase. Of the seventy activities with documented changes in product yield, sixty-eight reported increases; the average for twenty initiatives documented with specific data was 7 percent. These innovation offsets were achieved with surprisingly low investments and very short payback times. One-quarter of the forty-eight initiatives with detailed capital cost information required no capital investment at all; of the thirty-eight initiatives with data on the payback period, nearly two-thirds recouped their initial investments in six months or less. The annual savings per dollar spent on source reduction averaged three dollars and forty-nine cents for the twenty-seven activities for which this information could be calculated. The study also found that the two main motivating factors for source reduction activities were waste disposal costs and environmental regulation.

Innovation in response to environmental regulation can fall into two broad categories. The first is new technologies and approaches that minimize the cost of dealing with pollution once it occurs. The key to these approaches often lies in taking the resources embodied in the pollution and converting them into something of value. Companies get smarter about how to process toxic materials and emissions into usable forms, recycle scrap, and improve secondary treatment. For example, at

Table 1: Environmental Regulation Has Competitive Implications

Sector/Industry	Environmental Issues	Innovative Solutions	Innovation Offsets
Pulp and paper	Dioxin released by bleaching with chlorine	Improved cooking and washing processes	Lower operating costs though greater use of by-product energy sources
		Elimination of chlorine by using oxygen, ozone, or peroxide for bleaching	25% initial price premium for chlorine-free paper
		Closed-loop processes (still problematic)	
Paint and coatings	Volatile organic compounds (VOCs) in solvents	New paint formulations (low-solvent-content paints, water-borne paints)	Price premium for solvent-free paints
		Improved application techniques	Improved coatings quality in some segments
		Powder or radiation-cured coatings	Worker safety benefits
			Higher coatings-transfer efficiency
			Reduced coating costs through materials savings
Electronics manufacturing	Volatile organic compounds (VOCs) in cleaning agents	Semiaqueous, terpene--based cleaning agents	Increase in cleaning quality and thus in product quality
		Closed-loop systems	30% to 80% reduction in cleaning costs, often for one-year pay-back periods
		No-clean soldering where possible	Elimination of an unnecessary production step
Refrigerators	Chlorofluorocarbons (CFCs) used as refrigerants	Alternative refrigerants (propane-isobutane mix)	10% better energy efficiency at same cost
	Energy usage	Thicker insulation	5% to 10% initial price premium for "green" refrigerator
	Disposal	Better gaskets	
		Improved compressors	
Dry cell batteries	Cadmium, mercury, lead, nickel, cobalt, lithium, and zinc releases in landfills or to the air (after incineration)	Rechargeable batteries of nickel-hydride (for some applications)	Nearly twice as efficient at same cost
		Rechargeable lithium batteries (now being developed)	Expected to be price competitive in the near future
			Higher energy efficiency
Printing inks	VOCs in petroleum inks	Water-based inks and soy inks	Higher efficiency, brighter colors, and better printability (depending on application)

a Rhône-Poulenc plant in Chalampe, France, nylon by-products known as diacids used to be incinerated. Rhône-Poulenc invested 76 million francs and installed new equipment to recover and sell these diacids as additives for dyes and tanning and as coagulation agents. The new recovery process has generated annual revenues of about 20.1 million francs. New de-inking technologies developed by Massachusetts-based Thermo Electron Corporation, among others, are allowing more extensive use of recycled paper. Molten Metal Technology of Waltham, Massachusetts, has developed a cost-saving catalytic extraction method to process many types of hazardous waste.

The second and far more interesting and important type of innovation addresses the root causes of pollution by improving resource productivity in the first place. Innovation offsets can take many forms, including more efficient utilization of particular inputs, better product yields, and better products. (See the insert "Environmental Improvement Can Benefit Resource Productivity.") Consider the following examples.

Resource productivity improves when less costly materials are substituted or when existing ones are better utilized. Dow Chemical's California complex scrubs hydrochloric gas with caustic to produce a wide range of chemicals. The company used to store the wastewater in evaporation ponds. Regulation called for Dow to close the evaporation ponds by 1988. In 1987, under pressure to comply with the new law, the company redesigned its production process. It reduced the use of caustic soda, decreasing caustic waste by 6,000 tons per year and hydrochloric acid waste by eighty tons per year. Dow also found that it could capture a portion of the waste stream for reuse as a raw material in other parts of the plant. Although it cost only $250,000 to implement, the process gave Dow an annual savings of $2.4 million.[3]

3M also improved resource productivity. Forced to comply with new regulations to reduce solvent emissions by 90 percent, 3M found a way to avoid the use of solvents altogether by coating products with safer, water-based solutions. The company gained an early-mover advantage in product development over competitors, many of whom switched significantly later. The company also shortened its time to market because its water-based product did not have to go through the approval process for solvent-based coatings.[4]

3M found that innovations can improve process consistency, reduce downtime, and lower costs substantially. The company used to produce adhesives in batches that were then transferred to storage tanks. One bad batch could spoil the entire contents of a tank. Lost product, down-time, and expensive hazardous-waste disposal were the result. 3M developed a new technique to run rapid quality tests on new batches. It

Environmental Improvement Can Benefit Resource Productivity

Process Benefits

• materials savings resulting from more complete processing, substitution, reuse, or recycling of production inputs

• increases in process yields

• less downtime through more careful monitoring and maintenance

• better utilization of by-products

• conversion of waste into valuable forms

• lower energy consumption during the production process

• reduced material storage and handling costs

• savings from safer workplace conditions

• elimination or reduction of the cost of activities involved in discharges or waste handling, transportation, and disposal

• improvements in the product as a by-product of process changes (such as better process control)

Product Benefits

• higher quality, more consistent products

• lower product costs (for instance, from material substitution)

• lower packaging costs

• more efficient resource use by products

• safer products

• lower net costs of product disposal to customers

• higher product resale and scrap value

reduced hazardous wastes by 110 tons per year at almost no cost, yielding an annual savings of more than $200,000.[5]

Many chemical-production processes require an initial start-up period after production interruptions in order to stabilize output and bring it within specifications. During that time, only scrap material is produced. When regulations raised the cost of waste disposal, DuPont was motivated to install higher-quality monitoring equipment, which in turn reduced production interruptions and the associated production startups. DuPont lowered not only its waste generation but also cut the amount of time it wasn't producing anything.[6]

Process changes to reduce emissions and use resources more productively often result in higher yields. As a result of new environmental standards, Ciba-Geigy Corporation reexamined the waste-water streams at its dye plant in Tom's River, New Jersey. Engineers made two changes to the production process. First, they replaced sludge-creating iron with a less harmful chemical conversion agent. Second, they eliminated the release of a potentially toxic product into the wastewater stream. They not only reduced pollution but also increased process yields by 40 percent, realizing an annual cost savings of $740,000. Although that part of the plant was ultimately closed, the example illustrates the role of regulatory pressure in process innovation.

Process innovations to comply with environmental regulation can even improve product consistency and quality. In 1990, the Montreal Protocol and the U.S. Clean Air Act required electronics companies to eliminate ozone-depleting chlorofluorocarbons (CFCs). Many companies used them as cleaning agents to remove residues that occur in the manufacture of printed circuit boards. Scientists at Raytheon confronted the regulatory challenge. Initially, they thought that complete elimination of CFCs would be impossible. After research, however, they found an alternate cleaning agent that could be reused in a closed-loop system. The new method improved average product quality — which the old CFC-based cleaning agent had occasionally compromised — while also lowering operating costs. Responding to the same regulation, other researchers identified applications that did not require any cleaning at all and developed so-called no-clean soldering technologies, which lowered operating costs without compromising quality. Without environmental regulation, that innovation would not have happened.

Innovations to address environmental regulations can also lower product costs and boost resource productivity by reducing unnecessary packaging or simplifying designs. A 1991 law in Japan set standards to make products easier to recycle. Hitachi, along with other Japanese appliance producers, responded by redesigning products to reduce disassembly time. In the process, it cut back the number of parts in a washing machine by 16 percent and the number of parts in a vacuum cleaner by 30 percent. Fewer components made the products easier not only to disassemble but also to assemble in the first place. Regulation that requires such recyclable products can lower the user's disposal costs and lead to designs that allow a company to recover valuable materials more easily. Either the customer or the manufacturer who takes back used products reaps greater value.

Although such product innovations have been prompted by regulators instead of by customers, world demand is putting a higher value on resource-efficient products. Many companies are using innovations to command price premiums for "green" products and to open up new market segments. Because Germany adopted recycling standards earlier than most other countries, German companies have first-mover advantages in developing less packaging-intensive products, which are both lower in cost and sought after in the marketplace. In the United States, Cummins Engine Company's development of low-emissions diesel engines for such applications as trucks and buses — innovation that U.S. environmental regulations spurred — is allowing it to gain position in international markets where similar needs are growing.

These examples and many others like them do not prove that companies always can innovate to reduce environmental impact at low cost. However, they show that there are considerable opportunities to reduce pollution through innovations that redesign products, processes, and methods of operation. Such examples are common in spite of companies' resistance to environmental regulation and in spite of regulatory standards that often are hostile to innovative, resource-productive solutions. The fact that such examples are common carries an important message:

Today a new frame of reference for thinking about environmental improvement is urgently needed.

DO WE REALLY NEED REGULATION?

If innovation in response to environmental regulation can be profitable — if a company can actually offset the cost of compliance through improving resource productivity — why is regulation necessary at all? If such opportunities exist, wouldn't companies pursue them naturally and wouldn't regulation be unnecessary? That is like saying there will rarely be ten-dollar bills to be found on the ground because someone already will have picked them up.

Certainly, some companies do pursue such innovations without, or in advance of, regulation. In Germany and Scandinavia, where both companies and consumers are very attuned to environmental concerns, innovation is not uncommon. As companies and their customers adopt the resource productivity mind-set and as knowledge about innovative technologies grows, there may well be less need for regulation over time in the United States.

But the belief that companies will pick up on profitable opportunities without a regulatory push makes a false assumption about competitive reality — namely, that all profitable opportunities for innovation have already been discovered, that all managers have perfect information about them, and that organizational incentives are aligned with innovating. In fact, in the real world, managers often have highly incomplete information and limited time and attention. Barriers to change are numerous. The Environmental Protection Agency's Green Lights program, which works with companies to promote energy-saving lighting, shows that many ten-dollar bills are still waiting to be picked up. In one audit, nearly 80 percent of the projects offered paybacks within two years or less, and yet the companies considering them had not taken action.[7] Only after companies joined the program and benefited from the EPA's information and cajoling were such highly profitable projects implemented.

We are now in a transitional phase of industrial history in which companies are still inexperienced in handling environmental issues creatively. Customers, too, are unaware that resource inefficiency means that they must pay for the cost of pollution. For example, they tend to see discarded packaging as free because there is no separate charge for it and no current lower-cost alternative. Because there is no direct way to recapture the value of the wasted resources that customers already have paid for, they imagine that discarding used products carries no cost penalty for them.

Regulation, although a different type than is currently practiced, is needed for six major reasons:

• To create pressure that motivates companies to innovate. Our broader research on competitiveness highlights the important role of outside pressure in overcoming organizational inertia and fostering creative thinking.

• To improve environmental quality in cases in which innovation and the resulting improvements in resource productivity do not completely offset the cost of compliance; or in which it takes time for learning effects to reduce the overall cost of innovative solutions.

• To alert and educate companies about likely resource inefficiencies and potential areas for technological improvement (although government cannot know better than companies how to address them).

• To raise the likelihood that product innovations and process innovations in general will be environmentally friendly.

• To create demand for environmental improvement until companies and customers are able to perceive and measure the resource inefficiencies of pollution better.

• To level the playing field during the transition period to innovation-based environmental solutions, ensuring that one company cannot gain position by avoiding environmental investments. Regulation provides a buffer for innovative companies until new technologies are proven and the effects of learning can reduce technological costs.

Those who believe that market forces alone will spur innovation may argue that total quality management programs were initiated without regulatory intervention. However, TQM came to the United States and Europe through a different kind of pressure. Decades earlier, TQM had been widely diffused in Japan — the result of a whole host of government efforts to make product quality a national goal, including the creation of the Deming Prize. Only after Japanese companies had devastated them in the marketplace did Americans and Europeans embrace TQM.

THE COST OF THE STATIC MIND-SET

Regulators and companies should focus, then, on relaxing the trade-off between environmental protection and competitiveness by encouraging innovation and resource productivity. Yet the current adversarial climate drives up the costs of meeting environmental standards and circumscribes the innovation benefits, making the trade-off far steeper than it needs to be.

To begin with, the power struggle involved in setting and enforcing environmental regulations consumes enormous amounts of resources. A 1992 study by the Rand Institute for Civil Justice, for example, found that 88 percent of the money that insurers paid out between 1986 and 1989 on Superfund claims went to pay for legal and administrative costs, whereas only 12 percent was used for actual site cleanups.[8] The Superfund law may well be the most inefficient environmental law in the United States, but it is not the only cause of inefficiency. We believe that a substantial fraction of environmental spending as well as of the revenues of environmental products and services companies relates to the regulatory struggle itself and not to improving the environment.

One problem with the adversarial process is that it locks companies into static thinking and systematically pushes industry estimates of the costs of regulation upward. A classic example occurred during the debate in the United States on the 1970 Clean Air Act. Lee Iacocca, then executive vice president of the Ford Motor Company, predicted that compliance with the new regulations would require huge price increases for automobiles, force U.S. production to a halt by 1975, and severely damage the U.S. economy. The 1970 Clean Air Act was subsequently enacted, and Iacocca's dire predictions turned out to be wrong. Similar stories are common.

Static thinking causes companies to fight environmental standards that actually could enhance their competitiveness. Most distillers of coal tar in the United States, for example, opposed 1991 regulations requiring substantial reductions in benzene emissions. At the time, the only solution was to cover the tar storage tanks with costly gas blankets. But the regulation spurred Aristech Chemical Corporation of Pittsburgh, Pennsylvania, to develop a way to remove benzene from tar in the first processing step, thereby eliminating the need for gas blankets. Instead of suffering a cost increase, Aristech saved itself $3.3 million.

Moreover, company mind-sets make the costs of addressing environmental regulations appear higher than they actually are. Many companies do not account for a learning curve, although the actual costs of compliance are likely to decline over time. A recent study in the pulp-and-paper sector, for example, found the actual costs of compliance to be four dollars to five dollars and fifty cents per ton, whereas original industry estimates had been as high as sixteen dollars and forty cents.[9] Similarly, the cost of compliance with a 1990 regulation controlling sulfur dioxide emissions is today only about half of what analysts initially predicted, and it is heading lower. With a focus on innovation and resource productivity, today's compliance costs represent an upper limit.

There is legitimate controversy over the benefits to society of specific environmental standards. Measuring the health and safety effects of cleaner air, for example, is the subject of ongoing scientific debate. Some believe that the risks of pollution have been overstated. But whatever the level of social benefits proves to be, the private costs to companies are still far higher than necessary.

GOOD REGULATION VERSUS BAD

In addition to being high-cost, the current system of environmental regulation in the United States often deters innovative solutions or renders them impossible. The problem with regulation is not its strictness. It is the way in which standards are written and the sheer inefficiency with which regulations are administered. Strict standards can and should promote resource productivity. The United States' regulatory process has squandered this potential, however, by concentrating on cleanup instead of prevention, mandating specific technologies, setting compliance deadlines that are unrealistically short, and subjecting companies to unnecessarily high levels of uncertainty.

The current system discourages risk taking and experimentation. Liability exposure and the government's inflexibility in enforcement, among other things, contribute to the problem. For example, a company that innovates and achieves 95 percent of target emissions reduction while also registering substantial offsetting cost reductions is still 5 percent out of compliance and subject to liability. On the other hand, regulators would reward it for adopting safe but expensive secondary treatment. (See the insert "Innovation-Friendly Regulation.")

Just as bad regulation can damage competitiveness, good regulation can enhance it. Consider the differences between the U.S. pulp-and-paper sector and the Scandinavian. Strict early U.S. regulations in the 1970s were imposed without adequate phase-in periods, forcing companies to adopt best available technologies quickly. At that time, the requirements invariably meant installing proven but costly end-of-pipe treatment systems. In Scandinavia, on the other hand, regulation permitted more flexible approaches, enabling companies to focus on the production process itself, not just on secondary treatment of wastes. Scandinavian companies developed innovative pulping and bleaching technologies that not only met emission requirements but also lowered operating costs. Even though the United States was the first to regulate, U.S. companies were unable to realize any first-mover advantages because U.S. regulations ignored a critical principle of good environmental regulation: Create maximum opportunity for innovation by letting industries discover how to solve their own problems.

Unfortunately for the U.S. pulp-and-paper industry, a second principle of good regulation was also ignored: Foster continuous improvement; do not lock in on a particular technology or the status quo. The Swedish regulatory agency took a more effective approach. Whereas the United States mandated strict emissions goals and established very tight compliance deadlines, Sweden started out with looser standards but clearly communicated that tougher ones would follow. The results were predictable. U.S. companies installed secondary treatment systems and stopped there. Swedish producers, anticipating stricter standards, continually incorporated innovative environmental technologies into their normal cycles of capacity replacement and innovation.

Innovation-Friendly Regulation

Regulation, properly conceived, need not drive up costs. The following principles of regulatory design will promote innovation, resource productivity, and competitiveness:

Focus on outcomes, not technologies. Past regulations have often prescribed particular remediation technologies, such as catalysts or scrubbers for air pollution. The phrases "best available technology" (BAT) and "best available control technology" (BACT) are deeply rooted in U.S. practice and imply that one technology is best, discouraging innovation.

Enact strict rather than lax regulation. Companies can handle lax regulation incrementally, often with end-of-pipe or secondary treatment solutions. Regulation, therefore, needs to be stringent enough to promote real innovation.

Regulate as close to the end user as practical, while encouraging upstream solutions. This will normally allow more flexibility for innovation in the end product and in all the production and distribution stages. Avoiding pollution entirely or, second best, mitigating it early in the value chain is almost always less costly than late-stage remediation or cleanup.

Employ phase-in periods. Ample but well-defined phase-in periods tied to industry-capital-investment cycles will allow companies to develop innovative resource-saving technologies rather than force them to implement expensive solutions hastily, merely patching over problems. California imposed such short compliance deadlines on its wood-furniture industry that many manufacturers chose to leave the state rather than add costly control equipment.

Use market incentives. Market incentives such as pollution charges and deposit-refund schemes draw attention to resource inefficiencies. In addition, tradable permits provide continuing incentives for innovation and encourage creative use of technologies that exceed current standards.

Harmonize or converge regulations in associated fields. Liability exposure in the United States leads companies to stick to safe, BAT approaches, and inconsistent regulation on alternative technologies deters beneficial innovation. For example, one way to eliminate refrigerator cooling agents suspected of damaging the ozone layer involves replacing them with small amounts of propane and butane. But narrowly conceived safety regulations covering these gases seem to have impeded development of the new technology in the United States, while several leading European companies are already marketing the new products.

Develop regulations in sync with other countries or slightly ahead of them. It is important to minimize possible competitive disadvantages relative to foreign companies that are not yet subject to the same standard. Developing regulations slightly ahead of other countries will also maximize export potential in the pollution-control sector by raising incentives for innovation. When standards in the United States lead world developments, domestic companies get opportunities for valuable early-mover advantages. However, if standards are too far ahead of, or too different in character from, those that are likely to apply to foreign competitors, industry may innovate in the wrong directions.

Make the regulatory process more stable and predictable. The regulatory process is as important as the standards. If standards and phase-in periods are set and accepted early enough and if regulators commit to keeping standards in place for, say, five years, industry can lock in and tackle root-cause solutions instead of hedging against the next twist or turn in government philosophy.

Require industry participation in setting standards from the beginning. U.S. regulation differs sharply from European in its adversarial approach. Industry should help in designing phase-in periods, the content of regulations, and the most effective regulatory process. A predetermined set of information requests and interactions with industry representatives should be a mandatory part of the regulatory process. Both industry and regulators must work toward a climate of trust because industry needs to provide genuinely useful information and regulators need to take industry input seriously.

Develop strong technical capabilities among regulators. Regulators must understand an industry's economics and what drives its competitiveness. Better information exchange will help avoid costly gaming in which ill-informed companies use an array of lawyers and consultants to try to stall the poorly designed regulations of ill-informed regulators.

Minimize the time and resources consumed in the regulatory process itself. Time delays in granting permits are usually costly for companies. Self-regulation with periodic inspections would be more efficient than requiring formal approvals. Potential and actual litigation creates uncertainty and consumes resources. Mandatory arbitration procedures or rigid arbitration steps before litigation would lower costs and encourage innovation.

For an extended discussion of the ways in which environmental regulation should change, see Michael E. Porter and Claas van der Linde, "Toward a New Conception of the Environment-Competitiveness Relationship," *Journal of Economic Perspectives* 9, no. 4 (fall 1995).

The innovation-friendly approach produced the residual effect of raising the competitiveness of the local equipment industry. Spurred by Scandinavian demand for sophisticated process improvements, local pulp-and-paper-equipment suppliers, such as Sunds Defibrator and Kamyr, ultimately made major international gains in selling innovative pulping and bleaching equipment.

Eventually, the Scandinavian pulp-and-paper industry was able to reap innovation offsets that went beyond those directly stemming from regulatory pressures. By the early 1990s, producers realized that growing public awareness of the environmental problems associated with pulp-mill effluents was creating a niche market. For a time, Scandinavian companies with totally chlorine-free paper were able to command significant price premiums and serve a rapidly growing market segment of environmentally informed customers.

IMPLICATIONS FOR COMPANIES

Certainly, misguided regulatory approaches have imposed a heavy burden on companies. But managers who have responded by digging in their heels to oppose all regulation have been shortsighted as well. It is no secret that Japanese and German automobile makers developed lighter and more fuel-efficient cars in response to new fuel consumption standards, while the less competitive U.S. car industry fought such standards and hoped they would go away. The U.S. car industry eventually realized that it would face extinction if it did not learn to compete through innovation. But clinging to the static mind-set too long cost billions of dollars and many thousands of jobs.

To avoid making the same mistakes, managers must start to recognize environmental improvement as an economic and competitive opportunity, not as an annoying cost or an inevitable threat. Instead of clinging to a perspective focused on regulatory compliance, companies need to ask questions such as What are we wasting? and How could we enhance customer value? The early movers — the companies that can see the opportunity first and embrace innovation-based solutions — will reap major competitive benefits, just as the German and Japanese car makers did. (See the insert "The New Environmentalists.")

At this stage, for most companies, environmental issues are still the province of outsiders and specialists. That is not surprising. Any new management issue tends to go through a predictable life cycle. When it first arises, companies hire outside experts to help them navigate. When practice becomes more developed, internal specialists take over. Only after a field becomes mature do companies integrate it into the ongoing role of line management.

The New Environmentalists

Environmentalists can foster innovation and resource productivity by speaking out for the right kind of regulatory standards and by educating the public to demand innovative environmental solutions. The German section of Greenpeace, for example, noted in 1992 that a mixture of propane and butane was safer for cooling refrigerators than the then-prevalent cooling agents—hydrofluorocarbons or hydrochlorofluorocarbons—that were proposed as replacements for chlorofluorocarbons. Greenpeace for the first time in its history began endorsing a commercial product. It actually ran an advertising campaign for a refrigerator designed by Foron, a small refrigerator maker on the verge of bankruptcy. The action was greatly leveraged by extensive media coverage and has been a major reason behind the ensuing demand for Foron-built propane-butane refrigerators and the switch that the established refrigerator producers in Germany later made to the same technology.

Environmental organizations can support industry by becoming sources of information about best practices that may not be well known outside of a few pioneering companies. When it realized that German magazine publishers and readers alike were unaware of the much improved quality of chlorine-free paper, Greenpeace Germany issued a magazine printed on chlorine-free paper. It closely resembled the leading German political weekly, Der Spiegel, and it encouraged readers to demand that publishers switch to chlorine-free paper. Shortly after, Der Spiegel and several other large magazines did indeed switch. Other environmental organizations could shift some resources away from litigation to focus instead on funding and disseminating research on innovations that address environmental problems.

Among U.S. environmental groups, the Environmental Defense Fund (EDF) has been an innovator in its willingness to promote market-based regulatory systems and to work directly with industry. It supported the sulfur-dioxide trading system that allows companies either to reduce their own emissions or to buy emissions allowances from companies that have managed to exceed their reduction quotas at lower cost. The EDF-McDonald's Waste Reduction Task Force, formed in 1990, led to a substantial redesign of McDonald's packaging, including the elimination of the polystyrene-foam clamshell. EDF is now working with General Motors on plans to remove heavily polluting cars from the road and with Johnson & Johnson, McDonald's, NationsBank, The Prudential Insurance Company of America, Time Warner, and Duke University to promote the use of recycled paper.

Source: Benjamin C. Bonifant and Ian Ratcliffe, "Competitive Implications of Environmental Regulation in the Pulp and Paper Industry," working paper, Management Institute for Environment and Business, Washington, D.C., 1994.

Many companies have delegated the analysis of environmental problems and the development of solutions to outside lawyers and environmental consultants. Such experts in the adversarial regulatory process, who are not deeply familiar with the company's overall technology and operations, inevitably focus on compliance rather than innovation. They invariably favor end-of-pipe solutions. Many consultants, in fact, are associated with vendors who sell such technologies. Some companies are in the second phase, in which environmental issues are assigned to internal specialists. But these specialists — for example, legal, governmental-affairs, or environmental departments — lack full profit responsibility and are separate from the line organization. Again, the result is almost always narrow, incremental solutions.

If the sorts of process and product redesigns needed for true innovation are even to be considered, much less implemented, environmental strategies must become an issue for general management. Environmental impact must be embedded in the overall process of improving productivity and competitiveness. The resource-productivity model, rather than the pollution-control model, must govern decision making.

How can managers accelerate their companies' progress toward a more competitive environmental approach? First, they can measure their direct and indirect environmental impacts. One of the major reasons that companies are not very innovative about environmental problems is ignorance. A large producer of organic chemicals, for example, hired a consultant to explore waste reduction opportunities in its 40 waste streams. A careful audit uncovered 497 different waste streams — the company had been wrong by a factor of more than ten.[10] Our research indicates that the act of measurement alone leads to enormous opportunities to improve productivity.

Companies that adopt the resource-productivity framework and go beyond currently regulated areas will reap the greatest benefits. Companies should inventory all unused, emitted, or discarded resources or packaging. Within the company, some poorly utilized resources will be held within plants, some discharged, and some put in dumpsters. Indirect resource inefficiencies will occur at the level of suppliers, channels, and customers. At the customer level, resource inefficiencies show up in the use of the product, in discarded packaging, and in resources left in the used-up product.

Second, managers can learn to recognize the opportunity cost of underutilized resources. Few companies have analyzed the true cost of toxicity, waste, and what they discard, much less the second-order impacts that waste and discharges have on other activities. Fewer still look beyond the out-of-pocket costs of dealing with pollution to the opportunity cost of the resources they waste or the productivity they forgo.

There are scarcely any companies that think about customer value and the opportunity cost of wasted resources at the customer level.

Many companies do not even track environmental spending carefully, and conventional accounting systems are ill equipped to measure underutilized resources. Companies evaluate environmental projects as discrete, stand-alone investments. Straightforward waste- or discharge-reduction investments are screened using high hurdle rates that presume the investments are risky — leaving ten-dollar bills on the ground. Better information and evaluation methods will help managers reduce environmental impact while improving resource productivity.

Third, companies should create a bias in favor of innovation-based, productivity-enhancing solutions. They should trace their own and their customers' discharges, scrap, emissions, and disposal activities back into company activities to gain insight about beneficial product design, packaging, raw material, or process changes. We have been struck by the power of certain systems solutions: Groups of activities may be reconfigured, or substitutions in inputs or packaging may enhance utilization and potential for recovery. Approaches that focus on treatment of discrete discharges should be sent back to the organization for rethinking.

Current reward systems are as anti-innovation as regulatory policies. At the plant level, companies reward output but ignore environmental costs and wasted resources. The punishment for an innovative, economically efficient solution that falls short of expectations is often far greater than the reward for a costly but "successful" one.

Finally, companies must become more proactive in defining new types of relationships with both regulators and environmentalists. Businesses need a new mind-set. How can companies argue shrilly that regulations harm competitiveness and then expect regulators and environmentalists to be flexible and trusting as those same companies request time to pursue innovative solutions?

THE WORLD ECONOMY IN TRANSITION

It is time for the reality of modern competition to inform our thinking about the relationship between competitiveness and the environment. Traditionally, nations were competitive if their companies had access to the lowest cost inputs — capital, labor, energy, and raw materials. In industries relying on natural resources, for example, the competitive companies and countries were those with abundant local supplies. Because technology changed slowly, a comparative advantage in inputs was enough for success.

Today globalization is making the notion of comparative advantage obsolete. Companies can source low-cost inputs anywhere, and new, rapidly emerging technologies can offset disadvantages in the cost of inputs. Facing high labor costs at home, for example, a company can automate away the need for unskilled labor. Facing a shortage of a raw material, a company can find an alternative raw material or create a synthetic one. To overcome high space costs, Japanese companies pioneered just-in-time production and avoided storing inventory on the factory floor.

It is no longer enough simply to have resources. Using resources productively is what makes for competitiveness today. Companies can improve resource productivity by producing existing products more efficiently or by making products that are more valuable to customers — products customers are willing to pay more for. Increasingly, the nations and companies that are most competitive are not those with access to the lowest-cost inputs but those that employ the most advanced technology and methods in using their inputs. Because technology is constantly changing, the new paradigm of global competitiveness requires the ability to innovate rapidly.

This new paradigm has profound implications for the debate about environmental policy — about how to approach it, how to regulate, and how strict regulation should be. The new paradigm has brought environmental improvement and competitiveness together. It is important to use resources productively, whether those resources are natural and physical or human and capital. Environmental progress demands that companies innovate to raise resource productivity — and that is precisely what the new challenges of global competition demand. Resisting innovation that reduces pollution, as the U.S. car industry did in the I 970s, will lead not only to environmental damage but also to the loss of competitiveness in the global economy. Developing countries that stick with resource-wasting methods and forgo environmental standards because they are "too expensive" will remain uncompetitive, relegating themselves to poverty.

How an industry responds to environmental problems may, in fact, be a leading indicator of its overall competitiveness. Environmental regulation does not lead inevitably to innovation and competitiveness or to higher productivity for all companies. Only those companies that innovate successfully will win. A truly competitive industry is more likely to take up a new standard as a challenge and respond to it with innovation. An uncompetitive industry, on the other hand, may not be oriented toward innovation and thus may be tempted to fight all regulation.

It is not at all surprising that the debate pitting the environment against competitiveness has developed as it has. Indeed, economically destructive struggles over redistribution are the norm in many areas of public policy. But now is the time for a paradigm shift to carry us forward into the next century. International competition has changed dramatically over the last few decades. Senior managers who grew up at a time when environmental regulation was synonymous with litigation will see increasing evidence that environmental improvement is good business. Successful environmentalists, regulatory agencies, and companies will reject old trade-offs and build on the underlying economic logic that links the environment, resource productivity, innovation, and competitiveness.

FOOTNOTES

1. One of the pioneering efforts to see environmental improvement this way is Joel Makower's *The E-Factor: The Bottom-Line Approach to Environmentally Responsible Business* (New York: Times Books, 1993).
2. Andrew King, "Improved Manufacturing Resulting from Learning from Waste: Causes, Importance, and Enabling Conditions," working paper, Stern School of Business, New York University, New York, 1994.
3. Mark H. Dorfman, Warren R. Muir, and Catherine G. Miller, *Environmental Dividends: Cutting More Chemical Wastes* (New York: INFORM, 1992).
4. Don L. Boroughs and Betsy Carpenter, "Helping the Planet and the Economy," *U.S. News and World Report* 110, no. ii, March 25, 1991, p. 46.
5. John H. Sheridan, "Attacking Wastes and Saving Money. . .Some of the Time," *Industry Week,* February 17, 1992, p. 43.
6. Gerald Parkinson, "Reducing Wastes Can Be Cost-Effective," *Chemical Engineering* 97, no. 7, July 1990, p. 30.
7. Stephen J. DeCanio, "Why Do Profitable Energy-Saving Projects Languish?" working paper, Second International Research Conference of the Greening of Industry Network, Cambridge, Massachusetts, 1993.
8. Jan Paul Acton and Lloyd S. Dixon, "Superfund and Transaction Costs: The Experiences of Insurers and Very Large Industrial Firms," working paper, Rand Institute for Civil Justice, Santa Monica, California, 1992.
9. Norman Bonson, Neil McCubbin, and John B. Sprague, "Kraft Mill Effluents in Ontario," report prepared for the Technical Advisory Committee, Pulp and Paper Sector of MISA, Ontario Ministry of the Environment, Toronto, March 29, 1988, p. 166.
10. Parkinson, p. 30.

ACKNOWLEDGMENTS

The authors are grateful to Benjamin C. Bonifant, Daniel C. Esty, Donald B. Marron, Jan Rivkin, Nicolaj Siggelkow, and R. David Simpson for their extremely helpful comments; to the Management Institute for Environment and Business for joint research; and to Reed Hundt for ongoing discussions that have greatly benefited the thinking behind this article.

SUSTAINABLE DEVELOPMENT LEADERSHIP IN THREE CONEXTS: MANAGING FOR GLOBAL COMPETITIVENESS

Harrie Vredenburg
Research Professor of Competitive Strategy &
Sustainable Development
University of Calgary
and
Frances Westley
James McGill Professor of Management
McGill University

INTRODUCTION

Managers in many industries are coming to the realisation that in order to remain competitive in the rapidly changing world economy they must learn to think globally. In order to become more competitive through striving to achieve international standards of management performance, managers must factor in explicitly to their management processes the environmental and social impacts of their operations. The upsurge of concern for environmental and social risk management is global and now plays a major role in corporate strategic decision making in leading international firms in many industries.

In order to succeed in the global arena, certainly in North America and western Europe and increasingly in the 'developing' world, companies must increasingly turn the public's concern for the environment to their corporate advantage (Cairncross 1992, Hart 1992, 1997, Klassen and McLaughlin 1996, Reinhardt 1999, Russo and Fouts 1997, Shrivastava and Hart 1992, Sharma and Vredenburg 1998, Vredenburg and Westley 1997, Sharma, Pablo and Vredenburg 1999). The public's concern for the environment presents firms with market opportunities (Cairncross 1992, Reinhardt 1999, Westley and Vredenburg 1991), cost-saving opportunities (Porter and van der Linde 1995), or with actual or potential environmental legislation in the various jurisdictions in which the firm operates (Cairncross 1992, Porter 1991).

Porter argues that environmental protection and its proper corporate response can benefit a country's competitiveness. Countries with strong national public concern for environmental protection, or strict environmental regulations, often lead in export of affected products and services (Porter 1990, 1991). Companies whose home markets are relatively lax with respect to the protection of the natural environment have difficulty competing in the world's richest and most attractive markets where environmental concerns are highest. When in the late 1980's, for example, Germany set limits on residues of chlorinated organics in papers, its own producers could generally meet the standards but Canadian firms could not. Canadian firms expected similar limits in their domestic market and quickly switched to low chlorine techniques (Cairncross 1992). When a British publishing firm learned that their Canadian paper supplier was using virgin old growth forest, they cancelled their supply contract (CBC News, October 1992). British Columbia's environmentally-inspired Forest Practices Code, in effect for almost a decade, has motivated the B.C. forestry industry to achieve higher environmental standards. Two B.C.-based forestry firms, Canfor Corp. and Interfor Corp, both have environmental certification from the Geneva-based International Standard's Organization (ISO) (Gibbon 2000). This certification has resulted in increased market access to major markets and major retail chains in those markets, such as Home Depot, who demand that producers log in environmentally friendly ways (Gibbon, 2000).

Globally competitive companies will increasingly find themselves facing different environmental and social standards in different countries. World standards will, however, tend to be driven by the standards set in the larger, richer markets, which also tend to have the highest environmental and social standards. California's strict standards on car emissions have, after a lapse of time, become those of the U.S.; Germany's packaging laws increasingly have become Europe's (Cairncross, 1992). Multinational firms from the 'developed world' are finding, in a world of instant electronic communications and an increasingly active community of international non-governmental organisations (NGO's) (Economist, 2000) that they are expected to comply with the 'developed world's' highest standards regardless of where their operations are found. Nike, Shell, Enron, Monsanto, and McDonald's each were heavily criticised by critics abroad and in their home markets over the past few years for poor management decisions regarding environmental and social issues in their global operations (Economist, 2000). Even multinational firms entering foreign countries with the best of environmental and social intentions have found themselves embroiled in complicated NGO issues which spill over into legal approval issues, as U.S.-based Conoco found entering Ecuador in the early 1990's (Hall and Williams 1992).

Whether these environmental and social standards are to be enforced through a country's trade laws or through the marketplace is currently being debated and was the ostensible focus of the Seattle World Trade Organization (WTO) protests late in 1999 (Economist, 1999). Environmentalists and others argue that countries should enforce high environmental and social standards through trade law, banning the import of products produced by environmentally-unfriendly or socially-unfriendly means. Free-trade advocates maintain that such standards form a new non-tariff barrier, the establishment of which runs counter to the WTO's efforts to liberalise trade. They argue that labelling of products with respect to their environment-friendliness and social-friendliness will allow the marketplace to enforce environmental standards. (This of course leads to many thorny questions regarding labelling). However environmental and social standards are administered, they appear to be rising everywhere. To be globally competitive in the new millennium means to take environmental and social issues seriously and strive for the highest practicable standards, effectively embracing the concept of "sustainable development".

THE CONCEPT OF SUSTAINABLE DEVELOPMENT

With the publication of the Brundtland Commission Report (World Commission on Environment and Development, 1987), the term sustainable development became common currency for the tasks confronting the global community in the effort to protect the natural environment while sustaining a level of growth necessary for prosperity. Framed in this manner, attention shifted from the tasks of pollution control and prevention (output control) to processes of decision making, policy formulation and organization which predetermine the effects of human activity on the environment (input control). In addition, the Brundtland Report definition suggested a new role for business. It sees business as stakeholders or partners in an effort to integrate environmental, social and economic concerns, as opposed to business only being cast in the role of destroyers and polluters of the environment, as had been the case prior to the Brundtland Commission. The Brundtland Commission definition represents an opportunity for businesses to seek out a leadership role in innovating, not only new products and technologies, but also new processes or ways of doing business more compatible with sustainable development ideals. In order to do so, however, business organisations must seek out a proactive stance. We believe that the Brundtland Commission's re-definition of global environmental and social issues, and the Commission's prescribed expanded role that might be played by business in this domain, has given momentum to the prominence these issues have seized in business strategy over the past decade.

Many scholars and commentators, have, however, overlooked the fact that sustainable development proactiveness means different things in different contexts. We are still seeing studies which purport to seek a universal explanation of corporate environmental commitment based on managerial perceptions across industry categories (Henriques and Sadorsky, 1999). As Reinhardt has recently argued with respect to the question of whether corporate environmentalism 'pays', 'the debate has been framed in simplistic yes-or-no terms' (Reinhardt 1999). We argue here that being proactive with respect to sustainable development, as managers are increasingly required to be, may mean different things in different organisational contexts.

A number of papers and reports were published after the Brundtland Commission Report appeared in the late 1980's. Policy makers and researchers working to define criteria for sustainable development suggested that solutions to sustainable development problems should meet at least four criteria:

1) They should balance economic and environmental concerns, not only at the level of the specific policies, but in terms of a balance of power between organisational actors in finance and environmental roles. For example the chief financial officer should be made accountable for environmental policies of the organisation, or the chief environmental officer and the chief financial officer should have equal weight on policy making committees. The need to factor environmental costs into organisational balance sheets is also critical (McNeill 1989, Clark 1989, Commoner 1992, Denison, Hart and Kahn 1991, Kleiner 1991, Runnels 1990, World Resources Institute 1992).

2) They should recognise the cyclical nature of systems. For example, a production organization should not think in terms purely of input-throughput-output, but of the need to dispose or reuse the by-products of the production system. It should also be concerned with the ultimate disposal of the product, and be concerned with recycling materials as a form of sourcing, etc. (Frosh and Gallipolous 1989, Commoner 1992).

3) They should recognise the ways in which sustainable development problems are "domain" problems; i.e. affecting a variety of organisations and sectors. Collaborative action, which recognises these interconnections, is vital for problem solutions (Clark 1989, Brown 1991, Driscoll, Vredenburg and Westley 1992, Gray 1989, Sharma, Vreedenburg and Westley 1994, Vredenburg and Westley 1991, Westley and Vredenburg 1991a, 1991b, 1992, 1997). Within this context they should recognise the need for mutual adjustment, within organisations, between organisations and other stakeholders as opposed to unilateral interventions by single organisations. The former may require a willingness to depart from the speed and secrecy with which organisations in a highly competitive situation are encouraged to act. Openness of information and patience in the anticipation of change become critical

factors (Westley and Vredenburg 1991a, 1991b, 1996, Commoner 1992). 4) They should recognise a need for equity between industrial and developing nations and the inextricable link between economic production activities in the developed world and the environmental crisis in developing nations (World Commission on Environment and Development 1987, MacNeill et al. 1991, Clark 1989, Commoner 1992).

In order to exercise sustainable development leadership and respond to challenges in a proactive as opposed to reactive manner, all four of the above criteria need to be incorporated into the strategic processes of the organisation. This implies an overall shift in perspective. Managing for sustainable development requires a much higher tolerance for ambiguity and complexity on the part of managers (Cairncross 1992, Post and Altman 1991, Westley and Vredenburg 1996).

Cairncross (1992) in concluding her book on the subject asks, 'In practice, how does management differ in the most environmentally serious companies from the rest?' She states: "The answer is complicated by the fact that there is no single set of rules that tells managers how to be truly environmental. (This may be the case because it has taken business schools .... so long to grasp the importance of environmental management as a subject.) Certainly the number of packed conferences on the subject suggest that managers are eager to learn."

THREE CONTEXTS FOR SUSTAINABLE DEVELOPMENT LEADERSHIP

Just as there is no single set of rules that tells managers how to be truly environmental, the sustainable development challenges facing organisations will appear differently depending on the motivational context for leadership (Pettigrew 1988). It is possible to identify three such contexts: market-driven, regulation-driven and value- driven. In the first context, the organisation seeking to assume a position of environmental/sustainable development leadership is responding to a perceived market opportunity. In the second, the organisation is responding to threats of government regulation, consumer protests or protests from other stakeholders such as local communities, environmentalists etc. In the last, the organisation is responding to the internal values of organization members or the particular vision of the organisation's leaders. The ways in which organisations must operate in order to meet the above criteria for sustainable development is very different in these three different motivational contexts.

It should be noted that the three contexts are analytical categories, describing clusters of opportunities and threats which many organisations encounter. They are not mutually exclusive, and organisations with mixed motivations will be able to draw lessons from more than one context. In this paper we attempt to explore and conceptualise the differences between these three contexts in terms of organisational processes and dynamics.

RESEARCH DESIGN AND DATA COLLECTION

In-depth process oriented case studies of nine organisations were undertaken from a grounded theory development perspective (Glaser and Strauss 1967, Yin 1984). Organisations selected for study were those which appeared (in the public media and to environmental groups consulted) to have sought a proactive stance in relation to sustainable development. These nine different organisations may be classified in the three contexts described above. Procter and Gamble, and Loblaws Inc. are companies which initiated market- driven "green " strategies. Shell Canada, Ontario Hydro and Alberta Energy Company (Ecuador) sought to innovate in environmental/sustainable development areas, partly in response to threats of regulation or stakeholder protest. Body Shop, Bridgehead, Mountain Equipment Co-op and the Calgary Zoo are examples of organisations whose environmental policies are essentially value-driven.

Collection of the data involved extensive in-depth interviewing within the organisations as well in-depth interviewing of individuals in supplier organisations, competitor organisations, stakeholder organisations and individual customers (Glaser and Strauss 1967, Yin 1984). Interviews were tape-recorded, transcribed, and coded by the researchers. Altogether 71 respondents were interviewed, resulting in almost 130 hours of transcribed interview data. The compilation and analysis of secondary material supplemented this interview data. This material was drawn from trade journals, in-house and other publications.

On the basis of this qualitative data, we evaluated the organisations' strategies and analysed the reasons behind their successes and failures. These nine case studies provide us with the rich data necessary to start understanding the processes involved in sustainable development leadership leading to global competitive advantage.

CASE STUDY FINDINGS

Value-driven Organisations

Value Orientation and Consensus: Value-driven organisations are in many ways the epitome of what an environmentally oriented organisation can look like and do. The four organisations we examined which fell into this category all had major aspects of environmental action as the single raison d'etre of the organisation. In two cases the organisations were founded in order to effect environmental action. This central value of positive action on some aspect of the environment was a strongly and deeply held conviction on the part of the organisational leadership.

In the case of Body Shop its visionary founder and leader, Anita Roddick, initially envisioned a retail cosmetics chain that marketed cosmetics manufactured in an environmentally sound manner without testing on animals and using natural ingredients. This vision was subsequently broadened in concert with the initial vision. Although Body Shop has received its share of criticism, largely as a backlash reaction to its high profile visionary sustainable development–oriented leadership, it nevertheless was the first large commercial organisation to explicitly effect a value-driven organisation of this sort. The staff we interviewed specifically sought to work at Body Shop and subscribed to the organisation's values. They were there because it was 'more than just a retail job'.

Bridgehead was founded as a commercial division of Oxfam Canada, a development NGO. It operates as a catalogue retail operation on the principle of fair trade between indigenous small-scale environment-friendly producers of hand-crafted products that are organised as co-operatives in developing countries and retailers in developed countries.

The Calgary Zoo during the long time tenure of its visionary director Peter Karsten was transformed from a standard city zoo into an organization committed to endangered species and ecosystem conservation globally and locally. Employees throughout each of the organisations universally share the environmental and sustainable development conviction of the leadership and were attracted to work for the organisations because they shared the values espoused by the organisation.

Mountain Equipment Co-op (MEC) was founded as a co-operative by outdoor recreation enthusiasts in order to make available high quality recreational equipment at reasonable prices. As most outdoor enthusiasts, especially those engaging in self-propelled outdoor recreation which is the focus of MEC's retail operations, share environmental conservation values, these values have become suffused throughout the organisation. Employees from store sales clerks to head office buyers and accountants appear to believe in and espouse these values. As MEC has become commercially highly successful and hired a General Manager with an MBA and 20 years of general retail experience, this centrality of values seems to be surviving.

Collaboration on Core Competencies: Each of the value-driven organisations in the study collaborated extensively with other organisations in critical aspects of their operations. Unlike more traditional organisations which often view themselves as operating in an essentially hostile external competitive environment, these organisations appeared to see themselves as being embedded in the domain of organisations found in their organisational external environments. Both Body Shop and Bridgehead are intimately linked with and involved with the operations of their suppliers and consider them critical collaborators as well as stakeholders. The Calgary Zoo collaborates extensively with other zoos throughout North America through the American Zoological Association's Species Survival Program in exchanging animals from endangered species for breeding purposes. It also collaborates with the Canadian National Parks Service and provincial and national wildlife agencies on ecosystem preservation education. Mountain Equipment Co-op works closely with suppliers on design and improvement of products. MEC also works hand in glove with architects, engineers and designers to develop new stores in the most environmentally benign manner rather than simply purchasing or renting existing conventional retail facilities.

Fair Trade/Sourcing: Each of these organisations considered fair trade or sourcing to be a cornerstone of their organisational existence. Each recognised that historically the industry they were in had profited by taking advantage of channel power imbalances between retailers and suppliers. Both Body Shop and Bridgehead deal directly with developing country and developed country suppliers and look for indigenous or community-run co-operatives with whom to deal rather than private sector corporations. They will not deal with intermediaries or local wholesalers/distributors as these will prevent them from evaluating the production system. A fair price in local terms is paid for the product, and products are not unreasonably marked up at retail in the developed country, ensuring that the developing country producers get their fair share of the profit. Neither organisation will deal with any supplier who uses unfair labour practices, whether these be with regards to women or children or ethnic minorities. Mountain Equipment Co-op, although not having as explicit a strategy in this area as the other two organisations, nevertheless attempts to carefully inspect suppliers' operations for both environmental and social standards and to work with them on these matters as well as on quality control issues.

The Calgary Zoo will only display and breed animals which were obtained from the AZA's Species Survival Program (usually on an inter-zoo loan basis, in conjunction with the endangered species breeding program). The Calgary Zoo will not purchase animals from commercial animal dealers as these dealers might have obtained these animals from poachers in the animal's native country. There are only two types of wild-captured animals at the Calgary Zoo. There are those brought to the Zoo's veterinary clinic from their local natural habitat with injuries and who are unable to be re-released due to those injuries and there are some exotic animals who were captured because they continually wandered into human inhabited areas and caused problems. Two Siberian Tigers would have been shot if they were not captured and sent to the Calgary Zoo as they had been invading villages adjacent to their nature preserve in Russia. At the Zoo, as un-represented genetic lines, they became valuable contributors to the inter-zoo international tiger-breeding program.

Profit Sharing among Stakeholders: Value-driven organisations in our study shared profits among their stakeholders. Not only did they do this through ensuring fair prices to Third World suppliers but Body Shop, Bridgehead and Mountain Equipment Co-op directed a share of profits to their more indirect stakeholders, namely to environmental initiatives and Third World relief efforts. Individual staff in these organisations was also personally involved in these efforts. The Calgary Zoo directed a portion of their revenues and staff time to international wildlife/habitat conservation efforts, namely through voluntary contributions to organisations such as the Conservation Breeding Specialist Group of the Species Survival Commission of the IUCN (World Conservation Union).

Marketing as Education: Whereas most organisations employ the marketing concept, whereby the organisation is focused on identifying and meeting consumer needs, value-driven organisations see the role of marketing in their organisations much more as one of educating consumers to their environmental values. They do little in the way of market research to identify consumer needs and wants, instead, they are more like religious proselytisers, attempting to find opportunities to educate consumers to their point of view. Body Shop has environmental messages and descriptions on virtually all products carried in their retail outlets as well as on in-store posters. They also sell fashionable t-shirts with environmental messages on them.

Bridgehead uses their catalogue not only to display products and describe functional attributes of the products, but also to tell the story of the Third World people who produced the products in terms of their social and environmental setting. The focus of the story is usually on the need to promote indigenous craft industry as it provides a self-sufficient living and represents an industry, which is harmonious with the natural environment. The product is used as a stimulus to draw attention to the environmental/social issue and then the owned product becomes a symbol of the broader issue. Mountain Equipment Co-op is the least advocacy-oriented of our value-driven organisations although environmental messages are prominently displayed throughout their stores and many environmental books in their book section play this role.

The Calgary Zoo uses exhibits as stimuli for discussing species extinction and related issues of overpopulation and habitat destruction. This is done through signage and through interpretative programs by zoo staff. The Calgary Zoo has developed a large new part of the Zoo called The Canadian Wilds. Through major corporate donations and government grants, this accurate recreation of the seven major Canadian ecosystems was undertaken. Through collaboration with the National Parks Service and wildlife agencies, both indigenous fauna and flora are represented in these large exhibits. The development of the Canadian Wilds exhibits has sensitised the local community to the importance of protecting the natural heritage. International package tour companies visiting the Canadian Rockies are encouraged to start their tours at the Calgary Zoo's Canadian Wilds. The idea is that they will get an introduction to and appreciation of what they are about to see an hour down the highway in the mountains through interpretative programs focusing on native wildlife and habitat and the importance of preserving these. Through marketing, the Calgary Zoo in this manner hopes that international tourists will have a greater appreciation of conservation issues when they return home from their Canadian Rockies tour, while contributing to the Calgary Zoo's revenues as well as those of the broader Calgary business community.

High Commitment Culture: Employees who worked for the organisations because of what the organisation was doing staffed all four of these organisations. Salary, promotion, and status for these employees were clearly secondary to the fact that they had an opportunity to work at what they really wanted to do. In a word, all employees were committed to the cause and saw the organization as the vehicle, which allowed them to make a significant contribution and feel good about themselves. As such, these employees were prepared to make efforts well beyond the job description to further the cause. Whether they were sales clerks in a Body Shop or Mountain Equipment Co-op outlet or order fillers at Bridgehead or zookeepers or even concession stand operators at the Calgary Zoo, they considered themselves fortunate to be able to work for an organization they passionately believed in. They all worked tirelessly and personnel problems were minimal.

Socially Responsible Image: Value-driven organisations in our study were meticulous about maintaining their socially responsible image derived from their value-driven strategy. Activities or tactics which might negatively affect this image, however apparently innocuous or insignificant, were carefully avoided. The Calgary Zoo rejected an advertising campaign proposed by their advertising agency because it was inconsistent with their image as a conservation centre: the campaign was to have centred on the ferociousness of the gorilla — a portrayal which might have brought visitors in but was inconsistent with the conservation centre image carefully honed by the Zoo. Media relations are also carefully monitored by these organisations to ensure that the image is preserved. Anita Roddick of Body Ship regularly speaks at venues around the world on social responsibility issues which help burnish Body Shop's image in this area. Mountain Equipment Co-op has pro-environmental signage prominently placed at cashier checkout stations and has bulletin boards in the front of their stores available for pro-environmental messages and petitions on local environmental and wilderness issues.

Challenges: A major challenge faced by value-driven organisations is sustaining organisational commitment in a growth environment. As these organisations grow, will they be able to maintain their singular focus? As Bridgehead has grown, its volume increasing some 300% over a three-year period; the increasingly complicated logistics make it imperative that new systems be introduced for control and information purposes. Employees and managers, while recognising the need for such systems, are concerned that their impact will be increased bureaucracy as well as increased efficiency. Similarly, Anita Roddick has worked hard to keep the high commitment culture alive at the Body Shop. For example, she recounts that when the organization began to have too many meetings she established a set of meeting rules: (1) all meetings must take place after eight in the evening, (2) everyone must stand at meetings, (3) anyone who did not talk at the last meeting could not talk at the current meeting. Meetings, she recounted, were immediately cut down to a minimum. However apocryphal, the story indicates her concern that excessive routinisation may kill the spontaneity and commitment which have been critical to the success of the Body Shop.

The Calgary Zoo, on the other hand, is facing a challenge of limits to growth. Their difficulty has been in successfully fusing marketing and education in order to create a climate which is responsive to their new mission. The zoo is still viewed as recreation by many visitors; support is needed from the wider public to finance their conservation efforts.

Mountain Equipment Co-op has also faced the issue of the impact of growth and retail success on organisational culture. As the demand for staff has increased, some longer-term staff wonder whether newer staff share the same environmental values as the original staff or whether they see an MEC sales job like any other retail sales job. Offsetting this concern is the fact that in many areas of MEC's retail business the technical expertise required to sell backcountry ski equipment for example requires backcountry ski experience, which in turn almost guarantees strong environmental values. Where this challenge appears to be greatest is in the departments where MEC has made the greatest inroads into the 'general' retail market. For example, MEC backpacks, bags and hiking boots are increasingly sold to people who buy them for general purposes rather than backcountry recreation. This has been key to MEC's retail success but challenges its founding principles.

Regulation-driven Organisations

Regulatory Orientation: The regulation-driven firms in our study appeared to be motivated to effect environmental and social change by the prospect of tougher legislation or regulatory demands which could seriously affect their operations. Corporate leadership appeared to recognise that their industry belonged in the "dirty dozen" and that if they did not clean up of their own accord they would be forced to do so. Better to regulate yourself and pre-empt possibly tougher regulations. Among the regulation-driven firms, the concept and words of "sustainable development" were disseminated into the organization from corporate leadership who were in two of the cases personally involved in national and provincial 'Roundtables on the Environment and the Economy'. This is a factor possibly unique to Canada, but it meant that among these firms, the issues of sustainable development were handled with much greater sensitivity and complexity than had been anticipated.

Disjuncture Between Public and Private Initiatives: Unlike in the value-driven organisations and the market-driven firms, a full-fledged 'green' or sustainable development strategy was not articulated by senior corporate management. Instead the concept and mandate of "sustainable development" was disseminated as corporate strategic intent (Hamel and Prehalad, 1990) throughout the organization, leaving specific actions to individual managers. At Shell, one of the most environmentally active individuals was the manager of packaging for lubricants who was developing new recyclable plastic containers. The initiative for developing this program was his; the management allowed for such initiatives but did not specifically stimulate them. There was considerably more latitude for employees to experiment with these kinds of programs than in the market-driven companies studied. Some individuals appeared to have worked the sustainable development mandate into their functions as a result of their personal interest in it. Managers acted personally to develop and maintain network type relationships with environmental groups, for example, although this was not part of official company policy.

Similarly, at Ontario Hydro, much of the success of initiatives and programs (for example, the attempt to integrate both the environment and economics in decision making through a joint decision making committee) were the result of the influence of one "fast track" manager. His personal commitment to environmental and sustainable development issues and excellent process skills touched each position he passed through and left behind him a subtly transformed organization.

At Alberta Energy Company's Ecuadorian subsidiary, City Investing Ltd., an international development non-governmental organization (NGO) professional with more than 20 years of international field experience approached the general manager of the Ecuadorian operation with a proposal to set up a foundation funded by the oil company. This foundation would deal with sustainable development issues in the Amazon jungle where the oil activities were taking place. After using seed funding provided by the oil company to develop a feasibility study and proposal, Fundacion NanPaz was formally set up on the recommendation of the general manager with the foundation's NGO professional advocate being installed as executive director. The foundation has been highly innovative in pursuing the ideas of its executive director in community development and bio-diversity conservation with the support of the oil company.

Industry Standards as Doorways to Global Equity: Consistent with their orientation to pre-empting regulation, much effort was put into intra industry collaboration and agreement to standards. For example, Shell collaborated with other major oil companies in the two western Canadian provinces on used oil collection. Agreement was obtained on how many service stations in a geographic area should have collection facilities and how this responsibility would be shared between the major oil companies. This agreement was reached while there was pending legislation on the books in one of the provinces in which the companies operated. Shell was also involved with international standards setting through their European head office. It was through such industry organisations that companies like Shell and Ontario Hydro addressed issues of global equity. Ontario Hydro, like other utilities companies in Canada, found itself acting as a partner with native groups in preserving game and fish preserves in the north. Alberta Energy in Ecuador has attempted to establish an Amazon oil industry council to deal with regional sustainability issues. They have also made inroads to getting other North American oil companies operating in the region and the state oil company PetroEcuador to become involved in the bio-diversity conservation program.

Sourcing/Market Creation as System Perspective: Given the enormous market these large companies represent, they played an active role in creating markets for environmental products. For example, Shell agreed to purchase a volume of recyclable containers from a small start-up supplier, which would ensure its business survival. Other oil companies were contacted as well by Shell to broaden the market for the new supplier. Alberta Energy, through its affiliated Foundation, is training local people and local community-based entrepreneurial ventures to prepare them to bid on oil company business in the region. Some of these are low skill-based such as vegetation management, cleaning and catering while others are expected to be developed which will be higher skill-based.

Marketing as Education: Like the value-driven and market-driven organisations, the regulation-driven organization focused their marketing communications on environmental education. Shell publishes a booklet on environmentally sound driving and car care habits which is distributed at service stations. Ontario Hydro publishes a booklet on conservation and electricity use. Alberta Energy, through their Ecuadorean Foundation, publishes educational materials for people in their local communities. However, unlike the value driven organisations, regulation driven organisations use such marketing as advocacy advertising to defend their positions in the public arena in which they operate.

Value Commitment: The mindset of senior managers in regulation-driven organisations appears to be that environmental concerns are now a permanent fixture of business operations. Managers at Alberta Energy talk in terms of a 'social licence' to operate. It is not enough to have the requisite permits and approvals, local people at a regional and national level must be supportive of a company's activities. The history of oil development in the Andean region of Latin America is replete with stories of community and environmental opposition voiced through road blocks, vandalism and sabotage. These firms in regulatory-based industries appear to have a greater commitment to making real change than the market-driven organisations who are most concerned with market response but they have less commitment than the value-driven organisations. Shell seems to have maintained their commitment to their sustainable development mandate through the recession in the oil industry. Ontario Hydro, however, underwent a major organisational retrenchment and restructuring to deal with unsustainable debt loads. The corporation cut the budget of its $5 billion conservation programs nearly in half, despite the fact that Maurice Strong, the cost-cutting Chairman, was the Chairman of the Environment Summit in Rio de Janeiro.

Challenges: The major challenge facing the regulation-driven sustainable development-oriented firm is operating in the public arena. Because everything is so closely scrutinised, experimentation is viewed as risky. The firms discussed here have handled this by encouraging their employees to experiment beyond the publicly stated policy stance. Their activity is more radical than their policies. Alberta Energy's establishment of an organisationally separate entity, namely Fundacion NanPaz, could be seen as a way to distance the oil company's public stance from the Amazonian field activities carried out by the Foundation.

Market-driven Organisations

Market Orientation: These organisations are essentially successful consumer marketing organisations who have developed a sophisticated market research system and have become accomplished at responding to market trends. Corporate leadership of Loblaws and Procter and Gamble is not particularly personally committed to environmental change but is adept at recognising the importance of responding to consumer demand for environmentally friendly products. These organisations are particularly good at mobilising a strategic response to market conditions.

Loblaws, a grocery retailer, had previously responded quickly and successfully to market demand for low-priced staple grocery products with its introduction of a line of low-priced 'generic' brands. Subsequently it had responded to market demand for high quality (and higher price) in non-staple baked and deli products with its President's Choice brands. The line of Green products was simply another quick response to market demand. In each case, Loblaws was able to enjoy considerable first-mover benefits. After its Green line, Loblaws has responded to Southern Ontario shoppers' penchant for cross-border (U.S.) shopping with a line of low-priced cross-border challenge products.

Product Development/Marketing Collaboration: Market-oriented organisations in our study recognised that developing and marketing environmentally friendly products required collaboration with outside organisations. In order to make products environmentally sound and market them with the support of environmental organisations, input was required from the scientific and environmentalist communities. As collaboration called for new ways of managing a process, this was not without problems. Tensions arose because these market-driven organisations, organised as hierarchical business organisations in which those with authority can make quick decisions, had difficulty understanding why their collaborators such as democratically-run environmental groups could not make decisions as quickly. The market-driven organisations also had difficulty understanding why the leader of an environmental group could not bind his group to a secret agreement. The market-driven organisation considered it self-evident that in order to bring this new line to market, speed and secrecy were critical. On the other hand, organisations such as McDonalds have managed to work out more productive, longer-term relationships with environmental groups. And with their considerable resources and product development expertise, organisations such as Procter and Gamble stand a good chance of developing new products which will reduce damage to the environment. Procter and Gamble has also worked with communities in the Toronto area to start up a municipal composting program and financially supported the development of such composters.

Balance of Economic/ Environmental concerns in decision making: Whereas the value-driven organisations in our study were very concerned about their socially responsible image, the market-driven firms were prepared to suffer denigration of their environmental image (which was, in the first place, not well established) for the benefits accruing from first mover status in the market. This translated into a clear message that while environmentally sound product development was important, if the product did not make a profit in a short space of time, it was discontinued.

Marketing as Education: Like the value-driven organisations in our study, the market-driven firms used marketing as education. The environmental message and explanation is prominently displayed on products and in stores. In addition, senior executives, especially Loblaws' Vice President of Environmental Affairs, have regularly made themselves available for speaking engagements on environmental issues across the country. These speeches spend very little time talking about Loblaws' own efforts with respect to the environment, but rather focus on educating audiences about global environmental issues. Although the motivation appears to be the public relations benefits to be gained from associating the company's name with global environmental concerns rather than a deeply felt conviction with respect to the environment, the educational effects on audiences appear to be positive. Loblaws' Vice President of Environmental Affairs has also published a book (co-authored with a journalist) about the corporate advantages of environmentalism. It is also educational in nature and links the Loblaws company with positive environmental change.

Value Commitment: Leadership of the market-driven organisations in our study had no real commitment to the environmental cause beyond what their commitment might be to 'quality' when marketing a quality line, or their commitment to 'value' when marketing a generic low-price line. Employees in the market-led organisations were more cautiously committed to the environmental cause than those in the value-driven firms when asked the reason why they joined the organization and how long they had been interested in the environmental cause. It is interesting to note, however, that several employees appeared to have been personally affected by working on the green programs. Their sentiments might be described as discovering a way to give more meaning to an otherwise fairly ordinary corporate job. (This finding was also discovered among employees in regulation-driven firms). In many cases, employees held 'personal' environmental agendas, but they were hesitant to push these too far in the context of their jobs. They remained anxious to 'read' the message sent by upper management, based on the resources of time and energy they allotted to particular environmental projects, as a guide to how much they could push their personal views. On the other hand, corporate leadership of market-led organisations appeared to be least committed to environmental change. If market demand for environmental products should wane, so would their commitment to it.

Challenges: The major challenge facing the market-driven organisation is maintaining commitment to an environmental or sustainable development strategy in a highly competitive environment. The temptation will be to cut corners environmentally as soon as price competition heats up and consumers focus on another attribute as their critical decision-making factor.

CONCLUSIONS

It appears that environmental and sustainable development leaders have arrived at unusual functional strategies: innovative ways of defining marketing, new ways of accounting (Runnals 1990, Gray 1990), creative production and distribution strategies, and proactive human resource policies. In addition they are likely to have different decision criteria (Roots 1989), different time frames for product development (Westley and Vredenburg 1991) and return on investment, and models of stakeholder collaboration (Egri and Frost 1992), which redefine and stretch traditional recipes for operating a competitive business (Post 1991). This paper has described some of these from the perspective of value-driven, market-driven and regulation-driven organisations.

In particular we have noted that the different contexts demand different behaviour and different challenges for companies seeking a leadership position. Value-driven companies claim an institution-like role in society although they are often small, young companies. What they 'sell' is a way of doing business as well as a particular product or service. Evidence suggests there is a 'market' for such missions, as well as for the 'green' products produced. On the other hand, if this mission is not sold, as in the case of the Calgary Zoo, support for the product may decline.

Regulation-driven companies operate in the spot-light of the public arena. They tend to be large, well-established organisations and the cost of major redesign is high. They must also respond to the contradictory demands of a number of highly vocal stakeholders. The best of these organisations keep the best of their changes out of the public eye. They "piggy-back" environmental issues onto other human resource programs (such as total quality management, health and safety) to produce unusually participative cultures which allow individual employees much greater latitude for innovation along environmental and sustainable development lines. Their impact is important but subtle as they provide, through a variety of initiatives and programs, a huge incentive for the buyer-supplier network in which they are embedded to become more sustainability conscious.

Lastly, market driven companies seem to operate under the greatest constraints in meeting the criteria for leadership for sustainable environment. Operating from a traditional marketing perspective, with traditional definitions of meeting customer demand, it is hard to shift paradigms to a more "societal" marketing approach where meeting the needs of all stakeholders takes precedence over being first to market, operating with speed and secrecy, producing top performance products. In instances where real innovation seems to be occurring, it is because the organisation was like a value-driven organization in its public image of social responsibility or like a regulation-driven organization in that a core product was under threat of regulation. Still, leaders in this category may make a large difference with small changes. The emphasis on collaboration and on education as marketing in particular offers important models for other organisations in this category which seek to become more 'sustainable'.

Loblaws not only responded to market demand for green products but stimulated such demand with their 'green' strategy. They also create a market for green products for their suppliers. Shell Canada deliberately makes commitments to entrepreneurial start-up firms that they will buy a certain number (usually an economic production run) of recycled product. In order to ensure the viability of the 'green' market for the start-up firm and ensure its survival, contact is made with other oil companies in order to encourage them also to buy the green product.

These organisations would appear to envision their role as global competitors somewhat differently from more traditional organisations. They recognise that in order have access to the huge potential markets and resources in the developing world, they have to become actively involved in issues of third world development and environment (Shrivastava and Hart 1992, Perlmutter and Heenan 1986). Bridgehead positions itself as a market for small Third World producers of craft and gift items. Its role as a much-needed market as well as Bridgehead's commitment to fair trade with Third World producers and environmental protection is communicated clearly to its customers and is viewed as a competitive advantage. Shell Canada is actively involved both within Shell International and in industry associations in the establishment of global standards for sustainable development. Alberta Energy makes no apologies for being involved in community development in the Amazonian jungles of Ecuador where their oil operations are located.

REFERENCES:

Brown, L.D. (1991) "Bridging Organizations and Sustainable Development", *Human Relations*, Volume 44, No. 8, pp. 807-831.

Cairncross, Frances (1992) *Costing the Earth*, Harvard Business School Press, Boston, Massachusetts.

Clark, W.C. (1989) "Managing Planet Earth", *Scientific American*, Volume 261, No. 3, pp. 46-57.

Commoner, Barry (1992) *Making Peace with the Planet*, The New Press, New York, N.Y.

Denison, D., S. Hart and J. Kahn (1991) "From Chimneys to Cross-Functional Teams", paper presented at Strategic Management Society Annual Meeting, Toronto, Canada.

Driscoll, A., H. Vredenburg and F. Westley (1992) "Interorganizational Collaboration and Environmental Turbulence", proceedings, Administrative Sciences Association of Canada, Quebec, Canada.

Economist (2000), "A global disaster," December 9.

Economist (2000), "The world's view of multinationals," January 27.

Economist (2000), "Sins of the secular missionaries," January 27.

Egri, C. and P. Frost (1992, August) "The Power of Politics of Interorganizational Collaboration for Engendering Environmental Sustainability in Agriculture", paper presented at a Joint Symposium entitled "The Challenge of Collaboration in Interorganizational Initiatives to Resolve Environmental Issues", Academy of Management Meetings, Las Vegas, CA.

Frosch, R. and N. Gallopoulos (1989, September) "Strategies for Manufacturing: Waste from one industrial process can serve as the raw materials for another, thereby reducing the impact of industry on the environment", *Scientific American*, pp. 144-152.

Gibbon, Anne (2000), "The new BC forestry industry," *Globe and Mail*, March 15.

Glaser, B.G. and A. L. Strauss (1967) *The Discovery of Grounded Theory: Strategies for Qualitative Research*, Aldine, Chicago, IL.

Gray, B. (1989) *Collaborating: Finding Common Ground for Multiparty Problems*, Jossey-Bass, San Francisco, CA.

Hall, Susan E.A. and Charles Williams (1992) "Conoco's 'Green' Oil Strategy (A)", *Harvard Business School*, (Case No. 9-392-133).

Hamel, Gary and C.K. Prahalad (1989) "Strategic Intent", *Harvard Business Review*.

Hart, Stuart L. (1992) "How Green Production Might Sustain the World", University of Michigan, School of Business Administration, Ann Arbor, MI.

Hart, Stuart L. (1997, January-February) "Beyond Greening: Strategies for a Sustainable World", *Harvard Business Review*, (Reprint 97105).

Klassen, Robert D. and Curtis P. McLaughlin (1996, August) "The Impact of Environmental Management on Firm Performance", *Management Science*, Volume 42, No. 8, pp. 1199-1214.

Kleiner, A. (1991) "What Does It Mean To Be Green?" *Harvard Business Review*, Volume 69, pp. 38-47.

MacNeill, J., P. Winsemius and T. Yakushiji (1991) *Beyond Interdependence*, Oxford University Press, New York, N.Y.

MacNeill, J. (1989, September) "The Ages of Gaia: A biography of our living earth", *Scientific American*, pp. 155-165.

Perlmutter, Howard V. and D.A. Heenan (1986, March) "Cooperate to Compete Globally", *Harvard Business Review*, pp. 146-152.

Pettigrew, A. (1988) *The Management of Strategic Change*, Basil Blackwell, London, UK.

Porter, Michael (1990) *The Competitive Advantage of Nations*, The Free Press.

Porter, Michael E. (1991, April) "America's Green Strategy", *Scientific American*, p. 168.

Porter, Michael E. and Claas van der Linde (1995, September-October) "Green and Competitive: Ending the Stalemate", *Harvard Business Review*, (Reprint, 95507).

Post, J. and B. Altman (1991) "Corporate Environmentalism: The challenge of organizational learning", paper presented at Academy of Management, Miami Beach, Florida.

Reinhardt, Forest L. (1999, July-August) "Bringing the Environment Down to Earth", *Harvard Business Review*, (Reprint 99408).

Roots, E.F. (1989, May) "Decision Making and Sustainable Development", paper presented at the Manitoba Conference on the Environment and the Economy.

Runnalls, D. (1990) "Sustainable Development: Economics as if environment mattered", paper presented to the Economic Development Branch, Department of Finance, Ottawa, Canada.

Russo, Michael V. and Paul A. Fouts (1997) "A Resource-Based Perspective on Corporate Environmental Performance and Profitability", *Academy of Management Journal*, Volume 40, No. 3, pp. 534-559.

Sharma, Sanjay and Harrie Vredenburg (1998) "Proactive Corporate

Environmental Strategy and the Development of Competitively Valuable Organizational Capabilities", *Strategic Management Journal*, Volume 19, pp. 729-753.

Sharma, Sanjay, Amy Pablo and Harrie Vredenburg (1999), "Corporate Environmental Responsiveness Strategies: The Importance of Issue Interpretation and Organizational Context," *Journal of Applied Behavioral Science*, Vol. 35, No. 1, March, 87-108.

Sharma, Sanjay, Harrie Vredenburg and Frances Westley (1994), "Strategic Bridging: A Role for the Multinational Corporation in Third World Development," *Journal of Applied Behavioral Science*, Vol. 30, No.4, December, 459-476.*Shrivastava, P. and S. Hart (1992) "Greening Organizations"*, International Journal of Public Administration.

Vredenburg, H. and F. Westley (1991, November) "Interorganizational Collaboration and the Development of Green Tourism", paper presented at the 6th Annual Tourism Management Colloquium, McGill University, Montreal, Canada.

Vredenburg, Harrie and Frances Westley (1997), "Innovation and Sustainability in Natural Resource Industries," *Optimum: The Journal of Public Sector Management, Vol. 27, No. 2, Summer.*

Westley, Frances and Harrie Vredenburg (1991, March) "Strategic Bridging: The Collaboration Between Environmentalists and Business in the Marketing of Green Products", *Journal of Applied Behavioral Science*, Volume 27, No. 1.

Westley, Frances and Harrie Vredenburg (1991, October) "The Origins of Interorganizing: Three models of interorganizational linkages", paper presented at the 11th Annual International Conference of the Strategic Management Society, Toronto, Canada.

Westley, Frances and Harrie Vredenburg (1996, June) "Sustainability and the Corporation: Criteria for Aligning Economic Practice with Environmental Protection", *Journal of Management Inquiry*, Volume 5, No. 2, pp. 104-119, (Sage Publications Inc.).

Westley, Frances and Harrie Vredenburg (1996), "The Perils of Precision Managing Local Tensions to Achieve Global Goals," *Journal of Applied Behavioral Science*, Vol.32, No.2, June 143-159.

Westley, Frances and Harrie Vredenburg (1997), "Interorganizational Collaboration and the Preservation of Global Biodiversity," *Organization Science*, Vol. 8, No. 4, July - August.

World Resources Institute (1992) *Global Biodiversity Strategy: A Policy Maker's Guide.*

World Commission on Environment and Development (1987) *Our Common Future*, Oxford University Press, New York, N.Y.

Yin, Robert K. (1984) *Case Study Research: Design and Methods*, Sage Publications Inc., CA.

SHADES OF GREEN: COGNITIVE FRAMING AND THE DYNAMICS OF CORPORATE ENVIRONMENTAL RESPONSE

Charlene Zietsma
and
Ilan B. Vertinsky
Forest Economics and Policy Analysis Research Unit
University of British Columbia

INTRODUCTION

Degradation of the natural environment continues at a pace beyond that which the planet can sustain. Governments have historically attempted to curtail environmental degradation using regulation and economic instruments, but such interventions are usually not sufficient to bring about a sustainable development path. Policy instruments are subject to failures, as violations may not be detected, and regulations may fail to be sufficiently enforced. Furthermore, it is often not clear what kind of regulations or interventions will be most effective in an increasingly global and interdependent world (Rugman, Kirton & Soloway, 1997; Rugman & Verbeke, 1998). Market mechanisms are also subject to failure as consumers are largely unable to verify "green" claims by manufacturers, and media exposés of false claims lead all such claims to be suspect.

In the midst of such market and policy failures, the importance of voluntary efforts by firms to improve their environmental performance is increasing. There is growing recognition that "...changes in corporate organization, culture and procedures can yield environmental improvement in ways that a compliance-based [regulatory] approach cannot" (Roht-Arriaza, 1997:294).[1] We contend that a firm's commitment to pro-environmental values and actions is a good predictor of its long run environmental performance. It is thus important for those desiring sustainable development to understand what drives firms to commit to voluntary, pro-environmental efforts.

At least since Thompson's explanation of systems theory in 1967, the idea that firms must be aligned with their task environments has been a dominant assumption of organizational theorists and strategists. Firms that are out of alignment are expected to experience performance decrements, assessments of illegitimacy, and pressures for conformity. With severe misalignments, crisis can be the result. Yet there are different perspectives within the literature as to how these pressures for alignment come about and how they are experienced and responded to by firm members.

Economic explanations for the voluntary greening of firms point to incentives in the economic environment that reward pro-environmental behaviour and penalize behaviour that damages the environment (Baumol & Oates, 1988; Kneese & Schultz, 1975). For example, consumer markets that demand environmental responsibility force firms to adapt or forego sales, and firms that have greater consumer contact have been found to over-comply with environmental legislation (Arora & Cason, 1996). Firms in highly regulated industries have also been found more likely to over-comply with regulation (McKinsey & Company, 1991; UNCTAD, 1993), often in strategic attempts to influence the direction of future regulation such that it is more favourable to the firm (Porter & van der Linde, 1995). Given that firms in the same industry and geographical area often face similar consumer markets and regulatory regimes, we might expect similar environmental stances from these firms.

Sociological explanations from institutional theory also point to convergence among firms in the same industry/geographical space. Firms are expected to reflect the dominant forms, practices and interpretive frames (i.e. institutions) of the organizational field in which they are embedded (Meyer & Rowan, 1977), and these institutions are considered stable, enduring, and largely taken for granted by organizational field members (Scott, 1995). Institutional theory uses the "startling homogeneity of organizational forms and practices" (DiMaggio and Powell, 1983: 148), as its starting point. Norms, values, forms and practices are diffused within organizational fields by interaction among industry members (e.g., within trade associations), consultants who specialize in the industry, the common requirements of financial institutions and capital markets (Hoffman, 1997; Jennings, Zandbergen & Martens, 1997), and executive migration (Kraatz & Moore, 1998). Firms that are closely related in industry and location can also expect to face similar social pressures from stakeholders such as environmental groups, communities, employees, and others. Thus, both sociological and economic explanations suggest that firms in the same industry and location are likely to act in similar ways.

Yet, empirically, this is not always the case. Canfor and MacMillan Bloedel (MB) are two forestry companies operating in British Columbia that have faced similar regulatory, legal, industry, customer, raw material, economic, social, political and other environments, yet they have responded quite differently to the natural environment. Canfor reacted early to pressures to protect the environment, becoming an industry leader in environmental protection by the mid to late 1980s. By the late 1990s, Canfor retreated somewhat from this leadership position, focusing more on profitability issues.

MB's environmental record was subject to strong public criticism.

Targeted by Greenpeace and attracting international boycotts due to the clearcut logging of old growth forests in Clayoquat Sound, MB repeatedly resisted changes in environmental legislation and ignored, discounted, and prosecuted environmental protestors. As recently as 1997, MB leaders claimed publicly that an end to clearcutting would be the end of MB in BC. In 1998, MB graduated from being an environmental 'pariah' to a Greenpeace 'darling', by announcing an end to clearcut logging and a new commitment to sustainability.

These companies illustrate a dilemma for standard sociological and economic approaches. If a firm's economic and social environment determines its responses, why do firms facing similar environments differ so dramatically? Furthermore, if an organization's past largely determines its future through the inertia of stable and enduring institutions (Meyer & Rowan, 1977, Selznick, 1957), what causes these organizations to change their responses to the environment over time?

This paper addresses these questions by focusing on individuals as interpreters of their environments. Individuals in organizations focus on different aspects of the firm's external and internal environments, depending on the cognitive frame through which they look at the world. Cognitive frames are mental representations of a particular aspect of the world (Fiske & Linville, 1980), that are used by individuals to interpret and make sense of their world. Frames can come to be collectively held within organizations (Kitayama et al., 1997; Daft & Weick, 1984), especially through the influence of the organizational leader.

In this paper, we review the literature on frames and on the influence that a leader's frame has on the organizational frame. We then review previously published empirical work about organizations' responses to the environment, and use it to conceptualize a typology of frames that leaders of organizations hold about the environment. By focusing on leaders' cognitions, we can go beyond merely describing behaviours as they exist to focus on how change takes place. We predict pathways along which leaders can move from one frame to another. We propose that movements in leaders' frames correspond to changes in organizational responses to the environment, through direct actions and resource commitments by the leader, and through movement in the collective frame over time.

We end by returning to the stories of MacMillan Bloedel and Canfor, to examine how our concept of frames and frame dynamics holds up in light of their experiences. We conclude with a discussion of limitations of our model and directions for further research.

LITERATURE REVIEW

Framing In Organizations

Cognitive frames, cognitive maps, causal maps, schemata, and scripts all refer to conceptually similar constructs, but different terms and slight variations in focus are used by different researchers (Fiske & Linville, 1980; Laszlo, Artigiani, Combs, Csanyi, 1996; Laukkanen, 1998; Weick, 1995; Walsh, 1995). We will focus on cognitive frames. In general, these refer to the way knowledge is abstracted from examples and stored cognitively. Frames arise because repeated encounters with complex issues and conflicting pressures from the external environment to deal with such issues in certain ways result in both learning and the need to simplify complexities (Fiske & Linville, 1980). The abstracted knowledge in frames can consist of facts, affective responses, behaviours, attitudes, beliefs and values, and their interrelationships. The interrelated material adheres as a category, allowing simplified, heuristic decision making and speeding problem solving (Fiske & Taylor, 1984).

Frames are used to make sense of stimuli coming from the natural, economic and social environments (Weick, 1995). They signal what is to be attended to (White & Carlston, 1983), and allow individuals to anticipate what they are likely to see. When information is ambiguous or missing, frames provide default values based on past experience (Langer & Abelson, 1974). New information is perceived (or not perceived) and interpreted according to how it fits with existing cognitive frames. Frames therefore guide both search and perception, and not only represent individual realities, but also help to create them (Laszlo, et al., 1996). While not all cognition is accomplished via cognitive frames (theory-driven or top-down approaches), Louis and Sutton (1991) claimed that theory-driven processing may dominate for all but the most novel situations.

Shared frames develop within organizations (Daft & Weick, 1984; Weick, 1995). Kitayama et al. (1997) stress that the way a situation is defined and understood by group members depends on communication. One member (e.g., the leader) communicates a definition of the situation either by words or by actions, and the others understand and interpret the definition, confirming, modifying or challenging it by their responses. A common frame of reference emerges. As frames become enacted and reinforced by organization members, they become institutionalized into organizational knowledge, routines, values and norms (Daft & Weick, 1984; Weick, 1995).

Organization leaders play a powerful role in the development of the organization's shared frame: they make sense of issues for their members (Daft & Weick, 1984; Thomas, Clark & Gioia, 1993), legitimize them through attention and communication (Gioia & Thomas, 1996; Sharma, Pablo & Vredenburg, 1999) and shape collective frames and behaviour through strategies, budgets, and reward and control systems (Gioia & Thomas, 1996; Portugal & Yukl, 1994). By examining leaders' frames, we can understand firms' resource allocations and the shared frames that develop among employees. While the leader's frame does not solely determine the shared frame of the organization, in general we can expect the leader's frame to have the most prominent influence on the organization's collective frame. For example, Winn (1995) found that employees other than the CEO may also act as environmental issues leaders, however top management commitment to environmental improvements results in faster and more comprehensive diffusion of policy changes and a greater impact on the organization as a whole. Environmental issue leaders often work through the CEO to promote organizational greening.

Shared frames in organizations can be inferred from organizations' actions and communications. The communications of organizational leaders, and those who have leadership responsibility for a particular area (in this case, the relationship between the business and the natural environment) are especially important.

It is important to note that frames are not the same as actions. Frames indicate the cognitions behind actions, including the values, beliefs, intentions and assumptions. While we can examine actions and infer cognitions, different cognitions can motivate the same short-term behaviours. For example, a firm that is threatened with an impending consumer boycott may make the same sustainability decision as another firm that has internalized environmental values and is fully committed to sustainable practices. However, over the longer term, the first firm may revert back to its former practices as soon as the pressure is off, while the second firm may continue to improve its sustainability performance. Thus, examining cognitions provides additional information, allowing more accurate predictions about future greening behaviour.

An existing body of work, based on case studies and surveys, examines firms' actions and communications with respect to the natural environment. Firms' environmental approaches (or sets of actions), are classified by various researchers as belonging to one of a number of phases of greening. We will review this literature as a theoretical starting point to infer leaders' frames of the environment.

Phases of Greening

Several authors have developed typologies of the approaches of businesses to environmental issues, describing sequential stages of greening that each organization passes through en route to proactive environmental management. (Arthur D. Little, 1989; Gladwin, 1993; Henriques & Sadorsky, 1999; Hunt & Auster, 1990; Post & Altman, 1992; Roome, 1992; Schot, 1991; Welford, 1995). Welford (1995:19) defined a spectrum of greening of businesses: firms at one end respond to environmental issues in terms of add-on pollution controls, while firms at the other end place sustainability as a key priority.

Arthur D. Little (1989) identified a 3-phase framework based on 10 years of work with U.S. companies: (1) problem-solving – avoiding burdensome costs, but leaving the organization open to catastrophic environmental surprises; (2) managing for compliance, with little thought of the future; or (3) managing for assurance, where significant investments are made to reduce environmental impact and risk, despite limited financial payback potential. Hunt and Auster (1990) added 2 phases to the ADL framework: a beginner phase, in which no policies exist, and a pragmatist phase, where environmental policies are important but not a priority. Schot (1991) also proposed 5 phases, adding 2 innovative phases (either company-wide, or in pockets of the organization) to the ADL framework. Post and Altman (1992) characterize the phases as adjustment (reactive response to external demands), adaptation (limited environmental policy integration and external scanning), and innovation (deep integration of environmental policies, decision-making and performance objectives at the operations level.) Henriques and Sadorsky (1999) use the reactive/defensive/accommodative/proactive typology of Caroll (1979) and Wartick and Cochrane (1985) to describe a one-way path to sustainability. As firms seek environmentally-related competitive advantages, their strategic options ideally change from reactive-defensive (compliance-based pollution control) to proactive (eco-sustainable business practices).

Consistent with our focus on cognitions, we look behind the actions of firms to the cognitive frames that underlie them, providing us with information for prediction beyond that which is available from the phases of greening literature. Furthermore, while the phases of greening literature implicitly (and optimistically) suggests that firms progress along a linear path from less sustainable to more so, a focus on cognitions reveals the possibility of non-linear movements and even reversals among the phases. What the phases of greening literature does for us, however, is provide us with sets of correlated practices from which we can infer cognitions.

In the next section, we identify six frames that underlie environmental response and predict different environmental performance outcomes depending on leaders' frames.

THEORY DEVELOPMENT

Cognitive Frames Underlying Environmental Response

Based on the greening phase research and on a number of case studies of firms' environmental performance (e.g., Dechant & Altman, 1994; Post & Altman, 1992; Raizada, 1998; Sharma et al., 1999; Winn, 1995), we inferred six prototypical cognitive frames which correspond to the observed spectrum of corporate environmental response. Each frame represents a probable combination of characteristics that influences how environmental issues are perceived. Each frame is characterized by an interrelated attitude, value and belief set, a set of stimuli that the organization typically scans for information, and a set of typical responses towards the natural environment. Responses include communications, policies, practices, structures and resource commitments.

Specifically, environmental issues can be seen as: (1) not the firm's responsibility, (2) threats, (3) technical issues, (4) opportunities, (5) societal duties, and (6) a personal commitment. Each of these frames has implications for the cues actors attend to and the typical actions those actors will take (Weick, 1995). Below, we specify each frame in turn. Proposed cognitive frames and their associated greening phases are summarized in Table 1.

Frame 1: The environment is not the firm's responsibility. Some leaders do not perceive the natural environment to be part of the firm's area of responsibility. Firms in cleaner industries may not identify themselves as part of the problem. Similarly, leaders of very small businesses may feel that the business' impact on the environment is minor, or they may not even think about the environment in connection with their business. Firms in nations with low awareness or concern for the environment may not see environmental action as their responsibility. Firms whose leaders do not consider environmental action to be part of the firm's responsibility are unlikely to attend to any signals for environmental action and they are unlikely to take any environmental actions while in this frame. The firm's regular scanning of the business environment will include signals from sources such as customers, competitors, regulators, investors/shareholders, suppliers, etc., and unless signals for environmental protection come through these 'normal' stakeholder groups, they will not be noticed.

Frame 2: The environment is a threat. Jackson and Dutton (1988)

Table 1: Greening Phases, Environmental Frames and Their Effects

Phase of Greening	Environmental Frame	Signals Attended to for Environmental Action	Typical Actions
Beginner (H&A, 1990)	Not the firm's responsibility	None (Scan only 'usual' groups)	Inaction
Reactive/Defensive (H&S,1999) Problem-solving (ADL, 1989) Adjustment (P&A, 1992)	Threat	Regulations, Immediate problems, and strong pressures	Resistance strategies: lobbying, defiance, avoidance, bargaining (includes attempts to garner support from other organizational field members). Non- or minimal compliance - often with insufficient allocation of resources to meet requirements. Reactive adjustment to immediate problems and strong pressures.
Accommodative (H&S, 1999) Managing for Compliance (ADL, 1989) Adaptation (P&A, 1992) Pragmatist (H&A, 1990)	Technical Issue	Own technology, regulation and organizational field for least-cost practices	Delegation to a technical specialist function (e-unit), or outsourcing. Isolation of environmental unit from other functions. Just-in-time compliance. Cost/efficiency focus - incremental innovation in processes, materials.
Proactive (H&S, 1999) Innovation Pockets (Schot, 1991)	Opportunity	Market, and firm competencies, strategy and technologies	Environmental innovation (radical or incremental): new products and services. Environmental responsibility is found in marketing and strategic roles. Environmental performance may be spotty: excellent in close-to-market or highly visible areas, poorer in other areas.

Phase of Greening	Environmental Frame	Signals Attended to for Environmental Action	Typical Actions
Proactive (H&S, 1999) Managing for Assurance (ADL, 1989) Company-wide innovation (Schot, 1991) Innovation (P&A, 1992)	Societal Duty	Organizational field and stakeholders for legitimate practices; the firm's own practices and policies	Environmental values and goals are affirmed in mission statement, annual reports. Environmental implications considered in strategy process. E-unit linkages with other functions. Firm follows industry standards and may be involved in standard setting (voluntary over-compliance). E-unit and senior managers are involved in collaborative task forces. Some e-responsibility in most jobs within the company.
	Personal Commitment	Personal environmental values	Ecocentric paradigm. All jobs have responsibility for the environment. Firm is ahead of regulations and industry standards. Environmental innovation (radical) in processes, materials, products.

identified characteristics of issues that are consistent with a threat interpretation: decision makers feel (a) they can lose but not gain, (b) the situation is not controllable by them, (c) they are underqualified, and/or (d) the issue is personally aversive. Threats and opportunities both share the characteristics of having high stakes, high pressure, high difficulty, and high priority. Ambiguous information is more likely to be interpreted as threat (Jackson & Dutton, 1988).

It is easy to understand how environmental issues can be constructed as threats. Environmental regulations and responses to environmental groups seem to involve costs with no possibility of gains.[2] Managers facing new regulatory requirements may feel both underqualified to address them and resentful at the constraints on their own control.

When individuals and groups view situations as threatening, they constrict information acquisition and processing and revert to over-learned behaviors and routines (Smart & Vertinsky, 1977; Staw, Sandelands & Dutton, 1981; Weick, 1995). Firm leaders who see environmental protection as a threat are likely to focus on external signals from their 'usual' stakeholders, often ignoring or not even perceiving signals from other groups unless those signals are very strong and persistent. In the case of strong/persistent pressures, firms may engage in resistance strategies such as defiance, avoidance, lobbying, bargaining or others (Oliver, 1991). If the threat comes from regulation, firm leaders may not comply. Alternatively, they may engage in reactive compliance, doing just whatever it takes to ease the immediate problems and strong pressures they are experiencing. They may commit to action publicly, but fail to allocate sufficient resources to meet compliance targets. Pro-environmental actions are likely to be focused on the short-run only, lasting only as long as the pressure for them is expected to last. Firm leaders may undertake political, legal or public relations actions designed to reduce pressures for environmental response without undergoing fundamental change. Sanchez (1997) notes that firms perceiving the environment to be a threat are less likely to engage in innovation to counteract the threat.

Frame 3: The environment is a technical issue. When environmental protection is seen by the leader as a technical issue, firms treat it as any other operational problem. Environmental stimuli are treated as relevant. Firms attempt to meet their goals (e.g., compliance with regulatory requirements, better resource utilization) in a least-cost manner. Leaders who see environmental action as a technical issue will attend to regulation and the organizational field for the purpose of identifying least-cost environmental practices which can be adopted. They will delegate environmental responsibilities to a technical specialist function (e.g., an environmental unit), or an outside consultant, who will attend to regulations, incentives, and search the organizational field for least-cost practices that fit the firm's technology. The unit will usually be isolated from other functional areas and will focus initially on just-in-time compliance with environmental regulations and end-of-pipe pollution prevention. Isolating the environmental unit from production and line management means that the knowledge required to generate environmental innovation is separated from the responsibility to do it (Porter & van der Linde, 1995). While the formation of a specialized unit is likely to create some parochial objectives for environmental action, as long as the firm leader views environmental action as a technical issue, it is likely that the focus of environmental innovation will be on cost reduction/efficiency, and it will be only incremental in nature. As a result, technical efficiencies may be gained but radical innovations are unlikely to be generated because no one is looking for them.

Frame 4: The environment is an opportunity. When a leader sees environmental protection as an opportunity, he/she sees profitable market niches for environmentally-friendly products or services and/or opportunities to gain social legitimacy from environmental actions. In responding to market opportunities, the competencies, technologies and strategy of the firms are assessed in light of market signals to identify possible means of exploiting green opportunities. Efforts are focused on radical or incremental product or service innovations, with a view to increasing sales. Innovations in materials and processes are sought only if they are visible to consumers. Varadarajan (1992) labeled individuals who hold this frame 'enviropreneurs'. Menon and Menon (1997) suggest that enviropreneurial marketers attempt to create revenue while meeting their economic and social performance objectives. When the leader has this frame, environmental responsibility will be typically embedded first in R&D, marketing and strategic planning roles. Communication of the firm's environmental achievements will be directed primarily and extensively at customers. In responding to legitimacy opportunities, firms may seek to show a proactive environmental face to the world to give them latitude and credibility with regulators, environmental groups and the public. Environmental leadership may be situated within the public relations department. For both, environmental performance will be excellent in areas that are easily visible to interested observers, but may be spotty in other, more hidden areas. It is not necessary for leaders who use this frame to personally hold environmental values: they are capitalizing on business opportunities.

For example, Nick Mayhew, Director of Oikus, identified differences between the principles Shell Oil espoused and its actions in stakeholder consultations and environmental protection. He asked "whether all this work represents an especially sophisticated way for Shell to repair its battered corporate reputation, justify the continuation of its core business-as-usual, and renew its 'license to operate,'" adding that "the suspicion lingers that it [Shell] is more interested in using stakeholder consultation for 'issue management' purposes than for genuinely understanding the impact of its activities and perhaps changing its priorities" (Mayhew, 1998: 8).

Alternatively, firms with technological competencies may see regulatory changes as opportunities to develop process technologies to reduce compliance costs that may create immediate competitive advantage or be sold to others. When firms predict that regulatory demands are likely to increase, they may seek to develop technologies that lead to overcompliance so as to preempt rivals (Porter & van der Linde, 1995).

Frame 5: The environment is a societal duty. Leaders who hold Frame 5 see being a good environmental corporate citizen as part of their duty to society. The societal duty frame is a process frame: leaders who hold it will begin with good intentions and limited actions, but their cognitive commitment and its tangible result (firm environmental performance) will grow over time. As the firm's commitment to sustainability becomes more public, often identified in the firm's mission statement and annual reports, firm members become more aware of the impacts of their actions on the natural environment, and more linkages are formed between the environmental unit and other functions within the company. Firm members, including senior managers, may be involved in industry-government task forces on the environment, and in associations promoting environmental standards (e.g., ISO 14000). The environmental unit may be asked to assess the environmental impacts of potential capital investments in the strategic planning process. Environmental responsibility becomes embedded in most functions within the organization, though it may or may not be incorporated into every job description. As Frame 5's environmental commitments become embedded in the mission statement and enacted in strategy, organizational communications, standard operating procedures and external linkages, environmental values will be diffused and institutionalized within the organization.

As organization members' increasingly focus on environmental protection, they will be sensitized to environmental opportunities and improvements. When the environment is seen as a societal duty, the firm usually over-complies with environmental regulation, and regulation itself is not a principal signal scanned by the firm. Firm members attend to other members of the organizational field and society to identify the most legitimate environmental practices. The firm's own embedded commitments to the environment also become important signals scanned, as firm members compare the firm's environmental performance to its goals, values and norms.

Accepting that environmental issues are important socially leads to questioning environmental values, but not necessarily to the adoption of appropriate practices and the proactive search for solutions. The questioning process gives rise to the establishment of formal structures specializing in environmental issues within the organization. Often the specific practices which are adopted reflect imitation of other firms or inputs from other stakeholders in the organizational field. Practices receive legitimacy when they are endorsed by industry associations and customers.

Frame 6: The environment as a personal commitment. An entirely different paradigm underlies Frame 6: an ecocentric rather than an anthropocentric paradigm (Shrivastava, 1995; Purser, Park & Montuori, 1995; Jennings & Zandbergen, 1995). Ecocentrism involves a qualitative difference in the way the natural environment, with all its components, is viewed. Concern for the environment becomes paramount, dominating other values. The leader sees the environment both as a personal and a corporate responsibility. Typically, such a total commitment reflects a stage where environmental values are institutionalized in the organization's practices, policies, values and beliefs, and all jobs within the firm have responsibility for environmental protection. Underlying this cognitive frame is thorough knowledge of the environment and commitment to continuous learning and search for means to enhance the environment. Environmental issues dominate any other. Such an organization will resist economic or other pressures that may hinder the pursuit of environmental goals. There will be a constant search for new information about the environment and regular investment in generating new means to protect the environment. Radical innovation in processes, materials, and products can be expected. The strongest signals for environmental protection will come from within the firm, especially from the values of the leader him/herself.

Exclusivity of Frames. These frames are not necessarily mutually exclusive. For example, firms may respond to new regulation as a threat while treating old regulation as a technical issue. Similarly, pressures from environmental groups for a particular issue may be seen as threatening while customer pressures on another environmental issue may be perceived as an opportunity. A number of variations in frames may well signal an impending frame change. However, as prototypes with fuzzy boundaries, these frames are expected to represent dominant ways in which leaders and firms interpret environmental issues or respond to environmental stimuli. Characteristics of the stimulus or source itself may trigger variations in the evoked cognitive frame.

We have presented six possible cognitive frames that can be held by leaders and organization members, and which are associated with specific sets of firm actions and signals scanned. We have argued that frames are not exclusive, and that firms do not neatly and linearly progress from Frames 1 to 6, but that frames changes can be non-linear and even reversed. We turn now to a more detailed examination of how frames change.

The Dynamics Of Greening

We are interested in fundamental changes in organizational commitments to protect the natural environment. This process of "greening" is reflected in changes in the cognitive frames of organizational leaders. Some of the change is gradual, and represents shifts in societal institutions, as we become more aware of the fragility of the natural environment and, in industrialized countries, shift to post materialistic value systems (Dunlap & van Liere, 1978; Purser, Park & Montuori, 1995). A more abrupt change in organizational institutions can be induced by persistent pressures from stakeholders (Oliver, 1991).

Frames are not static: because they are based on experience they are subject to regular updates (Fiske & Linville, 1980). However, frames as cognitive heuristics limit the information that is noticed by frameholders. Frame-relevant sources will be actively scanned and frame-relevant information will be actively sought. Sources that don't fit the frame are likely to be ignored, however. Frame-inconsistent information may not even be perceived (Weick, 1995) or may be discounted (Fiske & Linville, 1980). For example, a firm which operates in Frame 1 ('the environment is not the firm's responsibility'), is unlikely to attend to environmental group claims for corporate environmental responsibility because they are considered irrelevant. When these claims affect profitability or the firm's legitimacy to groups it regularly scans (e.g., through boycotts or lawsuits), the firm is more likely to notice, since profitability and legitimacy (with the groups it scans) are relevant signals.

For change to occur, some frame-incongruent information must be noticed. Frame-incongruent information can signal a mismatch between the firm's frame (and corresponding actions) and key elements in its social, economic and/or natural environment. Jackson & Dutton (1988) suggested that threats to an organization may take a long time to become noticed, often building up to crises. Laszlo, et al. noted that "adherence to the classical cognitive maps of the recent past is increasingly counter-productive...it produces shocks and surprises" (1996: 103).

If mismatches are intense, persistent or made salient by others, they can result in incremental frame changes. In fact, they are the basic occasion for new efforts of sensemaking according to Starbuck and

Milliken (1988). Argyris and Schon (1978) similarly claim that organizational learning occurs when individuals detect mismatches in their environment which disconfirm their mental schemas. Once stimuli are perceived, those which are frame-incongruent will be most attended to (Fiske & Linville, 1980). Actors will attempt to find the sources of mismatches and identify new strategies to reduce them. If mismatches are intense and negative (e.g., threaten important organizational or personal values and involve a high degree of stress) they may be interpreted as "crises".[3] Whether positive or negative, intense interruptions will lead to changes in frames.

Examination of our typology of cognitive frames suggests several likely pathways along which these frames may change over time as a result of external stimuli. These pathways consider the endogenous feedback mechanisms that each frame has. Some frames have built-in mechanisms that encourage movement to another frame; others require exogenous input to facilitate frame change. Next, we describe our expectations with respect to the greening process.

Transition from Frame 1. In Frame 1, lack of attention to environmental events and information accompanied by minimal action to protect the environment implies that no organizational learning takes place. Events which increase the salience of environmental issues are key to a shift in the cognitive frames of leaders.

Organizational attention may be focused on the environment if an important stakeholder makes it an issue, or if environmental issues begin to affect the signals the firm regularly scans, including profitability and market signals. For example, new regulations that impact the organization may lead to shifts to Frames 2 or 3. Similarly, significant market opportunities may lead to shifts to Frame 4.

Proposition 1: Transition from Frame 1 occurs if an important stakeholder introduces environmental issues as key items in the organizational agenda or if environmental issues affect signals that the firm regularly scans.

Transition from Frame 2 to Frame 3 or 4. Firms moving from Frame 2 to Frame 3 or 4 face considerable coercive pressure from their economic environment. For example, as regulation tightens, continued avoidance of compliance has costs which include fines, loss of opportunities to bid on government business, withdrawal of licenses, loss of social legitimacy, etc. If the leader does not adjust his/her frame and firm actions, the firm could die or the leader could be replaced.

Pressures from internal stakeholders may also induce a frame change. If environmental responsibility is delegated to an environmental unit, the transition to Frame 3 begins. If the organization has built-in scanning mechanisms to prevent rigidities (Smart & Vertinsky, 1977), a transition to Frame 4 may be more likely. Thomas, Clark and Gioia (1993) suggest that an external scanning orientation is related to the perception of strategic issues as controllable and having the potential for positive gain, consistent with Dutton's (1992) description of opportunity interpretation. Open and decentralized organizations are more likely to have effective external scanning systems and notice environmental changes (Millikin, 1990; Sharma et al., 1999; Smart & Vertinsky, 1977). If threats become reinterpreted as opportunities, the firm will move to Frame 4.

Once a frame change is induced, organizational routines (planning, auditing, budgeting, etc.) can be focused on environmental action. Adaptation may occur sooner if a new leader is chosen, since the leader will often be selected based on the compatibility of his/her frame with the demands of the business environment.

Proposition 2: A persistent exposure to environmental threats may lead to reexamination of the resistance stance of the organization (Frame 2). If a unit specializing in environmental matters exists, the issue will be redefined as a technical issue (Frame 3). If the firm has a strong external scanning orientation and strategic opportunities are available from green action, a move to Frame 4 is likely.

Transition to Frame 4. Often the development of technical abilities to comply with regulation in Frame 3 provides the organization with new market opportunities. Generally, strong market signals that greening will lead to competitive advantage will encourage entrepreneurial organizations to innovate. Early success with green strategies will reinforce a Frame 4 orientation and lead to the search for even more opportunities. Alternatively, perceived increases in regulation may encourage some firms in Frame 1 or 2 to innovate quickly in order to gain negotiating leverage with regulators or advantage over competitors (see Sharma, et al., 1999). The exploitation of environmental opportunities does not depend on value commitments, but may encourage the development of such commitment as the salience of environmental opportunities and issues increases. Shifts to Frame 4 are most likely from Frame 3, but also could be realized from Frames 1 and 2.

Proposition 3: When opportunities for gaining competitive advantage from environmental protection are salient, transition to Frame 4 is promoted. Early success with green strategies will increase the salience of environmental protection opportunities.

Transition from Frame 3 or 4 to Frame 5. As firms implement environmental activities in Frame 3 and 4 to comply with regulation, influences build up which move firms incrementally to Frame 5. Compliance with regulations usually requires firms to engage in ongoing measurement of environmental impacts. By measuring them, their salience is increased (Porter & van der Linde, 1995). Measures become part of job descriptions and standard operating procedures. Measurements are communicated to other firm members, raising the salience of environmental issues within the organization (Sharma, et al., 1999).

Taking actions to protect the environment has a number of effects. First, when individuals without pro-environmental attitudes enact pro-environmental behaviors, they adjust their attitudes to match their behavior due to cognitive dissonance (Festinger, 1957) and retrospectively come to believe that dealing with environmental issues is necessary and important (Weick, 1995). Learning curve effects also improve the efficiencies of environmental protection, making it more attractive (Porter & van der Linde, 1995). Second, dealing with environmental issues becomes habitual and taken for granted. Incremental changes in institutionalized routines are easily established, since individuals and resources are already committed to dealing with environmental issues. Third, committing resources to environmental programs brings them into the mainstream of business activity as items to be budgeted for and objectives to be met in strategic plans. If costs of compliance become large and maintaining compliance becomes increasingly complex, strategic focus will shift to include environmental protection issues (Douglas & Judge, 1995). Pitney Bowes, for example, countered constantly changing regulations by developing a pro-active approach to product design (Dechant & Altman, 1994). Fourth, as other firms in the organizational field innovate to protect the environment, the most efficient innovations become observed and diffused, leading to their institutionalization in the organizational field.

Proposition 4: Organizations that commit substantial resources to environmental protection are likely to adopt Frame 5.

Proposition 5: Institutionalization of environmental protection in the organizational field increases the likelihood of transition to Frame 5.

Transitions to Frame 6. While movements to Frame 3 can be coerced and movements to and within Frame 5 can be subconscious and taken for granted, movements to Frame 6 involve a paradigmatic shift. The shift may be gradual, representing the culmination of a prolonged questioning process, or it may reflect a sudden conversion of beliefs (enlightenment). Because it is a fundamental shift in view, it is more difficult to reverse.

Proposition 6: The total commitment involving inseparable personal and organizational commitments to the environment characterizing Frame 6 makes transition to it almost irreversible. Pressures (economic or social) on the organization to violate its environmental commitment will result in exit (e.g., shift in product mix, exit of members or death of the firm).

While our discussion of frame dynamics focused on increasing organizational commitment to the environment, these pathways may be reversed. Recessions, fiscal crises, changes in government, international conflicts about environmental protection (such as those evident in the Rio Summit) and ambiguity in scientific information about the environment are but a few of the factors which may slow or even temporarily reverse the development of commitment to protect the environment. Particularly as other issues become salient to firms (e.g., deteriorating financial conditions), environmental commitments may be reversed.

Proposition 7: Regression to an earlier frame may result from shifts in the firm's attention to fiscal or other crises, or from information which increases the ambiguity of the effect of actions to protect the environment.

CASE ILLUSTRATIONS

We use two examples from the BC forestry industry illustrate the dynamics of frames. These examples are drawn from Raizada (1998), Stanbury (2000), interviews with corporate executives and analysis of company documents and media reports. In the early 1980s, both Canfor and MacMillan Bloedel (MB) were experiencing pressure from environmentalists and native groups to stop clearcutting old-growth forests in BC. Canfor was also experiencing pressure from the media and the public to clean up its pulp mill operations in Howe Sound, near Vancouver. Both Canfor and MB were subject to more stringent environmental regulations in pulp mill operations.

MB responded to more stringent regulation in the pulp and paper area as a technical issue (support for proposition 1). The head of the environmental division was an engineer, and pollution control and reduction issues were easily classified as engineering problems that could be solved technically (support for proposition 2). On the other hand, the pressure MB experienced on the forestry front was more social in nature – it came primarily from environmental activists and native groups. These groups were not part of MB's scanning horizon and thus the pressure was discounted. MB had considerable social legitimacy as the largest employer of the province, and it had close ties with the government. MB's dominant frame in the forestry business up to the early 1990s was that the environment was not its responsibility (frame 1), but instead the responsibility of the government. MB was committed to following environmental regulations as established by the government, but did not see any need to respond to other outside pressures. MB had been asked to sit on a task force with native and environmental group representatives, but it withdrew because it felt its interests were not being served (the task force was deemed irrelevant to MB's frame). The mismatches in the environment were ignored as MB continued with its economically-focused frame. In a public statement, the CEO of MB stated that there were too many interest groups trying to get 'a piece of the forest pie in B.C.,' suggesting that he was interpreting the claims of the other groups in economic terms, consistent with his own frame.

MB resisted change for over a decade, until it reached a crisis arising out of the Clayoquot Sound conflict with environmentalists from 1993 to 1995. Over 800 environmentalists were arrested when they violated legal injunctions to prevent them from blockading MB operations in Clayoquot Sound[4], attracting international media coverage. The company's legitimacy with the public was damaged. The government, facing its own pressures from environmentalists and the public, enacted more stringent legislation (the Forest Practices Code) in 1995, forcing great stress on BC forest companies as they strove to adapt.

Environmentalists began convincing customers to cancel their contracts with MB, using the power of the Clayoquot Sound issue and threats of direct action (e.g., consumer boycotts, letter campaigns, media stunts) against the customers themselves (Stanbury, 2000). Early cancellations were largely symbolic, accounting for a small percentage of sales. The crash of the Asian market in 1997 and the increasing success of environmental groups in pressuring more significant customers created problems for MB's profitability and legitimacy with customers. Combined with the pressures of responding to new environmental regulation and to public pressures, the environment became a threat to MB. These issues were within MB's scanning horizon, and they resulted in a change in frame (support for Proposition 1). An environmental vice-president, Linda Coady, was appointed in a public affairs function in 1994, during the Clayoquot Sound conflict (consistent with Frame 2). She gradually became 'the green voice for the company', creating enclaves of Frame 4 (opportunity), and generating Frame 4 pro-environmental actions in particular areas of conflict. Her influence was limited, however, by her isolation from the day-to-day operations of the company. Performance remained spotty elsewhere, and Frame 2 appeared to dominate.

As profitability and legitimacy continued to be affected, a shareholder's revolt led to the replacement of the CEO in 1997.[5] The new CEO had experience with radical environmental changes in the asbestos industry, and he strengthened MB's commitment to the environment, making structural and resource allocation decisions to support that commitment. In 1998, MB publicly committed to the elimination of clear cut logging of old growth forests. This announcement was favourably received by stakeholder groups, and received very positive media coverage. Following the announcement, MB continued to seek a position as a leader in sustainable forest management, supporting proposition 3. CEO Tom Stephens said the change was "driven by mainstream consumers in our key markets", not by extremists. He stated "you may be in total compliance with written rules and regulations, but totally out of sync with the social license that you need to be in business" (Truck Logger, June/July 1998: 18). Stephens' talk suggested that he and MB moved into societal duty Frame 5 (support for proposition 4).

The very rapid movement from a dominant Frame 2 to a dominant Frame 5 (contrary to proposition 2's predicted movement to Frame 3 or 4) was enabled by a change in leadership, by the enclaves of Frame 4 that already existed within the company, and by the radical changes that were taking place in all areas of the company. These radical changes required the destruction of old assumptions and the search for new solutions. The new CEO was precommitted to a societal duty frame ('social license' in his words), and he found ready converts among those within the organization who had already begun implementing pro-environmental actions. Many of the senior managers who had previously resisted environmental action were replaced in the turnaround.[6]

In 1999, MB was sold to Weyerhaeuser Ltd. During the weeks following the announcement, Weyerhaeuser executives were asked whether or not they would continue on with MB's environmental initiatives. They agreed to do so. In 2000, Environmental VP Linda Coady continued the former MB's environmental leadership role by leading a joint initiative by six logging companies and environmental groups to resolve environmental conflicts in the "Great Bear Rainforest", an area on the central coast of BC.[7]

Canfor's experience was substantially different. While the old growth forest issue affected all forestry companies, Canfor experienced more significant social pressure with respect to the pollution from its Howe Sound pulp mill, situated near the largest urban area in British Columbia. Health risks from air and water pollution were heavily featured in the media. The community pressured politicians to enforce environmental laws with which Canfor was out of compliance, threatening Canfor's very existence in Howe Sound (transition to Frame 2: the environment as a threat; support for proposition 1). Canfor also had a more open and decentralized scanning system than MB, better enabling it to notice environmental changes and perceive them as opportunities.

Canfor responded relatively quickly to the pressure, first initiating a joint venture to rebuild the Howe Sound plant to be both more environmentally and economically efficient (transition to Frame 4, support for proposition 2). More importantly, once organization members began to view the environment as a source of opportunities, Canfor enacted a series of proactive moves toward the environment (support for proposition 3). Environmental audits were instituted and environmental and sustainable forest management objectives were embedded in the corporate mission statement and performance measurement systems. Green products were developed and successfully marketed.

By the late 1980s, Canfor had established itself as an environmental leader, having dealt with both pollution and forestry concerns. Environmental values became institutionalized within the firm, and it operated in a societal duty frame (transition to Frame 5, support for proposition 4). From 1996-1998, economic threats and business losses caused a refocusing on profitability issues at Canfor. Emphasis on environmental leadership appeared to wane (regression to Frame 2, support for proposition 7), while a new leader was appointed to return the firm to profitability. Annual reports[8] focused less on environmental issues and were more likely to discuss the negative impacts of environmental regulation (see Table 2). CEO David Emerson's speech to shareholders at the annual general meeting in 1999 (fiscal 1998 results) discussed Canfor's four pillars of corporate strategy, which did not include environmental leadership. There is evidence that environmental performance had slipped by 1997: 23 forestry regulation contraventions were recorded that year, as compared to only 8 in the 18 months prior. The contravention record stimulated an internal review of environmental procedures that appeared to have some effect: forestry contraventions fell to 10 in 1998, despite heavy financial losses.[9] The company devoted considerably fewer words to environmental issues in annual and environmental reports in 1998 and 1999, and a larger proportion of those consisted of thorough listings of the company's contraventions of environmental regulations as well as statements about the negative impacts on firms of British Columbia's environmental regulations[10]. These years are not strictly comparable, however, since Canfor discontinued the production of a stand-alone environmental report in 1998, instead including environmental reporting in the annual report. Insiders claim that this was done to reduce costs, which is consistent with an emphasis on profitability issues over environmental ones.

By 1999, financial health had been restored, and the company returned to its environmental leadership. At the 2000 annual general meeting (for fiscal 1999 results), Emerson discussed the five pillars of corporate strategy, with safety and environment being lumped together as the fifth pillar. He also nearly doubled the proportion of words in his speech that discussed the environment, from 6% in 1999 to 11.2% in 2000[11]. He stated, "safety and environmental leadership make us more than a financial creature, they give us heart and soul. They are a means by which commercial value creation goes hand in hand with the creation of social value."[12] The first BC-based company to have all its operations ISO 14001 certified, Canfor introduced an ecosystem management approach to forestry, which involved "continuous improve-

Table 2: Proportion of words addressing environmental issues in three Canfor annual report sections from 1995-1999

Year	Net Income (in $ million)	A. Pro-environmental statements	B. Listing of environmental contraventions and negative statements about environmental regulation	Net positive words for the environment (A-B)
1999	$102.6	24.0	17.0	7.0
1998	-$203.7	20.7	27.3	3.4
1997	-$32.9	46.3	11.3	35.0
1996	-$56.9	42.9	9.5	33.4
1995	$45.6	58.6	6.2	52.4

ment, public involvement and third party verification of performance".[13] This re-commitment to environmental leadership suggests a return to Frame 5, though elements of criticism of environmental regulation (environment as a threat, Frame 2) and lobbying of the government persisted in 1998 and 1999. Thus Frame 5 was dominant but not exclusive.

DISCUSSION

In this paper we have identified 6 cognitive frames through which business leaders view the natural environment, and pathways of change among these cognitive frames. Analysis of 2 case studies in forestry provide preliminary support for our frame typology and for our dynamic propositions. We did not examine propositions 5 (dealing with the organizational field) or 6 (dealing with Frame 6) in our cases, nor did we definitively identify either organization as being in 6 (personal commitment), suggesting that further testing is necessary to either support or refute our conceptual framework.

The absence of a Frame 6 orientation in a sample of 2 firms over time is not surprising. In fact, some cynics would claim that a Frame 6 firm would not last long in a business environment, though some notable examples such as the Body Shop[14] might suggest otherwise.

The low incidence of a dominant Frame 3 (only in MB's pulp and paper operations) is more surprising, however. One might presume that many firms would begin with the environment as a technical issue — a part of doing business that is as 'normal' as production bottlenecks and quality control. The fact that Frame 3 dominated when regulation was the trigger may provide us with some clues. Regulation is coercive: it requires a response from organizations. If compliance is technically feasible and applies also to one's competitors, it is likely to be met with technical responses.

The triggers for change in MB's forestry case, and over all operations at Canfor were social pressures, involving significant controversy and conflict. Achieving a 'business as usual' orientation for environmental issues may be unlikely when the pressures are social and high emotions are involved. Social pressures seem to demand more social responses. Firms in other industries that have not experienced the same degree of social pressures may be more likely to jump directly from a Frame 1 to a Frame 3, as regulations are enacted and technologies improved. Alternatively, it may be that resistance to threats and sudden conversions to Frames 4 or 5 are more general across all firms. Further empirical testing in a number of industries is necessary.

Canfor's movement toward Frame 5 in 1998 despite heavy financial losses that year is problematic for proposition 7, which predicts a regression to an earlier frame during fiscal crises. While Canfor did indeed regress to an earlier frame, the company seemed to be uncomfortable there. With environmental scanning mechanisms still in place from its earlier Frame 5 (internal audits, employees and departments dedicated to environmental objectives, environmental reporting), the company was very aware of its failure to meet previously institutionalized values for beyond compliance environmental performance. It began its return to Frame 5 before it returned to profitability. This suggests that Frame 5 is relatively durable in the face of interruptions due to crisis because of the institutionalization of environmental values and practices among employees and within the firm.

The combination in Canfor of Frame 5 with statements critical of environmental regulation is also surprising at first glance. However, the company has long claimed that it emphasizes the protection of the environment over compliance with regulation. The company's critique has emphasized regulations that it suggests are ill-conceived or overly complex. Thus, the threat may be attributable more to government than to the environment.

Why do we care about cognitive frames? Frames allow us to go beyond static, cross-sectional data to identify why organizations act the way they do towards the environment. The coherent frameworks through which leaders and organization members make sense of issues prescribe which stimuli are relevant and which actions are appropriate. Furthermore, an understanding of the dynamics of frame changes can assist us in both predicting changes in organizations and in identifying levers for change in the corporate/natural environment interface. Firms wishing to improve their environmental performance, policy makers, and environmental activists can all benefit from a better understanding of what will move firms from one stage of greening to another.

A focus on frames provides the insight that proactive or voluntary efforts to protect the natural environment can be motivated by three very different orientations or sets of motivations (opportunity, societal duty, and personal commitment). When an opportunity frame (Frame 4) is dominant, corporate environmental performance may be superficial, spotty, or possibly short-lived (if the market doesn't value the pro-environmental actions), but significant and often radical innovation can be expected. When a societal duty frame (Frame 5) is dominant, corporate environmental performance is likely to be more consistent and longer lasting, but perhaps not as innovative as under an opportunity frame. When personal commitment (Frame 6) dominates, innovation, persistence and consistency can be expected. However, Frame 6 firms are rare.

A focus on frames in the area of business greening also has implications for other business issues. As noted in the MacMillan Bloedel case, greening was only one of a number of business issues that were problematic for the firm. Its failure to attend to green signals in its business environment was correlated with its failure to attend to other signals in its business environment. If failure to attend to signals is a more general corporate pathology, then a firm's environmental problems may be indicators of more general strategic problems. An understanding of triggers that enable firms to change their environmental frames may also inform us more generally as to those triggers than can stimulate other kinds of organizational learning. Future research is required.

Clearly, our research has some limitations. Our focus on only 2 firms in 1 industry seriously limits the generalizability of our conclusions. While our model was built based on general findings from the extant research, and it was intended to apply more broadly, it must be tested with a more general sample before firm conclusions can be drawn.

Second, our analysis is retrospective. While we suggest that the concept of frames can aid in prediction, it may be that there are too many influences in the environment and uncontrollable variables to reliably predict changes in environmental protection performance over time. Only further research can address this issue.

Third, our conceptual framework focused on the frames of organization leaders. When leaders are new and/or institutions within the organization are very strong, the leader's frame may not match the frame of employees. Given that implementation of the leader's commitments is subject to the will of employees (and the availability of resources), in many ways our focus is over-simplified. More contextualized models should be explored in future research.

Lastly, research in this area is necessarily complex. Identifying the leader's frame is difficult, since to the leader him/herself, it is largely taken for granted. Methods can include textual analysis of documentary data and/or analysis of interview transcripts (Laukkanen, 1998). Controlling for other variables is difficult. Because of the dynamic nature of our model, longitudinal or historical data is necessary to test it.

Despite these difficulties, however, we feel that the concept of the leader's frame will be useful in predicting the organization's environmental protection performance much of the time. Importantly, the understanding of leader's frames may lead to an increased ability to influence business leaders to make their organizations greener places.

REFERENCES

Andersson, L. 1998. "Framing green issues as greenbacks." In S.J. Havlovic (ed.), *Academy of Management Best Papers Proceedings*. Academy of Management.

Argyris, C. & Schon, D. 1978. Organizational learning: A theory of action perspective. Reading, MA: Addison Wesley.

Arora, S. & Cason, T. N. 1996. "Why do firms volunteer to exceed environmental regulations? Understanding participation in EPA's 33/50 program." *Land Economics*, 72: 413-432.

Arthur D. Little, Inc. 1989. State-of-the-art environmental, health and safety management programs: how do you compare? Cambridge: Arthur D. Little, Inc. Centre for Environmental Assurance.

Baumol, W. & Oates, W. 1988. *The theory of environmental policy*. Cambridge, U.K.: Cambridge University Press.

Carroll, A. B. 1979. "A three-dimensional conceptual model of corporate social performance." *Academy of Management Review*, 4: 497-505.

Clark, V. & Jennings, P.D. 1997. "Talking about the natural environment: A means for deinstitutionalization?" *American Behavioral Scientist*, 40: 454-464.

Daft, R. & Weick, K. 1984. "Toward a model of organizations as interpretation systems." *Academy of Management Review*, 9, 284-296.

Dechant, K. & Altman, B. 1994. "Environmental leadership: From compliance to competitive advantage." *Academy of Management Executive*, 8, 7-27.

DiMaggio, P. & Powell, W. 1983. "The iron cage revisited: institutional isomorphism, and collective rationality in organizational fields," *American Sociological Review*, 58, 147-160.

Douglas, T. J. & Judge, W. Q., Jr. 1995. "Integrating the natural environment into the strategic planning process: An empirical assessment." *Academy of Management Journal*, 38, 475-479.

Dunlap, R. & van Liere, K. 1978. "The new environmental paradigm." *Journal of Environmental Education*, 9, 10-19.

Dutton, J.E. 1992. "The making of organizational opportunities: An interpretive pathway to organizational change." In B.M. Staw, & L.L. Cummings, (Eds.), *Research in Organizational Behavior* (15): 195-226. Greenwich, CT: JAI Press.

Fiske, Susan T. & Linville, Patricia W. 1980. " What does the schema concept buy us?" *Personality & Social Psychology Bulletin*, 6, 543-557.

Fiske, Susan T. and Taylor, Shelley E. 1984. *Social Cognition*. Reading, MA: Addison-Wesley.

Festinger, L. 1957. *A theory of cognitive dissonance*. Stanford,CA: Stanford Univ. Press.

Gioia, D.A. and Thomas, J.B. 1996. "Identity, image and issue interpretation: Sensemaking during strategic change in academia." *Administrative Science Quarterly*, 41, 370-403.

Gladwin, Thomas N. 1993. "The meaning of greening: a plea for organizational theory," in Fischer K. and Johan Schot (Eds.), *Environmental strategies for industry*. Washington, DC: Island Press.

Henriques, I. & Sadorsky, P. 1999. "The relationship between environmental commitment and managerial perceptions of stakeholder importance." *Academy of Management Journal*, 42, 87-99.

Hoffman, A.J. 1997. *From heresy to dogma: An institutional history of corporate environmentalism*. San Francisco, CA: New Lexington Press.

Hunt, C.B. and Auster, E.R. 1990. "Proactive environmental management: avoiding the toxic trap." *Sloan Management Review* (Winter), 7-18.

Jackson, S.E. & Dutton, J.E. 1988. "Discerning threats and opportunities." *Administrative Science Quarterly*, 33, 370-387.

Jennings, P.D. & Zandbergen, P.1995. "Ecologically sustainable organizations: An institutional approach." *Academy of Management Review*, 20, 1015-1052.

Jennings, P. D., Zandbergen, P A., and Martens, M.L. 1997. "The adoption of environmental practices by organizations in one ecobasin: Variations in local interpretation." Paper presented at the annual meeting of the Academy of Management, Boston.

Kitayama, S., Markus, H.R., Matsumoto, H. & Norasukkunkit, V. 1997. "Individual and collective processes as construction of the self: Self-enhancement in the United States and self-criticism in Japan." *Journal of Personality & Social Psychology*. 72, 1245-1267.

Kneese, A., & Schultz, C. 1975. *Pollution, prices, and public policy*. Washington, DC: The Brookings Institute.

Kraatz, M.S., & Moore, J. H. 1998. "Executive migration and institutional change." In S.J. Havlovic (ed.), *Academy of Management Best Papers Proceedings*. Academy of Management, H1–H10.

Langer, E. & Abelson, R.P. 1974. "A patient by any other name...clinician group differences in labeling bias." *Journal of Consulting and Clinical Psychology*, 42, 4-9.

Laszlo, E., Artigiani, R., Combs, A., & Csanyi, V. 1996. *Human cognitive maps: past, present and future*. Westport, CT: Praeger Publishers.

Laukkanen, M. 1998. "Conducting causal mapping research: opportunities and challenges." In C. Eden and J.-C. Spender (Eds.), *Managerial and organizational cognition*. Sage, London, 168-191.

Louis, Meryl Reis & Sutton, Robert I. 1991. "Switching cognitive gears: From habits of mind to active thinking." *Human Relations*, 44:1, 55.

Mayhew, N. 1998. "Trouble with the triple bottom line." *Financial Times*, August 10, 1998: 8.

McKinsey & Company 1991. *The corporate response to the environmental challenge*. London: McKinsey & Company.

Menon, A. & Menon, A. 1997. "Enviropreneurial marketing strategy: The emergence of corporate environmentalism as market strategy." *Journal of Marketing*, 61, 51-67.

Meyer, J. & Rowan, B. 1977. "Institutionalized organizations: formal structure as myth and ceremony." *American Journal of Sociology*, 83, 340-363.

Millikin, F. 1990. "Perceiving and interpreting environmental change: an examination of college administrators' interpretation of changing demographics." *Academy of Management Journal*, 33, 42-63.

Oliver, C. 1991. "Strategic responses to institutional processes." *Academy of Management Review*, 16, 145-179.

Porter, M.E. & van der Linde, C. 1995. "Green and competitive: Ending the stalemate." *Harvard Business Review*, 5, 120-134.

Portugal, E. & Yukl, G. 1994. "Perspectives on environmental leadership." *Leadership Quarterly*, 5, 271-276.

Post, M. E. & Altman, B. W. 1992. "Models of corporate greening: How corporate social policy and organizational learning inform leading-edge environmental management." *Markets, Policy & Social Performance*, 13, 3-29.

Purser, R. E., Park, C. & Montuori, A. 1995. "Limits to anthropocentrism: Toward an ecocentric organization paradigm?" *Academy of Management Review*, 20, 1053-1089.

Raizada, R. 1998. "Corporate responses to government and environmental group actions designed to protect the environment." Unpublished Doctoral dissertation, University of British Columbia, Vancouver, B.C.

Roht-Arriaza, N. 1997. "Environmental management systems and environmental protection: Can ISO 14001 be useful within the context of APEC." *Journal of Environment & Development*, 6 (3), 292-316.

Roome, N. 1992. "Developing environmental management systems." *Business Strategy and the Environment*, 1, 11-24.

Rugman, A.M., Kirton, J. and Soloway, J.A. 1997. "NAFTA, environmental regulations and Canadian competitiveness." *Journal of World Trade*, 31(4), 129-144.

Rugman, A.M. and Verbeke, A. 1998. "Corporate strategies and environmental regulations: An organizing framework." *Strategic Management Journal*, 19: 363-375.

Sanchez, C. M. 1997. "Environmental regulation and firm-level innovation: The moderating effects of organizational and individual-level variables." *Business and Society*, 36 (2), 140-68.

Schot, J. 1991. *The greening of the chemical industry: an assessment.* The Netherlands, TNO Center for Technology and Policy Studies.

Scott, W. R. 1995. *Institutions and Organizations.* Thousand Oaks, CA: Sage.

Selznick, P. 1957. *Leadership in Administration,* Evanston, IL: Row, Peterson & Co.

Sharma, S., Pablo, A. & Vredenburg, H. In Press. "Corporate environmental responsiveness strategies: The role of issue interpretation and organizational context." *Journal of Applied Behavioral Science.*

Shrivastava, P. 1995. "The role of corporations in achieving ecological sustainability." *Academy of Management Review*, 20: 936-960.

Smart,C. & Vertinsky,I. 1977. "Designs for crisis decision units." *Administrative Science Quarterly*, 22, 640-657.

Stanbury, W.T. 2000. *Environmental Groups and the International Conflict Over the Forests of British Columbia, 1990 to 2000.* SFU-UBC Centre for the Study of Government and Business, Vancouver, B.C.

Starbuck, W. H. & Milliken, F. J. 1988. "Executive's perceptual filters: What they notice and how they make sense." In D.C. Hambrick (Ed.), *The executive effect: Concepts and methods for studying top managers.* Greenwich, CT: JAI, 35-65.

Staw, B., Sandelands, L., & Dutton, J. 1981. "Threat rigidity effects in organizational behavior: A multilevel analysis." *Administrative Science Quarterly*, 26: 501-524.

Thomas, J.B., Clark, S.M., & Gioia, D. A. 1993. "Strategic sensemaking and organizational performance: linkages among scanning, interpretation, action and outcomes." *Acad. Mgmt. J.* 36, 239-270.

Thompson, J.D. 1967. *Organizations in Action: Social science bases of administrative theory.* NY: McGraw-Hill.

Truck Logger, 1998. "New landscapes: In the boardroom and on the ground." June/July, 6-54.

UNCTAD. 1993. *Environmental management in transnational corporations: Report on the benchmark corporate environmental survey.* New York: United Nations Conference on Trade and Development, Programme on Transnational Corporations.

Varadarajan, P. R. 1992. "Marketing's contribution to strategy: The view from a different looking glass." *Journal of the Academy of Marketing Science,* 20, 323-43.

Walsh, J. P. 1995. "Managerial and organizational cognition: Notes from a trip down memory lane." *Organization Science,* 6, 280-321.

Wartick, S. L., & Cochrane, P. L.1985. "The evolution of the corporate social performance model." *Academy of Management Review,* 4, 758-769.

Weick, K.E. 1995. *Sensemaking in organizations.* London: Sage Publications.

Welford, R. 1995. *Environmental strategy and sustainable development, the corporate challenge for the 21st century.* New York: Routledge.

White, J.D. & Carlston, D.E. 1983. "Consequences of schemata for attention, impressions and recall in complex social interactions." *Journal of Personality and Social Psychology,* 45, 538-549.

Winn, M. 1995. "Corporate leadership and politics for the natural environment." In D. Collins & M. Starik (Eds.), *Sustaining the natural environment: Empirical studies on the interface between nature and organizations.* Greenwich, CT: JAI Press, Inc.

FOOTNOTES

1. Though Porter and van der Linde (1995) note that changes in regulation are often necessary to overcome organizational inertia and prompt action.

2. Though Porter and van der Linde (1995) provide several examples of situations where costs were overestimated and were more than offset by unforeseen gains.

3. Crises are a special case for frame dynamics. Firms may revert to over-learned behaviors in a crisis (Staw, Sandelands & Dutton, 1981). If these same behaviors contributed to the crisis initially, the firm may die, or the leader may be replaced. If firm's over-learned behaviors include environmental scanning or other activities supportive of organizational learning, they may respond effectively to environmental crisis and emerge greener than before. In either case, crisis will trigger change.

4. *Vancouver Sun*, December 3, 1993.

5. The shareholder revolt did not specifically address environmental issues, but merely profitability issues. The new CEO's mandate focused

on creating shareholder value, as he saw fit. He identified 3 key objectives for the firm: 1) worker safety, 2) respect, and 3) financial success, and turnaround efforts were focused on each of these objectives. Thus, environmental issues received attention in this turnaround as one of a number of business issues that required change. This is consistent with Andersson's (1998) finding that when green issues are framed as regular business issues, they are more likely to receive corporate attention.

6. The chief resisters to environmental change were also the chief resisters to other types of changes in the organization, and they were fired because they couldn't adapt to the new paradigm, according to sources in the company. More generally, it may be that firms and individuals that fail to notice signals for greening may also fail to notice signals in their environment for other types of changes. Environmental problems may thus be indicative of more general strategy failures.

7. As reported in *National Post*, March 16, 2000, pp. A1, A2. *Vancouver Sun*, March 16, 2000, pp. D1, D2. *Vancouver Sun*, March 17, 2000, pp. F1, F2. Canfor is also involved in this initiative.

8. Three sections of the annual reports were coded for each year. These included the CEO and Chairman's address to shareholders, the report on each of the corporate divisions, and the risks and uncertainties section of the management discussion and analysis. Other sections were not coded because they contained predominantly financial information, and did not mention environmental issues at all. The general format of these three sections remained largely the same over the period 1995-1999, ensuring comparability across years.

9. Canfor Corp. 1997 Annual Report.

10. Canfor Corp. 1998 Annual Report.

11. Speeches were found at www.canfor.com, and accessed on May 15, 2000.

12. CEO's address to the Annual General Meeting, April 28, 2000, from www.canfor.com

13. Canfor Corporation 1999 Annual Report, p. 24.

14. Of course, it is not clear without further study whether or not the Body Shop actually exhibits frame 6 or frame 4, and some of its claims remain controversial.

ACKNOWLEDGEMENTS

Earlier versions of this paper were presented at the Academy of Management Annual Conference, San Diego, CA, 1998, and the Sustainable Forest Management Network Conference, Edmonton, AB, 1999. The authors thank Dev Jennings, Oana Branzei, and anonymous reviewers for helpful comments on earlier drafts, Bill Stanbury for access to his forest chronologies database, and the Social Sciences and Humanities Research Council for generous funding.

WIN-WIN TRANSPORTATION MANAGEMENT STRATEGIES: COOPERATION FOR ECONOMIC, SOCIAL AND ENVIRONMENTAL BENEFITS

Todd Litman
Victoria Transport Policy Institute

INTRODUCTION

Environmental protection, social equity and community livability are often considered to conflict with economic goals. Critics often argue that policies to protect the environment and achieve social objectives reduce economic productivity. Climate change emission reductions strategies in particular are frequently attacked by industry groups because they would reduce employment and economic development.[1] Such claims are not necessarily true. Some policy changes help achieve environmental and social objectives and provide economic benefits. These are called "no regrets" strategies because they are justified regardless of uncertainties about environmental risks, such as global warming.

For example, a revenue-neutral shift from employment and general sales taxes to resource consumption taxes could reduce pollution while increasing economic productivity and employment.[2] One recent study found that increasing fuel taxes and using the revenues to replace more economically harmful income taxes could increase GDP by 7.7% and average household wealth by 5.5%, while reducing fossil-fuel use by 38%.[3] Similarly, the U.S. Congress Office of Technology Assessment concluded "...if a gasoline tax were coupled with an equal-revenue increase in investment tax credits, short-run macroeconomic losses resulting from motor fuel tax increases could be more than offset by the short-run macroeconomic gains."[4] These shifts provide economic benefits because higher fuel taxes encourage energy efficiency and technological innovation, reduce the economic costs of imported petroleum, and encourage employment and investment which stimulates economic development.

Our institute has identified many "no regrets" strategies in the transportation sector, many of which involved no new taxes or fees. They provide multiple benefits, including reduced traffic congestion, road and parking facility savings, consumer savings and accident reductions, and significant environmental protection. We call these "Win-Win Transportation Management Strategies."

WHAT ARE WIN-WIN STRATEGIES?

Win-Win strategies are cost effective, technically feasible changes in current policies and practices that help solve transportation problems by increasing consumer choice and encouraging more efficient travel behavior. Win-Win strategies are based on market principles. Most involve minimal regulation and some reduce existing regulations altogether. They remove barriers and market distortions that reduce consumer choice and encourage excessive motor vehicle travel (by "excessive" I mean driving above what would occur in a more efficient market).

If fully implemented to the degree that they are economically justified (from savings in facility costs, congestion reduction and road safety), Win-Win strategies could reduce motor vehicle impacts by 15-30%, or even more if implemented in conjunction with additional TDM policies.[5] This could achieve the Kyoto emission reduction objectives while increasing consumer benefits and economic development at the same time. Win-Win strategies are essential for sustainable transportation.

WHY WIN-WIN STRATEGIES WORK

These are, admittedly, big claims. To understand why such large benefits are possible, it is important to clarify a few basic economic concepts. Efficient markets have two basic requirements: Consumers must have viable choices, and prices for goods and services should generally reflect their full production costs. Most markets satisfy these requirements. Consumers have many choices when it comes to buying food, clothing and shelter, and the prices for most products and services cover production costs.

But the transportation market violates these market principles. Although consumers have many choices when it comes to purchasing a vehicle, they often have few alternatives to driving if they want to participate in common activities. In most North American communities walking and cycling conditions are poor, public transit is inferior, intercity bus and train service is infrequent and expensive. Employment, commercial, education and recreation centers are usually located for the convenience of motorists, which is often inconvenient for access by other modes. See for yourself – try living without an automobile for a few weeks. This is not a problem in a few communities that offer good transportation choices, but in most areas non-drivers are severely disadvantaged.

Another factor that contributes to excessive motor vehicle travel is that, although vehicles are expensive to own, they are cheap to drive, typically costing just a few cents a kilometer in out-of-pocket expenses. More than 70% of user costs are fixed, including most depreciation, insurance, registration fees and residential parking. Other costs are external, not borne directly by users. Motorists use the local street system that is largely funded through local taxes, they use free parking at most destinations, and they are not charged for congestion imposed on others, some accident costs, or environmental impacts. Figures 1 illustrates the distribution of these costs. Internal-variable costs, the costs that affect individual trip decisions, represent less than half of total cost.

Figure 1: Average Distribution of Automobile Costs[6]

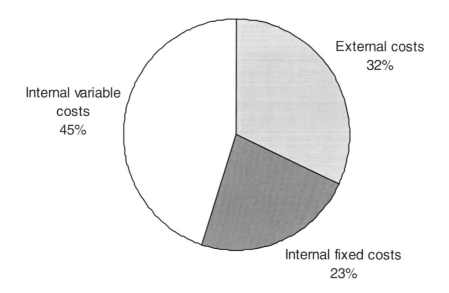

Figure 2 compares individual costs of automobile use. The largest costs are internal, including travel time and vehicle expenses. The externalities are significantly smaller, but numerous. If these external costs are considered individually they only suggest modest economic distortions that justify only modest reforms. However, when these external costs are considered together, as in Figure 1, they indicate that there are significant opportunities to benefit society by correcting these market distortions.

Figure 2: Magnitude and Distribution of Costs for an Average Automobile

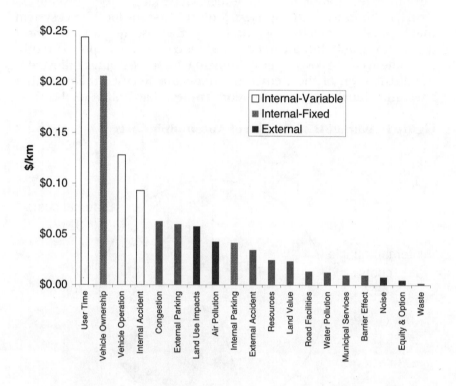

Motor vehicle use involves a number of costs. Although individually the external costs are modest, in total they exceed vehicle operating expenses.

In the language of economics, driving is "underpriced." This high fixed-cost, low variable-cost pricing encourages consumers to maximize their driving in order to "get their money's worth." A rich vocabulary exists to describe overpricing, which is said to "gouge" or "rip-off" customers, but there is no comparable vocabulary for underpricing. Yet underpricing is equally harmful to consumers and the economy since the costs must be borne elsewhere in the economy.

To put this another way, current pricing fails to return to individual motorists much of the savings that result when they reduce mileage. For example, commuters who shifts from driving to another mode usually reduce traffic congestion, parking requirements, accident risk (and therefore insurance costs) and environmental impacts, but these benefits would be widely dispersed rather than returned to the individuals who make the change. As a result, consumers lack the incentive to use each mode for what it does best. They are encouraged to drive even when other travel options are more cost effective and beneficial overall. This underpricing is also unfair because non-drivers, or anybody who drives less than average, receives less than their share of resources and benefits. For example, most employees who drive receive hundreds of dollars per year worth of free parking, while those who use other modes receive no comparable employee benefit.[7]

This is illustrated in Figure 3. When you make a transportation decision that reduces automobile use (for example, by riding transit, cycling, telecommuting or simply using a closer destination) you reduce external costs. Your neighbors benefit. An optimal market returns more of these benefits directly to you, increasing your incentive to choose the most efficient travel option for each trip. You would not give up all driving, but you would probably reduce some car travel to take advantage of these additional savings, just as many consumers respond to retail store sales and discount coupons.

Figure 3: Optimal Markets Return More Benefits of Reduced Driving to Individual Consumers

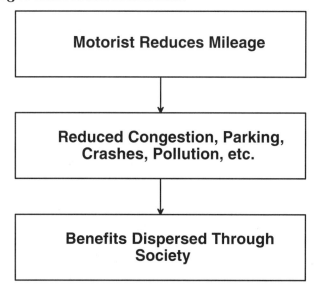

In current markets, when motorists reduce their vehicle travel (for example, by riding transit or telecommuting) they provide benefits that are widely dispersed through society

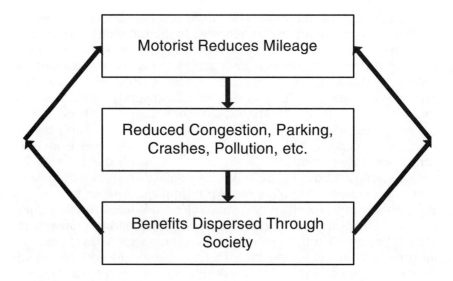

In a more optimal market, benefits are returned to individual motorist. This gives consumers an incentive to use alternatives when they are more cost effective overall.

Market distortions tend to be unfair and harmful to people who are transportation disadvantaged. They result in cross-subsidies from households that drive less than average to those that drive more than average, and reduce travel choices for non-drivers.

Market distortions also reduce economic productivity by increasing indirect and external cost burdens. Many people assume that since automobile use increases with wealth, it must contribute to economic development, but economic analysis indicates that beyond an optimal level, excessive automobile use reduces regional economic development by increasing transportation costs and because vehicles and fuel expenditures tend to provide few jobs or regional business activity in most regions.[8] This is particularly true in regions that do not produce vehicles and petroleum. International studies indicate that regions with balanced transportation are more economically competitive.[9] If properly implemented, transportation market reforms can increase equity and stimulate economic development.

This is not to ignore the benefits of driving, or to suggest that automobiles should be prohibited. It simply indicates that under a more neutral transportation market consumers would choose to drive less than they do now and be better off as a result. As an analogy, food provides tremendous benefits, since without it people die. However, this does not mean that increased eating is necessarily beneficial, that current diets are optimal, or that society should subsidize all food. If taxes subsidize food, we eat more but have less of things that are taxed, such as jobs, housing and clothes. Food subsidies may be justified for undernourished people, but since over-eating can be as unhealthy as under-eating, it is both economically and medically harmful to subsidize all food for everybody. At the margin (i.e., relative to current consumption) many people are better off eating less, both because overeating is unhealthy and because reduced food expenditures would leave more resources for other beneficial goods.

Similarly, that mobility provides benefits does not prove that more driving is better or that driving in general should be subsidized. Broad underpricing of transport is harmful because it requires subsidies from other economic sectors and results in excessive travel. Only if market distortions that encourage excessive driving are removed can consumers optimize their vehicle expenditures.

These inefficiencies are cumulative, so analysis that focuses on just one impact at a time underestimates the harm that results from market distortions and the potential benefits from market reforms. For example, underpriced parking not only encourages inefficient use of parking facilities, it also causes excessive traffic congestion, road costs, crashes and pollution. Similarly, underpricing road use does not simply lead to excessive congestion and road costs; it also increases parking costs, crashes and pollution. Over the long run, underpriced driving leads to automobile dependency, which increases the need to travel and further reduces travel choices.[10]

Win-Win strategies do not simply involve increased fuel taxes. There are a number of specific market distortions that favor excessive vehicle travel each of which requires corrective measures. If fully implemented, fuel taxes would probably stay about the same as they are now, or they might even decline.[11]

WHY WIN-WIN STRATEGIES ARE NOT BEING IMPLEMENTED NOW

Win-Win strategies are not implemented as much as is justified because most transport planning only takes into account a limited range of costs and benefits. Win-Win strategies provide a variety of benefits, but individual Win-Win strategies are not usually considered the best way to solve any individual problem. Solutions that provide many modest benefits tend to be overlooked, even if they are individually cost effective and could have large benefits if implemented as a package. Comprehensive analysis of costs and benefits recognizes the value of Win-Win strategies.[12]

Opposition to Win-Win strategies tends to come from resistance within existing institutions to changes in their administrative practices, even when the incremental costs are small compared with potential benefits. In such situations the challenge is to develop rewards for institutions that improve their practices. For example, transportation agency funding can be based in part on achieving TDM objectives, and businesses can retain a portion of the parking cost savings that result when they encourage alternatives to automobile commuting.

Because Win-Win strategies provide multiple benefits, they offer opportunities for cooperation and coordination between interest groups. People and organizations concerned with congestion, road and parking facility costs, road safety, economic development, consumer costs, environmental quality, community livability, and equity issues all have reasons to support these strategies. A first step toward broad implementation of Win-Win strategies is to develop coalitions to support reform programs.

EXAMPLES OF WIN-WIN STRATEGIES[13]

This section describes specific Win-Win strategies. How much each is implemented will vary depending on circumstances. They should be implemented to the degree that they provide direct economic benefits in terms of reduced congestion, road and parking facility savings, reduced crashes, and consumer savings.[14]

Federal

Remove Federal Subsidies To Oil Production and Internalize Government Costs

One study identifies five major federal tax exemptions provided to the petroleum industry, representing a total annual subsidy of $1.8 billion per year in the U.S.[15] These include Petroleum Research and Development program funding, deductions on drilling costs and on oil wells, and royalty waivers on deep-water offshore drilling leases. In addition, the cost of programs to benefit petroleum producers and consumers, such as the Strategic Petroleum Reserve and any environmental protection program costs, could be charged directly to users through additional taxes or fees.

Make Employer Provided Transit Benefits Tax Exempt[16]

Current Canadian federal tax policy allows most automobile commuters to receive untaxed free parking, while employer provided transit passes are fully taxed. Eliminating this bias increases transit commuting 5-20% among employees offered this benefit.

State/Provincial

Distance-Based Vehicle Insurance And Registration Fees[17]
Converting vehicle insurance and registration fees from fixed charges into per-mile charges approximately doubles variable vehicle expenses (for example, a motorist who now pays $900 per year for insurance and registration would pay about 4.5¢ per mile). This provides a significant financial incentive to reduce driving, while making these charges more fair and affordable. This is predicted to reduce vehicle travel by approximately 12%, reduce crash rates by a greater amount, increase equity, and save consumers money.

Least-Cost (Or "Integrated") Transportation Planning And Funding[18]
Least-cost planning means that programs to reduce demand are considered equally with programs to increase capacity, that all significant impacts are included in the analysis, and that the public is involved in developing and evaluating alternatives. This allows demand management strategies to receive appropriate consideration and investment.

Revenue-Neutral Tax Shifting[19]
Many economists recommend that taxes be increased on goods considered harmful or undesirable to consume, and reduced on socially desirable activities, such as employment and investment. Additional vehicle taxes are particularly justified to cover local road expenses. Although these costs result largely from motor vehicle use, they are currently funded by local property and sales taxes. Funding local roads through fuel taxes or weight-distance fees would be more equitable and economically efficient, and allow significant reductions in existing local taxes.

Reform Motor Carrier Regulations
Motor carrier regulations can be reformed to encourage competition and innovation in transit and ridesharing services. In particular, regulations can be changed to allow private companies to provide commuter bus services, and to encourage vanpooling (vanpools are currently limited to 6 passengers). Allowing more passengers would make vanpools more financially attractive and reduce the need for government subsidies.

Road and Congestion Pricing
Road pricing means charging road users tolls. Congestion pricing is road pricing with higher fees during congested time periods to encourage shifts in route, time and mode. Such pricing is an effective ways to reduce traffic congestion and encourage use of alternative modes.

Regional and Local

Local And Regional Transportation Demand Management (TDM) Programs[20]
TDM programs include a wide variety of services, including rideshare matching, transit improvements, bicycle and pedestrian facility improvements, parking management, and promotion of alternative modes. These can provide financial savings to governments, businesses and consumers, as well as environmental benefits.

More Efficient Land Use[21]
Current zoning and development practices tend to increase vehicle travel by separating land uses. More mixed-use and infill development can help reduce travel requirements and increase travel choices by placing common destinations closer together, such as having schools and small retail shops in or adjacent to residential neighborhoods.

More Flexible Zoning Requirements[22]
Parking and road requirements are often inflexible and over-generous. There are many ways to reduce the amount of land devoted to roads and parking without constraining mobility. Local governments can reduce parking requirements for businesses that have travel management programs or that are located in areas with good transit service. Shared parking allows significant reductions in parking requirements. This provides direct economic and environmental benefits, and helps support TDM objectives.

Parking "Cash Out"[23]
"Cashing out" means that employers who provide free parking also offer the cash equivalent to employees who use other modes. This is particularly appropriate for employers that have a shortage of parking capacity, that lease parking spaces, or that can lease excess parking spaces to other businesses. This typically reduces driving by 10-30%, and provides non-drivers with a benefit comparable in value to what drivers receive.

Transportation Management Associations[24]
Transportation management associations provide services such as rideshare matching, transit information, and parking coordination in a particular area, such as a commercial district or mall. This achieves more efficient use of resources and allows businesses of all sizes to participate in commute trip reduction programs.

Transportation Efficient Development and Location Efficient Mortgages[25]
Transportation efficient communities reduce motor vehicle travel by locating housing, services and employment activities in closer proximity, and by providing more travel choices. This allows households to reduce their automobile ownership expenses. Location efficient mortgages recognize the financial savings households enjoy when they locate in transportation efficient communities. Lenders can treat these transportation cost savings as equivalent to additional income, allowing households to increase their maximum borrowing limit. This gives home-buyers an added incentive to choose homes in communities with balanced transportation.

School and Campus Trip Management
These programs help overcome barriers to the use of alternative modes, and provide positive incentives for reduced driving to schools and college or university campuses. School trip management usually involves improving pedestrian and cycling access, promoting ridesharing, and encouraging parents to use alternatives when possible.[26] Campus trip management programs often include discounted transit fares, rideshare promotion, improved pedestrian and cycling facilities, and increased parking fees.[27] These programs give students, parents and staff more travel choices, encourage exercise, and reduce parking and congestion problems. They often reduce car trips by 15-30%.

Car Sharing[28]
Car sharing provides affordable, short term (hourly and daily rate) motor vehicle rentals in residential areas. This gives households convenient and affordable access to automobiles as an alternative to private ownership. Car sharing has much lower fixed costs and higher variable costs than private vehicle ownership, which encourages users to limit their vehicle use to those trips in which driving is truly the best option, and use alternative modes as much as possible. Drivers who join such organizations typically reduce their mileage by 50%.

Non-Motorized Transport Improvements[29]
Pedestrian and bicycle improvements are important for developing a more balanced transportation system. They encourage walking and cycling for a greater share of short trips, and provide access to transit. Research shows that residents of neighborhood with good walking and cycling conditions walk and cycle for more errands, and commuters will use transit or rideshare more frequently if they can conveniently walk from their worksites to restaurants and shops. There are many specific methods for accommodating and encouraging non-motorized transport, including improvements to sidewalks, trails and paths, street crossings, and bicycle parking facilities.

Traffic calming[30]
Traffic calming includes various strategies to reduce traffic speeds and volumes on specific roads. Typical strategies include traffic circles at intersections, sidewalk bulbs that reduce intersection crossing distances, raised crosswalks, and partial street closures to discourage short-cut traffic through residential neighborhoods. This increases road safety and community livability, creates a more pedestrian- and bicycle-friendly environment, and can reduce automobile use, particularly when matched with other TDM measures.

CONCLUSIONS

Existing market distortions reduce consumers' transportation choices and encourage more driving than would occur in a more neutral and optimal market. This exacerbates many economic, social and environmental problems. Although such distortions may individually appear modest and justified, their cumulative impacts are large. Most reflect decisions made with little consideration of their long-term transportation impacts.

Various technically feasible, cost-effective, market-based reforms, called Win-Win Transportation Solutions, could reduce these distortions. They expand transportation choices and encourage consumers to choose the most efficient option for each trip. The travel patterns that result would better reflect consumer preferences. They could reduce many existing transportation problems and are likely to increase economic productivity and development.

Such reforms are "no regrets" strategies that are critical for creating a more sustainable transportation system. Although some people suggest that technological improvements will allow unlimited increases in motor vehicle travel, more comprehensive analysis indicates that simply shifting to renewable fuels and zero-emission vehicles is insufficient;

true sustainability requires market reforms that increase choices and encourage more efficient consumer behavior.

Although vehicle operating costs would increase, this would be off-set by reductions in fixed vehicle costs, taxes and parking subsidies, resulting in overall savings to most households. Such reforms could stimulate economic development by increasing productivity, reducing burdensome taxes and public costs, and increasing the portion of consumer expenditures retained in the regional economy.

People may be skeptical that these strategies really make consumers better off. They ask, "If driving provides benefits, how can less driving increase benefits?" The answer is that these reforms return to individual consumers' more savings that result when they drive less. Consumers only forego travel when they value these savings more than a vehicle trip. Higher value vehicle trips would continue.

This is not to suggest that implementing Win-Win Solutions is easy. Most face substantial residence due to skepticism and ignorance (for example, many objections raised to per-mile vehicle insurance by participants in recent focus groups are simply not technically correct, indicating that education and marketing could significantly increase public support), and from entrenched interests that benefit in the short term from existing inefficiencies and inequities. However, they also provide a wide range of benefits that can attract broad support. It should be possible to build coalitions that include transportation professionals, consumer and equity advocates, public safety officials, environmentalists, economic development organization, and other interest groups to support implementation of Win-Win Solutions.

FOOTNOTES

1. For examples of these claims visit websites of coal and petroleum industry organizations.
2. Alan Durning and Yoram Bauman, *Tax Shift*, Northwest Environment Watch (Seattle; www.northwestwatch.org), 1998.
3. Douglas Norland and Kim Ninassi, *Price It Right; Energy Pricing and Fundamental Tax Reform*, Alliance to Save Energy (Washington DC; www.ase.org) 1998.
4. Office of Technology Assessment, *Saving Energy in U.S. Transportation*, (www.wws.princeton.edu/~ota), 1994, p. 225.
5. Todd Litman, *Potential TDM Strategies*, VTPI (www.vtpi.org), 1998.
6. Todd Litman, *Transportation Cost Analysis; Techniques, Estimates and Implications*, VTPI (www.vtpi.org), 1999.
7. Government transit subsidies can be considered to offset free employee parking and other subsidies to driving. On a per passenger-mile basis,

subsidies to automobile and transit travel are estimated to be about equal in Todd Litman, *Transportation Cost Analysis*, VTPI (www.vtpi.org) 1999. However, since motorists tend to travel much farther per year than people who are transit dependent, motorists receive far greater per capita subsidies.

8. Jon Miller, Henry Robison & Michael Lahr, *Estimating Important Transportation-Related Regional Economic Relationships in Bexar County, Texas*, VIA Transit (San Antonio; www.viainfo.net), 1999; Todd Litman and Felix Laube, *Automobile Dependency and Economic Development*, VTPI (www.vtpi.org), 1999.

9. Peter Newman and Jeff Kenworthy, *Sustainability and Cities; Overcoming Automobile Dependency*, Island Press (Covelo; www.islandpress.org), 1998.

10. Peter Newman and Jeff Kenworthy, *Sustainability and Cities; Overcoming Automobile Dependency*, Island Press (Covelo; www.islandpress.org), 1998.

11. Todd Litman, *Socially Optimal Transport Prices and Markets*, VTPI (www.vtpi.org), 1998.

12. VTPI, "Comprehensive Transportation Evaluation," Online TDM Encyclopedia (www.vtpi.org) 2000.

13. For more information on these strategies see the Online TDM Encyclopedia at www.vtpi.org.

14. Todd Litman, *Guide to Calculating TDM Benefits*, VTPI (www.vtpi.org), 1998.

15. Friends of the Earth, *Dirty Little Secrets, Oil & Gas*, (Washington DC; www.foe.org/DLS), 1998.

16. Todd Litman, *Income Tax Exemption for Employer-Provided Transit Passes Time for Action by the Government of Canada*, The Transit Advocacy Project of Transport 2000 Canada (Ottawa; http://ncf.davin.ottawa.on.ca/ freeport/orgs/civic/trans2000/menu), 1996.

17. Patrick Butler, *Operation of an Audited-Mile/Year Automobile Insurance System Under Pennsylvania Law*, National Organization for Women (Washington DC; www.now.org), 1992; Aaron Edlin, *Per-Mile Premiums for Auto Insurance*, Dept. of Economics, University of California at Berkeley (http:/ /emlab.berkeley.edu/users/edlin), 1998; Todd Litman, *Distance-Based Charges; A Practical Strategy for More Optimal Vehicle Pricing*, VTPI (www.vtpi.org), 1998; Todd Litman, *Distance-Based Vehicle Insurance*, VTPI (www.vtpi.org), 1998.

18. *What Is Least Cost Planning?* www.wsdot.wa.gov/regions/northwest/ planning/least_cost_planning.htm), 1999; ECONorthwest and PBQD, *Evaluation of Transportation Alternatives; Least-Cost Planning: Principles, Applications and Issues*, Metropolitan Planning Tech. Report #6, FHWA (Washington DC), 1995

International Institute for Energy Conservation, *The Integrated Transport Planning Beginner's Handbook*, (Washington DC; www.iiec.org), 1996; Phil Goodwin, *Solving Congestion*, University College London (www.ucl.ac.uk/~ucetwww/pbginau.htm), 1997.

19. Todd Litman, Charles Komanoff and Douglas Howell, *Road Relief; Tax and Pricing Shifts for a Fairer, Cleaner, and Less Congested Transportation System in Washington State*, Energy Outreach Center (Olympia; www.eoc.org), 1998.

20. Reid Ewing, *Transportation and Land Use Innovations; When You Can't Build Your Way Out of Congestion*, Planners Press (Chicago; *www.planning.com), 1997;* USEPA Commuter Choice Program *(www.epa.gov/oms/traq);* The TDM Resource Center *(www.wsdot.wa.gov/Mobility/TDMhome.html)* and Northwest Technology Transfer Center *(www.wsdot.wa.gov/TA/T2).*

21. Reid Ewing, *Best Development Practices; Doing the Right Thing and Making Money at the Same Time,* Planners Press (Chicago; *www.planning.org),* 1996.

22. Dan Burden, *Street Design Guidelines for Healthy Neighborhoods*, Center for Livable Communities (Sacramento; www.lgc.org/clc), 1998; Todd Litman, *Pavement-Buster's Guide; Why and How to Reduce the Amount of Land Paved for Roads and Parking Facilities*, VTPI (www.vtpi.org), 1998.

23. USEPA *Commuter Choice Program* (www.epa.gov/oms/traq); International Council for Local Environmental Initiatives, *Local Government Guide to Parking Cash Out*, , (www.iclei.org/us), 1998.

24. Association for Commuter Transportation (http://tmi.cob.fsu.edu/act/act.htm); Center for Urban Transportation Research, University of South Florida (http://cutr.eng.usf.edu).

25. Kim Hoeveler, "Accessibility vs. Mobility: The Location Efficient Mortgage," *Public Investment*, American Planning Association. (Chicago; www.planning.org), September 1997.

26. *Active and Safe Routes to School*, Ottawa; www.goforgreen.ca; *Way To Go! School Program*, www.waytogo.icbc.bc.ca; SUSTRANS *Safe Routes to School Project* www.sustrans.co.uk/srts.

27. Françoise Poinsatte and Will Toor, *Finding a New Way: Campus Transportation for the 21st Century*, University of Colorado Environmental Center (Boulder; ecology@stripe.colorado.edu), 1999; University of Washington U-PASS program www.washington.edu/upass; UBC TREK program www.trek.ubc.ca.

28. K. Steininger, C. Vogl and R. Zettl, "Car Sharing Organizations," *Transport Policy*, Vol. 3, No. 4, 1996, pp. 177-185; The Car Sharing Net (www.carsharing.net).

29.Steven Burrington and Veronika Thiebach, *Take Back Your Streets*, Conservation Law Foundation (Boston; www.clf.org), 1995; Todd Litman,

Quantifying the Benefits of Non-Motorized Travel for Achieving TDM Objectives, VTPI (www.vtpi.org), 1999; Oregon Bike and Pedestrian Planning (www.odot.state.or.us/techserv/bikewalk/obpplan.htm); Partnership for a Walkable America (http://nsc.org/walk/wkabout.htm); WSDOT Pedestrian Website (www.wsdot.wa.gov/hlrd/Sub-defaults/Pedestrian-default.htm).

30. PTI, *Slow Down You're Going Too Fast*, Public Technology Incorporated *(http://pti.nw.dc.us/task forces/transportation/docs/trafcalm)*; Portland Traffic Calming Website *(www.trans.ci.portland.or.us/Traffic Management/trafficcalming)*; Todd Litman, *Traffic Calming Benefits, Costs and Equity Impacts*, VTPI *(www.vtpi.org), 1999.*

MARKETING MIX DESIGN-FOR-ENVIRONMENT (DFE): A SYSTEMS APPROACH

Donald Fuller
University of Central Florida

INTRODUCTION

Sustainability can be visualized as a state in which the use of resources in consumption does not pollute and undermine the functioning of basic life-support ecosystems. To limit unfavorable ecosystem impacts and move towards sustainability, consumer societies have generally relied on the regulation of business facilities and processes as the primary ways and means of controlling waste, the antecedent of pollution. Through the mid-1990s, business interests generally dismissed voluntary initiatives to lessen pollution as unprofitable, altruistic exercises in social marketing. However, as we enter the 21st Century, the dimension of sustainability is exerting a much more direct influence on revenues and costs; the evaluation of sustainable marketing strategies under the standard "Total Profit = Total Revenues-Total Costs" equation is yielding more attractive results. Given marketing strategy is defined as the traditional "marketing mix-->target market" model, this suggests that the voluntary development of sustainable marketing mixes by private sector firms can play a much larger role in achieving environmental improvements in the future.

MARKETING MIX: THE DELIVERY VEHICLE

The marketing mix is the delivery vehicle through which strategy is actualized. Using available information and expertise, managers customize the marketing mix in relation to given target markets by making decisions concerning (1) product, (2) place (channels), (3) promotion (communications), and (4) pricing; a systems perspective is utilized to maximize effectiveness. The inclusion of ecosystem impact as a design factor (criterion) in this process is still somewhat novel to many marketing managers. However, in order to understand the direct linkage between marketing mix decisions and ecosystem impacts, one need only observe the former cause the latter. This cause-->effect assumption is valid because marketing mix decisions directly trigger conversions of natural capital/ resources, and all such conversions generate consumption waste. And, given the resource-intensive lifestyles of the western world's consumer societies, marketing mix-induced consumption waste represents a worthy target for environmental improvement.

310   *Bringing Business On Board*

Sustainable marketing is defined as ". . . the process of planning, implementing, and controlling the development, pricing, promotion, and distribution of products in a manner that satisfies three criteria: (1) customer needs are met, (2) organizational goals are attained, and (3) the process is compatible with ecosystems" (Fuller 1999, p. 4). Its environmental goal is to operationalize "low-waste, no-negative-discharge" product systems. Under the "marketing mix-->target market" model, this means that marketing mixes must be designed with the objectives of (1) significantly reducing the generation of waste, and (2) properly managing all remaining waste discharges into ecosystems. When this is the case, the production-consumption cycle becomes sustainable because it can be replicated over time without degrading ecosystems (i.e., the process is compatible with ecosystems/moderates pollution). This important result is necessary even if the broader goal is de-consumption (i.e., achieving a reduction in consumption level). However, sustainable marketing mixes must concurrently deliver genuine benefits to customers and financial rewards to firms; achieving compatibility with ecosystems is not an end in itself.

DECISION FRAMEWORK: PRODUCT SYSTEM LIFE-CYCLE (PSLC)

In order to capture a true picture of how marketing mixes impact ecosystems, and therefore be in position to implement decisions that support sustainability, a broad cradle-to-grave interpretation of where product systems begin and end is required. The product system life-cycle (PSLC) defines the appropriate decision framework. It represents the merger of two complimentary concepts: (1) the resource life-cycle (Tchobanoglous et al. 1993) and (2) the marketing channel network. The generalized PSLC for consumer products (see Exhibit 1) consists of five normative stages depicted as a set of linked channel networks. Stages 1-4 are aligned in series; Stage 5 represents concurrently functioning networks that process outbound waste streams at all levels of the PSLC. Also, the organizations and markets of the PSLC are bound by economic interest, which is designated by the marketing strategy symbol (MS) on Exhibit 1.

The PSLC demonstrates that waste generation is a holistic, interconnected phenomenon. The true ecological impact of any marketing strategy is a function of the collective decisions of all PSLC organizations and customers, which occur before, during, and after final consumption. For example, the life-cycle analysis for aluminum soft-drink containers must include the activities of all resource suppliers who precede and support finished products manufacturing (i.e., aluminum mining and smelting), actual soda-canning and wholesale/retail distribution, target customers, and final container disposal.

EXHIBIT 1: Product System Life-Cycle Model

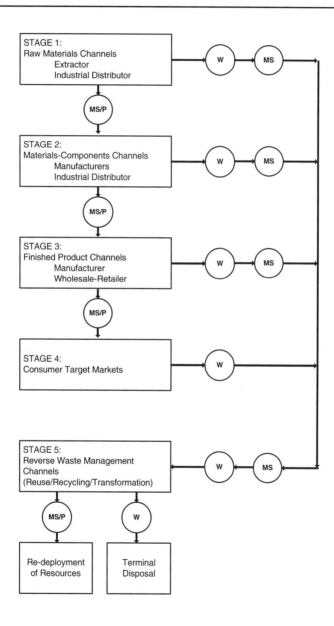

P = product; W = waste; MS = marketing strategy

Much environmental improvement strategy focuses on how to reduce the waste outputs and other impacts of industrial/commercial facilities and processes, without regard to the marketing mixes they support. This suggests that marketing mixes, which are essentially "solutions" to consumption problems, are a constant factor in the scheme of
things; merely "cleaning up" the waste generated by sets of apparently
independent manufacturing and distribution locations and customers
is the "environmental answer." Market-oriented PSLC analysis portrays a
different state of affairs. By first defining the ultimate benefits sought
by customers, the ways and means of delivering them in the marketplace become apparent. Therefore, marketing mix decisions determine
PSLC structure and processes. This places marketing managers in a
uniquely empowered position to address the environmental challenge
where it counts most - up front at the point of inception. The "environmental answer" is to (1) first develop innovative, ecologically sound
marketing mixes (i.e., solutions to the customers' problems that have
fewer unintended ecological consequences) that (2) trigger changes in
PSLC structure and processes which (3) deliver long-term environmental
improvements. Given the presence of significant profit incentives, marketing managers are very likely to take up the challenge. A recent example makes this point: Airlines typically spray 500 or more gallons of
glycol to de-ice the surfaces of an aircraft. The cost is between $1,500-
3,000 which includes the eco-costs of containing, recovering, and disposing of spent glycol, a severe water pollutant. Focusing on the problem (the de-icing airplane surfaces), Radiant Energy Corporation crafted
an environmentally-compatible solution: erect a pre-fabricated "hothouse
hanger" that uses infrared beams to remove the ice in three to six minutes at half the former cost. Although new energy sources now play a
role, glycol producers, and the unacceptable ecological impacts associated with their product's manufacture, distribution, and use have been
eliminated from the PSLC (Licking 2000).

ROLES OF MARKETING MIX ELEMENTS

The customization of the marketing mix is always situation-specific reflecting the demands/needs of customers, the nature of the product, the
technological setting, type of firm (i.e., manufacturer, supplier, distribu-
tor, retailer, etc.), and other unique local factors. When "compatibility
with ecosystems" (sustainability) is introduced as a decision criterion,
the firm's position in the PSLC will likely determine which marketing
mix elements are most actionable and what decisions may be most appropriate in a specific case. However, the general role played by each
element in achieving overall progress towards sustainability is relatively

constant (see Exhibit 2). Overall, the sustainability challenge centers on waste management issues, that is, reducing and remediating the wastes generated across the PSLC so as to moderate pollution. Two marketing mix elements are direct generators of wastes: (1) product decisions are the primary source, and (2) channel decisions are a secondary source.

However, given relatively "clean" products and channels exist, the work remains half done. This is because the total waste impact of any marketing mix is generalized as $I = (W)(Q)$, where I = ecosystem impact, W = waste per unit, and Q = units sold. Obviously, a low waste per unit (W) scenario must achieve adequate sales volume (Q) before a substantive contribution will be made to reducing total waste impact (I). Therefore, increasing Q becomes an important challenge, one that will be met only if targeted buyers (1) have reasonable access to the product, (2) are aware of the brand, and (3) perceive its characteristics and value to be line with their expectations and competitive offerings. This means that the potential to reap environmental gains will go unrealized unless complimentary, transaction-facilitating decisions in the areas of channels, promotion, and pricing are also implemented for the purpose of building Q.

As indicated above, the scope and depth of a firm's involvement in the sustainability aspects of each element of the marketing mix will vary. However, finished product manufacturing firms will likely find actionable "sustainability" opportunities in all elements of the marketing mix because they constantly must interpret the changing wants and needs of final customers. Such firms function as market gatekeepers controlling final "form and function," and are also instrumental in the other marketing mix decisions. In short, the marketing decision-makers in these firms occupy positions of great ecological empowerment. Similarly, heavily integrated firms (i.e., forward and/or backward) will likely have more "sustainability" opportunities to pursue across the entire spectrum of the marketing mix. In contrast, specialist firms, such as transportation/distribution firms, will likely have no direct involvement in product design activities; their decision-making will concentrate on developing low-waste forward channels, or efficient reverse waste management channels (Stage 5). Therefore, they are dependent on manufacturers to create the recyclable product and package designs that will allow them to achieve the high volume, low cost operations necessary to be profitable.

DESIGN-FOR-ENVIRONMENT (DFE) PERSPECTIVE

Design-for-environment (DFE) is a design management application that has evolved within the industrial/product design community (Graedel

---

EXHIBIT 2: Marketing Mix Elements — Roles in Sustainable Strategy

---

Sustainable Product Design Decisions

- Are the primary functional determinants of wastes (W), which derive from the types of resources and processes used in manufacturing and earlier life-cycle stages.
- Result in "low-waste, no-negative-impact" form and function product designs.
- Must protect customers' primary benefits.
- Must protect firm's revenue-cost relationship.

Sustainable Channel Design Decisions

- Are secondary functional determinants of wastes (W), which derive from the performance of forward and reverse channel move-store functions.
- Result in "low-waste, no-negative-discharge" forward and reverse channel systems.
- Facilitate reverse channel resource recovery volume and trippage rates by providing waste source access.
- Facilitate forward channel sustainable product sales (Q) by customer providing access.

Sustainable Promotion Decisions

- Are not significant functional determinants of waste (W).
- Facilitate reverse resource recovery participation by providing information.
- Facilitate sustainable product sales (Q) by providing information.

Sustainable Pricing Decisions

- Are not significant functional determinants of waste (W).
- Facilitate reverse resource recovery participation efforts through monetary incentives.
- Facilitate sustainable product sales (Q) by reflecting full costs and value added.

---

and Allenby 1995). Its purpose is to embed positive ecological attributes (eco-attributes) in product "form and function." As product components, eco-attributes reflect waste management enhancements, such as making packages easier to recycle, eliminating unnecessary quantities of materials from product construction, or designing durable products to be efficiently re-manufactured for a second marketing cycle.

In essence, DFE erects formal screening processes within the framework of the PSLC that insure that the various aspects of sustainability are fully taken into account during product design. When generalized beyond "product" to the other elements of the marketing mix (i.e., channels, promotion, and pricing decisions), the DFE perspective insures that each is scrutinized in regard to its potential to directly moderate waste impact and/or facilitate the sales (Q) of "clean" products.

POLLUTION PREVENTION (P2) AND RESOURCE RECOVERY (R2) STRATEGIES

DFE is operationalized through two proactive strategies: (1) pollution prevention (P2), and (2) resource recovery (R2). They are derived from the integrated waste management (IWM) hierarchy in which pollution prevention (P2) is the first priority followed by resource recovery (R2)(Freeman et al. 1992). Exhibit 3 defines these terms and provides a typology of sub-strategies. The essence of P2 is to engage in up-front preventative actions that eliminate waste before it occurs. In contrast, R2 focuses on devising efficient remedial actions that recover various resources (i.e., products, materials, energy values, etc.) from waste streams and re-deploy them in future production-consumption cycles, thereby closing the resources loop. R2 assumes waste streams will always be present because (1) all products wear out or become obsolete, (2) minimal packaging will always be required, and (3) conversion processes using best available technology (BAT) will never be 100 percent efficient.

The type and degree of change called for by P2 and R2 applications suggests the general sequence in which these strategies will be implemented by on-going firms. P2 involves significant change and investment in basic product design, manufacturing, and other support systems; it can be described as evolutionary, relatively high-cost, high risk, and long-term in nature. Implementing entirely new production technology, or re-inventing product form and function are examples. R2 often involves immediate, but often minimal, modifications to a firm's present systems; it can be described as incremental, reactive, low-cost, low risk, and short-term in nature. Adding-on a materials recycling system to a current manufacturing process to reduce waste disposal costs, or replacing outbound disposable packaging with a reusable system, are

---

EXHIBIT 3: Integrated Waste Management Hierarchy/Pollution Prevention (P2) and Resource Recovery (R2) Strategies

---

IWM Hierarchy	Sustainable Marketing Strategies Actualized Through Design-For-Environment
(1) Pollution Prevention (P2) - Process P2 - Product P2	**(1) Proactive Strategy: Pollution Prevention (P2)** Conserve resources and eliminate waste through up-front process and product design changes/decisions; eliminate after-the-fact waste processing costs.
↓ Waste Streams (Downsized)	
(2) Resource Recovery (R2) - Product Reuse - Materials Recycling - Materials Transformation	**(2) Proactive Strategy: Resource Recovery (R2)** Manage unavoidable waste streams by recapturing materials, energy values, and products for future use; enhance efficency-effectiveness of recovery functions through reverse channel and product design changes/decisions; build markets for recovered materials, energy, and reusable products.
↓ Waste Streams (Downsized)	
(3) Terminal Disposal (TD) - Releases into Air/Water - Landfilling	**(3) Default Option: Terminal Disposal** Wastes are released into ecosystems; this is not a strategy -- it is an occurrence/event often beyond the marketer's control; prior implementation of P2 and R2 strategies will reduce TD volume and also render benign products/wastes that undergo TD due to uncontrollable and varying local circumstances.

examples. When responding to the sustainability challenge, on-going firms are likely to first "green-up" present marketing mixes by implementing less disruptive R2 strategies. Success, and the institutional learning that occurs by doing so, then leads to the gradual introduction of potentially more disruptive P2 approaches over time. However, this P2-->R2 serial application is not the whole story. For, as noted above, all P2 approaches will continue to need an immediate R2 component to manage the inevitable waste/residual streams that will continue to exist.

Because the product and channel elements of the marketing mix are direct generators of waste, the applications made in these areas fall into a natural classification as either pollution prevention (P2) and resource recovery (R2) in purpose; the DFE discussions of these marketing mix elements utilize this dichotomy. However, promotion and pricing applications can not be naturally classified as either P2 or R2 in purpose; they are generally facilitative in character and can cover a variety of situations. The discussion of promotion DFE that follows is organized around the traditional components of the promotion mix. The discussion of pricing DFE is organized around a set of pricing policies that have linkages to sustainable practice.

PRODUCT DESIGN-FOR-ENVIRONMENT

Product decisions are the primary determinants of the quantity and character of waste generated by consumption because:

> Product design is a unique point of leverage from which to address environmental problems. Design is the stage where decisions are made regarding the types of resources and processes to be used, and these ultimately determine the characteristics of waste streams (Office of Technology Assessment 1992, p. 3).

This makes product design the core issue of sustainable marketing strategy and the cornerstone upon which all other sustainable marketing mix decisions are built. The design goal is to achieve low product ecosystem impact (W) by minimizing waste generation and maximizing remediation, while maintaining product efficacy in terms of customer benefits and financial returns to the firm.

Product Design-for-Pollution Prevention (P2)

Product P2 applications are double-edged. First, the nature of P2 is to "get more from less" resources. This translates into reduced demand for initial energy and materials inputs in Stages 1-3 of the PSLC due to gains in productivity, which also means less waste is generated "upstream." Second, this demand reduction, along with physical product enhancements, results in the downsizing of waste streams in the distribution and later stages of the PSLC, so future "downstream" waste management costs are also reduced ("Waste Reduction Works Like Magic" 1993; Freeman et al. 1992; Reilly 1991). Product design for P2 has two major substrategies: (1) manufacturing process-specific, and (2) product-specific (see Exhibit 4).

Manufacturing Process-specific. Products are accountable for the waste created by the total set of conversions up to and including the creation of final "form and function" (this can be visualized as all wastes left behind at the "plant" and earlier). The objective is to minimize resource inputs and the waste outputs of all manufacturing and inventory processes associated with product making. This is accomplished by reviewing production/inventory methods and modifying, or changing-out, technologies/procedures as necessary. The PSLC-orientation also requires scrutiny of the processes of a firm's suppliers as well.

Product-specific. Positive eco-attributes are incorporated directly into "form and function" (products) which then move forward into distribution. Any positive waste management gains then carry forward into the distribution, consumption, and post-consumption stages of the PSLC. Design enhances input resources productivity by: (1) reducing quantities of materials used in product/packages, (2) eliminating toxic/hazardous/radioactive/problematic materials, (3) extending product useful life, (4) reducing energy consumption and waste discharges (operating products), and (5) re-inventing the product's core benefit delivery system. These actions serve to de-materialize consumption and reduce waste management costs in later stages of the PSLC. In particular, product reinvention can take the form of eco-innovations, which utilize radically different ways and means to provide customer benefits (Fussler and James 1996; Ottman 1997).

Product Design-for-Resource Recovery (R2)

Resource recovery (R2) involves the continuous recapture of "already made once" products and materials and their re-deployment in future consumption cycles. This closes the resources loop and eliminates linear resources utilization (Neace 1995). For reasons cited earlier, R2 will remain a necessary follow-on to P2, but the scope and range of R2 activities are expected to narrow considerably as P2 becomes standard operating practice. R2 is focuses on making any future recovery options more efficient, and is accomplished through three sub-strategies: (1) product reuse, (2) materials recycling, and (3) materials transformation (see Ex-

---

EXHIBIT 4: Sustainable Product Applications

Pollution Prevention (P2)

• *Manufacturing process-specific*: Substitute hydrogen peroxide for chlorine bleaching systems in paper making; eliminate inventories of toxic chlorine and replacing them with benign materials.

• *Product-specific*: Light-weigth/downsize 12-ounce aluminum beverage containers by 25%; eliminate mercury, lead, and volatile organic compounds (VOCs) from paints; increase an appliance's operating life from 10,000 to 20,000 cycles; use "power down" technology to reduce computer energy use; replace traditional chemicals-based "wet photography" with digital imaging.

Resource Recovery (R2)

• *Product reuse*: Develop heavy-duty, multi-cycle reusable plastic containers with functional features such as collapsibility, nestability, stackability, side-door access, easy cleaning/sanitization, and standardized size/shape/cube.

• *Materials recycling*: Standardize container construction around one material (e.g., 100% aluminum, 100% polyethylene terephthalate – PET); design single-use cameras with two-way fasteners for quick tear-down; specify PET to compliment availability of DuPont's breakthrough Petretec recycling process; identify all the major metal and plastic appliance parts with industry standard codes; specify PET in package construction to compliment widely available recycling programs.

• *Materials transformation*: Use soy-based inks (eliminate heavy-metal based inks) in product labels and literature; replace nickel-cadmium batteries in non-recyclable hand-held appliances with benign battery technology.

---

hibit 4). In addition, it is important to note that all R2 strategies depend on complimentary reverse channel systems to accomplish their goals (see channels discussion below).

Product Reuse. Product reuse preserves original (already made once) product "form and function" and creates a series of back-to-back usage cycles. Reusable packaging systems employ "beefed-up" structural designs that withstand the rigors of multiple cycles. Achieving a high trippage rate (i.e., the number of times the package is cycled) radically reduces investment in materials per unit of delivered product. Complex products, such consumer appliances and office equipment, can be designed to anticipate re-manufacturing. This involves talking a "once-used" item and restoring it to new product specifications for re-sale. Design features include easy disassembly and the use of modular component systems to facilitate the restoration process.

Materials Recycling. In contrast, materials recycling involves re-capturing large quantities of "already made" products/packages and materials from diverse sources and physically reducing them to status of homogeneous raw materials/commodities; original "form and function" is discarded. This requires anticipating the type of future "reduction" (sorting-out) activities and technologies that will be involved, designing-in eco-attributes (features) that make it efficient to accomplish reduction from form and function to generic materials status. Design features include (1) materials simplification (reducing the number of materials in a product simplifies the sorting process), (2) easy disassembly (complex products), (3) use of materials compatible with recycling technologies, (4) adopting materials coding systems, and (5) specifying recycled-source materials to stimulate demand. Enhancing reduction efficiency is a critical issue because recycled-source raw materials/commodities are marketable products that directly compete head-to-head with virgin-source counterparts on price and quality.

Materials Transformation. Transformation involves chemical, biological, or thermal processes that are applied to waste streams for the purposes of harvesting energy values, or converting original materials/substances into different forms. Their application is particularly relevant to large mixed municipal waste streams that can not be economically sorted-out (reduced) for materials recycling purposes. The main product design feature is the avoidance of materials in product/ packaging construction will cause contamination of outputs or release pollutants during processing.

CHANNEL DESIGN-FOR-ENVIRONMENT

The move-store functions performed in forward (out-bound) channels are programmed to enhance customer access to products, thereby increasing potential sales (Q). In contrast, reverse channels perform recapture functions in support of the various product design-for-resource recovery strategies discussed earlier. Both forward and reverse channels continuously convert resources and generate wastes that can be described as significant, but of secondary importance. A common design goal of both forward and reverse systems is minimizing move-store wastes and maximizing the remediation of those that remain. An additional environmental goal associated with reverse channel operations is to enhance the efficiency of performing the resource recapture function.

Under the broadened DFE perspective, a finished product manufacturer must also look at reducing negative ecological impacts caused by (1) suppliers (input) channels, (2) wholesale/retail distribution (output) channels, and (3) end-customers. On the input side, "greening the supply chain" can occur when buyer organizations mandate supplier conformance with environmental management standards, such as those available through ISO 14000 certification. On the output side, "greening" wholesale-retail distribution is more of a two-way street with some manufacturers establishing environmental standards as a channel member selection criterion, while retailers sometimes turn the tables by mandating manufacturer (supplier) environmental conformance as an element of terms of sale. In addition, end-customers face final disposal decisions that can (and must!) be anticipated through PSLC analysis.

Channel Design-for-Pollution Prevention (P2)

Transportation and inventory holding are traditional move-store functions performed in both forward and reverse channels. Channel design-for-pollution prevention (P2) serves to minimize the wastes generated by the performance of these activities (see Exhibit 5).

Transportation Wastes Minimization. Because transportation vehicles consume energy (fuel) and discharge air emissions, the adoption of policies that stress fuel economy and the use of reduced emissions technology is an important consideration in achieving sustainability. Also, moving goods fewer times, utilizing large and/or consolidated shipments, and the avoiding distribution mistakes (i.e., wrong goods, wrong place) tends to lower waste per unit (W) of final delivered product.

Inventory Wastes Minimization. Minimizing inventory levels and associ-

---

EXHIBIT 5: Sustainable Channel Applications

Pollution Prevention (P2)

- *Transportation wastes minimization*: Utilize low-emission vehicles; minimize product movement by employing computer scheduling.

- *Inventory wastes minimization*: Reduce inventories and associated storage facilities through computer control systems such as electronic data interchange (EDI) and just-in-time (JIT) approaches.

- *Fugitive emissions minimization*: Design transportation equipment to reduce probability of spills/accidents (e.g., double-hulled oil tanker designs, and requiring collision-avoidance alert systems on all trucks).

Resource Recovery (R2)

- *Reverse channels for reusable packaging*: Utilize company-owned vehicles and reusable 4-gallon plastic "cases" for delivery and back-hauling in local retail food store distribution.

- *Reverse channels for remanufactured products*: Utilize third-party specialists nationwide to de-install complex computer systems and ship them to processing centers; provide the necessary packaging and postage as an incentive for customers to de-install and ship used toner cartridges to centralized locations for processing.

- *Reverse channels for materials recycling*: Use waste-hauler/public recovery/ curbside collection systems to separately recapture large quantities of pre-sorted plastic/aluminum/glass containers and newsprint; mandates require supermarkets handle returned disposable containers in bottle-bill states; specialized dealer-processors serve local manufacturers, shopping centers, and supermarket chains to recover corrugated packaging, newsprint, scrap metals, plastics, glass, and other materials.

- *Reverse channels for materials transformation*: Use waste-hauler/public recovery /curbside collection systems to recapture large quantities of mixed municipal solid waste (MSW) for input into local municipal waste-to-energy systems; employ separate curbside collection of post-consumer organic materials to support municipal composting operations.

ated storage facilities/space in relation to given levels of production, and minimizing damage/breakage, are factors that have hardly escaped scrutiny by logistics experts seeking to cut costs. Doing so also minimizes total resource requirements, thereby initiating parallel savings in waste (fewer resources must be converted to support given demand). Inventory minimization results from a more precise match between supply (inventories) and demand (sales). Computer-based techniques, such as electronic data interchange (EDI) and just-in-time (JIT) inventory systems, can help achieve this result.

Fugitive Emissions Minimization. Fugitive emissions result from transportation- and inventory-related accidents. This factor is of particular concern in PSLC's that routinely handle large quantities of hazardous or toxic materials. Given these materials are absolutely essential to operations, one minimization strategy is to reduce the quantities of these items being moved and stored in the first place which limits risk exposure. Another strategy is to redesign transportation equipment, facilities, and materials handling systems so that the probability of accidental discharges is reduced, while those that do occur are anticipated and immediately contained.

Channel Design-for-Resource Recovery (R2)

R2 strategies require logistics support to accomplish the task of diverting products/materials/wastes from terminal disposal, and re-deploying them in future consumption cycles. This closes the resource loop and eliminates the phenomenon of linear resource use (Neace 1995). The functional systems required to recapture resources are quite diverse and must meet the unique requirements imposed by specific situations.

Reverse Channels for Reusable Packaging. Reusable packaging is a product take-back system that can be employed in either industrial or consumer markets. Conditions that favor its use include (1) short channels (few participants), (2) short distribution distances (local, regional), (3) frequent, routine, and standardized transactions (time/place/quantity), (4) standardized package sizes/dimensions, and (5) motivated end-users. The presence of such conditions increases trippage, the number of times a package is cycled through a system. They generally characterize industrial transactions (including within-channel transfers of consumer goods), but are much less typical of consumer transactions. This is because the allure of disposal convenience has led to the almost 100% adoption of single-use packages in consumer food marketing in the United States. Additionally, the use of proprietary packaging to differentiate brands has also tended to dampen the use of standardized reusables in consumer markets. Marketing mix designers must first recognize when and where conditions favor deployment of reusable packaging, then, in collaboration with physical distribution specialists, work out the logistics infrastructure and processes necessary to accomplish the necessary recapture, back-hauling, and reconditioning/ inspection functions.

Reverse Channels for Remanufactured Products. Although re-manufacturing involves diverse types of products, everything from automotive radiator cores to copying machines and toner cartridges, most applications focus on relatively high-value items in which "take-back" (trade-in) also plays a major role in pricing. In contrast to the high volume and continuity that characterize materials recycling and reusable packaging systems, re-manufacturing recapture operations tend to be much more selective, sporadic, and low volume in nature. Equipment recapture likely involves a wide geographic array of user locations that must be serviced on an occasional, as-needed basis, frequently in conjunction with the sale of new equipment (i.e., an exchange/trade-in is part of the transaction). Various degrees of de-installation are involved, as well one-time, non-standardized packaging and transportation functions. In this context, manufacturers have a number choices including (1) using existing forward channel partners, (2) contracting with third-party specialists, or (3) having customers participate in de-installation and other tasks. The intermittent nature of the functional activities involved seems to explain the apparent lack of manufacturer corporate integrated networks to handle recapture (out-sourcing is the norm).

Reverse Channels for Materials Recycling. The availability of large quantities of disposal packaging from industrial and consumer sources, plus other potentially recyclable items (e.g., discarded appliances and electronic equipment, newspapers, production wastes, traded-in automobiles, automobile tires, lead-acid batteries, used oil, etc.) sets the stage for materials recycling. In all cases, Stage 5 materials recycling channels must be designed to perform functions that (1) continuously recapture relatively large quantities of materials, (2) process those materials to the required quality specifications of industrial buyers, and (3) maintain exchange continuity. Meeting the often quite demanding quality specifications of industrial buyers is particularly important because price and quality are positively correlated in recycled materials markets. In most cases, there is no ownership linkage between the initial producer of items recovered through reverse channels (i.e., containers, appliances, automobiles, etc.), the entity disposing of those items i.e., (industrial/consumer source), and the collector of those items. This is because passage of product title occurred in an earlier time period, and significant gaps have likely developed in terms of time and location of consumption and disposal in relation to point of manufacture. Reverse channels for post-consumer recyclables face the particular problem of collecting wastes from a large number of low volume sources; this intensifies channel coverage requirements. In contrast, industrial/commercial waste sources (operating locations) are typically few and tend to produce relatively large quantities of homogeneous materials; this simplifies channel design. In response, a number of basic reverse channel types have evolved that reflect the economic conditions, legal arrangements, the functional requirements associated with specific commodities, the strategies of specific industrial buyers, and public policy mandates (Fuller et al. 1996). They include:

Corporate integrated channels. A legitimate/ownership power base controls the required accumulation and sorting processes. This approach requires extensive investment in processing equipment/facilities, transportation equipment, and promotional programs to stimulate and maintain collection levels (Fuller 1991).

Waste-hauler/public recovery/curbside channels. This often the choice for solving the intensive post-consumer collection problem. Consumers provide the vital "first sort" of designated items from mixed wastes, a behavior that is usually mandated by local ordinances requiring the diversion of wastes from landfills (National Solid Wastes Management Association 1990).

Specialized reverse dealer-processor channels. These are independent wholesaler intermediaries who often perform heavy-duty processing functions such as dismantling, shredding, baling, and large quantity transporting. They often specialize by type of materials handled (e.g., metals, paper, glass, plastics).

Traditional forward retailer-wholesaler channels. These channels evolve where bottle-bill mandates require retailer-wholesaler participation in return bottle programs. Mandates may also cover items such as automobile tires, used oil and other automobile fluids, and lead-acid batteries.

Reverse Channels for Materials Transformation. These channels are supply sources for (1) waste-to-energy (WTE) and (2) materials composting systems. Mixed industrial and commercial waste streams are sources of combustible materials, such as food-related and agricultural by-products, and containers (all materials); households contribute all types of contaminated packaging and containers, yard wastes, and food-related items. Given it is uneconomic (or impossible!) to sort-out these items for recycling purposes, the opportunity exists to extract economic values by incineration in waste-to-energy (WTE) conversion processes. The high volume of mixed wastes required to "feed" such systems is generally available through public waste-hauler systems. In contrast, composting processes require separated, organic waste as feedstock. Consumer sources can be tapped through separate curbside collection programs. Industrial-commercial sources generate organics fewer locations such as schools, food service businesses/restaurants, supermarkets, food wholesalers, and food processors; each tends to generate relatively large quantities of presorted items. Prompt separation at the source is a basic requirement. Others factors influencing channel efficiency include: (1) refining routing to efficiently reach prime generators, (2) developing specialized collection vehicles (standard solid waste packer trucks are inefficient in this role), (3) utilizing specialized collection containers (to accommodate semi-liquid/putrefying materials), and (4) accounting for the seasonal variations in the composition of organic waste streams (e.g., lawn clippings in spring-summer; leaves in fall-winter) ("Hauling Food Residuals" 1995).

PROMOTION DESIGN-FOR-ENVIRONMENT

In contrast to the decisions that underlie product designs and channels, promotion is not a significant functional generator of wastes in and of itself. Rather, promotion's contribution toward reducing waste impacts is found in its capacity to increase the sales (Q) of sustainable products. The information made available through promotion makes it possible for customers to make more environmentally informed choices. The goals of sustainable promotion are two-fold: (1) establishing and maintaining the environmental credibility of both the product and firm behind it, and (2) educating a diverse set of stakeholders about the nature of environmental issues and solutions and how the firm's actions serve as positive solutions. In general, the environmental decisions/actions reflected by a firm's product and channel designs serve as valuable information resources for use in promotion. The implementation tools that translate these resources into marketing action are these traditional promotion mix elements: (1) advertising, (2) personal selling, (3) sales promotion, and (4) publicity/public relations. None of these tools is inherently P2 or R2 in character. Therefore, the designation of specific applications of these tools as support for either pollution prevention (P2) or resource recovery (R2) initiatives is simply a function of the "information contents" being communicated through them at the time (see Exhibit 6).

EXHIBIT 6: Sustainable Promotion Applications

- **Advertising**: Develop a product advertisement indicating the "percent of post-consumer recycled contents" in the package; create an institutional advertisement heralding the safety record of the firm's fleet of double-hulled oil tankers; support a multimedia campaign to improve the environmental image of products made from plastics; tri-venture a 30-second radio spot, with the U.S. Environmental Protection Agency and the Natural Resources Defense Fund, concerning the need for water conservation.

- **Personal selling**: Sub-contract sales training seminars in the specialized area of state-level environmental regulations; develop a detailed brochure explaining your firm's completion of ISO 14000 certification and what it means in terms of customer benefits (for use by the sales force).

- **Sales promotion**: Develop a "customer friendly" toner cartridge return-to-manufacturer program consisting of instruction brochure, mailer, pre-paid postage and labeling, and 1-800 information "hot line"; develop consumer brochures that explain the supermarket's role in recycling paper and plastics wastes.

- **Publicity/public relations**: Develop a quick-response information program that anticipates hazardous materials spills and provides factual and accurate information about the situation, and the actions being undertaken to remedy the problem; publicize corporate sponsorship of a national environmental organization.

Advertising Applications

Advertising provides the opportunity to communicate environmental information to large numbers of customers and other stakeholders. Specific types of advertising can serve different purposes in this process. The major objective of product advertising is to communicate relevant attributes and features. Because "environment" is not the primary consideration in most product purchases, experts suggest that eco-attributes be communicated in a low-key (understated/implicit) manner, while continuing to stress the primary product benefits the customer can expect. All other things equal, the presence of positive eco-attributes may represent a "tie-breaker" feature for many customers. Institutional advertising is designed for the purpose of positioning the firm as ecologically sensitive, responsible, credible, and trustworthy. Developing a positive environmental aura is consistent with the low-key product advertising approach mentioned above. Subject matter may include the company's environmental record, its alliances with activist groups, or its position on environmental issues such as global warming or air quality standards. Trade association advertising deals with how specific materials (e.g., plastics, petrochemicals, paper, ferrous and non-ferrous metals, etc.), and the products made from them, positively impact our lives. Pooling the resources of a number of producers and suppliers is a natural sustainable promotion application, the thrust of which is engender a positive environmental image for the material in question. Public service announcements represent a pooling of resources among private enterprise and public sector organizations (e.g., manufacturers, retailers, public interest groups, regulators, etc.) for the purpose of educating the general public about an environmental issue, such as air quality in urban areas.

Personal Selling Applications

Sales personnel are often the only contact intermediary organizations and end-customers have with a seller. The primary role of the sales force in sustainable promotion is to serve as a conduit for communicating the firm's environmental policies, profile, and commitment to its PSLC partners and customers. The importance of the sales force in this role will vary in relation to the types of sales tasks carried out at various levels within the PSLC. Those performing low level order-processing will be of limited usefulness in this regard. In contrast, those engaged in missionary and creative sales tasks represent a highly flexible medium through which important environmental messages can be delivered. These individuals, in particular, must be educated so they understand that environmental information can play a significant role in closing sales over the long run.

Sales personnel need to be knowledgeable about the following types of environmental information:

(1) Product environmental benefits: basic knowledge of ecological concepts, basic P2/R2 strategy, and applications to company brands.

(2) Regulatory/environmental compliance issues: basic knowledge of relevant environmental statutes that must be complied with by both the seller and buyer. "Compliance" must be treated as an eco-attribute that is sought by the buyer.

(3) ISO 14000 certification: when mandated as a buyer requirement, detailed knowledge of the firm environmental management system (EMS) will be necessary to get on the "to consider" list.

Because the above represent a variety of complex and highly technical issues, and are not included in the usual sales training curriculum, educational programs will be required to initially indoctrinate, and then constantly update sales personnel in these areas. This can be accomplished through formal sales training activities using in-house personnel and/or specialized vendors, sales meeting presentations, and sales personnel involvement on cross-functional teams (see Exhibit 6).

Sales Promotion Applications

Sales promotions are commonly directed at (1) customers (i.e., consumers and organizational buyers) and (2) internal and/or middleman marketing personnel. They attempt to induce immediate actions (e.g., increase quantity purchased by customers per transaction; increase the sales representative call rate per month), or serve as sales support devices. By imply adding "environmental contents," common sales promotion vehicles, such as catalogs/brochures, point-of-purchase displays, coupons/rebates, video presentations, allowances/trade-in programs, and trade show activities instantly assume the role of "communicator of sustainability" (see Exhibit 6).

Publicity-Public Relations Applications

The actions of firms sometimes lead to unintended environmental consequences: the Exxon Valdez Alaskan oil spill debacle is a case in point. This sort of negative publicity severely tarnishes the firm's environmental image and must be dealt with through responsive marketing communications that clear the air. Beyond the usual need to manage media relations (a public relations activity), advertising is also sometimes employed to accomplish public relations damage control by getting appropriate messages out to the general public. For example, Exxon ran full-page "Open Letter to the Public" advertisements in major daily U.S. newspapers shortly after the Exxon Valdez incident. On the positive side, well-designed out-bound public relations programs can have a positive impact on the firm's environmental image. Other proactive actions that can help a firm create and maintain a "sustainable aura" include entering into partnerships with environmental groups, developing a multi-stakeholder-oriented corporate environmental report (CER), and developing and documenting the firm's "environmental position" on the firm's web site (see Exhibit 6).

PRICING DESIGN-FOR-ENVIRONMENT

The setting and manipulation of price represents a major competitive weapon. Price is also usually the most important influence on the customer's purchase decision process. As with promotion, pricing decisions are not direct generators of wastes. Rather, pricing contributes to sustainability by increasing the sales volume of clean products (Q) through clean channels, while maintaining acceptable profit margins. Costs play a particularly important in sustainable pricing. One of the main issues is that environmental costs are often not allocated to the products that cause them; rather, they are categorized as non-allocated general overhead expenses where they have no impact on unit cost calculations. Because these costs can be significant, this practice tends to under-cost products that are incompatible with ecosystems and over-cost products that are compatible, thereby misstating profits, which is the key to retention in the product line. Therefore, one goal of sustainable pricing is to create the situation where the "Total Profit = Total Revenues - Total Costs" equation reflects a fair and full allocation of all relevant factors, including environmental costs. Again, the environmental decisions/actions reflected by a firm's product and channel designs can serve as valuable sources of information for developing cost accounting policies that result in more realistic cost allocations for guiding pricing.

A number of pricing practices have emerged that can be can be directly related to a variety of P2 and R2 strategies (see Exhibit 7). All face a general scenario in which most customers (both consumers and industrial buyers) assign much less importance to the relatively intangible benefits associated with eco-attributes than the usual primary benefits derived from product purchase (see Exhibit 7).

EXHIBIT 7: Sustainable Pricing Applications

- **Meet-the-competition/level pricing**: Maintain price at "look-alike" competitor levels while allowing positive eco-attributes to serve as the "tie-breaker."

- **Premium green pricing**: Develop a premium–priced electric village-transporter targeted at occupants of exclusive gated communities.

- **Larger quantity pricing**: Offer products in larger quantity packages at per unit discounts that reflect savings in packaging materials.

- **Complimentary product pricing**: Offer discounted remanufactured toner cartridges at discounted prices in association with new equipment purchases.

- **Service-life pricing**: Use price comparisons to show that compact fluorescent bulbs cost less than frequently replaced incandescent bulks when both energy costs and replacement costs are considered over time.

- **Take-back pricing**: Manufacturer offers a "back-end" discount coupon to be applied to a future purchase from that same manufacturer at some future point in time (loyalty discount).

- **Rent/lease pricing**: Execution of a non-title transfer contract that results in the product being automatically returned to the manufacturer at the end of service life or contract period.

Meet-the-Competition/Level Pricing

Many consumer products fall into a "commodity-convenience" category, where customers focus on traditional benefits offered by many look-alike brands, and price competition is intense. Matching the customary price level of competitors becomes the dominant consideration. Given basic benefits and price are equal, any positive environmental attributes offered by a brand can then serve as a transaction tie-breaker.

Premium Green Pricing

The belief in the assumption that large groups of customers will pay a premium to obtain for "green benefits" comes from self-response surveys reporting what customers say they will do. But, actions speak louder than words, and purchase actions generally reveal that consumers simply do not do as they say. The exception is a generally reported small and upscale segment of U.S. consumers reported by Roper Starch Worldwide Inc. (1997), called the "Green-Back Greens," to whom a higher than market price might appeal given the presence of significant eco-attributes. However, because even this segment is based on self-report data, the issue of premium green pricing remains shrouded in doubt. However, for products like General Motor's EV- electric car, which was lease-priced in the $30,000 to $40,000 range, the motive was likely to "skim-the cream" to achieve small sales while testing this strictly transitional technology in the marketplace ("GM Electric Cars. . ." 1996, p. E9).

Larger Quantity Pricing

Traditional packaged goods possess a unique eco-attribute: larger package sizes generally require less packaging material per unit of product, which translates into to less waste impact per unit of customer benefit. For example, the weight of paperboard packaging for a powdered detergent falls from 5.87 grams/load for an 18-load package to 4.55 grams/load for an 85 load package (a 23% difference)(Fuller 1999, p. 303). Although this reduced per unit price benefit is usually already passed along as a standard quantity discount, reporting the parallel environmental benefits of reduced packaging could serve as a low-key "tie-breaker" factor in some transactions.

Complimentary Product Pricing

When manufacturers link the sale of equipment to the long-term sale of replacement components, complimentary pricing can be employed.

When the component being continually replaced is relatively high-value, product design-for-re-manufacturing enhancements could make it profitable for the manufacturer to develop appropriate reverse channels to recapture and refurbish the component to "new" specifications. This would forge a long-term relationship with the customer and allow establishing long-term quantity discounts based on "buyer loyalty" over time. Remanufactured copier toner cartridges are an example.

Service-Life Pricing

Repetitive purchases of non-complimentary products over time set the stage for service-life pricing. One scenario is to use comparisons of costs/prices over time between "long-life, environmentally preferable" versus relative "short-life" products. Another scenario is to compare reusable and disposal product alternatives for the same applications. This has been done for many personal and medical products (e.g., diapers, surgical gowns, etc.) and brings into play life-cycle processes and associated total costs over time.

Take-Back Pricing

Take-back pricing involves pricing products, usually durable goods, in such a manner as to recover the future costs of disposal. The idea behind take-back is that involving the manufacturer at the end of product life will instigate changes in product design and distribution that will reduce ecological impacts significantly. However, this shift in functional responsibility entails costs that can be recovered through pricing considerations. Approaches include implementing a discounted future handling fee or a guaranteed trade-in discount system. In particular, this approach suggests opportunities for actualizing design-for-re-manufacturing and relationship marketing strategies.

Rent/Lease Pricing

Rent/lease pricing represents a shift in transaction format from outright ownership (title transfer) to the temporary transfer of property rights (product use) for a specified period of time, after which the product reverts back to the seller. For a sustainability perspective, this approach de-materializes consumption; customers obtain the benefits they need without accumulating large personal inventories of durable goods that are only occasionally utilized. Product take-back is also automatic, so disposal options for "taken-back" items (e.g., Remanufacture? Recycle?) must be considered during initial product design. Arrangements can be formally detailed in leases/contracts (e.g., automobiles, appliances, and furniture) or be quite informal in execution (e.g., 3-night video rental). The continuous customer contact associated with rent/lease tends to foster repeat purchase behavior over time; it is not single transaction focused. Because rent/lease pricing is essentially a relationship marketing approach, it has the potential to grow both brand loyalty and long-term customer continuity.

CONCLUSIONS

Sustainable marketing views ecosystems as a non-negotiable physical limiting factor in marketing strategy decisions. Because the preservation of clean and healthy ecosystems is a prerequisite for human survival, sustainable marketing must not be viewed as an exercise in corporate altruism. Rather, it challenges marketers to reinvent product systems so that they are "low-waste, no-negative-discharge" in character, while also delivering equivalent benefits to customers through products and meeting organizational goals (financial and other).

Marketing strategies are a major determinant of the use of natural capital/resources, the generation of wastes, and subsequent pollution. Sustainable marketing requires that marketing mix decisions be designed to be compatible with ecosystems; this mandates a systems approach when developing product, channel, promotion of P2 and R2 into the marketing decision-making process. P2 deals with preventive action; the point is to design product systems so that waste is eliminated from the start. R2 deals with remedial action; the point is to design product systems so that resources can be used over and over again. To attain these goals, sustainable marketing strategies are actualized through the design-for-environment (DFE) process. Within the marketing mix, product and channel design for-environment decisions directly serve waste management objectives. These decisions, in turn, provide valuable environmental information for use in promotion and pricing decision-making.

Because production-consumption processes and human well being are totally interconnected, the study of sustainable marketing cannot ignore social-moral issues. The ultimate answer to the question "Who is responsible for waste management?" will largely reflect the character and moral beliefs of the managers and customers who have to address it, as well as economic ramifications. The need for all parties to "cover their wastes" mandates that free riders cannot be tolerated; this includes customers, firms, and countries. Overall the prognosis for achieving sustainable marketing practice is positive: the changing values of individuals appear to be bringing pro-environmental beliefs to bear more heavily on business and customer decisions, and the economics of sustainable costs and prices are becoming more attractive when evaluated using traditional profit measures.

REFERENCES

Atlanta Journal/Constitution. 1996. "GM Electric Cars to Go on Sale in California, Arizona This Fall." January 5, p. E9.

BioCycle. 1995. "Hauling Food Residuals." August, p. 40.

Freeman, Harry, Teresa Harten, Johnny Springer, Paul Randall, Mary Ann Curran, and Kenneth Stone. 1992. "Industrial Pollution Prevention: A Critical Review." *Journal of the Air & Waste Management Association* 45:616-56.

Fussler, Claude and Peter James. 1996. *Driving Eco-Innovation.* London: Pitman Publishing.

Fuller, Donald A. 1991. "Recycling Post-Consumer Aluminum Containers: A Marketing Commentary." In: Robert L. King (ed.) *Developments in Marketing Science*, Vol. 14, Proceedings of the Academy of Marketing Science, pp. 101-5.

Fuller, Donald A. 1999. *Sustainable Marketing: Managerial-Ecological Issues.* Thousand Oaks, CA: SAGE Publications.

Fuller, Donald A., Jeff Allen, and Mark Glaser. 1996. "Materials Recycling and Reverse Channel Networks: The Public Policy Challenge." *Journal of Macromarketing* 16(1): 52-72.

Graedel, T. E. and B. R. Allenby. 1995. *Industrial Ecology.* Englewood Cliffs, NJ: Prentice Hall.

In Business. 1993. "Waste Reduction Works Like Magic." May-June, p. 1.

Licking, Ellen. 2000. "Hothouse Hangers to Fight Water Pollution." *Business Week*, March 20, p. 81.

National Solid Wastes Management Association. 1991. *The Future of Newspaper Recycling.* Washington, DC: NSWMA.

Neace, M. B. 1995. "Marketing's Linear-Hierarchial Underpinning and a Proposal for a Paradigm Shift in Values to Include the Environment." In: Michael J. Polonsky and Alma T. Mintu-Wimsatt (eds.) *Environmental Marketing: Strategies, Practice, Theory, and Research*, New York: Haworth, pp. 55-73.

Office of Technology Assessment. 1992. *Green Products by Design: Choices for a Cleaner Environment.* Washington, DC: Government Printing Office.

Ottman, Jacquelyn A. 1997. *Green Marketing: Opportunity for Innovation.* Lincolnwood, IL: NTC Business Books.

Reilly, William K. 1991. *The Next Environmental Policy: Preventing Pollution.* Washington, DC: U.S. Environmental Protection Agency, Office of Communications and Public Affairs.

Roper Starch Worldwide Inc. 1997. *Green Gauge Report.* New York: Roper Starch Worldwide Inc.

Tchobanoglous, George, Hilary Theisen, and Samuel A. Vigil. 1993. *Integrated Solid Waste Management: Engineering Principles and Management Issues.* New York: McGraw-Hill.

ECO-ACCOUNTING: HOW INDUSTRIAL ECOLOGY CAN PAY DOUBLE DIVIDENDES FOR BUSINESS

W. G. B. Smith
Environment Canada

THE PROBLEM

Human population growth and consumption now place unprecedented demands on the environment. Faced with these challenges, the Brundtland Commission recognised that the only way we would be able to continue to meet human needs was "by steadily reducing the energy and resource content of future economic growth" (WCED 1987: 213). In particular, Brundtland recommended that industrial operations should be encouraged "that are more efficient in terms of resource use, that generate less pollution and waste, that are based on the use of renewable rather than non-renewable resources, and that minimise irreversible adverse impacts on human health and the environment" (WCED 1987: 219).

Population and economic growth, and now more than ever, the lifestyles and consumption habits of more wealthy industrialised nations, draw massive amounts of energy and materials into the industrial system (Wernick et al. 1996). Studies show in North America that only seven percent of industrial throughput winds up as product and only 1.4 percent is still product after six months (Friend 1996). The waste generated per capita is now more than double that of the preceding generation (Davies & Mazurek 1997). Urban and industrial wastes are rapidly becoming potentially richer and more reliable material sources than naturally occurring ores and harvested fibres.

In nature, waste is the key to renewal. If we want to meet human needs and at the same time minimise the damage we do to the environment, then we will have to accept two challenges. We must steadily reduce the energy and material content of industrial production. At the same time, we must also increase our reliance on the use of industrial and post-consumer waste as the primary feedstock of future economic growth.

Canada's economy is characterised by a reliance on energy and natural resources. Because of the ready availability of energy, water, land and mineral resources, Canada is competitive in industrial sectors using these resources intensively. These industrial sectors (e.g., harvesting, extraction, food production, primary processing, energy generation and transportation) are generally more stressful to the environment than secondary manufacturing or service industries. The ratio of waste, contaminants, or resource recovery to useable product is very poor. Disposal, dispersion and dilution (end-of-pipe and end-of-stack solutions) are still the pollution and waste management approaches commonly in use. As long as Canada has a large backyard and under-prices its resources, there will not be much incentive for corporations to economise on the use of inputs or to minimise waste.

THE TRADITIONAL INDUSTRIAL PRODUCTION AND MARKETING MODEL

In the 19th and early 20th centuries, we managed industry as if we had unlimited resources and could produce unlimited waste without doing any harm. The traditional once-through model of industrial production depends on cheap abundant resources and waste disposal. Most industrial processes are fossil-fuelled, make intensive use of energy and materials, involve high temperature and pressures, and contain multiple steps where harmful substances can be discharged to the environment. Products are mass-produced, have limited useful lives, are not easily repaired and are cheaply discarded. Producers' responsibility for their products ended at the plant gate.

Since the 1970's, governments have forced industry to respond to growing public concern one pollutant at a time by imposing "command and control" regulations. Command and control regulations specify the allowable rates of discharge based on the use of a particular technology. To comply with these regulations, most companies have installed add-on pollution control devices. By definition these control devices cannot reduce risks to zero and may produce waste requiring safe disposal. As the stringency of control increases, the use of pollution control devices is sharply limited by rising costs. Moreover, the further removed from source, the more costly and less feasible pollution control and remediation options become. By relying on add-on control devices, increased economic activity invariably leads to decreased environmental quality. The command and control approach to regulation has diminished industry's capacity for adaptive learning and response. Industry has no incentive to innovate or to exceed the standards imposed by government.

WHAT IS INDUSTRIAL ECOLOGY?

More recently, public attention has shifted to more global concerns about the environmental effects of industrialisation and consumerism. We are entering a period where industry will have to make limited use of energy and resource inputs and to produce limited waste as an output. Industrial ecology has emerged over the last ten years as a distinct response to these concerns. It has been described as everything from a "metaphor" for looking at our society (Ehrenfield 1997, Socolow 1994) to "an agenda for management " (Tibbs 1992). The basic premise of industrial ecology is that the only way we can achieve a sustainable society is to redesign industrial production so that it emulates the workings of natural ecosystems. Industrial ecology suggests two lines of corporate self-improvement, centred on either the industrial plant or the products it produces.

Using nature as a model, industrial ecology views the industrial plant or system as an integrated set of cyclical processes in which the consumption of energy and materials is optimised, waste generation is minimised, and wastes from one process serve as feedstock for other production processes (Frosch and Gallopoulus 1989). Industrial ecology draws heavily on the work of Robert Ayres (1993) that views industrial production as a "metabolic" process. It attempts to close the "open materials cycle" characteristic of industrial society, whereby materials and energy are lost to economic use, and harmful toxic substances are released to the environment. Industrial ecology tries to "close the loop" in two ways: by eliminating waste from production processes, and by redesigning wastes as useful by-products that can be used in other processes.

Until recently, product design emphasised ease of manufacture and disposal over ease of repair and recycling. Stahel (1993) felt that designing durable and upgraded products with a longer useful life could further reduce the demand for energy and materials. Further, progress could be also made in closing the loop if producers developed customer service networks to support their products and to take back products at the end of their useful life.

The critical barrier to the internalisation of environmental costs and considerations by the firm is the lack of an all-inclusive environmental accounting system (Todd 1994). Moreover, managers lack the necessary market information about opportunities to turn waste into profit. In order to find new uses for waste or changing processes, so that the waste generated has some value to customers elsewhere in the industrial system, managers have to know who has what (supply), who needs what (market), who could use what (potential market) and who could produce something if somebody else wanted it (potential supply). Without a management information system functioning as a control feedback loop, we will be unable to identify the need for improvement in environmental performance or to assign the responsibility for change.

Industrial ecology asserts that an industrial system can be made to emulate a natural ecosystem through progressive modification of inputs, product design, production processes, and plant infrastructure. An agenda for action could include the following steps. First, products and production processes can be reformulated, through input substitution, so that scarce and harmful substances are replaced with plentiful and more benign substances. Second, production processes can be restructured so that waste is recycled and reused within the plant. Third, open production processes can be closed, so that harmful substances can be contained or reprocessed on-site. Fourth, infrastructure can be redesigned, so that waste from one process can be used either as feedstock in another process or as a saleable by-product. (An example of the application of this step would be co-generation.) Fifth, products can be reformulated and redesigned for decreased weight/mass and energy use as well as for disassembly and recycling after use. Sixth, product-life can be extended by improving durability and by redesigning for easy repair, part replacement and reassembly. Seventh, products can be marketed as services with lease and take-back provisions. Any of these actions would progressively reduce, but not completely eliminate, the throughput of energy and materials associated with economic growth.

Another development that will likely have a significant impact on the future of industrial ecology is the Zero Emission Research Initiative (ZERI) of the United Nations University in Tokyo (Heden 1995). ZERI was inspired by Gunter Pauli, a Belgian entrepreneur (manufacturer of the Ecover brand of environmentally benign cleansers), who found that in his own line of business he could reduce waste but not completely eliminate it. The trick in his view was to find the "missing links" to complete the cycle so that waste from one plant or process could be used as input to another. His vision was to establish multi-industry clusters of factories based on careful assessment of the missing links in their production processes. There are a broad range of "symbiotic" linkages that are only feasible now with government intervention in the marketplace, in the form of regulations or price adjustments. However, Pauli thinks that increasing demand for scarce commodities will ensure that in the near future, zero emissions will be beneficial from the firm's perspective even without public policy intervention. Pauli sees the elimination of waste solely as a way of obtaining maximum value from one's resources. If "zero inventory" (just-in- time delivery) or "zero defects" (total quality management) is possible, then "zero emissions" should also be possible. Pauli places zero emissions squarely in the realm of corporate strategy, and would clearly like to take the industrial system the next step to where virtually all material used or released by the industrial system would be cycled (Pauli 1997.)

DO WE HAVE THE BLUEPRINT FOR DESIGNING AN INDUSTRIAL ECOSYSTEM?

Life Cycle Thinking

Industrial ecology holds a considerably broader conception of industrial production than has been previously held by managers. It incorporates a life cycle approach to management, and a precautionary approach to decision making.

Life cycle thinking recognises that managers' responsibilities no longer end at the plant gate. Their responsibilities now extend upstream and downstream from the plant gate, encompassing a web of new relationships with suppliers and consumers. For example, through supply chain management, producers may try to make their purchasing habits more environmentally friendly. Lenders and insurers may force producers to incorporate the environmental liabilities associated with the construction, operation and closure of plants (i.e. brown field sites) in their business financial plans. Moreover, government authorities may force producers to take-back discarded or spent products at the end of their useful life. Generally speaking, life cycle thinking emphasises that the feasibility and benefit of environmental measures is greater, and the cost is less, when these measures are taken earlier in the life cycle. For example, in-plant recycling is more cost effective and has a greater environmental benefit than post-consumer recycling. Moreover, the positive effects of management actions taken early on in the life cycle are cumulative throughout the remaining phases of the product life cycle.

As a strategy, the precautionary approach tries to act on the sources of potential harm or hazards, rather than trying to determine acceptable or unacceptable levels of risk. The precautionary approach to decision making is imprecise about how to identify an adequate level of investment in technical or social change to prevent further environmental harm (Wynne 1993). The challenge is to provide a justification for policy decisions requiring efficiency gains (reduction in resource-use and waste-outputs). What the precautionary approach must provide are the motivation and incentives to seek out no-regrets solutions that are currently passed over under existing regulatory and profit-making regimes.

Industrial Metabolism

Every industry, regardless of sector or scale, can be characterised by its "metabolic processes"- a complex web of chemical, physical and biological processes that convert energy, raw materials, and labour into finished products and wastes. Industrial ecology tries to minimise total industrial throughput and waste, and to find beneficial uses for the by-products of industrial production in the metabolic processes of other industrial or living systems.

Managers face the daunting challenge of striking an optimum balance among improving process efficiency to minimise use of energy and natural resources; recovering waste created during production processes; re-using wastes created as by-products in other processes; and re-cycling materials from spent products at the end of their useful lives. Industrial metabolic efficiency can be measured through the reduction in material input per unit of economic output. Dissipative usage by which energy and resources are lost to economic uses is also a good measure of unsustainable consumption. By implication, this approach suggests that a "steady state" industrial economy would be characterised by near-total recycling of toxic or hazardous substances as well as a significant degree of recycling of materials whose disposal poses environmental problems.

Closing the Loop-From Product to Service

To "close the loop" industrial ecology tries to replace linear once-through industrial processes with cyclical processes that reduce the throughput of energy and materials and the need to use the environment as a sink for pollution and waste. Through "energy and material cascades" and "away grading", wastes become feedstocks for other processes. This strategy also calls for the production of more durable products, using recyclable materials and replaceable components. These products would be designed to be reuseable, possibly reconditioned, upgraded, and eventually recycled. The Four R's of appropriate technology include (see Stahel and Jackson 1993 Figure 4.1 p 267):
1) Reuse of products that are discarded;
2) Repair of goods that are malfunctioning, under-performing or broken;
3) Reconditioning or updating of products with new or second hand components;
4) Recycling the raw materials from durable products for local use in other goods.

At the bottom-end of the service hierarchy, the products may be sold as second-hand goods in lower value markets. The next grade of products may be reused after tune-up or cleaning. Minor damage may be repaired. At the next service level, the product could potentially be restored to its original functionality by a complete overhaul and the

Figure 1: Independence of the life-times of inter-compatible systems, proucts and components

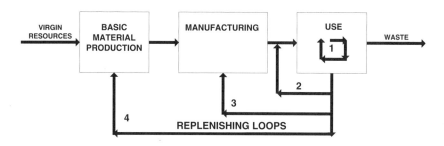

Loop 1: Re-use of goods
Loop 2: Repair of goods
Loop 3: Reconditioning/rebuilding of goods
Loop 4: Recycling of raw materials

replacement of component parts. At the highest service level, over-grading, the product would be adapted or updated to incorporate the latest technological advances or to meet current standards. Ultimately the raw materials from discarded products and components would be recovered and recycled for use in the manufacture of similar or lower grade products.

Although energy/material cascades will reduce the rate of industrial throughput they are still open, non-cyclical flows (O'Rourke et al. 1996). So far industrial ecology has paid more attention to options such as co-generation, the use of low-grade excess energy for heating, cooling or refrigeration, which presents limited opportunities for dissipating energy flows. The switch to renewable forms of energy should receive greater attention because the use of fossil fuels imposes a far greater burden on the environment than other energy sources. Hydrocarbons account for 86.8% of the pollution released to the environment (Wernick et al. 1996). Another consideration is that the transition from open to closed material cycles is often accompanied by significant shifts in energy consumption. For example, recycling aluminium cans results in significant energy savings; whereas recycling solvents from industrial waste streams will increase energy use. Finding sinks for existing waste streams will not be enough. Significant investments in separating and reprocessing technologies will be required to close material cycles.

Closing the loop also implies phasing-out the use, large scale production, and on-site storage of toxic or hazardous substances. Less harmful inputs would have to be substituted wherever possible. If toxic substances are used, they could be locally produced in small quantities on-demand, rather than transported long distances, and stored in large quantities on site for future use as we do now. For example, Mitchel (1992) suggested that where toxic substances must be used in a process, we could rely on the dynamic reaction of less hazardous precursors to create toxic substances that would be immediately transformed into benign final products. Another possibility is to produce waste streams from these processes in concentrated rather than dilute form, so that toxic substances may be reused. Closed-loop recycling and on-site containment may also be viable options for achieving zero-discharge.

Economies of scale discourage the design of products for long life and low maintenance, and make it uneconomical to repair broken or to upgrade worn out products. Demand for any product tends to increase as real prices fall due to economies of scale. Firms are thereby encouraged to increase sales and maximise profits by increasing output and capacity.

In the future, products would have to be positioned on service for industrial ecology to succeed in the marketplace. Growth could occur through finding new applications for current products or diversifying the product line. Extended producer responsibility and product take-back policies would have to become the norm.

Manufacturers would have to be willing to help develop the necessary local infrastructure and service networks necessary to recuperate and refurbish their own products. This network of local collection and recovery agencies could also become the source of new sales. As well, they could become service centres for the maintenance and repair of existing units.

Product life extension will inevitably lead to the replacement of relatively few large-scale, capital-intensive industrial plants with smaller-scale, labour- and skill-intensive production units. Any profits on the service component of the product line would have to more than offset the associated increase in overhead and labour to succeed. By implication, profit margins would come to depend not on the volume of sales but on the value of the services sold to the consumer.

Machines and durable goods may be treated as capital assets rather than as consumables - rented or leased but not sold. The producer retains the installed base of the product as an asset. This strategy makes it more costly for customers to switch to competitors, especially when the service offered is not standard. It works well with high-cost physical products. Customers may find this sales strategy attractive because it will free up their capital for other investments that may have potentially greater return or strategic value for their enterprise.

Building an Industrial Ecosystem

Industries tend to form spatial clusters in specific geographical regions. Their decision on where to locate is based on a combination of factors such as access to raw materials, convenient transportation and markets. In addition, firms have to consider the environmental constraints of various building sites.

Recent attempts to develop eco-industrial parks have shifted attention from product policy to a system-wide review of industrial production processes, and resulted in a growing realisation that, in many instances, greater economic and environmental gains can be made through collaboration than competition (Lowe et al. 1995, Côte et al. 1994.) In an ideal industrial system, all material inputs go into products and all energy is used to do work. Individual firms cannot "close the loop" on their own; that is to say, they can reduce but not completely eliminate pollution and waste. The trick is to find the "missing links" in their production processes needed to complete the cycle so that the waste from one plant or process can be used as input to another. An industrial complex could be built that would function as a virtual ecosystem, and would make use of the resulting waste by-products.

Eco-industrial parks are characterised by symbiotic relations between dissimilar firms. Industrial facilities can be clustered to minimise energy and material wastes through internal bartering and local sales of by-products. The total environmental impact of all the firms participating in an eco-industrial park should be less than the sum of the firms' individual impacts. The park infrastructure itself could also incorporate the best environmental practices in the choice of materials, energy use, waste reduction, and water management.

The strategy used to recruit new firms to the park should also reflect the potential for by-product exchange among the participants. Often the by-product from one firm and the input required by another firm are not a perfect match. Changes in process or technology used by the firms may have to be considered to make the match. Excess waste, heat and energy from one process may be used as feedstock in other processes. This may involve open loop or partial recycling where energy and waste is only partially recovered; closed loop recycling with near complete recovery; or synergistic relationships such as co-generation, where one process is dependent on the by-products of another. The success of these relationships depends on the scale of local demand, the efficiency of the conversion of waste to useable by-product, and the dependability of supply.

By establishing a waste exchange, eco-industrial parks help overcome informational barriers to transactions between firms. Firms may still face regulatory barriers and liability considerations.

By becoming linked to other firms by means of resource recovery loops, a firm's survival, growth, and expansion may become linked to the fate of other firms in the industrial ecosystem. Therefore the long-term reliability of these symbiotic supply relationships must be assured. Standby capabilities may have to be developed with other suppliers.

The creation of eco-industrial parks also creates many opportunities for partnering and networking. In a knowledge-based economy, small firms may not be able to achieve the critical mass of skills required to achieve break-through performance. Small- and medium-sized firms can achieve a competitive advantage over larger firms through their ability to create and explore new solutions by working together with other small firms. Networks of small- and medium-sized firms may also be more able to quickly reorganise the entire production cycle and value chain. A firm may obtain a competitive advantage by sharing common services or by technology transfers within the industrial park. Several types of networks could also emerge in response to other needs of the participants, including co-operative purchasing, production, marketing and learning networks. Factors influencing the development of networks include a common challenge, the benefits of collaboration, personal rapport or strong local community ties, and geographic proximity (Gertler 1995).

Waiting for the Next Industrial Revolution

Industrial production and mass consumption are still largely linear processes. Production, use and disposal often occur without substantial reuse or recovery of energy or materials. The industrial system is still driven by inputs of virgin materials, and waste continues to be generated and disposed of outside the economic system. As internal recycling is incorporated into production processes, the throughput of materials and energy will decrease. By integrating the lifecycles of diverse processes and products so that the waste stream from some become the feedstock for others, the materials and energy cycle may also be extended.

If every factory in the world shifted to the cleanest production available (or even the cleanest plausible technology), the larger environmental crises would be at best be deferred a few years....As long as the material component of products is still largely based on the use of virgin resources, while the energy is largely derived from fossil fuels, clean is an impossible dream...indeed sustainability will be a distant receding goal (Ayres 1993).

Much of the debate about sustainability obscures the fact that corporations, not individuals and households, are responsible for most of the decisions about energy and material use, waste disposal and pollution released to the environment. Industrial ecology allows us to focus on the role of technology, something we ignore at our peril. By helping to introduce more benign and less wasteful products and processes, industrial ecology could make a major contribution to reducing the flow of matter and energy per unit of economic activity. Short product life cycles with limited functional end-of-life value are also incompatible with sustainability. Moreover, the scale of industrial production must receive due consideration in the calculus of sustainability.

The transition from a resource-based to a service-oriented economy could be especially difficult in Canada. This transition will be further complicated by our lifestyle and consumption habits. If we accept Ayres' (1995) premise that "human welfare depends on the service, not the material content of production", it follows that the technological transformation of the economy promised by industrial ecology could allow us to increase human welfare without limits. The challenge to business is no more than "Find pollution and waste and you've found something you have paid for but can't sell....By striving to eliminate it we can grow a more efficient, competitive economy" (Lowe 1992).

CAN INDUSTRIAL ECOLOGY SUCCEED IN THE MARKETPLACE?

Current environmental rhetoric claims that win-win solutions should be the foundation of management strategy and that trade-offs can largely be avoided through smart decision making and technological innovation. Although there are many instances where managers have overlooked win-win solutions, they more commonly face decisions where there are trade-offs. The environmental "value chain" (Porter 1986) includes activities that occur throughout the whole product life cycle: out-sourcing ("supply chain" management), research and development ("green" design), manufacturing operations (industrial "symbiosis"), sales (service marketing, eco-labelling), packaging and waste disposal (extended producer responsibility). By improving their knowledge of the value-creating potential of efforts to improve their environmental performance, managers can strategically position their firms in the marketplace and differentiate their products from those of their competitors.

Corporate Buy-In

Although waste reduction and energy efficiency improvements are low-risk, overhead-reducing investments, they often receive scant attention from managers. When pollution prevention opportunities are found, corporate business priorities and decision making processes can pose significant barriers to acting on these opportunities (Porter & Van Linde 1995; Denton 1994; A.D. Little 1991). Managers are more likely to be rewarded for growing revenue than cutting costs. Up to now it is decisions about where to invest capital, what products to provide, and where to sell them that have been considered to be the most important determinants of long-term business success. Eco-efficiency projects have to compete with proposals to increase production capacity and sales.

Demand for energy and other inputs are a function of price. Raw materials are still so cheap that suppliers can often undercut the price of recycled materials. Even where waste disposal is problematic, disposal costs may be still too low to matter. Energy costs are routinely lumped together with other overhead costs and may be inconsequential relative to overall costs. As a result, energy conservation projects usually do not call for fundamental changes in production processes. Because waste disposal costs, energy, and resource prices are too low, they fail to induce input substitution, or technological innovation.

To an increasing extent, firms' access to investment capital, debt refinancing, and insurance now requires the full disclosure of their environmental liabilities. Only rarely are environmental issues associated with other business concerns such as loss of market share or damage to their corporate image and reputation. Under existing business conditions, firms are more likely to consider pollution prevention strategies when the:
·   costs of regulatory compliance and exposure to liability can be reduced;
·   cost increases cannot be passed on to the consumer;
·   thresholds of risk are very large;
·   exact location of risk thresholds are unknown;
·   potential damage is not reversible; or
·   the magnitude of the possible losses are unknown.

Managers also have many incentives to conceal poor environmental performance and liabilities. For example, the perceived risk to managers or the firm would outweigh possible long-term benefits:
·   when after all the associated environmental costs are attributed to the product, it is found to be unprofitable to produce;
·   the product in question accounts for a large percentage of the firm's revenue and its discontinuance would mean loss of market share; or
·   the mere existence of this highly sensitive information could result in potential contingent liabilities or the threat of regulatory restraints.

Consumer Demand

Green consumerism uses individual preferences to promote less environmentally damaging goods and services (Smith 1998). It is based on the belief that individuals in their everyday lives should help to save the planet. Although eco-labelling helps consumers make informed choices and verify product claims more cheaply than a comparable regulatory program, the very notion of green consumerism is itself problematic. Since the 1960's, the amount of solid waste disposed of per capita in North America has doubled (Davies & Mazurek 1997). The environmental loading from consumer use of goods and services now exceeds that from manufacturing processes in most advanced economies (Ayres 1993). This means that people are simply buying, consuming and disposing of more things. Uncoupling material wants from affluence may prove to be more difficult than reducing energy/material used to meet human needs (Wernick et al. 1996). Our goal should be to reduce consumption, not to redefine it according to consumer preferences or market forces.

"Green" consumer products typically are niche market products that have improved their performance in relation to one or more environmental attributes. Most green consumer products are the "less from less" variety. Their claim to environmental soundness is usually based on what they do not contain. They rarely generate significant market share because they simply do not do a good enough job - such products must have a lower overall environmental impact than alternatives and sell in place of products that have a greater environmental impact....Business is not fundamentally interested in increasing the physical volume of goods it makes and sells - its real interest is in profit - a business would be more than happy to increase its profit, while making and selling less tonnage of product - focusing efforts on product usage is the key to achieving more profit from less resources, i.e., provide a product that provides better results at lower cost than the competition (Hindle et al. 1993) .

Typically when firms develop environmentally sound products, the newer speciality product is sold in upscale markets to discriminating consumers who can afford to pay for it. Existing polluting products continue to be sold in mass markets at a discount. Experience has shown that except in narrow market segments, environmental soundness is not a substitute for basic product performance and quality, but only an additional benefit (see Fischer & Schot 1993).

Regulatory and market pressures to adopt eco-design and clean production practices are generally weak. Life cycle impacts with the exception of packaging or waste disposal are difficult to regulate. Other than in a few European countries, consumer demand for green products is generally weak. The experience of most firms to date has been that customers are not willing to trade off performance or to pay more for green products (Centre for Clean Design 1997; Hindle et al. 1993). Few firms have been active in this domain for more than three to five years. Most of the active firms are larger multinationals in the telecommunications and electronics sectors (Centre for Clean Design 1997). Eco-design and clean production practices can improve a firm's productivity and reduce the cost of compliance with environmental regulations. They could also be a significant source of competitive advantage. The real challenge to firms, however, is to get more value and performance in products that use fewer resources and produce less waste.

Investor Response

Research to date suggests that although environmental performance and financial performance appear to be correlated, not all firms or industrial sectors are equally well positioned to take advantage of environmental opportunities (Reed 1998, WBCSD 1997). For some industrial sectors such as forestry, mining, and utilities, environment performance is a core business concern because they need to protect their licenses to operate. For others, headlines risk may play a larger role in investment decisions. Event studies show that the market punishes negative headlines and disclosures (Reed 1998). Lending institutions also have a strong interest in performing extensive due diligence reviews of the environmental performance of prospective borrowers (Bisset 1995, Robbins & Bisset 1994). They are likely to be concerned about potential lender liability (e.g., for clean up costs), possible sudden drops in the firm's capitalised value, and the risk of loan default due to cash flow problems because of falling sales, litigation, insurance claims, fines or penalties (Weiler 1997). A more recent phenomenon are ethical investment funds. Traditionally these funds have been considered to be "green" because of what they do not contain. Portfolio studies show that these funds outperform the market. Nonetheless, it is not possible to say at this time whether these favourable preliminary findings are a function of low risk investments or better managed investments (Reed 1998, Adams 1997 WBCSD 1997). Portfolio managers have a fiduciary duty to maximise returns, minimise risks and conserve capital/assets for the beneficiary. Only when the linkage between environmental and financial performance is accepted will environmental considerations become a routine part of the selection process that any prudent investor would normally follow (Reed 1998). However, corporate managers would be foolhardy not to take action now to position themselves to take advantage of the increasing public and shareholder interest in the environmental performance of their firms.

Regulation

The belief that companies will act on profitable environmental opportunities without a regulatory push may be based on false assumptions: companies often have limited time and attention, and lack basic information and the incentive to act. Regulation may be needed to level the playing field and to force action when the cost of compliance is not offset by other advantages (Porter & Linde 1995). A firm has an incentive to go "beyond compliance" when it thinks it can improve its financial bottom line or more appropriately manage business risk (Reinhardt 1999, Estey & Porter 1998). The firm may be able to reduce the cost or quantities of inputs it must purchase, or capture a price premium for its products. It may also seek to minimise the risk of accidental failure and product liabilities, thereby reducing the threat of future litigation and government intervention. Through strategic interaction with regulators, a firm may obtain government sanction for a business solution in which they have a competitive advantage. For example, Dow exited from the CFC business prior to the phase out of ozone depleting substances because they had patented a more profitable substitute. Internationally co-ordinated regulatory action prevented Dow from being undercut in the market place.

Value Creation – The Key to Breakthrough Performance

For industrial ecology to succeed in the marketplace as a business strategy, it must contribute to the financial success of the firm. Industrial ecology contributes to the financial success of the firm by reducing costs, improving asset usage, increasing productivity, diversifying revenue growth, and reducing risk. Better environmental performance helps contain a firm's cost of doing business. For example, process improvements reduce resource input, overhead, operating, waste treatment and disposal costs, yielding many small earning improvements that may not appear to be significant unless aggregated. Improved environmental performance could also improve a firm's competitiveness by creating new product opportunities from waste by-products and new revenue from recycling. Product improvements may increase a firm's market share and pricing power by building retailer and customer loyalty. The firm must be able to protect itself from imitators long enough to recoup its investment or be able to target customers who are willing to pay more for a better product. A firm may diversify its product lines by increasing the service content of its offering or through extended product stewardship lock-in its customer base. However, the revenues from diversification must more than offset increased overhead and labour costs associated with this strategy. Environmental strategies that are not value-added are unlikely to be sustainable in the marketplace (Arnold & Day 1998, Reed 1998) .

Rappaport (1996) and Copeland (1996) have shown that business decisions can be assessed on the basis of value drivers. These include strategic, operating, investment, and financing considerations. Strategic value drivers include anticipated future costs and earnings potential. These drivers include opportunity costs and how long a better than market average return can be sustained. Operating value drivers focus on profit per unit sales. By increasing the product benefit or quality for the consumer (price leadership or product differentiation) and lowering costs of production through reduced use of inputs and waste, managers are able to increase their profit margins. Investment value drivers stress the ratio of sales to fixed assets. For example, end-of-pipe solutions are generally more capital-intensive and increase operating costs more than pollution prevention. Lower material throughput also reduces purchasing, storage and depreciation costs. Financing value drivers lower borrowing and insurance costs. For example, many environmental risks cannot be diversified and often the only way to reduce the associated costs or liabilities is to reduce the risk.

Table 1: Value-Added Environmental Strategies

ENVIRONMENTAL STRATEGY	Improve Production Processes	Redesign or Upgrade Products	Diversify Product Lines
Focus	Efficiency gains / Pollution prevention	Improved product quality	Increased service / Product stewardship
Business Value	Reduce costs and exposure to liability	Command a price premium or increase market share	Develop new products or lock-in customer base
Financial Impact	Increased profit margin and return on equity	Increased competitive advantage	Increased revenue

The overall contribution of industrial ecology to the corporate bottom line could be assessed on the basis of shareholder value - the expected cash flow minus any borrowing - the amount that would potentially be available to pay investors (Shaltegger & Figge 1998, WBCSD 1997). This approach has gained considerable support among those who feel that inaccurate expectations pose less of a problem than reliance on past events. It is also more manageable than other approaches because fewer variables need to be considered (forecast cash flow, discounting, interest and risk factors). Current management accounting practices reflect past performance, and are of little help in envisioning a company's future business success.

Table 2: Shareholder Value

(Future Discounted Cash Flow minus Debt Payments)

Free Cash Flow			Discount Rate
Strategic	**Operating**	**Investment**	**Financing**
Value growth	Sales growth	Working capital	Cost of capital
Opportunity costs	Profit margin	Fixed capital	(debt & equity)
	Tax rate		

DO WE HAVE THE TOOL KIT TO DO THE JOB?

Industrial ecology currently relies upon stand-alone decision tools such as Life-Cycle Analysis (LCA), Design for the Environment (DfE) and an assortment of environmental indicators. These tools have been developed to support product-oriented environmental policies and corporate reporting requirements.

LCA is used to evaluate the environmental burdens associated with all phases of a product's production, use, and disposal. LCA has mainly been applied to simple, low design, resource-intensive products. The materials in these products may be recycled as bulk commodities or may place excessive demands on waste disposal facilities. LCA has also been used to rate potential hazards and the impact of input substitution on the performance of products such as detergents. The most telling criticism of LCA has been that when different methods are used to evaluate the same product, substance or material, they often give inconsistent results

(Ayres 1995). LCA has failed to provide conclusive results because there are no commonly agreed-upon methods for comparing, valuing or weighting different environmental impacts. Moreover, use of LCA methods is often limited by cost or insufficient data. Although LCA does not provide a common denominator or bottom line comparisons of different product claims, it has been extensively used within firms to evaluate corporate progress towards policy targets. (For examples, see Nortel 1996, Kortman et al. 1994, Adriaanse 1993, Steen 1992, Braunschweig 1991).

Figure 2

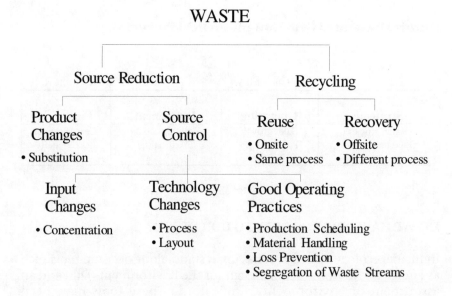

DfE first emerged in the 1980's as a generic response to concerns about the scale of technology, incineration and the amount of waste going to landfills. It deals with the potential environmental impacts of industrial processes and consumer products in a completely different way. It introduces the principles of pollution prevention into the design process before non-reversible choices have been made and while the selection of alternatives is still feasible and not cost prohibitive. DfE has been applied to structurally complex, high design products (e.g., electronics). These products usually contain valuable components or rare materials that are worth recovering.

DfE is a rule-based design system. First, the number of parts and assembly steps should be drastically reduced. Process chains should be shortened, bypassing as many intermediate steps as possible. These changes will reduce production, scrap, and rework costs. By reorganising production, there will also be savings in space, heating and lighting costs. Second, products and packaging should be redesigned to reduce their material content, size and weight. Third, the use of toxic and hazardous substances should be discontinued because of inherent dangers-in-use and potential liabilities. Fourth, products should also reformulated for durability, easy repair, eventual disassembly and recycling. This change can be achieved through modular design, standardisation and the use of materials that are easily machined or reprocessed. The bottom line is the reduction or elimination of potential hazards and waste: anything that does not add value to the product (Graedel and Allenby 1995; Ciambrione 1996). Although eco-design and clean production practices work well with heavily engineered products, they do not provide easily understood metrics that can be generally used in strategic business decision making.

Even though environmental reporting is based on the adage, "what gets measured gets done", no one has yet agreed on a common set of benchmarks or performance indicators that firms can use in decision making. Moreover, existing indicators generally do not clarify the relationship between the value of goods and services created and their associated environmental impacts. The recent Global Reporting Initiative (1999) has not materially advanced the state-of-the-art of corporate environmental reporting. Its primary concern has been the audit and verification of the facts and figures disclosed in the reports, not their usefulness in corporate decision making. Many critics feel that corporate environmental reporting is nothing more than a public relations exercise.

The World Business Council (1999) has been actively trying to promote the concept of eco-efficiency and to develop environmental indicators to evaluate the ratio of commercial value to the enviro-impacts created by business. In a recent survey of Canadian business, Vrooman and Beillard (2000) found that "eco-efficiency is recognised by some, endorsed by a few and not widely promoted." They encountered a general resistance by business to the use of "one size fits all" environmental indicators that could be used to compare different businesses lines, products or services. Their survey found that the four most important priorities for Canadian business were to reduce energy intensity (75%), material use (60%) and toxic dispersion (50%) and to improve material recyclability (36%).

ECO-ACCOUNTING FOR DOUBLE DIVIDENDS - THE NEXT STEP

Industrial ecology provides a coherent framework for strategic thinking about and testing of management options for the whole spectrum of environmental issues confronting an industry. Industrial ecology goes beyond mere efficiency improvements. By conceiving of environmental liabilities as potential assets and waste as potentially valuable products, industrial ecology could contribute a value-added perspective to environmental management. The value of an end product can be defined by the sum of the processes needed to make it, its properties in use and the possibilities of the end-product being reused and recycled. For example, the "greenness" of a consumer products could be determined from the percentage of inputs that are derived from recycled energy, materials and waste by-products. Industrial processes could be reassessed on the basis of the proportion of the inputs that wind up in useful products. Substitution of plentiful (renewable) for scarce resources and benign for harmful substances would also be an important consideration. Industrial ecology could guide the transition from fragmented and costly compliance with environmental regulations to more proactive programs yielding cost savings and new sources of revenue. It links the achievement of environmental quality objectives with continuous technological improvement and wealth creation.

It is no longer possible to ignore environmental costs and damages that fall outside the production process and to allow them to be borne by third parties, nature and future generations. Industrial processes and products must now start to incorporate environmental costs and damages in their financing, cost allocation, and pricing structures. The problem is how to do it.

There is no consensus about what constitutes an environmental cost or expenditure. Accounting systems often do not identify or assign environmental expenditures to corporate responsibility centres. Environmental costs are often lumped into overhead. In a recent Tellus survey (U.S. PCSD 1995) over 55 percent of the firms allocated environmental expenditures to overhead. In allocating overhead costs, firms used labour hours (58%), production volume (53%), and material use (27%). If environmental costs are ignored, left in a common pool or allocated incorrectly (say on a fixed percentage basis) to the various product lines, product managers do not have incentives to make improvements. An effort has to be made to capture the environmental cost elements associated with each activity or process and to use this information in business decision making.

Managers need a coherent accounting framework to guide environmental decision-making because they lack the means of assessing

the contribution of improvements in environmental performance to the financial success of the firm. It will help them direct their attention to high impact and high opportunity business units. Conventional bookkeeping systems do not track the environmental costs of their decisions. These decisions include: (1) the selection of raw materials and process technology; (2) product design and marketing; (3) pollution control (reducing leakages from the system); and (4) recycling of waste by- products. To achieve minimum waste at minimum cost, managers must strike an optimum balance among decisions to:
· Reduce the use of inputs
· Limit the creation of wastes during production
· Reuse wastes produced during production as raw materials in other processes, and
· Recover wastes from products at the end of their useful lives (Frosch 1996).

Figure 3

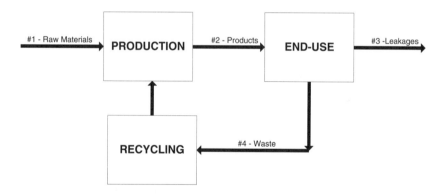

The first step in creating suitable environmental accounts is to implement activity- or transaction-based costing. Activity-based accounting provides the missing link between the demand for resources and value creation (Cooper and Kaplan 1991, 1988). Many important cost categories are not driven by short-term changes in output but vary over a period of years with changes in plant layout and design, production process, product mix and client services. Costs must be allocated to products/processes in order to ensure that the responsible managers have the necessary incentives to make needed improvements or to find creative alternatives. Then activity drivers (e.g., increased sales) and cost drivers (e.g., energy and materials used, waste disposal) must be identified for each product/process. Managers must account for conventional costs (such as increased use and more waste), for potentially hidden costs (such as siting and design, inspections, eventual plant closure and site decommissioning), and for contingent liabilities (such as potential claims, fines and penalties).

A product by process matrix could be created (see Figure 4) from the same information. As long as the units are consistent along rows, inputs and outputs may be measured in any convenient physical unit. The aggregate net resource requirements, direct and indirect outputs (including leakages) of a series of linked processes, may be determined by the application of matrix algebra. This simplifies the task of developing a process-based map linking activities, inputs, costs, revenues, impacts, and effects.

Figure 4

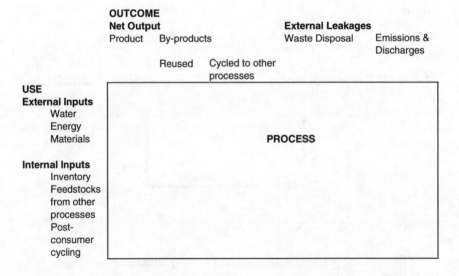

The next step would be to develop a series of environmental performance indicators, that could be based on the product-by-process matrix, and could be incorporated into a financial spreadsheets:

Industrial ecology simplifies environmental accounting considerably. By clarifying the relationship between the stocks and flows of resources required and identifying their fate in the environment, industrial ecology

W.G.B. Smith **359**

Table 3

INPUTS:	• Water - freshwater intake
	• Energy - renewable/fossil/nuclear
	• Raw material - renewable/non-renewable
	• Toxic or hazardous substances
	• Recycling -
	  • On site recovery (waste water, energy, materials)
	  • Feedstocks (by-products from other processes)
	  • Post-consumer recycling (components and materials)

THROUGHPUTS:	• Extractive waste or recovery ratio • Renewables - regrowth, restocking ratios • Process efficiency: $(Products+Leakages-Recycled\ by\text{-}products/_{New\ +\ Recycled\ inputs})*100$ • Cycle time (similar to inventory turnover) • Recovery rate - by-products and useable waste
OUTPUTS:	• Product - decreased weight/mass and energy use • Service life - (% of output that is replacement demand) • Packaging
LEAKAGES:	• Onsite storage/treatment - toxic/hazardous/radioactive • Other emissions and discharges to air or water • Waste disposal - landfills/incineration

makes it much easier to quantify the costs, revenues and potential liabilities associated with any product or process. By incorporating these measures within a financial spreadsheet we hope to facilitate the analysis of policies and market constraints limiting corporate environmental performance.

CONCLUSIONS

There is a need to rethink industrialism. Our prosperity and future depends upon it. Industrial ecology provides a useful way of thinking about the challenges that lie ahead. The blueprint and toolkit needed to build an industrial ecosystem need further work. Industrial ecology has the potential to succeed in the marketplace. It links environmental protection to other strategic management concerns such as growing the business, reducing risk, and increasing productivity. Industrial ecology provides the means of testing hypotheses about how things work, a reality check, to help us learn from experience and transform the marketplace.

REFERENCES

Adams, Roger. 1997. "Linking Financial and Environmental Performance." *Environmental Accounting and Auditing Reporter* 2 (10).

Adriaanse, Albert. 1993. *Environmental Policy Performance Indicators - a study on the development of indicators for environmental policy in the Netherlands.* The Hague: Netherlands Ministry of Housing, Spatial Planning and the Environment.

Arnold, Matthew B., and Robert M. Day. 1998. *The Next Bottom Line: Making Sustainable Development Tangible.* Washington D.C.: World Resources Institute.

Ayres, Robert U. 1993. "Industrial Metabolism - Closing the Materials Cycle." In: *Clean Production Strategies: Developing Preventive Environmental Management in the Industrial Economy,* edited by T. Jackson. Boca Raton, Florida: Lewis Publishers.

Ayres, Robert U. 1995a. "Economic growth: politically necessary but not environmentally friendly." *Ecological Economics* 15:97-99.

Ayres, R. U. 1995b. "Life Cycle Analysis: A Critique." *Resource Conservation and Recycling* 14:199-223.

Bisset, Doug. 1995. "Managing Risk: A New Responsibility for Banks." *The Bankers Magazine* 178 (2):55-59.

Braunschweig, A. 1991. "The new ecological valuation method based on ecological scarcity and its application to Switzerland." Paper read at SETAC - Europe Workshop on Environmental Life-Cycle Analysis of Products, December, at Leiden.

Centre for Clean Design. 1997. *Identification of Research Agenda and Issues in Relation to Clean Design (Eco-Design).* Farnham, Surrey: Surrey Institute of Art and Design.

Ciambrone, David F. 1996. *Waste Minimization as a Strategic Weapon.* Boca Raton, Florida: Lewis Publishers.

Cooper, Robin, and Robert S. Kaplan. 1988. "How Cost Accounting Distorts Product Costs." *Management Accounting* LXIX (10):20-27.

Cooper, Robin, and Robert S. Kaplan. 1991. "Profit Priorities from Activity Based Costing." *Harvard Business Review* (3):130-135.

Copland, T. 1990. *Valuation: Measuring and Managing the Value of Companies.* New York: John Wiley and Sons.

Côte, Raymond, Robert Ellison, Jill Grant, Jeremy Hall, Peter Klynstra, Michael Martin, and Peter Wade. 1994. *Designing and Operating Industrial Parks as Ecosystems.* Halifax, Nova Scotia: Dalhousie, School for Resource and Environmental Studies.

Davies, J. Clarence (Terry), and Jan Mazurek. 1997. *Regulating Pollution: Does the U.S. System Work?* Washington D.C.: Resources for the Future.

Denton, Keith. 1994. *Enviro-Management: How Smart Companies Turn Environmental Costs into Profits.* Englewood Cliffs N.J.: Prentice Hall.

Ehrenfield, John R. 1997. *Industrial Ecology: A framework for product and process design.* Cambridge MA: MIT Program on Technology, Business and the Environment.

Estey, D.C., and M.E. Porter. 1998. "Industrial Ecology and Competitiveness: Strategic Implications for the Firm." *Journal of Industrial Ecology* 2 (1):35-43.

Fischer, Kurt, and Johan Schot. 1993. *Environmental Strategies for Business: International Perspectives on Research Needs and Policy Implications.* Washington D.C. Island Press.

Friend, Gil. 1996. "A Cyclical Materials Economy: What goes around comes around...or does it?" *New Bottom Line*, March 12.

Frosch, Robert A. 1996. "Towards the End of Waste: Reflections on a New Ecology of Industry." *Daedalus* 125 (3):199-211.

Frosch, R. A, and N.E. Gallopoulus. 1989. "Strategies for Manufacturing." *Scientific American* 261 (3):144-152.

Gertler, Nicholas. 1995. *Industrial Ecosystems: Developing Sustainable Industrial Structures.* Masters, Civil and Environmental Engineering, Technology and Policy Program, Massachusetts Institute of Technology, Boston.

Global Reporting Initiative. 1999. *Sustainability Reporting Guidelines - Exposure Draft for Public Comment and Pilot Testing.* Boston: CERES.

Graedel, T.E., and B.A. Allenby. 1995. *Industrial Ecology.* Englewood Cliffs, New Jersey: Prentice Hall.

Heden, Carl-Goran. 1995. *The Zero Emissions Research Initiative.* Tokyo: United Nations University.

Hindle, Peter, Peter White, and Kate Minion. 1993. "Achieving Real Environmental Improvements Using Value Impact Assessment." *Long Range Planning* 26 (3):36-48.

Kortman, J.G.M., E.W. Lindeijer, H. Sas, and M. Spengers. 1994. *Towards a single indicator for emissions - an exercise in aggregating environmental effects.* Vol. nr 1994/2. The Hague: VROM.

Little, Arthur D. 1991. *Seizing Strategic Environmental Advantage: A Life Cycle Approach.* Cambridge, Mass.: Centre for Environmental Assurance - Arthur D. Little Inc.

Lowe, Ernest. 1992. *Discovering Industrial Ecology: An overview and strategies for implementation.* Oakland, California: Change Management Centre.

Lowe, Ernest A., Steven R. Moran, and Douglas B. Holmes. 1995. *Fieldbook for the Development of Eco-Industrial Parks V. II, Final Report, Indigo Development.* Research Triangle Park N.C.: Research Triangle Institute.

Mitchel, James W. 1992. "Alternative starting materials for industrial processes." *Proceedings of the National Academy of Sciences* 29 (February):821-826.

Nortel. 1996. "Northern Telecom Environmental Performance Index (EPI)." (http://www.nortel.com/cool/environ/epi): Northern Telecom.

O'Rourke, Dana, Lloyd Connelly, and Catherine P. Koshland. 1996. "Industrial Ecology: A Critical Review." *International Journal of Environment and Pollution* 6 (2/3):89-112.

Pauli, Gunter. 1997. *The Second Green Revolution*. Tokyo, Japan: United Nations University, Zero Emissions Research Initiative.

Porter, Michael. 1986. *Competitive Advantage: Creating and Sustaining Superior Performance*. New York: Free Press.

Porter, M.E., and C. van der Linde. 1995. "Green and Competitive: Ending the Stalemate." *Harvard Business Review* 73 (5):120-134.

Rappaport, Alfred. 1996. *Creating Shareholder Value: The New Standard for Business Performance*. New York: Free Press.

Reed, Donald J. 1998. *Green Shareholder Value, Hype or Hit - Sustainable Enterprise Perspectives*. Washington D.C.: World Resources Institute.

Reinhardt, Forest L. 1999. "Market Failure and The Environmental Policies of Firms: Economic Rationales for 'Beyond Compliance Behavior'." *Journal of Industrial Ecology* 3 (1):9-21.

Robbins, Lorne, and Doug Bisset. 1994. "The Role of Environmental Risk Management in the Credit Process." *Journal of Commercial Lending* 76 (10):18-25.

Schaltegger, Stefan, and Frank Figge. 1998. *Environmental Shareholder Value*. Basel: University of Basel, Center of Economics and Business Administration (WWZ), and Bank Sarisin & Co.

Smith, Toby M. 1998. *The Myth Of Green Marketing*. Toronto: University of Toronto Press.

Socolow, Robert. 1994. "Six Perspectives from Industrial Ecology." In: *Industrial Ecology and Global Change*, edited by R. Socolow, C. Andrews, F. Berkhout and V. Thomas. New York: Cambridge University Press.

Stahel, W. R., and T. Jackson. 1993. "Optimal Utilization and Durability: Towards a New Definition of a Service Economy." In: *Clean Production Strategies: Developing Preventive Environmental Management in the Industrial Economy*, edited by T. Jackson. Boca Raton, Florida: Lewis Publishers.

Steen, Bengt, and Sven-Olof Ryding. 1992. *The EPS Enviro-Accounting Method: An Application of environmental accounting principles for evaluation and valuation of environmental impact on product design*. Goteborg: Swedish Environmental Research Institute (IVL).

Tibbs, Hardin B. C. 1992. "Industrial Ecology - An Agenda for Environmental Management." *Pollution Prevention Review* 2 (2):167-180.

Todd, Rebecca. 1994. "Zero-Loss Environmental Accounting Systems". In: *The Greening of Industrial Ecosystems*, edited by B. R. Allenby and D. J. Richards. Washington, D.C.: National Academy Press.

U.S. President's Council on Sustainable Development. 1995. *Environmental Cost Accounting for Capital Budgeting: A Benchmark Survey of Management Accountants*. Boston, Massachusetts: Environmental Protection Agency, Pollution Prevention Division, Office of Pollution Prevention and Toxics - Tellus Institute.

Vrooman, Wally, and Cheryl Beillard. 2000. *The Status Of Eco-efficiency and Indicator Development in Canadian Industry - A Report on Industry Perceptions and Practices*. Ottawa: Industry Canada.

WBCSD. 1997. *Environmental Performance and Shareholder Value*. Geneva, Switzerland: Report of the World Business Council for Sustainable Development.

WBCSD. 1999. *Eco-Efficiency Indicators and Reporting*. Geneva: World Business Council for Sustainable Development, Working Group on Eco-efficiency Metrics and Reporting.

WCED, World Commission on Environment and Development. 1987. *Our Common Future - The Brundtland Report*: Oxford University Press.

Weiler, Edward, Brian C. Murray, Sheryl J. Kelley, and John T. Ganzi. 1997. *Report on Environmental Risk Management at Banking Institutions and the Potential Relevance of ISO 14000*. Research Triangle Park, North Carolina: Research Triangle Institute.

Wernick, Iddo, Robert Herman, Shekar Govind, and Jesse H. Ausubel. 1996. "Materialization and Dematerialization: Measures and Trends." *Daedalus* 125 (3):171-197.

Wynne, Brian. 1993. "Uncertainty and Environmental Learning." In: *Clean Production Strategies: Developing Preventive Environmental Management in the Industrial Economy*, edited by T. Jackson. Boca Raton, Florida: Lewis Publishers.

[Author's Note: The conclusions and opinions expressed are those of the author and do not necessarily reflect those of Environment Canada.]

CORRIDORS OF GREEN AND GOLD: IMPACT OF RIPARIAN SUBURBAN GREENWAYS ON PROPERTY VALUES

Stanley Hamilton
Professor of Urban Land Economics
Faculty of Commerce & Business Administration
and
Moura Quayle
Professor of Landscape Architecture
and Dean, Faculty of Agricultural Sciences
University of B.C.

The open space system like housing, transportation, education and economic development, like air, water and light is a fundamental building block of modern urban life, a physical, social, economic, and human necessity, day in, day out, year after year. - New York City Open Task Force, 1987

INTRODUCTION

Community builders, land developers, environmentalists, homeowners and politicians appreciate that land-use planning and management improves with better information and better understanding of the diverse interests involved. Behind concepts of growth management, sustainable development and new urbanism is a growing commitment to better understand ecological, social and economic factors in planning and managing our landscape.

This study is intended to contribute to our understanding of the role of greenways in residential property markets, with particular reference to greenway standards applicable to fisheries management along shorelines, rivers, streams and creeks. The focus of our research is on testing the general hypothesis that proximity to a greenway will have a positive impact on nearby property values. There is a widespread belief, supported by numerous studies, that the positive features associated with a greenway outweigh the negative features, and that on balance, tenants and owners are willing to pay for such proximity. To test this hypothesis, four different sample areas have been selected in the province of British Columbia; three in the metropolitan Vancouver area and one in the metropolitan Victoria area. The economic focus of the paper is the application of multiple regression analysis to isolate the impact of greenways on property values. A survey of property owners in the four study areas was also administered for insights about perceptions of values held by the residential owners and occupants related to their proximity to the greenways.

This study makes several important contributions to our understanding of the pricing dynamics associated with proximity to greenways. First, the empirical analysis relies on a comprehensive database that includes all sales within a sub-market, not just a sample as is the case in most other studies. As a consequence, issues associated with sample bias are overcome. Second, the database used in the study has a comprehensive set of property characteristics available for use. Finally, using current appraisal data from the provincial assessment authority provides a secondary rich database that can be used to augment the often small number of sales within an area. This is important since residential properties tend to turn over infrequently, resulting in a small number of sales. In British Columbia all residential assessment is market-based and intended to represent current values, hence these assessed values provide an independent second source of data to use as the dependent variable in the analyses.

Stepping back to define our term of reference, the term "greenway" is a relatively recent concept that may mean different things to different people. Generally, a greenway is characterized as a landscape corridor or linear open-space zone which is protected or regulated for public-interest purposes of balancing and enhancing the needs of natural systems and human experience. In its more natural form, a greenway could be a protected stream or wildlife corridor; in our cities it could be a carefully designed parkway or even a network of back alleys (Ministry of Environment, Lands and Parks, B.C. et al., 1995; City of Vancouver, B.C., 1995).

For the purpose of this study, the general concept of a greenway has been further defined by the following characteristics:

• the greenways are in or adjacent to suburban, residential neighbourhoods, and

• the greenways are natural or naturalized watercourse landscapes of importance to fisheries-related ecosystems with adjacent leave areas or 'no development/disturbance areas' and naturally vegetated undisturbed areas that are intended as buffers for protection of the aquatic feature and fish habitat.

Lands which form the banks of watercourses are called "riparian lands", and hence in this study we use the more specific reference of "riparian greenways".

This is a study of one aspect of economic value, that based on real-estate markets. We recognize that there are many aesthetic, cultural, ecological, health, political and social values and reasons for open space within an urban framework as part of the larger public interest. The greenway concept itself developed largely to promote environmental and social benefits: more diverse and sustaining ecological systems of plants, animals and water; social benefits of the calming effect of open space and passive recreation; educational opportunities and expanding awareness; and diversified transportation options which are consistent with the greenway's purposes. This study does not attempt to provide a comprehensive economic valuation of greenways over the long term. Rather it examines how a sample of communities respond to the presence of riparian greenways as indicated through community values reflected in real estate values at a given point in time.

Although the greenways concept may have been established for largely non-economic purposes, there is a trend to better understanding the economic value of open-space generally, and greenways in particular. Challenges to economic modeling have also started to address the difficulty of defining significant public or long-term values in economic terms, but currently few studies are available for comparable reference. Another aspect of this study is therefore to apply an updated method of economic analysis, and to update and augment the relatively sparse work on the economic impact of greenways in Canada.

BACKGROUND: OPEN-SPACE VALUE

Major research issues

In an economic assessment, some form of cost-benefit study is necessary to determine whether the benefits derived from a project outweigh the costs associated with creating the project. In most private enterprises or use of private property, the provider looks at the costs and benefits they could capture in either marketplace rents or prices. Public enterprises or the use of public property, on the other hand, make similar analyses; however the scope of public costs and public benefits frequently raises additional measurement problems. In many cases the economic value of a "public good" is only apparent through long-term analysis with attention to comprehensive costs and benefits, including effects on human health and welfare.

This study seeks to provide better information about decision-making, but focuses only on real-estate market information as an indicator of value. Economic studies recognize that there are some benefits which are not captured in the rents or prices charged for the project. Similarly there may be some associated costs which are not borne by the project. These benefits and costs are referred to as (positive or negative) externalities. For example, a golf course may provide valuable park-like views, cleaner air for the neighbourhood, and important ground-water recharge areas. The value of these benefits is not captured by the user fees for playing golf and using the clubhouse. A prudent developer may purchase a larger site and create both the golf course and development adjacent to the course. In this case the developer captures (internalizes) the benefits associated with the view of the golf course in addition to the user fees, but the developer does not capture the value of the clearer air associated with the green space for the golf course. Aside from some public tax, it is unlikely the value of the open space could be captured since it is not possible to give exclusive access to the cleaner air.

An example of a negative externality is pollution. The golf course may use dangerous or harmful chemicals in its maintenance operations, or create an eyesore of parking lots and ugly facilities, and these costs are not borne by the golf course. In this case the surrounding neighborhood pays the costs of the pollution, not the golf course.

Concerns relating to the economic valuation of externalities are not new. The principle seems clear: those who pay should capture the benefit and those who capture the benefit should pay. Governments try to better balance the effect of externalities through regulation. In our golf course example, governments may try such options as positive development incentives or tax concessions, or restrictive regulations such as chemical use and design controls. Good decision-making based on understanding economic implications often starts with problems with the availability and quality of data, including the historical lack of good data on property values, rents, and property characteristics. Given a set of quality data, there remains the problem of specifying a model that properly captures the valuation process for real property.

This study seeks to provide better information for informed decision-making, and to help owners, developers, and others better understand another aspect of the benefits of riparian greenways. While the empirical base for this study is British Columbia, the model and estimates will have wider applicability for similar situations, or for comparison purposes. Economic models are also limited by available resources for data and analysis, with the result of not being able to effectively value public goods due to a reliance on fairly narrow indicators of private valuation. Would there be National Parks, New York's Central Park, or Vancouver's Stanley Park, if only based on economic models of the time? However, economic models, like the one used in this study, are developing more sophisticated was to assess and attribute how prices paid in the market-place can reflect a broader range of values.

There is a growing body of literature that considers a variety of property and neighborhood characteristics and estimates their contribution to total value. Examples of studies on the impact of externalities

on property values include: (a) the impact of noise from major installations such as an airport (Uyeno and Hamilton, 1993); (b) the impact of
a positive or negative view from a given property (Maser et al., 1977); (c)
the impact of air or water pollution from major installations (Freeman,
1979); and (d) combinations of perceived nuisances such as traffic or
views from specific developments (Li and Brown, 1980). Perhaps the
closest type of study to the impact of the greenway is the impact of high
voltage transmission lines (Hamilton and Schwann, 1995). There is also
a shift to better understand important environmental and social values,
and long-term, life-cycle costs of land development to owners, taxpayers
and users. Land-use planning strategies adopted initially for environmental concerns have been found to not only improve the local environment and living conditions, but also to attract business and increase
economic value in the area (Brabec, 1992; Boerner-Ein, 1991; Gibbs et
al., 1996; Goldstein and Elliott, 1994).

Some costs and benefits of these externalities are reflected in property prices. The next step is to try to isolate what contribution is made
by each attribute. This step is always limited by available data and
subject to significant resource constraints. Even if data limitations and
resource constraints are minimal, there remains the significant problem
of designing the "correct" model of pricing which allows one to isolate
the contributions of each property or neighborhood attribute. Are the
contributions of each attribute linear (e.g., does the second bedroom
add the same value as the first bedroom in a house?) or non-linear (the
second bedroom adds less than the first bedroom[1]). Do property attributes interact? (e.g., is one bedroom plus larger backyard more valuable than two bedrooms and a smaller back yard?) A full specification
of a property valuation model is beyond the means of most research
projects. What one attempts to achieve is to design a simple model that
focuses on the attribute in question: What is the value of proximity to
greenways?

This study tries to draw credible conclusions from information gathered through on-site observations and a comprehensive set of price and
property characteristics. An accompanying survey of the property occupants, both renters and owners, provides supporting evidence for the
conclusions reached.

Greenways: An Economic Edge

Is it reasonable to attribute a component of the value of properties to
their proximity to a greenway? There are an increasing number of studies that indicate that there are many economic benefits associated with
open space generally, and greenways in particular, and that such value

is reflected in (i.e. capitalized into) rents and prices. Even before the recreation boom of the 1990s, studies identified economic benefits as including: (1) direct job creation from construction and management of a greenway, to recreation-oriented businesses including tourism, and indirect job creation from the greenway as an amenity which influences businesses or key personnel in making decisions as to where to locate or live; (2) increased local tax revenues as an incident of increased property value and business activity associated with greenways (with the added benefit of avoiding increased property tax rates); (3) increased retail sales, special events, recreation and financial services from the ripple effect of employment and business vigour; (4) frequent mitigation of the costs of other public expenditures, through safer transportation options, local climatic and aquifer recharge benefits, mitigated natural hazards, and support of important initiatives in the public interest, such as B.C.'s salmon-habitat preservation program; and (5) increased property values for owners through the above factors and the market recognition of the intrinsic value of environmental and recreational qualities of open-space for the human mind, spirit and body (Goldstein and Elliott, 1994; Little, 1990; National Park Service, 1990, updated 1995; Brabec, 1992; King, 1987).

A particular benefit of greenways is that as open-space corridors, they provide a long "economic edge" by touching on a number of smaller adjacent properties. Apart from more intrinsic environmental or social values, greenways have encouraged successful development strategies for local authorities because of this economic edge effect and the economic opportunities offered. As a result, greenways have become one of the most "rapidly growing conservation initiatives" (Diamond and Noonan, 1996). The economic effects are so strong that in some cases the greenway is specifically initiated as an economic revitalization project: for example, the River Park project in Chattanooga, Tennessee, and River Walk in San Antonio, Texas. Even greenways developed without specific economic motivation have been found to have "positive economic effect as an ancillary benefit" (Little, 1990).

Adjacent value - Greenway Gold

Is it possible to isolate the element of increased value in properties adjacent to greenways? Previous work confirms that positive economic effects have been identified for properties adjacent to and nearby greenway corridors. Higher real estate value and, in many taxation jurisdictions, higher property values which translate to higher real property tax revenue have been identified (Little, 1990).

For credible results, empirical studies must isolate the difference in the market value (or prices) of properties that are due to their proximity to the greenways, all else held constant. In other words, apart from the proximity to greenways, property, social and other characteristics must be relatively constant or clearly identified and measured in the underlying model. In this study, a cross-sectional database is used, hence changes over time are not a primary issue. Attention is focussed on those property and neighborhood characteristics which influence property values at one point in time, and which can be measured for the study areas selected.

Clarifying which other (uncontrolled) factors affect valuation will require a second generation of work to examine more critically what may have been over-simplified conclusions in the past. For example, Smith (1993) cites several other studies and observes:

> Pollard studied the aesthetic properties of water bodies and their influence on the heights of buildings in Chicago. Pollard concluded that residents of a lakefront apartment were paying 26% of their housing expenditure for consumption of amenities. Diamond found that living within 5 miles of a lake in Michigan increased the value of a house in Chicago by $2,219 (1970 dollars). Grimes indicates that land per square foot falls by and average of about 0.14% for every 1% rise in distance inland from the Lake Michigan shoreline and that the lake-distance variable alone explained 19% of the variation in land price for the sample as a whole.

Did the three studies referenced by Smith specifically address the implications of political, economic, cultural and land-use characteristics? Was there a way to assess whether such characteristics balance out over the reference area?

Two types of modeling for estimating the economic contribution of property and neighborhood characteristics have been used in the past. The more traditional approach has been to use appraisal or valuation models (generally the "market" or "comparative" method of appraisal) to isolate the contribution of a particular attribute. These traditional valuation models have been characterized by very small samples. An alternative traditional method is to use simple statistical analyses such as reporting and testing differences in the mean prices for two samples, one with proximity to a greenway and another without. Improved data and modeling permits improved estimates, and most modern studies rely upon more rigorous modeling such as the hedonic model. In this context, the regression analysis generally consists of relating the sales price of the property (the dependent variable) to the characteristics of the house and neighborhood (independent variables), including as one of the independent variables the specific attribute in question (proximity to a greenway).

Studies using regression analysis tend to be more credible by taking into consideration a more defined set of circumstances. Many statistical studies of this kind have concluded that greenways have a positive, or at least neutral, economic effect on property values for properties immediately adjacent to greenways or stream buffers. More recent studies have refuted concerns that proximity to open space encourages vandalism, loss of privacy or increased crime (Conservation Fund, 1995: 71).

Most examples of earlier studies are of U.S. urban areas, include greenways in Philadelphia (Hammer, Coughlin and Horn, 1974), Seattle (Little, 1990; Weicher and Zerbst, 1973); and the largely recreational community of Boulder, Colorado (Correl, Lillydahl and Singell, 1978). This last study, in a community built for a closer connection with nature, the average value of properties immediately adjacent to the greenbelt was 32% higher than those located 1000 m away, with commensurate increases in property tax revenues. On balance it appears that proximity to greenways is associated with increased property values, but the impact will be affected by local or neighborhood characteristics.

Our analysis differs from previous studies in three key respects. First, we were able to identify and use 100% of all sales in the study areas and did not have to rely on small samples of sales. Second, we are able to augment our results by reference to detailed property-tax assessment data as a second indicator of values. Third, this study has available an extensive list of property characteristics, although in the summary analysis described below, more simplified models are used.

VALUATION MODEL

Approach to estimating the contribution of a greenway to property values

A traditional and well-accepted method of measuring the implicit prices paid for housing attributes, including neighborhood characteristics, is the hedonic model. This model provides estimates of the marginal contribution of each property attribute to the total price. The underlying theory is well established (Follain and Jimenez, 1985; Griliches, 1971; Freeman, 1979a). In the theory of hedonic models, it is expected that the impact of property and neighborhood characteristics will be capitalized into property prices. For example, the positive effects of proximity to a greenway will be reflected in the prices (and rents) paid for properties enjoying the benefits.

With proper identification and pricing of such externalities, economic tools can be employed to mitigate or require compensation for costs, or to encourage or compensate for benefits. For example, an option to mitigate wear and tear of using something could be through the imposition of user fees; supporting something more in the general public interest may be through the application of general levy, cost-recovery fund-raising, or public incentives.

Major hypotheses

Two general hypotheses are addressed in this study:

H1: Properties adjacent to a greenway will exhibit positive and significant impacts on their value, all else being equal.
H2: As distance from the greenway to residential sites increases, the contribution to property value due to proximity to the greenway diminishes rapidly, all else being equal.

Using a survey instrument, we also examine whether resident property owners' estimates of the contribution of greenway proximity to property value are consistent with the results generated by our statistical analysis.

Multiple regression analysis, or hedonic modelling, is commonly used to estimate the value of individual property or locational attributes (Griliches, 1971; Rosen, 1974). These studies have been applied to a variety of valuation issues relating to real property as well as other assets. The studies relating to real property have been generally in residential markets where data are more readily available and the properties are generally more consistent in their characteristics.

The application of regression modelling raises two important and fundamental questions: (1) What pricing process or model is best for the particular research question; and (2) What variables (independent variables) are to be included in the model.

A variety of models have been employed in various real property related studies. The linear model is the most simple and has been commonly used in the past. This model assumes that each property characteristic adds to the overall value in a simple additive fashion; e.g., the fifth bedroom adds the same value as the first bedroom. However, previous work by numerous authors has indicated that the linear model, while a good first approximation, is not the best model. Some allowance must be made for interaction between variables and for non-linear contributions of the variables. To partially address some of these deficiencies, we have utilized a log-linear model in this study:

$$\ln P = \beta_0 + \beta_i \, (D) + \beta_i \ln X_i + \beta_g \, (Green) + u$$

where:

$\ln P$ = the log of property value, P, the dependent variable
β_0 = a constant term
β_i = estimated coefficients for other dummy variables
β_j = estimated coefficients for continuous variables
β_g = estimated coefficients for greenway variable
X_j = jth property characteristic
u = the error term (See, for example, Halvorsen and Palmquist, 1980).

Data

Four study areas were selected for the empirical analysis. A sample zone for data collection was chosen in each area. The selection of the specific sample zones was conducted by balancing the size of the sample zone and the time frame of sales or other statistics necessary for the analysis. Larger geographic zones create additional problems in the regression model, as it becomes necessary to measure and control for more neighborhood variables. The preference for using zones which represent small homogeneous neighborhoods would ideally be balanced by studying the context of many different situations along a greenway (time and resources permitting). In addition to variables reflecting the physical context, an adequate sample of sales is required. Including sales over extended time horizons creates problems of measuring and controlling for changing general economic conditions. Individual circumstances in each area determine the trade-off between larger geographic areas and longer time horizons.

In this study, the dependent variable is the sales price (or alternatively, the total assessed value of a property or the land component only). The choice of independent variables, which are intended to account for the major differences in property value, is more difficult. While a wide variety of property characteristics were available, previous research by numerous authors has shown that a few important variables account for a significant percentage of the differences in value. As with many previous studies, four or five independent variables captured much of the cross-sectional price variation for samples taken from small areas or well defined neighbourhoods. In this study, four independent variables are used, including (1) age of the building, (2) total floor area of the dwelling, (3) lot size (in square feet), and (4) the number of bathrooms. It is expected that the coefficient for "age" will be negative, and the coefficients for "lot size", "floor area" and "bedrooms" will be positive.

In addition to the analysis reported, alternative regressions were run using several different neighbourhood variables; but in most cases these other variables were common to all properties in the sample, hence added nothing to the explanation of differences in values. The effects of two particular neighbourhood variables (proximity to golf courses and schools) appeared to be important in two suburban areas only.

Sources of data included a review of market value statistics, site characteristics, and residential occupant opinions. The market-value statistics for this study were obtained through the British Columbia Assessment Authority and included all arms-length sales transactions for single detached dwellings in the study areas.[2] The timeframe was 1996, but sales going back to 1989 were used in one study area to increase the sample size. In addition, the assessed values of the properties were used in two study areas. Site characteristics were assessed using detailed maps and site visits; all properties which were adjacent to the greenway were labeled as "ADJACENT" and included in the sample. Next, all properties which were within a band of 150 feet of the greenway, but not adjacent, were labeled as "NEAR". Finally, all the properties located more than 150 feet, but not more than 450 feet, away from the greenway were classified as the "CONTROL" sample. A survey of residential occupants was also conducted and the results are discussed in more detail below.

Table 1 summarizes the key variables used in the regression models for each area. The sales price represents the actual price reported to the Lands Titles Office and includes all arms-length transactions as specified by the British Columbia Assessment Authority. British Columbia uses a Torrens-based land-title registry system — a model of effective computerized information management — and we are indebted to the Land Title Registry for this service. Sales for the year 1996 were used; however in some areas it was necessary to go back to 1995 or 1994 to obtain a sufficiently large sample of sales. The property characteristics were acquired from the Assessment Authority, along with the assessed values for the land component and the total property including improvements.

To provide a second estimate of the value of proximity to the greenways, the assessed value of each property was used as the dependent variable. Since real property assessments in British Columbia are at actual current value, they provide an important additional estimate generated by professional appraisers. In British Columbia, all properties are assessed annually for property tax purposes; and in the properties reviewed, the assessment authority provided highly credible market value assessments with an assessment-to-sales price ratio close to 1.0.

Site inventories were carried out at the beginning and the end of the survey period to first identify and then clarify or confirm physical

Bringing Business On Board

Table 1: Mean Values of Variables used in the Regression Models

Variable	Richmond	Delta	Maple Ridge	Saanich
Age (years)	22.3	20.1	7.0	18.4
Floor area (sq. ft.)	1375	1490	2239	1833
Prior Sale Price	$367,725	$288,578	$345,000	$190,347
Lot Size (sq. ft.)	7455	7807	7845	7834
Full Baths (count)	1.47	1.28	2.7	2.2
Assessed Value	$338,736	$289,970	-	-
Assessed Land Only	$315,892	$191,784	-	-
Adjacent (Count)	92	151	12	92
Near (Count)	79	99	28	164
Control (Count)	750	160	38	176
Sample size	921	410	78	432

site characteristics apparent on a visual inspection.

CHARACTERISTICS OF THE FOUR STUDY AREAS

Study Areas — Provincial context

The larger context of this study is the southwestern corner of British Columbia, Canada. This is a relatively small fraction of the land-base of British Columbia, but an area that includes the largest cities in the province, metropolitan Vancouver and metropolitan Victoria. Three of the four study areas are situated in metropolitan Vancouver, with a population of approximately 1.8 million, while the fourth is in metropolitan Victoria, which has a population of approximately 500,000. All four of the study areas could be described as middle-class, urban, multi-cultural communities with a mix of older and newer dwellings.

The study areas were selected after consultation with experts in fisheries management and real estate development for examples of riparian greenways which provide a cross-section of different greenway situations. The selection criteria were: (1) a reasonable sample of single detached dwellings in the immediate area of the greenway; (2) a reasonable volume of sales; and, (3) a difference among the study areas in some respect, such as age of property, price range, or other amenities.

Interestingly enough, in British Columbia at the time of this study, the final selection was not difficult since there were few areas that met these criteria.

Study areas – Overview

The four study areas are identified as follows:

(1) *Sturgeon Bank*, a mix of established, twenty-five-year-old and older streets with pockets of new construction, on a regional waterfront green corridor which serves as a buffer to the water at the mouth of the major watercourse, the Fraser River. It is located in Richmond, one of the larger municipalities experiencing rapid growth in metropolitan Vancouver (current population of Richmond is 150,000 and is expected to reach 220,000 by the year 2021).

(2) *Cougar Creek*, an established, twenty-year-old community which includes a greenway along the creek as part of a regional watershed and nature reserve network in Delta, a suburban community in metropolitan Vancouver.

(3) *Kanaka Creek*, a newer subdivision (seven years old) at the mouth of a meandering watercourse which is protected as a 15 km, narrow regional park in Maple Ridge, a suburban municipality in metropolitan Vancouver.

(4) *Colquitz Creek*, a more traditional municipal park setting as part of a municipal greenway surrounded by fifteen to twenty-year old neighbourhoods in Saanich, a suburban community in metropolitan Victoria.

RIPARIAN GREENWAYS STUDY: VALUATION BY STUDY AREA

Valuation analysis: Sturgeon Bank, Richmond

The property characteristics for the proximity to the greenway variables in the Richmond study area are summarized in Table 2. For the Sturgeon Bank greenway, both property sales prices and property-assessed values were available to be used as dependent variables for separate valuations.

The first model (Table 3) uses the log of the sales price as the dependent variable. The independent variables had the expected impact on sale prices: age has a negative impact; lot size, house size, proximity to the golf course, and number of bathrooms all had positive impacts. All coefficients are statistically significant at the 1% level. The base year was 1996. Sale prices from 1995 and 1994 were used to increase the sample size while keeping the geographic area small and contained. The coefficients for 1994 and 1995 were positive, suggesting that prices in 1994 and 1995 were somewhat higher than 1996, a finding which is consistent with comparable price information from a real estate multiple-listing service for Richmond. The overall explanatory power of the model is 0.66; within the range for many cross-sectional studies of this type.

The variables of interest are **Adjacent, Near** and **Control**. The coefficient for **Adjacent** is 0.145 and is statistically significant at the 1% level. This implies that properties adjacent to the greenway have prices that are 15.6% higher than otherwise similar properties in the control area.[3] The coefficient for **Near** is 0.024, but is not significantly different from zero.

The second model (Table 4) for Richmond used the log of the total assessed value of the property as the dependent variable. This model produces results that are very similar to those using the log of the sales price. Assuming assessors are reasonably accurate with their estimates of value, the total assessed values should be equal to the sales prices, hence produce similar results. What the results indicate is that the assessors also believe that proximity to this particular greenway contributes to value.

As a final model (not reported) the log of the assessed value of the land component only was used as the dependent variable. The lot size and proximity to the golf course and greenway are the only variables included since the assessors have removed the value of the improvements. The results relating to the proximity to the greenway remains the same. The coefficient for **Adjacent** is 0.14 (indicating that proximity to the greenway contributes 15% to the price).

Valuation analysis: Cougar Creek, Delta

Similar sets of regression models were used for the Delta study area. Table 5 summarizes the statistics for the study area. The only difference between the Richmond model and the Cougar Creek model is the inclusion of proximity to a school. The results of the first model using the log of price as the dependent variable are included in Table 6. The adjusted R^2 is 0.61, again within the range of similar studies.

As was the case with the Richmond study area, the signs on the coefficients are as expected, and all coefficients are statistically signifi-

Table 2: Mean Values of Variables by Zones in Richmond

	Adjacent	Near	Control
Age	19.7	13.3	23.7
Floor area	1560	1625	1325
Price	$473,644	$455,184	$354,904
Lot Size	9031	7539	7301
Baths	1.70	1.97	1.38
Assessed value: total	$460,065	$430,199	$375,054
Assessed value: land only	$356,427	$289,767	$313,447

Table 3: Model 1 - Sturgeon Bank, Richmond - Log of price as the dependent variable

	ß	Standard Error	t statistic
Ln (Age)	-0.034	0.004	-8.68
Ln (Floor area)	0.183	0.032	5.782
Ln (Baths)	0.141	0.019	7.22
Ln (Lot)	0.159	0.01	15.6
Year 1994	0.036	0.014	2.67
Year 1995	0.021	0.014	1.48
Golf	0.178	0.037	4.87
Adjacent	0.145	0.038	3.85
Near	0.04	0.02	1.19
Constant	8.758	0.212	41.263
Adjusted R^2	0.6602		
SEE	0.1289		
F	103.234		

Table 4: Model 2 - Sturgeon Bank, Richmond - Log of total assessed value as the dependent variable

	β	Standard Error	t statistic
Ln (Age)	-0.038	0.004	-8.59
Ln (Floor area)	0.195	0.035	5.54
Ln (Baths)	0.145	0.021	7.05
Ln (Lot)	0.178	0.011	16.07
Year 1994	-0.016	0.015	-1.08
Year1995	0.0061	0.015	0.397
Golf	0.134	0.04	3.34
Adjacent	0.127	0.038	3.31
Near	0.0081	0.022	0.37
Constant	8.31	0.234	35.59
Adjusted R^2	0.613		
SEE	0.136		
F	103.4		

cant at the 5% level except for the coefficient for the **Near** zone. The coefficient for **Adjacent** is 0.112 which implied that the greenway added 11.9% to the property values in this zone.

Using the log of total assessed values as the dependent variable produced results which were generally consistent with the first model except the coefficient for **Adjacent** is not statistically significant. Hence, it appears that the assessors in the area have not ascribed any additional value to otherwise similar properties adjacent to the greenways when, in fact, the market evidence suggests that some adjustment in the order of 12% is justified.

As in the case of the Richmond study area, a third model using the assessed value of land only was also tested. The results (not reported here) were inconclusive. This was not surprising given that the model using the total assessed value was also inconclusive.

Table 5: Summary Statistics for Cougar Creek, Delta

	Adjacent	Near	Control
Age	15.9	18.9	21.6
Floor area	1566	1450	1495
Price	$322,518	$260,960	$295,257
Lot Size	8229	6319	8504
Baths	1.53	1.31	1.21
Assessed Value total	$308,664	$275,428	$280,505
Assessed value land only	$198,480	$178,189	$193,171

Table 6: Model 1 - Cougar Creek, Delta - Log of sale price as the dependent variable.

	ß	Standard Error	t Statistic
Ln (Age)	-0.021	0.009	-2.22
Ln (Floor area)	0.246	0.032	7.64
Ln (Baths)	0.063	0.021	2.97
Ln (Lot)	0.102	0.024	4.23
Year 1995	-0.031	0.022	-1.49
School	0.062	0.028	2.21
Adjacent	0.112	0.047	2.41
Near	-0.044	0.027	-1.61
Constant	7.24	0.483	14.99
Adjusted R^2	0.611		
SEE	0.1437		
F	36.34		

Valuation analysis: Kanata Creek, Maple Ridge

Due to the limited sample size, only Model 1 (using the log of the sales price) was used for Maple Ridge. The sample is small because this area is mainly undeveloped larger parcels of land with few detached residential sales in recent years. There is an additional problem that the properties are reasonably homogeneous in terms of age, and the coefficients for both **Age** and **Baths** are insignificant and have the wrong sign; that is, the sign on the coefficient is not what theory suggests to be the case. The variable of interest, **Adjacent**, has a positive coefficient which is statistically significant at the 5% level. The results imply that proximity to the greenway adds 14.45% to the property value in this study area.

Valuation analysis: Colquitz Creek, Saanich

As with Maple Ridge, only one model was used — employing the log of sales price as the dependent variable. In order to capture an adequate sample of sales within the **Adjacent** and **Near** categories, it was necessary to include sales from the period 1989-1996. The results were disappointing in that we were unable to structure a model which was stable and produced reasonable results. These results reflect the sampling problems encountered in this study area. Having to use sales from previous years created additional problems in the regression model. Attempts to improve the sample by using larger study zones were not successful. In the final analysis, we were simply unable to identify a quality sample of properties in this one study area.

SURVEY OF RESIDENTIAL OCCUPANTS

A questionnaire was administered to residential occupants to identify their perceptions about the value of the greenway and its impact on property values. The questionnaire was developed and distributed to 500 residential occupants (owner-occupants and tenants) in each of the four study areas. The response rate was high for this type of questionnaire: 32.6% overall, from a low of 27.6% to a high of 40% in the four areas.

Each questionnaire included a schematic of the study area and the greenway under investigation. The questionnaires included several questions about the occupants: number of members in the household, age and gender for each member, whether they were renters or owners, and when they moved to the property. Key questions were designed to address the occupants' use of the greenway and their perceptions of the value that the greenways contributed to the enjoyment and value of their property.

Survey questions started with the broader issues and general decisions about what municipality to live in, and then sought to clarify the effect of the greenway on their decision to buy, their enjoyment of the property during occupancy, and finally as an advantage in the time or value on selling.

(1) Where to Live

QUESTION: Which of these factors were significant in prompting you to decide to live in this city or municipality?

Factors	Total
Proximity to work	42.3%
Proximity to family	23.0%
Affordability	55.5%
Access to greenway	51.2%

Affordability was the most commonly cited factor in the selection of the city or municipality in which to live; however, access to a greenway ranked second. There was no significant differences in the responses across the study areas in terms of the quality of access to the greenways, whether a more formal municipal park-like quality in one study area or largely unimproved, natural conditions in another.

(2) Where to Live within the Community

QUESTION: Which of the following factors played a role in choosing this particular dwelling? (First choice only reported here)

Factors	Total
Proximity to green ways	30.9%
Proximity to parks and play areas	11.6%
Proximity to schools	24.3%
Proximity to shopping	8.1%
None of the above	9.4%

Respondents were asked to rank the above factors by first, second and third priority as influencing their choice of their home. Proximity to the greenway received the most first priority votes; proximity to schools ranked second overall. In total, using a 3-2-1 weighting of first, second and third choices respectively, proximity to the greenways ranked significantly higher than any other factor.

(3) Willingness to Pay

QUESTION: Do you think the proximity to the greenways has affected your property value?

Factors	Total
Yes	75.0%
No	22.1%
If yes, positive?	98.6%
If yes, negative?	1.4%

Respondents were asked whether proximity to the greenways affected their property values: overall 75% said yes, of which 98.6% felt it was a positive effect. When the 73% who indicated a positive effect were asked to quantify it, the average impact of the greenway on property value was estimated at 20.6%, consistent across the four study areas. Interestingly, our statistical research indicates these estimates of positive price impacts appear to be higher than the sales data suggest; in two of the study areas our study's statistical research indicated no evidence of positive price impacts due to proximity to greenways. The survey results did indicate that more recent occupants felt that the price impact would be lower, perhaps because they were better-informed about market rents and prices in the area.

(4) Time to Sale

QUESTION: How do you think the proximity to the greenway will affect the time necessary to sell dwellings in your neighborhood?

Factors	Total
No impact on time to sell	30.6%
Properties sell more quickly	63.2%
Properties sell more slowly	2.7%

(5) Turnover Rate

QUESTION: How do you think that the proximity to the greenway will affect the turnover rate for dwellings in your neighborhood?

Response	Total
No impact on turnover	45.0%
Higher turnover rate	13.8%
Lower turnover rate	36.3%

The survey results suggest that approximately one-third of the respondents felt there would be no effect on time to sell due to proximity to a greenway, but two-thirds felt that properties would sell more quickly if they were close to a greenway. Respondents were next asked whether proximity to the greenway would affect the turnover rate of dwellings in the area. The average across the four study areas indicated that 45% felt the turnover rate would not be affected, 13.8% felt the turnover rate would be higher and 36.3% felt that greenways would reduce turnover. Subsequent comparisons with statistical data in this study indicated that turnover as a reference criteria is affected more by property characteristics and age than proximity to greenways.

(6) Use of the Greenway

QUESTION: What use do you normally make of the greenway?

Response	Total
Walking, jogging, byicycle	73.0%
Use as a view	53.1%
Use to protect fish, wildlife, water	22.9%
Place to dump refuse	5.5%

(7) Access

QUESTION: Do you find access to the greenway easy?

Response	Total
Yes	84.8%
No	12.1%
No opinion given	3.1%

Respondents were asked what use they normally made of the greenways. There was considerable variation in the responses across the four study areas, reflecting in part differences in accessibility. At Cougar Creek in Delta, where respondents had the least access to the greenway, they also assessed it the highest in abuse and lowest in constructive use. Interestingly, in Richmond, only a fraction of the respondents could actually see the greenway from their homes compared with other study areas, but it had the highest constructive use based on the responses in this study.

(8) Non-economic Value of the Greenway

QUESTION: Do you believe the greenways contribute to any of the following?

Response	Total
Vandalism	15.6%
Criminial activity	10.4%
Extra traffic in the area	27.6%
Walking	66.9%
Nature viewing	66.0%
Educational activities	54.7%

One of the surveyed areas, Kanata Creek in Maple Ridge, had the largest number of respondents concerned with a negative economic effect of the greenway on their property, but this did not translate to concerns with vandalism or criminal activity. On the other hand, the restricted access in Delta's Cougar Creek seems to correlate with increased concerns with such abuses.

When respondents later ranked the three most important benefits of greenways in their neighborhoods, general recreation was always in the top two benefits; control of flooding ranked higher in Richmond (30.6%), and preservation of wildlife ranked higher in Maple Ridge (42%), reflecting some local differences in the study areas.

Finally, respondents were asked whether they felt any "ownership" of the greenway. The intent of this question was to explore situations where individuals have moved from a sense of private to public responsibility, or the reasons why some greenways are better managed and used than others. The responses were positive and consistent across all four study areas: roughly two-thirds said they did feel some collective ownership; one-third did not. On the other hand, given the differences in access to and care of the greenways among the four study areas, this sense of "ownership" may not be translating through to an individual sense of responsibility for management. A much more detailed survey could be useful to explore this type of relationship further.

CONCLUSIONS

Our findings tend to support both the perception of increased economic value on the part of those living in the study areas, and an increase in real-property prices of residential suburban properties due to proximity to a greenway. The results indicated an order of magnitude of a 10% to 15% increase in value, after controlling for other factors such as age, location, and other adjacent amenities.

Two-thirds of the respondents believed that proximity to a greenway would result in quicker sales, and eighty-percent indicated a sense of either neutral or lower turnover. Quicker sales have an indirect economic benefit and also a very real personal benefit to the well-being and options of owners. Lower turnover means more stable neighborhoods, with all of the intrinsic and indirect benefits of greater sense of common ownership, comfort and security.

Our conclusions must also be weighed in the context of several general conditions that applied to all four-study areas:

- all areas are in middle-class urban communities;
- the timing of the study (1994-1996) coincided with the softening of a generally robust period of growth in the province;
- each of the communities has a relatively balanced job base;
- each of the communities remains fixated on automobile use and transportation, and
- greenway corridors remain the exception, not the norm.

While studies such as this are useful in estimating the impact of greenways on property values, it is also important to bear in mind that price effects for immediately adjacent properties are not the only economic effect of greenways, and focussing on economic effects or values is in itself limiting as economic models in many cases currently do not assess the broader range of personal, social and environmental values.

In the case of open space, its economic effect cannot be assessed entirely by the market since the benefits of the greenway are not restricted to the owners/occupants of the properties adjacent to them. Indeed, greenways offer benefits to communities in addition to increasing nearby property values. Unlike purely private land uses where the benefits can be internalized by limiting them to the owners, the benefits of open space may not be so completely internalized. Greenways produce externalities which may not be included in the price or market value that the owner-occupant is willing to pay: fresh air, bird songs, recharged water systems, recreational opportunities, opportunities to learn, see people, and enhanced community image.

Our study provides some evidence that greenways have a positive impact on property values and that current property owners tend to over-estimate the effects of greenways on prices. Our models base on assessed values produced roughly similar results to those based on recent property sales prices. These results should encourage further similar research in other urban areas with a broad range of potential location-specific explanatory variables. The ultimate goal of such research is to inform government, the real estate industry, and property owners of the contribution of greenways to private and public values.

REFERENCES

Boerner-Ein, Deborah. (1991) "Urban Open Space: Color It Valuable." *American Forests*. 97(1) at 61.

Brabec, Elizabeth. (1992) "Trees Make Cents," *Scenic America Technical Information Series*. 1(2).

Brabec, Elizabeth. (1992) "The Value of Preserved Open Land," *Scenic America Technical Information Series*, 1(2) at 4.

The Conservation Fund and the Colorado State Parks. (1995) "The Effect of Greenways on Property Values and Public Safety".

Correll, Mark R., Jane H. Lillydahl and Larry D. Singell. (1978) "The Effects of Greenbelts on Residential Property Values: Some Findings in the Political Economy of Open Space," *Land Economics*, 54(2) at 207.

Daugherty, William. (1996) "Economic Effects of Greenways", at: http://www.audubon.org/chapter/ca/buena vista.

Diamond, Henry and Patrick F. Noonan. (1996) *Land Use in America*. Island Press, Washington DC. Ch. 3, pp. 48-66 and Ch. 5. pp. 100-132.

Fisheries and Oceans, Canada and B.C. Ministry of Environment, Lands and Parks. (1997) "Urban Stream Protection: Restoration and Stewardship in the Pacific Northwest".

Follain, J. R and E. Jimenez. (1985) "Estimating the Demand for Housing Characteristics: A Survey and Critique", *Regional Science and Urban Economics*, v15 at 77.

Freeman, A. M. (1979) "Hedonic Prices, Property Values and Measuring

Environmental Benefits: A survey of the Issues," *Scandinavian Journal of Economics*, v81 at 155.

Gibbs, David, James Longhurst, and Clare Braithwaite. (1996) "Moving Towards Sustainable Development? Integrating Economic Development and the Environment in Local Authorities," *Journal of Environmental Planning and Management*, v39 at 317.

Griliches, Z. (ed.) (1971) *Price Indexes and Quality Changes: Studies in New Methods of Measurement.* Cambridge: Harvard University Press.

Goldstein Joel B. and Cecil D. Elliot. (1994) *Designing America: Creating Urban Identity.* Van Nostrand Reinhold, New York NY. Ch. 7. at 245.

Greater Vancouver Regional District. (1997) *"Greater Vancouver Regional Greenway Vision: An Environmental and Recreational Greenway Network and Assessment of the Potential Contribution of Existing and Future GVRD Rights-of-Way."*

Grove, Noel. 1990. "Greenways: Paths to the Future," *National Geographic* (June, 1990) at 77.

Hamilton, Stanley and Gregory M. Schwann. (1995) "Do High Voltage Electric Transmission Lines Affect Property Value?" *Land Economics.* November, 71(4), pp. 436 - 444.

Hammer, Thomas R., Robert E. Coughlin and Edward T. Horn I. (1974) "The Effect of a Large Urban Park on Real Estate Value," *Journal of the American Institute of Planners.* July, pp. 274-277

King, Caroline. (1987) "Is a Greenway Feasible Here?" *Land Trusts Exchange*, 6(2), pp. 14-15.

Li, M. M. and H. J. Brown. (1980) "Micro-Neighborhood Externalities and Hedonic Housing Prices," *Land Economics*, 56, pp.125-41.

Little, Charles E. (1989) "Making Greenways Happen," *American Forests.* January/February. pp. 37-40.

Little, Charles E. (1990) *Greenways For America.* Johns Hopkins University Press, Baltimore. Ch. 10, pp. 179-198. Segment found in Land Trust Alliance InfoPak Series. March 1994.

Maser, S. M., W. H. Riker and R. N. Rosett. (1977) "The Effects of Zoning and Externalities on the Price of Land: An Empirical Analysis of Monroe County, New York," *Journal of Law and Economics*, 20, pp. 111-32.

Ministry of Environment, Lands and Parks (B.C.) et al. (1995) "Community Greenways:
Linking Communities to the Country and People to Nature."

National Park Service (U.S.) (1991 and as amended, 1995) *Economic Impacts of Protecting Rivers, Trails and Greenway Corridors - A Resource Book.* US Department of Interior, National Park Service, Rivers, Trails and Conservation Assistance Programs.

Ohio River Basin Commission. (c.1994) "What's a River Worth? A

Valuation Survey of the Ohio River Corridor."

Rosen, S. (1974) "Hedonic Prices and Implicit Prices: Product Differentiation in Pure Competition," *Journal of Political Economy*, 82, pp. 34-55.

Smith, Bruce H. (1993) "The Effect of Ocean and Lake Coast Amenities on Cities," *Journal of Urban Economics*, 33, pp. 115-123.

The Trust for Public Lands (U.S.) (1994) *Rediscovering Urban Rivers.*

The Trust for Public Lands (U.S.) (1997) *Green Sense: Financing Parks and Conservation.*

Uyeno, Dean, Stanley Hamilton, and Andrew J.G. Biggs. (1993) "Density of Residential Land Use and the Impact of Airport Noise," *Journal of Transport Economics and Policy.* January. pp. 3-18.

Weicher, John C. and Robert H. Zerbst. (1973) "The Externalities of Neighborhood Parks: An Empirical Investigation," *Land Economics,.* 49(1), pp. 99-105.

Yinger, John A., Borsch-Supan, H. S. Bloom and H. F. Ladd. (1988) *Property Taxes and House Values*, Academic Press, Toronto.

ACKNOWLEDGEMENTS

The authors wish to thank Cecilia Achiam, Jorge Alvarado, and Sara Muir for their research assistance. We also wish to credit Brian Tutty with the inspiration for the title of this paper. This study was supported by funding from the Fraser River Action Plan of the Department of Fisheries and Oceans (DFO) and from the Real Estate Foundation of B.C. This report is intended to be another in the urban initiatives series that focusses on research and evaluation of fish habitat/land use conflicts in urban and suburban settings. Thanks to the scientific authority, Melody Farrell of DFO, for her support and assistance.

FOOTNOTES

1. It is possible that the second bedroom could add more than the first, but this is not found to be the case in any major study.

2. In British Columbia, the Assessment Authority collects sales data for all transactions in the province from the Provincial Land Titles Office. Property owners are required to declare the actual sales price. In addition, annual assessments are prepared at "actual value", which in the majority of cases reflect current market value. The quality of assessment in the province is very reliable.

3. In a log model, the interpretation of the coefficient for a dummy variable, such as Adjacent, must be modified in the following manner: percent change= $(100 * (e^{0.145} -1)$.

SUSTAINABLE DEVELOPMENT: IN SEARCH OF A LEGAL RULE

Bruce Pardy
Faculty of Law, Queen's University

THE QUESTIONS TO BE CONSIDERED

Should sustainable development be a domestic legal rule? What role could it play? What would it mean? Before considering these questions, I will briefly describe their legal context.

THE LEGAL CONTEXT

The emergence of the concept: international environmental law

In 1983, the United Nations established the World Commission on Environment and Development.[1] In 1987, in its report *Our Common Future*,[2] the Commission recommended sustainable development as a strategy to combat the world's accelerating environmental problems and the growing divide between rich and poor countries. Sustainable development was defined as "development that meets the needs of the present without compromising the ability of future generations to meet their own needs."[3] The report identified the objectives of sustainable development as reviving growth, changing the quality of growth, meeting essential needs for jobs, food, energy, water, and sanitation, conserving and enhancing the resource base, reorienting technology, managing risk, and merging environmental and economic decision making.[4] It was described as a multi-faceted concept consisting of ecological, social, and economic sustainability, and encompassing the ideals of environmental health, social justice, and qualitative improvement in living standards.

Since then, sustainable development has become one of the dominant concepts in international environmental law. The 1992 Rio Declaration on Environment and Development[5] articulated 27 principles directed at achieving sustainable development. Several environmental conventions and other international instruments refer to sustainability and sustainable development as guiding principles.[6] The Preamble of *Agenda 21, A Global Programme of Action on Sustainable Development*[7] drafted at the United Nations Conference on Environment and Development in 1992 states:

1.1. Humanity stands at a defining moment in history. We are confronted with a perpetuation of disparities between and within nations, a worsening of poverty, hunger, ill health and illiteracy, and the continuing deterioration of the ecosystems on which we depend for our well-being. However, integration of environment and development concerns and greater attention to them will lead to the fulfilment of basic needs, improved living standards for all, better protected and managed ecosystems and a safer, more prosperous future. No nation can achieve this on its own; but together we can - in a global partnership for sustainable development.

International versus domestic law

International law governs relationships between states.[8] It does not directly govern the actions of persons within those states. In contrast, domestic law is intra-national law. It is the law that exists within a country that proscribes certain behaviour from individuals, and governs relationships between persons, including corporate entities, and between persons and the government of that state.

International law is dependent upon voluntary submission and observance. International conventions and treaties are essentially agreements between or among countries that are entered into voluntarily, as a result of political negotiation. They are statements that define how signatory states are expected to behave. When a treaty is breached, the consequences are largely political and symbolic. Other countries may retaliate in an economic or political manner; or the offending state may be challenged in an international forum, such as the International Court of Justice. Such bodies do not have the coercive power to enforce their judgments. If the regime includes binding arbitration, as in the case of international trade law, there may be consequences for the terms of the offending country's continued participation in the pact. But whatever the consequences, there is no supreme authority with the power to make laws and enforce them unless states voluntarily submit themselves to that authority.

Unlike the non-coercive nature of international law, domestic laws are rules with sanctions imposed by the state. Obedience to these rules is mandatory, not voluntary. Any breach can result in some form of liability, leading to criminal punishment like a fine or imprisonment, or a civil order to pay compensation. Both types of order may be enforced by the coercive power of government. Not all breaches lead to liability, since minor breaches may be ignored or overlooked by enforcement agencies, or not sued upon by people whose rights have been injured. But such circumstances do not change the basic definition that laws are rules that have sanctions enforced by the state. Governments create and enforce laws without seeking the consent of those who will be subject to them, except in the most general way by holding elections. An election can be seen as the delegation of coercive law-making authority from the populace to the elected legislative body.

Domestic environmental law

Identifying the central features of domestic environmental law is difficult for at least four reasons. First, it is not a formal legal category. Domestic law can be split up into distinct subject areas, such as contracts, commercial law, family law, and the law of restitution, but environmental law is not one of these. Instead, it is a somewhat haphazard collection of statutory provisions, regulations, common law rules and principles. Some statutes and regulations have been created specifically for the purpose of environmental protection, but there are also many other laws that have some role to play in the environmental arena. The term "environmental law" is merely a label used to refer to the group of laws that impact upon environmental matters in some way. Second, explanations for environmental problems differ in science, philosophy, economics and politics, and environmental law is the place where the explanations collide. A way to reconcile the different perspectives has not yet been developed. Third, environmental law exists in both the international and domestic spheres, described above. Because of the fundamental differences in the nature of international and domestic law, it is not a simple matter to take a concept from one area and apply it to the other.[9] This problem is related to the fourth difficulty, which is that there is a gap between "soft" environmental law, which consists of philosophical and jurisprudential writings and much of international environmental law, and "black letter" environmental law, which consists of provisions in statutes, regulations, treaties, and judgments from courts. As a discipline, environmental law has yet to confront, much less resolve, its central dilemmas, and its core principles are in a state of flux.

Sustainable development in federal and provincial statutes

Sustainable development is not yet a core principle of domestic environmental law, but in Canada it has been incorporated into some environmental statutes. For example, one of the purposes of the *Canadian Environmental Assessment Act* is "to encourage responsible authorities to take actions that promote sustainable development and thereby achieve or maintain a healthy environment and a healthy economy."[10] The *Canadian Environmental Protection Act, 1999* declares that "the protection

of the environment is essential to the well-being of Canadians and ...
the primary purpose of this Act is to contribute to sustainable
development through pollution prevention."[11] The purpose of
Manitoba's *Sustainable Development Act*[12] is to "create a framework
through which sustainable development will be implemented in the
provincial public sector and promoted in private industry and in society
generally."[13] These statutes define sustainable development in the same
way as the Brundtland Commission: "development that meets the needs
of the present without compromising the ability of future generations
to meet their own needs."[14]

   In other statutes in other jurisdictions, "sustainable development"
does not appear, but the words "sustainable" and "sustainability" are
used. In British Columbia for instance, these terms appear in a variety
of statutes. The purpose of the British Columbia *Water Protection Act* is
"to foster sustainable use of British Columbia's water resources in
continuation of the objectives of conserving and protecting the
environment."[15] In the *Forest Practices Code of British Columbia*,
"sustainable use" includes "managing forests to meet present needs
without compromising the needs of future generations."[16] One of the
purposes of the B.C. *Environmental Assessment Act* is "to promote
sustainability by protecting the environment and fostering a sound
economy and social well-being",[17] and in both the B.C. *Budget
Transparency and Accountability Act*[18] and the *Auditor General Act*,[19]
"sustainability" means "the integration of environmental, social and
economic considerations to ensure that the use, development and
protection of the environment enables people to meet current needs,
while ensuring that future generations can also meet their needs."

   As will be seen below, the mere appearance of sustainable
development in a statute does not necessarily make it a legally binding
standard of behaviour.

SHOULD SUSTAINABLE DEVELOPMENT BE A DOMESTIC LEGAL RULE?

Non-legal analyses of environmental problems: voluntary behaviour

Why does it matter if sustainable development is a domestic legal rule?
After all, many discussions about environmental issues are not focused
on rules at all. Instead, they consider the historical, social, economic,
political, or scientific causes of environmental problems. The solutions
proposed in some of these commentaries call for transformation of
personal beliefs, social values, or economic behaviour. Consider for
example the advocacy of former U.S. Vice-President Al Gore, who wrote

in his book *Earth in the Balance*:[20]

> When considering a problem as large as the degradation of the
> global environment, it is easy to feel overwhelmed, utterly helpless
> to effect any change whatsoever. But we must resist that
> response, because this crisis will be resolved only if individuals
> take some responsibility for it. By educating ourselves and others,
> by doing our part to minimize our use and waste of resources,
> by becoming more active politically and demanding change –
> in these ways and many others, each one of us can make a
> difference. Perhaps most important, we each need to assess our
> own relationship to the natural world and renew, at the deepest
> level of personal integrity, a connection to it. And that can
> only happen if we renew what is authentic and true in every
> aspect of our lives.[21]

Many other analyses have been written in a variety of disciplines.
They often differ in their conclusions, but have at least one thing in
common: the diagnosis is not about the content of rules. Where
commentators recommend a course of action, the change can often
only be achieved voluntarily and outside the boundaries of the legal
system. Gore, for example, suggests that the situation will change only
if individuals take responsibility, by educating themselves and by
minimizing their use of resources. Such an approach has credence only
if it is possible for people and organizations to make such voluntary
behavioural changes. I will describe the argument below that voluntary
change of the degree required to solve or prevent environmental problems
is not possible. Western-style economies demand certain kinds of
behaviour from their participants. The tragedy of the commons
illustrates why this is so.

Tragedy of the Commons: the need for coercive environmental rules

The tragedy of the commons is an environmental allegory. Garrett Hardin
tells the story of the commons this way: "Picture a pasture open to all.
It is to be expected that each herdsman will try to keep as many cattle as
possible on the commons."[22] Any herder with access to the commons
must make a choice between using the commons to graze her animals or
feeding them herself. Each herder does the following mental calculation:
"If I feed my animals myself, I must pay that expense, either in the form
of purchasing feed or buying or renting land for grazing. If I put the
animal upon the commons, I pay nothing to feed the animal. Therefore,
my cost of producing the animal for market is reduced. Therefore, I

must place the animal to graze upon the commons."

Every herder does the same calculation for every animal she owns, and the answer is always the same. Soon there are more animals upon the commons than the pasture can support, and eventually the pasture deteriorates and is finally destroyed. Thus, the individual decisions made by the herders have the effect of removing the resource from their use altogether. They would all individually be better off if they made less use of the commons to preserve its use over the long term. But it is impossible for them to decide to behave in a "sustainable" manner because they are all acting individually. Consider what happens if one environmentally enlightened herder perceives what will happen to the commons. He says to himself, "This common pasture has a limited carrying capacity. If I place my animals to graze upon the pasture like all the other herders, it will hasten the pasture's collapse. Therefore, in the interests of preserving the environmental resource, I will not place my animals on the pasture, but will feed them myself." By taking this approach, the herder imposes upon himself costs of doing business that none of his competitors have. When he takes his animals to market at the end of the season, he has more costs to recover, and therefore the price for his product is higher than that of any other herder. Therefore, nobody buys from him. He loses money and eventually goes out of business. The other herders, in the interests of their own competitive survival, continue to place their animals upon the pasture. The demand placed upon the commons exceeds its carrying capacity in spite of the self-restraint practiced by the now bankrupt, enlightened herder. Again, the pasture eventually deteriorates and is destroyed. The only difference between the two scenarios is that one of the herders failed to remain competitive and went out of business in the process. (Unless, of course, that herder can persuade consumers to purchase his higher priced goods because he has caused no harm to the commons – "green" marketing saves the day.)

According to Al Gore, one person can make a difference. If that one person is a herder with an impending tragedy on the commons, that herder can make a difference only by encouraging the creation of a coercive rule for protection of the land, or by selling customers his higher priced products. What he cannot do is make a difference merely by changing his own behaviour. Compulsion is the key to the tragedy of the commons. Individuals do not overuse natural systems because they are greedy and uninformed. They are compelled to do so in order to secure economic survival. Their competitors do the same. Industrial manufacturers dispose of effluent into waterways not because they are evil or stupid, but because they must sell their goods in the marketplace. Those goods must be offered at a competitive price. If they incur costs to prevent the pollution of the nearby stream, they increase the costs of producing their product, costs which their competitors have not experienced. Like the lone herder, they price themselves out of the market and eventually cause themselves to go out of business.

The commons allegory can be applied to any situation in which private interests use public resources including air, water, land, trees, and so on; and can be applied whether the resource is being consumed, such as in the case of grazing on pasture, harvesting lumber, or extracting water; or whether the resource is being used for depositing waste, such as emissions into air, effluent into water, or waste disposal on land. Any use of a public resource by a private interest externalizes the cost of that use, and thus is not reflected in the private cost of the activity.

Instead of a rule imposed by some coercive authority, the herders could all agree amongst themselves to take care of the pasture, especially if there are only a handful of herders with access to the resource. However, in the real world, environmental decline is caused by the simultaneous actions of millions. Coming to a consensus on how to behave as individuals is not feasible. No agreement can possibly be reached. The alternative is some kind of coercive rule imposed by the state.[23]

Almost thirty years ago, Francis Carney described a Los Angeles version of the tragedy of the commons:

> Every person who lives in this basin knows that for twenty-five years he has been living through a disaster. We have all watched it happen, have participated in it with full knowledge just as men and women once went knowingly and willingly into the "dark Satanic mills." The smog is the result of ten million individual pursuits of private gratification. But there is absolutely nothing that any individual can do to stop its spread. Each Angeleno is totally powerless to end what he hates. An individual act of renunciation is now nearly impossible, and, in any case, would be meaningless unless everyone else did the same thing. But he has no way of getting everyone else to do it. He does not even have any way to talk about such a course. He does not know how or where he would do it or what language he would use.[24]

Although Los Angeles is still dependent on the automobile, and still suffers from poor air quality, the smog has improved. The improvement has come about not because of individual acts of renunciation, but because of more stringent emission controls – that is, because of rules imposed by the state. That is not to say that societal beliefs about what constitutes appropriate behaviour is irrelevant. The more widespread the support for environmentally sustainable behaviour, the more likely it is that rules will be enacted to require it.[25] The more people consent to the rule, the greater the degree of their compliance, and the state will require less direct action to enforce it. On the other hand, agreement with the rule among the populace is not necessary for its legal validity.

The tragedy of the commons demonstrates that it is to the advantage of resource users to have a clear and consistently enforced rule that preserves the resource. Economic competitors who use public resources would be better off with a coercive rule that limited the use of the commons in a fair and equitable way so that each one individually and all of the them together could make use of the resource over the long term. That is, it benefits all of them to have a coercive rule that requires the resource to be used sustainably. Such rules ensure fair competition by subjecting all competitors to the same limitations; sustain natural resources by preventing a tragedy of the commons; and relieve commercial operations from dependence on the inconsistently exercised discretion of bureaucrats and the voluntary compliance of their competitors.

Prioritizing interests: win-win versus win-lose scenarios

Law is required to resolve disputes. It is not required where no conflict exists. That is, a legal rule is required when there is a "win-lose" scenario in which two or more interests struggle on opposing sides of a dispute. For instance, there might be one party taking action to which another objects, or there might be property that two parties claim as their own. Whatever the nature of the dispute, victory for one party entails defeat for the other. Where such disputes exist, it is necessary to apply a legal rule or principle to determine which interest takes priority.

Not all disputes involve win-lose scenarios. Sometimes parties are able to resolve their differences by finding a "win-win" solution, a scenario that puts them all better off than they would have been otherwise. For example, consider the case of an employee whose work is substandard because he lacks the training and experience for the position that he holds. If the employer and employee together can find an alternative role within the company, one that is more suited to the individual's training and experience, and one in which the employee will thrive and do excellent work, both the employer and the employee will benefit. The employer will not have to dismiss the employee, and a lawsuit for wrongful dismissal can be avoided. While the laws of wrongful dismissal form the backdrop for the interaction between the employer and the employee, they do not determine the win-win solution that the parties may develop on their own.

The concept of sustainable development can be effectively applied to develop win-win scenarios. By integrating environmental, social and economic considerations, it is possible to find solutions that have environmental, social, and economic advantages. For example, making changes to methods of natural resource extraction, production of manufactured goods, or waste management practices can produce environmental benefits and enhance the bottom line. Recycling waste products may lower requirements for expensive and environmentally sensitive raw materials, thereby lowering the cost of production and conserving the natural resource. Manufacturing products in an environmentally appropriate manner may increase the demand for those products while reducing the environmental impact of the manufacturing process.

In legal terms, these are easy situations. There is no irreconcilable conflict. Everybody's interests push in the same direction, and legal rules are not required. Legal rules are needed where win-win outcomes are not possible. If the reason for an employee's substandard work is not lack of experience but pure incompetence, his employer will not want him in the company in any capacity. In an action for wrongful dismissal, will the court find that the employer is entitled to dismiss him, or that the employee is entitled to compensation? The law must choose between the parties – the rights of one must prevail over the other.

Where environmental interests and short-term commercial interests pull in opposite directions, genuine conflict exists. Where there is an irreconcilable clash of interests, can the concept of sustainable development be applied to resolve the dispute? Does it tell us what to do?

THE LEGAL ROLE OF SUSTAINABLE DEVELOPMENT

There are at least three legal roles that sustainable development could play in a statute. From strongest to weakest, they are the following. First, sustainable development could be used as a general standard of behaviour; that is, it could define a limitation that applies to everybody, everywhere. Anyone who acted contrary to the rule could be subject to civil liabilities or criminal penalties. Second, sustainable development could play a narrower, and therefore more limited, role as a factor for administrative decision makers to consider when exercising their discretion and making their decisions. Third, in its weakest form, sustainable development could be neither of these things, and instead function merely as a guide to interpretation of the rest of the statute.

Below are three alternative provisions about sustainable development that illustrate these three roles. There are many other variations, but these three reflect the basic possibilities.

Provision 1: "No one shall act in a way that is inconsistent with sustainable development."

This provision is stated in the form of a blanket prohibition. It is a rule that would govern the behaviour of everyone. Elsewhere in the statute would normally appear provisions describing the consequences of breaching the rule. A breach might result in regulatory (or "quasi-criminal") prosecution by the state, and/or a civil action for compensation might be available to persons harmed by the breach. For example, if such a rule was in place, no one would be permitted to develop land in any way inconsistent with sustainable development, and anyone who built a parking lot on a wetland could be required to pay for restoration of the site.

   Environmental provisions do presently exist in the form of blanket prohibitions in Canada,[26] but they do not incorporate sustainable development.[27] Blanket prohibitions have the advantage of general application. They apply equally to all competitors, and thus create a level playing field in which no one is subject to more advantageous environmental rules than any other player.[28] However, their effectiveness depends in part upon whether their meaning is clear. If a rule incorporated sustainable development as the standard, would it be possible to understand what actions the rule prohibited? The question will be considered later.

Provision 2: "In conducting environmental assessments, a review panel shall consider whether a proposed project is consistent with sustainable development."[29]

At first glance, this provision appears to mean that no development would be approved unless it was consistent with sustainable development. However, the provision would not actually demand that result. Instead, it would require the panel merely to "consider" whether a proposed project was consistent with sustainable development. Generally, this means that decision makers would be required turn their minds to the issue of sustainable development, and to the social, economic and environmental effects that the project would produce.[30] For example, an environmental assessment board could be required to inquire into whether a proposal to build a dam would be consistent with sustainable development before recommending whether the dam should be built. As long as this question was considered, there would be a significant degree of discretion in the decision about whether the project would be recommended to proceed. Decisions of this kind are difficult to challenge. Generally, they cannot be appealed, but must be challenged by judicial review,[31] which means that a court must find some significant error in the manner in which the decision makers exercised their jurisdiction under the statute.[32] The statutory provision would not prohibit any particular kind of environmental or social effect.

Provisions directing decision makers "to consider" or "have regard to" environmental factors in their deliberations can be even weaker than the example. The provision could have said, "…the panel *may* have regard to…", in which case contemplation of the factors in question would not be mandatory. Also, such provisions typically enumerate a list of factors, which means that they may be weighed and balanced against each other, increasing the degree of discretion in the decision.

Provision 3: "The purpose of this statute is sustainable development."

Statements of statutory purpose, which often appear in a preamble to a statute or in one of the statute's first few sections, are weak provisions. No one could refer to such a statement alone as the basis for imposing any kind of restriction on anyone. An environmentalist could not bring an action to prevent the building of a dam or the cutting of a forest on the grounds that there was a statute in existence whose purpose was sustainable development. It is no coincidence that the most generous use of the words "sustainable development" and "sustainability" in environmental statutes is in preambles and statements of statutory purpose.

Even though such statements do not impose legal standards of conduct, they may have a legal role to play. When courts apply provisions in a statute that are ambiguous, they must interpret those provisions to decide what they mean and how they should be applied. One of the sources of information they may use to resolve ambiguity is the preamble to the statute. Statements of purpose also help to define the boundaries of delegated decision-making authority. For example, a fishery protection statute could identify sustainable development as its purpose. The statute could grant a government department the authority to pass regulations. If that department creates regulations for the purpose of maximizing government revenue by encouraging the unlimited sale of fishing licences, and not for the purpose of sustainable development or environmental protection, the validity of those regulations may be challenged. A court could refer to the statute's purpose of sustainable development to determine that the statutory power has not been validly exercised.[33]

THE LEGAL MEANING OF SUSTAINABLE DEVELOPMENT

Sustainable development could be effectively employed in the above roles if its requirements were clear. They are not. The meaning of sustainable development is a mystery.[34] Consider the original and standard definition: sustainable development is "development that meets the needs of the present without compromising the ability of future generations to meet their own needs." If sustainable development is to be applied as a legal rule, it is necessary to be able to apply it to real situations and decide whether the facts are consistent with the rule. Assume the following scenario: a proposal is developed by Canadian Pacific Hotels to develop a meeting facility at the Chateau Lake Louise in Banff National Park.[35] Parks Canada must decide whether the project should be allowed to proceed. If the standard to which the project is to be evaluated is "sustainable development", then Parks Canada must decide whether the construction and operation of the meeting facility is consistent with the rule. If sustainable development is "development that meets the needs of the present without compromising the ability of future generations to meet their own needs," does the project meet that standard?

The first step in answering this question is not to consider the details of the proposal, but to interpret the test to be applied – what does the definition mean? It says that development is sustainable when it does two things. First, it meets the needs of the present generation. And second, it does so without compromising the ability of future generations to meet their own needs. What are the needs of the present generation? The definition does not say "wants" of the present generation, but its "needs". Does this mean that there is a difference between wants and needs? Are needs more fundamental than wants? Are needs limited to survival requirements, such as food, water, shelter, and clothing? Are all other things wants and not needs? Is development that satisfies desires for aesthetics, comfort, luxury, or convenience inconsistent with sustainable development? If so, the scope of acceptable activities would be severely limited: only those actions that satisfied basic survival needs would meet the test, and the expansion of Chateau Lake Louise to provide a meeting facility would fall outside the rubric. On the other hand, Canadian Pacific Hotels "needs" to expand the hotel and build a meeting facility so as to enhance its business, bring in more revenue and increase its profit. Future employees "need" the jobs that the expansion will create. In fact, without those jobs, perhaps some of those employees would be unable to provide food, water, shelter, and clothing for themselves and their families. The use of the word "needs" does not provide a sense of which actions should be permitted or prohibited.

Let us ignore the ambiguity in the first limb of the definition and proceed to the second, since arguably it is the second limb that really provides the limitation on what kinds of activities qualify as sustainable.

Sustainable development means any activity that does not compromise the ability of future generations to satisfy their own needs. Unfortunately, similar interpretative problems arise in this limb as in the first. How are we, in the present, to know what the "needs" of future generations are going to be? How many future generations are to be accounted for? We do not know how many people there will be in those generations. We do not know what the aspirations of all those individuals are going to be. What if the population of those future generations is so large that the earth in its present state could not satisfy all their needs? What if future technological developments make it easier to satisfy their demands? How are we to calculate how many resources will be required? Should the earth's environment be unchanged from the way it is today? Should it be in better shape than the way it is today, since it is likely that future generations will be larger than our own? If the expansion of Chateau Lake Louise will use up wild space in Banff National Park, there will be less wild space for future generations. How much wild space do they require? If the expansion is acceptable because it will only use up a little bit of wild space, would it also be all right to build three more hotels around Lake Louise? Where should the line be drawn? The definition offered by the Brundtland Commission is vague and unhelpful in answering these questions.

Since the meaning of sustainable development is not apparent in the basic definition, let us refer elsewhere for more help. The Brundtland report identifies the main components of sustainable development as ecological, social, and economic sustainability. The definition of sustainability adopted in the B.C. *Environmental Assessment Act*, to take one example, is consistent with this description. The purpose of the Act is "to promote sustainability by protecting the environment and fostering a sound economy and social well-being".

This version of sustainable development does not establish a predictable idea about where the line is to be drawn between conflicting interests. It incorporates environmental, social, and economic concerns, but it does not prioritize them, or define their relationship. Where environmental, social, and economic interests are in conflict, sustainable development does not say which interest should prevail. If harvesting an area of forest creates 100 jobs and adds $10 million to the local economy but destroys the forest, is that sustainable? If replanting trees to replace the ones that are cut will replenish the supply of trees but forever change the forest ecosystem, is that sustainable? If preserving the forest means that the logging company will have to go out of business, is that sustainable? If the only choices are to cut down the forest or shut down the company, which of those choices does "sustainable development" require?

The ambiguity is inherent in the term itself. "Sustainable development" is an oxymoron. To sustain means to continue, to last indefinitely. To develop means to grow and change. Is it possible to grow and change while keeping the environment in its present state? Or is the environment not what is to be sustained? Does sustainable development mean that development should be sustained? That is, does it mean that there should be continuing and steady growth, without regard for the environment? That interpretation would encourage the kind of behaviour that produced environmental problems in the first place. Sustainable development emerged because of the recognition that business as usual – that is, economic growth without regard for environmental limitations – creates environmental degradation. Therefore, sustainable development must mean something other than growth that is sustainable in the short or medium term.

Because environmental, social, and economic well-being are all included within sustainable development, and because the priority among them is not identified, it is possible for interests and organizations with vastly different objectives to endorse the concept. It does not commit them to any particular course of action. Sustainable development, writes Phil Elder, "is a flag under which many armies are marching."[36] Wolfgang Sachs describes the difficulty:[37]

> ... since 'development' is conceptually an empty shell that may cover anything from the rate of capital accumulation to the number of latrines, it becomes eternally unclear and contestable just what exactly should be kept sustainable. This is the reason why all sorts of political actors, even fervent proponents of economic growth, are today able to couch their intentions in terms of 'sustainable development'. The term has become inherently self-referential, as a definition offered by the World Bank neatly confirms: 'What is sustainable? Sustainable development is development that lasts.[38]'

When the Brundtland Commission sat down to do its work, it found itself on the horns of a dilemma. A significant percentage of the world's population, particularly in Third World countries, lived in poverty, without access to basic necessities of life such as clean water, food, and adequate shelter. At the same time, environmental problems were increasing, and causing an even further deterioration of the living conditions of the poor. Either of these problems alone would have been much easier to solve than both of them together. One approach to solving poverty is to encourage economic growth. Indeed, some would say that the fastest route to prosperity is unrestrained economic expansion with as little state regulation as possible. On the other hand, environmental decline is a symptom of industrial activity. Unregulated industry is compelled to make maximum use of common resources such as air and water to externalize its costs. The Commission decided that neither of these problems could be given priority over the other. It attempted to articulate a concept that would address both. As described by the Commission, sustainable development attempts to encourage three things simultaneously: environmental protection; economic development; and social equity, particularly in the sense of alleviating poverty. A catch-22 scenario results: Industrial growth causes environmental harm. Environmental harm increases and accentuates poverty. Environmental protection is costly; thus, poverty prevents environmental protection. Alleviating poverty requires industrial growth. Industrial growth causes environmental harm. Sustainable development does not describe how to solve the problem.

CONCLUSION

Without a legal rule, disputes between conflicting interests cannot be resolved, and common resources cannot be sustained. Without a clear meaning, sustainable development cannot be effectively applied as a legal rule.

Business leaders are not always the first to argue in favour of broad, generally applicable environmental laws, but they should be: where those laws are clear and evenly applied, a healthy business environment can result. Such laws would allow commercial enterprises to understand, with predictability and certainty, the rules of the game; provide the confidence that the same rules apply to competitors, and so create a level playing field; and reduce the need for discretionary, ad-hoc decisions of administrators and bureaucrats, who may have their own, idiosyncratic visions of what is meant by sustainable development. Clear, coercive rules are required to preserve common resources, so that those resources are available to all for the foreseeable future. As an aspirational concept with a vague meaning, sustainable development does not yet accomplish these objectives.

FOOTNOTES

1. Also known as the Brundtland Commission after its chair, Gro Harlem Brundtland, then Prime Minister of Norway.
2. Oxford: Oxford University Press, 1987.
3. *Ibid.*, at 43.

4. *Ibid.*, at 49. The report stated, *Ibid.*, at 37, that "economics and ecology must be completely integrated in decision-making and lawmaking processes not just to protect the environment, but also to protect and promote development."

5. 13 June 1992, U.N. Doc. A/CONF. 151/26; 31 I.L.M. 874 (1992).

6. See, e.g., *Convention on Environmental Impact Assessment in a Transboundary Context*, 25 February 1991, 30 I.L.M. 800 (1991); *Convention on Biological Diversity*, 5 June 1992, 31 I.L.M. 818 (1992) (entered into force 29 December 1993); *United Nations Framework Convention on Climate Change*, 29 May 1992, 31 I.L.M. 849 (1992) (entered into force 21 March 1994); *Kyoto Protocol to the United Nations Framework Convention on Climate Change*, 11 December 1997, FCCC/CP/1997/L.7/Add.1.

7. A/CONF.151/26 (1992).

8. This kind of international law is commonly referred to as "public international law". There is another category of law called "private international law" or "conflict of laws" that governs relationships between persons in different states, such as a commercial transaction between a company in British Columbia and a company in Germany. Contrary to its label, this is not really "international" law at all but domestic law: it consists of the rules of particular states that govern such situations. For example, if the German company brought a civil action against the B.C. company, and the action was commenced in the Supreme Court of British Columbia, the Court would refer to the "conflicts of laws" rules of British Columbia to decide what law ought to be applied to the dispute.

9. For a discussion of the application of sustainable development and related concepts from international environmental law to common law doctrines, see D. VanderZwaag, "The Concept and Principles of Sustainable Development: 'Rio-Formulating' Common Law Doctrines and Environmental Laws" (1993) 13 Windsor Yearbook of Access to Justice 39.

10. S.C. 1992, c. 37, s. 4(b).

11. S.C. 1999, c. 33, Declaration.

12. S.M. 1997, c. 61. See J. Krowina, "Manitoba's *Sustainable Development Act*" (1998) 25 Manitoba L.J. 385.

13. *Ibid.*, s. 2.

14. *Canadian Environmental Assessment Act, supra* note 10, s. 2; *Canadian Environmental Protection Act, 1999, supra* note 11, s. 3; *Sustainable Development Act, supra* note 12, s. 1.

15. R.S.B.C. 1996, c. 484, s. 2.

16. R.S.B.C. 1996, c. 159, Preamble: "sustainable use" includes (a) managing forests to meet present needs without compromising the needs of future generations, (b) providing stewardship of forests based on an

ethic of respect for the land, (c) balancing economic, productive, spiritual, ecological and recreational values of forests to meet the economic, social and cultural needs of peoples and communities, including First Nations, (d) conserving biological diversity, soil, water, fish, wildlife, scenic diversity and other forest resources, and (e) restoring damaged ecologies.

17. R.S.B.C. 1996, c. 119, s. 2.

18. S.B.C. 2000, c. 23, s. 1.

19. R.S.B.C. 1996, c. 23, s. 1.

20. New York: Houghton Mifflin Company, 1992.

21. *Ibid.*, at 366.

22. G. Hardin, "The Tragedy of the Commons" (1969) 162 Science 1243 at 1243.

23. Another possible solution to the tragedy of the commons is to privatize the resource, thereby internalizing the cost of its use and removing the incentive to exploit it as intensely and quickly as possible. Privatization is not always an equitable or feasible policy option, since privatization would eliminate public access to the resource, and transient environmental elements such as air and water are not capable of being privately owned in any event. The creation of tradable emission permits is an attempt to introduce a private right to dispose of waste into public resources.

24. F. Carney, "Schlockology", *New York Review of Books* (1 June 1972) 26 at 28-29, quoted by W. Ophuls, *Ecology and the Politics of Scarcity* (San Francisco: W.H. Freeman and Company, 1977) at 150.

25. Law and culture have a relationship too intertwined to easily determine cause and effect. Laws express cultural norms. New social conditions may produce legal change, but new laws may also help establish new social beliefs. "The social sciences are divided as to whether legal change necessarily contributes to social change. The belief that laws shape popular beliefs and actions is widely shared by legal theorists. On the other hand, the bulk of recent sociological and anthropological studies suggest that judicial opinions and new laws, in themselves, will not necessarily lead to behavioral changes." J. Moffet and F. Bregha, "The Role of Law Reform in the Promotion of Sustainable Development" (1996) 6 J.E.L.P. 1 at 14-15 (footnotes omitted).

26. For example, section 14(1) of the Ontario *Environmental Protection Act,* R.S.O. 1990, c. E.19, states: "Despite any other provision of this Act or the regulations, no person shall discharge a contaminant or cause or permit the discharge of a contaminant into the natural environment that causes or is likely to cause an adverse effect." Section 36(3) of the federal *Fisheries Act*, R.S.C. 1985, c. F-14, states: "Subject to subsection (4) [allowing deposits authorized by regulation], no person shall deposit or permit the deposit of a deleterious substance of any type in water

frequented by fish or in any place under any conditions where the deleterious substance or any other deleterious substance that results from the deposit of the deleterious substance may enter any such water."

27. The title of Manitoba's *Sustainable Development Act, supra* note 12, suggests that the statute could be expected to prohibit conduct inconsistent with sustainable development, but it does not.

28. Except where the competitors are located in other jurisdictions where there are more demanding or more lenient environmental rules.

29. An example of such a provision is section 16(1) of the *Canadian Environmental Assessment Act, supra* note 10, which does not list sustainable development as a factor but does include other environmental considerations: "Every screening or comprehensive study of a project and every mediation or assessment by a review panel shall include a consideration of the following factors: (a) the environmental effects of the project, including the environmental effects of malfunctions or accidents that may occur in connection with the project and any cumulative environmental effects that are likely to result from the project in combination with other projects or activities that have been or will be carried out; (b) the significance of the effects referred to in paragraph (a); (c) comments from the public that are received in accordance with this Act and the regulations; (d) measures that are technically and economically feasible and that would mitigate any significant adverse environmental effects of the project; and (e) any other matter relevant to the screening, comprehensive study, mediation or assessment by a review panel, such as the need for the project and alternatives to the project, that the responsible authority or, except in the case of a screening, the Minister after consulting with the responsible authority, may require to be considered."

30. See, e.g., *Friends of the West Country Assn. v. Canada (Minister of Fisheries & Oceans)*, [2000] 2 F.C. 263 (C.A.), application for leave to appeal to the Supreme Court of Canada dismissed [1999] S.C.C.A. 585.

31. See, e.g., *Taku River Tlingit First Nation v Tulsequah Chief Mine Project*, [2000] B.C.J. No. 1301 (S.C.) at paragraph 22: "A fundamental premise of judicial review is that a court in exercising the powers of judicial review does not act as an appellate body. The court's role is to determine whether the impugned decision was made within the statutory jurisdiction of the person or body making the decision."

32. See, e.g., *Union of Nova Scotia Indians v. Canada (Attorney General)* (1996), 22 C.E.L.R. (NS) 293 at 320 (F.C.T.D.): "The very nature of the decision means that in judicial review proceedings the court must inevitably defer to the statutory decision maker, unless persuaded that the decision is patently unreasonable, in the sense that it cannot rationally be justified in light of all the information available to the

decision maker at the time of the decision. So long as there is information on which the decision could be rationally based, the court will not intervene."

33. In some circumstances, the statement of statutory purpose in the form of Provision 3 can have a similar role to a section in the form of Provision 2. The purpose of the statute can be explicity incorporated as a factor that must be considered (see, e.g., section 9(2) of the Ontario *Environmental Assessment Act*, R.S.O. 1990, c. E.18), or even where not explicitly referred to, can be implied as a requirement (see, e.g., *Taku River Tlingit First Nation v Tulsequah Chief Mine Project*, [2000] B.C.J. No. 1301 (S.C.), para. 37 and sections 2, 10 and 30 of the B.C. *Environmental Assessment Act,* R.S.B.C. 1996, c. 119). Thus, if one of the purposes of an Act is "sustainability" or "sustainable development", decision makers under the statute can be required to consider whether their decision will achieve that purpose.

34. "(T)he concept of sustainable development, rather than offering firm groundings or a clear blueprint for the future, is cloaked with various interpretive, definitional and terminological mists." D. VanderZwag, "The Concept and Principles of Sustainable Development: 'Rio-Formulating' Common Law Doctrines and Environmental Laws" (1993) 13 Windsor Yearbook of Access to Justice 39 at 41; "(I)t is by no means easy to identify the meaning of 'sustainable development'. The concept is often exemplified and instantiated but rarely, if ever, defined...At best, 'sustainable development' looks like a convenient umbrella term to label a group of congruent norms." V. Lowe, "Sustainable Development and Unsustainable Arguments" in A. Boyle and D. Freestone, eds., *International Law and Sustainable Development: Past Achievements and Future Challenges* (Oxford: Oxford University Press, 1999) 19 at 25-26.

35. See *Bow Valley Naturalists Society v Canada (Minister of Canadian Heritage)*, [2001] F.C.J. No. 18 (C.A.).

36. P. Elder, "Sustainability" (1991) 36 McGill L.J. 831 at 834; "Sustainable development is open to a wide range of interpretations, not all of them compatible. Not surprisingly, the particular interpretation chosen tends to vary according to the interests of the group identifying itself with the concept." J.O. Saunders, "The Path to Sustainable Development: A Role for Law" in J.O. Saunders, ed., *The Legal Challenge of Sustainable Development* (Calgary: Canadian Institute of Resources Law, 1990) 1 at 1.

37. W. Sachs, *Planet Dialectics: Explorations in Environment and Development* (London: Zed Books, 1999) at 81.

38. World Bank, *World Development Report 1992* (Oxford: Oxford University Press, 1992) at 34.

ACKNOWLEDGMENTS

I would like to thank Rosemary Rayfuse, Faculty of Law, Queen's University; Helen Colebrook, Law Commission of New Zealand; and Jane Ashford, Corporate Controller, A.G. Simpson Automotive Inc., Toronto, for their helpful comments on an earlier draft.

THE JOURNEY TOWARD SUSTAINABLE ENERGY DEVELOPMENT – THE EXPERIENCE OF SUNCOR ENERGY

David Coglon
Calgary, Alberta

The roots of Suncor Energy's enterprise as an innovative developer of hydrocarbon energy go back many years. In the late 1890s the Canadian government sponsored investigations of northern Alberta's Athabasca "tar sands" as a potential source of petroleum. Then, in the 1920s, Alberta scientist Karl Clark found a practical way to separate the bitumen from the sand. After adding hot water and caustic soda to the tarry sand using makeshift equipment that included the family washing machine, he discovered that the bitumen floated to the surface as a frothy foam, ready to be skimmed off. Clark's method was clearly workable. Yet the idea languished for decades until Suncor's precursor, the Great Canadian Oil Sands Ltd., began commercial development of oil sands at Fort McMurray, Alberta in 1967. Even then it was described as a "daring venture into an unknown field." But the company persevered with positive results.

Today, oil from northern Alberta's oil sands, including Suncor's Oil Sands operations, accounts for about one quarter of Canada's daily crude oil production. [See Figure 1] This figure is expected to continue to increase as oil from oil sands replaces declining conventional oil production.

Headquartered in Calgary, Alberta, Suncor has grown to become one of Canada's major integrated oil and gas companies, with assets of C$6.8 billion and approximately 3,000 employees. The company's Oil Sands operation, which achieved an average of 114,000 barrels of oil per day in 2000, continues to be the largest part of the business. But in addition, the company has a conventional natural gas exploration and production business in Western Canada and a refining and marketing operation in Ontario under the Sunoco brand name.

The company's growth strategy is focused on building on its existing assets while expanding globally and strengthening its presence in new segments of the energy business. A $2.8-billion expansion, called Project Millennium, is designed to more than double current oil sands production in 2002. Suncor's longer-term vision is to increase this to 400,000 to 450,000 barrels per day in 2008.

In 2000, Suncor also announced plans to invest $100 million in alternative and renewable energy by 2005. Suncor's vision for this business is to be a full-service developer of renewable energy, providing consumers with energy options that have environmental benefits and are competitively priced.

Figure 1: Location Of Suncor's Operations

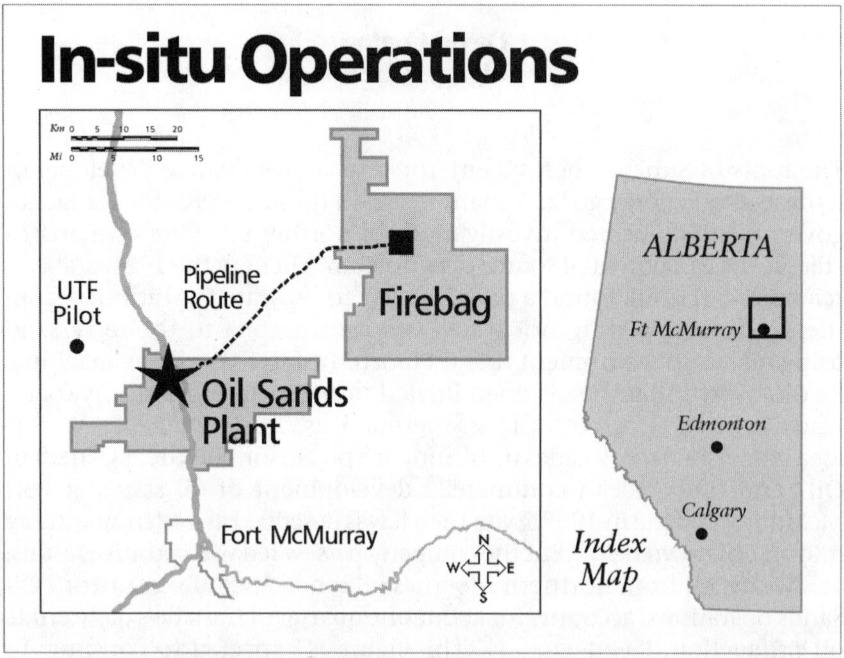

Underlying this vision of growth is Suncor's commitment to the principles of sustainable development.

"Business success isn't just about money," says Suncor CEO Rick George. "Our society has changed. In today's world a truly successful – and sustainable – business is one that makes a profit, and protects our planet and cares about people."

"More than 30 years ago, Suncor helped to pioneer commercial development of Canada's oil sands when many said it could not be done," says George. "This same pioneering spirit guides us on our journey to becoming a sustainable energy company."

The commitment to sustainable development reflects the company's desire to survive and prosper in a changing world. It also reflects some of the lessons learned after the company successfully reinvented itself during the early 1990s.

THE TURNAROUND AT SUNCOR

In the mid-1980s plunging world oil prices made Suncor's oil sands production uneconomic. The company's mining technique, based on giant bucket wheels and conveyor belts, was prone to breakdowns. The company was also burdened by under-performing operations in the conventional upstream and downstream businesses.

The crisis surrounding the future viability and sustainability of Suncor's operations caused the company to make important changes. In the early 1990s, under newly appointed CEO Rick George, Suncor embarked on an ambitious program to enhance existing operations and to pursue growth activities, with the aim of improving its long-term financial picture.

Ambitious plans and targets were established to increase shareholder value. Renewed emphasis was placed on a set of core business directions that included safety, environmental care, productivity and production volume, product value, customer relations and shareholder return. A new core purpose statement, supported by values and beliefs, was developed to reflect these business directions.

During this period, the emphasis at Suncor was on survival by improving operations, reducing costs and maximizing current assets. The company changed its technological approach to oil sands development. The massive bucket wheel mining system at Oil Sands was replaced with a more efficient and reliable truck and shovel operation.

As the company retooled itself for the 1990s, it also began to pay closer attention to environmental performance. At Oil Sands, air emissions such as sulphur dioxide were high and, increasingly, regulators and community stakeholders were demanding environmental improvements from the company. It was clear to the company's management that Suncor would be unable to successfully pursue growth without improvements to its environmental performance.

In 1992 Suncor's Board of Directors voted unanimously to create the company's first standing committee of the Board exclusively devoted to monitoring the company's environment, health and safety performance. The company also introduced its first "We Care" environment policy to employees, outlining their environmental responsibilities. In 1995 the company backed this policy commitment by issuing its first public We Care progress report. In the preface, George said: "Quite simply, responsible management of the environment, is not just a good way to do business – it is the only way. At Suncor, we have integrated environmental principles into our business plans."

As part of its growing commitment to sustainability, the company was increasingly aware of the importance of stakeholder concerns. Suncor began to develop a community involvement process for its existing projects and long-range development plans. Working with aboriginal communities, government and other groups in northern Alberta, the process enabled the company to pursue mutually beneficial solutions that addressed concerns about the environment, employment, business development and industrial growth. The company also gained stakeholder input that improved its operations and accelerated regulatory approval for projects such as the company's new Steepbank mine in 1997.

Through community involvement, Suncor broadened its approach to operations to reflect a wide range of economic, environmental and social needs and concerns. The concept of sustainable development began to increasingly enter key discussions at the corporate level and in long-range planning exercises.

In a relatively short time, Suncor has successfully transformed itself into a successful enterprise. It has modernized its operations and dramatically improved its financial performance. Since 1992, Oil Sands production has almost doubled. Suncor's bottom line has improved from a loss of $228 million in 1992 to earnings of $377 million in 2000. In that time frame, Suncor's stock price has increased significantly, going from $4.75 per share in 1992 (adjusted for a 2-for-1 split in 1997 and 2000) to $38.30 per share at year-end 2000.

During this period, the company has gained increasing public recognition as a leader in environmental management and sustainability. In 2000, Suncor maintained its position for the second year in a row as one of 200 elite companies that constitute the Dow Jones Sustainability Group Index. This is a new global index of companies that are committed to the principles of sustainable development. The company is also a member of the World Business Council for Sustainable Development, Canadian Business for Social Responsibility and Alberta Ecotrust.

Suncor continues to build on this success as it pursues its vision of being a sustainable energy enterprise. It plans to achieve this vision by providing energy solutions that meet or exceed the environmental, economic and social needs and expectations of its customers and other stakeholders.

"There is a lot at stake in this for Suncor – real risks and potentially huge rewards," says George. "If we don't act responsibly, we will lose our right to operate and grow. On the positive side, I believe that, if this company pays attention to the environmental and social needs of our stakeholders, we will not only succeed, but we will have a distinct competitive advantage."

SOME GUIDING PRINCIPLES FOR ACTION

In undertaking this vision, Suncor's management recognizes that sustainability is a challenging goal that requires a clearly defined path. At a 1999 senior management conference on sustainable development, George summarized the company's approach to sustainability into six principles for action:

1. Continue to enhance environmental and social practices

Suncor's policy commitment is to continuously improve the environment, health and safety (EHS) performance of its operations and products. In this way the company's goal is to exercise responsible use of resources, provide a safe and healthy workplace and enhance the competitiveness of the business.

Suncor's We Care policies, introduced in 1992 and updated in 1997, describe the company's commitment to excellence in EHS performance. An EHS management framework supports these policies within each operating business. The framework is designed to achieve compliance with regulations, manage risks to the business and environment, and encourage continuous improvement in all areas of Suncor's EHS performance.

The company is also committed to maintaining and improving the quality of life in society, particularly in communities where its employees work and live. This commitment includes investing in communities, encouraging employee volunteerism and building mutually beneficial relationships with stakeholders. Suncor is developing a strategic framework to more effectively manage and measure its performance as a socially responsible company.

2. Adopt a parallel approach to energy development

As an energy company, Suncor is known for taking a phased approach to resource development. This reflects prudent financial management as well as a desire to carry out development that addresses stakeholder needs and concerns. The company has adopted a similar philosophy in building Suncor as a sustainable energy company. This is reflected in the company's "parallel path" approach to energy development, which calls for developing hydrocarbon resources responsibly to meet current needs and, at the same time, taking action now to support the diversification of energy sources over the longer term.

"We see the need for parallel paths to achieve sustainable development," says George. "By pursuing this approach, we will be better positioned to make the right choices at the right time and in the right way to ensure our continuing success as an energy company."

3. Consciously apply values

Suncor believes that the logic of sustainable development is not enough to drive change within an organization. It believes that sustainable development must be supported by a strong declaration of support at the top of the organization and reflected in decision-making and innovation that occurs at different levels throughout the company.

4. Broaden the company's approach to decision-making

The company understands that the challenge of sustainability will cause it to test conventional wisdom in its own organization and industry. As a result, Suncor looks for new tools and practices that encourage employees to think about their business from "outside the box" and enhance business decision-making and business planning. This includes the use of life-cycle value assessment, a systematic method of evaluating the economic, environmental and social effects of business activities.

5. Continue to pursue technological innovation

The company and its management believe continual technological innovation is essential to reducing its environmental impacts in a sustainable way.

"Technology can be applied to produce positive results, in many cases, far beyond what we imagined possible and without destroying our economic prosperity," says George. "I'm not saying that technology is the answer to all our sustainability dilemmas, but I'm a real optimist that technology will be a key to long-term solutions and will be an important starting point for action."

6. Contribute to new models for action.

Suncor believes industry can lead by example by participating in early actions and initiatives that promote an understanding of sustainable development and contribute to positive results.

"In pursuing sustainability, we have two options as a company," says George. "We can wait until the rules of the game are all established. Or we can get involved early and show what can be done. I think the latter approach is more responsible."

As it works toward becoming a sustainable energy company, Suncor is striving to apply these principles. The following examples illustrate these principles in action.

PROGRESS TOWARD SUSTAINABILITY: SOME EXAMPLES

Climate change

A major focus of Suncor's environmental management efforts is the issue of global climate change.

In late December 1997, on the same day an international global climate change conference opened in Kyoto, George outlined the company's approach to the issue. He said Suncor took the risk of global climate change seriously and that the company would commit to discovering new and innovative ways to deal with its greenhouse gas emissions.

"We believe we can significantly reduce our emissions of greenhouse gases without sacrificing the economy," he said. "And we need to act now, not because we're certain the global climate is changing. We need to act now because we can't ignore the scientific consensus that the balance of evidence suggests that there is a discernible influence on the world's climate."

In his speech, George announced a comprehensive action plan that included:

- management of the company's own greenhouse gas emissions;
- development of alternative and renewable sources of energy;
- environmental and economic research;
- domestic and international offsets;
- constructive public policy input;
- employee and public education; and
- measurement and public reporting on progress.

While the plan emphasized management of Suncor's own emissions as a key priority, the company also announced that it would look outside its own operations for greenhouse gas reductions through offsets [See Figure 2].

"If we are committed to the goal of spending money to reduce our overall emissions in the atmosphere, we want to get the biggest environmental and economic bang for our buck," George said. "And because this is truly a global issue, in some cases we might be better to spend our money somewhere else – even in another part of the world. So, at the same time as Suncor is working to improve its own performance, we are looking at other solutions."

Suncor demonstrated early commitment to the action plan by announcing that it would participate in a pilot project developed by the U.S. Nature Conservancy to acquire and preserve endangered forests in Belize. Under this project, Suncor committed to a contribution of US$400,000 to add 7,000 hectares to the country's Rio Bravo Conservation Area. Without this acquisition, the area, which is home to jaguars and other rare animals and plants, would have been cleared and converted to agriculture. Suncor's participation is estimated to prevent the

Figure 2: Greenhouse Gas Emissions

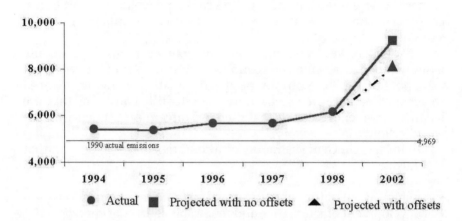

release of 400,000 to 500,000 tonnes of CO2 into the atmosphere over five years.

Since then, Suncor has taken further actions to implement its climate change plan. The company's actions to date on internal efficiencies have resulted in a cumulative reduction of more than 10 million tonnes of carbon dioxide equivalent over 1990 to 2000. The company has also begun to invest in alternative and renewable energy opportunities, and has participated in other offset projects, including an initiative to reforest previously cleared land in Australia and the purchase of greenhouse gas emission reductions from U.S.-based Niagara Mohawk Power Corporation. Through these and other actions, Suncor's goal is to meet or exceed relevant national and international commitments to limit greenhouse gases emitted to the atmosphere. In the context of the current Canadian commitment to meet the targets of the Kyoto Protocol, this means lowering net greenhouse gas emissions to 6 percent below 1990 levels by the year 2010.

"The entire senior management team is very engaged on the climate change issue and has established the direction of the organization," says Gordon Lambert, Suncor's Corporate Director, Sustainable Development. "Each of Suncor's businesses assumes ownership and responsibility for the bottom line results for greenhouse gas performance in their areas. And this performance is encouraged and supported by employee incentives."

The timing of the 1997 speech attracted attention of business and government leaders in Canada and elsewhere. By taking a bold strategic position on the issue, Suncor gained a seat at the policy development table in important climate change initiatives in Canada. In 1999, the company participated in the development of a Canadian Early Emission Reduction Program (CEERP). Through this collaboration, the company has contributed to the design of a credit for early action program that promotes greenhouse gas reductions while respecting Canada's needs for economic growth. Governments, stakeholders and other industry players from as far away as Japan have also begun to seek out the company's advice and opinion on emissions trading and other implementation issues.

Emission reduction trading

Under an emission trading system, a company that achieves more reductions than is required can be rewarded by selling the surplus reductions to another company. The purchaser can use the reductions to offset some of its own greenhouse gas emissions in a cost-effective and efficient manner. Suncor recognizes that policy makers will only take a broader perspective to climate change solutions, such as emission reduction trading, if they see results.

In October 1999, Suncor helped to pioneer one of the world's first cross-border emission reduction trades when the company completed a purchase of 100,000 metric tonnes of greenhouse gas emission reductions from Niagara Mohawk Power.

The transaction marked the first part of a trade agreement between the two companies originally announced in March 1998 and having a potential value of approximately C$10 million. Under the agreement, Suncor has an option to buy up to an additional 10 million tonnes of greenhouse gas emission reductions over a 10-year period, starting in 2001. This option will depend on U.S. and Canadian government recognition and credits for the emission reductions. The companies hope their trade agreement will be the first step toward the creation of an international trading system for reductions in greenhouse gas emissions.

"While many countries and companies have expressed an interest in the concept of an emissions reduction trading system, many of the rules are not in place," says George. "We see our transaction as providing an international case study of what's required to design, carry out and measure emission reduction trades."

The agreement is designed to help Suncor achieve its voluntary emission reduction targets, while providing Niagara Mohawk with additional funding for new projects that will further reduce global concentrations of greenhouse gases in the atmosphere. Under the terms of the agreement, a minimum of 70 per cent of the net proceeds from the sale will be re-invested by Niagara Mohawk in new greenhouse emission reduction projects, creating additional environmental benefits from the trade.

Under separate agreements with the Environmental Resources Trust (ERT), a U.S. non-profit organization, the two companies report all greenhouse gas emissions to the ERT, including emissions reductions from individual projects and transfers of emissions reductions. The agreements provide a mechanism for credible third-party review of the methods used in measuring and monitoring greenhouse gas emissions and for reporting of the actual greenhouse gas emissions performance of the two companies.

Investing in alternative and renewable energy

Through its climate change action plan, Suncor is also pursuing development of alternative and renewable sources of energy. The company believes that over the long term renewable and alternative sources of energy offer important potential as alternatives to traditional hydrocarbon energy.

Suncor's announced plans in 2000 to develop an alternative and renewable energy business by 2005 include investments in wind power, solar power, run-of-river hydroelectricity and energy production from biomass and municipal solid waste. To help determine which renewable energy projects Suncor should invest in, the company evaluates the project's "green" potential. Criteria for investment include:

- reduces greenhouse gas emissions to the atmosphere
- stands up to life-cycle value assessment as efficient energy conversion technology
- not associated with oil, natural gas or coal sources
- lowest energy-intensive process
- minimal environmental impact
- economic return
- positive social impact

Since that annnouncement, Suncor has created a long-term strategic plan, reviewed more than 700 opportunities and, in April 2001, took a major step forward in harnassing wind for power in Canada by partnering with Enbridge Inc. to build a $20-million wind power project in Gull Lake, Saskatchewan. When fully commissioned, the wind power project will generate the province's first major supply of renewable energy and will increase Canada's generation of power from wind by approximately 10 percent.

Ethanol-enhanced gasolines

Suncor's goal is to provide cleaner energy over the longer term and to be a leader in the evolution of the energy industry. In 1997, Sunoco became the first major fuel retailer to offer ethanol-enhanced gasolines in the Ontario market.

The ethanol-enhanced gasolines provide environmental advantages when compared to conventional gasolines. Ethanol is a high-octane, alcohol fuel that boosts the oxygen content of gasoline. The result is a cleaner burning fuel that reduces emissions of carbon monoxide and volatile organic compounds (VOCs). Based on a life-cycle value assessment and third-party verification, the company estimates the program will also reduce greenhouse gas emissions by 100,000 tonnes each year.

In 1998, the fuels were introduced to all Sunoco retail outlets. The company is investigating the potential use of ethanol and other renewable fuels in diesel reformulation.

Focusing on natural gas

As part of diversifying its energy portfolio, Suncor's goal is to build its natural gas business. This strategy is expected to increase revenues while decreasing air emissions, as cleaner burning natural gas replaces other fossil fuels.

Suncor's natural gas business pursues growth from conventional natural gas sources in Western Canada, focusing on finding and developing reserves that can be brought on stream economically. The company is also exploring the potential to recover natural gas from coal beds in the form of methane.

Coal bed methane (CBM) is a clean form of natural gas that is produced in underground coal seams. Suncor is developing CBM operations in the United States, Australia and Canada, and production is planned for the fourth quarter of 2001.

In addition to increasing the company's natural gas production, Suncor's pursuit of coal bed methane may also provide an opportunity to prevent greenhouse gases from entering the atmosphere. Carbon dioxide (CO_2), one of the largest greenhouse gases produced in Suncor's operations, can be injected into underground coals seams for storage, potentially creating a valuable offset for the disposal of CO_2 emissions.

Suncor is one of six global energy companies that have joined forces to research and develop effective methods to capture significant amounts of CO_2 emitted from power generation and industrial sources and store the gas in geological formations below the earth's surface. If successful, the project could lead to a notable reduction in greenhouse gas emissions across a wide range of industries, not just the energy sector.

Turning traditional wastes into value

As part of its ongoing drive to improve environmental performance, the company has continued to look for innovative ways to create new efficiencies. This has involved opportunities for "byproduct synergy," where traditional wastes can be sold and used to create valuable products.

At Oil Sands, petroleum coke is formed as a byproduct when bitumen is heated to create hydrocarbon vapors. Over three decades of oil sands development, some of Suncor's coke has been used as a fuel source at the Fort McMurray plant to produce steam and energy. The rest has been stockpiled.

In 1995 Suncor began pursuing the possibility of selling coke, dealing with marketing companies in the Far East, Europe and North America. In 1998 this search led to Suncor completing an agreement with Ube Industries of Japan. Under the agreement, Ube Industries will purchase a total of one million tonnes of petroleum coke over five years for use in the production of ammonia. The purchase represents about 17 per cent of the company's six-million-tonne stockpile of coke.

Before the agreement, Ube had relied on suppliers in the United States, Venezuela and Japan for the coke it requires for ammonia production. Then the Japanese company decided to diversify its supply source and stabilize the price it pays for coke. In Suncor, Ube found a high quality, economic and long-term source of supply.

The company continues to look for other opportunities for byproduct synergy. In 2000, Suncor and Williams Energy Canada, Inc., began construction of the Hydrocarbon Liquids Conservation Project to recover natural gas liquids and olefins from "off-gas," a byproduct of oil sands upgrading that is currently used as a fuel. The plant, scheduled for commissioning in 2001, will recover propane, propylene and other commercial products from the off-gas.

The company has also helped to form the Alberta Byproduct Synergy Initiative. In partnership with the International Institute for Sustainable Development, the company has been involved in collaboration with other industries to identify new opportunities to turn wastes into valuable products.

Tools for change

In considering its future, Suncor has concluded it must look for new tools and practices that will help its decision-making and business planning. In consultation with the Pembina Institute for Appropriate Development, Suncor has adopted the use of life-cycle value assessment (LCVA). LCVA provides the company and its employees with a systematic method of evaluating the economic, environmental and social effects of business activities in an integrated manner. [See Figure 3]

Analyses include capital and operating costs as well as environmental impacts, such as greenhouse gas emissions. Suncor has adapted LCVA on a project-specific basis and now uses a range of methodological approaches. Depending on the size of the project, the method chosen may range from the use of a LCVA checklist to a full LCVA study.

In 1998 LCVA was used to assess options for an oil sands in-situ project near Fort McMurray, Alberta. The LCVA method helped Suncor to choose between a direct route for a pipeline over undisturbed terrain or a longer route along an existing right-of-way. After consideration of the long-term effects of using the longer pipeline route, the analysis indicated that the shorter route was preferable, both environmentally and economically. More energy would be required to pump product along the longer route, resulting in higher emissions.

Encouraged by this early experience, Suncor has adopted a policy that promotes the use of LCVA and plans to expand the use of this method to all significant business decisions by 2001. A company-wide initiative is under way to train employees and to incorporate LCVA into the evaluation of development projects, the implementation of green purchasing policies and other business activities.

The assignment of internal monetary values to emissions from operations can also be an effective tool for incorporating environmental impacts into decision-making. In 1999 Suncor assigned monetary values to emissions from all current operations and new projects. These values will be considered in all corporate investment decisions as well as the planning and development of environmental improvements and alternative and renewable energy.

Community involvement

Suncor strives to involve community members affected by its operations and facilities and solicits public and community input into the company's long-range development plans. For example, the company has used an extensive stakeholder consultation process to guide expansion of its Oil Sands operation.

In 1997 Suncor commissioned an environmental impact assessment for its Project Millennium oil sands expansion project, with input from government, environmental organizations, aboriginal people and other community groups. Through this study, Suncor identified key issues and developed plans to mitigate adverse impacts. The consultation led to

Figure 3: LCVA Methodology Overview

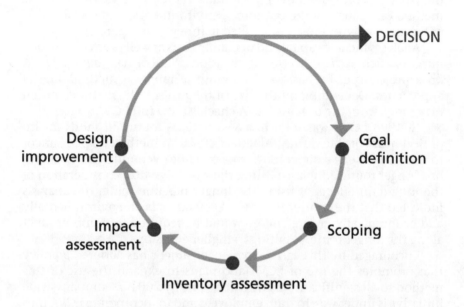

design improvements that are expected to reduce emissions per unit of production and contribute to more efficient use of energy and water.

Consultation plans have also been developed with local aboriginal communities. In 1998 Suncor helped to establish the Fort McKay Industrial Relations Corporation (IRC). Through the IRC, Suncor and the community are pursuing mutually beneficial solutions that address concerns about the environment, employment and business development. So far, the IRC has led to increased employment, a greater volume of contracts for Fort McKay businesses, and quarterly consultations with community elders.

Suncor's consultation process considers the impact of Project Millennium and other development on the Regional Municipality of Wood Buffalo. Working with government and industry, Suncor has helped to address increasing demand for transportation, education and other services, which are affected by industrial growth.

Since 1997, Suncor has also helped to lead an initiative to assess and manage the cumulative environmental effects of Project Millennium and other planned development in the region of Wood Buffalo. In 2000, Suncor helped to found the Cumulative Environmental

Management Association to examine and manage the cumulative environmental effects of large-scale industrial development in the region. Members of this multi-stakeholder organization include native groups, environmental and public-interest groups, all levels of government, and key industry sectors such as forestry and oil sands.

Social responsibility

As its business grows, Suncor recognizes that public expectations for the company to contribute to corporate social responsibility will continue to increase. Suncor is committed to maintaining and improving the quality of life in society, especially in communities where its employees work and live.

"Creating value at Suncor means adding value to the communities in which we do business," says George. "For Suncor, corporate social responsibility complements economic performance and environmental responsibility."

In 1998 the company established the Suncor Energy Foundation to manage financial donations to charitable organizations. In 2000, the Foundation gave almost $3 million to 293 organizations, compared with $2.5 million in 1999 and $1.5 million in 1998.

The Foundation focuses its grants on environmental initiatives, education in science and technology, and community activities and programs. These support a wide range of initiatives, including promoting trades as career choices in Alberta schools, eco-efficient practices by Alberta communities, university programs on sustainable development in Alberta and Ontario, and Earth Day activities in Ontario.

Through the Suncor Energy Foundation Community Service Grants Program, the company awards grants to charitable organizations where employees and retirees volunteer. Over 1999 and 2000, this program contributed a total of $292,000 to more than 200 charitable organizations.

The Foundation also provides matching grants to Canadian post-secondary institutions, and matches employee donations to the United Way. In 2000, total employee and Foundation donations to the United Way reached nearly $950,000.

The company further promotes socially responsible and sustainable business practices through its Values and Beliefs statement. These values include:

- treating coworkers and customers fairly and with respect;
- being highly ethical and professional;
- encouraging open, honest communication that fosters a climate of trust between the company and its stakeholders;

- valuing the judgment of employees;
- being progressive in its health, safety and environmental practices;
- earning customer loyalty with superior products and services; and
- caring for and working to improve the communities in which Suncor operates.

The company's objective is to ensure that business is conducted in an honest and fair manner and that respect is shown for the cultural and business customs of every community in which Suncor operates.

Suncor values the strengths that diversity of thought, perspective, culture and talent can add to its business. It also strives to achieve a workforce that is representative of the labor market and appropriate to local, regional or national interests. In 1998, the company's Oil Sands operation was selected by the Women in Trades and Technology National Network as one of a few Canadian sites to pilot a new employment strategy to increase the number of women in non-traditional roles. Suncor also plans to increase the number of aboriginal people employed full-time at Oil Sands to about 12 per cent by 2002. At the end of 2000, more than 9 percent of the Oil Sands workforce was aboriginal compared with 3 percent in 1996.

CONCLUSIONS

The pursuit of sustainability requires Suncor to continually search for opportunities to improve its environmental, economic and social performance. This pursuit has played an important role in the company's past development and its current success. Since the 1990s, Suncor has evolved into a major Canadian energy company with a recognized commitment to sustainable development. This commitment has earned the company awards and enhanced its reputation within industry, in Canada and internationally. It has also driven the company to increase productivity, to pioneer the use of new environmental tools, to develop new stakeholder alliances and to increase emphasis on corporate social responsibility.

While achieving considerable progress toward sustainable development in a short period of time, Suncor also recognizes that it still faces a number of significant challenges. Suncor recognizes the need to reduce the environmental impacts associated with the ongoing development and use of hydrocarbon energy. These include climate change concerns, urban air quality, and cumulative environmental and social impacts of industrial development. While the company doesn't have all the answers, it is working hard to address these issues through initiatives such as implementing its comprehensive climate change action plan, reformulating fuels, the development of alternative and renewable energy, and consulting with stakeholders in the planning of its projects. As the company discovers new ideas, sees new opportunities and invests in new technologies, Suncor's approach to energy development will continue to develop over time. This in turn will help the company to define and redefine itself as an energy business.

"At Suncor, we are very clear that we don't have all the answers," says George. "This is entirely appropriate, since sustainable development is a journey, not a straight line from A to B. Our first steps on our journey have been intense and demanding. They have required us to think about the nature and future of our business from challenging and new perspectives."

The company is actively participating in the World Business Council for Sustainable Development. It is using this experience to learn from other leading companies and to benchmark its performance against global standards of excellence for sustainable development. This will be especially important as it uses its energy expertise and reputation for sustainable performance to enter new markets.

"We can't be complacent," says George. "What has worked in the past may no longer be good enough. We must now aspire to world-class standards of economic, social and environmental performance."

In looking to the future, the company remains clearly focused on its goal of sustainable growth. "We will strive to grow shareholder value in ways that balance and integrate the economic, environmental and social needs and expectations of our stakeholders," says George. "We may not be able to meet the expectations of all stakeholders, but we are prepared to give it our best try. This, we believe, is how will achieve our vision of being a highly successful and caring business enterprise now and in the future."

IKEA: "NOTHING IS IMPOSSIBLE"

Brian Nattrass and Mary Altomare

Sustainability is the key word for the future. Our ambition is to work step by carefully thought-out step, and with great respect, towards a business based on sound ecological principles. It is not enough to be friendly toward the environment — we must adapt to it. Anders Moberg — President, IKEA

Riding the intercity express into the beautiful lake and forest country of southern Sweden, we found it difficult to imagine that we were approaching the center of operations for the world's largest retailer of home furnishings. As the pine and birch trees, lakes, and farm lands sped by the rushing train, we could imagine ourselves in the countryside of Wisconsin, Minnesota, or Ontario, where, indeed, tens of thousands of Swedes had settled in the great out-migrations of the 19th century. Today, the outflow is millions of Scandinavian-designed household products destined for the global market place. Founded in 1943 by then 18-year old Ingvar Kamprad as a simple mail order business operated from a farm in this same Swedish countryside, by 1997 IKEA had achieved annual worldwide sales in excess of US $7 billion. One could not help wondering by what intriguing interplay of personality, market and historical forces this home furnishings colossus had arisen from the unlikely and aptly named area of Småland ("Small Land") in this land of forests and farms in the south of Sweden.

IKEA's Swedish founder, Chairman, and still dominant presence, Ingvar Kamprad has stated many times over the more than half-century life of his creation that the soul of his company is to be found in the traditional and enduring handmade stone fences characteristic of rural Småland. Each of these solid fences is built from thousands of individual rocks, each lifted one by one from the rocky soil of the Swedish countryside. Rooted in the soil, built one stone at a time, made with intention and much effort over the years, these solid stone walls serve as a continual symbol of IKEA's spirit.

The very name, IKEA, helps co-workers remember their roots as the four letters of the name are derived from the first letters of four words: Ingvar Kamprad Elmtaryd Agunnaryd. Elmtaryd is the name of the farm on which Ingvar Kamprad was raised and Agunnaryd is the name of the village in which the farm was located. IKEA's driving purpose is "to provide a better everyday life for the majority of people." As the company's far-flung operations extend in product lines, complexity, and geography far beyond its humble beginnings in Småland, its mission statement and the vision of its founder are familiar landmarks by which to navigate through new opportunities, challenges, and markets.

The founding values of the IKEA culture are outlined in a booklet written by Kamprad called Testament of a Furniture Dealer given to every IKEA employee. These values include simplicity, humility, and honesty in internal relations among co-workers and in external relations with suppliers and customers; risk-taking, daring to be different, always questioning assumptions and asking "why"; and daring to take responsibility. For IKEA, grown in the soil of frugal Småland, doing more with less and providing value for money are key foundation stones. Today this is called "resource efficiency," obtaining good results with minimum inputs. Waste of resources is considered a "mortal sin" at IKEA. In the IKEA family, the core values are to support one another and to exercise freedom of action and the responsibility that goes with it.

Kamprad believes that the fear of making mistakes is the "enemy of evolution." The challenges of a rapidly changing world and expanding markets are viewed as opportunities; the word "impossible" is absent from IKEA's dictionary. "Strategic mistakes", i.e., unsuccessful initiatives in pursuit of the company's goals, are regarded as "learnings." There is a realization and an acceptance that mistakes not only happen, but are necessary in an entrepreneurial company such as IKEA.

IKEA TODAY

In the lifetime of its founder, IKEA has successfully grown into a profitable and complex global system of more than 40,000 co-workers with 150 stores in 28 countries, 14 major distribution centers, and approximately 2,300 suppliers in more than 64 countries. Worldwide, more than 168 million people visited IKEA stores in 1998. Clearly a robust company, IKEA has seen its revenues grow steadily (Figure 1).

The IKEA group is owned by a Dutch foundation, Stichting Ingka, of which Ingvar Kamprad is Chairman. The management services to the IKEA Group are provided by IKEA International A/S located in Humlebaek, Denmark, the international headquarters for IKEA, which is managed by the President of the IKEA Group, Anders Moberg. The operations of the IKEA Group are based on four basic functions: the product range (design and development), trading (purchasing), wholesale (distribution), and retail (sales).

The product-range company, IKEA of Sweden, often referred to as the "heart of IKEA," has overall responsibility for the competitiveness and effectiveness of the entire IKEA product range in all IKEA markets. It also has the overall responsibility to ensure goods availability in the

Figure 1: IKEA Turnover

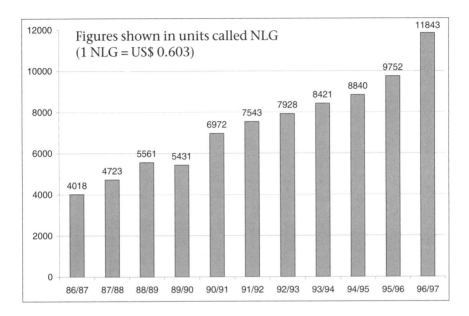

stores and warehouses. Trading has the overall responsibility for purchasing activities including relationships with suppliers, product quality, service levels, and delivery information. The functions of wholesale and retail are organized into three regions: North America, Europe, and Asia Pacific. Wholesale with its commercial and supply-support function has the overall responsibility for all warehousing activities, the phasing in and out of products, delivery information, and the transportation of goods within IKEA. Retail companies are responsible for marketing and sales in each local market.

In general, IKEA does not manufacture its own products, but works through a complex network of suppliers around the world. However, in the past few years, IKEA has acquired a number of its own factories, some of which function as training units and set standards for other suppliers for production economy, quality, and environmental awareness. To secure supplies and help suppliers develop, IKEA is also partnering as joint owners or financiers in a number of countries including Poland, Slovakia, Russia, Romania, and Bulgaria.

CRISIS IN THE MARKET

Signals from the marketplace initially raised IKEA's environmental awareness. In the mid-80s, customers, especially in Germany, IKEA's largest market, began to ask new questions, such as: "Are IKEA's bookshelves made from wood from tropical rainforests? Is there anything toxic in the lacquers IKEA used? Do IKEA's halogen lamps cause cancer?" According to Karl-Olof Nilsson, Group Staff Environmental Affairs, IKEA's product and material experts initially thought these questions were "sometimes strange." In fact, what IKEA personnel ultimately discovered was that questions such as these signalled that the "majority of people" were starting to worry. They were becoming more concerned about the environmental and health effects of products.

IKEA hit its first environmental wall in the mid-80s. In 1981, Denmark established a new law regulating the maximum emissions allowed from formaldehyde off-gassing in particleboard, which is a core component of many IKEA products. According to Nilsson, although the law seemed very strange to IKEA at that time, they simply requested that their suppliers follow it. The Danish authorities decided to test compliance with the new law and found that furniture companies were paying very little attention to it. Being one of the largest companies operating in Denmark, and with headquarters located there, IKEA became the focus of a new and aggressive public campaign. The government tested products from IKEA and found that some products had formaldehyde emissions above the legislated limit. A television program drew dramatic attention to the issue. IKEA was sued for violating Danish laws and assessed a fine. The fine, however, was minimal compared to the damage done to IKEA's image and sales, which temporarily dropped by about 20 percent in the Danish market.

The formaldehyde issue was quickly referred to IKEA's quality department. Russel Johnson, then head of quality moved into action. IKEA immediately set up a large testing laboratory for its products, that today is one of the most sophisticated of such facilities in Scandinavia. They began testing samples from their suppliers and introduced stringent new requirements for suppliers to meet. For suppliers to meet those standards, the investigation had to go deeper. IKEA's suppliers, scattered throughout the world, use particleboard and plywood from numerous manufacturers. IKEA went to these manufacturers and was advised that they could not solve the problem alone because they, in turn, used numerous manufacturers of the glue, which turned out to be the source of the formaldehyde. IKEA took the investigation to the glue manufacturers and still could not find a satisfactory solution. Eventually they ended up going directly to chemical giants such as ICI and BASF in Germany to find a way to reduce the level of formaldehyde off-gassing in IKEA products. In the course of this investigation, Johnson believes that IKEA actively contributed to finding solutions for the entire European furniture and particleboard industry.

In addition to the formaldehyde crisis, IKEA became aware in the late 1980s that it was being criticized more often for more environmentally-related issues. For example, IKEA began to receive criticism for its packaging waste and for the use of PVC plastic which had become a big issue in Germany. PVC, once considered to be an excellent material, had come under environmental scrutiny particularly after a large fire in the plastic industry traced dioxins to the combustion of PVC. Unexpected criticism was also launched against IKEA's famous catalog, then the biggest circulation color catalog in the world. Criticisms were voiced about the number of trees felled each year for pulp to make the catalog's paper, and for the use of chlorine in bleaching that pulp because the chlorine residues released into rivers and seas endangered marine life, particularly in the Baltic Sea. The company was also criticized for the amount of waste produced in the making of the catalogs and from discarded catalogs. These environmental issues were new and confusing for the company. IKEA began to recognize that environmental concern was a new market reality.

Then in 1992, IKEA faced yet another and totally unexpected formaldehyde crisis. This time it was in IKEA's largest market, Germany, and with one of its biggest sellers, the globally popular Billy bookshelf, which represented many millions of dollars per year in revenue to IKEA. Tests conducted by an investigative team from a large German newspaper and television station found formaldehyde emissions for the Billy bookshelf to be just slightly higher than the legislated requirement. This time the culprit was not the particleboard itself —which was the part of the bookshelf that was actually regulated by law — it was the lacquer on the bookshelves. The regulatory details did not matter to the press. The impact of the coverage mattered a great deal to IKEA. Glenn Berndtsson, current head of IKEA's quality division, recalls: "It was in all the newspapers and all the television stations throughout the world: 'the deadly poisoned bookshelves.' From Hong Kong to Australia. We had to put a stop on all sales of Billy bookcases. We stopped production worldwide."

Berndtsson estimates that the direct cost just to track the bookshelves and correct the situation was between US $6 million and US $7 million at that time, not counting the cost for diverted manpower, lost sales, lost production by suppliers, or the costs and time it took to persuade customers to return to IKEA to buy the bookshelves. Altogether, this one incident cost IKEA and its suppliers tens of millions of dollars to correct. IKEA was learning an important and costly lesson. As Erik Linander, former Environmental Coordinator for IKEA of Sweden, reflects:

IKEA was top of the line in Europe, and I think one of the best companies in the world, with regard to formaldehyde problems. But from that day on, we realized that the environment is not only a technical and a legal affair but an emotional media affair. We were prepared for the technical. But when the media put in the headline 'the deadly poisoned bookshelves,' I think that day we woke up.

Johnson explains that early on, Kamprad defined the mission of the company: to create a better everyday life for the majority of people. If environmental problems such as pollution and health effects are becoming more of a worry for everyday people, they must also be a concern for IKEA. "If people see IKEA as a company that is polluting the environment, creating wastes or emissions, or wasting resources, then we are not living up to our mission as it is understood by people now in the late 1980s and 1990s. That's a very strong matter. We are meeting customers face-to-face every day. As a company built on the mission to create a better everyday life for the majority of the people, of course we must take environmental issues seriously."

IKEA AND THE NATURAL STEP

Prior to the 1992 German formaldehyde incident, IKEA had already begun to examine its stand on environmental issues. In 1989, Anders Moberg, President of the IKEA Group, asked Russel Johnson, head of quality for the IKEA Group, to take on the task of mapping out which environmental questions were relevant to IKEA, which might affect their operations, and conversely, what impact IKEA might have on the environment. Moberg told Johnson: "Environment is not just a new fashion, it will not just fade away, it is the new reality and we have to adapt to it." He asked Johnson to draft an environmental policy as a basis for discussion for the IKEA Group management.

Johnson had no knowledge in the environmental area nor did the members of the environmental task force that he pulled together to work on the environmental policy. Nilsson, a member of that pioneering group, recalls that when the task force was formed, they realized that they had to go outside the company to learn more about environmental issues. They went to authorities in several countries where IKEA does business, particularly Germany and Sweden, to learn about anticipated regulation. They conferred with environmental organizations, universities, and scientists that were involved in research relevant to IKEA's business. Finally, they learned from other companies that had already started to work with environmental issues in a structured way. Altogether it took more than a year for the task force to complete the analysis.

In January 1990, Johnson presented his first report to the group management. The report detailed a number of environmental issues relevant to IKEA and presented a first draft of the environmental policy. Johnson told the group management that he realized that neither he nor IKEA had the competence to address these environmental issues. IKEA could not sort these issues out alone. He proposed that the environmental task force would organize an environmental day for the IKEA group management and group staff with someone who could help them make sense out of these issues. Johnson decided that Dr. Karl-Henrik Robert, then working as a medical doctor and director of cancer research at a major hospital in the Stockholm area, was the appropriate person for this task. At that time, although still practising medicine, Robert had a growing reputation for balanced environmental thinking after the well-publicized launch of his Natural Step organization in 1989 under the patronage of the King of Sweden.

IKEA's first environmental day was held at the beginning of June, 1990. Johnson recalls that a number of the corporate executives present at the meeting were quite suspicious. They were accustomed to environmental activists talking only about problems and blaming industry. Robert, however, was different. Johnson explains: "He presented a quick story of how the Earth looked three billion years ago, how it has evolved, and how we are now running the evolutionary picture in reverse. He showed us that the situation is really serious, but that it's not too late, and that we can change it. It is companies, enterprises, that can make the difference."

The group management agreed that environmental issues were becoming more important to IKEA's business. They adopted the first environmental policy for a one-year trial period in 1990. In 1991, IKEA's Board approved the current IKEA environmental policy.

The challenge remained to make the environmental policy an operational reality. The next assignment of the task force was to develop an environmental action plan. By early 1992, it was ready. In April 1992, Moberg hosted a two-day environmental seminar for IKEA's top management to increase their environmental awareness and to get their acceptance of the proposed environmental action plan. At this seminar, IKEA's environmental task force presented its analysis of IKEA's relationship with the natural environment. Nilsson recalls:

"We stated that we had discovered that we at IKEA were environmental gangsters, that we were a threat to the environment. We were violating the possibilities of having a sustainable society." The task force used only three overheads to present the results of their analysis. One slide contained IKEA's success figures such as increased sales and new stores opened the previous year. The second slide pointed out that IKEA had distributed some three million cubic metres of future waste in the previous year. The third slide was a hand-drawn illustration of IKEA's relationship with the environment. Nilsson describes it as follows:

It showed how IKEA takes natural resources such as fossil fuels, minerals, metals, etc. and transports these resources, often in many stages and often in many directions, to a facility where they are transformed into products. The transport process uses fossil fuels, produces emissions, and requires roads that take up green spaces. The production process also produces other effects such as emissions into water, air, and soil; the use of energy; and the production of other wastes. Then again, the products are transported, in many cases to a central warehouse and in some cases to a store. The IKEA store, where the product goes, uses energy, takes up land, and produces wastes. In that store, IKEA markets its products and the customer brings him or herself to the store, hopefully buys IKEA products, and transports him or herself and the product back home. Again polluting transport is used. The first thing the customer must do is get rid of the packaging material, so that becomes waste rather quickly. And, at some stage, hopefully later rather than sooner, the product itself becomes waste.

The environmental task force summarized their findings by telling IKEA's top management that when they analyzed how IKEA works, how other companies work, and how society works, they realized that "what we are doing is actually transforming resources into waste. The process is measured at the cash register where we measure turnover. What we are actually measuring there is the rate at which we are transforming resources into waste." After the task force analysis was presented, Robert introduced The Natural Step framework as a way to begin reconceptualizing and redesigning the relationship between IKEA and the natural environment.

IKEA's environmental task force had conducted significant research on environmental issues with numerous organizations covering a range of approaches and knowledge. The reason they chose The Natural Step approach is summarized by Johnson: First, Robert delivered a positive message, that IKEA could make a difference because it influences people in countless ways. It is an important value in the IKEA culture to make a difference in the world. The second factor is structure. Johnson remarks, "The Natural Step provided a compass, a means to orient us to move ahead. We can use these System Conditions to test the changes we want to make, to see how the proposed change relates to these System Conditions."

After the seminar, the group management approved IKEA's first environmental action plan beginning with education and training.

EDUCATION AND TRAINING

As part of its new environmental action plan, IKEA's senior management elected to use The Natural Step as the foundation for developing an environmental training program to be given to all employees. In consultation with The Natural Step, the environmental task force developed training material geared specifically to IKEA's business and culture. A video was created to deliver a message from Anders Moberg about the importance of incorporating environmental matters into IKEA's business strategy and operations. This message reinforced that environmental issues were important to IKEA and that this was consistent with IKEA's culture. The training was designed as either a 10-hour or a 16-hour program over two days. The 10-hour program was designed for co-workers working in the sales organization, and the 16-hour program was for co-workers working with product development and purchasing. Specialized training was designed to meet the demands of specific work areas.

IKEA decided on a "train-the-trainers" approach to disseminating the environmental education. Trainers were chosen from each IKEA department. They attended an intensive week-long trainers' seminar and received a trainers' kit consisting of a manual and overhead slides. The seminar curriculum included the principles of The Natural Step and descriptions of IKEA's environmental policy and action plan together with information about how different aspects of IKEA's operations were affecting the environment.

Although the training design team made every effort to simplify the language in the materials so that it was applicable at all levels of the organization as well as at all educational levels, the first trainers' seminar revealed the need to simplify even further. At the end of the seminar, each trainer had to present a component of the training for a practice session. Some of the trainers were assigned the task of giving The Natural Step portion of the training. Nilsson reports that they came back with swollen eyes after a sleepless night and said "No, we'll skip that part, it's much too complicated." He comments: "I started to think about this and very spontaneously came up with a description that has helped us very, very much."

A three-part approach was developed to learning the fundamentals of The Natural Step. First, a summary of the scientific principles behind The Natural Step in four short statements; second, the four System Conditions expressed in action language;[1] and third, an outline of eight key concepts that are related to the four System Conditions and that can be used to guide day-to-day decisions. He summarized these three components as follows:

Four fundamental scientific principles underlying the four System Conditions

1. Everything spreads.

2. Nothing disappears.
3. Concentration and structure give value.
4. Green cells concentrate and give structure.

Four System Conditions

1. Cease using resources from the Earth's crust.
2. Stop using unnatural, persistent substances.
3. Allow space for nature and the natural cycle.
4. Harmonize use of resources with natural regeneration.

Eight key concepts to translate the System Conditions into possible actions or bases for decisions

1. Renewable: Change over to renewable raw materials and energy sources (System Condition one).
2. Degradable: Use substances and materials that are easily broken down in nature and converted into new resources (System Condition two).
3. Sortable: Construct products so that the constituent materials can be easily separated for recycling (System Condition four).
4. Nature: Refrain from all unnecessary intrusions into nature and the ecocycle (System Condition three).
5. Save: Always ask yourself whether you can avoid or cut back on your use of resources (System Condition four).
6. Quality: Choose products with a long useful life, which can be repaired if they break (System Condition four).
7. Efficiency: Plan use of materials, energy, technology, and transport to achieve maximum benefit for minimum expenditure of resources (System Condition four).
8. Reuse: The greatest savings in our use of resources can be achieved by reusing them (System Condition four):
   a. Reusing products (i.e., using the same product several times).
   b. Recycling materials (i.e., using used material as raw material for a new product).
   c. Incinerating materials to release the energy content, such as using for heating purposes. This is only acceptable if the gases emitted are such that nature can deal with them. Dumping waste on garbage tips or pumping it into rivers, lakes, and seas is not an alternative in a sustainable society.

According to Nilsson, "the four fundamental principles provide the scientific background. They address why we have the situation we have today. The four System Conditions describe what we have to do about it. The eight key terms provide guidance on how to do it." Once these distinctions were made and discussed, Nilsson recalls, "all of a sudden everything, to everybody's big surprise, was quite clear!" Participants could see the functional use of the information and the way it related to IKEA. For the training to become effective, it was essential, first, to connect the various components of the training material, and second, to link that material to IKEA's daily business decisions and activities.

IKEA's initial company-wide environmental training strategy in the early 1990s was three-fold:

1. The training would proceed in the company's four functional areas, starting with product development, then purchasing, and finally wholesale and retail.
2. It would be a "top-down" training strategy where management would receive training first. For example, Anders Moberg ensured that his management team was trained. Each member of the management team was to ensure that his or her management team was trained. Then each member of those management teams was responsible for seeing that his or her area of responsibility received training.
3. The training applied what IKEA calls the "grandfather principle." This meant that when IKEA of Sweden (product development and product range company) had their training session for their management team, it was convened by the managing director of that company, and Anders Moberg, as president of the company and each managing director's boss, provided the introduction to the training. This process, showing the support at the highest executive levels of the company, was duplicated at all levels to communicate that this training and these issues were highly important to IKEA and to be taken seriously by each worker.

IKEA's goal was to provide full training to all co-workers directly involved in product development or in direct contact with suppliers or customers — about 90 percent of IKEA's 20,000 employees at that time. All other co-workers were offered the opportunity of attending a shorter version of the training. They started with their major environmental training in 1993, and, including the retail side, the majority of the training was done by 1995. However, by the end of 1997, the coverage of the training program in IKEA stores around the world was uneven. In general, where there was higher demand and higher interest about environmental issues in the market, such as in Germany, the training rate was as high as 90 percent of the co-workers in a store. In other cases, it was closer to 50 percent.

In the process of launching a worldwide education campaign in this area of new learning, IKEA has learned some valuable lessons. In the beginning, the education team was so involved in providing the training to all co-workers that little emphasis was placed on what steps should occur after the training. Nilsson reflects that they counted on the training to be the stimulus for action, but it was not that easy. Training had to be reinforced through practice and action. That is, workers needed opportunities to experiment with different ways to do their jobs and management needed to support suggestions and ideas generated after the training about how IKEA could conduct business with more environmental responsibility. Another lesson they learned was to make sure concrete results can be shown very quickly to co-workers to keep the fire of their enthusiasm burning. It is important to take advantage of "low hanging fruits" to demonstrate that something is being done, that progress is taking place.

After five years of experience, IKEA is developing its Natural Step-influenced environmental education in three general categories:

1. Basic training for all co-workers to create awareness, understanding and know-how, and refresher training for co-workers who took part in the extended training in 1993-95 that will include information on what has occurred in IKEA since that time and what is being planned for the future.
2. Professional training for (a) specialists to increase knowledge about the environmental aspects in IKEA's functional areas. (For example, IKEA has developed a program for transport buyers and transport planners who need to know more about the environmental aspects of the transport sector); (b) environmental coordinators and environmental trainers. It develops more extensive environmental knowledge, and greater capacity to help co-workers see the connections between their day-to-day work and the natural world; and (c) for suppliers.
3. Master training, which is more advanced training for co-workers that support the professionals, to develop either a very deep knowledge in one or a few areas, or a very broad general knowledge.

INITIAL STEPS

For most companies, working with the concept of sustainability and the fostering of an environmental consciousness is a new area requiring the development of new knowledge and new competencies. IKEA is no exception. In the course of IKEA's journey, the company has made mistakes as well as built upon its many successes. IKEA's environmental concerns are clearly connected to signals received from a changing marketplace, but they go beyond that. IKEA's vision involves a better everyday life for the majority of people. Originally that vision meant that the majority of people should be able to afford attractive and durable home furnishings. Today the vision embraces choosing a path that will help achieve a sustainable society in ecological balance.

It was easy to recognize the need for integrating environmental concerns into business thinking. It was more difficult to imagine how the changes would actually happen. As early as the April 1992 presentation of the environmental task force to the top management at IKEA, the challenge was obvious. When Robert presented The Natural Step framework at that meeting, one of IKEA's top managers responded: "Thank you very much, you have just ruined our business idea." The discussion that followed acknowledged that IKEA would clearly have to start changing direction, but environmentally friendly products were known to cost more money and thus were out of the question for IKEA. Then one manager suggested that IKEA start by producing an "eco-range" that might be more expensive than other parts of the range, but that would still be less expensive than what anyone else could produce. People began to come to agreement around this idea.

IKEA set out to create a line of products under the new name of "Eco-Plus", consisting of products that had one or more environmental advantages. Erik Linander, at that time Environmental Coordinator for IKEA of Sweden, was deeply involved in this effort. He went out to all of IKEA's business areas to initiate the program. He quickly learned that it was an extremely difficult task. Immediately questions arose about how to compare different products such as a sofa and a glass, and what criteria should be used. Linander started building up criteria, looking for something that went beyond ISO 14000 "because ISO 14000 doesn't explain how you find the product criteria that have environmental value." The more Linander searched, the more questions arose.

Despite the many problems, the project team identified several possibilities to be included in the Eco-Plus line working with The Natural Step System Conditions as the core criteria. After they selected the product line, questions arose as to how they were going to market the product, how long the products were likely to remain environmentally adapted, what would happen in one or two years when technology or knowledge changed? In addition, by creating a more expensive eco-line, IKEA was in danger of inadvertently drawing negative attention to the rest of its product range. Linander recalls that internally, people remarked: "That's good, you're talking about a hundred products, that's good. How about the other 7,000? Aren't they good?" Without intending to, the more expensive Eco-Plus line had, in a sense, created an elite line of furniture that was contrary to IKEA's guiding vision to provide a better everyday life for the majority of the people. Despite its merits and IKEA's best intentions, the Eco-Plus line was not the way to proceed. IKEA was not being forced to produce the collection. They had time to experiment, time to learn.

AN EVOLUTIONARY MOMENT

Part way into the development of the new Eco-Plus line, IKEA decided to reassess and change its strategy. Putting marketing aside for a moment, they asked how IKEA could make the best contribution to a better environment. They concluded that a few products of a very high environmental standard would not make much of a contribution. The best thing to do was to focus on the products already in the range or being designed for the range that had potential to be the best sellers. They reasoned that everything that IKEA could do to reduce their environmental impact in those products would make a greater contribution than if they sold 10,000 eco-sofas. According to the new strategy, it is not a matter of taking five or 15 percent of the product range and making it environmentally the best, it is taking the whole range and improving it step-by-step.

In retrospect, we can see that this fundamental insight marked IKEA's evolutionary shift toward true ecological sustainability. This change in strategy meant that environmental thinking would be integrally connected with the IKEA business vision and operations. It needed to be connected with daily work, with product design and specification, with analysis of the environmental effects of a product through its whole life-cycle, with choice of suppliers and supplier relations, and with the hundreds of thousands of daily decisions made by tens of thousands of IKEA co-workers around the world. According to Linander, this meant that environmental improvements would occur in a much less dramatic way, but would take place in many, many small steps integrated into daily planning and operations. Everyone needed to be involved because these "small green steps" needed to occur at all levels of the organization. In this way, environmental thinking would be interwoven into how IKEA co-workers conducted the company's business.

STAIRWAY TO SUSTAINABILITY

One of the most practical sustainability initiatives arose from co-workers in IKEA of Sweden where the product range is designed, specified, and developed.

As a result of the mandate to integrate environmental thinking into operations, Björn Frithiof, head of law and standards at IKEA of Sweden, helped innovate an approach that has since been adopted by all business areas as a basic IKEA operational model. Originating in the textile division, the model presents a way of operationalizing the idea of "small green steps."

Textiles represent between 15 and 20 percent of IKEA's entire product range. In a US $7 billion dollar company, this represents a significant business item with potentially important environmental impacts all the way down the supply chain. As Figure 2 illustrates, the step model developed by textiles is a system that classifies the entire textile range into four groups based on the environmental standard that each product or supplier has attained.

The first step, or level, ensures that all of IKEA's textile products are tested in internationally recognized textile laboratories to verify compliance with IKEA's basic requirements. This assures that there are no harmful substances in the products and that the customer can feel safe using them. This is the minimum requirement that all IKEA textile products must meet. All IKEA suppliers of textiles must comply with this requirement. The standards of the first green step mean that all textiles produced for IKEA must meet the following minimum criteria: lead free, cadmium free, no PCPs, no AZO-dyestuffs, strict limitations on formaldehyde, no PVC, and no moth-proofing except per International Wool Society recommendations.

The second step calls for tougher production standards. This step begins to incorporate a lifecycle view of the product. The first step specifies that there is nothing toxic or harmful in the product that will affect the customer. The second step applies criteria concerning the way the product is produced to reduce any negative affects on the environment at the production stage. At this level, IKEA requires that no chlorine bleach and no organic solvents are used in the production process, that heavy metal residue is kept to a minimum, and that the pH stays within a range of 4.5-7.5.

The third step demands minimal environmental impact throughout the product's entire lifecycle. It takes into consideration factors such as waste-water treatment at the manufacturing site, the use of PCBs, and the reduction or elimination of other harmful emissions. It also takes into account what happens when the product has served its lifetime, ensuring that it can be recycled and that it won't be harmful if it is deposited or incinerated.

The fourth step goes back even further in the chain to the source of

Figure 2: IKEA Textiles

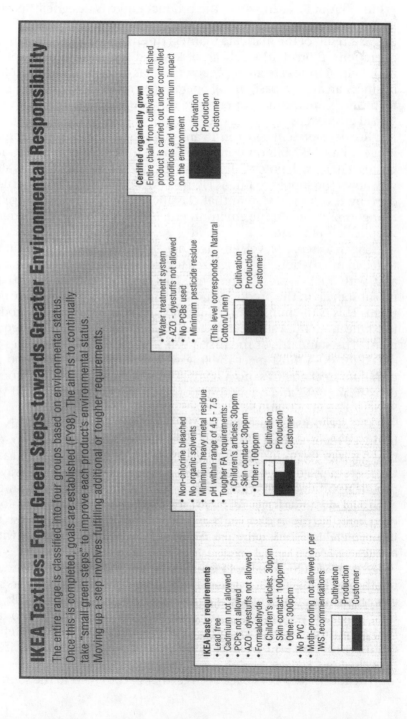

IKEA Textiles: Four Green Steps towards Greater Environmental Responsibility

The entire range is classified into four groups based on environmental status. Once this is completed, goals are established (FY98). The aim is to continually take "small green steps" to improve each product's environmental status. Moving up a step involves fulfilling additional or tougher requirements.

IKEA basic requirements
- Lead free
- Cadmium not allowed
- PCPs not allowed
- AZO - dyestuffs not allowed
- Formaldehyde
  - Children's articles: 30ppm
  - Skin contact: 100ppm
  - Other: 300ppm
- No PVC
- Moth-proofing not allowed or per IWS recommendations

Cultivation
Production
Customer

- Non-chlorine bleached
- No organic solvents
- Minimum heavy metal residue
- pH within range of 4.5 - 7.5
- Tougher FA requirements:
  - Children's articles: 30ppm
  - Skin contact: 30ppm
  - Other: 100ppm

Cultivation
Production
Customer

- Water treatment system
- AZO - dyestuffs not allowed
- No PCBs used
- Minimum pesticide residue

(This level corresponds to Natural Cotton/Linen)

Cultivation
Production
Customer

Certified organically grown
Entire chain from cultivation to finished product is carried out under controlled conditions and with minimum impact on the environment

Cultivation
Production
Customer

raw materials. At this step, IKEA seeks sources of organically grown material such as cotton and flax. This is an ideal toward which IKEA is aspiring.

Originally, the four-step process developed by textiles was configured in three steps: the first step safeguarding the customer; the second step ensuring environmental and human safety during production; and the third step going back to how the fibers are originally grown. Textiles extended it to four steps because suppliers complained that it wasn't possible to make the kind of leaps IKEA required. So IKEA made two steps out of the second step. By working with all suppliers to move them progressively up these steps, textiles is working with its entire product range rather than singling out just a few articles to be environmentally friendly.

The stair model is now being adapted to, and adopted by, other functional areas within IKEA and is being applied to IKEA's relationship with suppliers outside the textile area. It is an example of how education led to involvement, innovation, and operational integration.

EMPLOYEE PARTICIPATION

Because IKEA's culture provides so much room for autonomous action, no single model of involving employees was applied after the initial company-wide environmental education process. The level of engagement of co-workers turned out to be quite variable and depended upon the initiative of the workers in any particular operating unit. Through experience, IKEA has learned that for them to build a shared mental model and language, education is a necessary but not a sufficient condition to stimulate involvement. In addition, a company operating in many countries must take different societal and cultural contexts into account.

In 1993-94, for example, IKEA North America developed a strategy to make the core IKEA values relevant to the North American setting. IKEA's environmental values were not presented as a separate program, but as fundamental to IKEA's core values. According to Göran Carstedt, then President of IKEA North America and member of the IKEA Group executive committee, The Natural Step-influenced environmental education provided for all co-workers in the United States and Canada was a powerful vehicle for blending these cultural values. As a result of the largest training program IKEA North America has ever implemented, co-workers became energized, environmental ambassadors were designated in every store, and numerous activities were initiated. Co-workers developed a sense of pride and convergent values with their company. However, despite the success of the initial launch, interest and energy waned over time. As a result, IKEA North America learned that to keep co-workers energized, it is necessary to constantly re-launch and renew initiatives, and to view change as a step-by-step process, each development acting as a step to the next level.

In 1998, IKEA North America re-launched its environmental education initiative. The general philosophy behind the new initiative is, first, to make IKEA's environmental action plan and policy credible internally to its own employees. Second, it is not part of IKEA North America's plan to advertise itself as environmentally friendly. According to their business plan, their overall goal is to be perceived as an environmentally responsible company without necessarily advertising themselves as such. According to Didi Malabuyo, Assistant to the Sales and Marketing Manager for North America, who has been centrally involved in the re-launch activities, it is essential that IKEA employees believe in the company's efforts and that this must be demonstrated not just in words, but also in actions. Once employees are convinced of IKEA's intentions and actions, it will become natural to convey this information to the customer.

As part of the environmental re-launch, every IKEA facility, store, and warehouse in North America designated an environmental coordinator who participated in an intensive training course. The intensive training was done in June 1998 in three locations: Philadelphia, Toronto, and Los Angeles. The local environmental coordinator was then responsible for training his or her co-workers. To facilitate this process, IKEA North America staff in Philadelphia developed a simple training tool, including a set of PowerPoint slides, that covers IKEA's approach to the environment, The Natural Step framework, and examples that make the information relevant to everyday life.

These training activities are also based on a staircase model: at the first step, as part of their orientation, all new employees learn that IKEA has an environmental policy, what that policy is, and what it means. They receive an introduction to the environmental action plan. They learn who the environmental coordinator is and where they can go for information. The second step, which takes place within the first month of employment, is the basic environmental training. At the third level, if additional environmental training is desired, people can attend the intensive training provided to environmental coordinators.

In addition to the training, environmental coordinators form a North American network and meet monthly by teleconference. The purpose behind the network is to provide the support that was lacking in the first launch of the education program, to link the coordinator in the store to the Environmental Coordinator for North America and through that linkage to connect them with the overall IKEA Environmental Network coordinated through IKEA's international headquarters in Humlabaek, Denmark.

Another important difference in this re-launch is that IKEA North America has made the environmental coordinator a full-time position, whereas previously it was only part of the position handled by the customer service manager. Besides monthly teleconferencing, John Zurcher, the Environmental Coordinator for North America, is working with the local environmental coordinator in each store to set up a working committee in the store to create an environmental action plan and to provide support, generate ideas, and encourage on-going action.

INTEGRATION: ACTION AND RESULTS

The key to operationalizing sustainability is to integrate it into daily decisions and practices, to make environmental aspects a normal part of working methods. Education is the necessary foundation for the effective integration of environmental considerations into the frame of business reality. However, without actual involvement of the workers, education remains in the realm of theory. These two ingredients, education and involvement, are essential for success. Building on these, IKEA has identified five key areas to focus the task of integrating environmental criteria and awareness into its business operations.

1. The Environmental Adaptation of the Product Range

IKEA has become increasingly aware of how much there is to learn about how the materials and substances in their products can affect health and the environment. Currently, IKEA is working with Chalmers University in Goteborg, Sweden, to produce a material inventory of all their products using the four System Conditions and lifecycle analysis as their framework. The goal is, first, to identify what material is being used today and, second, which materials they will need to eliminate over both the short and long term. The knowledge gained through this initiative will be used to improve the environmental performance of existing products as well as to inform the design of new products. Because the IKEA product range is so extensive, with more than 10,000 product lines currently, the project is expected to take between one and two years. IKEA is also working with Kingston University in the U.K. to look at designing furniture from an environmental perspective, including the concepts of dematerialization and design for disassembly.

The stair model for the adaptation of the product range can be summarized as follows:

First, inventory the materials in the product. Second, analyze the

material and determine what needs to be, or can be, eliminated and by
when. Third, increase the percentage of products that use fewer materials and materials that are not harmful to the environment. Fourth,
ensure that the materials used are 100 percent recyclable or are third-
party certified, and that the product can be easily disassembled for future recycling.

Producer responsibility legislation — regulation that makes producers liable for taking back products at the end of their lifecycle — is of
particular concern to IKEA, particularly with respect to furniture. IKEA
believes that eventually the majority of countries will introduce some
form of voluntary or legislated producer responsibility for furniture. In
Sweden, discussions about the parameters for producer responsibility
for furniture have been taking place since May of 1995, and some form
of producer responsibility legislation is expected. In Germany it is no
longer legal to dispose of old furniture at dumpsites. IKEA is working on
the product development side to design and construct furniture for future disassembly and recycling. In Switzerland, IKEA's store in
Spreitenbach has been offering customers the service of recycling their
old sofas and armchairs since 1994. This service is offered at a charge
that is less than customers would have to pay for disposing of the furniture at a dumpsite. In 1996, this service was expanded to allow customers purchasing home furnishing articles at IKEA to return all types of
furniture including kitchen units, white goods, and flooring. In both
Sweden and Switzerland, IKEA is working with local recycling companies to explore the feasibility and logistics of recycling materials from
discarded furniture. The discarded furniture will be recycled for use as
raw material for new products. What cannot be recycled will be used for
energy recovery.

2. Sustainable Forestry

Approximately 75 percent of the raw material for IKEA's products, packaging, and catalogs comes from forests. This makes sustainable forestry
a very important issue to IKEA. IKEA has become actively involved with
various organizations in establishing principles for sustainable forestry.
It is a founding member of the Forest Stewardship Council and was a
member of the working group for the Swedish Forest Stewardship Council
in developing their criteria for sustainability. IKEA has dedicated one
full-time position to making an inventory of IKEA's current use of wood,
including how much wood IKEA uses and from what sources. IKEA's
ultimate goal is to use wood products sourced only from sustainably
managed forests.

3. Environmental Work with Suppliers

The manufacturing of products creates some of the greatest environmental impacts. IKEA directly manufactures less than 10 percent of the products it sells. The balance is produced by some 2,300 suppliers in more than 60 countries. IKEA is initially focusing its environmental lens on its largest suppliers as it estimates that approximately 20 percent of IKEA's suppliers provide about 80 percent of its product line. Although individual suppliers are directly responsible for any harmful effects on the environment, IKEA understands its role as the purchaser for deciding which suppliers it will use. Many suppliers, particularly in Eastern Europe and Southeast Asia, have lower environmental standards than in Western Europe or North America. In IKEA's view, sourcing products in those countries provides an opportunity to advise suppliers of suitable technical solutions to reduce environmental impact. IKEA's responsibility includes providing information about IKEA's environmental policy, environmental action plans, and environmental requirements on products. IKEA's policy is to adopt and apply the strictest standards found anywhere in the world to each specific component in their entire product range. So rather than seeing low environmental standards in a country as an opportunity to avoid responsibility for its environmental impacts, IKEA takes this as an educational opportunity to bring a higher level of awareness and understanding to the particular situation.

IKEA now accepts that its role extends far beyond simply providing information to its suppliers. IKEA is working with a definite goal of reducing its environmental impact while maintaining low cost and value for money for its customers. To do this, IKEA works closely with its suppliers as illustrated in the four-step process developed by textiles. Wherever possible, suppliers are encouraged to practice active, preventive environmental work.

Until recently, each of IKEA's trading regions has developed its own method of working with suppliers with respect to the environment. Now they are synchronizing and coordinating these activities and one person has been made responsible for environmental coordination for IKEA Trading. The stair model for working with suppliers is being developed and will be applied to suppliers in all regions.

Currently, IKEA Trading Northern Europe has an environmental checklist with 10 questions about the supplier's environmental work. It has defined a number of prioritized areas to be given special attention by the supplier, such as surface treatment in all forms, degreasing processes, leather preparation, chemical use in the textile industry, and waste handling. IKEA Trading North America has included questions about the supplier's environmental status in the form of a checklist in the supplier assessment document that is filled out on new and existing supplies. IKEA Trading Asia Pacific has begun compiling a register of the laws and regulations governing their suppliers' operations. They are also carrying out a comprehensive study of the most important suppliers to verify that they fulfill all applicable laws and standards as well as IKEA's specific requirements. The results of the study will be stored in a database which will be updated as environmental improvements are made by the supplier.

IKEA Trading Southern Europe has started an environmental program called "4SEA": Supplier Environmental Assurance built around four points. The program is an environmental management system invented at IKEA and is not very different from the ISO 14000 approach except that it places more emphasis on the current situation and the needed steps than on documentation. The program is designed to assure that the supplier is aware of the environmental impact of its operations and is working for continual improvement. The four points are:

1. The supplier must establish an environmental policy that is relevant to its own organization and in line with that company's environmental ambitions. The supplier must also describe how the work is organized and who is responsible for aspects of the program.
2. The supplier must establish procedures and documentation for areas of its own operations that have an impact on the environment. This involves having systems for laws and regulations that concern the organization, approval from authorities, follow-up of emissions, incident reporting, requirements on sub-suppliers, etc.
3. The supplier must establish and document targets for reduced environmental impact from its operations, for example concerning energy consumption, waste, and emissions to the air and water. Targets must be quantified and measurable.
4. The supplier must establish documented procedures and instructions for handling incidents.

IKEA is encouraging its suppliers to institute environmental management systems in their operations, and many suppliers have already fulfilled the requirements according to ISO 14001, an international standard for environmental work; EMAS (Eco Management and Audit Scheme) which has been developed by the European Union; or BS7750, a British Standard. IKEA is not demanding that its suppliers be certified according to these standards but that they work toward continuous improvement.

The management for IKEA Trading Northern Europe has initiated regional meetings with all of its approximately 400 suppliers. The aim of these meetings is to communicate IKEA's views on the environmental issues facing industry and to learn about suppliers' views, experiences, and needs. A number of suppliers have expressed a desire for receiving help from IKEA in developing their environmental program, particularly with respect to environmental training. To address this need, Trading Northern Europe is offering its suppliers training based on IKEA's environmental training program, which is founded on The Natural Step.

4. Transport and Distribution

Transport is crucial to IKEA because it is a heavily transport-dependent company. In 1996, IKEA produced the booklet Moves in the Right Direction which makes an open and honest assessment of the environmental impact of transport. The booklet points out: "Of all society's present-day activities, transport has perhaps the greatest single impact on the environment. If we were to look at total impact, i.e., do a lifecycle analysis, we would have to include a multitude of factors in the calculation — from extraction of raw materials, construction of ships, cars, planes, roads, etc., to consumption of energy, emissions, and finally reuse and recycling of vehicles."

In fact, the complexity of transportation networks for a modern multinational corporation such as IKEA and their manifold impacts on the environment is quite extraordinary. Considering that IKEA has approximately 2,300 suppliers around the world manufacturing approximately 10,000 different products, with each product made of perhaps dozens of parts themselves made and shipped by dozens of sub-suppliers, the environmental ramifications are significant. And this is just from one company in a global economy of millions of suppliers, transporters, and users. It is easy to understand why decreasing the environmental impact of their transport needs is one of IKEA's fundamental goals.

Therefore, environmental considerations are now an integral part of IKEA's transport purchasing. According to Peter Olofsson, Freight Purchaser for IKEA Northern Europe, environmental impact is now one of the four criteria upon which transport decisions are made. The other three are capacity, flexibility, and cost. IKEA has outlined several priorities for action in the transport area:

1. Competence development of all co-workers directly and indirectly involved in transport or transport-related activities, through a specially designed internal training program covering trans-

port methods and their environmental impacts.

2. Efficiency through better planning and planning systems to minimize the number of transports and to ensure that each is used optimally. Continuing development of packaging and aids to further reduce the transport volume.

3. Transport methods that increase the volume of goods transported by rail, including a combination of road-rail transport. IKEA is monitoring the development of new transport concepts, techniques, methods, and fuels, and actively supports and participates in research in these areas.

4. IKEA is formulating environmental requirements that are communicated to its carriers. These requirements are being made a condition for contracting and will be reviewed and updated annually in consultation with the carriers.

IKEA realizes that there are limits to what they can do to reduce their transport-related environmental impact. Beyond that they must depend upon their transport carriers who are also limited by existing transportation infrastructure, availability of alternative fuels, etc. These are areas where IKEA is building collaborative relationships to move the system in the right direction. Wherever possible, IKEA plans to use rail transport and combined road-rail transport. In the long-term, this requires influencing railway companies and public opinion about the economic and environmental benefits implicit in these choices.

IKEA is working in close co-operation with its carriers to discover ways to reduce the environmental impact of transport. The company has developed a program called "IKEA, Transport, and the Environment" to develop ideas with their carriers for making transportation more efficient. An IKEA "Environment Day" was held regionally in Northern Europe in which nearly 100 European carriers participated. The first part of the day included presentations about why IKEA is now focusing on the environment in all aspects of its business using The Natural Step framework as the conceptual model. The second part consisted of collaborative work with the carriers to generate ideas about how IKEA and its carriers could work together in a more environmentally responsible way.

The transport staircase, which is under development, currently has the following steps: First, require environmental policies from all carriers; second, require an environmental action plan from all carriers; third, construct an environmental audit covering such items as policies, the level the carrier is at according to IKEA's environmental criteria, information on their action plan, equipment, tires, fuels, possibilities for rail or combi-transport etc.; and fourth, divide the carriers into A and B carriers based on a point system from the audit. Carriers wishing long-term contracts would have to quickly reach the A level.

5. Meeting the Customer

This goal is very much an internal process, which includes the environmental adaptation of all IKEA stores, training or retraining of co-workers, and communications with customers. All IKEA stores are conducting material balance inventories to determine the throughput of material and energy in their stores. All new IKEA stores are to be built with environmental criteria in mind. It is the policy in North America, for example, that every new store that is opened from now on will take environmental impact into account in the building design and construction. One of IKEA North America's goals is for that policy to be part of the investment proposal for every new store. As IKEA North America plans to add several stores and to renovate several more in the next few years, this policy has important ramifications for IKEA's investment and planning. To encourage stores to participate in this initiative and to make it more enjoyable, IKEA is considering instituting a friendly competition among stores, and perhaps even among countries.

In the U.S., IKEA is working with the Environmental Protection Agency on their Green Lights Program which encourages the use of energy-efficient lighting. IKEA has partnered with the EPA for about three years. Partners to the program agree to survey 100 percent of their facilities lighting systems and within five years of joining the program to upgrade 90 percent of that square footage to energy-efficient lighting, as long as the upgrade achieves a minimum internal rate of return of 20 percent and there is no compromise of lighting quality. IKEA U.S. has made excellent progress in the program. As of November 1998, they had reduced their kilowatt demand by 781 kw and their kilowatt hour usages by more than three million. The expected annual savings from lighting load reduction, air conditioning reductions, and reductions from lower lighting system maintenance costs is estimated to be more than $500,000, with a simple payback period for all projects of 1.9 years. Environmentally, IKEA in North America has avoided more than four million pounds of annual carbon dioxide emissions, over 17 million grams of annual sulphur dioxide emissions, and almost seven million grams of annual nitrogen oxide emissions equivalent to planting 982 trees, removing 482 cars from U.S. roadways, and preventing the combustion of 313,500 gallons of gasoline.

The goal for the future is to carry out lighting retrofits for three IKEA stores in the U.S. that have not yet been done and to ensure that future facilities within the U.S. are designed to include the most energy-efficient lighting systems possible.

IKEA's philosophy is to become known as an environmentally responsible company by actually being one. It does not intend to advertise itself as a "green" company and is particularly wary of any actions that can be misperceived as greenwashing. IKEA also has a long tradition of informing its customers about the contents of its products to facilitate the making of informed decisions in purchasing. IKEA is working to ensure that its products can withstand environmental scrutiny and that its co-workers can be the best ambassadors for the environment through education and communication of what IKEA is really doing for the environment. In addition, to further inform its customers, IKEA has recently developed Green Steps, an informative booklet on its environmental policy and actions. With customary IKEA understatement, the booklet will not be put in stands by the front door, but will be available for customers who ask for it, or who show interest in how IKEA is dealing with environmental issues.

IKEA's catalog is one of its most important tools of communicating with its customers. Once a source of considerable pride as the largest color publication in the world, IKEA began to receive considerable criticism for the environmental impact of the catalog. The company set out to create an environmental action plan for the catalog. The first step was to identify the environmental concerns involved and to figure out how to improve them. One of those issues was the use of chlorine bleach. By working in partnership with Swedish Greenpeace, IKEA identified a way to produce its catalog on totally chlorine-free paper starting in 1992. IKEA identified paper sources with the help of the Greenpeace network. During that first year, the company purchased most of the world's supply of totally chlorine-free paper and, by doing so, helped push demand for the product. By the second year, IKEA was able to find sufficient supply with no problem. Currently, the catalog contains some 10 to 20 percent recycled paper, which is considered to be the maximum range for that quality of paper. Other catalogs, such as the summer and winter brochures, are made from 100 percent recycled paper because they are not required to have the same durability as the main catalog. IKEA requires a guarantee from its suppliers that the paper in their catalogs is not made from old-growth forests.

In 1997, IKEA launched a campaign to provide Swedish customers with low-cost, low-energy light bulbs. Kamprad decided that he wanted to encourage people to change from the old kind of inefficient incandescent bulb to the modern low-energy, or compact, fluorescent bulb. These produce the same light level for just 20 percent of the energy consumption of the conventional bulbs. Eleven watts of electrical energy give the same light as 60 watts in an ordinary bulb. IKEA found a Chinese manufacturer for the bulb and was able to sell it at a price one-third that of other compact fluorescent bulbs on the market in Sweden

— the equivalent of US $5 instead of $15. To encourage people in Sweden to try them, IKEA in 1997 gave away 532,000 compact lamps to Swedish households. Each household could receive one free bulb by redeeming a coupon at an IKEA store. It was estimated that if every Swedish household exchanged 20 of their bulbs, total Swedish energy consumption could be reduced by an amount equal to the production of one nuclear reactor's power. Considering that Sweden has a population of only nine million people compared to a North American population of roughly 300 million, one can calculate the enormous savings in electrical consumption, and therefore the lowered environmental impact, if the populace of North America converted to low-energy light bulbs.

JUST THE BEGINNING

There are many, many other green steps, both small and large, that IKEA has taken and plans to take. There is IKEA's experimentation with solar energy and its hopes to ultimately be able to build new stores at least in part powered by solar panels. There is the list of materials that IKEA has eliminated, or nearly eliminated, including lead, PVCs, cadmium, and chrome. There is IKEA's children's furniture line that meets a long list of environmental criteria. There is the new range of "a.i.r." sofas and armchairs filled with an inexhaustible, free, and environmentally friendly material: air, in terms of its materials and manufacturing the air sofa uses only one-sixth of the resources of a conventional sofa. There is the North American Recovery program and the Christmas tree recycling program. The list goes on and is growing.

FINAL REFLECTIONS

IKEA occupies a special place in the development of The Natural Step as an effective instrument for business. It was the first major corporation to engage with The Natural Step, that being in 1990. It has the longest continuous business relationship with The Natural Step of any corporation, now a continuous ten-year relationship. It has trained more of its employees in The Natural Step than any other corporation, i.e., approximately 30,000. Many of the most effective environmental management tools, methodologies, and concepts utilizing The Natural Step were pioneered at IKEA over the past decade and continue to be pioneered today. IKEA was the first company to bring the natural step framework to North America and to begin to link the strengths of organizational learning with The Natural Step framework for sustainability. Finally, IKEA has a culture of entrepreneurial innovation, risk taking, forgiveness of mistakes and learning from them as well as caring for all of its stakeholders, and has come to an understanding of the business relevance and importance of sustainability. This has been fertile soil to create an effective dialogue between The Natural Step and business.

Several factors have facilitated IKEA's process of integrating sustainability as a core value of its business. The foundation of this is the link between The Natural Step framework and the values of IKEA's founder, Ingvar Kamprad, who has always detested waste in any form. Furthermore, exciting product innovation has resulted from seeking to balance environmental criteria on one hand with a low cost structure on the other. The integration of sustainability as a core value also owes a great deal to the tremendous drive of a small group of dedicated and enthused individuals, most notably Anders Moberg, IKEA Group President. In addition, the enthusiasm and pride with which many co-workers throughout the company have embraced the inclusion of environmental concerns in their work has been very important. Still another significant factor is that IKEA focused its environmental lens on the heart of its business — product design and development — and on supplier relations through educating them about IKEA's sustainability vision, values, and plans.

In reflecting upon the ongoing ten year intellectual and commercial relationship between IKEA and The Natural Step, there appear to us to be at least five main benefits to the company.

First, The Natural Step has been very helpful to IKEA in creating awareness, understanding, and enthusiasm for environmental issues among IKEA's senior management, middle managers, and co-workers. The Natural Step provides a key part of the environmental education programs used to train all co-workers. It provides the scientific core of the three different types of environmental training programs offered in IKEA today (as described above).

Second, The Natural Step has given IKEA management and co-workers a means to understand their relationship as a company and as individuals, to the natural world, and how IKEA in its widespread operations affects, and is affected by, the natural environment. By embedding The Natural Step framework into IKEA's strategic and day-to-day operations, through environmental policies, environmental action plans, environmental training, and through making environmental factors a core consideration of investment, supplier, transport and product design and specification decisions, IKEA is approaching a more ecological worldview. In effect, in terms of its corporate identity as it relates to the natural world, it knows who it is, what it stands for, and why.

Third, with respect to the attacks of critics and the media, sometimes highly emotional, about the safety and environmental impacts of its products and operations, The Natural Step framework empowers and enables IKEA to analyze its products and operations and respond knowledgeably to criticism. IKEA does not claim to be environmentally pristine, far from it, but it at least has a much clearer understanding than most corporations of its inconsistencies and it has a step-by-step vision for their eventual solution.

Fourth, The Natural Step stimulates innovation and out-of-the-box thinking. It provides a framework for design innovation that empowers designers in all media to innovate for the betterment of profits, people, and planet. A recent example of how sustainability considerations stimulate innovation is the new "a.i.r." sofa from IKEA which exemplifies dematerialization in terms of volume of space to factor six.

Fifth, The Natural Step provides a rational, common language and mental model for IKEA and its suppliers to create a shared basis for understanding IKEA's environmental vision and enables them to better and more efficiently implement IKEA's purchasing policies. IKEA and its thousands of suppliers around the world comprise a very complex system of relationships, languages, and cultures. So far hundreds of IKEA suppliers in Northern Europe have received training in IKEA's Natural Step-influenced environmental policies.

Despite many advances in both sustainability thinking and action, co-workers at IKEA are noticeably humble and honest as they describe their ten-year environmental odyssey. They are the first to say how far IKEA still needs to go. Moving toward sustainability is recognized as a very long path, consisting of thousands and thousands of small green steps. Often it is a frustrating road when the pace of change does not seem to match the urgency that is felt by many people. However, by any standard, IKEA has made remarkable progress. Perhaps most importantly, the senior leadership of the company and a large body of co-workers understand the basic issues of sustainability and the reasons it is so relevant to IKEA's global operations, both today and in the future, and are motivated to continue IKEA's march towards a sustainable world — a world where IKEA will continue to pursue its mission to help provide a better everyday life for the majority of people.

FOOTNOTE

1. It is important to note that IKEA's abbreviated adaptation of the System Conditions does not fully or accurately convey their meaning. For example, System Condition One does not suggest that society should stop using resources from the Earth's crust, but that society should use these resources in such a way that concentrations of substances from the Earth's crust do not systematically accumulate in nature. The IKEA version is included to illustrate their learning and communication pro-

cess, not to suggest that this is a preferred presentation of the System Conditions.

Excerpted from *The Natural Step for Buisness: Wealth, Ecology and the Evolutionary Corporation*, by Brian Nattrass and Mary Altomare, New Society Publishers, 1999.

BY-PRODUCT SYNERGY: A CASE STUDY OF TAMPICO, MEXICO

Rebekah Young
Hatch Associates
and
Susana Hurtado Baker
Frederico Ortiz Lopez
Cosejo Empresarial para el Desarrollo Sostenible - Golfo de Mexico

INTRODUCTION

In October 1997, the Business Council for Sustainable Development – Gulf of Mexico (BCSD-GM) launched a demonstration By-Product Synergy project in Tampico, Mexico with a group of 21 local industries. The goal was to promote joint commercial development among economic sectors so that one industry's wastes became another industry's inputs. The project demonstrated that by working together, industries can maximize use of potentially profitable materials which otherwise may be treated as "waste". By reusing by-products as raw materials rather than disposing of them as waste, companies save energy, reduce environmental damage, and gain potential trade opportunities. They may also lower their greenhouse gas emissions, while cutting the demand for raw materials and landfills. The Tampico project provided an opportunity to put those ideas into practice. The goals of the demonstration BPS project were to identify a minimum of five synergies, foster greater understanding of eco-efficiency, and create a new community of companies with greater industry leadership. This summary report documents and disseminates the project's successes, shares the lessons learned, and recommends ways to overcome barriers in future by-product synergies.

BACKGROUND

Several member companies of the American chapter of the Business Council for Sustainable Development for the Gulf of Mexico (BCSD-GM) have experienced individual successes with by-product synergies. These have been documented in the primer, "By-Product Synergy: A Strategy for Sustainable Development – A Primer" (April 1997). The American and Mexican chapters of the BCSD-GM wanted to test the idea of approaching by-product synergy in a systematic manner. Rather than stumble upon synergies haphazardly, the idea was to seek these potentially profitable synergies among a group of industries.

The Tampico-Cuidad Madero-Altamira region offered an ideal location for a demonstration by-product synergy project. Most of the major industries in the area were already linked for other business purposes through the powerful network of the Asociación de Industriales del Sur de Tamaulipas (AISTAC). Eighteen of the twenty-one companies are members of this association; the demonstration project was able to take advantage of the association's structure and relationships.

The region has recognized that it must set a zero waste - 100% product goal, if it is to shift to a sustainable industrial economy. Eco-efficiency has been an ongoing pursuit within these companies; most companies are ISO 9000 certified and several are ISO 14000 certified. The BCSD-GM is advancing these efforts a step further by identifying and capitalizing on opportunities to promote eco-efficiency *across* industries, not just within a given industry.

The Tampico region with a population of approximately 800,000 is located on the Gulf of Mexico. It is one of the busiest ports in Mexico. Most of the participating firms were chemical and petrochemical companies (see Appendix 1).

The driving forces behind the project were the BCSD-GM, (American and Mexican chapters) AISTAC, and the strong leadership and support of Mexican industrialist Ing. Eduardo Prieto Sanchez M., director general of GRUPO/PRIMEX, and president of the BCSD-GM Mexican Chapter. The US Environmental Protection Agency, NAFTA's Commission for Environmental Cooperation (CEC), the AVINA Foundation, and the Ford Foundation also supported the project, which was managed by Susana Hurtado, a local facilitator.

THE PROCESS

The entire process took approximately fourteen months, plus the evaluation period. The proposal for a generic BPS Project estimates that it should take nine to twelve months, with two additional months to evaluate the results.

Awareness

Project organizers began by seeking the support and commitment of a core group of participant companies. Ing. Prieto and Susana Hurtado worked together to sell the idea to the CEOs of major industrial companies in the area. BCSD-GM representatives explained the BPS concept to more than forty company executives responsible for industrial facilities in the Tampico-Altamira region. Mexican and American businesses and research organizations provided background information on previous BPS successes, industrial ecology, available resources, and the status of current waste management and clean-up efforts in Tampico.

Participants were asked to commit to a yearlong BPS demonstration during which they would systematically seek out profitable synergies among their operations. Their response was enthusiastic. More than twenty companies signed a Declaration of Intent detailing their commitment to the demonstration project. The local project manager then began working down the corporate chain to explain the process. This step involved meeting with plant managers and engineers who would be likely representatives of their companies during the project. A successful BPS project requires "sources" and "sinks" for materials, which dictates a diverse selection of participants. Extensive communication was required in order to gain broad company participation.

Data Collection

The objective of this phase was to account for each company's in-flows and out-flows of materials, commodities and utilities. Each company was given a data template which process and environmental engineers could use to identify material flows. Many of the participants found the templates difficult to complete. Also, most industries aren't accustomed to sharing information, and Tampico was no exception. Despite a signed confidentiality agreement, many companies chose to give only rough material quantities with no cost information. Complementary on-site plant visits by the BCSD-GM project staff helped build trust and rapport among the group.

Analysis

Materials were analyzed in two ways. Bechtel, a San Francisco-based engineering and consulting firm, was contracted to provide an overall view of materials within the group and a list of potential synergies. The program first matched raw material and waste flows within the Tampico group. It then matched raw material and waste flows from Tampico against company profiles that Bechtel has collected around the world.

While data collection was still in progress, the BCSD-GM scheduled bi-monthly meetings with the group where facilitated brainstorming was carried out to maintain and advance the momentum that had been established during the awareness stage. These sessions were assisted by outside consultants Hatch Associates. This second method of analysis identified all but one of the synergies that Bechtel had pinpointed; it also found 10 additional synergies. A major reason for the success was that the brainstorming process established confidence and trust and generated a great deal of enthusiasm for the project.

RESULTS

Cumulative Material Flows

Materials input/output profiles were generated for 27 separate processes in 18 regional Tampico companies. A total of 373 materials flows were documented: 199 inputs and 174 outputs. Of the output data, 120 were waste flows consisting of 78 different materials, and 54 were finished and semi-finished products and by-products. The first step was to look at the group's overall waste production. Table 1 shows relative quantities of reported wastes.

Table 1: Classification Of All Waste Flows

Gases and gaseous waste	50.90%
Water	30.04%
Soil, clay, sand, etc.	13.52%
Plastics	1.86%
Other inorganic chemicals	1.61%
Other organic chemicals	1.02%
Metals	0.49%
Oils, fats and waxes	0.25%
Wood and paper	0.14%
Alkalis	0.05%
Food products	0.04%
Solvents	0.03%
Glass and ceramics	0.02%
Biomass, agricultural waste	0.01%
Finished agricultural products	0.01%
Textiles	small

This first analysis highlights the biggest problems in terms of quantity. Table 2 summarizes the flows of the five greatest waste quantities by mass in tons per year.

It is beneficial to view relative waste quantities excluding these major items. Table 3 presents a similar summary for the 8,255 metric tons remaining after excluding water, gases, and contaminated soils. Clearly, there is significant potential for taking advantage of economies of scale to recover various plastics and chemicals as a group.

Table 2: Five Largest Waste Flows

WASTE	FLOW (tons per year)
Wastwater	44,820
Carbon monoxide	44,397
Carbon dioxide	26,716
Tailings	17,000
Oxygen	4,534

Table 3: All Waste Flows (Excluding water, gases & soils)

Plastics	33.66%
Other inorganic chemicals	29.06%
Other organic chemicals	18.49%
Metals	8.94%
Oils, fats and waxes	4.49%
Wood and paper	2.58%
Alkalis	0.97%
Food products	0.66%
Solvents	0.48%
Glass and ceramics	0.29%
Biomass, agricultural waste	0.24%
Finished agricultural products	0.10%
Textiles	0.03%

Selected Synergies

The Bechtel analysis highlighted 19 material flows that had potential users within the participating group. On a global scale, 44 potential uses for the materials of 29 streams were identified, yielding a total of 63 identified synergies. Thirteen synergies were selected for further investigation based on criteria of quantity, toxicity, control cost and lost opportunity cost. The timeframe for implementation was also an influential factor in selection; those with relatively easier and shorter implementation were favored. Of the thirteen chosen synergies, seven were identified by both the Bechtel analysis and group brainstorming. Five were identified only by the working group, while one synergy was identified by the data analysis alone.

Six of the thirteen synergies were one-to-one relationships: the by-product of one company can be used by another individual company. Seven synergies involved more than two companies. These are identified wastes that are common to a majority. Although it may not be feasible for individual companies to recover these products, a group of companies may be able to afford to do so. The role of the BCSD-GM helped facilitate dialogue among the companies.

Figure 1 summarizes major Tampico regional synergy opportunities. Research focussed on the following opportunites: (1) recovery of CO_2; (2) use of spent butadiene, used in the polymerization reaction of polymers such as polybutadiene, styrene-butadiene rubbers and lattices, and nitrile-butadiene rubbers; (3) recuperation of Hydrochloric Acid; (4) use of polymer resins for construction materials; (5) cryogenic rehabilitation of polymer resins; (6) cleaning and recycling of empty chemical drums and barrels; (7) recuperation of ferric chloride for external sale; (8) producing loading platforms from polyethylene/polypropylene bags; (9) use of stock chemicals resulting from process changes; (10) use of fiberglass fabric; (11) use of mine tails in cement manufacture; (12) use of PVC residual for shoe soles; and (13) waste-to-energy conversion.

BARRIERS TO BY-PRODUCT SYNERGY

The BCSD-GM's Primer on By-Product Synergy outlines a number of potential barriers toward implementation. These include technical, economic, geographic, regulatory, legal, business, social, time and informational barriers.

Technical: *Is conversion of the by-product technically feasible?*

In the Tampico case, this barrier was manageable. Technical solutions for many of the by-products are available. For example, the PVC residuals can readily be converted into shoe soles while the polyethylene/polypropylene bags can be transformed into plastic shipping palettes. The technology is also available for the other medium-term projects such as the polymer recycling, gasification and chemical recovery. When project participants weren't familiar with the technological options, they

Figure 1: Major Tampico Synergy Opportunities

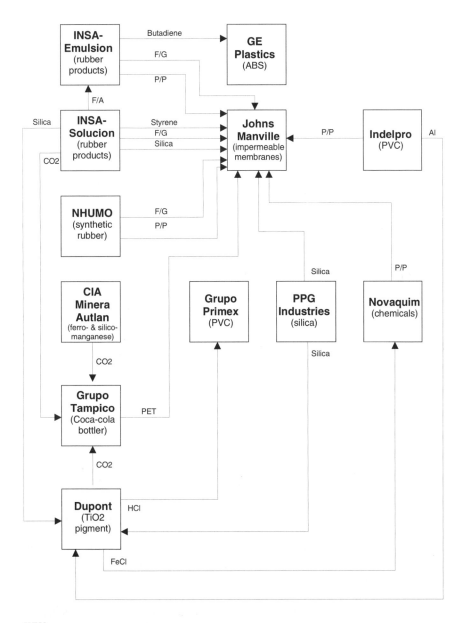

KEY:
Al = aluminum; CO2 = carbon dioxide; F/A = fatty acids; FeCl = ferric chloride; F/G = fiberglass; HCl = hydrochloric acid;PET = ; P/P = polyethylene/polypropylene.

brought in outside technical help. For example, specialists from Cryoinfra from Mexico City were invited to one of the working sessions where they presented their nitrogen reprocessing technology for plastics recovery.

Economic: *Is it economically feasible?*

Implementation of many of the identified synergies will depend largely on economics. Companies use their in-house cost-benefit analysis to decide which projects to pursue. Ferric chloride and hydrochloric acid recoveries provide examples where economics may be the impediment. The technology is available, but given today's market for these chemicals, the supply/demand may not be favorable for the investment in recovery. The costs of polluting are not reflected in the economic structure. As long as polluting costs are low, companies will not prioritize waste reuse or reduction. Taking the large quantities of waste streams of high calorific value as an example, each industry is permitted to discard these by-products in a common landfill for a low tipping fee. As long as those fees remain low, there is no incentive to investigate other long-term options such as waste-to-energy projects.

Business: *Is it competing against other investment opportunities?*

Most synergies require an up-front investment in the form of laboratory research, technology change, process modification, or treatment processes before a saving or profit is realized. Before deciding to invest, company managers will compare the benefits of by-product synergy with those of other investment choices, such as expanding capacity. Even if the project has a net positive value, the rate of return on other options may be more favorable. Logic would suggest investing in the higher rate of return when the investment funds are limited. Sustainable practices are increasingly being viewed as ethical investments, thus making financing and liability insurance more readily available. NAFIN, a Mexican national bank, described its special financing options for corporate investments meeting certain environmental criteria. Many other institutions and development agencies will lend money at attractive rates only for these types of projects. Such incentives will promote large-scale investments that may have longer rates of return than other investment opportunities.

Corporate practice: *Is the company's decision-making process hindering investment?*

Other benefits of by-product synergy are measured indirectly. Sustainable behavior can improve a company's public image, leading to more productive relationships with community and environmental organizations. Participation can improve safety and morale in the work place, which can minimize shutdown time and increase worker productivity. Suppliers and consumers are expected to pay more attention to the life cycle costs of materials, and rewarding those companies that do the same. Some proactive companies are beginning to take these other factors into account in a systematic way. An example is Grupo Primex's sustainability index, a diagnostic tool designed to evaluate sustainable development in all its dimensions. As companies adopt these practices more widely they will gain an advantage over those using traditional methods.

Regulatory: *Are there government-created barriers to synergies?*

Classification of wastes was identified as a significant regulatory barrier. Once something is defined as a waste, it is subject to a unique set of regulations governing its transportation and disposal. The concept excludes the consideration of re-use, thus it is a cumbersome process for an industry to gain permission to adopt approaches other than those outlined in the regulations. For example, in Tampico, used chemical drums were classified as hazardous wastes, so companies wishing to reuse these materials would have to clear many legal and regulatory hurdles. In another case, the by-products from a state-owned company are considered "national property". Therefore, a private facility wishing to reuse them would have to consider all of the legal ramifications.

Risk: *Could use of or transportation of a "waste" lead to increased liability? Who is responsible?*

Companies are more comfortable making decisions after analyzing potential risks. They usually tackle liability questions after surmounting technical, economic and regulatory barriers. It is not always clear who is liable for the re-use of the by-product: the producer or the consumer? This means both parties in a by-product synergy transaction must take a calculated risk based on incomplete information. Conservative companies would be reluctant to do this. Companies that are storing wastes or by-products on site rather than using them face greater liability because of the potential for leaks and spills. Transporting the waste poses its own risks of accidents during shipping and handling. Most companies will not take the risk of transporting if liability during transport is greater (or more uncertain) than the liability for property damage on site. Regulatory institutions should clearly and consistently define and enforce liability laws to reduce this uncertainty and allow companies to make informed decision**s**.

Geographic: *Can the by-product be economically transported from its generator to its consumer?*

The geographic region was confined to the Tampico-Altamira area, based on the assumption that the easier or more economically feasible synergies will be confined within a certain radius. However, in certain cases where the by-product has a higher value, the radius may expand. Mineral Autlan has two million tons of mining slag available on site. CemStar has demonstrated that a synergy between a cement company and a steel company can be profitable up to a transportation distance of 250 miles. This company can seek a possible partner in this larger radius since there is no cement company in the immediate vicinity. For some materials the radius is reduced. Carbon dioxide is relatively expensive to transport. Producers and users must be located in relatively close proximity to one another to make a synergy involving this gas viable. In Tampico, a synergy of this type is being developed. One source of the gas, PEMEX, was already established in the area. The user, Cryoinfra, decided to select a new site within the PEMEX compound.

Trust: *Are companies comfortable working together?*

Building a sense of trust among the companies in Tampico took some effort. Facilitated brainstorming sessions promoted increased group interaction, which in turn helped build a sense of comfort and confidence. The signing of a confidentiality agreement encouraged submission of more comprehensive data on waste streams.

Time: *Is by-product synergy a low priority in the organization?*

Most companies assigned only one person, and in some cases two people who shared responsibility for the project. In their questionnaire responses, many of the contact people said their work responsibilities left them little time to carry out their commitments to the project within the agreed time frame. The companies most strongly committed to the project voiced the greatest concern regarding insufficient human resources. This is logical since those companies were involved in the majority of synergies. Clearly a company will gain more from the BPS process if it allocates the resources to follow through with ideas. Inaction or low participation on the part of other companies resulted from assigning the project to a person who lacked sufficient influence in the company. It was important that the person had the ability to take decisions on behalf of his company, or have the influence to successfully promulgate the ideas within his company following the meetings.

ADDITIONAL BENEFITS

Fostering a greater understanding of eco-efficiency

The project strengthened the concepts of sustainable development and eco-efficiency in a number of companies. Eighty percent of the participants reported that they found opportunities to bring the concepts back to their respective companies as a result of the process. For companies that had already begun exploring sustainable development, the project strengthened their commitment and gave them an opportunity to put those ideas into action. A performance analysis of each company revealed that 65 percent of companies were strongly committed to sustainable development throughout the process. They supported the project without restrictions, adopted it as an integral part of their philosophy and are always searching for new synergies. The most committed participants identified the most synergies and learned the most from the project. Sixty-five percent of the companies are taking part in at least one synergy directly derived from the project. These companies had some prior knowledge of sustainable development and were eager to put their theories into practice. They were open to new ideas and eager to share their experiences with other participants. Not surprisingly, the successful companies had strong support from upper management. CEO's and plant managers considered it a priority within their company; this was demonstrated in the commitment of necessary resources during the project. Only 10% of companies reported that their upper management was disinterested.

A new agenda for the community of companies

The existence of a strong and organized association (AISTAC) was essential in getting the project started. It lent structure and familiarity to the group since most of the participant companies were accustomed to meeting as a group. While they were accustomed to discussing economic and industrial development, some were initially reluctant to openly discuss waste and waste disposal processes. Going into the project, the participating companies recognized they shared a common goal, but they were not entirely clear on how companies from completely different sectors could help one another. As it became apparent that there were significant opportunities to work toward sustainability together, they began communicating more effectively as a group. One of the shared project conclusions is that the participation of the 21 companies in the by-product synergy project is creating a competitive advantage for the region as a whole.

THE NEXT STEP

Although the initial phase of the demonstration project is complete, the involved parties can still take steps to ensure sustainability of by-product synergy projects.

Business Council for Sustainable Development - Gulf of Mexico

Clearly, companies that go into the project strongly committed to sustainable development will benefit most. Disseminating success stories is one way organizers can win over skeptics. The demonstration project provides concrete evidence of the benefits sustainable-development efforts provide. Although most companies recognize the importance of environmental protection in theory, the primary motivation for participation in the majority of cases was economic: the continuous search for new opportunities and sources of revenue. The BCSD-GM must explore ways to measure and report the economic benefits derived from Tampico. This will be the key in promoting similar practices in other areas. Clearly many of the lessons learned in Tampico would be valuable to similar initiatives in the future. A new company, Applied Sustainability LLC, was formed by a number of members of the BCSD to take this model for sustainable development around the world. It will take the lessons from Tampico and apply them to future projects. The process will be refined continually with experience. Applied Sustainability has helped launch similar projects in Alberta, Canada and North Texas, USA in February 1999 and July 1999 respectively. Although the process is industry-led, other institutions will play a role in making implementation possible. Applied Sustainability LLC must act as facilitator in bringing other parties to the, such as academic, research, technological, regulatory, public and financial institutions. Applied Sustainability provides the link among these future by-product synergy initiatives as it continues to expand the range of participating companies in its global databank. It can also help facilitate links between companies from different regions.

Industry

Having an influential leader "champion" the project in an industrial community is invaluable. By publicly announcing his commitment to the effort, he is taking the first step forward and providing leadership within the industrial community. His confidence encourages his peers to participate. This was clearly the case in Tampico, where Ing. Eduardo Prieto spent considerable time leading the project to its successful conclusion. Similarly within each individual corporation, commitment from top management is important. The CEO or director general can change corporate attitudes towards sustainable development throughout the organization. Ideas for by-product synergy should come from all areas of operation, from the head office to the plant floor. If, on the other hand, companies relegate sustainable development to a single office or staff member, they miss valuable opportunities. The managing director's commitment must be substantiated with adequate resources assigned to the project. During the first phase of the project man-hours are required. Ultimately the industries will implement those ideas judged feasible; but it will require investment of time, effort and money. The initiative in Tampico has been self-sustaining; the companies have recognized the enormous potential of by-product synergy. At the conclusion on the BCSD-GM's involvement, 80 percent of the companies stated their wish to continue taking advantage of the benefits that sustainable development generates both for the industries and for the environment. AISTAC is considering institutionalizing the by-product synergy effort now that the structure and methodology are in place for working collaboratively.

Government

The most significant regulatory barrier affecting by-product synergy implementation is the classification of materials. In the past, regulatory and industry relationships have been adversarial; regulators assumed industry would abuse any flexibility in regulations. From a regulatory point of view, by putting all waste materials under an umbrella regulation, monitoring and enforcing regulation was most cost-effective. Participants of the by-product synergy project stressed that there should be avenues for de-classifying waste materials based on their potential future use. There is no mention of "waste" in by-product synergy, only by-products, inputs and raw materials. As industry recognizes the tremendous opportunity presented by by-product synergy, regulators' attitudes should also change. At a follow-up discussion of the "Intergovernmental Task Force in Conjunction with the Tampico By-Product Synergy Project" (February, 1999) the project participants highlighted opportunities for government to use fiscal incentives to promote by-product synergy. In particular, companies were interested in financial programs that would help update technologies or launch environmental projects. Carbon credit trading is another promising financial incentive, particularly on an international scale. In cases such as CO_2 recovery and reuse, where economics are the major barrier, the reused carbon units would be valuable. U.S. industry is under pressure to reduce CO_2 emissions. If the United States were to buy CO_2 credits from Mexico; it would benefit the U.S., and generate revenue for the Mexican industries selling the credits.

APPENDIX 1: LIST OF PARTICIPANTS

COMPANY	PRODUCT

Plastics

Indelpro S.A. de C.V.	PVC
G.E. Plastics	ABS
Grupo Primex	PVC resin and dust, phtalic anhydride
Policyd	PVC
Polioles	Polystyrene
Pecten Poliesters	Polyethylene

Industrial Minerals

PPG	pure silica
Dupont	TiO2 pigment

Chemical / Petrochemical

Novaquim	chemicals for rubber industry, herbicides
NHUMO	synthetic rubber
INSA-Emulsion	rubber products (tires, hose)
INSA-Solucíon	rubber products (roads, shoes)
Pemex	petroleum refinery products
Petrocel-DMT	dimethyl terephtalate
Petrocel-PTA	phteraphtalic acid

Metallurgical

Sulfamex	manganese sulfate
Minera Autlan	ferromanganese, siliocmanganese

Miscellaneous

Cryoinfra	industrial gases
Grupo Tampico	Coca-cola bottler
Johns Mansville	impermeable membranes
Enertek	electric power

CHEMICAL INDUSTRY INTEGRATION

T.J. McCann
T.J. McCann and Associates
Calgary, Alberta

INTRODUCTION

Clustering of chemical plants to maximize interchange of feedstocks and utilities has long been a practice. However, similar integration amongst most other industries has been slow in development. While we consider only Canadian examples in this chapter, U.S. Gulf Coast and Dutch chemical industry examples are much more advanced and larger in scale. Through eco-industrial (economic sustainable) development activities, similar interchanges are being developed in light industrial parks and between various industries often of quite different nature and philosophies.[1]

Many regions are promoting integration to improve regional economics following losses of one or more major industries. This is especially true in at least five well-defined European chemical clusters. In several cases, divestiture and even shutdown of certain operations has opened the way to new synergies with existing industry and utilities.

In this chapter, our emphasis is on Shell Canada and Shell Chemicals/Air Liquide complexes in Alberta. Data for this case are largely from the public domain, but comments and interpretations are those of the writer, who is solely responsible for the contents.

CHEMICAL INDUSTRY AND INTEGRATION

Chemical companies are continually redefining their core products and spinning off non-core production and services, often to new companies fitting many such pieces together. There have been so many of the latter and so many changes in ownership and corporate names that it is often difficult to decipher articles in the major industry journals such as Chemical Week unless one has kept up to date on the specific industrial sector.

The chemical industries have been leaders in the process of integration. Sometimes this includes competitors, but more usually incorporates suppliers of non-core services and selected processing of feedstocks and products.[2] Cogeneration of steam for at-site use and electricity for at-site and sale to others is a typical example where chemical companies are 'farming out' activities to other companies specializing in such facilities. Supply of industrial gases - oxygen, nitrogen, carbon monoxide and hydrogen — are almost invariably purchased from others today. Even waste treatment services are being provided by municipal and other agencies serving numerous plants in a given area.

Sarnia

In Canada, the Sarnia refining/chemical cluster started in 1942 with the construction of the Polymer synthetic rubber complex. That complex of five groups of integrated units, with a common coal-based utility core, was operated by different U.S. chemical companies based on feedstock from the existing Imperial Oil refinery, then the largest in the British Empire. Imported benzene and coal were received by Great Lakes ships. The Sarnia area provided a well-trained process-plant-oriented working force and construction labour came mostly from northern Quebec. (By that time, local crude supply had dropped to a low level and U.S. crude was the primary supply for the refinery.)

For many years, Dow Chemical used the vast salt beds under Sarnia and other local feedstocks to produce a variety of chemical and plastic products. Over the years, there have been many changes in ownership, number of plants and products produced. The availability of feedstocks and trained labour brought in DuPont and Nova (both now NovaChem). Canadian Oil (now Shell) and Sunoco built refineries and Imperial added a variety of chemical and polymer operations. In recent years Dow reduced its operations by over 1,000 staff, and Imperial and Dow Canada head office operations were ultimately transferred out of the area.

In the past, utility interchange was not economic except on the original Polymer site. Even there such interchanges dropped over time, but is now picking up again with a 500-MW cogeneration facility to be operated by TransAlta, expanding upon a smaller system based on surplus Dow generating facilities.

The Sarnia regional economy has tended to rise and fall with the construction industry, and economic diversification has proved difficult due to high labour rates and no special advantages — such as low feedstock, utility costs or location incentives — compared to the U.S. Gulf Coast and other chemical clusters. Rate concessions have recently been made by unions to permit several new projects to proceed.

Quebec

The Quebec government has been trying for many years to develop the Montreal area into a major chemical center, but aside from 3 or 4 dispersed plants, has not achieved its objective despite incentives. (In the most recent cases - for example, a petrochemical detergent plant - the government of Quebec has taken a share of ownership and continues majority ownership of a large ethylene plant.) Electricity cost subsidies brought in some industries, but these subsidies are now gone due to international trade complaints. Montreal is on the fringe of North American markets and has no unique feedstock cost advantages.

Alberta's Industrial Heartland (AIH)

In Alberta, the region 50 kilometers northeast of Edmonton around Fort Saskatchewan, now called Alberta's Industrial Heartland (AIH), has Canada's largest chemical cluster in terms of sales value and number of plants. [See Map Below] Three counties, one city and industry jointly promote the AIH, and regional planning is proceeding to build on an eco-industrial (network) logo. AIH industry is based on Alberta natural gas processing, oil sands to the north, Ontario phosphate rock, Cuban nickel/cobalt ores, and local salt and water. Feedstocks and gas costs are generally the lowest in Canada and the U.S., and electricity costs prior to 2000 were well under those of competitive regions in the U.S. The area covers roughly 500 square kilometers in a heart-shaped region, spanning the North Saskatchewan River.

AIH industry is well supported by Edmonton's service industry and educational facilities and the approximately 900,000 process-industry-knowledgeable regional population. The Edmonton area also serves

Canada's oil and gas and oil sands industries; AIH industry is only a portion of total industrial activity in the service area. AIH industry started in the 1950's and is reaching a mature stage. A $2 billion project at the Shell Canada refinery is proceeding and a $500 million petrochemical facility and cogeneration plant were recently completed next door by Shell Chemical and Air Liquide, respectively.

While not formally part of the AIH, the Strathcona Industrial Association (SIA) industry cluster on the east edge of Edmonton and 40 kilometers from the AIH has two large oil refineries, two petrochemical plants, one large 'mini' steel mill, large asphalt roofing and fiberglass plants. As well as being one of the world's largest oil pipeline centers with over 10 pipeline systems, collecting and dispatching gasoline/jet fuel/diesels, natural gas liquids, conventional crude oils and synthetic crude oils, the SIA is a very important adjunct to the AIH.

AIH capital costs are at or below those of virtually any competitive chemical process cluster worldwide. Canada leads the world in modular and cold climate construction. AIH operating costs are also at or below those of the U.S. Gulf Coast and most other competitive sites. Due to location, natural gas costs will continue below those of competitive North American centers. Electricity costs have been below those of most competitive centers worldwide. Alberta deregulation will increase costs at least over the next 3 to 5 years for most plants without cogeneration, but these will still be below competition. In the past, electricity was largely provided by coal-fired plants west and east of Edmonton; however, gas-based cogeneration will shortly supply about 70% of AIH's own electricity needs.

Salt is the only local feedstock underlying most of the AIH. Over 25 large such storage chambers store hydrocarbons, including natural gas. Two plants use salt as their primary feed as does a major unit in the AIH's largest single owner complex run by Dow Chemicals.

While natural gas, natural gas processing-derived ethane and its derivative ethylene, salt and synthetic and other crude oils are the primary chemical plant feeds and are all available from relatively close and low-cost sources, these costs are often higher than those in certain developing countries with lower gas and natural gas liquid prices.

The AIH has few examples of competition - two sodium chlorate plants, two air separation plants, four natural gas liquids fractionators being the principal examples. Most plants produce unique products. However, while ethylene is available from Dow in the AIH, it is also available via pipeline from NovaChem at Joffre, 200 kilometers to the south. AIH plants are all large-scale, except for several small metal derivatives and special chemical plant sites. Most plants are world-scale and the key ethylene unit of Dow was the world's largest until a new

Joffre unit came on stream in 2000. AIH industry is not as highly integrated as many European and U.S. chemical clusters. The Alberta sites are more geographically dispersed, and fewer small-scale secondary products are produced.

Except for fertilizers going to prairie agriculture and pulp and paper chemicals, the vast majority of AIH products move to distant markets. Even 70% of gasoline/jet fuel/diesel production in the AIH and the SIA moves to Calgary, Vancouver, Saskatoon, Regina and Winnipeg via pipeline. The AIH is about the only major chemical cluster worldwide without marine transport and is the most northern; both CN and CP Rail serve the AIH, with unit trains to Vancouver and other centers. AIH industry transport costs are slightly higher to the U.S. Midwest than those of U.S. Gulf Coast competition. Costs to California are similar and less to Asia.

AIH and Sustainable Development

The selection of an Eco-Industrial logo for the AIH - the first time a major chemical cluster has done so - was largely a marketing decision. There is no general agreement on what Eco-Industrial development means. Steven Peck's 'Economic Sustainable Network' definition is particularly compelling, but everyone has his own definition of sustainable and it changes over time. Minimization of wastes is one target in light industry Eco-Industrial Parks, but wastes are generally minimal in most advanced chemical plants. Underutilized byproduct utilization is a more appropriate term.

Only 25% of allowable river water withdrawals are used and return water is similar to river ambient quality levels. Two or three multi-unit plants are starting to route process wastes to a major municipal sewage plant - one plant has carbon-rich wastewaters, the other very complementary nitrogen-rich waters. Air pollution is minimal and well within provincial regulations. However, it will be necessary to consider the entire area as new industrial emissions are added - regional sustainable development plans will be necessary and cumulative emissions will be very important.

Due to flat terrain, except for the river valley, there is some noise and visual pollution (primarily steam plumes in winter) from industry and one rail line. Better control of rural residential development should preclude new problems. Tree belts may be needed to overcome sound reverberation along the river valley.

Formal worst case emergency scenarios have not been published for AIH industry, but certain integrated emergency planning is evident - a new fire hall will serve the east side of the AIH, for example. The newer plant sites are quite dispersed - there are good safety clearances, but these preclude most steam exchange except with adjacent sites.

SHELL OIL

We have selected two Shell related examples from AIH industry for more detailed discussion. Air Liquide and ATCO also come into the picture and both plant sites depend on many others in and outside the AIH. Unfortunately, economic data are not available to illustrate the dollar value of integration or lack thereof. However, different corporate approaches by Shell Canada and Shell Chemical will become apparent.

Shell in Canada

Shell Canada was a relatively conventional integrated Canadian oil company prior to the 1990's with minority public ownership and an independent board. In 1980 the Scotford (AIH) synthetic crude oil refinery was built to serve Shell prairie markets. This was a billion-dollar project - massive for any company at the time. A parallel styrene chemical plant was also built at Scotford, using benzene from the new refinery and ethylene from one of two Alberta sources.

Shell Canada had a series of chemical plants in Montreal and later Sarnia, generally oriented towards derivatives of propylene produced in conventional refinery cracking. However, petrochemicals were usually not at the top of the priority list. In the rationalizations of the past five years, Shell Canada sold its chemical operations to Shell Chemical, wholly owned by Royal Dutch/Shell. Shell Canada got out of conventional crude oil production and is moving ahead on a several billion-dollar oil sand mining project with upgrading at the Scotford site in the AIH.

Shell Chemicals selected Air Liquide to provide over-the-fence electricity, steam and oxygen for their Scotford petrochemical site and that operation was just going on-line at time of writing as a new Shell glycol plant went through its commissioning. (Styrene is the other product at their site). Air Liquide will also be producing oxygen, nitrogen and argon for truck and rail delivery to others and is converting 200 to 300-tonnes/day of CO_2 byproduct stream from Shell Chemicals into high-quality merchant grade product for Air Liquide regional markets. Excess electricity production will be sold into provincial markets.

Conversely, the Albian Joint Venture (upgrading bitumen from the oil sand mine) finally selected ATCO Electricity to operate its new Scotford cogeneration facility. That facility will use gas turbines to produce electricity, with their waste heat producing steam to be added to byproduct steam from the hydrogen unit in the upgrader to generate more electricity.

Shell Canada and Partners

Figure 1 depicts the current and proposed Shell Canada/Albion complex. The refinery and the Edmonton terminal and interconnecting pipelines are all that exist today with construction just starting on the rest. As Figure 1 illustrates, the ownership picture is crowded. The new upgrader facilities will be complementary to those of the refinery; hence the jagged line between the Albian Joint Venture and Shell Canada in that complex. The size can be gleaned from the $3 billion price tag - even the pipeline costs are in the order of $700 million.

The Muskeg River tar sands mine will produce approximately 150,000 barrels a day (24,000 cubic meters) of a partially processed heavy crude; some very poor hydrocarbons will be removed and returned to the mine at site. This oil will be mixed with a gasoline-like diluent to allow movement to the upgrader in the new corridor pipeline systems owned by Transmountain Piplelines. At Scotford, the oil -- in combination with a heavy byproduct from an Edmonton refinery and some natural gas processing-derived, naphtha-like hydrocarbon -- will be converted into refinery-usable synthetic crude oil.

The Shell Scotford refinery was the world's second all-hydrogen refinery and the first for synthetic crude oils, which have some characteristics poorer than conventional crude oils. These factors make the upgrading/refining integration very attractive, both technically and economically. About half of the feed will end up in gasoline, jet fuel, diesel and benzene from the refinery and half will be a synthetic crude oil for sale and/or use elsewhere by the partners.

ATCO's north and south cogeneration facilities differ in several respects. At the Muskeg River mine, the waste heat from the gas turbine generators all goes to mine process heating, whereas at Scotford one unit in the upgrader has a large quantity of byproduct steam available to be combined with cogen waste heat-derived steam to produce even more electricity. Roughly 30 MW of this will flow to the electricity grid.

While there will be a large new hydrogen (from natural gas) generation unit on-site, Dow Chemical will supply roughly 30% of the upgrader's hydrogen. This will be replaced in Dow's fuel gas system with natural gas. This introduces interesting challenges related to greenhouse gas (GHG) emissions. Dow's GHG emissions will increase but the Joint Venture will minimize emissions - there is an overall hydrogen system GHG saving of about 15 to 20% through such hydrogen interchange. (This example points out the need to have GHG offset clauses in all over-the-fence transfer system agreements. Such agreements would address the issue of who gets what credits and who pays any/all carbon charges in whatever controls that evolve.)

The very appreciable hydrogen use in the upgrader (as in the exist-

Figure 1: Shell Canada / Albian Complex

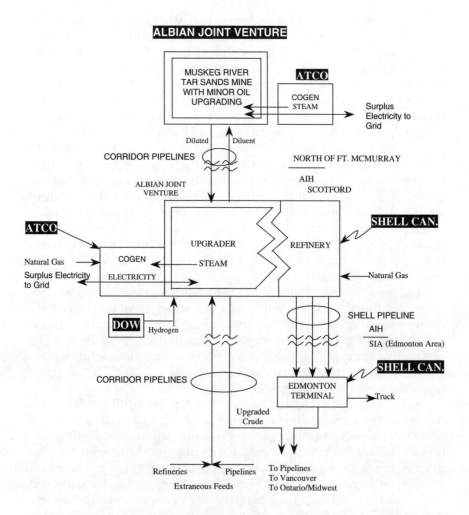

CORRIDOR PIPELINES
(TransMountain PipeLine, B.C. Gas Subsidiary, as Operator)

ALBIAN JOINT VENTURE
60% Shell Canada, 20% Chevron, 20% Western Oil Sands

ing refinery) requires a significant quantity of natural gas at the upgrader and at Dow. An increase in natural gas cost of $1 per GJ will roughly equate to an increase in upgraded crude and refined product costs by as much as 0.5 cents U.S. per litre, or approximately 10% of cash costs. The project economics are thus very sensitive to natural gas costs. While the cogeneration systems protect against external electricity price changes, the sensitivity to gas price is apparent.

Shell Chemicals

The Scotford site produces the bulk liquid chemical styrene and ethylene glycol. The styrene facility originally started operations in 1981 and the glycol unit came on-line in mid 2000. There are very limited local markets for both products. The 450,000 plus tonnes per year of styrene are shipped to U.S. and Canadian markets by rail and occasonally onto river barge. The 400,000-tonnes a year of ethylene glycol will be moved to markets via the same modes. The vast majority of styrene and ethylene glycol will be shipped to Pacific Rim and other markets via rail and, when offshore, then by ships. Shell Chemical is concentrating its operations worldwide on a selected group of bulk chemicals where it has extensive production, technical and marketing strengths and these two product groups are identified as 'core'. At time of writing, the dollar value of products are roughly $430 million Canadian ($300 U.S.). This assumes U.S. Gulf Coast prices in May 2000 less 4 cents a pound. The latter is approximately the freight cost to the U.S. Gulf Coast, as the default market area.

Styrene

Styrene is produced in a two-step operation from benzene and ethylene:

- Benzene + Ethylene ————-> Ethylbenzene
  Catalyst
- Ethylbenzene ——————> Styrene (+ Hydrogen)
  Catalyst Net

The styrene is shipped in rail cars, primarily to polystyrene and related polymer producers, with one minor exception outside Alberta. Figure 2 briefly illustrates the interrelationships of the styrene unit with other AIH and Alberta industry.

There are two principal feedstocks utilized in the production of styrene: benzene and ethylene. Roughly 0.78 tonnes of benzene is required per tonne of styrene - supply is primarily via pipeline from the adjacent Shell Canada refinery. Roughly 120 KTA of benzene is obtained via the Shell refinery from a raw benzene stream from the Imperial Edmonton (Strathcona) refinery. Aside from some benzene in ethylene byproduct streams leaving Alberta, no significant new Alberta benzene supply opportunities are apparent. The Shell Canada refinery will be concentrat-

Figure 2: Simplified Shell Canada Styrene Ins/Outs and Ethylene System

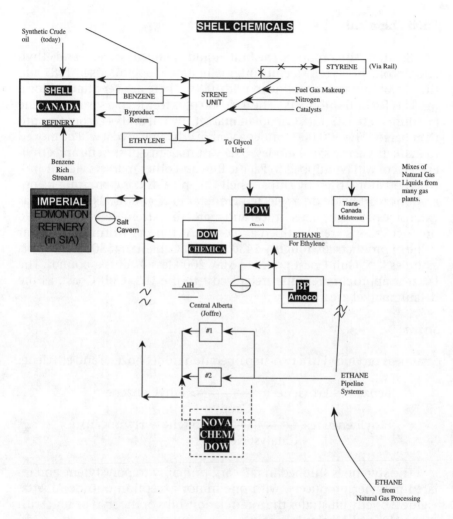

ing on its new upgrader addition discussed later.

In addition, roughly 0.28 tonnes of ethylene is required per tonne of styrene - supply is now available from two sources: Dow's AIH ethylene production and from NovaChem's two existing smaller units at Joffre near Red Deer. Late in 2000, the world's largest new unit started up at Joffre - half owned by NovaChem and half by Dow.

As Figure 2 shows, major salt cavern storage in the AIH is available for both ethylene and ethane. Such storage is much less expensive than surface storage.

In recent years, natural gas pipeline capacity out of Alberta has increased dramatically and the newest line will also carry ethane (and propane) with minor transport costs. This latter development will reduce new ethane supply and reinvigorate a sagging ethylene/ethylene derivatives industry in the Chicago area, which is very competitive with Alberta industry in Midwest markets.

Electricity deregulation in Canada and the U.S. is resulting in many new gas-based generating stations - these can be built much faster and at lower capital than coal-fired plants, and economics are favourable at much smaller-scale, allowing geographic dispersion. These plants also fit the 'drive' to reduce greenhouse gas and other emissions. There is a growing acceptance of the need for GHG reduction even in the U.S., and that the momentum is expected to increase over time (with the Kyoto protocol only one step on the way - ratified or not).

Ethylene Glycol

Ethylene glycol is the principal product of a two-step plus purification operation:

- Ethylene + Oxygen ————> Ethylene Oxide (+ some CO_2)
- Ethylene Oxide + Water ———-> Ethylene glycols

The Shell route does not include ethylene oxide as a marketable product - ethylene glycol is the sole target. Roughly 0.8 tonnes of ethylene oxide are used per tonne of ethylene glycol. Aside from ethylene as a feedstock, oxygen is also needed. It is now almost universal practice to buy oxygen - 0.3 tonnes per tonne - from a traditional industrial gas company. In this case, Air Liquide was the selected partner and was provided land for an air separation unit, carbon dioxide purification system and the cogen facility.

Air Liquide Complex

The industrial gas companies are normally interested in cogeneration of electricity and steam for other companies only when there are significant parallel oxygen, nitrogen, hydrogen and/or carbon monoxide sales. Industrial gas companies and even utilities these days can often consider slightly lower returns than their over-the-fence partners due to the ability to take the payment "to the bank." The Shell Chemical/Air

Figure 3: Shell Chemical / Air Liquide

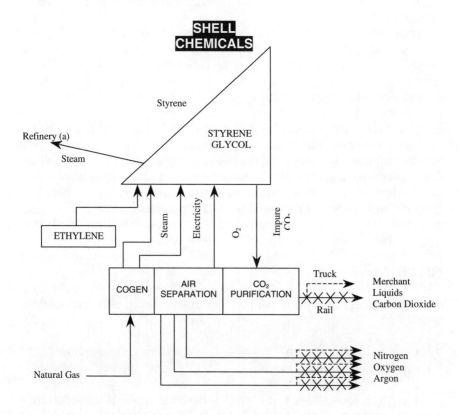

(a) An existing small line probably kept hot for emergency.

Liquide interfaces are ideal examples of very synergistic integration of quite different industries, but with similar economic goals. (See Figure 3). Shell is interested only in gaseous oxygen, but needs an assured supply. Air Liquide will produce gaseous and liquid oxygen. The latter will move by road and rail to other customers and its tank(s) will provide gaseous supply to Shell whenever the air separation unit shuts down. The air separation plant is also designed to provide gaseous and liquid nitrogen and liquid argon for sale to others.

Air separation requires appreciable electricity, but the Air Liquide complex has very little steam demand, while Shell Chemical needs both. Thus, a simple 80-MW cogeneration plant supplies steam to Shell, electricity to both plants and 20 to 30-MW for sale through the Alberta electrical grid. During gas turbine shutdowns, electricity can be backed in from in the grid, but Shell will only have existing styrene unit steam capacity.

Air Liquide will process most/all of Shell's 80 to 90,000-tonnes a year of raw CO_2 for sale to merchant markets via truck and rail. The economic synergies of the Shell Chemical/Air Liquide interface are apparent. Each concentrates on its own specialties. The overall energy efficiency of the cogeneration facility will be roughly the same as a high quality steam boiler, thus electricity generation will result in very low CO_2 emissions per unit of electricity — much less than if coal-based electricity were purchased. It should be noted that electricity and steam variable costs will be directly related to natural gas costs - and these are rising. However, both Shell Chemical and Air Liquide are protected against peak hour charges from grid-based electrical supply and such cogeneration facilities have the highest energy efficiencies. Fuel costs may rise above those for coal-based electricity, but with much lower non-fuel variable and fixed costs.

SECURITY OF SUPPLY AND PLANT

Security of supply and/or market is of major importance in all industrial interchanges. In the past, it was considered best to produce on site all utility and even industrial gas needs, such as hydrogen, oxygen, etc. It was felt that reliability could be better controlled in-house. The steel industry started the move to third party supply with all oxygen supplied offsite. The chemical industry has moved even farther in accepting fully qualified third party suppliers with nearby plants. The oil refining industry has been slower, but in the U.S. most new hydrogen supply is from third parties and cogeneration is often by others. The Shell Canada joint venture will be producing its own hydrogen, but with a third party operator on the cogen.

Two years ago a Malaysian air separation unit blew up, shutting down the market - a Shell natural gas to liquids plant — for many months. About the same time, a California over-the-fence hydrogen production facility went out of service for several months. These examples show that reliability is not 100% even for very highly qualified operators and there is a major need to fully assess the risks on both ends of any trade. This usually means that a detailed economic uncertainty statistical analysis is essential. Similar analyses are used for chemical plant process/ utility system definition during design, but seldom to the degree used for over-the-fence supply. The Turkish earthquakes of 1999 showed the pinball potential of fires spreading from one chemical plant site to another. Nevertheless, AIH spacing - industry and even unit-to-unit in most cases - is generous and risk of spread of fire or other disaster minimal.

Maintenance shutdown schedules are all meshed in AIH and most other process industry clusters to insure labour supply. However, this does mean that plants often run a 'little' longer than appropriate, increasing emergency shutdown potential.

OTHER INTEGRATION RISKS AND OPPORTUNITIES

There has been very little discussion in the literature about the risks of integration. It is very easy to point to major savings with one cogen serving two plants; particularly, where the plants have varying electricity-to-thermal-heat demand ratios. The integration of cogen by Air Liquide at Shell Chemicals probably saves $30 to 50 million in capital and $3 to 5 million in annual operating costs, compared to individual cogeneration systems. Hydrogen purchase by the Joint Venture saves approximately $30 million in capital, with possibly a minor saving in operation of marginally more hydrogen production facilities. (The operating savings are dependent upon the premium Dow puts on its hydrogen above its heating value.)

It is very common to overestimate integration opportunities; for example, what is the cost of backup electricity supply in the case the Air Liquide generator goes down and how will Shell Chemical manage without its related steam? But industries are learning how to get around such challenges - this is generally easier the more plants of similar nature there are in any region. The chemical industry is leading the way in integration, but this stems in large part from the emphasis on core products only - anything else is a service operation, and depends on the availability of experienced, well-financed service operators.

In the AIH most industries operate continuously, there are few batch operations. The latter are very difficult to integrate due to variability of utility and/or feed needs. In the AIH, individual plants are generally one-half kilometer or more from each other - these buffers are ideal for isolation of fire and other emergencies and providing/preserving an almost rural setting. But in Alberta's cold winter climate, such buffers preclude interplant steam transfer unless directly over-the-fence. Even on the Dow plant site, a main steam line had to be oversized and provided with added insulation to span almost a kilometer.

The integration/distribution of ownership is noteworthy in these examples. Shell Canada chose to add Joint Venture partners directly along with pipeline and cogen operators. Funding the Joint Venture has gained appreciable mining expertise through one partner - a target of Shell Canada from the beginning. Innovative financing/partnering appear essential in virtually all cases of good industrial integration. Partners in such integration must continue to be fully economically viable along with their plants. The AIH and the example facilities are generally blessed with high value-bulk products with long market lives and the ability to easily modify to extend market life.

In the AIH, generally we see the following major challenges over the next few years:

* Economic stresses due to rising natural gas costs affecting virtually all but two plant sites;
* Economic stresses due to rising electricity purchase costs at those two and other sites; and
* Capital costs rising due to a very tight construction labour market in Alberta.

Environmental challenges are not major, but worst disaster scenarios integrated with emergency planning will be interesting.

SUMMARY

Integration of industrial facilities offers appreciable capital cost reduction opportunities, but does add many risks not common to light manufacturing plants. Detailed analysis of all interrelated flows and facilities and their related risks and opportunities is essential in order to develop economic data for corporate decision making. Mitigation of certain risks, for example spreading plants apart, may well preclude certain synergies such as steam exchange.

FOOTNOTES

1. Some general eco-industrial development websites are listed in the Appendix.
2. In the pharmaceutical industry, over 60% of chemical intermediate production and a significant quantity of actual product manufacture are already 'farmed' out to third party operations.

APPENDIX: ON-LINE INFORMATION ABOUT EXISTING ECO-INDUS-TRIAL NETWORKS

• Burnside Industrial park - Dartmouth, Nova Scotia
www.mgmt.dal.ca/sres/eco-burnside/index.htm

• Cabazon Resource Recovery Park - Indio, California
www.cabazonindians.com/recoverypark.html

• Cape Charles Sustainable Technology Park
www.sustainablepark.com

• 7Civano - Tucson, Arizona
www.civano.com

• Fairfield park - Baltimore, Maryland
www.buildfairfield.com/ffhome.htm

• Kalundborg, Denmark
www.symbiosis.dk

• Londonderry Eco-Park - Londonderry, New Hampshire
www.londonderry.org

• Oko-Tech-Park Windelsbleiche - Bielefeld, Germany
www.windel.de/english/index.html

• Sault Ste. Marie Eco-Industrial Network - Sault Ste. Marie, Ontario
www.sault-canada.com/eco-ind/ecoindex.html

• The Green Institute - Minneapolis, Minnesota
www.greeninstitute.org

• Triangle J. Council of Governments Industrial Ecosystem Development Project
www.ticog.dst.nc.us/TJCOG/indeco.htm

SUGGESTED STUDENT CASE ANALYSIS

HYDROGEN TRANSFER (1,000,000 cubic meters)

Your plant site has 35,300,000 standard cubic feet of hydrogen available daily for sale to others, but you would require added natural gas to replace it in your fuel gas system and capital expenditures of $12,000,000 to purify, compress and deliver to a proposed new hydrogen consumer a few kilometers away at the same pressure he would have if he built his own hydrogen generation facility. develop and discuss your proposal for hydrogen supply to that potential customer under the following assumptions:

- 0.273 volumes of natural gas are needed to replace one of hydrogen in fuel systems.
- Cost of natural gas delivered to you is $5.00 per gigajoule ($5.25 per 1,000 standard cubic feed - 30 cubic meters), but is expected to rise at about 2% a year for the next 10 years.
- The potential end-user could build its own hydrogen generation facility for approximately $40,000,000, including all costs before commercial production. Your estimate has annual cash costs exclusive of natural gas at $2,000,000 and his gas needs for hydrogen generation at 13,000,000-scfd (corrected for heat to byproduct steam from the hydrogen operation), probably purchased at the same unit cost.
- Your hurdle rate is 16% before taxes and depreciation - say 11% after taxes and depreciation. Assume his will be the same - at least for your initial analysis. (But you should consider an alternative where, with your guarantee take a pay contract, his hurdle rate will be 2% lower).

GREENHOUSE GAS IMPLICATIONS

In the above example, the sale of hydrogen will increase your plant site's greenhouse gas emissions by approximately 190,000-tonnes a year as carbon dioxide equivalent (CO2E), allowing for increased emissions due to added compression energy, but the potential end user's greenhouse gas emissions would be roughly 235,000-tonnes a year less. In today's very informal greenhouse gas trading, CO2E reductions are worth approximately $5 a tonne, but as countries establish regulatory and trading protocols, the value may rise to $10 by 2010.

Discuss how you would handle the greenhouse gas issue in your proposal.

COGENERATION OPTION

Your plant requires 30 megawatts of electricity at a constant rate and 50 megawatts of thermal energy as steam. (Your boiler is old and needs replacing and you would like to minimize your utility costs and avoid open-market electricity prices.) A natural-gas-fueled gas turbine plus waste heat boiler system will cost approximately $32,000,000 in capital and $1,600,000 in annual cash costs, exclusive of gas and consume 7,200,000-scfd (204,000 cubic meters) of natural gas.

Assuming the same cost bases as in the preceding cases, discuss how you will consider your company building and operating such a system versus having a third party, now owning and operating many such facilities, do so on your site. Note that in practice there will be some excess electricity for sale either way. Again, note greenhouse gas issues, although the total CO_2 emissions will be essentially the same regardless of who owns/opens the new facility.

DOING SUSTAINABILITY - THE ECOS CORPORATION STORY

Murray Hogarth
Ecos Corporation

This is the case history of the evolution of Ecos Corporation, a business strategy consultancy that shapes its advice based on principles of sustainability. The fast-growing Ecos practice, based in Sydney, Australia, aims to make its clients more profitable while simultaneously achieving better outcomes for the economy, society and the environment. The firm's story is told through its people and its clients. How does Ecos operate? What attracts paying customers? Where have the firm's employees come from, and where are they going? Ecos Corporation staff writer Murray Hogarth, a former environment editor of the Sydney Morning Herald, gives an insider's account.

"Activist in a suit" was the eminently predictable headline waiting to be written when Paul Gilding became a corporate consultant. The young Australian's personal re-invention followed back-to-back stints running Greenpeace in Australia and then internationally as Amsterdam-based executive director. Gilding had wanted Greenpeace to engage more with the business world to help drive a global environmental rescue. Others in the hierarchy of Greenpeace — the guardians of the planet's best green action brand name — were not ready. Gilding was ousted. He had something to prove.

Days after he departed Greenpeace, Gilding addressed a conference of business leaders in Zurich. He spoke as a long-time social activist — but one no longer shackled by Greenpeace correctness circa 1994. His optimistic topic was "The Role of Enterprise in Creating a Just and Sustainable Society." "Business faces the exciting opportunity to redesign itself into being a positive force for society, leading the way forward from the social and ecological crises we presently face," he concluded. "It is an opportunity to release the enormous positive human energy we need if we are going to turn the situation around." The activist had become enchanted with the potential for business to save the world, highlighting its power, its adaptability and its positive culture. The big question, then and still, was whether business was ready to take up the cause.

Six years later, Gilding still believes passionately that business can lead the world to sustainable solutions. Like-motivated and similarly minded individuals have gathered around him, forging a team drawn from the ranks of high-level environmental and social activism, industry, the corporate advisory world, information technology and journalism.

After taking stock of his life, Gilding and his partner Michelle

Grosvenor established the firm that is now Ecos Corporation — initially in partnership with the British-based consultancy group, Paras. It was 1995. The Internet was only just starting to attract attention in the wider community, outside of the cloistered world of academia. The "new economy" was still in gestation. The Kyoto summit on climate change was two years off. In Australia, and around the developed world, the environment had slipped down the political priority list after the fervour of the late 1980s and the early 1990s, culminating at the Earth Summit in Rio de Janeiro in 1992.

In Australia, business was lagging well behind North America and Europe in terms of environmental awareness and commitment to eco-efficiency. It was in fully-fledged denial about global warming. Sustainability — and the notion that corporations should focus on the community's social and environmental "values", as well as hard-nosed financial value — was nigh on invisible on the national corporate agenda. While there was considerable talk about post-Rio commitments to ecologically sustainable development (ESD), it seemed that everyone had their own ideas about what this meant. Few, if any, were prepared to "walk the talk". In this climate, Paul Gilding was trying to make the leap from being commodore of the protest boat fleet to boardroom insider.

For the first few years the business often struggled. Headquarters was a converted former church in an inner city Sydney suburb. Staff came and some went. The balance sheet ebbed and flowed. There were good clients, though rarely enough, and notable successes. Ecos conceived the idea of making the Athletes Village for the Sydney 2000 Olympics and Paralympics — the so-called Green Games — into the world's biggest solar suburb. It helped a major mining company to produce the Australian industry's first environment report. And it created the blueprint for an historic forest peace deal in the State of Queensland, with industry, government and environmentalists agreeing to phase out native forest logging by 2025. But despite this and other significant achievements, in 1999 Ecos Corporation had to question its own future. Success was coming as strategizing for sustainability entered the business mainstream, especially in the U.S. But the challenge to change whole companies and industry sectors demanded new skills and more people. The choice was get bigger or get out; and Ecos voted for growth. The old church was left behind as Gilding and a small team moved to the Sydney CBD.

By May, 2001, Gilding and his team were riding the wave of transition from the old industrial economy to the new knowledge-based economy, a resurgence of the environment as a major public issue and unprecedented pressure for corporations to exhibit greater social responsibility. Over the previous 12 months, Ecos had doubled in size, including hiring in America, and was focusing heavily on its major U.S.-based clients, DuPont and the Ford Motor Company. In Australia, present and past clients included big miners BHP, Placer Dome Asia Pacific and WMC, Lend Lease, Pacific Power, BP Australia, Toyota Australia, Suncor Energy, Cotton Australia, the Queensland Timber Board and state and federal government agencies.

So how did Ecos Corporation do it? How did it break through corporate ignorance and apathy among potential clients to achieve its own version of sustainability? The answers to all of these questions highlight the challenges that still confront those pursuing sustainability. For the record, Ecos defines sustainability as a future society where: *our ecological systems will be preserved; quality of life will improve for all humans; and the capital, democratic market place will evolve to support a stable transition to a better future.*

At times the company's people wish there were another word than sustainability — one with less syllables — or, perhaps, a snappy acronym. But, at the moment, sustainability is the best we have. Ecologically sustainable development, or ESD, is clumsy and contradictory. Greens prefer ecological sustainability with a big E, while business favours sustainable development with a big D. Sustainability is the cleanest compromise and — in the financial sense at least — business people know the unfortunate consequences of being unsustainable.

Promoting change in corporations, the core mission that Ecos Corporation has set itself, is a multi-faceted challenge. Awareness of the need for change is just a first step. Even being provided with a well-thought out strategy is only the beginning for a company. Driving organizational transition — by actually changing attitudes, behaviour and overall culture at all levels of an enterprise -- is a huge and crucial part of the job. And when progress is being made, or alternatively if the process is failing, then companies need to be able to measure it. Similarly, if other companies are to follow — and the financial markets are to recognize the value being created — then the "metrics" have to be in place. Ecos seeks to cover the change trajectory from awareness, to strategy, to cultural transformation, to measuring the outcomes. For success, hearts, minds and hip-pockets have to be won over, and success is what Ecos needs. What the firm seeks to achieve is what Gilding calls "symbols of change" — primarily corporate examples that will in turn drive changes in others.

As demand for Ecos Corporation's strategic thinking and other services has grown, so has Paul Gilding's firm. Those who come aboard share the desire to drive change. Each brings new insights into how it can be achieved, and new passions for the task at hand. To know Ecos,

Case history No. 1:

CLIMATE CHANGE – A BOOST FOR SELLING SUSTAINABILITY

The growing profile of climate change as a challenge and an opportunity for business has been a major driver for Ecos Corporation's growth. It is likely to be the most pivotal sustainability issue that the world has faced. Some companies will be transformed and will prosper, while others will decline and even collapse.

Ecos Corporation has advised a number of clients on the implications of climate change and on strategising to turn the challenges to advantage. Examples include DuPont, Australian electricity generator Pacific Power, the State of NSW's Sustainable Energy Development Authority and Canada-based oil producer Suncor.

From 1999 to 2001 the firm published a weekly electronic journal, carbonmarket.com, providing world news on carbon trading, climate change and renewable energy to both clients and a wider audience. But the publishing experiment failed to establish itself commercially.

Ecos also sought to drive the formation of a business leadership group on climate change in Australia, similar to the Pew Centre grouping in the U.S., but found that its home territory corporations were not ready.

and to tap its values-to-value equation, clients need to know the team.

One of the key figures in the Ecos growth story from 1998 until he left in 2000 was American Ben Woodhouse who'd wanted a change of life when he retired from Dow Chemical in 1997 after 33 years. A toxicologist by training, he'd risen to the position of Vice President for Global Issues and Crisis Management. The Dow where Woodhouse learned his trade was never short of issues and crises. Dow was a chemical company in a post-Rachel Carson (author of the landmark environmental expose The Silent Spring) world. Over many years Dow grew big, powerful and arrogant. It became hated by many and a target for activists. Sustainability was a theme that Woodhouse learned — and in a real sense helped to pioneer — as he, the renowned David Buzzelli and others steered Dow back towards a degree of community acceptance. Beyond Dow, he helped to start U.S. President Bill Clinton's Council on

Sustainability, and the World Business Council for Sustainable Development, making him a genuine leader in the field.

Woodhouse has a nice turn of phrase to describe one of the main paths by which corporations find their way to taking on sustainability as a strategy to underpin their business plan. "They have a 'significant emotional experience'," he observes dryly. That means a scarifying crisis: something like what Royal Dutch Shell faced in 1995 over the Brent Spar controversy in Europe. Shell had wanted to dump an old oil-drilling platform at sea. It found its service stations being boycotted and attacked. In the same year, internationally acclaimed writer and Ogoni tribal independence champion Ken Saro-wiwa and eight others were executed by the military regime in Nigeria. They had been fighting for their homelands where Shell was extracting vast quantities of oil at a huge environmental cost. Shell was accused of doing nothing to check the ugly and murderous regime.

In their former lives, Paul Gilding and Ben Woodhouse were more likely to be on opposite sides of a fight. Gilding had led a Greenpeace that excelled at inflicting "significant emotional experiences" on recalcitrant companies — or exploiting self-inflicted ones — while Woodhouse had to manage the fallout in such circumstances and strive to avoid any repeats. At Ecos Corporation, a belief in sustainability, and the potential for the market to be mobilized towards it, brought them together.

So crisis is a part-answer to how Ecos Corporation gets its foot in the door of at least some new clients. It can be a crisis already unfolding, or the fear that one is imminent. It is always open to question whether crisis-driven clients are truly committed to change through embracing sustainability. They are, logically enough, far more focussed on avoiding short-term pain than achieving long-term gain. But for Ecos Corporation and other purveyors of sustainability advice, the entrée is crucial. This is the "Trojan Horse" principle. Once the values, the vision and the language of sustainability are pulled inside the walls of the corporate fortress, they start to take over. The conservative chief executive of one former Ecos Corporation client — a major resources company — saw this as a threat, fearing that a "virus" was being unleashed within his company. That particular client-consultant relationship was not a long-term one, given that Ecos wears its own agenda to drive change openly on its corporate sleeve (right alongside its agenda to increase its clients' profits via sustainable growth).

Woodhouse speaks the language of big and sometimes bad business, as well as that of sustainability. He warns companies not to embrace sustainability simply because they think it's the right thing to do. "Feel good" is never enough. Ecos Corporation advocates taking the plunge because it is actually good business. Doing the right thing, and doing it

Case history No. 2:

GENETICALLY MODIFIED FOODS – THE MOTHER OF ALL CRISES

In 1999, an extraordinary consumer reaction against genetically modified foods swept around the world — starting in Europe, enveloping Asia and finally hitting the biotechnology heartland in North America.

Ecos Corporation clients with a big exposure to GM issues included a major "life sciences" company in the international arena, as well as a rural industry association and a State Government in Australia. In response to the GM controversy, Ecos mobilised to expand its own expertise on biotechnology.

The firm's services to clients included analysing global trends, interpreting concepts like the precautionary approach, forecasting movements in the debate, facilitating stakeholder engagement exercises and advising on appropriate responses through business and communications strategies. Ecos is continuing to work in the biotechnology field as part of its growing focus on the wider issue of sustainable agriculture, covering everything from organic farming, through gene technology, to the future of the commodities system.

the right way, means a better chance of getting the right result. That can manifest itself in several ways, including margin improvement in current business, a robust growth strategy to boost future cash flows, increased competitive advantage and minimizing of exposure and risk. In a global marketplace, with Internet interconnectivity, the risks for the mega brand names of the 21st Century are just as great as the opportunities.

"We used to worry about obtaining the social licence to operate," says Woodhouse. "But in the new economy, that licence has been overtaken by the absolute need to earn the licence to grow — that is to expand and to prosper. Those who stay in the old economy thinking will suddenly find their licence to operate equates to mere survival. If that's where they stay, they will eventually perish." Woodhouse's high-level industry background proved to be the perfect foil to those who saw Ecos as a bunch of "greenies in suits".

At 24 years of age, Cath Bremner switched from her first consultancy job with a global purveyor of hardcore business strategies, McKinsey and Company, to join Ecos Corporation. In her third year at university in Australia, Bremner took a trip to Alaska and visited the scene of one of the greatest pollution disasters of the 20th Century, the oil spill from the Exxon Valdez supertanker into the beautiful Prince William Sound. The spill had happened several years earlier, but the massive environmental damage was still in evidence. In her final year of university, studying chemical engineering, her major topic was sewerage. Between Alaska and sewerage studies, Bremner had pollution and the environment on her mind. But her first job took her to McKinsey. "It was a divergence, but it helped me to understand business," she says. "And there were projects at McKinsey that created value in a traditional sense and also helped the environment."

"After two-and-a-half years at McKinsey I was tired," says Bremner. "I was not feeling like the work had soul. A partner at McKinsey suggested that I meet with Paul Gilding." Bremner's leap into a values-driven organization like Ecos Corporation — a firm that takes decisions about who it works for very seriously — hasn't obliterated the lessons she learned at McKinsey. She probes for answers to the questions that the financial world has to ask — answers that have to be articulated before business people will endorse sustainability as a set of tools for creating value. How do funds that focus on socially and environmentally responsible investments perform against the wider market? Where are the productivity gains? Do consumers really care when they make buying decisions? Everyone at Ecos Corporation has perceived the need for proof that sustainability performs, and for tools to capture the how, why and what of that performance. But Bremner has driven the process of assembling the evidence, and locking in the methodology. In 2000, she went back to visit McKinsey with Paul Gilding in tow, helping with his latest presentation on *Sustainability and the New Economy.*

She thinks that Ecos Corporation is "very challenging" for its clients. "But I do not think that we are perceived as being able to give hardcore business advice like a McKinsey," she says. "Clients also view Ecos mostly as being its figureheads, Paul Gilding and Ben Woodhouse, and as people who are connected to worlds that they do not know a lot about — social movements and NGOs. But they have a lot of fun with us. They laugh a lot. And it is a learning experience. Paul and people like Rick Humphries and Sheena Boughen understand that change does not just happen with accounting profit and loss sheets. Change is something that is dynamic and does not fit in boundaries. They can understand because of the organizations that they come from. That is a niche

Case history No. 3:

**INTERPRETING THE TRAN-
SITION FROM OLD
ECONOMY TO NEW**

Understanding the challenges and the opportunities in the transition from the old, polluting industrial economy to a cleaner new knowledge economy has become another core area of Ecos Corporation's client work. This is taking the firm further and further away from its environmental origins, and deeper and deeper into a broader role advising on business strategy to integrate social, environmental and economic priorities. To this end, Ecos has identified six drivers of the new economy. They are:

1. Globalization. The globalization of the economy, of values and of expectations, which has already led to a far more competitive and fast moving economy, but will in future lead to even more dramatic shifts.

2. Sustainability. The recognition of the economic, security and human threats posed by ecological change and social inequality, along with a recognition that the changes needed to address them are as daunting as they are crucial to our future health and prosperity.

3. Connectedness. The way individuals are connected, and communities are created, through new technologies, economic forces and the media, and the implications for how change occurs and how risk is created and managed.

4. The Retreat of Government. The changing and decreasing role of government in a globalized, fast-moving, connected economy as it adapts to the challenges posed by globalization and the rising power of transnational corporations.

5. The Victory of the Market. The way liberal, market-based democracy has become the dominant way to organize society, with implications for the role of the market and the power of corporations, but also societal expectations of corporate performance.

6. The Rise of Civil Society. Coupled with the victory of the market, civil society is evolving into a connected, yet distributed, powerful and market making/breaking force. As such, it can hold corporations globally accountable.

market and a niche understanding. When companies hire Ecos, there generally are one or two people inside who passionately believe that there is a need to change. Ecos comes in to incubate that change."

For Rick Humphries, two decades of environmental activism has been the training ground for a new career at Ecos Corporation. His passion and specialty is high-level strategy. In his time with Greenpeace, the Australian Conservation Foundation and the Wilderness Society, this meant applying strategic thinking to effectively attack corporations, industries and governments that were presiding over environmental destruction. Now the same skills and a new mindset are being applied to foster sustainability thinking inside the same kind of groups — his former targets — and to promote the products and advantages of a sustainable approach.

He says that he felt constrained inside "the movement" he has left behind. "They can do the toolbox for change, but they cannot articulate how you make it happen," he says of traditional environmentalists. "Unless we try something radically new we are buggered," says Humphries. "Clearly governments and the Left-wing view of the world have failed. Our economic behaviour is what got us in trouble. Unless we change that and make corporations a force for doing good things, then there is no hope." He says he is "beyond ideology now", explaining: "I am a social ecologist I suppose." His focus is turning overwhelmingly towards the five-sixths of the world's population who don't share the wealth and lifestyle of the high-consuming, heavy-polluting, one-sixth who live in the First World countries. Ecos increasingly shares this focus as a key direction for the years ahead. "The 'five-sixths' is a huge thing that is emerging for the corporates," says Humphries. Half of the world's six billion people are yet to make their first phone call. The U.S. has four percent of the world's population, but takes a 25 percent share of resources being consumed. If everyone is to get the same, two extra planets are required. And, perhaps most importantly, for the first time in history "the disenfranchised know they are disenfranchised". They see wealth on TV, and they want it too.

He and Ecos believe that generating clean solutions to meet the demands of the "five-sixths" is the major challenge and a matter of survival for the democratic capitalist market system. "We have to be more aggressive and up front and say to companies 'You guys all rely on a stable growth-oriented system. You have to invest in elevating the five-sixths' — governments cannot do it alone, and nor can NGOs. Business has to change its culture. They have to keep pace with what is happening in the real world. The threats are real, and we all have to respond. The trick is to combine society's values with the vision to create value. Ecos is all about the process to identify the buttons to press for change. We have consciously decided that corporations are the driver,

Case history No. 4:

A CORPORATE GIANT SEEKS MORE VALUE FOR LESS FOOTPRINT

Sustainable growth champion DuPont Corporation — once known as the world's biggest polluter — celebrated its 200th birthday in 2002. It operates in 70 countries, has 90,000-plus employees and turnover of more than $27 billion a year. In the late 1990s it spent $US 14 billion on the world's biggest seed company, Pioneer Hi-Bred, while remodelling itself as a "life sciences" company with a big exposure to biotechnology. For decades it wrestled with chemical issues such as CFCs and toxic waste, and now has emerged as a clear international leader in the management of health, safety and environment.

Ecos Corporation has worked with DuPont's international management on broadening their focus into sustainability – and especially on "sustainability metrics" to guide investment and business development. DuPont, under CEO Chad Holliday, is now vowing to reduce greenhouse gas emissions by 65 percent by 2010 while increasing revenues by 35 percent. In the same time frame it also wants to source 10 percent of energy use from renewable sources such as solar and wind, and to earn 25 percent of revenues from non-depletable resources such as plants, rather than from petrochemicals.

In an interview with *Sky* magazine, Ecos Corporation chairman Paul Gilding said of Holliday: "His vision of sustainable growth is about a fundamentally different way of doing business, not just dealing with the environmental and social impact of the company. Chad is asking why the company exists, and how to integrate its businesses into society in ways that generate greater shareholder and societal value." During 1999 Holliday became chairman of the World Business Council for Sustainable Development. In a speech to the Global Roundtable on Environment and Business in May 2000, he explained DuPont's application of a sustainability metric to its 80 business units.

Holliday said: "As we work on improving both shareholder value and societal value while reducing environmental footprint, we have found a useful metric to help guide our thinking and decisions. This metric is 'shareholder value added per pound of production' or 'SVA/lb'. SVA/lb is the shareholder value created above the cost of capital, which typically is 10-12% for corporations in the U.S. On a simplistic basis, shareholder value can be created with both material and with knowledge.

"The higher the SVA/lb, the greater is the use of 'knowledge intensity' and the lower is the use of 'material intensity' to create economic value. Coupled with the more traditional financial measures like 'return on invested capital' and 'cash flow', the SVA/lb metric provides a useful and additive guide for portfolio management, and one that is an indicator of the longer term sustainability of different growth strategies.

"At DuPont, we have evaluated the SVA/lb for all of our 80 business units with some of our businesses beginning to set goals to increase SVA/lb over the next five to 10 years. For DuPont as a total corporation, we believe that a stretch, but reasonable, target is a four-fold increase in SVA/lb over the next decade. While each of the values – environmental, societal and shareholder – are important in their own right, the real objective of sustainable growth is to develop business strategies that integrate improvements in all those areas."

not governments."

Sheena Boughen is a teacher by early profession and by instinct. But her classes now are business professionals in Ecos-client companies like DuPont, based in Wilmington, Delaware. While Rick Humphries is a strategist, Boughen's expertise lies in cultural change and organizational development. Many people assume, says Boughen, that achieving change around an issue is about "getting the content right". In fact, she believes that designing the content — in effect the strategy — is the easy part. "The hardest part is shifting people, their attitude and behaviour," says Boughen. "It's 20 percent content, and 80 percent 'what does it mean for how we act'. We believe in the strategy and we guide you. We give people the tools, the motivation and the content so that they can do it themselves. If you no longer need us, then you are succeeding at change."

Her key focus is on "action learning". Every lesson is based on a real project, small, medium or large. Consciously or otherwise, this mirrors the Ecos bigger picture formula of seeking whole corporations or industry sectors to transform as examples for others to follow. Seeing really is believing — in business as much as anywhere else. "If you have a community of learners in the workplace, you have people who are confident to ask questions and to inquire," says Boughen. "I work towards creating a learning organization where inquiry and reflection are used and people feel confident and comfortable with them. Sustainability forces people to look at the impact they are having in all aspects of business — social, environmental and economic. It forces you to deal with complexity."

As Boughen sees it, being comfortable with complexity is a key factor: "The single financial bottom line is about making the complex simple by denying the rest." This is fertile territory for her recipe of action learning. "People need to be given security within complexity, so they need specific projects," she says. "People are often in denial with difficult social and environmental issues." Sustainability can help to set

---

Case history No. 5:

COTTONING ON -- SUSTAINABILITY THINKING FOR FARMERS

Cotton Australia represents the interests of Australian cotton farmers to governments, non-government organizations and the public. The cotton crop is worth more than $A1 billion a year, but the industry faces strong challenges to its future over issues like pesticides use, genetically modified crops, land degradation and water consumption.

In 1999-2000, Ecos Corporation helped Cotton Australia with:
· Implementing a stakeholder engagement strategy
· Developing a code of sustainable practice
· Establishing policies on biotechnology, land use and water

The industry's future relies on showing a genuine commitment to reducing environmental and community impacts. In a major breakthrough, Cotton Australia in June 2000 came out in support of controversial official action to curb broad acre clearing of native vegetation in the State of Queensland.

them free, Boughen asserts, adding: "Most people say that they never understood that working in sustainable development would give them such a personal experience and fulfilment. People say to us, 'What is it about you people from Ecos that makes you so excited?' The DuPont people see our passion. If you want to change a health system, or an environmental system, or yourself, you can do it — it is just a matter of working out how."

As a journalist for two decades, senior partner Alan Tate's approach to his role at Ecos Corporation has been shaped by a profession that prizes persistent inquiry and clear analysis. His specialist focus is climate change and the challenges that it poses for the corporate world. For the decade before he joined the firm in 1998, Alan was one of Australia's foremost environmental journalists. He established the environmental reporting arm of ABC-Television, Australia's publicly funded national broadcaster, in 1989. From then until joining Ecos, Tate was the ABC's National Environmental Reporter, focussing on national and international environmental issues. He is a recipient of numerous awards for his reporting and analysis. With such journalism credentials, it is hardly surprising that Tate is sought out for media and communications strategy advice as well as for more general business strategy advice.

Ecos faces its share of critics and detractors. Most notably, perhaps, Australian academic Sharon Beder — author of a book called *Global Spin* — who has written extensively on Ecos. She has been published in the U.S., particularly in John Stauber's *PR Watch* journal. Beder's attack centres around accusations that Ecos is an agent for PR spin-doctoring, and "greenwashing", rather than for real and positive change through its clients. There is no denying that Ecos works with clients that have done much that is harmful and wrong for the environment and society. Equally, if change is the target, then there is little point in preaching to the converted. "I just think it is something that we have to wear and the only recourse we have is to show our successes," says Tate. "I understand the difficulty that some of our close associates in the green movement have in understanding that we have moved out of our former occupations and have decided to work inside business for change. It is very easy to make the accusation that this is PR and spin-doctoring, but because of confidentiality requirements, the only thing that we can do is to respond with our successes."

When Tate wanted to depart journalism to engage more directly in the battle for sustainability, he found that his options were very limited. "At that time, Ecos was really one of the few places in the world to go," he says. At the Rio Earth Summit in 1992 he witnessed enormous enthusiasm among world leaders for action in the face of "such enormous need". Then he watched that enthusiasm evaporate. At the report-back on Rio "plus-five" in New York in 1997, he watched world

Case history No. 6:

PLANNING AN END TO THE LOGGING OF NATIVE FORESTS

In 1995 Ecos Corporation began working with the Queensland Timber Board (QTB), which represents the logging industry in one of Australia's major states. The QTB and Ecos co-developed a new approach for the industry's future against the background of decades of anti-logging protests in Queensland and around Australia.

The new strategy brought about a dramatic change in attitude – from the QTB seeing environmentalism as a threat, to seeing it as presenting new commercial opportunities. Examples include the areas of biodiversity protection, climate change (carbon sequestration/ trading) and eco-labelling. Subsequently, Queensland adopted Australia's most innovative regional forest agreement with the aim of phasing out native forest logging in favour of plantations by 2025. This was applauded by industry and environment groups. The QTB acknowledged Ecos' key role.

leaders admit that environmental problems had escalated in the face of international inaction, and then fail to agree on a better way forward. A similar story of government failure is looming for Rio+10, set for Johannesburg in September 2002.

"I decided that governments would not lead us towards the solutions," says Tate. "It was too much to expect that governments alone would create the fix. At the same time, there were clear signs that business was seeing opportunity at long last in solving environmental problems. Ultimately, business does have more self-interest in the solutions than governments might," he says. "And business can take a long-term view. Becoming a global brand like a Nike or a McDonalds is fraught with danger. But becoming a global brand in partnership with the global community provides both strength and security." There are dangers, however, and leadership requires bravery. "We at Ecos frequently advise companies that if you seek leadership in this area that you have to do extraordinary stuff," says Tate. "That frequently requires you to do new stuff —set precedents, create icons and do things that are memorable. That also requires bravery."

Case history No. 7:

PLACER DOME INC – QUEST TO BE THE WORLD'S 'GOLD MINER OF CHOICE'

Canada-based Placer Dome Inc is the world's fifth largest gold miner, employing more than 12,000 people at 16 mines in six countries on four continents. Since the late 1980s Placer has been seeking to lift its environmental and social performance, and for the past several years has been embracing sustainability as a core framework for building its future.

Ecos Corporation worked with Placer from 1997 to 2000. A key theme of its approach to sustainability is the desire to be the "gold miner of choice" for governments and local communities – including indigenous landowners – thereby gaining increased access to new mine sites and competitive advantage over less-attentive industry rivals. Placer's then Vice President for Global Sustainability Leadership, Gavin Murray, has the job of integrating sustainability throughout the company. He says of Ecos Corporation:

"From our experience what Ecos has done for us is create awareness and understanding that the world is different. That we need to think differently about what we do and how we do it. It is really that strategic advice and the ability to influence and engage a broad range of people within the corpora-tion around this 'the world is a different place' theme. To me, the value that Ecos brings is that it has got a group of people that have come from many different walks of life, who have seen the world through different lives, and who have come to see the myopia that looking through only one set creates. To me it is helping the corporation to really open its eyes and understand that there are different perspectives out there and that they are important ... and that it is no good arguing that people 'don't understand', because perhaps they do but they just see things differently.

"Driving that change is

very difficult to do internally. You are a symptom of the problem yourself. You are part of the situation. Ecos allows us to bring people in who have credibility and status, and who are able to challenge the organization, challenge the corporation at senior levels. At the same time it is a matter of having people stand up and say: 'Look, we have been through this. We understand the sort of cultural change issues this brings upon a corporation. We understand and we can help you support that process.' Like a lot of things the engagement itself – this is the process verses outcomes debate – the process becomes far more valuable than the outcomes because you actually have a whole range of people starting to think differently."

Blair Palese, the U.S.-born manager of Ecos' Knowledge Team, has mixed her career between the commercial world and green activism over the past decade. Prior to joining Ecos in 1998, Palese was Head of Public Relations for The Body Shop International in the UK and Director of Communications for Greenpeace International. Blair works with a group of researchers and writers at Ecos to keep up to speed with information on sustainability issues and to meet client's information needs. As a virtual company, with people on both sides of the Pacific joined by e-mail traffic, telephone conferences and frequent flyer points, internal communications has become a key challenge for Ecos. Blair also works as a consultant on a number of Ecos projects and is a member of Ecos' management team.

The Ecos Knowledge Team carries out research and writes on sustainability issues and trends and publishes its work via its Web site and in a range of international publications. Key areas of interest include the value case for a sustainable business approach, climate change and approaches to addressing it, and trends in biotechnology. The "knowledge" work has become critical to the Ecos approach. "Ecos plays a unique role in bridging the gap between NGOs who can identify global problems and how companies can positively contribute to solving them," says Palese. "Yes, it's risky not knowing whether companies will take the kind of action we hope they will, but if we can achieve some success it can have a huge impact."

Case history No.8:

GOING FOR GOLD AT THE GREEN OLYMPICS IN SYDNEY

Ecos Corporation's home city was the host for the so-called Green Games – the Sydney 2000 Olympics and Paralympics. In 1996 Ecos was strategic adviser to Lend Lease Corporation, the multi-national finance and property giant that led the winning consortium to build the $A500 million Athletes Village project. Ecos conceived of and negotiated the cornerstone environmental outcome, making the village the world's largest solar-powered suburb. The firm also aided the Australian Government in profiling Sydney 2000's green achievements and the nation's environmental technology and services sector for a global audience.

In April 2000, Ecos welcomed Michael Ward as its latest high-level recruit. His role as managing director is to oversee the rapid growth of a boutique consultancy with global influence and to revolutionize the firm's use of information technology as a tool for driving change. Ward came to Ecos from a background of several years with one of Australia's earliest and most successful "new economy" companies — an Internet service provider called OzEmail. In several years with OzEmail, he helped it to grow from about 100 staff to more than 800, and to be sold to the MCI WorldCom company, UUNET. His last role before joining Ecos was that of Vice President Corporate Relations for UUNET in Australia.

Ward has come from a sector driven by the convergence of technologies — information, communications and broadcasting to name a few — to one driven by the convergence of ideas. This includes the convergence of economic, social and environmental challenges for business, civil society and governments everywhere. Ward is planning to grow the Ecos information services division from a small base of online journals, and will also use IT to archive Ecos' growing store of intellectual property and manage client services and contract delivery.

He feels that without significant change in large companies, there could be little hope for addressing the world's social and environmental crises. But is the time right? "Fashion in business is like fashion in most other places," says Ward. "You can create it. The question is whether you can sustain it. We have all heard of other fashions like TQM and continuous improvement. Most of the rhetoric has no long-term impact unless companies are rewarded for the effort. We have to be about creating the effort and creating the reward. We need to create positive reinforcement."

One of the keys to the Ecos modus operandi is Gilding's personal ability as a communicator. Being heard and being noticed were two of the great challenges that confronted the fledgling consultancy. His advocacy for sustainability is couched in language that business relates to, and his prescriptions for action are often acceptable even to the most hard-headed of business people. In the frontline of the battle to convert business to sustainability, that ability to translate is crucial. It means translating ideas into words, words into action, and passion into pragmatic progress. In 1997, two years after he founded Ecos Corporation, Gilding was awarded *Tomorrow* magazine's Environmental Leadership Award. "You can't deny business its roots," explained Gilding to the magazine. "It has to have growth and profit to succeed against its competition in society. If you want to make it do something different, then make it more profitable for business to do good things or less profitable to do bad things."

The transformation of Ecos Corporation and its leader over the past few years has been marked by the convergence of sustainability with the other great themes and drivers of business at the start of the 21st Century. Information technology (IT), the Internet itself, biotechnology, globalization and world trade are all examples. Gilding is heavily focussed on the transition process from the old, polluting industrial economy to a new and cleaner knowledge economy. In this transition, IT and biotechnology may emerge as great enabling tools for sustainability (just as they may do great harm). If they are positive factors, they will allow new approaches to all levels of production — from the farm and the mine to the factory and the office — and will facilitate economic growth without an escalation of environmental destruction. The quest is now on for sustainable solutions that were beyond the imagination of most people even a few years ago.

While there are a relative handful of corporations around the world that are surging ahead in the pursuit of sustainability, most are still struggling to understand the basic concepts involved. A key component of the Ecos role is to translate the challenges of a transition from the old economy to the new for its clients and for the wider business community. It also means establishing beyond question that value will be generated. When they catch up and "get it" in terms of sustainability, their superior knowledge of their own industries and businesses will take over. At that point, a role for Ecos is likely to end, and the company will move on to new clients and new challenges.

Case history No. 9:

PLUGGING THE MARKETS – ACTIVISTS GET SAVVY

Ecos Corporation clients expect the firm to provide them with a deeper understanding of the green and social movements, and to help them to communicate across the activist-business divide. In the early '90s activists "plugged the pipe" to put pressure on polluters. By the late 1990s their successors had learned to "plug the markets".

A prime example that Ecos uses is the way that the extraordinary global campaign against genetic engineering was built on crucifying "life sciences" giant Monsanto in the United Kingdom and Europe. Eventually this devastated the Monsanto reputation and its share price, forcing it into a merger with Pharmacia & Upjohn. Strategically, Monsanto faced an activist movement enemy that was united as never before by Internet-style connectivity.

In the old economy, a business tended to see itself as a separate entity from the society around it. There was a simple set of interactions between "the business" and its external stakeholders in government, civil society and the marketplace. These other players were influential, but nonetheless were outside the core business. This scenario assumed an element of creative tension with the other players, a series of "enforced relationships" through negotiation and/or fighting to establish desired outcomes, and inherently a number of trade offs. For the business, the old economy meant certainty for investments in bricks-and-mortar, machines and lifelong careers. The new one is characterized by uncertainty, speed and chaos. And knowledge is the key commodity.

The biggest challenge of all is to make the business value case for corporate action on sustainability. While a growing number of corporations have learned that sustainability can be good for business as well as being the right thing to do, the financial markets have been slow to take any notice. So even if value is being created, Wall Street often fails to recognize it and to reward leadership companies. "We talk value and we talk business," says Gilding, identifying why he believes Ecos has achieved what it has. "Our reputation is that we understand value. That is the most powerful thing that we have ever done. We are also a client-focused company. That is what we exist for; to generate value for our clients and, through that, drive change." The value that corporations can create through focusing on sustainability is both shareholder value and societal value. Gilding is adamant that not only is the value often there for business, as well as society, but that it will normally translate into traditional shareholder value — through familiar areas such as margin improvement, risk reduction, capital efficiency and, most importantly, growth enhancement. If societal value is not being created as well, however, then the business model won't be robust enough to survive in the longer term, and value will cease to flow to shareholders. At that point, a corporation is in danger of losing its capacity to change anything, its own fate included. In many ways, his faith that business, not governments, will be the crucial force that will drive sustainability in the 21st Century is being borne out. Many in the activist world that rejected Gilding and his ideas in his Greenpeace days are now focusing their campaign efforts on corporations, rather than governments, precisely because they now believe that this is the fastest way to drive change. Sometimes they punish, and sometimes they engage constructively; but regardless, it is now corporations, their brands and their markets that are the main game. "Let us reiterate our main point over and over," says Gilding. "Sustainability strategies will not be successful or sustainable unless they deliver shareholder value. While this may seem obvious, it is often a focus missing from debates around strategy in this area. We argue it should be front and center — that the potential to generate shareholder value or not should be the key criteria in making decisions on the right strategies to follow in the pursuit of sustainable growth. This is campaigning. We're here not just to come up with ideas. The world doesn't need any more ideas on sustainability. We need to provoke a debate in which they get adopted and acted on!"

One of Ecos Corporation's main tools to assist in navigating in the new economy has been dubbed the "value web". Developed by Paul Gilding with Cath Bremner and Rick Humphries, the value web portrays a new economy world where the business entity is enveloped by a complex series of interactions between companies, governments, civil society and the marketplace. In this scenario, the corporation is a prime force for making things happen. But it cannot sit apart from the other stakeholders and needs a series of business relationships with others. These relationships need to deliver mutual benefits for all players — giving rise to that much used expression, the "win-win" scenario. This is how value is created. "In this new sustainability-focused economy, that value may be economic, social and environmental," says Gilding. "Inherently, therefore, it is about adding value rather than trading off competing interests like in the old model."

The value web model provides a framework in which business can apply concepts that it understands — value creation and negotiating for mutual value — to the context of a new, more complex and global marketplace. "It expands traditional approaches in two directions," explains Gilding. "Firstly it assumes that 'value' is expanded, to include value beyond commercial transactions such as social value and environmental value. Secondly, it assumes that the partners with whom value is created are not just other commercial entities — members of a more traditional value chain — but also are individuals and organizations with non-commercial interests, such as NGOs, governments and communities."

The value web has led Ecos in its redefining of the old economy concept of businesses requiring a "licence to operate". "The new economy has new requirements," says Gilding. "We've moved beyond the licence to operate, which is a compliance-based approach. That is just 'paying the rent' and earning only the 'right to exist'. Success in the new economy requires a 'licence to grow'. This is support from the market (community) to grow faster than the competition. The way to achieve this is to add value to as many partners as possible, and that requires knowledge, relationships and reputation. This is a new way to create shareholder value. It does not replace the need to keep costs low, but that is now a base line, not a growth line." For Gilding a focus on sustainability principles is a core part of doing business in the new economy, not an add-on or a trade-off. "It can be seen as the new expectation of business," he says. "So the challenge is not how to integrate sustainability into the business, but rather to integrate the business into the new societal reality."

For the foreseeable future, the concept of truly sustainable growth is likely to be a dream — even for the most enlightened of corporations. What can be achieved by many, quickly, is growth that is more sustainable. Gilding has built a business strategy designed to inspire action before all the answers are known. He calls it "doing" sustainability, because there is no time not to. "It is not that the 'doing' is more important than developing the theory around sustainability," says Gilding. "It's because that is the business we are involved in. We work with major corporations around the world trying to apply sustainability in practice." The "activist in a suit" has come a long way from Greenpeace, moving from the protest boat to hitching rides on the corporate jet in just over a decade.

WHAT DOES SUSTAINABLE DEVELOPMENT MEAN FOR A FOREST PRODUCTS COMPANY?

Michael J. Bradley
Director, Technology
Canfor Pulp and Paper Marketing
Vancouver, BC, Canada

Canfor is an integrated producer of forest products headquartered in Vancouver, British Columbia, Canada. We produce solid wood from the bole of the tree, engineered wood and panels, and pulp and paper products from the residual materials. We have manufacturing facilities at sites in BC, Alberta and the north-western United States. These operations are primarily based on publicly owned forestlands in BC and Alberta where we harvest softwoods under a variety of tenure arrangements between provincial authorities and ourselves. Under these tenure arrangements we must harvest within precisely defined limits which are determined on the basis of ensuring a fully sustainable operation. We also have full responsibility for restoring every forest site harvested to a healthy free growing state. This reforestation is accomplished with native species only.

With the acquisition of Northwood Inc. in November 1999, Canfor became the largest producer of both softwood lumber and softwood pulp in Canada. The products which we produce possess unique properties which are highly valued in construction applications and by papermakers world-wide. These unique attributes arise directly from the combination of climatic conditions and species types, making forest products from BC highly prized industrial raw materials. When compared with other developed countries, commercial forestry in Canada is a relatively recent activity and, as a result, the majority of the harvest is still conducted in primary forests. This is especially so in the western part of the country where Canfor operates exclusively.

BACKGROUND

Forest products have many inherent advantages when viewed from an environmental perspective; they can be renewable, recyclable, biodegradable and carbon neutral. They have the potential to be among the few truly sustainable products, but they do also have some associated environmental burdens and we believe that it is important that these are fully understood and quantified. Many of our corporate activities are directed at understanding and mitigating these impacts and at communicating our progress in doing so.

In our mission statement, Canfor expresses a commitment to

enhancing the forest resource, ensuring environmental stewardship and protecting human health and safety. We also commit to working closely with our customers. These commitments are not new; they date back to the founding of the company in 1938. This paper will deal with some of the more recent initiatives we have undertaken, but environmental initiatives are not a new "flavour of the month". For instance, in 1973 we were the first company in BC to employ a wildlife biologist in our forest operations. In 1991 we were the first company in North America to produce totally chlorine-free wood pulp (TCF). In the last decade of the nineties, we fully embraced the doctrine of Sustainable Development, and it is this topic that the balance of this paper will address.

The main centre of our forestry operations is the community of Prince George in central British Columbia. (See Figure 1 and Table 1) Situated in a central plateau between the coastal mountains and the Rockies, the area is home to slow growing forests of mostly white spruce and lodgepole pine. We have operations also on the BC coast and Vancouver Island which are situated in the coastal rainforest zone, with western red cedar, western hemlock and Douglas fir among the dominant species. All of these regions are parts of important ecosystems, and all of

Figure 1: Canfor's Operating Locations

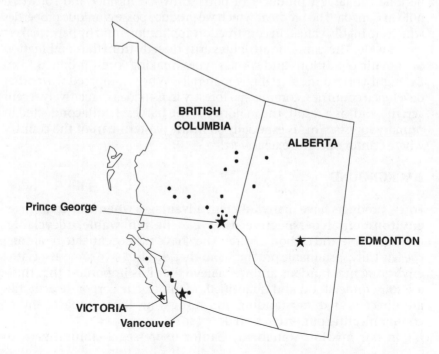

Table 1: Canfor Manufacturing Sites (2000)

Lumber Manufacturing Production		Lumber Remanufacturing		Pulp and Paper Production	
Chetwynd	180,000 Mfbm	Bellingham, WA	125,000 Mfbm	Intercontinental Pulp Mill	Pulp: 297,500 t
Clear Lake	135,000 Mfbm	Clear Lake	40,000 Mfbm	Northwood Pulp Mill	Pulp: 553,000 t
Fort St. James	232,000 Mfbm	Grande Prairie	16,000 Mfbm	Pr. George Pulp & Paper Mill	Pulp: 160,000 t / Kraft Paper: 120,000 t
Fort St. John	174,000 Mfbm	Northern Specialties	11,112 Mfbm	Howe Sound Pulp & Paper**	Pulp: 340,000 t / Newsprint: 210,000 t
Grande Prairie	199,000 Mfbm	Kyahwood Forest Products JV	66,000 Mfbm		
Hines Creek	82,000 Mfbm				
Houston	430,000 Mfbm				
Isle Pierre	171,000 Mfbm				

Plywood Production

Prince George Sawmill	216,000 Mfbm	North Central Plywood	167,000 Msf
Polar	158,000 Mfbm		
Rustad	237,000 Mfbm		
Taylor	76,000 Mfbm		
Upper Fraser	268,000 Mfbm		

our forestry activities must be evaluated with consideration for the unique local nature of these ecosystems. Coastal temperate rainforests world-wide are viewed by many as an especially threatened ecosystem. As custodians of a quarter of the area remaining, British Columbians have a uniquely important conservation role to play. Canfor fully accepts this role.

WHAT IS SUSTAINABLE DEVELOPMENT?

The definition of Sustainable Development is well known[1] dating back to the world commission on Environment and Development in 1987:

> Development that meets the needs of the present without compromising the ability of future generations to meet their own needs.

While this is a simple statement, it is one with profound consequences. Upon analysis it emerges that the concept of sustainability has three distinct components, economic, social and environmental. This realisation has led many authors on the topic to use the ubiquitous Sustainable Development Venn diagram seen in Figure 2. This view of sustainable development has been likened to a three-legged stool; if any

Figure 2: The "Classic" SD Venn Diagram

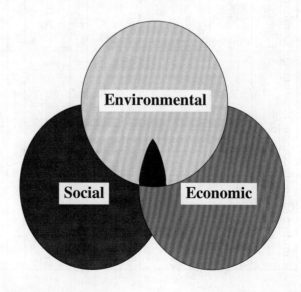

one of the legs is missing, the stool falls over. But what happens if one leg has a different length from the others? A more recent vision of Sustainable Development is an ecosystem-based one.[2] This vision still has the three components, but the ecosystem is represented as all encompassing, and the other components exist within it. This is illustrated in Figure 3. In this model the ecosystem is recognised both for the services it provides (clean air, pure water, etc.) as well as for the resources it contains (timber, fish, etc.) Critical to this model is the recognition that the human economy must not only extract resources from the ecosystem, but it must re-invest in the ecosystem too. If it does not, then the overall system will be depleted and it will not be sustainable. An important consequence of this vision is that if the ecosystem is allowed to degrade, then both the *quantity* and the *quality* of the ecosystem and its resources will decline.

We are long past the point in time when governments, citizens and companies were concerned about what impact the economy was having on the environment. Today we are collectively concerned with what impact severe environment stresses are having on the economy. Fisher-

Figure 3: The Sustainable Development Ecosystem

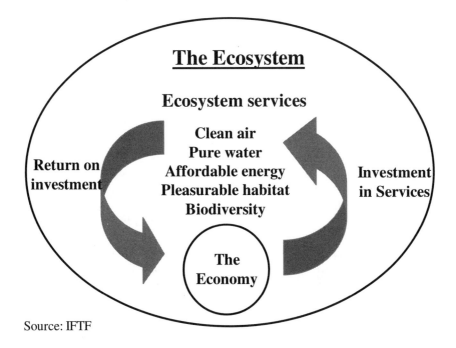

Source: IFTF

ies have collapsed, climate is changing and forests in many countries have been over-exploited. The results of anthropogenic change are apparent in many areas.

Not everyone in the business world sees sustainable development as an obvious way forward however. To some, the concept is either unclear or the premise is unproven. William Ruckelshaus, former director of the US EPA and now CEO of Browning Ferris, was referring to this sceptical constituent of managers and leaders when he stated:

> Sustainability is as foreign a concept to managers in capitalist societies as profits are to managers in the former Soviet Union.

This view is not found everywhere however, and the recent introduction of a "Sustainability index" as a subset of the broader Dow Jones is a clear testament to this. In recent years the business community has seen the emergence of environmentally motivated initiatives such as "Natural Step".[3] or management techniques such as "eco-efficiency".[4] [5] The recent rapid growth in "Green" ethical funds and "Green" power is further evidence that the concept of sustainable development is gaining wide acceptance within the business community.

Companies whose entire enterprise is based on the use of a renewable natural resource, as are forestry companies, can understand and relate to a sustainable line of reasoning. It is in this context that I would like to lay out some of the activities that we have engaged in at Canfor.

What is the scope of our activities?

The activities of Canfor start in the forest. They involve the extraction of timber, the manufacture of wood, pulp and paper products, and the transportation of these materials to destinations both local and global. We extract resources from and release various materials into the biosphere, air water and soil. Customers use our products in the creation of consumables or shelter. Our customers, and theirs, want assurances that the products they buy are safe and that they carry no environmental shadow, either directly or indirectly. Our areas of concern for sustainability therefore span the entire supply chain, from forest to consumer. (Figure 4 illustrates one of these chains for paper).

Canfor has a corporate VP for Environment and Forestry, and this department is responsible for setting the corporate standards, initiating forestry certification activities, and conducting in-house auditing of the various activities. Beyond this corporate involvement, it is the responsibility of the manufacturing units themselves to comply from day to day

Figure 4: The Paper Chain - From Cradle To Grave

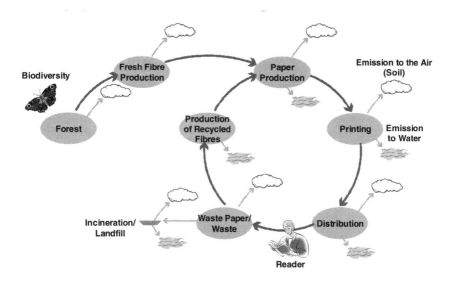

with legislation, meet corporate policies and objectives, and meet health and safety objectives. The performance objectives of key company personnel include an environmental component based on meeting corporate objectives. Unlike many companies, we have no single person charged corporately with responsibility for "Environmental Affairs"; rather, a cross-functional group including forestry, pulp, paper, solid wood and regulatory compliance is intimately involved. So far this approach has served us very well.

The forest

As mentioned earlier, our activities take place on publicly owned land in the provinces of BC and Alberta. The majority of the forest areas in which we are harvesting are primary forests; i.e. this is the first time they have been harvested for industrial purposes. This is in contrast to parts of the US, Scandinavia or central Europe where forests have been managed over many rotations, and where in some cases very little of the original forests exist today. In western Canada we have a wide range of ecosystem types to consider. The various ecosystem regions have been divided into major biogeoclimatic zones within which additional sub-zones are further defined. The major zones are outlined in Figure 5. To

Figure 5: Biogeoclimatic Zones Of BC

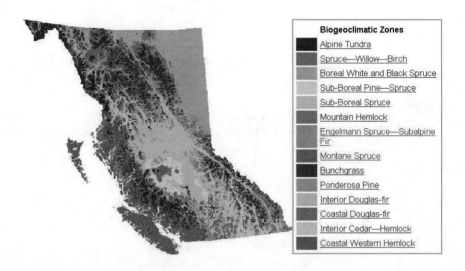

have any expectation of practicing sustainable forestry, Canfor must define its sustainable forest management activities in a manner which respects this ecosystem complexity.

For several decades, the forests of British Columbia and Alberta were managed under a policy of sustained yield of timber. Forest tenures were designed to yield a continuous harvest of timber in perpetuity through the practice of sustained yield forestry. This approach enabled the development of a globally significant integrated forest products industry. Today our awareness has grown of how critical are all of the ecosystem functions of the forest. This has happened at the same time as citizens both locally and globally have been expressing their concerns over how forests world-wide are managed.

In 1998 Canfor set up a process that defined a set of ten Forestry Principles, our Ten Commandments. These principles attempted to define how we could ensure a truly sustainable forestry operation. The team assembled to develop the principles included foresters, academics, marketers and researchers. In addition, we had a review panel that included two different Environmental Non-Governmental Organisations (ENGOs), First nations and customers. The fundamental tenet which underscores these principles is one of *Ecosystem Management*, defined as attempting to manage the forest resource in a manner which does not compromise its essential functioning. The concept is extremely complex to implement, and the holes in our knowledge will always be significant, but it is a manageable task, and one which is well underway today.

The concepts that the Ten Forest Principles cover are:

1. Ecosystem Management - ecological response to disturbances
2. Scale - stand, landscape and forest
3. Adaptive Management - continually improve forest management
4. Old Growth - conservation and old growth attributes
5. Timber Resource - continuous supply of timber
6. Forest Land Base - forest land as an asset for the future
7. Health And Safety - protect human health and safety
8. First Nations - mutual social, cultural and economic benefits
9. Communities - engage the public and communities
10. Accountability - third party verification

The company formally adopted the principles in June 1999. In the announcement and roll out of the principles to our employees, David Emerson, our CEO, indicated his senior level support when he said:

> These principles have to become part of our day-to-day thinking and be embraced by all. Staff at all levels and in all areas will have a role to play and must be dedicated to these principles.

The process of implementing the principles is a time-consuming one, but is now well underway throughout our operations. We have also used the principles as the basis of a successful application to the BC government to participate in an experiment implementing "innovative forest management techniques".

As we have seen, Sustainable Development has a social dimension, and one manifestation of this is the health and safety of employees. This is reflected in our Forest Principles by having one of them devoted exclusively to the subject. Protecting health and safety will always be a core value for Canfor.

For the balance of this paper, I will concentrate mostly on the environmental aspects of sustainable development.

Certification

The last two decades has been a period in which public confidence in the claims of government and corporations has been profoundly shaken.

Examples range from Bhopal, Exxon Valdez, the Canadian blood supply, dioxins in the Belgian food supply, and there are many others. In such a world, the claim of sustainable development by any corporation is met with scepticism at best. Additional proof is necessary. Organisations such as the World Business Council for Sustainable Development and the Swedish Environmental Agency have called for communication of environmental data to consumers and the public. To be credible, such communication must be based on valid criteria and be independently verified by a third party. We believe so strongly that this is an important issue that it appears as one of our Forest Principles:

Accountability

We will be accountable to the public for managing forests for present and future values. We will use credible, internationally recognised, third party verification of our forestry operations as one way of demonstrating our performance.

The most widely used form of environmental certification is undoubtedly the ISO14001 Environmental Management Systems (EMS). This internationally recognised certification verifies that an organisation has developed a valid set of environmental criteria and that procedures exist to ensure that the environmental issues are being managed in a responsible manner. ISO14001 is a voluntary standard. It is sometimes criticised because the standard itself does not define specific targets or criteria, but that is the role of the company or organisation preparing their policies. ISO14001 does require full compliance with all local regulations, laws and permits as a minimum standard for registration. Furthermore, any system of auditing or certification must have a basic management system within which to operate, and ISO14001 is a perfect platform on which to base any other environmental certification standards. In 1998, all of the Canfor pulp and paper mills were registered under ISO14001, and in 1999 all of the 3 million hectares of forestlands where we operate were registered. We have now extended this ISO certification to the forest and pulp operations of Northwood Inc. a company we purchased in late 1999. All of our forest operations and all of our pulp lines are registered under ISO14001. All company sawmills were prepared for audit during 2000, although audit dates have not been set.

When it comes to specific forestry certification systems, there is considerable debate about which standard should be used. One, called the Forest Stewardship Council standard (FSC), has support from some well known environmental groups, most notably World Wide Fund for Nature (WWF), while others such as the Canadian Standard for Sustainable Forest Management (CSA Z808/809) have so far gained more support from the industrial community. It is the opinion of the author that the reasons for different groups favouring different standards are much more closely related to the pedigrees of the different standards than they are to the quality or integrity of the standards per se. Different standards may in fact be more appropriate for different constituencies and markets. Customers in Europe may favour an FSC certification accompanying the products they buy, while groups of concerned citizens in BC may be more interested in seeing that all forestry activities were conducted under the Canadian standard. In an attempt to streamline the certification process and minimise confusion, international efforts are underway to negotiate some equivalency agreements between the various certification schemes. Until such time as these agreements are reached however, some companies, including ours, have announced their intentions to embrace a combination of the appropriate forest certification standards in the coming years. (See Table 2)

So far I have discussed certification in the context of providing assurance by a third party that certain standards are being met. We should not forget however that certification systems such as FSC or CSA are

Table 2: Forestry Certifications In Canada (by April 2000)

COMPANY	LOCATION	AREA (million ha)	VOLUME (million cubic metres)	STANDARD
Canfor	BC & Alberta	3,000,000	5,800,000	ISO
Interfor	BC & Alberta	2,900,000	3,300,000	ISO
Abitibi-Consolidated	Newfoundland	1,860,000	600,000	ISO
Weyerhaeuser	BC Interior	1,250,000	1,670,000	ISO
Spruce Falls/Tembec	Ontario	1,000,000	750,000	ISO
Weldwood	Alberta	1,000,000	2,000,000	ISO
StoraEnso	Nova Scotia	630,000	300,000	ISO
TimberWest	BC	600,000	3,700,000	ISO
Weldwood	BC	250,000	400,000	ISO + CSA
Weyerhaeuser	BC Coast	230,000	1,400,000	ISO + CSA
JD Irving	New Brunswick	191,000	650,000	ISO + FSC
Haliburton Forest	Ontario	19,200	-	FSC
Tembec Huntsville	Ontario	1,000	-	FSC
BC Woodlot W)588	BC Interior	700	-	FSC
Pictou Landing First Nation	New Brunswick	400	-	FSC
Alen Hopwood Enterprises	BC	130	-	FSC

looking not only at the forestry activities, but also at the broader social and economic framework within which the forestry activities exist. It is therefore readily apparent that third party certification of sustainable forest management practices is an enormous undertaking, with ramifications which can ripple throughout a forest company and the communities where it operates. The concept of certification goes right to the heart of what Sustainable Development means for a forest company.

Our impacts on the receiving environment

Life cycle Assessment is the name given to a technique of looking objectively at the environmental impacts associated with the creation of a functional unit of product. It is defined in the current ISO standard as:

> Compilation and evaluation, according to a systematic set of procedures, of the inputs and outputs and the potential environmental impacts of a product system throughout its life cycle.

In 1994 we conducted a small life cycle assessment (LCA) of the impacts of our wood, pulp and paper operations. In our initial study we looked at all of the "industrial" impacts, energy, forest road building, water use, air emissions, transportation, etc. We did not look at our forest ecosystem impacts because we had no way to measure them, nor did we look at the downstream impacts associated with our products once customers had used them. This first attempt to quantify our impacts demonstrated that fossil fuel depletion and photochemical smog creation were amongst the largest potential impacts across our product supply chain. In 1995 we launched on a second, more detailed LCA, this time focussing closely on the forest ecosystem, the carbon chain, and also extending the study into key papermaking plants of one of our customers and into the plants of a key printer also. This second study spanned the entire supply chain from the forest, through paper use, reuse and disposal. It took 3 years to complete, and remains one of the most thorough such studies ever undertaken of a paper chain.[6] To date we have not conducted such a detailed study on our wood products, mainly because their subsequent processing is expected to be so much less "process-intensive" than the production of pulp and paper. However, such a study may still be done one day.

It is not my purpose here to explain the methodology of conducting an LCA. Nor will I explain the entire scope or the conclusions from the LCA; readers who wish to learn more can follow up the references below. I will however use some of the LCA results to illustrate the relative environmental significance of various aspects of our operations and those of our customers.

Life Cycle Impacts – Forestry

In Figure 6 we see the relative impacts of the various stages in the paper chain involved in the production of the weekly magazine we studied (a TV Guide - Horzu) and Figure 7 shows the impacts for the daily newspaper we studied (Bild). One key observation evident in these figures is that the ecological impact of the forestry activities, while quantifiable, is relatively small when compared to the overall impacts. The proportional ecological impact of forestry is higher in the case of the newspaper, simply because the industrial processing of the newspaper is much "lighter" than that of the magazine. A message which Canfor takes from this study is that even though the ecological impact of the forestry operations is low, it is definitely not zero, and it can be done well or done badly. Our objective is at all times to do it well or better. The LCA methodology allows us to quantify our activities.

Ecotoxicity to water

Pulp production involves the bleaching of coloured compounds in the wood fibre using various chemical agents. Until the 90's, chlorine gas had often been used for this purpose, but as environmental concern for the by-products of chlorine use grew, so alternatives were sought. Canfor ceased using chlorine gas in 1996 and adopted an Elemental Chlorine Free process (ECF). (Canfor was the first company in North America to produce Totally Chlorine Free pulp in experimental campaigns in 1991.) The LCA evaluated the environmental impacts of these different options and concluded that the differences between them were small, and were in fact not related to the particular bleaching chemistry in use. This is shown in Figure 8. This figure clearly highlights one of the uses of LCA as an environmental decision making tool. Most of the concern expressed about the pulp production process has centred on the bleaching stages, whereas in fact the biggest impacts are actually associated with the energy and raw material use. It is to these areas that investments should be directed for the best environmental effect.

A carbon balance

One of the environmentally benign aspects of wood or paper products is that they are renewable. Their constituent material is cellulose, a hydrocarbon material produced naturally from carbon dioxide and water by living plants under the influence of sunlight. But how efficiently does the paper industry utilise this renewable resource and how much

Figure 6: Environmental Impacts Of *TV Guide*

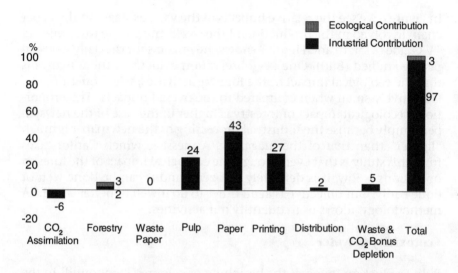

Figure 7: Environmental Impacts Of The Daily Newspaper

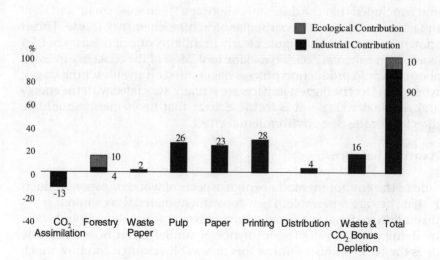

Figure 8: Environmental Loads (Ecotoxicity Water) And The Impact Of AOX-Emissions

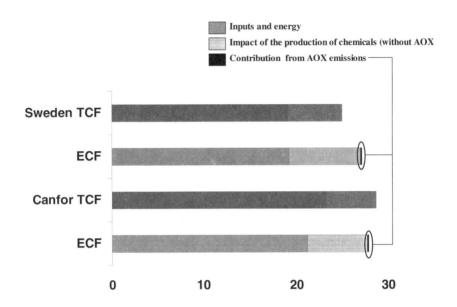

non-renewable energy do we use in the process? We obtained the answer from the LCA. Figure 9 shows the balance for 1kg. of newspaper. The amounts of carbon dioxide initially shown below the zero line are those sequestered by the tree growing in the forest. As the tree is processed, some of its material constituent is consumed as energy or lost as waste from the system. Non-renewable energy sources are also utilised in the processing. The overall balance of renewable and non-renewable carbon is shown in the figure. It is such that the newspaper in the hands of a reader still has a "positive" carbon balance. While not studied, a similar profile would undoubtedly exist for any lightly processed forest product; important information for us to have in a world about to embark on an era of post-Kyoto carbon trading.

Opportunities revealed by the Life Cycle

Many opportunities for each of the partners were revealed by the study. At Canfor we discovered that producing a stronger fibre would allow papermakers to utilise weaker recycled materials, and in certain circumstances this would lead to an overall reduction in impacts across the chain. We also observed how sensitive was our claim of the carbon neu-

Figure 9: CO_2 Balance For Newspaper (1 kg)

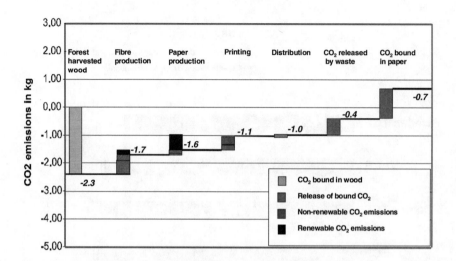

trality of forest products to whether the forest was truly being renewed, and the initial conditions at harvest. The overall carbon balance was significantly altered by the efficiency of energy cogeneration at the pulp mills.

The Canadian Voluntary Challenge and Registry (VCR)

The VCR is a Canadian initiative to encourage the voluntary reduction of greenhouse gas emissions. Canfor has participated in this program since its inception in 1995. Figure 10 shows our progress to date. The large reduction seen after 1990 followed the rebuilding of one of our pulp mills.

Communication across the paper supply chain

Groups such as the World Business Council for Sustainable Development, and the UN Economic Commission for Europe have called for better communication across supply chains.

> ..exchange of relevant environmental information on the life cycle of products must be improved...[7]

The Canadian Pulp and Paper Association has instituted a voluntary

Figure 10: Canfor Greenhouse Gas Reductions

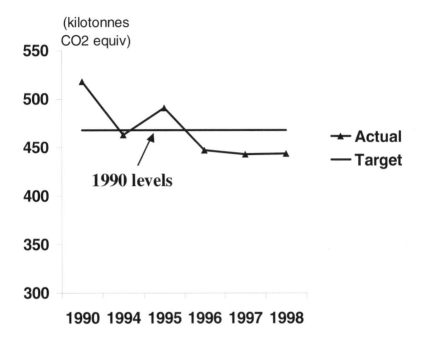

product declaration that covers all of the environmental impacts of a pulp or paper product. This declaration, an Environmental Profile Data Sheet (EPDS), can be applied to a specific product, and is very detailed, covering over 50 distinct environmental aspects of the production of pulp or paper. The EPDS sheets are completed annually and are audited by an external auditor. We were the first company to implement these data sheets and Canfor has used these data sheets since their introduction in 1997. We continue to find them a very effective way of communicating with our customers and their customers on the environmental attributes of our products. They are now in use by a majority of the major Canadian pulp exporters, and at least one European based manufacturer. A sample data sheet is provided in the Appendix to this chapter.

What does it all mean?

Canfor accepts the responsibility of being a steward of the forest resource. We understand why there is a global concern over how the world's remaining forests are managed. As one of Canada's largest forest companies, we recognise that we have a responsibility to be one of the best, not one of the worst, in how we go about our business in the forest. Paper and wood products have the potential to be among the most environmentally benign products, provided that they are harvested and produced in a sustainable manner. We must demonstrate this sustainability. The activities outlined above show how Canfor has acted at various points along the chain to ensure that our impacts are known, always the first step towards improving them. I have also tried to show how the entirety of the environmental attributes is being communicated with customers and others around the world. More work is ongoing, notably in the area of harmonisation of the various certification standards and adding yet another level of detail to our carbon balance.

Why do we do it?

We believe that there is a corporate ethic at Canfor that supports doing the environmentally sustainable thing. This is evident in our Corporate Environmental Policy:

> We are committed to responsible stewardship of the environment throughout our operations.
>
> We will:
>
> • Comply with or surpass legal requirements.
> • Comply with other environmental requirements to which the company is committed.
> • Set and review environmental objectives and targets to prevent pollution and to achieve continual improvement in our environmental performance.
> • Create opportunities for interested parties to have input to our forest planning activities.
> • Practice forest management that recognises ecological processes and diversity and supports integrated use of the forest.
> • Promote environmental awareness throughout our operations.
> • Conduct regular audits of our environmental management system.
> • Communicate our environmental performance to our Board of Directors, shareholders, employees, customers and other interested parties.

But there are also good sound business reasons for doing business sustainably. For one thing, in markets such as Europe, and increasingly the USA, significant customers have set their own sustainable development standards. Publishing companies such as *Time, Der Spiegel,* BBC Publications, or retail stores such as Home Depot, have announced or are developing purchasing guidelines that include environmental considerations. As these are major accounts that Canfor may want to supply, it is not in our commercial interests to be excluded from their list of potential suppliers. Our best commercial success will occur when we can select our customers for optimum benefit across the supply chain. This commercial success is evidenced by better loyalty from preferred customers and better margins as a result. In a business as notoriously cyclical as pulp and paper, the stability alone is an important benefit.

Finally, a "resource-based" company such as Canfor requires a social licence to operate. These are not empty words, for the citizens of BC own the forestland on which the company operates. It is essential to the continued operation of my company that these citizens remain satisfied with the performance of Canfor. Recall the social, economic and environmental dimension of sustainable development and the interrelatedness between them (Figure 3). The citizens of BC are an important subset of the overall ecosystem. If any one of these dimensions is compromised, the quality and the quantity of the "output" will suffer. This is a risk we cannot run.

FOOTNOTES

1. World Commission on Environment and Development (WCED) 1987, *Our Common Future,* Oxford: Oxford University Press.
2. Institute for the Future 2000, *Sustainable Resources: Moving from Commodities to Ecosystem Services, Ten-Year Forecast,* IFTF, Menlo Park, CA.
3. Brian Nattrass and Mary Altomare 1999, *The Natural Step for Business - Wealth, Ecology and the Evolutionary Corporation,* New Society Publishers.
4. World Business Council for Sustainable Development 1995, *Eco-efficient Leadership for Improved Economic and Environmental Performance,* Geneva.
5. Livio D. DeSimone and Frank Popoff 1997, *Eco-efficiency: The Business Link to Sustainable Development,* The MIT Press, Cambridge, MA.
6. LCA Graphic Paper and Print Products, Parts 1 and 2, Axel Springer Verlag, Stora, Canfor, 1998. Available from the author or by download from www.canfor.com.
7. UN Economic Commission for Europe, Committee on Environmental Policy, Brussels and Geneva.

APPENDIX

Environmental Profile **Data Sheet (EPDS)**^{M}	Pulp, Newsprint and Other Uncoated Mechanical Printing Papers

To develop a better informed marketplace in the pursuit of sustainable development

Product

Description: **Intercontinental fully bleached sulphate softwood woodpulp, bleached with total CIO$_2$ substitution (ECF).**

Product unit: for pulp: one air dry metric ton; for paper and paperboard: 1000 square metres

HS commodity code[1]:

Production period: January 1st to December 31st 1998

Mill location:

Manufacturer

Company: **Data For Example purposes only**

Address:

Contact person:

Corporate Environmental Management Attributes[2]

Environmental management systems	All operations are required to comply with corporate policies on environment and forestry practices. In addition they must comply at all times with all official codes and permits. Performance against official and corporate standards is reported publicly. All company pulp and paper mills are registered to ISO14001.
Environmental / sustainable development report	We produce an annual environment report that is included in our annual report, which is distributed to customers, shareholders and other interested parties. It is also available to the public. Copies may be obtained from http://www.canfor.com.
Sustainable forest management system	During 1999, we expect to complete preparations for registration of all our forestry operations to the ISO 14001 Environmental Management System standard. This EMS will provide the foundation for registration /certification of our forestry operations to standards of forest management, such as those of the Canadian Standard Association or the Forest Stewardship Council.

Forestry Attributes of Raw Fibre Sources[3]

		Comments
Forest Land Managed by Company		
Public ownership (% of total)	100%	Canfor operates on 4 Forest Licences (FL) and 1 Tree Farm Licence (TFL) granted to us by the provincial government.
Private ownership	0%	
Forest Management Plans		
Type and term		The TFL Management Plan has a 5-year term and specifies management to establish, tend, protect and harvest timber resources, and protect and conserve non-timber resources. In some areas Land and Resource Management Plans (LRMP's) having a 10-year term have been completed and provide land use objectives for broad areas covering numerous forest operators. All harvest areas are covered by annual Forest Development Plans, accompanied by Silviculture Prescriptions, that specify timber harvesting and reforestation activities and measures taken to identify and protect non-timber resources..
Public participation		The public is an active participant in LRMPs, with the goal of identifying values and developing management objectives. We consider the public to be any individual or organisation with an interest in the forest management activities in the area, such as communities, aboriginal groups, unions, recreational and environmental groups. Notice of the preparation of Management Plans and Forest Development Plans is published in newspapers to provide opportunity for the public to review and comment on these plans before they are finalized. All comments must be addressed.

Non-timber values		Examples of the non-timber values we protect in our plans include aesthetics, biodiversity, cultural heritage (incl. aboriginal peoples), and fish and wildlife. Programs include the reservation of deer winter range areas and spotted owl habitat conservation areas within our operations.
Government approval required		The BC Forest Practices Code requires that all our activities have provincial government approval, at all stages from planning to execution.
Performance inspections / audits		Our operations are inspected and audited by provincial Ministry of Forests officials against the objectives established in the plans above and the Forest Practices Code. Canfor is working with a consultant to revise the Canfor EMS - Corporate Audit Checklist to more closely reflect the requirements of ISO 14001.

Forest Renewal / Regeneration

Natural	(%of total)		
Planted and / or seeded			
• native species		100%	We only plant with species native to BC. For the Prince George Region, where Canfor operates, these species are chiefly white spruce, lodgepole pine and sub-alpine fir.
• non-native species		0%	

Resource Attributes

		Comments
Fibre Use		
Efficiency (ADMT fibre / product unit)	2.48	In kraft pulping the extracted non-cellulosic materials are burnt as a carbon-neutral fuel in recovery boilers.
Chemical oxygen demand (COD)[4] (kg COD / product unit)	46	Chemical Oxygen Demand is reported here as an indication of the degree of close-up of the mill system.
Fibre content (% of total product weight)	>99.8%	
Non-fibre content	<0.2%	The typical ash content of this pulp is <0.2%
Fibre Type		
Raw fibre (% of total fibre weight)	100%	This pulp is produced primarily from white spruce, lodgepole pine and sub-alpine fir fibres (SPF).
• roundwood	1%	This proportion of the fibre was from roundwood logs that were not appropriate for use as saw logs.
• chips	99%	These woodchips are residues from sawmilling.
Recovered fibre	0%	
• planer shavings / sawdust	-	
• other pre-consumer	-	
• post-consumer	-	
Non-wood fibre	0%	
Raw Fibre Source		
From land managed by company (% of total fibre weight)	42%	A major part of the balance of our fibre supply comes from sources in BC, where harvesting operations are covered by the BC Forest Practices Code.
From other sources	58%	Primarily from other licensees operating on provincial tenures, also covered by the BC Forest Practices Code.
Under certified / registered sustainable forest management system	0%	We are in the process of preparing our Northern BC operations for audit against the ISO 14001 Environmental Management System standard.
Energy Use		
Efficiency (GJ/product unit)	39.5	All energy is included in this figure, whether renewable or

			non-renewable. This value includes an allowance for offsite wood chipping and chemical production, and the transport of the wood and chips from sawmills to pulp mill.
Hydroelectric	(% of total)	9.7	Power purchased in BC from the provincial utility is primarily produced from hydroelectric sources. During 1997 a proportion (ca. 7%) was produced by natural gas. This natural gas component has been included in all energy and emission calculations.
Biomass		78.3	Biomass energy is obtained from black liquor, a by-product of our kraft pulp production, plus purchased waste wood 'hog' fuel. Hog fuel includes sawmill waste, wood residues and bark.
Fossil Fuels		12.0	Natural gas purchased by the mill, plus a proportion of the purchased hydro power is included in this figure. Fuels used in the transportation of wood and chips are also included.
Nuclear		-	
Other sources		-	
Water Use			
Process water	(m³ / product unit)	88.0	This is the total water <u>extracted</u> from the environment to produce 1 tonne of pulp. While high for a modern pulp mill, this figure is typical of pulp mills of this vintage. Permitted provincially, monthly average flow must be less than 215 ML/d.
Cooling water		0	No cooling water is lost.

Process Attributes

		Comments
Liquid Effluent[5]		
Sublethal toxicity (TER$_{sub}$) (units TER$_{sub}$ /m³ effluent flow)	Ceriodaphnia d. reproduction 26 Selenastrum c. inhibition 13	Sub-lethal toxicity testing of all mills is required under the Canadian federal Environmental Effects Monitoring program (EEM). The IC$_{25}$ results obtained during Cycle 1 of the EEM have been reported here.
Acute lethal toxicity (for rainbow trout and daphnia magna)	100% pass	Mill effluents entering the receiving environment are not toxic at 100% concentration. During 1998 we conducted xx official tests and no failures were seen. Permitted provincially, effluent must be non-toxic to trout.
Environmental effects monitoring[6]	Cycle 2 in progress	Cycle 1 testing has been completed, and Cycle 2 is still in progress, Cycle 1 provided a benchmark for reference. EEM action plans could follow completion of Cycle 2. Compliance with the EEM program is mandatory.
Biochemical oxygen demand (BOD) (kg BOD$_5$/ product unit)	2.4	Permitted provincially, monthly average must be less than 7.5 kg/ADt.
Total suspended solids (TSS) (kg TSS / product unit)	7.9	Permitted provincially, monthly average must be less than 11.25 kg/ADt.
Polychlorinated dioxins (PCDD) and Polychlorinated furans (PCDF) (ppq 2,3,7,8-TCDD equiv./ product unit)[7] (ppq 2,3,7,8-TCDFequiv./ product unit)[7]	0.3 pg/l 0.09 pg/l	The values reported here are toxicity equivalents, combining the 8 main congeners of dioxin and 10 of furan. These levels are equivalent to values of 3.2 pg/l of dioxin TEQ and 0.95 pg/l of furan TEQ respectively. The detection limits for both TCDD and TCDF were 2 pg/l. Permitted federally under the Canadian Environmental Protection Act (CEPA), and also provincially, pulp mill effluent must be less than 15 ppq 2,3,7,8-TCDD and 50 ppq 2,3,7,8-TCDF.

Solid Waste

Volume	(m³ / product unit)	?	Permitted provincially, annual total from the mill site must be less than 94000 m³.
Landfilled	(%)	?	10% of our solid waste is incinerated with energy recovery.
Incinerated without energy recovery		?	
Diverted		?	

Air Emissions[8]	Grid Breakdown	Marginal fuel	Comments
Total reduced sulphur compounds (TSR) (kg TRS / product unit)	0.20	0.20	The figures described as 'Grid' represent the actual fuels used in the manufacturing processes of this pulp. Permitted provincially, daily average from recovery must be less than 9 mg/m³, and yearly averages from other sources less than 0.225 kg S/ADUt.
Total suspended particulates (TSP) (kg TSP / product unit)	2.40	2.40	The figures described as 'Marginal' represent the theoretical case that would occur if additional energy was required. In BC this would be generated by natural gas. Permitted provincially, yearly average must be less than 0.2 kg/ADUt at the Smelt tank, 230 mg/m³ at the lime kiln, and 41.4 kg/hr at the power boiler.
Global warning potential (kg CO_2 equiv. / product unit)	617	935	Calculated from standard emission factors for carbon dioxide and methane.
Acidification potential (kg SO_2 equiv. / product unit)	3.0	3.0	Calculated from direct measurements on-site, plus an allowance for the acidification emissions from purchased electricity.
• SO_2 (kg / product unit)	2.43		Permitted provincially for Intercon recovery boiler, monthly average must be less than 200 mg/m³.
• NO_x (kg / product unit)	0.80		This value was calculated from the actual fuel mix used.

Other Information

		Comments
Absorbable (total) organic halogens (AOX)[9] (kg AOX/product unit)	0.35	It is now widely recognised that for ECF effluents from mills with secondary effluent treatment, AOX levels below 2.0 kg/ADMt do not correlate with toxic, bio-accumulating or persistent environmental effects. Permitted provincially, monthly average must be less than 1.1 kg/Adt. This parameter is required by some eco-labeling schemes.
Phosphorous in effluent (kg P / product unit)	0.05	This parameter is required by some eco-labeling schemes.
Nitrogen in effluent (kg N / product unit)	0.04	This parameter is required by some eco-labeling schemes.
Organic halogens in pulp (ppm)	140	Tested at ISEGA to the DIN method. Some end-use product categories require a knowledge of the organic halogens in the product.

WHAT I SAW OF THE REVOLUTION:REFLECTIONS OF A CORPORATE ENVIRONMENTAL MANAGER IN THE 1990'S B.C. COASTAL FOREST INDUSTRY

Linda Coady
Vice President, Environmental Enterprise
Weyerhaeuser
B.C. Coastal Group

INTRODUCTION

British Columbia is on the cutting edge globally when it comes to new approaches to the changing relationship between natural resources, the environment and people. You can tell it's the cutting edge by all the blood on it. And, as MacMillan Bloedel's experience indicates, when it's your own blood, it tends to concentrate the mind wonderfully.

What we choose to do with our forests here in BC, and how we choose to handle the increasingly complex biological and social relationships around them, will have enormous implications—for ourselves, and for people and forests in many other parts of the world.

This is the story of MacMillan Bloedel's struggle to adapt to change. The change we had to struggle to adapt to was, in general, a shift in social values in North America and Europe on environmental issues and, in particular, the globalization of concern about the world's remaining coastal temperate old-growth forests.

PREVIEW: THE TRUTH ABOUT THE TRUTH

What exactly happened at MB? Well, imagine there's a movie version of the whole story about to be released, and what follows is the coming attractions preview.

We open in the fall of 1993 with a wide shot of a giant inflatable chain saw—big enough to reach up to the fifth floor of the Hotel Vancouver. Traffic is blocked on West Georgia while environmental activists hang a huge anti-clearcut banner from the side of a 23-storey building across the street. Other activists chain themselves to the desks of senior executives in MacMillan Bloedel's corporate headquarters.

Then we cut to a logging road in Clayoquot Sound, with the Mounties hauling away some 800 people in the biggest display of civil disobedience in Canadian history.

Next we hear a voice-over of colourful Toronto lawyer Clayton Ruby reading his *Globe and Mail* column, in which he regularly characterizes

MB as Canada's expression of the Evil Empire.

Then we go to the Hull headquarters of Environment Canada on a snowy winter's day in 1994. Into an elevator gets a 30-something woman. She is on her way up to the departmental boardroom to make a presentation to the senior bureaucrats on behalf of MacMillan Bloedel, having recently been hired as the company's government relations rep. Two female bureaucrats get onto the elevator. One says to the other, "What are you up to today?" The second woman says, "I'm meeting with the barbarians from MacMillan Bloedel."

The screen fades to black as we fast-forward to 1998. We close in on a shot of Greenpeace International's annual report. Amazingly, it shows MacMillan Bloedel's promise to end clearcutting as one of Greenpeace's top achievements of the year.

Next we cut to the cover of *Tomorrow Magazine*, a European business journal that covers the environment. It names MB the 1999 "Company of the Year."

Then we cut to an annual meeting of Home Depot vendors in 1999 and MB receiving an award for "Environmental Partner of the Year."

Then, finally, a close-up of forestry professor Jerry Franklin—the father of ecosystem-based "New Forestry" in the Pacific Northwest—as he returns from touring some of MB's new variable retention logging sites. Franklin looks into the camera and says, "I have to begin by complimenting MB. The learning here is obviously in an exponential phase—these [logging sites] are extraordinary. They were excellent. I have never seen any better retention harvest prescriptions and actual implementations."

Now this is a fairly stark contrast. And if all your information comes from the mass media or the internet, what appears to have happened is that in the space of a couple of hours in June 1998, MB was transformed in some Orwellian maneuver, no doubt involving a lot of smoke-and-mirrors, from a corporate environmental criminal into a corporate environmental hero.

But as someone who stood on both sides of this divide, I can certainly testify that although there was significant change at MB in the late 1990s when it came to environmental issues and policies, it occurred over a much longer period of time than most people think. And the truth is, of course, that MB was not the villain it was previously made out to be. Nor in all modesty, was it ever the environmental "star" it was sometimes portrayed to be. Truth is not only stranger than fiction, it's also way more complicated.

As the 20th century draws to a close, we have come to appreciate that forest management and conservation are extremely complex tasks. Probably the single largest impediment to our collective ability to perform these tasks well is a tendency to deny that complexity.

It is always easier to reduce issues to a struggle between good guys and bad guys, between right and wrong, between a life-sustaining natural environment or some life-destroying corporate agenda. Or—to do a paradigm shift on the semantics—between uncompromising, single-issue special interest groups and socially-responsible economic development.

If you want to tease apart the multiple truths about what happened at MB during the mid 1990s, you need to be not only a good forester, biologist and resource analyst, but a political scientist, an economist, a shrewd international trade and business analyst, a psychologist, and a sociologist. Most of those disciplines were, in fact, represented on the highly diverse Forest Project team that designed MB's new forest management strategy in 1998.

At the end of the day, the most important aspect of what happened at MB really wasn't the company's public pledge in 1998 to end clearcutting, voluntarily increase the conservation of old growth, and achieve independent certification that the products it produces come from well-managed forests. Certainly, the shift in corporate forest policy embodied by those three things is what captured all of the attention. But the underlying drive behind that shift in corporate forest policy was the fact that in the late 1990s, MB came unstuck from an old, linear, compartmentalized and hierarchical system of management. What those of us working in the company learned, and continue to learn via the things we are doing, is significant; but, perhaps more importantly, we *unlearned* a decision-making style that was blocking us from making all kinds of necessary changes.

The actual changes we ended up making involving forest practices, conservation and certification were really less significant than the fact that we learned how to change, and the fact that we got reasonably good at it. You might liken it to a move from a religious or ideological perspective to a scientific perspective. We gave up a comfortable system that was based on fixed, eternal absolutes, and got used to a world built on theories and hypoteses, where you learn by doing—where truth is what you can make of the best available knowledge, and where evolution by constant testing and verification can mean continual change. Another way to look at it is that we moved toward an adaptive management system that is aimed at achieving particular objectives, and away from a prescriptive management system with an emphasis on rules and compliance. In other words, we put the emphasis on product instead of process.

For example, if I'm a logging division manager, is it my job to ensure that there is a 15-metre forested buffer retained along each side of a stream? Or is it my job to ensure that logging doesn't damage the quality of habitat in the area of the stream? There's a big difference. The former approach is about complying with the rules; the latter approach is about effective outcomes. The former says, "Do the job this way and in most instances it should get this result." The latter says nothing about how to do the job, but stipulates what must be the effective result.

MB's HISTORY: THE BIG PICTURE

The roots of MacMillan Bloedel in coastal BC extend back to three pioneer logging companies which merged in two separate deals in the 1950s. These companies were established back in the time when what brought down big timber was steam and sweat. They evolved through the age of diesel into the era of computers. The history of MacMillan Bloedel's Franklin River division near Port Alberni exemplified this evolution. During the 1930s, Franklin River boasted the world's largest logging operation. It was here that Canadian loggers were introduced to the steel logging spar, the chainsaw and the first logging truck fleet.

HR MacMillan, a company founder, became a BC legend. He served as the first Chief Forester of the BC Forest Service from 1912 to 1916. He continued to have a profound influence on provincial forest policy, even while he was building MacMillan Bloedel into the premier forest company of British Columbia.

Through the 1960s and 1970s, the company rapidly expanded into the U.S. and elsewhere in Canada. As the '70s came to an end, the company had a workforce of 24,500 people, largely concentrated on Vancouver Island, where 10,000 men and women worked. In BC, MB's major facilities included 17 logging camps, 9 sawmills, 3 panelboard plants, 2 newsprint mills, 3 pulp mills, 1 fine-paper mill and 1 paper bag plant.

It was also operating a panelboard plant in Saskatchewan, two panelboard plants and one corrugated medium plant in Ontario, a newsprint mill in New Brunswick (in which MB held a 65% ownership) and 1 lumber mill, 2 panelboard plants and a linerboard mill in Alabama. Of its 24 corrugated container plants, 7 were in Canada, 11 in the United States and 6 in the United Kingdom.

Although the 1980s had started out looking hopeful, it became evident in the latter part of 1981 that the forest industry was experiencing its worst recession since the 1930s. MacMillan Bloedel reported a net loss for 1981 of $26.7 million. In early 1982, the company was restructured into three regional business units in an effort to make it more responsive to the marketplace.

For most of its 75-year history, MacMillan Bloedel had been more volume-driven than value-driven. Success meant pushing big logs through the sawmills at the fastest speed and the lowest cost. The company was slow to recognize that some others here in BC and elsewhere in North America, as well as in Asia and Europe, were doing better by processing smaller logs more efficiently.

When the recession of the early 1980s crippled the Canadian forest industry, MacMillan Bloedel moved into survival mode. Managers realized they had to get more value from logs and move into specialty markets. New challenges called for new strategies. "Value-added" became the theme for the next decade. Throughout the '80s, new mills were built and old ones retooled in an effort to capture the beauty of the province's old-growth coastal timber and make it a selling point, especially in the Japanese market.

During the '70s and '80s, the company maintained a very active and highly-regarded Research Centre. It was here that MacMillan Bloedel researchers invented two new engineered wood products, Parallam and TimberStrand. MacMillan Bloedel researchers also developed SpaceKraft, a disposable, recyclable bulk container which could replace steel barrels for transporting and storing liquid foods and non-hazardous chemicals.

The company built manufacturing plants in Georgia and Indiana in the late 1980s. As the '90s began, it continued to close down or divest itself of unprofitable operations. In the first part of this decade came a series of new investments, mainly outside British Columbia, aimed at expanding the company's manufacturing base and marketing capabilities, particularly in the area of composite wood, while building its value-added manufacturing capability in BC. The company's solid wood business performed very well in the mid-90s, but by 1996, markets were falling off and the company was once again facing challenging times, mainly due to increased competition for the Japanese market.

In September 1997, the board brought in a new CEO to restructure the company. Tom Stephens, a native of Arkansas, had recently retired as CEO of Manville Corporation, a building materials company based in Denver. He had successfully brought Manville back from the brink of bankruptcy and a disastrous exposure to class action lawsuits stemming from asbestos manufacturing operations owned by the company. Stephens immediately began to reshape and reposition MB. His strategy was founded on further focusing MB on its core building materials business and aggressively addressing the areas that were hampering cost-competitiveness in its BC base and limiting market access for the company's products.

Stephens also initiated a program to make safety a first priority, and to make the company the kind of place that people would feel good about having their kids work at. He led MB through a revolution in labour relations by encouraging a process of employee involvement called co-management and co-design. This process breaks down the traditional roles of staff and hourly employees to bring everyone to the decision-making table. By working closely together, union and management representatives designed new ways of running sawmills and woodlands operations in BC to cut costs, increase efficiency and, ultimately, make the operations more competitive.

As 1998 came to a close, MB had sold its paper business and was trying to sell its packaging business, so it was smaller than it used to be. But with sales of $4.5 billion Canadian it was still one of the biggest forest companies in this country. Although Canada as a whole is a major forest products-producing nation, on the international scale our companies are relatively small. MB was not even one of the world's two dozen largest forest companies. And when you compete in global commodity markets on an international scale, size does matter.

MB's HISTORY: CLOSE-UP ON FOREST & ENVIRONMENT ISSUES

To a significant extent, the environmental campaign against MB that began in the early 1990s was attributable to factors other than company's actual environmental performance. Historically, the company was one of the better performers in complying with regulatory legislation — not necessarily the best, but easily within the top quartile in BC. Moreover, the company's harvesting and silvicultural practices were virtually indistinguishable from those of other BC coastal companies—everyone pretty much used the same recipes in those days.

So I think it's accurate to say that our notoriety was owed to something other than our performance. That something was primarily *where* we operated—on the BC coast, primarily on Vancouver Island, in some of the most dramatic examples of BC's old- growth forest.

So as public appreciation of the non-timber values of BC's old-growth forests increased, along with a general increase in public concern over environmental quality, MB's forest tenures received a lot of focus. MB's size and history also often made it the first corporate name most people thought of when they thought about BC's forests. In addition, it was also a company that sold into European and U.S. markets, where there was growing public sensitivity to environmental issues.

The mid-80s to the mid-90s was a period characterized by plenty of environmental controversies in BC, and MB was at the centre of most of them. But they were controversies that mostly stayed within the borders of our province; they were essentially home-grown disputes among British Columbians: forest companies, the provincial government, First

Nations, local environmental groups, BC labour unions and resource-based communities.

The provincial government responded, under an NDP government, with a commitment to double the total land dedicated to parks and protected areas to 12% of the provincial land area. There was a series of public stakeholder processes devoted to defining those new protected areas, followed by a new *Forest Practices Code*. The responsibility for responding to the controversy landed primarily on the provincial government because it owns the Crown lands—adding up to 94% of BC's land area—on which most of the forests grow.

Although these responses were all substantive ones, they didn't stop the controversy. Environmental groups decried every action as a wholly inadequate compromise. And in fact, the province's attempts at compromise not only failed to end the controversy, but in 1993 the disputes heated up even more when Greenpeace International invited itself into the fray.

Greenpeace was born in Vancouver in the '70s, but they'd long since moved away, becoming a substantial force in Europe and elsewhere in the world, while leaving the field in BC to other provincially-based groups. Attracted by the situation in Clayoquot Sound, Greenpeace took up the battle with enthusiasm, organizing a coalition of groups to mount a marketplace boycott of MB paper products, first in Europe and then very aggressively in the U.S. Suddenly, BC forest issues had gone global.

When you look back at those years—particularly 1994 and 1995—economically, those were the best years the forest industry almost everywhere, including MB, had enjoyed in more than a decade. As a result, when those of us embroiled in countering the market campaign dared to suggest internally that "We may have a significant problem here!", it was hard to get anybody's attention. Our intuitive sense that things just might be heading for a crunch was buried beneath an avalanche of positive economic indicators.

Similarly, it was difficult for company ecologists who may have had some misgivings about aspects of our forest management to exercise much internal influence. The same situation faced the marketing analyst who tracked the relationship between consumer demand and social values. This was because people with those kind of skills had no role to play in the zero-sum game that was being waged in those years by both the BC forest industry and the environmental movement.

A zero-sum game is one in which the only acceptable outcome is for one side to win at the expense of the other. By the mid-1990s, the environmental movement and the BC forest industry were nose-to-nose in a zero-sum game. By the mid-1990s, the majority of the industry, for which MB was an icon, and the majority of the environmental movement, for which Greenpeace was an icon, were firmly on the zero-sum page. But since neither one faced any realistic risk of suffering the sort of outright defeat that the other was seeking to inflict, the only strategy that either side could conceive of was to continue pouring more and more resources into the battle.

Meanwhile, however, something interesting was happening in Clayoquot Sound. A third force stepped into the middle of the battle-field. The First Nations in Clayoquot had found themselves caught up in the war of wills between the big corporation and the big environmental lobby. And they didn't like it. It didn't serve their interests at all. But significantly, they did not see themselves as helpless bystanders. And they certainly weren't about to accept any collateral damage as a result of clashes between other interests.

With a modern-day treaty process having recently begun in earnest in BC, the aboriginal peoples of Clayoquot Sound suddenly found themselves with the moral authority to cast the swing vote in that whole controversy. They had the effective political power to either discredit Greenpeace's international market campaign or to blow MB's defences to smithereens. To their everlasting credit, the First Nations in Clayoquot opted to do neither. They called in the company and the environmental groups, and they said in essence: "You guys are both out to lunch. You get your act together and find some solution that we can all live with, or we're going to intervene in a way that neither of you is going to like."

That focused everyone's attention. And the ability of First Nations to focus the attention of other stakeholders in Clayoquot was subsequently strengthened in December 1997, by the *Delgamuukw* decision of the Supreme Court of Canada affirming the existence of Aboriginal Title. What it led to was a long, difficult journey in which both MB and the environmental groups were like the two convicts who escaped from the chain gang manacled together. Like it or not, they had to work out a solution both could live with.

All of this happened well out of sight of both the media and the public. Greenpeace's boycott campaign and MB's defence against the campaign kept on rolling. MB's industrial logging operations in Clayoquot were a casualty of the dispute. More than 100 loggers lost their jobs, and a local community lost a big part of its way of life. There was a lot of confusion and bitterness. The politics of blame ruled.

But as time went by, whether we wanted to or not, the people on both sides got to know each other a lot better. Consequently, much of the theatre and some of the bitterness fell by the wayside. At some point, we all began to put more time and energy into achieving a shared goal— a goal that each side knew it could not achieve on its own—than into fighting with each other.

It is important to note that this shared goal was a new outcome in the sense that it didn't really belong to either side when the dispute began. Nor would it likely ever have been foreseen as a viable option by either side when the dispute began. So it wasn't really a product of consensus or compromise. Instead, it was an outcome of continual interaction and constant redefinition of the situation and the options for dealing with it. And so began the makings of a very different dynamic.

What was the exact nature of that dynamic? It is such simple and obvious stuff that it sounds silly to recount. But, for the record, it went something like this:

- The First Nations required that both the company and the environmental groups recognize their right to make decisions on matters that affected their traditional territory or interests; in return for which they committed to use that right in a way that would respect the interests of others.

- The company required that the environmental group recognize its economic interests; in return for which the company committed to pursue its economic objectives in a way that respected the conservation interests of the environmental groups.

- And the environmental groups required that the company recognize their interest in conservation; in return for which they committed to pursue their conservation objectives in a way that respected the economic interests of the company.

Of course there were many more groups involved in this situation, including the provincial government, labour, local communities and international customers of MB's forest products, so it really was much more complicated than this. But, looking back on it now, I would say that this fundamental pattern of realignment around relationships and interests was the dynamic that eventually pushed the situation beyond a standoff and into unfamiliar and uncomfortable territory for everyone involved. And unfamiliar and uncomfortable territory is fertile ground for new ideas and approaches.

What the Clayoquot First Nations did was to effectively transform an irresolvable battle between conflicting absolutes into a process driven by a need to reach shared objectives. I don't think there was, or is, any other party in BC than the First Nations who is capable of doing such a thing. What it required was one player with the political power to not only hold everyone at the table, but to ensure that failure was not an option.

So when I say that MB's transformation from environmental villain to environmental hero didn't happen overnight, this is what I'm talking about. Well before any of us at the company ever dreamed we would have the opportunity to work on a project aimed at revamping our corporate forest policy in BC, there had been several years of quiet relationship-building with other interests, accompanied by an ongoing search for new solutions to concerns about clearcutting and old-growth logging.

Clayoquot—that mother of all environmental conflicts—had borne "children" that took the form of several limited but special initiatives, such as the Clayoquot Sound Scientific Panel, variable retention logging, UNESCO Biosphere Reserve status, forest certification and a joint venture company with First Nations. Some of those children were now alive and growing up inside MB. Moreover, other things at MB were also quietly changing. As a result of a decade of exposure as a constant target for environmental activists, there was generation of managers at MB who were far less inclined than any of their forebears or most of their current industry colleagues to put their faith in either government policy or regulations or industry solidarity when it came to dealing with environmental conflict.

We didn't know it at the time, but there was only one place left to turn to for help, and that was to ourselves. But doing that meant we had to accept accountability for the problem.

THE BC COASTAL FOREST PROJECT

By late 1997, the economic bubble had burst, and MB was beset by some fundamental structural problems that had been largely obscured by the market upswing. And while the campaign against MB products had been quieted by progress in Clayoquot, the elements that nurtured it were all still in place.

Our new CEO, Tom Stephens, told the company's 9,000 employees to throw away the corporate policy manuals and let everything they did be guided by three basic principles:

Principle #1 was safety. Even though MB's safety performance had been well within the industry norm, Stephens said that record was abysmal, totally unacceptable, and he wouldn't work for an organization that injured people. He linked pay incentives for both managers and workers to safety performance.

Principle #2 was respect. Stephens said that one of MB's key goals must be to become the most respected forest company in North America.

Principle #3 was to make money—lots of it.

Tom Stephens called this "outrageous success." And he also linked financial performance to pay incentives. It wasn't lost on most of us in the company that if we ever did indeed manage to become the safest and most respected company in North America, odds were good we would also be one of the most financially successful. Any business journal will tell you that really good companies usually perform well across a range of indicators.

So these three principles were linked and formed the genetic code from which MB was to adapt and evolve. The co-management process embraced them. Training and leadership courses for salaried and hourly employees were developed around them. Performance indicators were agreed upon and yearly personal goals were derived from them. We were all accountable, and it was very clear exactly what we were accountable for.

Quickly enough, within the company the quest to achieve "most respected" status came to be seen as code for ending the environmental controversy. And lest anyone think it was a prescription for pouring on more PR, Stephens invited the environmentalists into his office for a get-to-know-you talk. On the same afternoon he gave the company's Chief Forester $1 million to undertake a special project to come up with a recommendation for ending the old-growth clearcutting problem on the BC coast.

Just like the Nuu-Chah-Nulth chiefs in Clayoquot Sound, Stephens had swept away the notion that MB should rest its case exclusively on compliance—even 100% compliance— with regulatory requirements. It wasn't enough to be law-abiding, we also had to have something called "social license."

The idea of social license holds that there are social expectations beyond the law that a corporation—or, for that matter, everyone—has to meet. And because Tom Stephens was a businessman, he said that a company doesn't want social license only because it's the right thing to do. Depending on how sensitive your business is to social values, you can also want it because if you don't have it, you're going to lose business in the long run. Or, conversely, you want it because it may give you a competitive edge in gaining business over the long run.

As a result of that afternoon, MB's Chief Forester quickly assembled a project team, and those of us on the team were thrust into a six-month quest that, for the longest time, felt dangerously like a career-terminating misadventure. It was frequently argumentative and unproductive. As one member noted, MB had taken a controversy that had always been "out there," and moved it right into our own corporate living room. Greenpeace wasn't on the street or chained to anyone's desk anymore. The point is, none of us cared. We were too preoccupied dealing with the arguments and debates now being waged within the company.

A key member of the team, who is now our Woodlands VP, later acknowledged that he thought the project was the stupidest thing he'd ever heard of, and the only reason he joined the team was to put the poor misguided thing to death as quickly as he could. His term for the ecologist and silviculturist leading those aspects of the project was "the blue- sky guys." Naturally, the "blue-sky guys" meanwhile were complaining about the intransigence of certain "redneck loggers." Meanwhile, our resource analyst, who was supposed to quantify the economic impacts of our green schemes, studiously refused for months to have anything to do with the project at all.

I was the leader of the so-called social aspect of the project, and I went around telling people that I couldn't define what would or wouldn't allow MB to achieve the much-sought-after prize of social license until I had a proposal to assess—a position that my colleagues said was nothing more than the old chicken-or-the-egg cop-out.

As a team we were organized into six "aspects": effectively six separate research projects: ecology, silviculture, harvesting, economics, growth and yield, and social concerns. Each aspect had a leader, and the six of us constituted the core team. We each employed a variety of consultants and other resources.

In retrospect, it is clear to me that the challenge for the leaders of our company during this time was to manage the conflict that was now breaking out within the company in a way that did not inhibit innovation, but still protected the process from ending up in gridlock or breakdown because of clashes between personalities or ideologies. In the style of leadership they exhibited, our CEO and Chief Forester were key to this. But so were other managers in the company, who would occasionally pull some of the more fractious protagonists out of the game and quietly combine personal suasion with good old-fashioned linear authority in a way that effectively ensured none of us lost sight of the bigger picture.

Somehow, in the final weeks things started to come together in a way that none of us probably ever anticipated they would or could, and it all came out looking something like the following figure.

This figure is essentially an input-output diagram. If you think of the Forest Project as some kind of a conversion mechanism or facility, what you see is the "raw materials" being fed in at the bottom and the "product" emerging from the top. While this is a linear diagram, in many respects the process it describes is actually a cyclical one.

The raw materials are our logging practices at the site level (replac-

Key Elements of the Forest Project

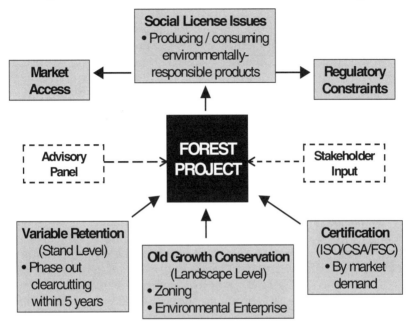

ing clearcutting with variable retention), our conservation initiatives at the landscape level (zoning and environmental enterprise) and independent, third-party certification under systems designed by the International Standards Organization (ISO), the Canadian Standards Association (CSA) and the Forest Stewardship Council (FSC). All of these inputs are subject to influence by outside advisors and other stakeholders, as well as ongoing modification based on various feedback loops within the company that are not shown here.

You might think of the product from the Forest Project as the value-added output of the various inputs. That product is our response to the social license demands that originate in the marketplace. If we are effective in responding to those demands, we will maintain unimpeded access to markets capable of placing the most amount of value on our products, and we will minimize the pressures that would otherwise build for further regulatory control—and, of course, increased operating costs that inevitably reduce competitiveness and profitability.

The Forest Project stressed economic margin rather than harvest volume. A core assumption was that it would be possible to offset additional costs with technological innovation and improved performance. It established three zones for the company's private and public forest tenures on the coast of BC. The zones were designed to manage for different objectives: old-growth conservation, habitat conservation and timber production. The intensity of logging varies by zone designation, and harvesting is done under a system known as "variable retention" which protects biodiversity by retaining a portion of the original forest as individual trees or in groups of various sizes.

I want to comment more on the conservation initiatives input box since this is the element of the Project that I am most involved with. It is important to note that when we talk about additional conservation within the context of the Forest Project we are not talking about establishing more parks or protected areas, since that is obviously not something a private company operating on crown land in BC has the authority to do.

Rather, what we are aiming for here is managing for conservation in areas *outside* of parks and protected areas. That is not going to happen in British Columbia as a result of guidelines published by the government that inevitably translate into economic barriers for companies attempting to follow them. Instead, it requires making a business case for conservation, or stated differently, creating a commercial *incentive* for conservation because it produces benefits for employees, customers and shareholders.

That is what we were trying to convey with the term "environmental enterprise." It is an attempt to acknowledge the potential for business innovation and growth as a result of forest conservation, and to begin the process of developing business strategies to realize the potential of both timber and non-timber products and services from forests.

While the move away from clearcutting is the aspect of the Forest Project that has tended to capture the most attention, for me the truly radical, most exciting and, of course, completely untested and unproven aspect of the Project is the commitment to advance a commercial case for conservation management. From my perspective, this is the leading-edge issue, at least when it comes to natural forests that are publicly-owned. While we are too new at it to know exactly what it requires, our experience to date suggests that one thing it requires is a completely different mindset than the existing one in Canada when it comes to issues involving ownership and investment in timber and non-timber values.

This is an area that is ripe for leadership in the global forest sector, and British Columbia is extraordinarily well-positioned to provide that leadership. Perhaps, just as significantly, it is an area that cries out for collaboration between aboriginal and non-aboriginal interests in an effort to derive greater value from the interaction between modern science and technology and the traditional environmental knowledge of First Nations people, as well as the historical wood-using traditions of coastal aboriginal communities.

I have certainly come to believe that developing globally-recognized expertise in conservation management is one of the keys to the future of the BC forest sector. This is not to say that all of our forests should be managed for conservation. Rather, the point is that managing some forests for conservation, and thereby expanding our toolbox for landscape-level planning, can expand opportunities for other types of management in other types of forests. Admittedly this concept places traditional thinking on its head, which has tended to hold that conservation diminishes opportunities for commercial management. But while on a given hectare that may be true, across several hundred thousand hectares it may not be. This is an area where we in industry need to suspend disbelief and establish the kind of collaborative relationships with First Nations and environmental groups that will allow us all to learn by doing.

Let me go back to the chart and try to explain why this fairly simple-looking plan was so hard to get at, and why it achieved the consensus it did in our fractious team. The easiest way to do that is to briefly itemize some of the main reasons that for years were the standard explanations why we couldn't do something like this, and then tell you what caused us to change our collective mind.

Let's start with safety. We used to say that we couldn't safely employ non-clearcut systems in BC's coastal old-growth forests. If you walk into one of those forests and look up into the canopy, you'll see that it's frequently a mass of broken-off tops and limbs. It's a life-threatening exercise trying to fall one tree among standing timber in that environment. Even if nothing hurtles down on top of you, there's always a chance that this enormous tree is going to get hung up midway to the ground, and then you've got another life-threatening exercise to finish the job.

We dealt with that objection by rejecting the idea of single-tree selection harvesting for most of those situations. For the most part, the silvicultural systems we endorsed tend to retain trees in patches or as widely-dispersed individuals. The ecological study we commissioned gave us some help here. It strongly endorsed the habitat benefits of aggregate over dispersed retention. We worked closely with the provincial Workers Compensation Board throughout the project to make sure that nothing we recommended was going to jeopardize worker safety. Let the record show that the company's safety performance so far under variable retention has been better than its record under clearcutting.

Then there was the economic argument. Everybody knows that non-clearcut systems cost more. On a per cubic metre basis, they cost more to design in the planning phase, and they also cost more in the yarding phase when you're recovering felled trees from a setting. And coastal BC is already the highest-cost jurisdiction in North America.

How much more do these variable retention systems cost? The answer is – it depends. It depends on the site, it depends on the trees, it depends on exactly which system you're talking about, it depends on things that a faller might or might not do. What we finally concluded was that given the shape of our final recommendation, and averaged out across all three zones, it might add 4-5 percent to our current costs.

But then we began finding ways to mitigate that cost increase. As one example, what if you could design an opening to favor recovery of a particular species? True enough, you're not likely to have all your fir or hemlock or cedar nicely organized into discrete little patches, but some areas may run heavier to one species than another. What if you could concentrate on cedar when market demand was high, and then make a second pass some years later for the hemlock when that was fetching a good price? This is as opposed to cutting everything in the area at once, even if it means that some of that timber can't be sold for the cost of logging it.

Or maybe, "I've got a couple of old fir veterans here that are twisted and half-rotten to the extent that they're no good for anything but pulp. I'll never make a profit on those. But the ecologists, speaking on behalf of the world's cavity-nesting birds and animals, love those trees. What if I built my retention patch around them? Or around the less than commercially-valuable trees on this ecologically-important rock outcrop?"

You have to be careful in all this not to veer into the rightfully-disparaged practice of "high-grading": taking the best and leaving the rest, with negative consequences for the genetic health of future forests. But if you're mindful of that concern and if you understand that you are also going to have to leave behind some commercially- valuable trees, you can nevertheless begin to see some interesting possibilities. The more we looked, the more possibilities we began to find.

What was happening was not that we were trading one system for another, which is how the old debate had always been scripted. Instead, we were trading an old cookie-cutter system for an apparently inexhaustible range of variations or tools. And we were finding enough flexibility in those variations to accommodate safety, our new ecological objectives and improved profit margins.

Here again, we found some synchronicity between the economic and ecological requirements. The ecologists told us that the key to biodiversity is diversity of habitat. It's not that clearcutting is necessarily such a bad thing, they said. The problem is that it's been the only thing that the industry in BC has done. The solution is not to substitute another homogenous approach; the solution is to do many different things.

With this strategy, there is no question that we are giving up a certain amount of volume: perhaps as much as 8–10% of our Annual Allowable Cut, or maybe less. Either way, that's not an irrelevant factor for the mills and their employees who rely on that wood. But when we look back over the last decade, we find we've been steadily losing that volume anyway to parks and more stringent regulations. And the prognosis was for more of the same.

The Forest Project offered us an opportunity to try to move ahead of the curve, to effectively address via non-regulatory initiatives some of the environmental and social concerns that were driving the decline in AAC. Besides, you have to remember that we went into this project because it was our strong belief that the status quo was not an option.

Another in the list of old arguments against getting out of clearcutting had to do with regeneration. Some coastal species such as Douglas-fir require virtually full sunlight to regenerate successfully. Douglas-fir is prevalent in those few areas of the Coast where fire is a relatively common part of the natural disturbance regime. But the public won't tolerate big forest fires. Given this popular prejudice, clearcutting is how you let the sun shine in. Other species may be more shade-tolerant, but they all do better in sunlight. Their growth is retarded roughly in direct relation to the percentage of shade-generating retention. Slower growth would mean a further reduction in what constitutes a sustainable harvest.

This concern was addressed to some extent by placing the drybelt Douglas-fir area of southeast Vancouver Island mostly within our Timber Zone—the zone with the least amount of retention and therefore the least shading. (This also happens to be the area where we have the largest concentrations of mature second growth and the largest percentage of our private lands.)

But this issue is not fully resolved. The growth and yield specialist on our team was and remains our least enthusiastic member. He also has concerns about the future of control strategies for certain endemic diseases and pests. These are areas that are subject to monitoring, further research and perhaps adaptive strategies.

The last old argument against giving up clearcutting was the question of social impacts. It seems curious now that we at MB ever offered social impacts as a defence for clearcutting, but that is exactly what we did when the debate, at least in the way we used to frame it, coupled any retreat from clearcutting with an enormous job-destroying reduction in harvest levels. And not only lost jobs, but lost profits, lost shareholder value, lost government revenues, lost community stability—in short, a veritable catastrophe, a zero sum.

Two important ideas helped us pull ourselves out of that game. One idea came from Paul Hawken, who wrote *The Ecology of Commerce*. We read his book, attended a public lecture he gave in Vancouver and asked him for advice about how to deal with conflict on environmental issues. Hawken said that no matter how many significant points of divergence there are on a given issue, there are also, simultaneously, points of convergence. The trick is to find them. Hawken believes that most people's values come from similar sources, and that if you "swim upstream"—away from the points of divergence—you'll be heading toward those sources. You'll begin to find things that everyone believes in and can agree on. He predicted that if we started to build on those points of agreement, and if we devoted as much time and energy and resources to them as we were all devoting to the points of disagreement, then the dynamic of the situation would, over time, change.

He also predicted that from our collective work on the points of convergence would come new tools or options for dealing with the points of divergence, which would not necessarily eliminate them altogether, but would change them. Hawken's advice certainly struck a chord with those of us within the company who had worked on Clayoquot.

The second idea came from three people: David Suzuki, Daniel Botkin and Dee Hock. David Suzuki is an internationally-known scientist and broadcaster from British Columbia. Daniel Botkin is an American ecologist who wrote a book called *Discordant Harmonies*. And Dee Hock is the American businessman who founded the international system of VISA cards. Granted, this is an eclectic combination of thinkers, but all of these individuals are passionately committed to the environment and to the premise that diversity is the built-in mechanism that allows us to adapt to change.

Suzuki and Botkin see biodiversity—or the discordant outcome of never-ending and simultaneously-occurring competition and cooperation between the different biological participants in an ecosystem—as the basis for vitality and evolution in nature. Dee Hock took these principles, applied them in the marketplace, and created a highly-successful economic organization, VISA International, that is now owned by 20,000 financial institutions in 200 countries and territories, and used by hundreds of millions of people every years for the purpose of conducting a couple of trillion dollars worth of transactions. VISA International is the financial equivalent of an ecosystem.

We came to understand that if biological diversity is nature's tool for adapting to change in ecosystems, then perhaps a diverse array of opinions and ideas is necessary for adaptation and evolution in social and economic systems. Once we loaded that concept into our belief system, the whole situation began to look a bit different. We came to see discord in a less negative light. In fact, as long as it wasn't totally destabilizing, we came to see diversity between all the different interests as being a good thing. In fact, we came to see diversity as the catalyst that causes a system to mobilize its collective intelligence and evolve in ways that no individual component could ever conceive of, let alone do, on its own.

So we moved away from the metaphor of a game—or a war—in which one side wins and the other loses, into the metaphor of an ecosystem, where survival is the end result of simultaneous cooperation and competition among the various elements. And then came the dawn.

As our economist quickly reminded us, ecosystems aren't the only thing characterized by simultaneous cooperation and competition. Markets are as well. We created a social model that we used to help us understand forest issues and options in BC. That model held that the application of traditional linear authority simply doesn't work when it comes to forest issues and policy in this province. It doesn't work because relationships among the various interests involved are so complex and interdependent that no one can really be in charge. Instead, the situation behaves much more like an economic marketplace (or an ecosystem), in which outcomes are the product of constant interaction among various forces.

The concept I am talking about here is not "win-win," nor is it a "stakeholder consensus" model. The dynamic I am describing is both more complex and more variable. *But whether or not you agree with it, the important thing is that it inspired us to want to move away from the old simplistic, adversarial relationships into new relationships that would allow us to deal with complexity.* Interestingly, in this respect, the social model we created to help us come to grips with the perspective of various interests on BC forest issues was really very similar to the one being employed within the company by labour and management in the co-management initiative on productivity.

On one level, the Forest Project was about applying ecosystem management principles to commercial forest management within the context of coastal temperate old-growth forests. But in and of itself this is not exactly revolutionary. Either of their own volition or as a result of regulatory pressures, most industries these days are looking for ways to reduce their ecological footprint. And ecosystem management is a concept that was in vogue in the US Forest Service back in the 1980s.

I want to stress that although this particular combination of initiatives and the circumstances surrounding its evolution may have been unique to MB, other forest companies in BC and elsewhere in Canada and North America have their own journeys and stories to tell on the environmental side, many of which involve the application of similar tools at the site and landscape level. Moreover, the forest certification trail is getting so crowded these days that it is difficult to find room to walk on it. There isn't a company on the coast of BC right now that isn't considering FSC certification—yet further proof, if any were needed, that the coast is the leading edge, or perhaps even beyond the edge, on some of this stuff.

Looking back now, it is clear to those of us who participated in the Forest Project that it was essentially an exercise in adaptive management and organizational learning. As I said before, the most significant result is not so much the particular changes we came up with. *It is the fact that we learned some new ways to learn.*

ONE YEAR LATER

June 1999 marked the one-year anniversary of the Forest Project. When I consider what happened during that first 12 months, I am certainly reminded of the old adage in politics that timing is everything. In many ways the attention that the MB Forest Project received was considerably out of proportion to the changes it actually wrought. It certainly exceeded anything we ever expected. I am not sure how to explain this, except to say that somehow this initiative became a symbol for something else that people care about.

For battle-weary customers of BC forest products, it was a sign that the coastal BC industry was coming to grips with the need to address demand for a wider range of forest products aligned with a wider range of values. And for some battle-weary British Columbians, it was a sign that there are new approaches out there that may ease some of the social controversy and polarization that has existed around forest and environmental issues in this province. At the most basic level, it sent a signal that change was appropriate, and reshaped at least some of the political landscape in BC on forest issues.

A special scientific panel conducted a two-day review of our first year's implementation program. The participants were recognized experts in their various fields, but what makes the gathering particularly unusual is that half of them were nominated to the panel by MB and half by environmental groups including Greenpeace, the Sierra Club, the Natural Resources Defense Council, the Western Canada Wilderness Committee, the World Wildlife Fund and others. The review was jointly organized by MB and the NRDC, and it was independently facilitated.

The panel and the environmental group representatives who attended the review by no means offered uncritical support of the Project, but their criticisms were constructive ones—a sure sign of growing mutual acknowledgment of complexity. I believe that we are—tentatively, and with some caution, but nevertheless indisputably—past the zero-sum barrier.

In the Canadian context, particularly in British Columbia, this represents an enormous achievement for all the parties involved. Will it last? Can we sustain it? I honestly don't know. There are enormous pressures against it from many sides. Zero-sum politics is a tried and true tradition in public life in North America. It may not produce the most socially-equitable or environmentally-sustainable results, but there is lots of evidence that in the short term at least, individuals and groups skilled in its application can wield considerable power and upset established orders, be they social or ecological. The internet and the nature of media coverage in our society create endless opportunities for those who are prepared to be self-righteous and impossible in pursuit of a specific objective, regardless of where on the ideological spectrum that objective might fall.

Some of these people and groups accomplish remarkable things that are later heralded as much-needed reform. Others leave havoc in their wake and pieces that have to be picked up and put together by someone else. But like them or lump them, agree with them or disagree with them, their presence in the system drives change. It is one of the great strengths and equally great vulnerabilities of democracy. A paradox, if you like, that lies at the heart of it.

But paradox is a familiar phenomenon in the BC coastal forest sector. Coastal BC forests continue to be at the centre of a lot of seemingly-conflicting demands. There are tensions between the demand to have a forest industry capable of representing British Columbia's interests in a competitive global marketplace, and the demand for more local variety, involvement and autonomy in forest resource management and manufacturing. There are tensions between the demand for more commercially-productive or intensive management of forests and the demand for more conservation of old growth and more community-based eco-forestry. And there are tensions between Crown and Aboriginal title.

If there is one thing I hope you take away from the MB story, it is that reconciling these kinds of complex paradoxes requires new approaches and new accountability on the part of everyone involved. We at MB learned, sometimes the hard way, that if we want to unlock value in coastal forests, we had to be willing to:

• take risks;

- invest in specialized resources and capacities; and, perhaps most difficult of all for a large corporation,
- be prepared to let the people we're involved with—including our
employees, First Nations, local communities and our customers—
find new ways to exercise more personal control in an increasingly
impersonal global economy.

What's the prize? All the trendy articles on the benefits of empowerment and micro-enterprising aside, why would any private company in
its right mind ever be interested in doing such a thing? Quite simply
because a company that can do these things—and do them well—is a
company that will be highly valued.

IISAAK: A NEW ECONOMIC MODEL FOR CONSERVATION-BASED FORESTRY IN COASTAL OLD GROWTH FORESTS, B.C.

Linda Coady
Vice President, Environmental Enterprise
Weyerhaeuser
BC Coastal Group

BACKGROUND

During the 1970's public concern began to build regarding industrial forestry operations on western Vancouver Island. In 1979, the Nuu-chah-nulth Tribal Council (NTC) was asked by its member First Nations to address the declining employment of First Nations in the forest sector, and the damage poor logging practices were causing to fisheries and other resources. In the mid1980's concern focused on Meares Island in Clayoquot Sound, when Tofino residents organized a boat blockade of Meares Island. The Tla-O-Qui-Aht and Ahousaht Nations declared the Island a Tribal Park.

In 1993 opposition to logging in Clayoquot Sound led to widespread civil disobedience and the arrests of over 800 people for blockading logging operations. In reaction to the controversy, the provincial government established the Clayoquot Sound Scientific Panel, composed of scientists and representatives of First Nations, with a mandate to recommend special forest practices appropriate for the area. The Scientific Panel submitted a series of groundbreaking reports in the spring of 1995.

In the interim (March 1994) the provincial government and the five First Nations of the Nuuchah-nulth Central Regions, located in the Sound, signed the historic Interim Measures Agreement, which established joint management of their traditional territories until current treaty negotiations are completed. The Central Region Board (CRB), a unique board with equal aboriginal and non-aboriginal membership, was created as a bridge to treaty. One responsibility of the CRB is to promote sustainability in Clayoquot Sound. Meetings began at this time to discuss the possibility of a joint venture between MacMillan Bloedel, holder of one of the Tree Farm Licenses in Clayoquot Sound, and the five First Nations.

In April 1996 the Clayoquot Interim Measures Agreement was extended, notably with a commitment by MacMillan Bloedel Ltd. and the five First Nations in Clayoquot Sound to examine creating a joint venture forest company. The declared purpose of the venture was to not only conduct forestry and logging operations consistent with the Scientific Panel recommendations, but seek to make Clayoquot Sound the leading global example of ecologically-sensitive harvesting techniques to maintain old-growth attributes and biodiversity.

In 1998 MacMillan Bloedel closed its logging division in Clayoquot Sound, resulting in the loss of over 100 jobs in the Ucluelet area, and significant impacts on the local community. The company worked with Forest Renewal B.C. to partially mitigate those impacts, but the employment and economic losses were nonetheless substantial.

From 1997 through 1999 the Central Region First Nations and MacMillan Bloedel pursued the development of the new joint venture. The CRFN formed Ma-Mook Natural Resources Limited (MNR) to represent their collective economic interests, while MacMillan Bloedel undertook the transfer of the Clayoquot Sound portion of their Tree Farm License 44 into a new TFL to be held by the joint venture. In 1998 both parties entered into a shareholders agreement detailing terms of the partnership. The First Nations ownership interest is assigned through the agreement with Ma-Mook Development Corporation, a subsidiary of MNRL. The parties selected the name "Iisaak", which means "respect" in the Nuu-chah-nulth language.

In July 1999 a Memorandum of Understanding was signed between Iisaak Forest Resources Ltd. and: Greenpeace Canada, Greenpeace International, Natural Resources Defense Council, Sierra Club of BC and Western Canada Wilderness Committee. In September 1999 a Memorandum of Understanding was signed between Iisaak Forest Resources and community interests and displaced forest workers in Ucluelet.

In November1999 Weyerhaeuser Company purchased MacMillan Bloedel, creating the Weyerhaeuser BC Coastal Group out of MB's former BC operations and pledged to honour the commitments made by MB in Clayoquot.

In August 2000 Iisaak Forest Resources began harvesting in Clayoquot Sound.

Introduction to Iisaak Forest Resources

The Clayoquot Sound area (Figure 1) has many unusual features that provide a high degree of profile both in Canada and internationally as a consequence of both natural and political history. These features include:

• Designation as a world heritage site under the UNESCO Biosphere Reserve program
• Formal agreements between the aboriginal community and the government of British Columbia that support a modern day Treaty Process

Figure 1

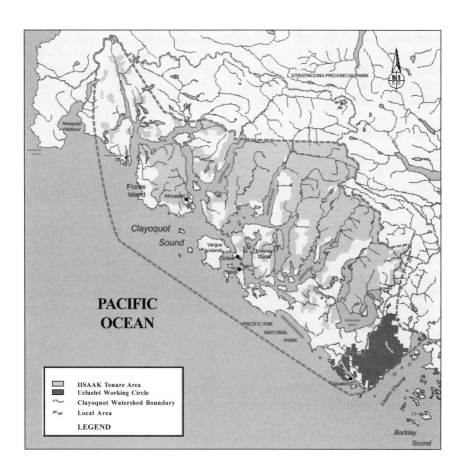

for reconciliation of aboriginal title issues for local indigenous peoples
• The first Tree Farm License tenure on the coast of B.C. controlled by
First Nations
• An ecological approach to forest management and resource use based
on recommendations from a panel of internationally recognized scientists and aboriginal Elders
• A high level of local community involvement in land use decision
making through customized processes.

Corporate Structure

Iisaak Forest Resources (IFR) is owned by the five Central Region First
Nations (CRFN) of Clayoquot Sound and the Coastal Group of
Weyerhaeuser (formerly MacMillan Bloedel Limited). Ma-Mook Development Corporation, with 51% ownership of Iisaak Forest Resources, is
a non-profit development corporation created by the CRFN to manage
their business and economic development interests.

The principal corporate asset is Tree Farm License 57, an
area-based timber harvesting and forestry tenure with the government
of British Columbia covering approximately 87,000 hectares in Clayoquot
Sound. Iisaak began timber-harvesting operations this summer with a
harvest of approximately 10,000 m3.

Strategic Intent

As a First Nation joint venture, Iisaak embraces two core principles from
the Nuu-chah-ninth language and culture that we believe to be critical
for restructuring the economic, ecological and social elements of forest
resource management in Clayoquot Sound:

• Iisaak - (E-soc) - Respect
• Hishuk-ish ts'awalk - (He-shook-ish-sa-walk) - Recognition of the limits of what is extracted and the interconnected of all things

The strategic intent of the company is to be a global example of
leadership in the development of successful approaches to the management of forests with high conservation and cultural values, and the
production of forest products and services. Iisaak is in the early stages of
building capacity through a management strategy, which in turns supports a business strategy aligned with these values.

Stakeholder Agreements

Iisaak is also supported by two stakeholder agreements that are critical to the long-term stability and success of operations. In the spring of 1999 a Memorandum of Understanding (MOU) was signed with five major environmental NGOs. The MOU promotes the resolution of the historic land use conflict in a way which respects First Nations' traditional ownership of their territories, enhances local sustainable economic development opportunities, provides stability for local communities, and protects the natural beauty and biodiversity of Clayoquot Sound. A second MOU was signed with the community of displaced workers of the Clayoquot South Community that recognizes the need to generate economic and social benefits for other local communities.

Conservation-based Forestry

Iisaak defines conservation-based forestry (CBF) as practices and operations designed to achieve conservation as a primary management objective. It features a unique approach to ecosystem planning and operations, in which Iisaak commits to:

• Implement the unique Clayoquot Sound Scientific Panel recommendations for sustainable forestry in the Sound
• Maintain a continuous reserve network
• Emphasize non-timber opportunities in the eehmiis areas (defined as "very, very precious" in the Nuu-chah-nulth language)
• Apply variable retention harvesting systems in developed watersheds
• Certify forest operations with the Forest Stewardship Council
• Monitor and adapt management practices.

However, conservation-based forestry is also designed to enhance the social and economic values from the forest by undertaking to:

• Create employment and training opportunities
• Cooperate to develop non-timber enterprises
• Obtain the highest possible value from the volumes harvested.

Green Investment Strategy

Iisaak's Green Investment Strategy is a critical component of both the general business strategy and long-term financial management.

Business Strategy

The strategy begins with the practice of conservation-based forestry in all aspects of forest management. These operations are founded on the proactive management of relationships with both public stakeholders and governments - local, First Nations, provincial and federal.

This framework creates the conditions for financial sustainability through development of three business segments:

• Timber-Commercial (T-C). Timber operations - production of sawlogs to be used in the manufacture of specialty products featuring premiums based on a unique Clayoquot brand.
• Non-timber-Commercial (NT-C). Non-timber businesses based on harvest of secondary forest (i.e. botanical) products, and recreation or ecotourism.
• Non-timber- Conservation Values (NT-CV). Developing and marketing conservation values such as carbon and biodiversity in order to generate a source of financing. We refer to these activities as the Green Investment Strategy (GIS).

The business segments are described in Table 1.

Table 1: Description Of Business Segments

SEGMENT	SUMMARY
Timber-Comercial	Maximize value from low-volume; create "brand" value along entire supply chain, from raw material to final solid wood product based on: FSC certification reputation for innovation niche market position based on conservation-based management
Non-timber-commercial	Create opportunities for new, non-timber enterprises linked to: conservation-based management participation on planning process and regulatory reform agreements with new non-timber enterprises which enhance Iisaak value and brand Examples: Secondary forest products; botanicals Recreation, ecotourism
Non-timber-conservation Value	Leverage additive environmental benefits of Iisaak's approach to forest management to offset additional operating costs. Execute Green Investment Strategy by creating asset value from conservation values, including: Carbon Biodiversity

The Finance Concept

Iisaak's Green Investment Strategy is part of a fundamentally different approach to managing and capitalizing forest assets. Iisaak's business requires integrated *financial* strategies that mutually support both conservation-based and timber-based lines of business. In Iisaak's case, this is to be achieved in part by realizing a certain premium on timber products, which arises from marketing and promoting a form of Clayoquot "brand". However, in addition Iisaak will need to generate investment flows in various forms, which are derived from, and support, the high-conservation values of this temperate rainforest. This financing is to be applied to:

(i) additional operating costs, including timber harvesting and transportation
(ii) the relatively high forest planning, development and approvals costs, and
(iii) research, development and other capacity building specifically related to conservation-based forestry practices.

The Green Investment Strategy is designed to *primarily* address long-term capitalization of the enterprise, including capital requirements for growth and potentially acquisition. We recognize that there are various sources and programs for shorter-term funding for sustainable forest management programs. The capital requirement for Iisaak Forest Resources is roughly in the order of $15 million.

Cash Flow Profile

Table 2 illustrates the cash flow profile of Iisaak that arises from conservation-based forestry practices combined with the Green Investment Strategy and compares this profile to the cash flow of a traditional forest products company.

The Economic Model - A Private-Public Partnership

The economic model for conservation-based forestry in Clayoquot Sound must be based on some form of partnership between public and private sector parties with aligned interests. The reasons for this are:

• Iisaak's current operations on Tree Farm License 57 cover only about a third of the total area.
• Conservation-based forestry involves the development of non-timber

Table 2: Comparison Of Cash Flow Characteristics

CASH FLOW	CONSERVATION-BASED FORESTRY	TRADITIONAL FORESTRY
OPERATIONS		
Revenue	Commercial timber-premium Partnerships with non-timber enterprises	Commercial timber-commodity
Cost	Incremental harvesting costs Incremental development costs	Standard harvesting costs Standard development costs
INVESTMENT	Operating assets, land and specialized capacity	Principally hard assets - PPE
FINANCE	Limited corporate finance - debt/equity reflecting *conservation-based* production Green Invesmtent flows reflecting conservation values	Standard corporate finance - debt/equity reflecting *industrial* production

enterprises distinct from, but likely partnered with, Iisaak.

• The forest land base in Clayoquot Sound is public, Crown land. The rights and obligations of Iisaak and other forest tenure holders in the area pertain to timber harvesting and forestry operations only. The province of British Columbia holds all other significant property rights.

• To some extent both forms of rights may be altered or transferred through the current treaty negotiations between the provincial government and the Central Region First Nations.

• The drivers for conservation-based forestry in the region include not only Iisaak's desire for corporate success, but other high-value social objectives associated with communities and the Biosphere Reserve. Any new investment vehicles will require alignment of government and investor support.

The design of this project must fit a context for Iisaak and Clayoquot Sound that is different from many other forest conservation projects elsewhere. There is interest on the part of the First Nations, Weyerhaeuser, the government of Canada and the government of British Columbia in designing appropriate green investment vehicles. The basic approach Iisaak is promoting would re-configure and bundle existing rights held by the relevant public and private entities so that tangible value is derived from the underlying environmental benefits and services resulting from conservation. The new values thus created are then packaged through a financial mechanism to support the transition to financial strategies that sustain both conservation- and timber-based lines of business. We believe there are three basic steps to structuring the partnership and financing:

1. Establish the form of the PPP and underlying agreements in order to:
   • Consolidate selected resources and rights in the PPP
   • Provide long-term security for resources and rights.
2. Create asset value through a financial instrument consisting of bundled conservation values. In the Clayoquot context, the broad range of values includes:
   • Environmental services - climate change mitigation and biodiversity protection
   • Ecological integrity for Pacific Rim National Park'
   • Community economic development projects and opportunities.
3. Undertake a financing program to sell to investors.

Creating Asset Value

The financing instrument is based on the environmental services of (i) climate change mitigation through carbon sequestration and storage, and (ii) biodiversity protection that are derived from conservation-based forestry practices. In order to bundle these values, measures have to be derived for both services. The bundling is facilitated by the fact that while they can not be measured in commensurate units, both biodiversity and carbon storage can be calibrated to impacts on old-growth in the forest land base. The intention in bundling, therefore, is to create what we refer to as a "Conservation Credit Unit" (CC/U) that represents a combined unit.

While Iisaak operations will contribute to the mitigation of climate change, the forestry activities would not currently qualify as a projects that could generate an emissions reductions credits under the framework of the Kyoto Protocol. The market for "biodiversity", apart from acquisition of genetic resources, is also not established. These CC/U's are, therefore, not intended to be traded in an established market, although opportunities for private sales may develop depending on perceived value. After issuance, these units would more closely represent the purchase of "development rights".

Characterization and Measurement

The underlying asset values of units will be generated from:

• Preservation - exclusions from the harvestable land base (protected areas)
• Retention - maintaining old-growth structure through variable retention silvicultural systems that maintain existing forest structure and age distribution.

Iisaak's initial timber supply analysis indicates that the forest management constraints applied to the area will actually increase significantly the proportion of old-growth forest over time.

To measure carbon, Iisaak proposes to model the carbon sequestration and storage that is projected given appropriate harvest and management scenarios, adapting the forest inventory and harvesting data to an ecosystem carbon accounting model prepared for Weyerhaeuser operations elsewhere.

To assess the creation of biodiversity values, it makes sense to focus on the elements that sustain biodiversity such as habitat, rather than the biodiversity itself. Because biodiversity is not a thing, but a "cluster of concepts" (Bunnell 1998), one cannot purchase an amount of it. Managing for habitat becomes a surrogate for protecting and managing species (Scientific Panel 1998). The structural diversity of old-growth forests - with their abundant coarse woody debris snags, uneven canopies, gaps, and mix of tree ages - supports ecosystem function and provides habitat for many species of plants, animals, and microorganisms (Scientific Panel 1998).

Both carbon and biodiversity can be linked to the age-class structure and composition of the forest, expressed in variables that can be measured and linked to area. The CC/U investment unit could therefore be primarily defined in terms of the number of hectares of old-growth preserved or retained within the area under management, currently TFL 57. The units could potentially be structured in two-tiers:

• Preservation Units - arising from certain categories of exclusion from harvestable land base (reserves, pristine watershed or eehmiis areas, etc.)
• Conservation-based Forestry Units - arising from variable retention and other constraints additional to those required strictly by existing forest regulation.

There are other options involving timing of offering in design of the transaction. The entire stream of benefits could perhaps be capitalized in one major public offering, or alternatively a series of offerings could be designed consisting of an initial offering reflecting the current land base, and additional units offered as they are manifested either through corporate growth or maturing of second-growth forest.

Monitoring and Verification

Independent verification of results would be required for purposes of providing security to investors, and Iisaak is continuing research on the approach. To some extent security is provided by the existing framework including the Scientific Panel recommendations, which are incorporated in the Tree Farm License document, the M.O.U. with ENGOs, and FSC certification. An ongoing program of quantification through assessment and modeling would also be added.

The Transaction

Target Proceeds and Pricing

The first issue in design of the transaction is to establish the desired proceeds and allocation from the financing. Since it is a public-private partnership, funds must be generated for public programs as well as Iisaak's corporate requirements. Table 3 provides an example of how the target financing might be derived from specific public-private proponents and programs. It must be emphasized that this is just one scenario, and is not based on any policy decision either by Iisaak, government or other non-profit entities, nor are the estimates and targets established in any current negotiation.

Table 3: Example Of Target Proceeds From Financing

CATEGORY	PROPONENT	PROGRAM	AMOUNT ($ CDN MM)
Private	Iisaak Forest Resources	Capital Expenditures	$10
Private	Iisaak Forest Resources	Operating Costs - CFB	$5
Public	Community-based organizations	Non-Timber Enterprises	$3
Public	Government Agencies and Local Planning Authorities	Landscape Level Planning	$5
Public	Clayoquot Biosphere Trust Society	Research, Education, Monitoring	$7
TOTAL			**$30**

The pricing of the transaction is simply derived by the number of units generated. For example, if 100,000 units are created, the target pricing per unit is $300.00 per CC/U. Note that each CC/U represents an "interest" in the entire package of benefits and opportunities created by the partnership. While the underlying asset is based on conservation and biodiversity, investors would also be supporting the wider range of activities, including the social benefits of community economic development, enhancement of First Nations capacity and holdings, etc.

Placement

The transaction as contemplated is a private placement marketed to selected categories of green investors. Additional research, including testing ideas with this group for specific feedback, will be required as part of this program.   Possible investors who might value participation include:

• Corporate investors - from perspective of environmental mitigation; desire offsetting investment relevant to corporate lines of business (e.g., domestic energy companies, mining).
• Corporate investors - from perspective of social responsibility; desire regional investment which enhances corporate social responsibility profile.
• Non-profit (Foundations, etc.) - with predominant interest in sustainable development and environmental issues.
• Non-profit (Foundations, etc.) - with predominant interest in community economic development and social justice/aboriginal rights issues.

Structure of Transaction

The features of the structure that might be in place as a result of the financing include: (1) Pledges, covenants and agreements among public-partners create basis and security for investment mechanism; (2) Terms and pricing of conservation credits ("CC/U's") are established for issuing entity; (3) Information memorandum and/or prospectus is prepared for marketing to and negotiation with potential private investors; (4) Transaction is executed with investors purchasing units, capitalizing operations of the partnership; (5) Partnership operations are conducted according to the terms and conditions of agreements that create security for investors. The partnership structure also yields specific performance measurements to be monitored according to terms of the transaction; and (6) Results of independent monitoring and verification are submitted routinely through the issuer to private sector unit-holders.

CONCLUSION

Significance for B.C.

We believe that the success of conservation-based forestry in Clayoquot Sound, centered on the operations of Iisaak Forest Resources, is critical for British Columbia. An economic model that supports conservation in areas that are not formally protected not only advances forest management and policy in B.C., but helps the province controls it owns destiny. Active development of the model allows B.C. to:

• put the question of "what non-timber values are worth" to international markets
• assume leadership in global arena by pioneering reconciliation of global and local demands for some types of old growth forests
• diversify and strengthen forest policy portfolio
• generate international interest and support
• assist with conservation of key forest values in advance of final Treaty resolve in a way that can achieve support from local First Nations.

A viable economic model for conservation in areas requiring special management also represents an important addition to provincial resource management options and strategies. There are significant limitations to special management and zoning prescribed elsewhere in B.C. by regulation. Unresolved issues around the economic viability of low-impact forestry are a contributing factor to forest conflict on the coast. Under these conditions, timber operations must still cover the cost for conservation of non-timber values. With few exceptions (non-commodity products), forest product markets will not bear the premium necessary to support operations with a smaller ecological footprint.

Clayoquot is also the ideal place to develop a CFB model of global significance. Clayoquot is a new frontier as a consequence of history. The traditional, industrial model failed some time ago in the region, and the losses in terms of reduced harvest and associated economic activity have been taken. This past liability is now an open field for experimentation. There is a great deal of energy, in the absence of intense conflict, for change. The area is recognized internationally as a special place, and is a positive setting for generating investor interest in a fresh start with a new approach.

Issues and Questions

The designation of Clayoquot Sound as a UNESCO Biosphere Reserve
and Iisaak's crafting of a green investment strategy are in many respects
responses to the difficult issues and questions that arose both locally
and globally during the late 1990s regarding the future of coastal old
growth forests in Clayoquot Sound. Ironically, the effort to resolve one
set of difficult issues often leads to others. This is particularly the case in
British Columbia where forests, like those in Clayoquot, are both publicly owned (Crown land and resources) and the focus of unresolved
issues regarding aboriginal rights and title.

For this reason, some of the solutions surrounding our proposal
for new conservation-based partnerships are unlikely to be found within
existing government policy or legislation. The willingness of governments,
both federal and provincial, to go beyond current policy frameworks is
critical to the emergence of a viable economic model for the type of
business strategy envisioned by Iisaak. It is recognized that this necessarily
places government in a position where it will have to balance risks
(foregone revenue from forestry and environmental services) with the
potential benefits (ecological, economic and social) created by a new
and untested approach.

Indeed, the suggestion that Iisaak and Clayoquot could represent a
winning model will remain a major issue in British Columbia. The international controversy that erupted over logging in the Sound in the
early 1990s is associated with the failure of both government and corporate policy and significant social and economic dislocation at the local
level. It is also recognized that this failure occurred despite the infusion
of large amounts of capital and resources. Both government and industry are wary of any further investment in the absence of a significant
cash stream from new sources given previous losses. And while the recent designation as a UNESCO Biosphere Reserve creates a logical platform from which to argue for customized solutions and/or pilot projects,
government has a natural aversion to non-routine, special-case solutions. This applies even to innovation to create broad, long-term benefits.

The development of a business model for timber and non-timber
values in coastal forests is therefore unlikely to be at the top of any
government's list of priorities given competing pressures. Unlike Iisaak,
government likely does not have the same incentive to invest significant time or resources in such a project; hence the need for partnerships.

Iisaak's corporate structure - a joint venture between local indigenous people and a large multinational corporation - raises further is-

sues and questions, particularly regarding the responsibilities of corporate shareholders seeking to derive benefit from non-timber values. For this reason, the proposal may raise an obligation for existing shareholders to enhance their own investment and/ or be willing to limit returns on equity in the early stages. The will and capability of both Central Region First Nations and Weyerhaeuser to successfully see a new model through design and implementation will be a critical success factor.

The issue of legal and fiscal instruments to maximize benefits at the local community level, and methods to quantify such benefits, will also be an equally important consideration in any assessment of this proposal.

Uncertainties in British Columbia regarding the current Treaty process to resolve outstanding issues around aboriginal rights and title also present opportunities and constraints.

Finally, the value of a credit for conservation, environmental services or mitigation in the Clayoquot context is largely uncertain. The value is affected by the ongoing debate among, governments and within the environmental movement regarding forestry projects under the Kyoto Protocol, the future of emission trading, and the ultimate value for the carbon that lies beneath the old growth forests of Clayoquot. We have therefore chosen to emphasize the biodiversity aspect of our proposal. The development pathway for biodiversity offers the advantage of being less traveled than the carbon pathway, and is probably more relevant to old growth forests on the coast of BC. However, the unknowns surrounding measurement, valuation and securitization of biodiversity are perhaps even greater than the ones surrounding carbon. Private sector demand for related investment products, bundled in this fashion with other social benefits, is also uncertain.

The challenges are obviously formidable. In the end, they can only be addressed by individuals and groups determined to meet them and capable of meshing together policies, action and financing at both the local and global level in order to achieve a shared goal.

PATAGONIA, INC.

Jacquelyn A. Ottman
CEO, J. Ottman Consulting, Inc

At Patagonia, Inc., headquartered in Ventura, California, catering to Alpine and other outdoor enthusiasts means much more than just designing and selling the highest-quality outerwear. It means making a deep commitment to pressing environmental and social concerns as well. By developing an environmentally conscious corporate culture and supporting the environmental causes and groups its customers care most about, Patagonia has hit upon a winning business formula that sets it apart from all other outerwear marketers, and stands as a shining example for all environmentally minded businesses. Their "doing well by doing good" strategy is paying off in stellar sales and fiercely loyal customers.

Patagonia's reputation for innovative social and environmental responsibility extends back to the company's roots. Founder Yvon Chouinard started Patagonia in the late 1960s as a sister to the Chouinard Equipment Company, purveyors of hardware for Alpine climbing and other outdoor activities. When Chouinard realized that climbing equipment adversely affected the pristine wilderness setting in which it was used, he decided to make his equipment environmentally responsible, offering an innovative alternative to the bolts that were traditionally used.

Although Chouinard Equipment Company has since been sold, the environmentally responsible tradition lives on at Patagonia. The company takes environmental issues into consideration in all aspects of its business, from the materials in its clothing and the construction details in its retail stores to supporting various environmental causes of concern to its customers.

Edible Landscaping

Patagonia's commitment starts with an internal assessment that helps the company understand and prioritize opportunities to minimize environmental impact. Everything from the wood and lighting in Patagonia's retail stores to the food in the corporate cafeteria has been scrutinized for possible environmental harm. The company now maintains an extensive recycling program, composts its food waste, uses low-flow toilets, and participates in the U.S. Environmental Protection Agency's voluntary Green Lights energy-efficient lighting program. Even the grounds around company headquarters feature edible landscaping --

banana trees.

Outerwear with Minimal Environmental Impact

Patagonia works closely with suppliers to minimize the environmental impact of its clothes. In 1993, Patagonia was one of the first customers for Wellman's EcoSpun fiber, which they incorporated into fleece jackets and pants redubbed Synchilla PCR (for post-consumer recycled). Anxious to help build the market for this innovative material, Patagonia spread the word on "PCR Synchilla" within the industry and, today, the use of recycled materials in various types of fabrics is widespread, helping to keep costs low for all.

To help cut down on the pollution of soil, air, and water associated with cotton farming, which is chemically intensive despite its benign image, Patagonia uses only organically grown cotton, effective with the spring 1996 line. To avoid letting the relative expense of organic cotton stand in its way, Patagonia chose to "split the difference" with consumers, reducing its margin while asking them to accept a $2-$10 price increase on each garment. To help enlist their support for the more sustainable alternative, Patagonia educated their consumers about the environmental imperative of growing cotton organically. Educational efforts included extensive customer communications including an essay in the Spring 1996 catalog by Yvon Chouinard, and an interactive display in its Ventura headquarters.

As part of its attempts to reduce the environmental impact of its products, Patagonia simply makes fewer of them. Supporting the company's corporate goal to be a model sustainable enterprise, in 1993 the company decided to limit its product line to 280 styles. In Chouinard's words, this decision stems from the desire "to avoid cluttering the world with a lot of things people can't use." High-quality, durable products don't have to be replaced often, and when outgrown can be passed along for further use. He dubs the idea of capping the size of the company "Natural Growth," because it mimics a principle of nature -- if something gets too big for the community, it will die. Likewise, if the size of the company gets out of control, it can outgrow its consumer support.

Support for Environmental Groups and Causes

Patagonia reinforces its strong ties to consumers by supporting the environmental groups and causes they care most about. Each year, Patagonia pledges 1 percent of its sales or 10 percent of pre-tax profits, whichever is greater, to groups actively working in such areas as biodiversity, old-growth forests, environmentally preferable methods of resource extraction, alternative energy, water, social activism, and environmental education. Referring to this commitment as an "Earth Tax," Patagonia donates primarily to the smaller environmental groups and organizations working on local environmental protection initiatives which may have difficulty receiving funds from other sources. As an example, Patagonia supported the "Friends of the Ventura River" group to clean up an unofficial bird sanctuary bordering the Ventura River near the corporate headquarters. Among its commitments, Patagonia is a founding member of the Conservation Alliance, an organization of like-minded companies seeking to give back to the outdoors.

Contrary to the more conservative sentiments of many a mass marketer, Patagonia is not afraid to support controversial groups and causes such as Planned Parenthood (the company views population growth as a critical environmental problem), or the now-defunct Earth First! group. While acknowledging that such efforts will offend some would-be customers, Patagonia believes its most loyal patrons support the same causes, or will at least respect the company for taking a stand.

Through April 1997, Patagonia contributed more than $8 million to hundreds of organizations including the Access Fund, the Surfrider Foundation, and the Earth Conservation Corps.

Communicating with Customers

Patagonia communicates environmental messages to its consumers through essays in its seasonal catalogs, in-store communiqués, and paid advertising. Ads placed in select outdoor-oriented magazines inform customers of product developments as well as emerging environmental issues and Patagonia's activities. In addition, the company publishes an annual "Green Report" detailing progress against all key environment-related goals.

Business Success-Public Recognition

Patagonia's commitment to quality and its pioneering environmental and social practices add up to more than just business success. In little more than a decade, Patagonia has amassed $150 million in annual sales throughout the United States, Japan, and Europe. In addition, the company has won numerous awards, including the American Marketing Association's 1995 special Edison Award for Corporate Environmental Achievement, a listing in *The Nation's* Top 100 Companies, and a nine-year stint on *Working Mother* magazine's 100 Best Companies for Working Parents. Yvon Chouinard was also invited to participate in a

Corporate Responsibility Roundtable held at the White House in 1996.

While sales and accolades are important at Patagonia, it is clear the company manages with an eye on a double bottom line, measured by a strong corporate culture and recognition as a force for social and environmental change. Their success provides a lesson to other businesses looking to garner profits while furthering environmental and social priorities.

INTERFACE, INC.

Jacquelyn A. Ottman
CEO, J. Ottman Consulting, Inc

According to Ray Anderson, CEO of Atlanta-based Interface, Inc., a leading maker' of commercial carpet, carpet tile, and other interior furnishings, responsible management of Earth's resources is a question of business survival. In Anderson's words, "Sustainability is the key to achieving the resource efficiency that will be necessary for manufacturing companies such as ours that hope to survive, much less flourish, in the 21st century." Setting his a4-year-old, $i-billion company on course "to become the first name in commercial and industrial ecology worldwide," Anderson is encouraging Interface, with products sold in more than no countries, to incorporate environmentalism into every corner of the firm. Despite a product line based heavily on petrochemicals, Anderson is determined to make his company the paradigm of sustainability and zero waste. He believes that Interface's own impact can be magnified by influencing others, so Interface's example has infinite potential to make the world a better place to live.

Interface's first step toward sustainability begins with the implementation of a three-part educational program. The first is the adoption of environmental training for the entire workforce, to include training in the principles of The Natural Step for all 5,000 employees worldwide. The second is an internal "EcoSense" program which outlines a seven-front approach to sustainability and focuses on resource depletion, landfill use, pollution, and energy waste. The third part aims to increase employees' overall environmental awareness at home as well as in the workplace. By extending positive environmental steps beyond the office walls, Interface hopes to affect attitudes and extend the impact of the internal environmental program-QUEST (Quality Utilizing Employee Suggestions and Teamwork).

At Interface, education translates into profitable innovation. As of 1995, the company entered a revolutionary new phase, and raised the environmental bar in the process-they began leasing carpets through a unique Evergreen Lease Program. Under the program, Interface actually retains ownership of its carpet tile, making itself, the manufacturer, responsible for the maintenance, repair, and ultimate recycling of the carpet tile. By assuming full life cycle responsibility for its products, Interface not only ensures that the recycling loop will be closed, but also maximizes the potential to reuse natural resources while preventing a voluminous and potentially hazardous source of waste from going into landfills. The Evergreen Lease is especially effective with carpet tile because only worn tiles are replaced, thus eliminating the need to install a whole new carpet, but providing a rolling, progressive face-lift that goes on theoretically as long as the building stands.

If Interface has its way, one day its carpeting may be not just recyclable but biodegradable as well. In 1995, the R&D division developed a fully compostable carpet made of natural and degradable fibers, now undergoing testing. Meanwhile, the company continues to explore other initiatives and technologies brought about by heightened awareness internally for responsible and profitable management of environmental issues.

Interface may be in the earliest stages of its journey toward becoming a sustainable company, but it is already profiting significantly in the process. Through QUEST, part of the company's overall environmental initiative, Interface has saved more than $20 million. Thanks to QUEST, the company now produces 100 percent post-industrial recycled nylon carpet, enjoys a 25 percent unproved efficiency of turnover for beams of yarn, a 16 percent reduction in hexane solvent usage with the implementation of a new carpet-drying procedure, and a 75 percent reduction in scrap yarn from beams at one of their manufacturing sites. In addition, Interface has retrofitted machinery that consumes less energy, and steam water used for dyeing is starting to be recaptured.

These, along with many other efforts, have boosted efficiency and waste reduction while lowering operating costs and thus increasing profits. The company encourages employees to identify new ways in which the company can achieve its 1997 goal of reducing their waste by 50 percent relative to the amount produced in 1994 By the company's own calculations, this represents a possible savings of approximately $35 million.

THE COST OF CRIME IN NOVA SCOTIA

Colin Dodds
GPI Atlantic
and
Ronald Colman
Director, GPI Atlantic

Crime conservatively cost Nova Scotians more than half a billion dollars in economic losses to victims; public spending on police, courts and prisons; and private spending on crime prevention in 1997 (Table 1). This amounts to nearly $600 for every man, woman and child in the province, or $1,650 per household. When losses due to unreported crimes, insurance fraud and shoplifting are added, as well as the costs of shattered lives due to crime, the loss is nearly $1.2 billion a year or $1,250 per person ($3,500 per household). These crime costs amount to between 3% and 6.3% of the provincial GDP. The distribution of these costs is demonstrated in Figures 1 and 2. Per capita crime costs in Canada are estimated to be 20% - 25% higher than crime costs in Nova Scotia.

These estimates do not include deaths, injuries and property damage due to impaired driving; non-hospital medical, drug and counseling costs; private spending on criminal lawyers; non-retail business spending on alarms, electronic surveillance and other crime prevention and detection equipment; most white collar crime; and a wide range of indirect crime costs. Also, monetary estimates clearly convey only a small part of the true costs of crime, which include the trauma of being violated, pain and suffering, fear and insecurity, and lost opportunities to undertake activities because of crime risks.

In our conventional economic accounts, most crime costs are perversely counted as contributions to economic prosperity and well being. The higher the crime rate and the more we spend on prisons, police, criminal trials, burglar alarms and security systems, the more our economy grows, which in turn is taken as the primary sign of progress.

By contrast, the Genuine Progress Index (GPI) regards crime as a liability rather than an asset, and its costs as an economic loss rather than a gain. Unlike the GDP, lower crime rates make the GPI go up, and higher crime rates make it go down. Reduced crime costs are seen as savings that can be invested in more productive activities that build communities and enhance well being. Higher costs to maintain a given level of security indicate a decline in the quality of life.

Unlike current measures of progress based on the GDP, the GPI does not view all economic growth as an unqualified good. Crime, pollution and other "regrettable" costs point to sectors of the economy where

Table 1: Costs of Crime in Nova Scotia, 1997

Conservative Estimate

Victim Losses: Reported Crimes [fn. 1]

Direct Victim Losses due to Property Crime	$102.4
Direct Victim Monetary Losses in Assaults and Sexual Assaults	$0.6
Cost of Hospitalization due to Violent Crime	$1.6
Lost Potential Economic Production due to Homicide	$23.4
Lost Production due to Absenteeism resulting from Criminal Attack	$4.2
Subtotal	**$132.2**

Public Justice Costs

Police Expenditures, incl. N.S. share of RCMP expenditures	$143.3
Courts, Legal Aid, and Prosecutions	$39.5
Corrections: Provincial, N.S. share of Federal, and Youth	$74.8
Subtotal	**$257.6**

Private Defensive Expenditures on Crime Prevention/Detection

Home Security Systems	$45.5
Private Security Guards and Private Investigators	$56.3
Retail Business Defensive Costs (Store Surveillance, Alarms, etc.)	$37.0
Theft Insurance (Premiums minus Claims)	$25.0
Subtotal	**$163.8**
Total Conservative Estimate	**$553.6**

Comprehensive Estimate

Total Conservative Estimate (from above)	*$553.6*
Victim Losses due to Unreported Property Crime	$165.2
$ Losses, Hospitalization, Absenteeism: Unreported Violent Crime	$5.2
Unpaid Household Work Losses	$8.2
Unpaid Voluntary Work Losses	$1.4
Voluntary Work: Crime Prevention, Legal Aid, w/Victims,Offenders	$16.0
Business Shrinkage due to Shoplifting, Employee Theft: Retail Only	$113.8
Insurance Fraud (higher premiums)	$66.4
"Shattered Lives" (based on court awards for serious violent crimes)	$249.0
Total Comprehensive Estimate	**$1,178.8**

The following costs are not included: (1) deaths, injuries and property damage due to impaired driving; (2) health, lost production and other costs associated with drug offences, prostitution and other crimes not classified as property or violent crimes; (3) most white collar and corporate crime, fraudulent professional service claims, tax fraud, employment insurance fraud, etc. (except for cases reported and prosecuted; (4) non-hospital medical costs, drugs and counseling due to violent crime; (5) non-retail business and government defensive expenditures including alarms, electronic surveillance, etc., and non-retial shrinkage due to employee theft; (6) private spending on criminal lawyers; (7) civil justice costs, including courts, legal aid and litigation costs; and (8) indirect and induced crime costs, such as property value losses, foregone economic activity due to fear of crime, etc.

Figure 1: Conservative Crime Estimate: Distribution of Costs, Nova Scotia, 1997

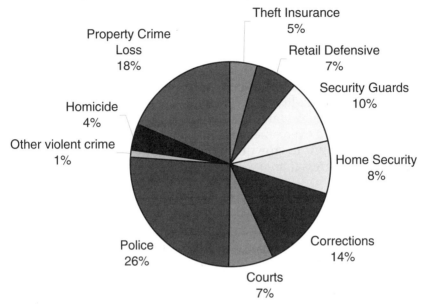

Figure 2: Comprehensive Crime Estimate: Distribution of Costs, Nova Scotia, 1997

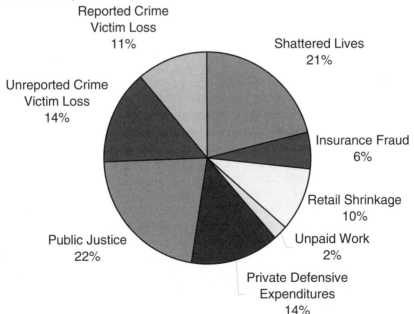

limits to growth may signify well being, prosperity and progress more accurately than continued growth.

A peaceful, harmonious and secure society is therefore valued as a vital and profound social asset that directly benefits the economy and the quality of life of its citizens. Conversely, high crime rates signify a depreciation of that asset and an erosion of the social and economic value that derive from personal security and social stability.

By registering crime costs as an economic loss to society, the GPI demonstrates the inability of market statistics alone to provide adequate benchmarks of progress, and can signal the need for policy initiatives and investments to overcome the causes of crime.

In this case limits to growth in crime rates and crime costs are more indicative of progress than unlimited growth.

CRIME IN COMPARATIVE PERSPECTIVE

From the perspective of conventional market statistics, the Atlantic provinces are generally seen as economically disadvantaged by comparison to the rest of the country. But the reliance on market statistics nationally and internationally produces faulty and misleading comparisons. If a peaceful and secure society is viewed as an important social asset making a vital contribution to the quality of life, and if crime costs are seen as an economic drain eroding the standard of living, then Nova Scotia and its neighbouring provinces have a significant comparative advantage.

The Nova Scotia crime rate for serious violent crimes is just 63% of the Canadian rate; it is 82% of the national property crime rate, and less than half the rate for robberies and motor vehicle thefts. Nova Scotians therefore require less police per capita to keep the peace, they imprison fewer of their citizens than any other province, and they spend significantly less on locks, alarms, electronic surveillance and other crime prevention and detection devices. These hidden savings may actually show up as a disadvantage in comparative GDP measures, which see more spending of any kind as a contribution to economic growth.

While crime costs have not been separately calculated here for Canada and the other provinces, it is possible to extrapolate from comparative crime rates, incarceration rates, police to population ratios, and victimization surveys to estimate that average per capita crime costs are probably 20% to 25% higher for most Canadians than the figures given here, and about 30% higher in the western provinces.

This would produce an annual overall crime bill of more than $20 billion for the country as a whole by conservative estimations, and nearly $45 billion according to the more inclusive "comprehensive" method.

This translates into a per capita cost of between $730 and $1500; or $2,000 to $4,300 per household in Canada. The extra $400 to $700 Canadian households pay annually for crime over Nova Scotians, amounts to an additional hidden "crime tax" for a correspondingly less peaceful and secure society.

Again, it must be emphasized that these Canadian estimates are simply extrapolations derived from the Nova Scotia results and from comparative crime statistics. It would certainly be possible to use the methods and data sources in this report to calculate the Canadian crime bill more precisely, and to construct a comparative estimation of crime costs across the provinces. It would also be desirable for such comparative studies to include major crime costs currently omitted from the estimations, such as the costs of impaired driving; non-hospital medical, drug and counselling expenses due to crime; private spending on criminal lawyers; non-retail business defensive expenditures; health costs of drug offences; and other excluded costs.

The contrast is even more marked by comparison with the United States, which has nearly six times the crime rate for serious violent crimes as Nova Scotia, including 3.5 times as many homicides per capita, five times as many robberies and ten times as many forcible rapes. The U.S. also jails more people than any other country in the world except Russia, and imprisons more than 10 times as many of its citizens per capita as Nova Scotia. More than one out of every 150 Americans is behind bars, compared to one out of every 900 Canadians, and just one out of every 1,600 Nova Scotians. A black male in the U.S. has a 28.5% chance of landing in a federal or state prison in his lifetime, and an even higher chance if local and county jails are included.

It costs more than $44,000 a year to keep an inmate behind bars in Nova Scotia. Every person kept out of prison due to lower crime rates therefore represents a significant economic saving that can be used to hire an extra teacher or to send a student to university for three years, including full-time tuition, accommodation and meals. Nova Scotians spend only a quarter as much per capita on corrections as Americans, but the cost saving does not show up in the conventional market statistics, which record every extra prison, court case, security guard, police officer and burglar alarm as a contribution to the economy and a sign of progress.

Imprisonment is today one of the fastest growing sectors of the American economy, with an average growth rate of 6.2% per year throughout the 1990s, significantly outpacing overall GDP growth. The U.S. spends almost $U.S. 50 billion a year to keep nearly 2 million of its citizens in prison. Per capita spending on corrections has more than tripled in that country in less than 10 years, helping to fuel the "robust"

U.S. economy.

From the GPI perspective, crime costs lower the standard of living by diverting precious resources from health, education, environmental protection, and other activities that enhance human and social welfare. Though the "dynamism" of the U.S. economy is frequently held up as a model to Canadians, the GPI also records the social costs of that growth and the fact that it is driven in part by factors that signify a serious decline in the quality of life.

A DEPRECIATING ASSET

While Nova Scotia maintains a significant comparative advantage in crime costs relative to Canada as a whole, the advantage cannot be taken for granted. It is in fact eroding markedly as the province's crime rate converges rapidly towards the national average. Twenty-five years ago, Nova Scotia's overall crime rate for all reported criminal code violations was less than two-thirds the national average. Today it stands at 98% of the national average. In 1972, Nova Scotia's property crime rate was 60% of the Canadian rate; by 1982 it had climbed to 72%; and by 1997 to 82%.

While serious violent crimes are still less than two-thirds the national average, a substantial increase in common assaults has raised the official violent crime rate in the province above the national average. A substantial portion of the increase in the official crime rate is due to higher reporting rates for assaults, sexual assaults, domestic violence and other crimes, a positive sign signifying reduced social tolerance for violent behaviour once considered socially "acceptable."

But there is also no doubt that Nova Scotia today is a markedly less peaceful, harmonious and secure society than it was a generation ago. Considering only police-reported crimes, the average Nova Scotian is today four times as likely to be a victim of crime as his parents. In 1962, according to the official statistics, the chances of being a victim of crime in Nova Scotia were one in 49. In 1997, they were one in 12,[1] though a portion of this increase must clearly be discounted to account for higher reporting rates. The long-term rise in crime has also been ameliorated by a 16% drop in the provincial crime rate since its 1991 peak.

Homicides and robberies, because of their seriousness, are considered less susceptible to changes in reporting rates than minor crimes like common assaults, and thus may give a more accurate picture of actual changes in the provincial crime rate over time. There are 80% more homicides per capita in the 1990s than there were in the 1960s and 300% more robberies. The rate of break and enter incidents in the province has increased by 330% since 1962, rising from two-thirds the national rate to 80% today.

Higher crime rates translate into higher economic costs. Hospitalization costs due to crime have increased markedly since 1962, due in part to higher violent crime rates and in part to much higher hospitalization costs. Absenteeism due to crime cost the provincial economy an estimated $4.25 million in lost production in 1997, a three-fold increase since 1971. And 452 potential person-years of production were lost to the economy in 1997 due to past homicides, at a cost of $23.4 million. Victim property losses have probably increased in direct proportion to the property crime rate.

Public justice costs have also increased, necessitating higher taxes. We now need nearly 50% more police per capita than we did 30 years ago. Compared to Canada as a whole, Nova Scotia had 94% the number of police officers per 100,000 as the rest of the country, up from 74% 20 years earlier. Spending on home security systems likely parallels the increase in break and enter incidents. Per capita spending on theft insurance has more than doubled in the province since the early 1970s, an indicator of public perceptions of crime risk.

Business crime costs also translate directly into higher consumer prices. Spending on in-store crime prevention and detection equipment, business losses due to shoplifting and employee theft, and salaries of private security guards, are all passed on to the consumer. Based on Retail Council of Canada surveys, it is estimated that Nova Scotian households each pay about $800 a year in higher prices due to crime, amounting to 2.6% of their annual consumption budget. Nationwide, the figure is closer to $900 a year. Insurance fraud costs Nova Scotian households an additional $200 a year in higher premiums, amounting to about 15% of total insurance premiums, according to the Canadian Coalition Against Insurance Fraud.

While all this extra spending makes the GDP grow and is taken as a sign of growing prosperity, the GPI counts these expenditures just as the average householder does – as costs rather than increases in welfare. If increases in the official crime rate are discounted by one-third to account for higher reporting rates, and if crime costs are roughly proportional to crime rates, then Nova Scotians would have saved $350 million in 1997 if crime rates were still at 1962 levels, according to the conservative estimate. Using the more comprehensive estimate, the saving would have been $740 million, money that would have been available for more productive and welfare-enhancing activities.

Returning to the comparative perspective, it is clear that the crime rate in all three Maritime provinces has increased faster than the national rate. Because all three provinces started from a considerably lower base, they are all still below the national crime rate average, but they are catching up rapidly. Explicit recognition of this eroding advantage can prompt policy changes designed to arrest the decline and restore the value of a vital social asset.

POLICY CONSIDERATIONS

In this study we have hypothesized that a growing divergence between crime rates and crime costs may signify an erosion of civil liberties. As police states have demonstrated, it is possible to keep crime rates down by spending more on police, prisons and other repressive measures. In the United States, for example, the gap between crime rates and crime costs has been growing throughout the 1990s, as an ever larger percentage of the population is imprisoned. If civil liberties were to remain constant, crime costs should rise and fall in rough proportion to crime rates.

Because civil liberties are recognized as an important social asset, because the GPI is concerned to reduce rather than increase crime costs, and because a full cost accounting framework naturally points to social, economic and demographic linkages, this study clearly favours policy options that deal with the social causes of crime rather than its symptoms. The GPI approach supports the National Crime Prevention Council's contention that crime prevention rather than incarceration is the key to reducing crime, and is not only "the right thing to do and the effective thing to do, but the cost-effective thing to do."

To this end, the full report notes that crime is not an independent variable but is highly correlated with gender, age, marital status, drug addiction, employment status, educational level, a history of abuse, and prior convictions. These correlations point to potentially cost effective investment strategies that can improve the standard of living and quality of life while yielding additional dividends in crime reduction.

One recent study, for example, found that every dollar invested in residential drug treatment programs yielded a seven-dollar dividend in savings from reduced crime costs, incarceration, property damage, production losses and health costs. And a long-term longitudinal study in the United States found that every $5,000 invested in high quality pre-school education in high crime inner city areas yielded an estimated $28,000 return to society, including lower crime rates.

Nova Scotia's restorative justice initiative could be an important and powerful model of cost-effective intervention that deals far more effectively with the causes of crime than the conventional adversarial system that focuses on punishment, is plagued by high rates of recidivism, and deals only with symptoms.

By contrast, it would be a serious misuse of the data in this report to ignore the social correlations with crime and to argue that more costly, punitive and repressive measures are the answer to high crime rates. The very purpose of the GPI is to elucidate social, economic and environmental linkages to encourage a deeper understanding of the fundamental roots of progress and decline. Short-term symptomatic treatments cannot provide long-term solutions to social problems like crime.

For this reason, the GPI approach is very much in line with the goals of the restorative justice initiative. Similarly, social investments in education and job creation may have a crime reduction function, and lower crime levels in turn produce savings that become available for further investments in education and job creation, a positive feedback loop that produces social benefit in several areas. The cost of incarcerating one inmate for one year can produce a $34,000 a year job and an additional $10,000 educational investment.

While detailed cost-benefit analyses of alternative investment strategies are beyond the scope of this study, the 35-year time series do indicate a remarkable correlation between crime rates and the business cycle nationwide. Across the country, crime rates rose dramatically during the recession of the early 1980s and then declined during the economic recovery, peaking at record high rates during the early 1990s recession and easing off again during the recovery.

After each recession in the last four decades, unemployment rates have not fallen back to their pre-recession levels, and crime rates have also remained correspondingly higher. From 1962 to 1997, each decade saw higher average unemployment rates and higher average crime rates throughout Canada. When discounted for higher reporting rates, the chances of being a victim of crime and the chances of being unemployed in Nova Scotia were both about three times greater in 1997 than in 1962.

The correlation between crime and employment status is confirmed by profiles of prison inmates. In Nova Scotia 58% of inmates were unemployed at the time of admission, and only 22% had full-time jobs. When these statistics are further correlated with the high proportion of young males convicted of offences, the data strongly suggest that investments to reduce high rates of youth unemployment may be a cost-effective crime prevention strategy.

The gender dimension of crime is also important in that women, who are charged with only one-fifth the number of offences as men and who account for only 5% of prison admissions, are effectively subsidizing the costs of male crime from an economic point of view. Though women earn just 66 cents to the male dollar for full-time work in Nova Scotia, female tax dollars pay for prisons and police, and women bear substantial costs of victim losses, theft insurance, higher prices, and home security expenditures, - costs mostly incurred because of male crime. From the GPI perspective, women would have a case for arguing for a public justice tax rebate in proportion to their lower crime rates.

These examples are simply illustrative of the broad range of potential policy applications of the GPI approach, and are not intended as definitive recommendations. Detailed benefit-cost analyses of alternative crime reduction strategies are necessary to determine the most cost effective policy options.

CONCLUSION

A peaceful and secure society has been a powerful social asset in Nova Scotia and the Maritimes, that has traditionally signified a high quality of life. As the GPI demonstrates, it has also produced substantial economic cost savings that have perversely appeared as a disadvantage in the conventional economic accounts. Nova Scotia and the Atlantic region today retain a significant comparative advantage, with lower crime rates than the rest of the country, particularly for serious violent crimes and property crimes.

But the gap is narrowing and the advantage slimming. Even accounting for higher reporting rates, Nova Scotians are about three times as likely to be victims of crime as their parents, and the crime rates are converging rapidly towards the national average, with higher crime rates apparently correlated with higher unemployment rates. The trend has led to higher taxes for public justice expenditures, higher shopping bills to pay for in-store theft and business crime prevention costs, higher insurance premiums, higher rates of personal spending on locks and alarms, and more victim losses.

If the province is to retain its important advantage, personal security and a peaceful and harmonious society must first be reaffirmed as core values in our measures of progress, a commitment that is lacking in our current reliance on market statistics. With such a commitment, the Genuine Progress Index can then monitor progress towards these and other important non-material goals that are vital for our well being and prosperity. Those measures in turn will stimulate cost effective policy actions designed to attain these goals, a stimulus that is lacking when market statistics and related measures of progress mistakenly count costs as gains.

At a deeper level, the GPI inevitably calls into question the current fascination with the "robust" and "dynamic" American economic model, driven in part by high crime costs and extraordinarily high levels of incarceration. With its substantially lower levels of serious crime, Nova Scotia retains a powerful, currently unvalued, advantage over the U.S.

model that can only be protected and developed by limiting growth in this sector of the economy.

The explicit recognition that limits to growth in certain economic sectors may signify progress more accurately than unlimited growth provides a stark contrast to the current reliance on market statistics that confuses quantitative expansion with qualitative improvements in well being. From a full cost accounting perspective, it is highly questionable whether growth in crime, lawsuits, pollution, sickness, war, divorce, gambling, road accidents, drug use, overeating, stress, and natural resource depletion enhances social welfare. Building on social and environmental liabilities in the name of growth will likely produce an accumulation of long-term economic costs that overwhelm apparent short-term gains and undermine genuine prosperity.

It is the hope of the authors that this case study of the costs of crime will encourage the adoption of a more comprehensive index of progress that integrates economic, social and environmental realities. It is also our conviction that Nova Scotia is well placed to take the lead in this important development and thereby to help create the accounting basis for the new economy of the 21st century.

FOOTNOTES

1. The figures are derived by dividing the number of reported criminal code incidents by the population. This does not mean that one in 12 people is a victim of reported crime, since some individuals are victimized more than once in a year. The authors wish to thank John Turner, Chief, Policing Services Program, Canadian Centre for Justice Statistics, for his assistance in clarifying this issue (personal communication, 6 April, 1999). Risk is also not equally distributed in the population, with young males (18-29) most at risk, and females over 65 least at risk.

2. Average victim losses per crime category are derived from victim surveys, and therefore include both reported and unreported crimes. The same average loss per crime is applied to both reported and unreported crimes in this study, because separate estimates are not available. Because reported crimes are likely to be more serious, the reported crime victim losses are therefore likely to be underestimated and the unreported losses to be overestimated. As an aggregate, however, the two categories correspond to the victim survey results.

[**Authors' note**: all footnotes, references, sources, and calculation methodologies are cited in the full GPI report (223 pages), *Cost of Crime in Nova Scotia*, which can be obtained through the GPI website at: www.gpiatlantic.org].

GPI: ALBERTA'S SUSTAINABILITY TRENDS

Mark Anielski
Director, Green Economics
Pembina Institute for Appropriate Development
Edmonton, Alberta

WHAT IS THE GPI ACCOUNTING PROJECT?

The GPI (Genuine Progress Indicators) accounting project is a pioneering research effort to develop a new system for measuring the total well-being and sustainability of nations or states. This project, led by the Pembina Institute for Appropriate Development with research funding from Western Economic Diversification, selected Alberta as the first region in the world to construct a full set of GPI accounts using the new GPI System of Well-being Accounting architecture. The development of this new system is presented as an alternative to the current measures of economic progress like the GDP (Gross Domestic Product). The Alberta GPI project addresses these long-standing concerns by explicitly measuring the quantity and quality of all living capital or real wealth. Real stewardship is about carefully managing the wealth of our households and nature, as well as our money.

In the Spring 2000 federal budget, Finance Minister Paul Martin committed $9 million over three years to research and design a national set of environmental and sustainable development indicators to guide decision making. In his budget speech, Mr. Martin noted:

> In the years ahead, these environmental indicators could well have a greater impact on public policy than any other single measure we might introduce.

The GPI sustainable well-being accounting system is currently being considered along with several other alternative approaches for measuring and monitoring sustainability for Canada.

MEASURING GENUINE PROGRESS

The GDP makes no distinction between expenditures that contribute to genuine well-being and those that many might view as regrettable costs associated with environmental or social degradation. The GDP and the UN System of National Accounts in fact violate basic financial accounting principles by treating the liquidation of assets, such as oil and gas, coal and timber, as income rather than as a reduction in the inventory of natural capital.

The GPI pilot for Alberta is a significant step towards providing an alternative to an outmoded system of accounting for economic well-being. The GPI accounts for Alberta show how the province is doing in relation to its sustainable development objectives -- development that embraces social and environmental objectives as well as economic ones. As a starting point, this requires an adjustment in our perspective-how we define and measure wealth, equality and progress -- and a return to the origins of the words "economy" and "wealth.

WHAT IS GPI ACCOUNTING?

The GPI accounting system is built on the traditional application of common bookkeeping systems, including ledgers, a balance sheet and a net sustainable income statement that can be used to prepare a sustainability report to citizens. The GPI accounts measure progress and changes in the condition of all living and built assets, similar to the way in which a business measures its financial health. The main features include:

• **GPI Balance Sheet**. The GPI Balance Sheet is a set of measures or indicators that describe the many facets (physical, qualitative, monetary) of the state of well-being of individuals, communities and the environment over a specified period of time. The GPI balance sheet is similar to a traditional accounting framework in that it shows assets, liabilities and shareholder (citizen) equity of all capital or wealth.

• **GPI Net Sustainable Income Statement**. This is a national or provincial income statement that differs fundamentally from the GDP in that it subtracts from our gross output (i.e., GDP) the human, social, ecological and natural resource costs that were incurred to generate that income. It also recognizes the positive contributions of unpaid work, such as volunteering, childcare and housework that lie outside the market yet contribute to well-being. Finally, it recognizes that not all expenditures in the economy represent positive contributions to our well-being; some things like automobile crashes and suicide should be treated as costs, not revenues as they are in current national income accounts and GDP.

The GPI accounts for Alberta consist of an integrated set of 51 indicators of well-being based on raw data drawn from various statistical sources including Statistics Canada, the Alberta Government and other sources (see Appendix A). The Genuine Progress Indicators (see Table 1) track the changes in the condition of all capital for roughly 40 years, from 1961 to 1999. In constructing the GPI accounting system we reviewed a number of the best sustainability, quality of life and performance indicator frameworks available, including the Alberta Government's *Measuring Up* performance reporting system, the United Nations Human Development Index, the World Bank's Total Wealth accounts and many others.

This benchmarking exercise enabled us to integrate the best features of several models, resulting in the GPI System of Sustainable Well-being Accounts for Alberta. Because we attempted to construct the accounts and indicators to align with the quality of life values most important to Albertans and Canadians, we believe the GPI accounts will inform citizens about the condition of many of the values they hold most dear. Moreover, the accounts are flexible and transparent, allowing for customization as values change.

The GPI System of Sustainable Well-being Accounts, which includes

Table 1: The Alberta GPI Indicators for Economic, Personal-Societal and Environmental Well-being

ECONOMIC	PERSONAL-SOCIETAL	ENVIRONMENTAL
• Economic growth	• Poverty	• Oil and gas reserve life
• Economic diversity	• Income distribution	• Oilsands reserve life
• Trade	• Unemployment	• Energy use intensity
• Disposable income	• Underemployment	• Agricultural sustainability
• Weekly wage rate	• Paid work time	• Timber sustainability
• Personal expenditures	• Household work	• Forest fragmentation
• Transportation expenditures	• Parenting and eldercare	. Parks and wilderness
• Taxes	• Free time	• Fish and wildlife
• Savings rate	• Volunteerism	• Wetlands
• Household debt	• Commuting time	• Peatlands
• Public infrastructure	• Life expectancy	• Water quality
• Household infrastructure	• Premature mortality	• Air quality-related emissions
	• Infant mortality	• Greenhouse gas emissions
	• Obesity	• Carbon budget deficit
	• Suicide	• Hazardous waste
	• Drug use (youth)	• Landfill waste
	• Auto crashes	• Ecological footprint
	• Divorce (family breakdown)	
	• Crime	
	• Problem gambling	
	• Voter participation	
	• Educational attainment	

both physical and monetary measures of well-being, are structured along the following capital themes:

- **Time-use accounts**: measures of how individuals and households allocate their time for paid work, parenting, eldercare, commuting, housework, volunteerism and free time.
- **Social capital accounts**: measures of the condition of households and communities, including measures of poverty, inequality, family breakdown, crime, democracy and social cohesion.
- **Human health and wellness accounts**: measures of the condition of our health and wellness, including life expectancy, premature mortality, suicide, obesity, and lifestyles.
- **Natural resource and environment accounts**: measures of the condition of natural capital, natural ecosystems, and the environment, including ecological footprints, forests, agriculture, peatland, wetlands, non-renewable energy, energy efficiency, fish, wildlife, parks and wilderness, air quality, water quality, carbon budgets, hazardous waste, and landfill waste.
- **Economic accounts**: measures of traditional financial and built capital conditions including the GDP, trade, disposable income, weekly wages, consumption expenditures, taxes, savings, debt, and public and private infrastructure service values.

The time-use, social capital and human health and wellness accounts were clustered into a personal-societal well-being account from which a composite GPI societal well-being index could be derived. Natural resource and environmental accounts were consolidated to derive a GPI environmental well-being index, and the economic accounts were used to derive a GPI economic well-being index. See Table 1 for the indicators in each of the three categories.

The aggregation of GPI indicators of economic, social, human health and environmental sustainable well-being into composite indices is similar to the Dow Jones Industrial Average Index or the United Nations' Human Development Index. Indicators were aggregated using an equal weighting formula for the economy, society and environment indicators whose indices could then be compared directly with the GDP and other monetary measures of economic progress, such as stock market indices. Individual Genuine Progress Indicators can also be compared directly with trends in the GDP, which may provide important visual and statistical correlations between economic growth and changes in the conditions of personal well-being, societal and environmental conditions.

The GPI accounts also include a revised national or provincial net sustainable income statement that accounts for the full monetary costs and benefits, which are currently treated as additions to economic growth (i.e. GDP), or not included as either benefits or regrettable costs. The GPI net sustainable income line starts by adjusting the GDP[1] for changes in income inequality, then adding estimates of the value of unpaid work. Next, various social and environmental costs, seen as either regrettable expenditures or depreciation costs of living capital, are deducted from the GDP. This includes the depreciation costs of depleting natural resource stocks and degrading the environment. The resulting GPI income statement is a common-sense measure of the net beneficial output of a society.

THE ALBERTA GPI RESULTS

The Alberta GPI accounts tell a different story from the more familiar one we hear about a booming economy, government surpluses, and other Alberta advantages. By combining all 51 Genuine Progress Indicators, we derived a composite index -- the GPI Well-being Index.

Figure 1 compares Alberta's GDP per capita as an index with the composite GPI index of 51 indicators. From 1961 to 1999, Alberta's GDP (in constant 1998 dollars) increased by over 400 percent, or 4.4 percent per annum, while the Alberta GPI Well-being Index declined at an annual rate of 0.5 percent per year. The GPI Index was highest in the 1960s then declined to reach a plateau in the 1990s despite continued economic growth. Our study indicates that the best GPI Index was recorded in 1961 and the lowest in 1998. In the 1990s, the GDP per capita grew at an annual rate of 2.4 percent while the GPI per capita was virtually stagnant, growing a mere 0.43 percent per year, on average.

We can also present an integrated portrait of sustainability and well-being by showing the 51 Genuine Progress Indicators in a Sustainable Well-Being Circle Index (Figure 2). The GPI Sustainable Well-being Circle Index for 1999 could be compared to a balance sheet for a company where the condition of each type of living and produced capital is reported as an index score relative to historical conditions. The figure shows the condition of all capital in Alberta in 1999, with each indicator having a score. The scores were derived by converting the original raw data for each indicator to an index using a scale from 0 to 100, with 100 set as the best condition of the indicator during the time period for the study; that is, 1961 to 1999. Deviations from that year were measured as movement toward zero. In Figure 2, the higher the score, the closer its point is to the outside edge of the circle. For example, in the years between 1961 and 1999, GDP per capita was highest in 1999; thus the score for economic growth in that year was 100, and this point is at

Figure 1: The Alberta GPI Well-being Index versus Alberta GDP Index, 1961 to 1999

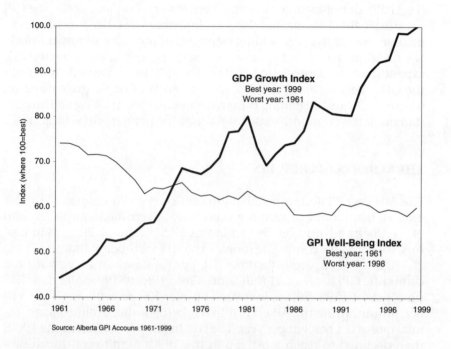

Source: Alberta GPI Accouns 1961-1999

the outside edge of the circle. In contrast, suicide rates were high in 1999 compared with 1964, which had the lowest rate and was thus assigned the "best" or "target" score of 100. Therefore, relative to the best year in the study, the 1999 score for this indicator was lower and its point on the circle is closer to the centre.

The GPI Circle Index is a powerful visual image of the overall condition of economy, society and environment that could be applied at the local, provincial or national level. It provides an alternative to trend lines and shows clearly the contrast between the condition of the factors that contribute to quality of life. For example, health indicators such as life expectancy, premature mortality and infant mortality are in good condition; that is, their scores are close to 100 points. Many social and environmental indicators, on the other hand, were in an unhealthy condition in 1999 compared with the previous 40 years. While individual indexed Genuine Progress Indicators shown on the GPI Circle Index cannot be compared directly with each other (for example, timber sustainability cannot be compared with agricultural sustainability), they do show relative conditions for any point in time. Moreover, each indicator can be shown as a trend in condition using either indexed

Figure 2: The Alberta GPI Sustainable Well-being Circle Index for 1999

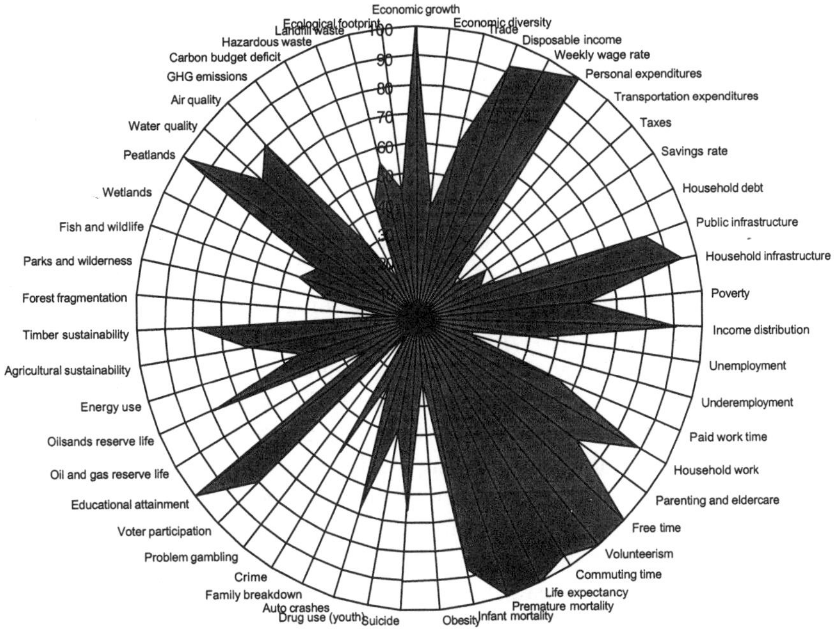

data or raw data.

The results of the GPI accounts can be presented in a number of different ways, including in the form of a "Sustainable Well-being Condition Report Card". The report card shows the current condition of well-being for each indicator in 1999, the best and worst performing year for each index, and the long-term (40-year) trend in the indicator. The highest composite GPI Index occurred in 1961, with 74.0 points out of a possible 100.0, while the lowest index of 58.4 was recorded in 1998. However, in 1961, only 42 indicators were available, as opposed to 51 for 1998. The GPI Sustainability Circle for 1961 is thus more "full" than the one for 1998. We can also compare the top performing indicators with the lowest.

A GPI NET SUSTAINABLE INCOME STATEMENT

The Alberta GPI accounts contain a full benefit-cost assessment of economic growth by accounting for the costs or benefits associated with several components of living and produced capital. The original U.S. GPI (Cobb et al., 1995) and, more recently, the Australian GPI (Hamilton and Denniss, 2000) both use a full cost approach to measuring sustainable economic welfare. Such analysis allows decision makers to identify the costs (or expenditures) of, for example, crime, auto crashes, oil and gas depreciation, climate change, and unsustainable agricultural or forestry practices that either count as contributions to GDP or are ignored as potential regrettable costs of economic growth. Benefits such as the value of unpaid housework, parenting and volunteer time can also be estimated then added to or compared with the GDP.

The notion of sustainable income is the bottom line being estimated in the Alberta GPI net sustainable income statement. British economist John Hicks used the term "Hicksian income" to mean the maximum amount that a person or a nation could consume over some period of time and still be as well off at the end of the period as at the beginning (Hicks, 1946).[2] Thus income is synonymous with maximum sustainable consumption; that is, sustaining consumption over a given period by maintaining the productive potential of all capital stocks that generate the flow of goods and services needed for consumption.

Sustainable economic well-being can be estimated by adjusting gross output (GDP) for unaccounted benefits and for social, human and natural capital depreciation costs. This gives us, in effect, a full benefit-cost statement of genuine progress for the nation or province. We thus explicitly account for the sustainability of consumption by incorporating monetary values of capital stocks and their consumption. The GPI income statement adjusts for the shortcomings of the GDP and the System of National Accounts.

Even if adjustments to the GDP are not made using these human, social and natural capital cost and benefit estimates, simply accounting for their magnitude is an important exercise. It allows us to distinguish between those contributions (expenditures) to economic growth that are genuine improvements in well-being of society and those that are regrettable detractors.

Starting with the GDP or with personal consumption expenditures (a component of GDP), an adjusted GPI income statement that measures net sustainable income can be derived (see Appendix B). Like the U.S. and Australian GPI estimates, the Alberta GPI starts by adjusting personal consumption expenditures for changes in income inequality, assuming that higher inequality between income groups detracts from the well-being and social cohesion of a society. This new income (or expenditure) statement then identifies the magnitude of real costs or expenditures that contribute to a rising GDP but might otherwise be identified as regrettable costs and detractions from genuine progress. These could include, for example, the costs of crime, family breakdown, problem gambling, and the depletion of finite stocks of non-renewable energy resources. Making such adjustments to GDP will always be controversial since some value judgment is needed about which expenditures should be treated as regrettable (i.e. a form of capital depreciation that requires a negative adjustment to the GDP), and which should be viewed as genuine contributions to the money measure of progress.

We offer this preliminary GPI net sustainable income statement as the basis for future development of annual full cost-benefit reporting of economic growth. In future, policy analysts and citizens will be better informed about the key contributors to economic growth by knowing the magnitude of either the dollar value of expenditures or the value of the unaccounted benefits. Adjusting the GDP for the value of unpaid work and for societal, human, and environmental capital costs provides a revised provincial income statement. The result is a more complete picture of Alberta's sustainable economic performance measured in money terms.

Figure 3: Alberta GDP per capita versus GPI net sustainable income*
per capita, 1961 to 1999 (1998$)

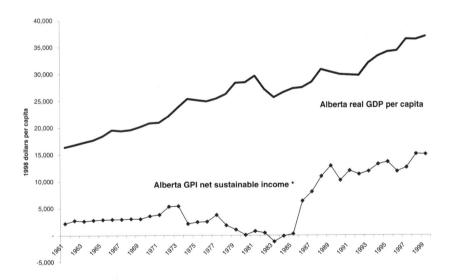

* The GPI net sustainable income is a measure of net economic welfare based on the original ISEW/GPI model of Cobb and Daly (1989) which takes personal consumption expenditures and then adjusts for income inequality, the value of unpaid work, value of services (and depreciation) from public/private infrastructure, social and human capital costs (depreciation), natural capital depreciation and environmental degradation costs.

With these adjustments, the Alberta GPI net sustainable income statement attempts to account for the full monetary value of benefits and costs associated with consuming living and produced capital. This is consistent with previous GPI studies in the U.S. and Australia, with some of our own modifications. The monetary expression of the GPI can then be compared with Alberta's GDP (Figure 3).

When we add the benefits of unpaid work, deduct various social and environmental costs (including depreciation costs of depleting oil and gas reserves), and adjust for the cost of servicing household debt, the trend in sustainable income (i.e. the monetary-based GPI) looks much different from the trend in GDP. From 1961 to 1973, the monetary-based GPI rose only slightly while the GDP showed considerable growth. From 1973 to 1983, the monetary-based GPI declined even as the GDP continued to rise. From 1986 to 1990, the GPI rose sharply, but remained relatively constant throughout the 1990s while the GDP continued to increase.

Estimating the monetary expressions of the GPI is of interest and is important to public policy and to budget decision making. However, it is more challenging than creating composite GPI indices from raw physical data of capital conditions. Methods for estimating these money values can be complicated and controversial. Tracking money flows through an economy for such things as auto crashes or crime will require careful study and analysis. Some may view putting money values on social, human and natural capital as repugnant. Some correctly identify both the methodological difficulties in accurately estimating costs and the problems associated with double counting and mixing stock and flow value estimates. Other concerns relate to whether non-market values should be introduced in the equations. Notwithstanding, we have drawn upon the best available academic work, methods and other research to estimate the full costs and benefits associated with sustainable economic well-being in Alberta. We recognize that this particular component of GPI accounting represents a significant work-in-progress that should be subjected to considerable debate and forensic analysis.

CONSTRUCTING THE GPI NET SUSTAINABLE INCOME STATEMENT

Drawing from Canadian research, from the U.S. and Australian GPI work, and from the work of Dr. Ron Colman at GPI Atlantic, we have constructed an Alberta GPI net sustainable income statement. Our methodology includes several important modifications to the original U.S. GPI and ISEW (Index for Sustainable Economic Welfare) models developed by others (Cobb and Cobb, 1994; Daly and Cobb, 1989; Cobb et al., 1995; Anielski and Rowe, 1999a and b), as well as the new Australian GPI (Hamilton and Denniss, 2000) by the Australia Institute.

First, we measure the depreciation of natural capital based on the estimated value (depreciation costs) of drawing down (finite oil and gas stocks and on the cost of unsustainable forestry and agricultural practices. Second, we include estimates of the liability costs of greenhouse gas emissions to global climate change, plus the liability costs of the cumulative impact of toxic waste production and storage (net of disposal), and the potential cost (i.e. risk) to the environment from cumulative municipal landfill waste. Third, we estimate the costs of debt servicing by households as a regrettable cost to well-being; individuals and households experience financial stress as a result of debt and we view this as regrettable and a cost to sustainable well-being.

To understand economic systems and sustainability, one must first understand money and how it is created (Daly and Cobb, 1994; Anielski, 2000). Virtually all money in our current debt-interest-based system is created in the form of debt with little or no relationship to living capital management. Thus, the GPI accounting system treats interest payments on cumulative debt of households as a regrettable cost to genuine well-being and also as a hindrance to sustainability objectives. No other GPI accounting research has considered the nature of money creation and household debt in this manner, although both the U.S. and Australian GPI work regard net foreign borrowing as a cost to national well-being. Discussions of sustainability and well-being must include an analysis of the role of money creation in modern economies and its relationship to economic growth (Daly and Cobb, 1994). The Alberta GPI net sustainable income statement considers sustainable income, with household debt servicing costs both included and excluded (as seen previously in Figure 3).

The result is a different perspective on economic progress than that traditionally measured by the System of National Accounts and the GDP. The Alberta GPI Income Statement shows the full benefits and costs associated with our management of living and produced capital, expressed in money terms. It explicitly corrects for the shortcomings of the System of National Accounts and the GDP in measuring total well-being by assessing the full benefits and costs of human, social, natural and built capital consumption. Thus, the GPI income statement provides a more comprehensive look at the real costs of economic progress as well as the unaccounted benefits such as unpaid work.

While the GDP is not an effective measure of economic well-being it does provide a useful measure of the economic transactions of the economy. Indeed, although it has grown to be used for much more than that, the GDP as it was originally intended is still useful.

Appendix B shows the real costs and benefits of the consumption of all capital and provides a new bottom line of genuine progress. The GPI income statement begins with gross personal consumption expenditures by households, because it is the economic well-being of the households of the nation with which we are concerned, including the unaccounted benefits and social and environmental costs that affect welfare. We then adjust consumption expenditures by the change in income distribution, using an index derived from the Gini coefficient for after-tax income distribution.[3] In 1999, there is no adjustment to consumption expenditures since income was most evenly distributed in that year compared with the other years in the time series.

The next step is to add the estimated monetary value of unpaid work, the value of services (less depreciation) of public and private infrastructure, and the value of net capital formation (growth in capital stock per worker). For example, in 1999, the value of unpaid work was estimated at $38.8 billion (1998 dollars) or 35.4 percent of Alberta's GDP ($109.7 billion). We also include an estimate of the value of public expenditures that represent genuine investments in improved economic well-being of the nation or province and exclude so-called defensive expenditures that were made to mitigate regrettable damage to human, social and natural capital.

We then subtract estimated social costs of unemployment, underemployment, auto crashes, commuting, crime, family breakdown, suicide and problem gambling. The social costs of human and social capital erosion, which is treated as a deduction against gross output (GDP), are estimated at $13.4 billion (1998 dollars), or 12.3 percent of GDP.

We also deduct several environmental costs to account for the depletion of natural capital (oil, gas, unsustainable timber resource use, unsustainable agricultural practices) as well as the costs of environmental pollution and degradation (greenhouse gas emissions, air pollution, loss of wetlands, toxic waste liability costs, and estimates of municipal landfill liabilities). The estimated cost of depleting oil and gas finite reserves (a reduction of inventory) is $10.6 billion (1998 dollars) or 9.7 percent of GDP; this would be a deduction in our GPI income statement. As indicated above, total environmental costs of pollution, environmental liabilities and depletion of natural capital stocks (both non-renewable and renewable resources) are estimated at $26.4 billion (1998 dollars) or 24.0 percent of GDP; thus we would adjust Alberta's provincial income accounts (GDP) downward by these estimated costs.

The resulting GPI net sustainable income estimate for 1999 is estimated at roughly $37.0 billion (net of household debt servicing costs) or $43.4 billion (without household debt servicing costs), compared with $52.8 billion in personal consumption expenditures (the starting point in the GPI net sustainable income statement) and $109.7 billion in GDP.

SO WHAT? POLICY TOOLS FOR SUSTAINABLE MANAGEMENT

The GPI accounts tell us whether Alberta is better off or worse off-not just in traditional economic terms like changes in the GDP, but also in terms of how we use our time; the condition of our stocks of natural resources; and the health of individuals, households, communities and the environment. Understanding these conditions is critical to Alberta's future. The Alberta GPI Accounts (1961-1999) suggest that while more money has changed hands, the price in this growth in GDP has been an erosion in the condition of many forms of living capital.

These accounts can be used to develop annual "state of sustainability trends" reports to citizens about the changing conditions that affect their lives. With better information, people would be empowered to participate more fully in the democratic process of shaping their future. The strength of the GPI accounts is their open architecture. The accounts are a "work-in-progress" and are intended to be transparent and flexible to accommodate the changing values of citizens.

GPI accounts are a powerful tool for public policy development, strategic planning and budgeting. They allow decision makers to compare many different measures of sustainability and well-being using a common measuring system. As we did in this analysis, raw data can be indexed in relation to benchmarks of best-case scenarios for a province or community. Provincial or community data can also be examined in relation to targets of other jurisdictions. Both approaches are valuable and meaningful ways for setting public policy objectives. The flexibility of GPI accounting allows for comparison against oneself, as well as assessment of progress over time or against other jurisdictions or organizations.

Because GPI accounts give such a comprehensive perspective on long-term trends in sustainable well-being, they are ideal for measuring sustainable development. They can be used in any organization for measuring "triple bottom lines" of economic, social and environmental performance. GPI accounts can be used for non-partisan reporting to citizens on their overall "state of well-being" in accordance with their quality of life values. It is the ideal 21st century navigational tool for charting a sustainable future -- one in which stewardship of real wealth takes priority over making money.

CHARTING A SUSTAINABLE FUTURE

The GPI Alberta project raises several fundamental questions about how to chart a sustainable future for Alberta and other jurisdictions. How are we doing as stewards of the households and of the natural environment of Alberta? A sustainable society could be defined as one in which all four forms of capita -- human, social, natural and produced -- are managed so they are in equilibrium; that is, they are stable at sufficient levels over time. The focus would thus be to maintain the stock, flow and quality of all capital. The challenge is to understand and define the equilibrium or threshold for each form of capital, on an individual as well as a collective basis. At the very least, one principle would be to ensure that the integrity of each form of capital is maintained in terms of its quality and the services it generates. This is where GPI accounts could provide guidance as a measure of the health and integrity of each form of capital and as a tool for designing a sustainable future.

Alberta's prosperity over the past 40 years or so has relied heavily on the development and export of natural capital. This continues even now with oil, gas, forest products and agricultural product exports. A sustainable future might consider several important questions. How much of our natural capital do we need or want to export beyond Albertans' or Canadians' basic needs for living? Are we currently getting maximum value or service from using natural capital? Could we improve the eco-efficiency of resource and energy use from natural capital? Should we be using today's oil and gas revenues to invest in sustainable, renewable energy capacity at the household, business or industrial level? What are the thresholds or limits to how much natural capital can be developed in our industrial complex without negatively affecting the integrity of nature or ecosystems to sustain a continuing flow of natural resources and environmental services? Is there such a thing as "enough"? Can production from agriculture, forests, and energy resources be pushed further without compromising long-term sustainability and ecological integrity? These questions must be addressed.

On the level of personal lifestyles, how could Albertans change their consumption habits to reduce their ecological footprint? If Albertan consumption habits were to be the world norm, the total footprint of all human activity would be more than five times the Earth's carrying capacity. Can we reduce our energy and food footprint to live within the carrying capacity of Alberta's natural environment? This would require some serious choices about what constitutes a level of sustainable self-sufficiency in food, clothing, homes, energy and other materials that are consumed. Do we have a responsibility to other global citizens with whom we share the Earth's carrying capacity to ensure our lifestyle does not jeopardize or preclude others from enjoying benefits of the Earth?

When it comes to human and social capital, sustainability might be defined in terms of how we spend our time -- do we have a healthy balance of work time, family time and free time? Are we enjoying the time "dividends" of a more productive and efficient society and economy? Or are we working harder and feeling more stressed than ever, while eroding the time we have to spend with our families and friends? While we may be living longer, various stresses seem to be showing up in the form of disease, injuries, suicides and family breakdown. Is the drive for greater economic prosperity coming at personal and social cost? Are we as a society investing enough in our intellectual capital to build a knowledge legacy? Do we have an effective ratio of teachers to students in primary school? Are we graduating university and college students with unreasonable levels of financial debt? Why aren't all Albertans earning a fair living wage? Are food banks really necessary? Are we building a fair and just society by investing in alternative methods of resolving conflict and healing the hurt from crime? Are companies operating in a socially and environmentally responsible way? These are some of the important human and social sustainability issues.

In terms of sustaining produced or manufactured capital, the question of maintaining the integrity and services of household, business and public infrastructure is fundamental. Are we investing enough in the maintenance and refurbishment of our infrastructure to ensure that the services continue now and for future generations? Or have we let some of our infrastructure erode so that future costs will be that much higher?

If we agree that these are some of the key issues concerning well-being, then the GPI accounts can guide us as we seek to chart a sustainable future. If we are serious about pursuing sustainable well-being then we must develop clear visions, policies, goals and performance targets. This will mean tackling many tough questions about our consumer lifestyle, trade policy, economic policies, social policies, and our approach to stewardship of nature. Charting a sustainable future is an exciting task that will require the collective energy and spirit of all Canadians.

FOOTNOTES

1. Specifically, the personal consumption expenditure component of the GDP is adjusted, as was done in the U.S. GPI and the Australian GPI.
2. Hicks also wrote that "the practical purpose of income is to serve as a guide for prudent conduct" (Hicks, 1946: 172), a comment that has particular relevance for today's concern with ecological sustainability (Hamilton and Denniss, 2000).
3. The Gini coefficient is a measure of income inequality among income groups, expressed as a ratio from 0 (no income inequality) to 1.00 (maximum income inequality). It measures the dispersion within a group of values (usually income), calculated as the average difference between

every pair of values divided by two times the average of the sample. The larger the coefficient, the greater the dispersion.

REFERENCES

Anielski, M. and J.Rowe. 1999a. *The Genuine Progress Indicator – 1998 Update*. Redefining Progress. San Francisco. http://www.rprogress.org/pubs/pdf/gpi1998_data.pdf

Anielski. M and J. Rowe. 1999b. *The US Genuine Progress Indicator: Summary Report*. Redefining Progress. San Francisco. (www.rprogress.org)

Cobb, C. and J. Cobb. 1994. *The Green National Product: A Proposed Index of Sustainable Economic Welfare* (University of Americas Press: Maryland).

Cobb, C., T. Halstead and J. Rowe. 1995. *The Genuine Progress Indicator: Summary of Data and Methodology*, Redefining Progress. San Francisco.

Daly, H. and J. B. Cobb. 1994. *For the Common Good: redirecting the economy toward community, the environment, and a sustainable future*, 2nd edition. Beacon Press, Boston.

Hamilton, C. and R. Denniss. 2000. *Tracking Well-being in Australia, The Genuine Progress Indicator 2000*. The Australia Institute. Number 35. December 2000.

Hicks, J.R. 1946. *Value and Capital*, 2nd ed., Oxford University Press. Oxford

APPENDIX A: THE ALBERTA RAW GPI DATA

GPI INDICATOR	Description of Indicator	1960	1970	1980	1990	1999
Economic growth	GDP at market prices, expenditure based (1998$ per capita)	$18,371	$24,333	$28,196	$33,315	$37,005
Economic diversity	Economic Diversification Index based on Hachman Index (closer to 1.00 means closer to national average)	*	0.28	0.137	0.275	0.228
Trade	Trade balance (exports less imports) per capita (1998$)	$800	$1,801	$2,950	$2,963	$3,219
Disposable income	Personal disposable income per capita (1998$)	$10,386	$14,977	$20,361	$19,762	$20,147
Weekly wage rate	Weekly wage rate (1998$)	$438.07	$593.95	$699.57	$694.10	$718.15
Personal expenditures	Alberta personal consumption expenditures per capita (constant 1998$)	$9,736	$13,253	$16,650	$17,112	$18,389
Transportation expenditures	Direct expenditure per capita on transportation in Alberta, including public transit (1998$)	$204	$343	$422	$485	$530
Taxes	Taxes on persons per capita (1998$)	$1,286	$2,481	$3,533	$4,099	$5,172
Savings rate	Savings rate as percentage of after-tax disposable income	4.40%	6.60%	12.60%	6.80%	4.70%
Household debt	Household debt per capita (1998$)	$6,891	$11,566	$14,517	$18,975	$21,172
Public infrastructure	Value of services from public infrastructure, $ per capita (1998$)	$503	$543	$659	$676	$612
Household infrastructure	Value of services from household infrastructure, $ per capita (1998$)	$964	$1,432	$1,737	$1,782	$1,866
Poverty	Percentage of all persons living below LICO (poverty line)	11.90%	13.40%	14.90%	16.40%	15.50%
Income distribution	Gini Coefficient (after-tax-and-transfer income, all families)	0.41	0.367	0.324	0.304	0.316
Unemployment	Unemployment rate in Alberta over the study period	2.70%	4.70%	8.20%	7.60%	5.70%
Underemployment	Underemployment rate (underemployed as a percentage of those employed)	0.60%	1.00%	2.60%	3.90%	3.50%
Paid work time	Hours of paid work per person in the labour force per year	2,403	1,991	1,683	1,475	1,463
Household work	Household work hours per person per year	985	983	938	1,004	1,032
Parenting and eldercare	Parenting and eldercare hours per person per year	197	178	138	137	137

GPI INDICATOR	Description of Indicator	1960	1970	1980	1990	1999
Free time	Leisure hours per person per day	*	5	5.2	5.5	5.8
Volunteerism	Volunteerism hours per person	69.3	69.2	63.4	68	75.4
Commuting time	Average minutes per day per worker (includes both automobile and transit users)	24.25	25.74	28.39	27.13	25.04
Life expectancy	Estimated blended life expectancy (years) for men (50%) and females (50%)	72.7	74.4	76.5	78.6	79.3
Premature mortality	Person years of life lost per 100,000 population from all causes of death	5,385	5,469	4,411	3,628	3,373
Infant mortality	Infant mortality (deaths per 1,000 live births)	*	14.7	9.1	6.5	5.6
Obesity	Percentage of adults (15 years or older) with Body Mass Index (BMI) greater than 27	*	*	17.40%	27.70%	32.90%
Suicide	Suicide rate for both sexes per 100,000 population	11.5	15.5	16.3	16.2	14.4
Drug use (youth)	Youth drug use (% of youth)	*	0.08%	0.10%	0.11%	0.15%
Auto crashes	Total auto crashes per Alberta adult (15+ years)	375	475	571	446	408
Family breakdown	Divorce rate (percent of marriages that end in divorce)	13.50%	29.10%	41.20%	43.70%	40.90%
Crime	Crime incidents per 100,000 people in Alberta	3,799	6,353	7,386	6,889	5,624
Problem gambling	Estimated cost of problem gambling per capita (1998$ per capita)	$42.08	$55.74	$74.63	$407.35	$731.11
Voter participation	Composite voter participation rate (federal provincial municipal), % of eligible voters	56.60%	55.60%	49.80%	50.90%	48.60%
Educational attainment	Percentage of population (15 years and over) with some postsecondary education or university degree	12.10%	31.20%	43.70%	50.50%	53.80%
Oil and gas reserve life	Average reserve life for conventional crude oil and natural gas, excludes oilsands	39.59	23.32	19.04	11.39	8.46
Oilsands reserve life	Average reserve life for oilsands	*	*	40.2	27.4	23.1
Energy Use	Total energy demand GJ per capita	367	491	592	720	754
Agricultural sustainability	Composite agriculture index, includes summerfallow, soil organic carbon, pesticide use, salinity, yield	49.2	48.7	49.8	58	61.5

GPI INDICATOR	Description of Indicator	1960	1970	1980	1990	1999
Timber sustainability	Timber Sustainability Index, the ratio of annual increment (growth) divided by total harvest, energy and agriculture depletions	4.08	3.63	1.68	1.32	0.87
Forest fragmentation	Percentage of Alberta's forests (Boreal and Foothill) that remain unfragmented based on World Resources Institute report	92.50%	80.40%	54.50%	24.00%	10.90%
Parks and wilderness	Area protected, sq km	*	55,400	56,350	58,070	63,570
Fish and wildlife	Average of caribou (benchmark year = 100), bears (target of 2500 bears in province) and sport and commercial fisheries (benchmark year = 100)	58.15	53.61	63.11	51.64	44.77
Wetlands	Wetlands area remaining in square kilometres	17,253	16,309	15,315	14,362	14,051
Peatlands	Peatlands, area change per annum (million ha)	0.21%	0.21%	0.21%	0.21%	0.21%
Water quality	Average water quality Index (100 = best)	*	50.5	48.67	58.91	72.73
Air quality	Average Air Quality Index, includes SO2, CO2, VOC, NOx	63.67	65.75	74.99	81.76	80.34
Greenhouse gas emissions	Total greenhouse gas emissions (tonnes) per capita	24.25	35.57	53.81	68.22	68.7
Carbon budget deficit	Annual greenhouse gas emissions as a percentage of sequestration capacity	57%	105%	205%	313%	338%
Hazardous waste	Tonnes of hazardous waste produced per annum	*	*	*	28,806	46,850
Landfill waste	Per capita disposal rate, tonnes per person per year	*	*	1.02	0.85	0.75
Ecological footprint	Total Ecological Footprint (hectares per capita)	7.14	9.49	10.05	10.37	10.74
GDP (gross 1998$ millions)		$26,711	$44,564	$67,281	$91,548	$109,708
GPI net beneficial output (1998$ per capita)		$10,505	$16,507	$19,792	$29,557	$34,234
GDP (1998$ per capita)		$18,371	$24,333	$28,196	$33,315	$37,005

Source: Alberta GPI accounts from various sources including Statistics Canada, Alberta Government and others.

Note: * not available

APPENDIX B: ALBERTA GPI NET SUSTAINABLE INCOME STATEMENT

		million (1998$)	% of GDP
Gross Domestic Product (expenditure-based)		109,708.43	
Personal consumption expenditures		52,838.59	48.2%
Consumption expenditures adjusted for income distribution		47,957.49	43.7%
Non-defensive government expenditures		7,727.89	7.0%
Value of services of consumer durables		5,532.50	5.0%
Value of public infrastructure services		1,660.96	1.5%
Net capital investment		(864.64)	-0.8%
Cost of household and personal debt servicing		(6,433.77)	-5.9%
Value of unpaid time use			
Value of housework	32,907.30		30.0%
Value of parenting and eldercare	3,291.54		3.0%
Value of volunteer work	2,631.30		2.4%
Value of free time	0.06		0.0%
		38,830.19	35.4%
Social Costs			
Cost of consumer durables	(7,998.17)		-7.3%
Cost of unemployment and underemployment	(3,823.98)		-3.5%
Cost of auto crashes	(3,026.43)		-2.8%
Cost of commuting	(4,406.03)		-4.0%
Cost of crime	(1,833.23)		-1.7%
Cost of family breakdown	(147.96)		-0.1
Cost of suicide	(2.43)		0.0%
Cost of gambling	(2,167.50)		-2.0%
		(23,405.73)	-21.3%
Environmental Costs			
Cost of non-renewable resource use	(10,656.30)		-9.7%
Cost of non-timber forest values due to change in productive forest	(23.78)		0.0%
Cost of unsustainable timber resource use (loss in pulp production)	(14.60)		0.0%
Cost of erosion on bare soil on cultivated land (on-site only)	(12.78)		0.0%
Cost of reduction in yields due to salinity on dryland and irrigated cropland	(58.15)		-0.1%
Cost of air pollution	(3,666.00)		-3.3%
Cost of greenhouse gases (damage of climate change)	(4,073.33)		-3.7%
Cost of loss of wetlands	(7,682.01)		-7.0%
Environmental cost of human wastewater pollution	(0.57)		0.0%
Non- market cost of toxic waste liabilities	(4.71)		0.0%/0
Non-market cost of municipal waste landfills	(190.10)		-0.2%
		(26,382.33)	-24.0%
GPI (Net Beneficial Output), with debt servicing costs		36,999.62	
GPI (Net Beneficial Output), without debt servicing costs		43,433.40	
GPI (with debt) per capita		12,480.10	
GDP per capita		37,005.04	

WASTE TO PROFITS: THE CASE OF CONSOLIDATED MINING AND SMELTING LTD.

Peter N. Nemetz
Professor, Strategy and Business Economics
Faculty of Commerce and Business Administration
University of British Columbia

The Consolidated Mining and Smelting Company (renamed Cominco in 1966) was formed in 1906 and four years later bought the Sullivan Mine, the world's largest silver-lead-zinc ore body, located at Kimberley in the Southeast corner of British Columbia. The complex sulphite ore was shipped to the company's newly acquired and redesigned smelter in Trail, B.C., some 160 km to the southwest, in the Columbia River valley. As the lead and zinc concentrates contained from 17-33% sulphur (anon., c.1948), their smelting produced significant quantities of sulphur dioxide as a waste product which was off-gassed from a 409-foot tall stack (Murray, 1972, p. 72). By 1930, these releases had reached a high of 651 tonnes per day of SO_2 (or 325.5 tonnes as sulphur).

The topography of the Trail region presented some unusual challenges and problems:

> The Trail Smelter lies in a deep gorge cut out by the Columbia river. The region is decidedly rugged and the Columbia is flanked on either side by mountains sufficiently high to preclude a diffusion of smoke fumes to east or west, except in cases of gorges formed by creek tributaries (Howes and Miller, 1929, p. 6). [See Figure 1]

> The distance from Trail to the [international] boundary line is about seven miles as the crow flies or about eleven miles, following the course of the river . . . . At Trail and continuing down to the boundary and for a considerable distance below the boundary, mountains rise on either side of the river in slopes of various angles to heights ranging from 3,000 to 4,5000 feet above sea-level, or between 1,500 to 3,000 feet above the river. The width of the valley proper is between one and two miles (Trail Smelter Arbitration Tribunal, 1935, p. 8).

The net result of this topographical configuration was a funneling of SO_2 waste gases down the Columbia River valley into Northeast Washington state. [See Figure 2] In 1926, citizens of the town of Northport in Stevens County, Washington complained that the toxic fumes were de-

Figure 1: Cominco's metallurgical complex on the Columbia River at Trail, B.C.

Figure 2: Map of Columbia River valley near Trail, B.C.

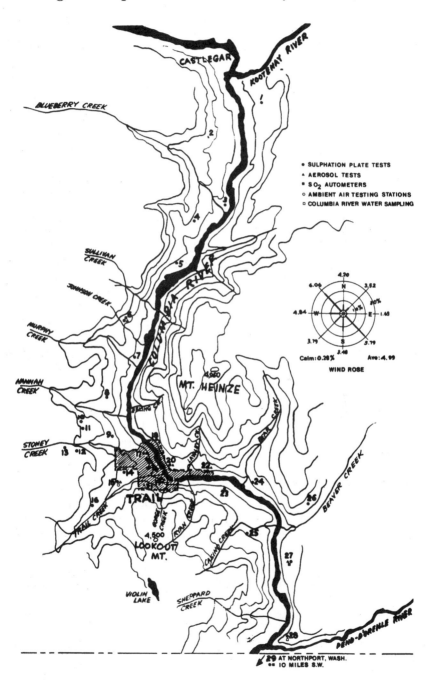

stroying crops, killing their cattle, corroding their barbed wire fences and galvanized roofs and peeling building paint. The U.S. government complained in turn to Canada and both countries agreed to take the case to arbitration under the International Joint Commission, marking the first time that an issue of air pollution came before an international tribunal (Murray, 1972; see also Agent for the Government of Canada, 1936).

The IJC found against the smelter in 1931, recommending that financial compensation of $350,000 be paid and that the company be required to reduce the massive amounts of SO_2 released into the atmosphere (IJC, 1931). The U.S. government rejected the Commission's recommendations as inadequate, and the issue was not finally settled until March 1941 when a special panel (the Trail Smelter Arbirtation Tribunal), established in 1936, issued its "Final Decision." Well before the date of settlement, the Consolidated Mining & Smelting Company had hit upon a answer to the problem and had installed several new industrial processes at their site in Trail. The solution was to extract sulphur from the gaseous emissions and produce sulphuric acid which could then be used to manufacture fertilizer.

On the face of it, being forced to expend large sums of money on the control of waste products, estimated in excess of $20 million (Read, 1963, p. 221), posed a significant financial challenge to the smelting company. Fortuitously, the system to use sulphur dioxide to produce fertilizer addressed a number of critical issues facing the Consolidated Mining & Smelting Company at the time: (1) most importantly, the new control procedures essentially removed a threat to the continued operation of the smelter; (2) it provided a more diversified product base which allowed the company to weather falling metal prices in the Great Depression; and (3) it allowed the company to capitalize on an emerging market for synthetic fertilizers, both nationally and internationally.

The production of fertilizer was largely based on the conversion of SO_2 to H_2SO_4 which was used, in turn, to produce fertilizers such as ammonium sulphate, ammonium phosphate and superphosphate. Figure 3 presents a simplified schematic representation of part of the company's extensive industrial complex as described in the immediate post-WWII period. Not shown here are separate components devoted to the production of nitric acid (and subsequently, ammonium nitrate), a chlor-alkali plant and facilities for iron and steel production.

To quote from an early internal corporate history:

It was recognized early in the game that the Canadian Prairies represented a large potential market for phosphate fertilizers. Whereas in 1930 the Canadian Prairies used negligible quanti-

Figure 3: A Simplified Schematic of Fertilizer Production at Consolidated Mining & Smelting

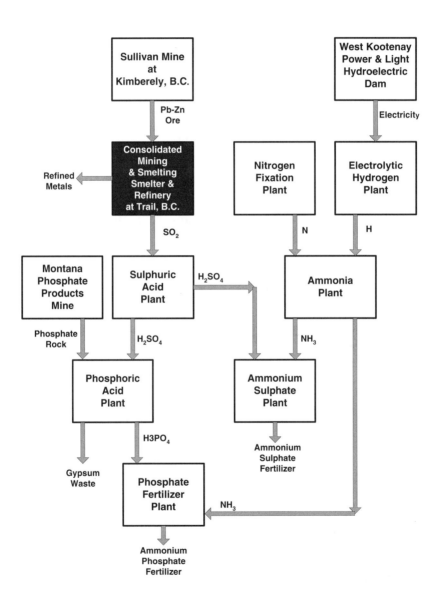

ties of phosphate fertilizers, today [c. 1947] they are using more than 45,000 tons per annum and the demand for these phosphates continually grows.

Following investigation of Canadian sources of phosphate rock, it was found that the best source of rock for our purpose was located in Montana. A sufficient acreage of phosphate rock deposits are now owned and rock is mined by Montana Phosphate Products Limited to supply our requirements for many years to come.

With these two basic materials, acid and phosphate rock, it was decided at that time to round out the picture by the construction of nitrogen fixation plants at Trail. As a result of such developments in 1931, a large electrolytic hydrogen plant, ammonia plant, phosphoric acid and phosphate fertilizer plant, and an ammonium sulphate plant were built at Warfield, in addition to several large sulphuric acid plants at Trail. As considerable power was available from hydroelectric installations of the West Kootenay Power & Light Company on the Kootenay River, the electrolytic hydrogen process was chosen as a source of hydrogen for ammonia. The production of ammonia demands pure hydrogen and pure nitrogen which are combined in a ratio of 3 volumes to 1 volume, under high pressure and high temperature conditions. The nitrogen required is obtained from the liquefaction and fractional distillation of air by the standard liquid air process. The two gases are then mixed and compressed to over l.5 tons per sq. in. and are passed through a complicated cycle of heat exchange, catalytic reaction, and cooling to produce liquid anhydrous ammonia. In the phosphoric acid plant, phosphate rook containing 32% P_2O_5 (but unavailable to the soil in that form) is treated with sulphuric acid to produce phosphoric acid in solution and gypsum or the waste part of the phosphate rook, as a mud. Filtration separates the gypsum from the acid and the acid is then neutralized with ammonia to produce ammonium phosphate which is produced in a dry granular, highly concentrated form which can be drilled into the ground along with wheat seed, at planting time. This form of P_2O_5 is readily available as plant food when put into the ground.

As all markets or soils do not require the very high P_2O_5 present in this form of ammonium phosphate, namely 48% P_2O_5, and as more sulphuric acid was made than was then required for ammonium phosphate production, a sulphate plant was included in the original construction programme which produced, by the neutralization of ammonia by sulphuric acid, the white crystal-line ammonium sulphate product containing 21% nitrogen. This material, a fertilizer of world-wide use, found a ready sale throughout the world but not to any extent in Canada where the major demand was for phosphorus.

In order to make a phosphate product of lower phosphorus and higher nitrogen content than the 11-48-0 material, ammo-nium sulphate can also be introduced into the circuit, so that another product containing 20% P_2O_5 is produced known as ammonium phosphate sulphate. This material in also granular and drillable, and contains 16% nitrogen and 20% P_2O_5, whereas the 48% ammonium phosphate contains only 11% nitrogen. The 16-20-0 ammonium phosphate finds a ready sale through-out the world, particularly in California and the Western States.

In addition to ammonium sulphate, made by neutralizing ammonia with sulphuric acid, and the two types of ammonium phosphate mentioned previously, some single super phosphate was made containing 16% P_2O_5. This was made by the simple reaction of sulphuric acid on phosphate rock, in a den, by batch process. It did not long remain a standard product of the com-pany because of its low plant food content and the Company's decision to produce mainly fertilizers of high plant food con-tent. From these smallish beginnings whereby about 800 tons of sulphuric acid, 50 tons of ammonia, 200 to 800 tons of am-monium phosphate, and 125 tons of ammonium sulphate were produced, our production has grown to the point where more than 1,000 tons of sulphuric acid, 450 tons of ammonia, 600 tons of ammonium phosphate and 500 tons of ammonium sul-phate and 550 tons ammonium nitrate or over 1,650 tons of fertilizer, are the rule of the day (anon, c. 1948).

On a volume basis, Cominco's historical metal production has been largely dominated by lead and zinc [Figure 4] and this has also been reflected in corporate metal-based revenues [Figure 5]. Metal prices are notoriously erratic, and the effects of price declines in the Depression [Figure 6] are evidenced in Cominco's revenues.

The unusual set of circumstances which forced the smelter to under-take extensive and costly pollution control led to a transformation in the strategic direction of the company. Once fertilizer production was underway in 1930, it continued an almost steady increase until the mid 1960s [Figure 7]. Figure 8 details the extraordinary changes in sulphur emissions and feed that occurred at the Trail smelter over the period from 1900 to 1999. Figures 9 and 10 summarize the contribution of

Figure 4: Cominco metal production (tons)

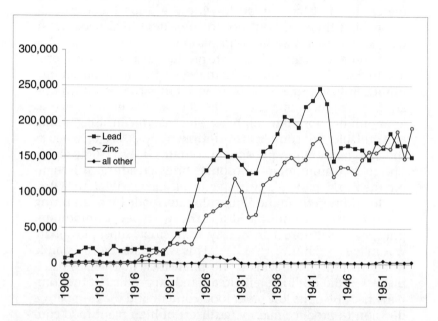

Figure 5: Cominco Metal Product Revenues (million CDN$)

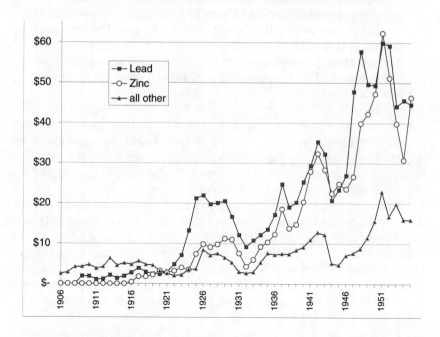

Figure 6: Prices for Lead and Zinc (CDN$/lb.)

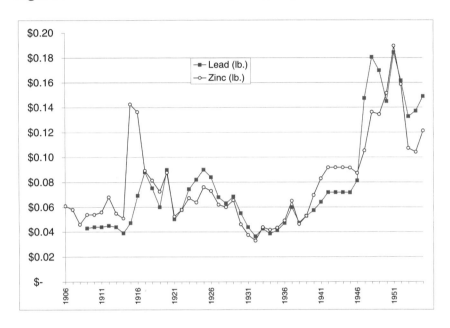

Figure 7: Cominco Fertilizer Production

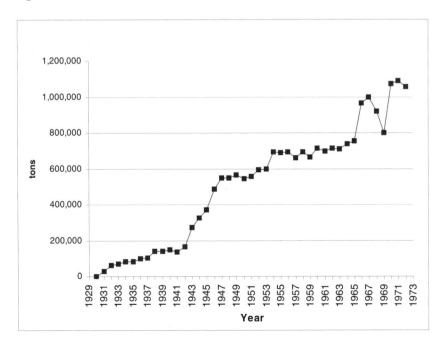

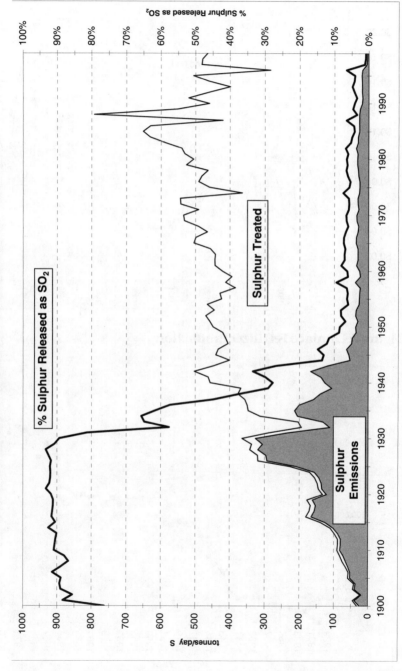

Figure 8: Cominco's Sulphur in Feed & Sulphur Emissions

Figure 9: Cominco Fertilizer Production - Contribution to Total Revenue

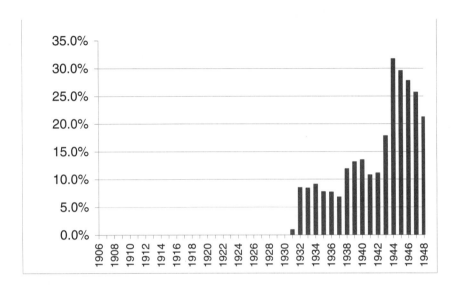

Figure 10: Cominco Fertilizer Production - Contribution to Total Profit

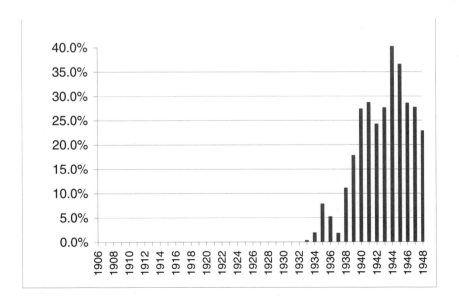

fertilizer production to company finances. These contributions peaked in 1944 with fertilizer revenue as as percentage of total revenue at 31.7 percent, and the comparable percentage for profit at 42.7 percent.

While numerous examples have been produced of recent efforts by companies in a broad range of industrial acitivites to convert waste to profits, less attention has been paid to Cominco's pioneering experience from seven decades ago. This unusual historical example provides a cogent argument for reconceptualizing the opportunities which may lie hidden in ostensible threats to corporate profitability and survival.

As a parenthetical note, an internal corporate document from 1938 indicated a concern over levels of costs and profits from sulphur and fertilizer production resulting from inadequate accounting separation of the finances of distinct but related production processes. The letter concludes:

> If elemental sulphur production had not taken place in 1937 our metal production must therefore have been curtailed approximately 30,000 tons, and the great overall advantage and economy to us of the sulphur operation is, of course, apparent (RWD, 1938).

It seems clear that even if waste product recovery had not made a contribution to profit at Consolidated Mining and Smelting, pollution control would still have be justified -- as it essentially permitted the continued operation of all other corporate activities.

POSTSCRIPT

As Figure 9 illustrated, the release of Sulphur Dioxide from Cominco's operations at Trial has declined steadily since the company instituted waste gas recovery in the late 1920s. Table 1 summarizes Trail's Sulphur emission history at the start of each decade since the peak year of 1930. Despite the enormous reductions in SO_2 emissions, the nature of the ore and smelting technology precluded the total elimination of this pollutant. As a result, Cominco instituted a unique system of air pollutant monitors located downwind of the smelter [see Figure 2] to provide telemetric feedback on ambient SO_2 levels which vary by season and time of day, depending on temperature, winds and other atmospheric conditions. Any levels of SO_2 deemed excessive lead to a temporary curtailment of smelting operations (B.C. Ministry of Environment, Lands and Parks and Environment Canada, 1993,p. 79).

Table 1: Trail Smelter Sulphur Emission History

Year		Avg. Emissions		Efficiencies	Emissions
	S in Feed	t/day S	t/day SO_2	% S Fixed	% S as SO_2
1930	364.3	325.5	651.0	10.6%	89.4%
1940	457.0	126.6	253.2	72.3%	27.7%
1950	448.8	37.8	75.6	91.6%	8.4%
1960	421.6	26.3	52.6	93.8%	6.2%
1970	534.9	35.2	70.4	93.4%	6.6%
1980	505.6	33.0	66.0	93.5%	6.5%
1990	460.2	19.4	38.8	95.8%	4.2%
1999	465.0	4.2	8.4	99.1%	0.9%

Source: Cominco

REFERENCES

Agent for the Government of Canada (1936) "Statement of Facts Submitted by the Agent for the Government of Canada, May 3, 1936," in *Trail Smelter Question*, Government of Canada, King's Printer, Ottawa, 1936.

Anon (c.1948) "Producing of Chemical Fertilizers by The Consolidated Mining and Smelting Company of Canada Limited."

B.C. Ministry of Environment, Lands and Parks and Environment Canada (1993) *State of the Environment Report for British Columbia*.

Howes, Dean E.A. and Dean F.G. Miller (1929) "Trail Smelter Question, Appendix A1, The Deans' Report. Final Report to the International Joint Commission," King's Printer, Ottawa.

International Joint Commission (IJC) (1931) "Report of the International Joint Commission, Signed at Toronto, 28th February, 1931,"Appendix A3, *Trail Smelter Question*, Government of Canada, King's Printer, Ottawa, 1936.

Murray, Keith A. (1972) "The Trail Smelter Case: International Air Pollution in the Columbia Valley," *BC Studies*, No. 15, Autumn, pp, 68-85.

Read, John E. (1963) "The Trail Smelter Dispute," In: Charles B. Bourne (ed.) *The Canadian Yearbook of International Law*, Volume 1, pp. 213-229, UBC Press.

RWD (1938) "Memorandum to Mr. S.G. Blaylock, Vice-President & General Manager," Consolidated Mining and Smelting Company, March 14, V.F. No. 661.12.

Trail Smelter Arbitration Tribunal (1941) "Decision reported on March 11, 1941 to the Government of the United States of America and to the Government of the Dominion of Canada by the Trail Smelter Arbitration Tribunal, under the convention signed April 15, 1935."

ACKNOWLEDGEMENTS

The author would like to express his appreciation to the following individuals for their advice, provision of data, and permission to research corporate records at head office in Vancouver, B.C. and the provincial archives in Victoria: David A. Thompson, President and Chief Executive Officer, Cominco; Norman Anderson, former President and CEO, Cominco; and Keith Low, corporate librarian. Any errors remain the responsibility of the author.

BUSINESS AND SUSTAINABLE DEVELOPMENT IN SOUTH EAST ASIA

Simon S.C. Tay
National University of Singapore,
Member of the Singapore Parliament,
Chairman of the Singapore Institute of International Affairs

INTRODUCTION: CRISIS AND NEW CONTEXTS

Businesses face a new context in opportunities and regulations in South East Asia. Many indicators suggest that the crisis that affected many countries in the region since mid 1997 has bottomed out. Leaders of the Association of South East Asian Nations (ASEAN) at their 1999 Informal Summit, held in Manila, spoke confidently of a recovery.

There are good reasons to question whether sufficient reforms have been undertaken to prevent a recurrence of the crisis. Most, however, would tend to agree that the worst seems to be over. New opportunities arise in the wake of the crisis.

In many countries, more sectors have been opened to foreign investment. Many large local conglomerates, affected by the crisis, are rationalizing their operations and seek to sell parts of their holdings, either by shares, or in whole companies and plants. In some countries, liberalization is proceeding at the advice and behest of international agencies, such as the International Monetary Fund. In one or two others, such as Singapore, liberalization in the financial and other sectors (e.g., telecommunications) is proceeding as part of national strategies to meet the growing international competition.

Economic cooperation and promotion within ASEAN as a whole has been increased by the acceleration of the ASEAN Free Trade Area (AFTA) and ASEAN Investment Area (AIA). Throughout the crisis, government leaders have been prompt in declaring their abiding commitment to liberalization. Continued liberalization, together with AFTA and the AIA, promises to increase the ease of cross-border business, and hope to attract foreign businesses to think of investment in the ASEAN area more as a single entity, rather than as 10 different states.

Concurrent with these opportunities, there are new concerns and approaches in the region concerning regulation. In large part, this is a healthy response to the crisis. Liberalization without sufficient regulation in some sectors, especially in banking, contributed to the Asian crisis. There is now a search for good governance, in both corporate and public sectors, with an accompanying concern with the appropriate institutions, attitudes and instruments for such regulation. Despite the recovery in the major macro-economic indicators for most of the region, this search should continue. Reforms are required and may bring about substantial changes that will affect businesses.

What has happened in the ASEAN countries in the crisis? What further changes will come as part of that search for reform? There are good reasons to be cautious about analyses that generalize the causes of the crisis and the changes and policy responses that are arising in its wake. The specific financial and economic positions of the ASEAN countries are quite different, both before, during and after the crisis. So too are their social and political systems.

Despite the contagion of the crisis, the ASEAN countries have quite greatly differed in their responses. This is, in some regards, a caution against much commentary about where the crisis will take the region. Change in political and economic systems is more complex and difficult to predict. This is especially so given that ASEAN has traditionally been seen as a way for member states to work together, despite considerable differences and diversity among themselves. There are, as such, good reasons to be sceptical about any analysis that suggests the different countries will all, and necessarily, evolve quickly and peaceably into free market democracies.

Similar cautions must be expressed about predicting the changes for business and for environmental governance, the focus of this essay. There is little prospect for a heightened and harmonized code concerning environmental standards in the region. Nor is there any strong indication that individual ASEAN states will take the same general approaches and directions. What can be seen with more certainty however, is that, just as new opportunities have arisen in the wake of the crisis, a new context for the environmental regulation of businesses is also emerging.

Concerns with the environment and sustainable development did not received much attention in the crisis or the preceding decades of growth. The implicit policy of governments in the region was, according to many analysts, "grow first, clean up later" (Bryant and Parnwell, 1996). During the extended period of growth in the East Asian "miracle", there were noticeable impacts on the environment (ESCAP, 1995; Hetttige and Wheeler, 1997). The crisis did nothing to alleviate this and, indeed, tended to worsen the situation (Tay, 1998a; World Bank, 1998).

In the post-crisis period, however, there are a number of reasons to argue that the environment will feature more highly on the agenda of many countries in the region. This is not so much because governments have changed their minds. Rather, it is the effect of actors within the state such as civil society and non-governmental organizations, as well as institutions and groups above the state. These forces, this essay argues, will likely press businesses to give more attention to sustainable development.

How they react to and interact with these new driving forces of course remains to be seen. Some may be defensive and continue with an attitude of "business as usual". They run the risk of failing to recognize the new driving forces and will face growing obstacles to their work and profitability. Others may be more proactive and responsive. They would seek to better understand, accommodate and even benefit from the changes. It is in this context that this essay will survey the changing dynamics of business and sustainable development in South East Asia.

There has been a growing amount of writing about the intersections between business and concerns with sustainable development. Many have been severely critical of the environmental and human impacts caused by international business, trade and investment, seen in the phenomena of globalization (Nader et al., 1993; Grieder, 1997). Some seem almost to regard businesses as an evil that the region would do better without. In some other writings, there is a recognition of the possibility that businesses can help promote sustainable development, with both economic growth and good standards in the protection of the environment. However, much of this has tended to assume that businesses will adopt the necessary habits and changes of mind to do so, or there is a certain tendency to preach, in moral terms, why they should do so.

This essay has different aims. By focusing on the driving forces that promote sustainable development, it sees the connections between businesses and sustainable development as a matter of policy and choice. Such choice, as with much of business, is driven by a mix of laws and regulations by the state, as well as by the businesses' own estimate of public opinion and profit concerns. In so doing, the essay hopes to contribute to the growing understanding of how private capital can make decisions that sufficiently take into account the public concerns over the environment and the promotion of public good.

The essay is structured in four parts. First, the pre-crisis approaches to sustainable development will be surveyed, together with the effects of the crisis on the environment. In the second part of this paper, we will give attention to the forces that bring greater attention to sustainable development, within the nation-states of South East Asia, and to the growth of civil society and non-governmental organizations (NGOs). In the third part, we shall survey the role of the broader, international community as driving forces for better environmental governance. Finally, the essay will consider different company choices in response to the changes and new driving forces.

PRE-CRISIS APPROACHES TO SUSTAINABLE DEVELOPMENT

The theoretical relationship between economic growth and the protection of the environment is both settled and yet controversial. It is settled in that the concept of sustainable development is well established in the aftermath of the Brundlandt Report and the UN Conference on Environment and Development (or Rio Summit). The promise of sustainable development is that we should decide and take action for our progress in such a way that we do not diminish the ability of future generations to pursue their development. The concept of sustainability reconciles the imperatives of both economic growth and environment protection.

But beyond this concept, the connections between economic growth and the environment remain controversial however in practice, in specific, concrete situations. Some feel that the concept of sustainable development has been misused to "skillfully disguise a step backwards" for environmental protection because it justifies the priority given to development (Pallamearts, 1993).

There continues to be concern among many environmentalists that economic growth and business activity worsen the environment. In the area of trade, some environmentalists believe that increased trade leads to the depletion of natural and environmental resources. As such, the wish to curb trade that harms the environment has led to many controversies, such as the Tuna-Dolphin case and Shrimp-Turtle cases in the WTO. Environmentalists are concerned that trade rules are being used to strike down rules intended for better environmental protection. There also continues to be suspicion that trade and increased demand will, without such improved environmental protection, lead to further deterioration of nature and natural resources (Tay, 1997).

As regards investment, there have been concerns that the competition between countries to attract foreign direct investment will lead to a cut in environmental standards (and therefore costs) in a race to the bottom. South East Asia has not witnessed a single industrial accident of the scale of Bhopal in India, or of the Sandoz and Chernobyl incidents in Europe, but the role of foreign capital and transnational companies (TNCs) has nevertheless been suspect. Some studies point to examples in which TNCs extract natural resources in non-sustainable and callous ways.

One example of this is the role of Japanese TNCs in forest, wood pulp and other wood related products (Dauvergne, 1997). Another has been the exploitation of minerals, especially in the Philippines and Indonesia. There are also examples in the industrial sectors, where pollutants in production are difficult to monitor. In the Asian Rare Earth case, Malaysian authorities did not properly control the use and disposal of low level radioactive wastes by a company jointly owned by Malaysian and Japanese interests, with the result that pollution was suffered by the local and largely poor community (Harding, 1996). In many such cases, these TNCs have acted in concert with large companies controlled by elites or even governments. The environmental and health costs are then visited on local peoples who may have little power and voice to resist.

Worse, there are concerns that governments cannot respond with higher environmental standards without provoking TNCs and foreign capital to relocate to another country with lower standards. This fear of a race to the bottom continues to be raised despite the fact that empirical studies show mixed evidence of industrial migration in response to environmental standards (Esty, 1996; Revez, 1993).

On the other hand, some assert that economic growth is not harmful to the environment but actually creates the wherewithal to allow greater environmental protection. They believe that free and open market economies are the best basis for sustainable development and the environment. This belief, as regards free trade, can be seen in Principle 21 of the Rio Declaration.

Certainly, there is no clear evidence that closing the economy to foreign trade, investment and business is an alternative that benefits the environment. Indeed, closed economies have tended to be among the worst cases, as seen in Eastern Europe and South Africa, under apartheid. In Asia, there is anecdotal evidence that foreign investment can also bring in higher standards of environmental protection as foreign multinationals in developing countries conform with their own standards and practices that are higher than those set by the host governments (Pangestu et al., 1996). Indeed, countries such as Singapore, that have experience in attracting foreign investment, the ability to monitor their activities and the administrative and legal capacities to enforce their laws, have shown that open economies and good environments can be reconciled (ESCAP, 1995).

A number of studies point to a conclusion somewhere in between the extremes that economic growth is wholly bad or wholly good for the environment. The experience of the OECD and East Asian NIEs has been that pollution is likely to first increase with economic growth, when starting up from low income levels, before then decreasing with further economic growth to higher levels of income. This is the observation of what is known as the inverted "U" or Kuznets curve of environmental quality. A recent study exemplifies this changing relationship between economic growth and environmental protection in the area of water pollution, finding considerable improvements as income levels reach US$6,000 per capita, and then remains stable thereafter (Hettige and Wheeler, 1997).

It is significant that, before the crisis, Japan and the NIEs had passed the US$6,000 per capita mark, whereas the second tier NIEs and others in Asia had not; second tier NIEs such as Thailand had per capita incomes in 1996 of less than US $4,000 and per capita incomes in China, Indo-China and most of South Asia were less than US$1,000 per capita.

Transposing these income levels onto the inverted "U" pattern of pollution, we might hypothesize that much of the region was going through the lower and more pollution intensive section of the development pattern. Some facts support this supposition.

Air pollution in Asian capitals, as measured in average levels of air particulates from 1991-95, were five times higher than those in the OECD and twice the world average. Water pollution, as measured in BOD levels and levels of suspended solids, were also substantially above world averages. The depletion of natural resources in water, arable land, timber and oil in Asia are also high, especially in SE Asia. For example, estimates are that the region will go from being a net exporter of oil, to becoming energy importers. For timber, deforestation and the end of the timber export industry in Indonesia and Malaysia are also envisaged in coming decades, just as Thailand and the Philippines have previously been commercially overlogged. With growing populations, some studies suggest increasing environmental and food insecurity in the region.

These environmental impacts of growth in Asia are not only in absolute terms, but also relative to GDP. Asia's energy demands only doubled every twelve years from the 1960s up to the crisis and, with an estimate at $1.40 output per kilogram of oil equivalent of energy, was much more energy-intensive and inefficient than corresponding figures for the USA (40%) and Japan (15%).

For most of the region, like many developing countries, while politicians spoke of sustainable development, there was a de facto policy of, "pollute first, clean up later" (Bryant and Parnwell, 1996). Much of Asia experienced rapid economic growth prior to the present crisis. But this "Miracle" exacted a high price on the region's environmental qualities and natural resources (ESCAP, 1995). The economic crisis that started in mid 1997 has also had impacts on the environment.

THE ENVIRONMENTAL IMPACTS OF CRISIS

There have as yet been few empirical studies to evaluate its precise environmental impacts. Trends however can be seen. There are three major reasons to believe that the environment in South East Asia has been worse off. These are: (1) decreased funds for environmental protection and infrastructure and weakened regulatory agencies and efforts to ensure compliance; (2) a resurgence of environmental problems associated with poverty; and (3) negative environment impacts from attempts to restart economic growth.

Decreased Funds and Weakened Regulation

Prior to the crisis, the newly industrialized economies (NIEs) of East and South East Asia strengthened their environmental laws and regulation, in response to growing public concern. In the decade before the crisis struck, Asia and especially the East Asian NIEs, made substantial investments to improve pollution control. Infrastructure investment in water supply and sanitation systems and, to a lesser extent, in mass transit systems had environmental benefits. Prior to the crisis, there were also some signs of improved and effective regulation over industrial activity, with a strong record in some countries, such as Singapore and improvements in some others, including Taiwan and Malaysia. The Asian Development Bank predicted that air and water quality would improve in the higher income countries of the region (Desai and Lohani, 1998).

The crisis has seen a slow down in the provision of such infrastructure. Investment in improved and less polluting technology has also been cut back generally.

There are concerns that environmental regulations and the regulatory agencies have been weakened. The Asian crisis was blamed, at least in part, on Asia's weakness in the governance of public sector, financial institutions and corporations. In many cases, environmental laws on the books were not enforced because of the lack of capacity or the prevalence of corruption. The crisis further weakened the regulatory reach of the public system on environmental compliance, worsening an already poor situation.

The Problems of Poverty

Second, the crisis has meant vastly reduced circumstances for many individuals and poverty for a considerable percentage. Alongside the profound human dimensions of the crisis are the environmental impacts that accompany poverty.

Even leading up to the crisis, the Asian Miracle displayed a number of negative social and human impacts in South East Asia. This included the increasing disparity in wealth distribution between elite and the masses, visible in the migration of people from rural areas to the cities, where they were very often confined to low-level employment or the informal sector, and lived in shanty-towns (Rigg, 1997).

The crisis has seen the return migration of urban poor to the countryside. While urban poverty has attendant problems, the reversal of this phenomena was no solution. The push factors that caused the initial migration still remain, especially landlessness. Consequently, many who returned to the countryside have sought new lands to cultivate.

Many helped themselves by clearing forest, belonging to the state or held in common, under traditional rights. Some take lands previously set aside for agro-industry or luxury elite uses, such as golf. Others turned to illegal hunting of endangered species of flora and fauna, or to illegal logging.

Such activities may be understandable where starvation is the alternative. The environmental impacts of such uncontrolled activities may however be considerable. This is especially where the landless turn to fire to clear land or drive out animals; a method that is polluting and often illegal, but always cheap and quick. The situation has been compounded when such land takings are unauthorized and give no secure title to its occupants. In such cases, the landless have the immediate imperatives to clear and use land, but not to maintain and sustain it over the longer term.

The industrial sector too has faced difficulties. The lower level jobs and informal sector in the region are most often associated with poor environmental and health standards. In many countries, there was a domestic sector of medium to smaller enterprises whose production was often low on technology and international competitiveness, and high on natural resources inputs and polluting by-products. Firms in these sectors have been unable to conform to higher environmental standards, especially as demanded by Western or international communities (Vossenaar and Jha, 1996). The crisis tended to make this worse as focus was on reducing cost and increasing market share, rather than sustainability.

Negative Environmental Impacts from Policy Responses

The third trend is that policy responses to the crisis may lead to negative environmental impacts. This may be intentional, if the environment is seen as a luxury concern that can no longer be afforded in the crisis. Or it may be unintentional, given that policy responses are driven by economic agencies, with little or no knowledge of environmental concerns and costs. While there has been difference and notable change in economic policies prescribed in the crisis, there have been three general edicts.

The first is the prescription for countries to export themselves out of the crisis. The second is to attract foreign direct investment. The third, and most general, is the aim to re-start the economy. Such prescriptions re-trigger the environmentalists' concern that Asia's growth, or in this case, its recovery will be at high environmental cost.

This is especially so in the case of trade. Many of the exports in the region (e.g., oil, timber, minerals) are extractive or otherwise high on natural resource input. Many are high also on polluting outputs, especially given lower standards in regulations and weak systems to enforce such regulations. The international trade system in the WTO does not assist in this regard. It has pointedly and repeatedly set aside environmental conditions imposed by importing countries, in favour of unfettered free trade. The regional trading systems such as APEC and AFTA have yet to conjoin their agendas for trade and investment with their environmental undertakings, and may not have the will to do so (Tay, 1996).

As for investment, there is no international system of supervision. As such, it is up to the national systems in the region to screen foreign investment for environmental impacts. Most countries in the region have laws or policies to do so and to undertake environmental impact assessments before deciding on foreign investment. But their track record has been mixed, and exceptions or absences are notable even before the crisis. What more now, when the hunger for FDI has increased and the competitiveness and stability of the region is in doubt.

In this context, it is of considerable concern that economists have tended to see the task in the aftermath of the crisis as being to "re-start" the stalled economies. For if the progress of the Asian Miracle consoled environmentalists it was that, with faith in the inverted U pattern of pollution, continued growth would drive the Asian countries into that part of the curve in which the environment would come increasingly into the picture and with increasing resources to meet the environmental concerns.

As such, with the drop in the per capita income of most countries, it would seem that the region is being driven through another round of the lower end of that inverted "U", when growth coincides with pollution. The search for environmental protection and sustainable development seems like a game of snakes and ladders. And the crisis has brought the Asian economies back to the bottom of the inverted "U" shaped snake.

The three concerns for the environmental impacts of the crisis that have been discussed have been expressed in general terms. One example that may assist to focus the concerns is that of the South East Asian fires and the haze experienced in 1997 and 1998, coinciding with the economic crisis (Tay, 1999). This may be briefly considered to illustrate the environmental dimensions of the crisis.

These fires centred in Kalimantan and other parts of Borneo, and in Sumatra. Their effect was however both regional and global. The haze suffered by Singapore, Malaysia and parts of Thailand and the Philippines cost the region more than US$1.1 Billion in 1997, estimated in terms of lost tourism, and increased health costs alone. The global costs are almost immeasurable: climate change gases released in the months of the fires are estimated to equal those of industrial Western Europe, and the fires resulted in the loss of biodiversity rich areas of Kalimantan and the death of endangered species, such as the orang-utan. UN Environment chief, Dr Klaus Toepfer called the fires a global environmental disaster.

The cause of the fires was partly climatic: the El Nino weather pattern created dry conditions in the rainforests and other vegetation. However the primary and initial cause was manmade. The fires were started for land clearing operations, mostly by large scale, agro-industry companies in oil palm plantations and timber concessions. The use of fires, while illegal, could not be stopped by the regulatory system. This failure was because of corruption and cronyism, and also because even those agencies that had the will, lacked capacity.

The danger of fires in the region and the failure to avert or deal with the threat are systemic and persistent. Although the fires of 1997 and 1998 were the worst on record, large scale fires and haze also occurred in 1994, 1991 and further back into the 1980s. At root are not only climatic and geographical factors, but economic. The fires are used as the cheapest method for clearing land. The land clearing is central to the development of Indonesia's oil palm and timber industries. These industries reaped large profits, and continue to do so in the midst of the crisis. Those profits have accrued largely to elites associated with the ruling regime, and with some foreign investment and trade. The lands, moreover, are often appropriated from locals and become a focal point for resistance and contention (Barber, 1997).

In this situation, it is easy to see how the economic crisis might disable any real attempt to deal with future fires. The crisis focuses attention of limited resources on economic and political reforms, driving the environmental problems — even a global disaster such as the fires — to the bottom of the agenda.

Further, it is also possible that the remedies prescribed for the crisis will worsen matters. The call to increase exports as a means to increase revenues will, without sufficient regulation and effective implementation of regulations, tend to increase land clearing and the use of fires. The call for fresh capital in the form of FDI and for export credits is unlikely to give pause to whether the investments and exports are linked to fires or other environmental harms. The lack of jobs, social safety nets and other factors that drive people back to the countryside will increase competition for land, and may provoke locals to revenge by setting fire to estate lands. Without attention to the specific problems, the crisis both diminishes the capacity to respond to the environmental problems of the fires and may continue and strengthen the underlying factors that cause it.

Yet while these factors are of real concern for the environment and sustainable development in South East Asia, they are not the entire picture. In a number of cases, studies are beginning to suggest that the effects of the crisis on the environment and on the poor were not as severe as originally feared. Local communities and social forces may have been better able to cope than anticipated. There are also grounds for some optimism.

New driving forces are emerging that may promise a greater emphasis on the protection of the environment and the search for sustainable development. These forces will not of themselves determine the outcome. As noted earlier, interactions of political and economic systems in the ASEAN countries, both in and after the crisis, are diverse and complex. It can be seen, however, that these new driving forces do set a new context for environmental governance in the region and the regulations and regulatory processes that can potentially affect businesses. What are these new driving forces?

IMPROVING ENVIRONMENTAL GOVERNANCE: DRIVING FORCES IN THE REGION

The world movement for improved environmental protection has come from many different sources. The driving forces have included ethical and religious beliefs as well as the immediate and visceral reaction to large and well publicized environmental disasters that have killed or severely affected human and animal life. The environmental movement has been driven by a growing science that has begun to uncover the complex interdependence and possible fragilities of life on this shared planet. It has also been driven by the simple and basic need of many to obtain safe and sufficient access to the most fundamental resources of food and potable water. The drive for better environmental protection has also come through different players and institutions, such as the mass media, small groups of citizens and local communities, government leaders, non-governmental organizations, businesses, indigenous peoples, and international organizations.

These driving forces of environmental concern have not been completely absent in South East Asian countries. From a variety of reasons, Asia has witnessed the gradual emergence, since the 1980s, of an increasing environmental consciousness among the people of the region (Lee and So, 1999). In the pre-crisis days of rapid growth, however, they were often shut out and marginalized. National development plans were instead given priority.

The part played by civil society and NGOs has also been controversial and contested in much of the region. Governments in South East Asia have been among the most jealous in the international community of their monopoly in representing the state and reluctant to admit the legitimacy of such groups. Where they have relented, in the pre-crisis days, was where NGOs and civil society groups consciously dedicated themselves to supplementing the state and taking on a complementary role in promoting development (de Fonseka, 1997). This was the general nature of state-civil society relations in Asia up to the mid 1980s. The main tasks given to civil society in this minimal state conception were to promote production and market activities; deliver services to communities and groups beyond the reach of the state; and foster participation in the development process.

Only towards the start of the 1990s, did Asia experience a second and different wave of civil society. This conceived its role as being an autonomous and countervailing power to the state. This concept, drawing its roots from Western liberal thought, as well as events in Eastern Europe, witnessed non-governmental organizations and civil society more generally play a greater role in calling Asian governments to account for a wide range of issues, such as the environment, poverty alleviation, women's rights and human rights.

The second wave of civil society has, in some countries, fostered new arrangements and forms of political organization upon the existing political parties. This was often marked by cross-cutting alliances among different sectors of civil society such as students, the media, the middle class and even business interests. A stark example of this was seen in events in Thailand following the aftermath of the May 1992 protests, and the push for democratic reforms. States have reacted to this trend by seeking to place legal controls on NGO activities and efforts to co-opt and demobilize civil society.

The third wave in Asia has been characterized as a reaction by governments to moderate the growing pressures from civil society groups and to incorporate them as an instrument of state. Observers have noted the trend for governments in Asia to place legal controls on NGO activities and efforts to co-opt civil society and demobilize the more political, policy advocacy groups (Riker, 1995). Other studies by country or by region also reconsider the balance between the state and civil society. This is often seen in the context of globalization, which poses a pressure on existing systems of governance. In general, country studies in South East Asia, and in Asia more broadly, perceive the growth of civil society and predict a change in the functions of government and civil society, and also for the private sector of business (Yamamoto, 1995).

The nature of the relationship between civil society and NGOs to government on one hand and to business on the other, varies from country to country. In many cases, it is changing and evolving in the context of the crisis and the response taken by governments. Broadly, speaking, however, we can see both differences and similarities in the second and third waves of civil society and what they mean for environmental governance.

The second wave seems more to correspond with the conception of a civil society opposed to the state. In the third wave, civil society cooperates with the state and is said by some to be compromised or co-opted in so doing. Yet they share a similarity in looking at state and civil society as being opposed to each other. The main difference between them is which of the opposing entities — state or civil society — is in the ascendant. There is, of course, a difference between opposing the state and of demanding that governments properly account to the people. However, in the minds of governments unaccustomed to being questioned, the difference is not felt. To those in power, strict and public accountability is often viewed as an erosion of their power, and a confrontation.

Present and unfolding developments since the advent of the economic crisis in 1997 have revitalized the interest in civil society. In the crisis, these actors have grown stronger, both generally and with particular regard to the environment.

Partly, this has been because of the emphasis on the need for systems of better governance and to root out cronyism, corruption and nepotism, or "KKN" as the Indonesian reformers call it. This general desire for good governance has particular importance for the environment. Accountability, greater and more widespread participation in decision making and aspects of democracy are all factors that potentially impact environmental protection.

In many cases, such as the Indonesian fires discussed briefly, environmental degradation in South East Asia has been linked to "KKN" practices. Elites collude with agencies of the state to monopolize access to natural resources such as forests and land. Together, these elites and businesses over exploit the country's natural resources for personal gain, without regard to longer term sustainability. The state's gain, moreover, in terms of taxes and payment for the use of the land, is relatively small. In some cases, there are even state incentives given to promote the unsustainable exploitation. In many cases, the over-exploitation leads directly to harms that are suffered by local populations. These harms include severe floods, or smoke haze, or soil erosion, or the expropriation of lands they have traditionally used (Tay, 1999). This has been strongly evident in the case of Indonesia. (Barber, 1997). It is also true of a web of legal and illegal logging that links the countries of Indo-China and Myanmar (Bryant, 1997). Weak systems of governance and those that are closed to participation and opaque to inspection have tended to be mired in unsustainable practices that overexploit environmental resources.

This link brings the agenda of environmental protection closer to the agenda for good governance. Additionally, there is a stronger link between environmental protection and other aspects of sustainable development, such as the rights of participation. The link from environmental protection to human rights and other aspects of social responsibility is, in this regard, strengthened .

An important part in the push for better governance and an end to KKN has been played by civil society and by non-governmental organizations (NGOs). They have been active in supporting forces of change and have in some cases, such as Indonesia, become closely involved in the broader reform movement.

In South East Asia, the changes have been dramatic, especially in Thailand, Indonesia and Malaysia. Some observers see the final vindication of their thesis that democracy and civil society will come to the region. They see events in Thailand, the Philippines and, further afield, in South Korea as consolidating democracy. Others, to the contrary, are concerned with the failure of governance and a rising tide of anarchy, especially in Indonesia. They may also not be so sanguine about the strength and capacity of these democrats to govern effectively and therefore to deal with possible back-lash.

The longer term consequences of these trends has yet to become clear. What is clear however is that the crisis has provided a further opening for civil society actors and NGOs. In many South East Asian countries, civil society and NGOs seem now to be in the ascendant, or (at least) to be playing a bigger role than ever before. This is the situation in Thailand and Indonesia, clearly, as well as the Philippines, as the site of the original "people's revolution" that pushed former President Marcos from power. In many cases, the movement and actions of civil society actors and NGOs have been significantly amplified by a media that is increasingly independent and varied.

This growth in NGOs and civil society has included environmental groups. Indeed, in some cases, such as Thailand and Indonesia, environmental groups have been among the vanguard of civil society and NGOs. The crisis has created an opportunity for them.

In Indonesia, the growth of environmental civil society organizations and NGOs changed. In the pre-crisis days, they had tended to focus on around particular issues, such as opposition to dams, or for conservation. (Hirsch and Warren, 1998). In the crisis and immediately prior, local environmental struggles were often linked to broader politics and calls for political reform. This has led to a local challenge to the elite's monopoly over access and ownership to natural resources. Indonesian NGOs such as WALHI, the umbrella coalition for environmental NGOs, achieved considerable prominence in the crisis period as did the Indonesian chapter of the Worldwide Fund for Nature.

In such circumstances, the calls for political change and for greater environmental concern have tended to reinforce each other. This is particularly where, as in Thailand and Indonesia, a reformist or avowedly democratic government has come into power in the wake of the crisis.

Yet also in countries that have gone without such widespread reform, such as Malaysia and Singapore, there are also some signs of greater civil society and NGO movements, both generally and particularly for environmental concerns.

In Malaysia, NGOs that focused on environment and sustainable development witnessed considerable growth from the late 1970s. Examples of this are the Consumer Association of Penang and the Malaysian chapter of the Friends of the Earth. Another Malaysian NGO of note is the Third World Network, which has achieved some prominence internationally, especially in its work on the World Trade Organization and its relationship to sustainable development concerns of developing countries.

The growing strength of Malaysian NGOs is evidenced by their participation in several high profile cases that involved public protest or litigation in the courts against government agencies. An earlier example of this was the Asian Rare Earth case in which NGOs supported a suit brought by local villagers against a company for health and other damage that arose from the improper storage and disposal of hazardous materials. The government agency that approved the company's activities was also implicated (Harding, 1996). A more recent highlight of the growing role of NGOs in Malaysia has been their participation in the controversy surrounding the building of the Bakun Dam in East Malaysia. The dam, which would impact traditional and indigenous lands, was approved by government authorities without an environmental impact assessment. On this basis, the court initially ordered that work be stopped and, although this has since been circumvented, the issue remains contested between government and NGOs.

In Singapore, the growth of NGOs has been less dramatic. In large part, this is because NGOs have eschewed public law suits. Using either private suasion or public petition, they have nevertheless been of increasing significance in the decision making process. A relatively early example of this was the role of Singapore NGOs and especially the Singapore Nature Society in the early 1990s in opposing the use of a nature reserve for a golf course.

More recently, NGOs, including the Singapore Environment Council, have sought to inform and involve NGOs about the Indonesian haze. Notwithstanding the political sensitivity between Indonesia and Singapore, the Council hosted an international dialogue on the issue in 1998. The dialogue included not only Singaporean activists but also regional and international NGOs, such as the WWF. This was followed by a presentation of the chairman's statement from the meeting to the ASEAN Senior Officials for the Environment, perhaps the first such presentation by an NGO (Tay, 1999).

These brief examples point a growth in the strength of NGOs and civil society actors during the crisis years. This drew from activities and progress made in the decades prior to the crisis. In many cases, however, their growth in the crisis years was exponential. This was a result not just of greater political space and change, but more fundamentally for some, it was a recognition of the connections between economics and environment, and the broader and more inclusive concerns of sustainable development.

Will these groups continue to be important in the post-crisis period? Their rapid growth and the underlying factors behind their growth suggest they may well endure and continue to grow. The actors in South East Asian countries have therefore increased, bringing new and locally, nationally and regionally sited forces for sustainable development.

Yet while these indigenous forces are of increasing importance, they are not the only driving factors in calling for improved environmental governance. There has been an increase in the international factors that push in this direction as well.

INTERNATIONAL DRIVING FORCES

Environmental concerns have risen steeply on the international agenda. From being a new and relatively obscure concern, interest peaked with the 1992 Rio or Earth Summit, which was attended by the highest number of leaders ever to converge on a single international meeting. Many governments, especially but not only the developed countries of the West, have subscribed to an increasing number of environmental declarations and treaties. There has also been a real growth in international NGOs that push for greater environmental protection.

Events in the late 1990s demonstrate the continuing and increasing strength of such non-state international actors. The case of the Brent Spar witnessed Greenpeace and other NGOs forcing Shell to change its plans for the disposal of this oil platform. The 1999 WTO Ministerial meeting in Seattle was disrupted by NGOs and other protesters, including those who felt that increased trade would harm the environment. Such headline cases demonstrate the increasing ability of NGOs and civil society actors to cajole large and powerful transnational companies and even block governments (Wapner, 1996).

The role of NGOs and civil society in the international community has also widened beyond environmental issues. Within the region but even more so in North America and Europe, sectors of society have voiced disquiet over the adverse costs of globalization. Many focused on the outflow of jobs, from their developed and more expensive economies to cheaper centers of production in Asia and elsewhere. Additionally, others voiced concern of the accompanying social and cultural costs in environmental pollution and degradation, or the lack of protection of human and labour rights, and the exploitation of vulnerable sectors of the populace, such as undocumented migrant workers, women and children. Globalization threatened, in this analysis, a "race to the bottom". In this debate, one focal point was the environment and its connection to international trade. The US sought to close its markets to goods that harmed species it wanted to protect, such as canned tuna that resulted in the accidental killing of dolphins, and shrimp imports that killed sea turtles. In human rights, the Asian values debate generated controversy, as did the use of Western sanctions against China and Myanmar.

There has been an increasing coalition of environmental groups with those concerned about other issues, such as labour and human rights, the social responsibility of transnational corporations and the effects of globalization generally. The coalition on these issues is strongly associated with non-governmental organizations (NGOs). In environmental protection, NGOs such as Greenpeace and the Worldwide Fund for Nature have become household names and, in human rights, so have Amnesty International and Human Rights Watch. NGOs have also organized around other specific areas that can be seen as relating to human rights or the environment, such as humanitarian emergencies, the women's movement, the anti-nuclear movement, and the campaign against land mines. Such NGO movements have become increasingly strong and acknowledged sources of influence in the international sphere, with established roles in fora such as the UN.

Yet while NGOs may be the core of non-state actors, a newer phenomenon seems to be emerging with globalization. This is the rise of an "international" or "world civil society". The idea of an international civil society is wider, including NGOs but also networks of scholars and individuals, trade unions, religious and other voluntary organizations, research institutes, media. This "society" is not confined to any state, but relies upon the global telecommunications of media and the internet as well as the supporting symbols and values of such systems. Some counterpose the concept of "globalization from above" that favoured the movement of capital and multinationals, with "globalization from below", by which networks of citizens organized themselves for common cause, across borders.

These tensions in institutions, policies and conceptions of international order ignited at the 1999 World Trade Organization (WTO) Ministerial Meeting, held in Seattle. The mass and partially violent demonstrations against the WTO meeting displayed a frustration with a globalization that the demonstrators perceived as undemocratic, bad for the environment, and bad for their individual economic prospects.

The emergence of civil society in Asia and the new approaches to governance it bodes is taking place in this context of globalization. This has two major implications for the role of civil society in environmental governance. First, it suggests that the evolution of environmental and social norms will be determined by both internal and external forces. Most analysts think of globalization primarily or even solely in economic terms: trade, investment, finance, corporations, technology, information—these are the bedrocks of globalization. However, with economic integration, as well as access to information technology and travel, NGOs are themselves becoming international. Even if they never leave their communities, they have access to international news on the Internet, they communicate regularly with people throughout the world, and of course, they feel the effects of economic globalization in their day to day work and social lives.

The growing international consciousness of NGOs helps to spur the globalization of norms, especially human right and environmental norms. In addition, coalitions between international and local NGOs create commonalities of language and philosophy. Interestingly, in Asia, the process of globalization of norms is generating a common critique of globalization primarily based on what the UNDP calls the "grotesque gap" between winners and losers (UNDP, 1999). In the future, civil society in Asia is likely not only to call for better environmental performance and protection of human rights but also for new economic and social policies which promote equity. There will be a struggle between forces seeking to withdraw from and those seeking to reform the processes of globalization.

It is also likely that trans-Pacific environmental partnerships and NGO coalitions will blossom in the next decade based not only on ethics but ecological self-interest. In March, 1999, a new report found that airborne chemicals from Asia—carbon monoxide, radon, aerosols, hydrocarbons, and other chemicals—were reaching the West Coast of the United States. Rising concern and activism in the U.S. is likely to give rise to both new governmental and civil society action.

The second implication of globalization for environmental governance civil in Asia is that local policymakers will feel a range of external pressures on policymaking. On the one hand, they will be pressed to not unilaterally raise industry standards for fear of loss of foreign investment. On the other hand, they will be pressed to accept standards set by the U.S. or Europe as conditions of market entry. Environmental issues will continue to be on the agenda for global and regional trade diplomacy—and NGOs will press to have their voices heard.

Yet while international factors have pushed for greater consciousness and attention to the environment, they are not the only determinants in how states actually behave. This is especially as international law and policy-making on the environment has often been characterized by a North-South divide. The South has, generally, been skeptical of the environmental agenda put forward by the international community. This is so even where they have recognized the relationship between environment and development, and increasingly participated in many environmental declarations and treaties In many cases, their environmental performance has lagged behind their statements.

In the North-South divide on the environment, the countries of South East Asia have almost always been on the side of the South. Either individually or collectively under the umbrella of ASEAN, they cast doubt over the appropriateness of environmental initiatives proposed by Western countries. Indeed, in the run up to the 1992 Earth Summit, countries such as Malaysia and Indonesia took a leading role to defend and justify their rights to continue logging trees as part of their national patrimony, and to limit the possibility of a world convention on forests. ASEAN too acted together to lobby to force Austria to back away from attempts that the latter had made to restrict the imports of tropical timber. The Malaysian prime minister, Dr. Mahathir Mohammed, was a leading spokesman against increased environmental protection, often denigrating them as "neo-imperialism" and ways of trying to stem the rise of developing countries by imposing new strictures on their growth.

This does not mean that Malaysia or other South East Asian countries can isolate themselves from globalization, and the increased transactions in trade, investment and between peoples, or that they wish to try to isolate themselves. However, many in the region have advocated globalization for economics, but regional or national particularities for culture and society. The Asian values debate that doubted human rights and "Western-style" democracy was emblematic of this. Asian spokesmen in this debate posited a world of convergence in economics but of essential (and essentialized) differences in social norms, culture and politics (Tay, 1996; Bauer and Bell, 1999).

By these means, many governments in the region have sought to partake of economic globalization through international trade and investment without agreeing to global standards and supervision in other areas, such as environmental protection and human rights. In contrast, international civil society have sought to meld the two together, and to otherwise reject the present models of globalization. Some governments from North America and Europe (but not all and not always), have tended to support this movement. They have generally sought to amend the WTO to allow for greater coherence with environmental protection, although the preferred means of doing so has been debated. They have also sought to foster greater adherence and compliance to international treaties and norms in the areas of environmental protection and human rights by pressing other states through international diplomacy or by measures relating to trade and aid.

There are other, additional means of pressure that are used to promote greater environmental protection and sustainable development. These are often the tools of NGOs and civil society groups, either directly or working through the governments of sympathetic, often Western states, and bear at least a brief mention.

One of these tools is the use of consumer boycotts, or the threat of such boycotts. In the field environmental protection, the Brent Spar case and the actions threatened against Shell is a prime example. In other areas of concern, companies that are thought to have invested in countries with poor human rights records or have overseas production facilities that fall short on labour rights are also targeted. The impact of potential consumer reaction on Nike operations in Asia is one example of this. One shortcoming of consumer boycotts, however, is that by their nature, they are only potent against recognizable consumer brands and companies.

A second and connected tool for NGOs and civil society in promoting environmental protection is the use of international standards, such as the ISO14000. This seeks to evaluate the product's content, production method and use for their impact on the environment and to guide management processes within the producer to minimize their impact. In a number of different product lines, ISO14000 has also sought to generate minimum standards. A similar attempt is seen in eco-labels. These have been adopted by many developed and developing countries to help consumers distinguish products that are relatively benign to the environment. Eco-labels however employ criteria that differ, one from another, rather than the internationally agreed approach of the ISO14000. Both ISO14000 and eco-labels depend on consumer preference to have an impact. They are also limited in that labeling that is compulsory or discriminatory may well be considered a violation of international trade rules under the GATT.

A third tool that is used is to seek control through the laws of the home country of transnational companies, where the laws of the host country provides no adequate remedy. For example, in the 1980s, litigation was brought against Union Carbide in the USA, its home country, for toxic pollution caused by a plant in India. Although this suit was ultimately unsuccessful, it demonstrated the real concern that transnational companies faced in accounting for their overseas operations. Other litigation has also been tried for environmental harms committed abroad, such as in the case of the exploitation of the Oriente in Ecuador by oil companies.

More recently, Unocal of the USA has been successfully sued in the USA for its continuing operations in Myanmar (Burma). The basis of the suit was that Unocal has collaborated with the Myanmar regime in human rights violations against the people of that country. The fact that the events happened in South East Asia and not on US soil was not an obstacle in view of the US Alien Torts Act, which allows for universal jurisdiction by American courts over human rights cases. While the Unocal case shows how such actions can be effective tools, there are several limitations, not least that the case concerned human rights, rather than environmental harm, which does not enjoy universal jurisdiction under US law. However, given the convergence between environmental harm and governance that this essay has pointed to earlier, there can be an increasing number of cases in which environmental harm and human rights violations may run together (Sachs, 1995).

Access to finance is a fourth important tool that can be used to try to affect the behaviour of developing countries and transnational companies in environmental protection and sustainable development. For countries, international finance by the World Bank and other inter governmental agencies now comes with conditions attached. These conditions go beyond economic terms, narrowly defined, to include environmental impact assessment and mitigation. Increasingly, social impacts and governance issues are also considered in loan approval. Private international finance is also taking similar approaches. Banks, insurance companies and accounting firms have also come to see how the lack of proper environmental protection has to be factored in as possible future liabilities. (French, 1998).

With these tools and the broader coalition between environmental and other interests, the driving forces at the international level that push for sustainable development have been growing stronger. Their strength, moreover, is not only in pressing at the international level against the states that they think are in default, but in their ability to pursue transnational companies that invest in such states through consumer action and in the courts of their home countries.

How have businesses reacted? What should they do in the changing context of South East Asia in the post-crisis years?

RESPONSES FOR BUSINESS

For many states in Asia, the first reaction to international civil society is to deny them. The reaction of businesses can be much the same, and some say has been so. Transnational companies may not move to a developing country to cynically exploit lower standards in environmental and other protections, or to benefit from lax enforcement. Many companies, however, may believe that their duty is met if they meet the laws of the land. If there are no laws, some feel they have no duty to meet. Increasingly, however, this has begun to change.

There is a sense that corporations face new rules on their conduct. After decades of highly publicized industrial disasters, management groups have begun to internalize environmental concerns. This is especially in Europe and America. Markers of this change in mindset include the spread of codes of conduct, such as the principles adopted by CERES (the Coalition of Environmental Responsible Economies) and the work of the Business Council for Sustainable Development. More than two-thirds of larger US corporations now have codes of business ethics, many of which include the environment. This is, in increasing cases, more than a matter of public relations (Wilson, 2000). Some commentators believe that concern with the environment and sustainability is a "megatrend" that companies must consider (Hanson, 1995). If not, they will fail themselves and humanity (Hawken, 1993).

Companies have responded better to market based instruments to regulate environmental performance (such as pollution trading permits), rather than the old command and control mode of supervision. Some have begun to look at longer term phenomena, such as global climate change, to see how they can anticipate and help take precautions to prevent the consequences (Wilson, 2000). In a number of instances, and particularly in Europe, companies in a particular industry have come to see the benefit of concluding voluntary and self-regulating environmental agreements (ELNI, 1998).

Increasingly, companies have also been able to reframe environmental concerns as questions of efficiency, leading to systemic efforts to reduce waste and resource use, while increasing productivity (Von Weizsacker, Lovins and Lovins, 1997; Romm, 1994). Some see that environmental management methods and technology alone cannot deliver sustainability; ethical and ecological concerns must instead be incorporated into strategic management (Welford, 1995; Crosbie and Knight, 1995). This shows a striking shift in corporate mindsets, from reactive thinking that sees environmental regulations only as an increased costs, to proactive thinking that sees them as challenges to innovation and reasons to improve productivity.

In this effort, companies have given much more attention to environmental monitoring as well as to audit and disclosure. Pioneering work in this respect was done by Shell in the summer of 1998, when it released its first environmental audit that was externally verified and covered its worldwide operations. Other companies too have improved their environmental reporting. There is a notable trend towards a more widespread practice, with greater standardization; mandatory requirements set by government or the industry itself; independent external verification and environmental benchmarking (Elkington, 1998). This is an outgrowth of business ethics and the recognition of "reputational risk" that a company run in public opinion that will affect its standing, profitability and sustainability. The risk is not just moral, but also has legal and financial implications (Case, 1999; Speeding, 1996). This applies, additionally, to associated companies and firms that lend, ensure and service the corporation. This has led to greater recognition of environmental concerns among banks and accountants too (Elkington, 1998).

Such a view, with openness and transparency from greater accountability by companies to the community, strives to change the relationship of the company to the state and community. No longer is the company to be a closed entity, narrowly pursuing the narrow profit calculations of its shareholders and management. Stakeholders in the community and the states that host these businesses are recognized.

After the calls of the 1980s for the minimalist state that would not interfere, many leading corporations have begun to redefine their relationship to the state. Rather than an absent state or an interfering one, the need is for the state to set the standards for environmental protection adequately and rationally, for which there are suitable and supportive ways of fostering compliance among companies. There is a similar need to engage develop partnership models between businesses and civil society.

The regulations, laws and social context for these movements have to date however largely been American or European (Speeding, 1996). There has also been some comparisons with Japan (Wallace, 1995). What is happening in the developing countries of Asia and more particularly South East Asia has been less closely studied. This is needed as, even in the developed economies, the responses of business corporations in responding to the challenges of environmental protection and sustainability are relatively new and still evolving. The observations of this article however point to a number of trends that will likely bring environmental concerns to Asia that ally with business concerns, especially for foreign investors.

The first factor is that, as surveyed, there is increasing knowledge of business practices and efficiencies, a body of business ethics and new ways of looking at business strategy to support this. Frameworks are changing in boardrooms worldwide, and especially in the USA and Europe. There are also clear wishes expressed by shareholders, consumers and civil society in their home countries. For these reasons, and even without the laws and regulations of their home governments or their Asian hosts, there is good and growing reason for companies to bring this mindset into South East Asia, apply their codes of conduct and principles on a worldwide basis.

The second factor is the trend in the region towards a stronger civil society and NGOs. Such a civil society and NGOs, that are better linked internationally and can act more surely locally, will drive towards better environmental practices in business. The more traditional way of doing this, especially for NGOs, is by using public protest and the media to make demands upon the state to better regulate such businesses. This is will continue and likely grow in the freer and more democratic South East Asian societies. Consumer boycotts and shareholder activism will also likely emerge in a recovering Asia that has learnt to be more concerned with private sector governance.

The third (and connected) factor is the drive to end corruption and collusion between business interests and the state. The reforming state in Asia is under pressure from both its citizens and the international community to address these issues in the wake of the crisis and to evolve better and more effective forms of governance. In this context, the callous exploitation of natural resources and uncontrolled pollution from industry can no longer be protected by vested interests. The state in Asia will seek to reassert its regulatory role.

In this, there is a danger that traditional views of command and control by the state will return. This should be avoided because of the higher cost and inefficiencies of such methods. Market based instruments and financing will need to be emphasized, with the requisite knowledge and capacity (Asian Development Bank, 1994). This would give a lighter touch to regulation and a helping hand in environmental protection that would assist both environmental performance and business performance.

Companies and investors in the region can help in this by responding not just to their bottom lines and government directives. They need to engage civil society at both the national and international levels, and the stakeholders in their host countries. This would include not just those in the capital cities, but also the local communities in their area of investment. Such engagement will need, of course, to go beyond an exercise in public relations. More effort is needed to shape strategy in relation to the concerns expressed. By such means, civil society and NGOs in Asia can interact with business in a "stakeholder" or partnership model.

If this can be done, the danger of protests, boycotts and "reputational risk" can be lowered for companies. For environmentalists, there would be the benefit of moving beyond sporadic protests over incidents of pollution, to help shape policies that can prevent such pollution in the first place. It is also a means to keep businesses in their communities on a sustainable basis, and to grow from such businesses.

The means and opportunities of doing so will necessarily differ from sector to sector and from business to business. The clean up of natural resource sector companies, such as those engaged in forestry and mineral exploitation, will clearly be different from the sustainable routes in the field of energy generation and use. Further, as South East Asia is a diverse region, there will be some variation between different countries as well.

The key strategic challenges for business, the environment and sustainable development in the region however are clear and universal. Companies will need to embrace the challenge of pursuing environmental protection, working at both the level of strategy and in the details of particular businesses (NCE, 1995). They must find ways to do so that will include reforming states or re-energized communities and citizens as partners and stakeholders, and not opponents, to recognize their common interests. They must seek paths and practices that will reconcile better environmental protection and profitability, working towards sustainable development.

REFERENCES

Asian Development Bank (1994) *Financing Environmentally Sound Development*, Manila; ADB.

Barber, Charles (1997) *Environmental Scarcities, State Capacity, Civil Violence: The Case of Indonesia*, American Academy of Arts and Sciences.

Bauer, Joanne R. and Daniel A Bell (1999) (editors), *The East Asian challenge for human rights*, Cambridge, UK; New York: Cambridge University Press, 1999.

Bryant, Raymond L. (1997) *The political ecology of forestry in Burma, 1824-1994*, London: Hurst & Co., 1997.

Bryant, Raymond L. and Michael Parnwell (1996) "Politics, Sustainable Development and Environmental Change in South East Asia," in: *Environmental Change in South-East Asia* (Parnwell and Bryant, eds.), New York, Routledge.

Bullard, Nicola et al. (1998), *Tigers in Trouble* (KS Jomo, editor), New York, Zed Books.

Case, Phil (1999) *Environmental Risk Management and Corporate Lending: A Global Perspective*, Woordhead Publishing, Cambridge, England.

Crosbie, Liz and Ken Knight (1995) *Strategy for Sustainable Business: Environmental Opportunity and Strategic Choice*, London; New York: McGraw Hill.

Dauvergne, Peter (1997), *Shadows in the forest: Japan and the politics of timber in Southeast Asia*, Cambridge, Mass.: MIT Press.

de Fonseka, Chandra (1995), "Challenges and Future Directions for Asian NGOs," in: *Government-NGO relations in Asia: prospects and challenges for people-centred development*, Noeleen Heyzer, James V. Riker, Antonio B. Quizon (eds), Kuala Lumpur: Asian and Pacific Development Centre; Houndmills, Basingstoke, Hampshire: Macmillan Press; New York: St. Martin's Press.

Desai, Vishvanath V. and Bindhu Lohani (1998), "Asia's Environment: Challenges and Opportunities," in: *The future of Asia in the world economy*, edited by Colm Foy, Francis Harrigan and David O'Connor; Asian Development Bank; Development Centre of the Organisation for Economic Co-operation and Development, Paris, France: Organisation for Economic Co-operation and Development.

Eccleston, Bernard and David Potter (1996), "Environmental NGOs and Different Political Contexts in South-East Asia: Malaysia, Indonesia and Vietnam," in: *Environmental Change in South-East Asia* (Parnwell and Bryant, eds.), New York: Routledge.

Elkington, John (1998) "The 'triple bottom line' for twenty-first-century business," in: *Companies in a world of conflict: NGO's, sanctions and corporate responsibility* (John V. Mitchell, ed.) London: Earthscan, 1998..

ELNI (Environmental Law Network International) (1998) *Environmental Agreements: The Role and Effect of Environmental Agreements in Environmental Policies*, London: Cameron & May.

ESCAP (1995) *State of the Environment in Asia and the Pacific*, New York: UN.

Esty, Daniel (1996) "Environmental Regulation and Competitiveness," in: *Asian dragons and green trade: environment, economics and International* (Simon S.C. Tay and Daniel C. Esty, editors)Singapore: Times Academic Press.

French, Hilary (1998) *Investing in the Future: Harnessing Private Capital Flows for Environmentally Sustainable Development*, Worldwatch Paper 139, Washington, D.C.: Worldwatch Institute.

Greider, William (1997) *One world, ready or not: the manic logic of global capitalism*, New York: Simon & Schuster.

Hanson, Jon Lun (1995) *Invisible Patterns: Ecology and Wisdom in Business and Profit*, Westport, CT: Quorum Books.

Harding, Andrew (1996) "Practical Human Rights, NGOs and the Environment in Malaysia," in: *Human rights approaches to environmental protection* (Alan E. Boyle and Michael R. Anderson, eds) Oxford: Clarendon Press; New York: Oxford University Press.

Hawken, Paul (1993) *The Ecology of Commerce: A Declaration of Sustainability*, New York, NY: Harper-Business.

Hetttige, Mani and David Wheeler (1997), *Industrial Pollution in Economic Development: Kuznets Revisited*, Washington DC: World Bank Development Research Group.

Hirsch, Philip and Carol Warren (1999) (editors) *The politics of environment in Southeast Asia: resources and resistance*, London; New York: Routledge, 1998.

Lee, Yok-shiu F. and Alvin Y. So (1999) (editors) *Asia's environmental movements: comparative perspectives*, Armonk, N.Y.: M.E. Sharpe, c1999.

Nader, Ralph et al. (1993), *The Case against "free trade": GATT, NAFTA, and the globalization of corporate power*, San Francisco, CA: Earth Island Press; Berkeley, CA: North Atlantic Books.

NCE (National Council on the Environment of Singapore, now Singapore Environment Council) (1995) *Greening the Bottom Line*, Singapore: NCE.

Pallamearts, Marc (1993) "International Environmental Law from Stockholm to Rio: Back to the Future," in: *Greening International Law* (Sands, ed.), London: Earthscan Publications.

Pangestu, Mari, and Kurnya Roesad (1996) "Experiences from Indonesia and Other ASEAN Countries," in: *Asian Dragons & Green Trade* (Tay & Esty, editors), Singapore: Times Academic Press.

Revez, Richard (1992) "Rehabilitating Interstate Competition: Rethinking the Race to the Bottom," *New York University Law Review*, 67: 1210.

Rigg, Jonathan (1997) *Southeast Asia: The Human Landscape of Modernization and Development*, London: Routledge.

Riker, James V. (1995) "From Cooptation to Cooperation and Collaboration in Government-NGO Relations: Toward an Enabling Policy Environment for People-Centred Development in Asia," in: *Government-NGO relations in Asia: prospects and challenges for people-centred development*, Noeleen Heyzer, James V. Riker, Antonio B. Quizon (eds), Kuala Lumpur: Asian and Pacific Development Centre; Houndmills, Basingstoke, Hampshire: Macmillan Press; New York: St. Martin's Press.

Romm, Joseph L. (1994) *Lean and Clean Management: How to Boost Profits and productivity by Reducing Pollution*, New York: Kodanshu America.

Sachs, Aaron (1995) *Eco-justice: linking human rights and the environment*, Washington, DC: Worldwatch Institute.

Speeding, Linda (1996) *Environmental Management for Business*, New York:

John Wiley & Sons.

Tay, Simon S.C. (1996) "The Way Ahead in Asia," in: *Asian Dragons & Green Trade* (Tay and Esty, editors), Singapore: Times Academic Press.

Tay, Simon S.C. (1997) "Trade and the Environment: Perspectives from the Asia-Pacific," *World Bulletin*, Vol. 13, No. 1-2 (Jan-Apr).

Tay, Simon S.C. (1998), "SE Asian Fires: A Haze over ASEAN and International Environmental Law," *Review of European Community and International Environmental Law*, Vol. 7 Issue 2.

Tay, Simon S.C. (1998a) "Asia's Economic Crisis: Impact and Opportunities for Sustainable Development," special report to the 4th Asia Pacific NGOs Environmental Conference, 26-27 Nov 1998, *Proceedings*, edited by Chou LM et al, and published by the Dept of Biological Sciences, National University of Singapore, Jan 1999.

Tay, Simon S.C. (1999) "SE Asian Fires: The Challenge to International Law and Sustainable Development," *Georgetown International Environmental Law Review*, Winter 1999.

UNDP (1999) *Human Development Report*, New York: Oxford U Press.

Von Weizsacker, Ernst, Lovins, Amory, and Lovins, Hunter (1997), *Factor Four: Doubling Wealth, Halving Resource Use*, London: Earthscan.

Vossenaar, Rene, and Veena Jha (1996) "Competitiveness: An Asian Perspective," in: *Asian Dragons & Green Trade* (Tay and Esty, editors), Singapore: Times Academic Press.

Wallace, David (1995) *Environmental Policy and Industrial Innovation: Strategies in Europe, the US and Japan*, London: Royal Institute of International Affairs and Earthscan.

Wapner, Paul Kevin (1996) *Environmental activism and world civic politics*, Albany: State University of New York Press , c1996.

Welford, Richard (1995) *Environmental Strategy and Sustainable Development*, London; New York: Routledge.

Wilson, Ian (2000) *The New Rules of Corporate Conduct: Rewriting the Social Charter*, Westport, Connecticut; London: Quorum Books.

World Bank (1993) *The East Asian Miracle: economic growth and public policy*, New York, N.Y.: Oxford University Press.

World Bank (1998) *East Asia: The Road to Recovery;* Washington, DC: World Bank.

Yamamoto, Tadadhi (1995) (editor) *Emerging civil society in the Asia Pacific community: nongovernmental underpinnings of the emerging Asia Pacific regional community,* Singapore: Institute of Southeast Asian Studies.

Zarsky, Lyuba and Simon S.C Tay. (2000) "Civil Society and Environmental Governance in Asia," in: *Asia's Clean Revolution: Industry, Growth and the Environment* (David Angel and Michael T Rock, editors) Sheffield: Greenleaf Publishing, forthcoming.

ACKNOWLEDGEMENTS

Parts of this paper draw on work commissioned by the US-Asia Environmental Partnership (US-AEP) for policy papers that frame the current state of environmental regulation in Asia and a future agenda for work and research and, in particular, the work of Simon Tay with Lyuba Zarsky of the Nautilus Institute, on Civil Society and Environmental Governance. Their work appears as a chapter in *Asia's Clean Revolution: Industry, Growth and the Environment* (David Angel and Michael T Rock, editors) Greenleaf Publishing, UK, 2000.

EMISSIONS TRADING: U.S. EXPERIENCE IMPLEMENTING MULTI-STATE CAP AND TRADE PROGRAMS

Brian J. McLean
Director, Clean Air Markets Division
U.S. Environmental Protection Agency

INTRODUCTION

In order to reduce the cost of compliance with air pollution reduction requirements, several flexibility mechanisms were introduced in the United States in the late 1970's. Referred to generally as emissions trading, they included emissions offsets, plant-specific "bubbles," and emission reduction credits. The offset mechanism was introduced to permit economic growth in areas that were not meeting air quality goals. For example, a new source could locate (or an existing source could expand) in a nonattainment area by reducing emissions at another source (usually by more than the increment of new emissions). In this way, the economy could grow and the environment could improve.

Under the bubble concept, limitations on individual emissions points within a facility could be adjusted upward and downward to minimize compliance costs as long as the total emissions at the facility remained below the level that would have occurred under the original command and control regulations and there were no adverse impacts on air quality.

Emission reduction credits (ERCs) were the most flexible of the three because they allowed a facility to earn credits by reducing its emissions below the required level and to sell those credits to another facility, either directly or through an emissions credit broker. The use of the credits, however, needed to cover the same time period as that for which the reductions occurred, i.e., generation and use of credits needed to be contemporaneous.

A derivative of ERCs, called "discrete emissions reductions" (DERs) allows credits earned during one period of time to be "banked" and used by a source in lieu of a required emissions reduction during a future period. This further flexibility is a feature of "open market" trading introduced in the late 1990's.

Although emissions offsets and emissions credit trading have been used for over 20 years to reduce the cost of complying with command and control regulations, the underlying regulatory infrastructure had not originally been designed with the intent of supporting emissions trading, and the marriage raised environmental concerns and incurred transaction costs that inhibited more extensive use of emissions trading.

CONCERNS WITH EMISSIONS TRADING

Traditional air pollution control regulations focus on source-specific requirements to reduce the rate at which pollutants are emitted (e.g., pounds of pollutant per quantity of heat input) but generally do not limit the use of the facility. Therefore, neither mass emissions on a source-by-source basis, nor overall area-wide emissions are usually established as enforceable limits. Coupled with the tendency of sources to aim for slightly lower rates to ensure compliance, this has the desired effect of reducing air pollution, but it does not provide a very precise level from which to determine emissions reduction credits, nor does this system assure that emissions will not increase as facilities are utilized more (or expanded) or as new facilities are built in the future. In fact, regulators informally have relied on the extra control to provide a margin of safety for the environmental uncertainty of the command and control system.

Consequently, environmental concerns arose when facilities wanted to receive "credit" for emitting below their required levels in order to sell those credits to another facility (so that it could emit more) or to permit new sources of pollution to locate in an area. First, were these credits (or portions of these credits) a result of the over-control inherent in the traditional program, and not "real" or "additional" reductions? Was the source simply commoditizing the safety margin and allowing other sources to use the credits to emit more with the environment being worse off as a result?

Second, when a source sought credit for taking actions that actually reduced emissions, might those actions have happened "anyway" (or eventually) as part of modernization efforts, and therefore, were they not already being relied upon to temper the growth in emissions allowed under the traditional emissions rate approach to regulation? Third, a lack of rigor and consistency in emissions measurement and the uncertainties regarding projected emissions (the product of future emissions rates and future activity levels) contributed to the difficulty in establishing current and future baseline emission levels from which credits could be earned.

Fourth, since emissions trading per se did not reduce emissions (or reduce them significantly), was it simply moving emissions around, and perhaps making air quality in some areas worse? Assurance of no harm often required air quality modeling which introduced additional analyses and costs.

Addressing and resolving these concerns took time, added to the transaction costs of emissions trades, and consequently, limited the application of emissions trading.

CAP AND TRADE

During the 1980s, the United States was confronted with the problem of reducing acid rain–a regional air pollution problem caused not by a single source, but by the collective emissions of SO_2 and NO_x primarily from hundreds of electric power plants in the eastern half of the country. In 1989, a new program was proposed that would replace the combined command and control and trading approach and address the problems identified above. The new approach would:

- establish limitations on sources in terms of allowable mass emissions rather than emissions rates and express those allowable emissions in terms of tradeable "allowances" (each allowance being an authorization to emit one ton of a pollutant)

- require a significant reduction in emissions for an entire industrial sector

- place a "cap" or limit on total emissions, requiring any emissions increases by new or existing sources to be offset

- require accurate and consistent measurement and reporting of all emissions from all sources

- establish automatic and significant penalties for exceeding allowable emissions

- allow sources total flexibility in selecting and revising control approaches, including using emissions trading; i.e., government approval would not be necessary

- retain source-specific emission limitations designed to protect local air quality; i.e., buying "allowances" would not entitle a source to exceed limits established to protect public health

This new approach, which became known as "cap and trade," was the centerpiece of Title IV of the Clean Air Act Amendments of 1990. The goal of Title IV was to address the problem of acid rain by reducing annual SO_2 emissions in the contiguous 48 states and the District of Columbia by 10 million tons from the 25.9 million ton level that had been emitted in 1980. This would represent a 40% reduction. Of the 10 million ton reduction, an 8.5 million ton reduction was to come from electric utility plants by using the new cap and trade approach. The cap, or permanent emissions limit, would be introduced in phases by first requiring the 263 largest and highest emitting electric utility boilers to reduce their collective emissions by 50 percent beginning in 1995. From 2000 through 2009, emissions from all existing electric utility boilers and turbines serving generators larger than 25 megawatts (approximately 2000 units) and all new units would be limited by receiving no more than 9.48 million allowances per year. Finally, in 2010 and thereafter, emissions from all affected electric utility units (including new units) would be limited by receiving no more than 8.95 million allowances per year. This would result in a reduction of almost 50 percent in annual utility SO_2 emissions from their 1980 level of 17.5 million tons.

Figure 1 shows the location of the affected sources and the geographic scope of the program. Figure 2 shows the emissions expected from utility sources with and without the Acid Rain Program as well as the emissions allowed each year. Because sources may save or "bank" allowances not used in one year and use them to comply in a future year, the figure shows how such behavior is expected to smooth the actual reduction in emissions over time.

OPERATING RESPONSIBILITIES

Responsibilities for implementing the program are clear and somewhat different from existing command and control programs and previous trading programs. Sources are free to choose their compliance strategy (and to change it as circumstances require) without needing government approval. However, all sources must install, operate, and quality assure emissions monitoring equipment and must report emissions data and test results periodically to the government. In addition, sources do not need government approval to transfer allowances, but they must hold sufficient allowances in their accounts at the end of each compliance period to cover their emissions. A fluid, active market is assisted by the government's issuance of allowances for 30 years into the future.

In contrast to traditional command and control programs, the government does not tell the source how to comply or even collaborate with the source in determining a compliance strategy. The government is responsible for ensuring that each source accurately accounts for all its emissions, for tracking allowance transfers and holdings, for enforcing penalties for noncompliance, and for making all emissions and trading information publicly available. This last function enhances accountability and public credibility of the program.

Figure 3 shows how the emissions monitoring and reporting process works under the Acid Rain Program. A source submits its SO_2, NO_x, and

Figure 1: Scope Of SO₂ Program (Over 2,000 sources affected)

Figure 2: Goal Of SO₂ Program

- Reduce SO2 emissions by 10 million tons from 1980 level-- 8.5 million tons from power generation through "cap and trade" mechanism

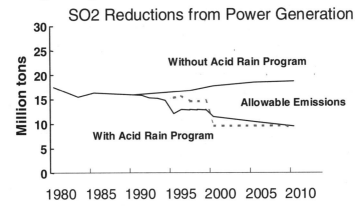

CO_2 emissions data via the internet to the Emissions Tracking System (ETS) operated by the U.S. Environmental Protection Agency (EPA), and EPA provides electronic feedback so that the source can correct errors quickly. EPA and State personnel also visit the source to witness tests and to conduct audits of equipment and operations. EPA posts emissions data on its web site quarterly.

Figure 4 shows the steps involved in completing an allowance transfer. Currently, EPA enters each transfer into its Allowance Tracking System (ATS) and posts all transfers recorded each day on its web site. This notification of the official transfer of allowances is often used by parties to signal payment for allowances purchased. In 2001, EPA expects to provide online transfer capability for traders via the internet to further speed transactions and reduce administrative costs.

PROGRAM RESULTS

In the first 5 years of the Acid Rain Program, SO_2 emissions from the 263 Phase I sources were reduced substantially and all sources were in compliance with respect to their allowable emissions (see Figure 5). It is also apparent that Phase II sources, which were not subject to the emissions cap until 2000, did little to reduce emissions during this period. However, data for 1999 and preliminary data for 2000 indicate that Phase II sources are reducing their emissions (EPA, 2001). Figure 6 shows the geographic distribution of the SO_2 emissions reductions under the Acid Rain Program with significant reductions taking place in the Midwest where emissions have historically been the highest and where the cost of reducing emissions is most economical.

Through a 200-station wet deposition monitoring network it is possible to assess the impact of these emissions reductions on the chemistry of rain and snow. Figure 7 shows the changes in wet sulfate deposition across the eastern United States from the 1989-1991 period to the period from 1995 through 1998. Reductions of up to 25 percent in the concentrations of sulfate ions in wet deposition occurred throughout a large portion of the northeastern United States.

When the full SO_2 reductions are achieved in 2010, a significant benefit to public health is expected because of the reduction in airborne fine particulate matter, much of which is due to sulfates. Monetized benefits, due largely to reduced premature mortality, are estimated at $50 billion per year (Ostro, 1999). Figure 8 shows the distribution of those benefits across the eastern United States.

In stark contrast to the benefits of the emissions reductions is the cost of compliance shown in Figure 9. When the Acid Rain Program was being considered by Congress in 1989 and 1990, the estimated cost

Figure 3: Emissions Monitoring And Reporting

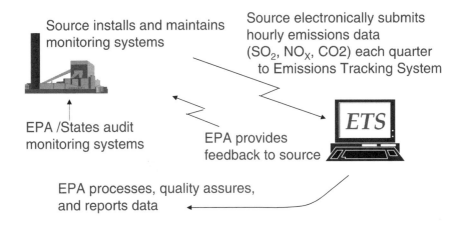

Figure 4: Allowance Transfer Process

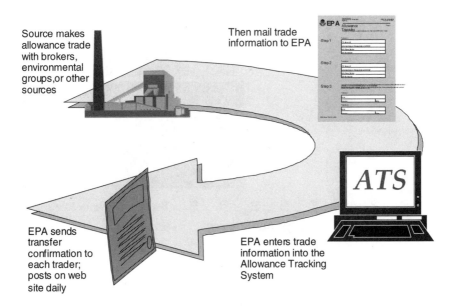

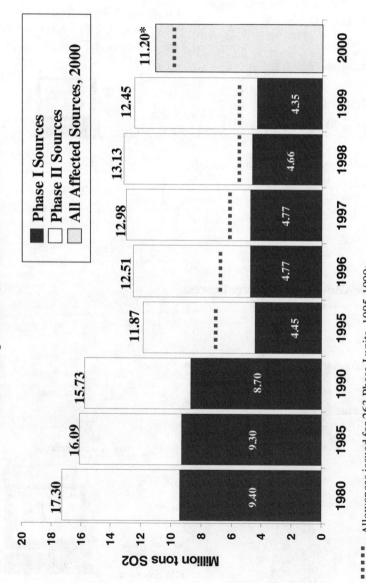

Figure 5: SO$_2$ Emissions From Title IV Sources

Allowances issued for 263 Phase I units, 1995-1999;
Allowances issued for all affected sources in 2000.
*Estimated 2000 emissions.

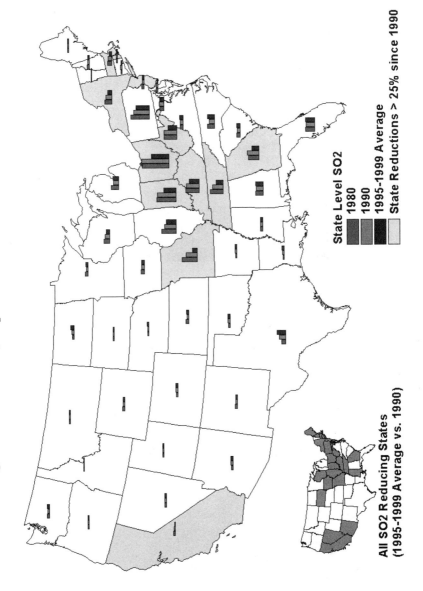

Figure 6: Total Utility SO$_2$ - 1980, 1990, 1995-1999 Average

State Level SO2
1980
1990
1995-1999 Average
State Reductions > 25% since 1990

All SO2 Reducing States
(1995-1999 Average vs. 1990)

Figure 7: Sulfate Deposition Reduction (kg/ha) Since Start-Up Of Acid Rain Program

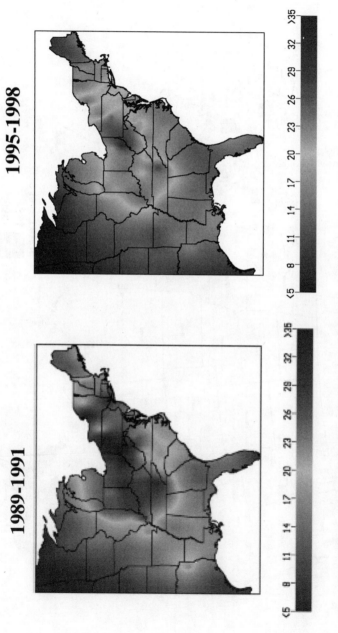

Lynch, J.A., Bowersox, V.C. and Grimm, J.W., 2000. Changes in Sulfate Deposition in Eastern USA Following
Implementation of Phase I of Title IV of the Clean Air Act Amendments of 1990. *Atmospheric Environment*, 34(11) 1665-
1680. Updated by the principal author to include data for 1998, as published in the GAO Report: Acid Rain, Emissions
Trends and Effects in the Eastern United States, March 2000 (GAO/RCED-00-47). (Units are in kilograms per hectare).

Figure 8: $50 Billion In Health Benefits From Title IV SO$_2$ Reductions

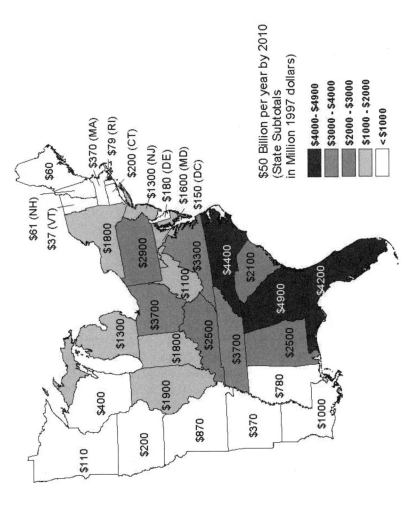

Figure 9: SO₂ Trading Program: Expected Costs By 2010

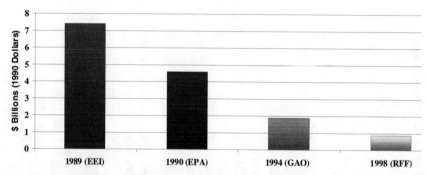

Estimated Annual Cost of Full Acid Rain Program in 2010

EEI = Edison Electric Institute (assumes no trading)
EPA = Environmental Protection Agency
GAO = General Accounting Office
RFF = Resources for the Future

of the program ranged from over $4 billion per year (EPA, 1990) to over $7 billion per year (utility industry estimate). But four years after its enactment, an audit of the program by the U.S. General Accounting Office concluded that the cost of full implementation was likely to be closer to $2 billion per year (GAO, 1994). More recent estimates have placed the cost closer to $1 billion per year (Burtraw, 1998).

As cost estimates came down, questions arose. Why were the earlier estimates so far off? Studies revealed that the flexibility of the program allowed companies to take advantage of numerous cost saving opportunities as multiple methods for reducing SO_2 emissions competed with one another (Ellerman, 2000). Competition among railroads shipping low sulfur coal led to significant reductions in transport costs, a major component of coal cost; flexibility in the operation of flue gas desulfurization equipment ("scrubbers") coupled with design and equipment advances significantly reduced the cost of scrubbing high sulfur coal; and medium sulfur coal became marketable now that there was no arbitrary sulfur content for "compliance coal" as existed under the traditional regulatory program. Also, the ability of sources to bank allowances earned from extra control actions allowed them to reduce future expenditures. Finally, the allowance market, in addition to providing a compliance option for sources, also provided a benchmark price against which companies could better evaluate compliance alternatives.

Figure 10 summarizes activity in the SO_2 allowance market over the past seven years. While allowance prices have ranged from under $100 to a little over $200, volume has steadily increased. As of the end of the year 2000, over 111 million allowances had been transferred through over 12,700 official transactions. Although many of these transfers have occurred between units owned by the same companies, an increasing number have been taking place between unrelated companies, reflecting an increasing acceptance and reliance on the trading mechanism.

EXTENDING CAP AND TRADE

In 1993, the South Coast Air Quality Management District (SCAQMD), which is the air pollution control agency for the Los Angeles metropolitan area of California, instituted a cap and trade program for SO_2 and NO_x called RECLAIM (the Regional Clean Air Incentives Market). It has many of the same characteristics outlined above, but with a few differences. For example, there are two zones with trading of allowances into the zone with the more severe air quality problem is restricted. Also, there is no banking of allowances from one year to the next. This paper is not reporting on the details or results of this program, but information can be obtained from the SCAQMD (www.aqmd.gov).

In 1994, 11 of the 12 Northeast States of the Ozone Transport Region (OTR) signed a Memorandum of Understanding agreeing to reduce and cap NO_x emissions in that region. In 1996, EPA agreed to administer the multi-state cap and trade program for the OTR. EPA constructed a new Allowance Tracking System with features specific to the OTR NO_x Program and augmented the Emissions Tracking System to accommodate NO_x mass emissions data as well as several hundred additional sources in preparation for start up of the program in 1999.

Figure 11 shows the 1990 baseline emissions for the eight states participating in the program in 1999 along with the allowable emissions and actual emissions for 1999. In 2003, the allowable emissions will be reduced again. As with the SO_2 program, actual emissions were significantly less than allowable emissions. However, from Figure 12 one can see that trading volume was lower and prices spiked just prior to the first compliance period.

As is the case with the SO_2 cap and trade program, the NO_x program for the OTR has a single allowance and emissions tracking system to promote fungibility and minimize transaction costs. However, there

Figure 10: The SO₂ Allowance Market

- Since 1994, over 111 million SO₂ allowances have been transferred

- EPA has executed over 12,700 transactions, 80% within 24 hours of receipt

- Approximately 41% of all SO₂ allowances have been traded between different companies

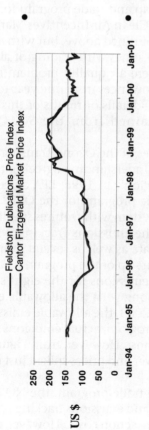

Source: Clean Air Markets Division

Figure 11: Ozone Transport Commission (OTC) NOx Budget Program

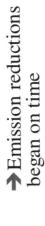

→ Emission reductions began on time

→ Sources have achieved over 99% compliance

→ Emissions reduced by 242,400 tons in 8 participating states

→ Source emitted 20% below 1999 allocations

OTC NOx Emissions

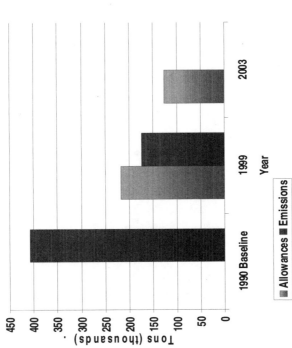

Sources: Cantor Fitzgerald (MPI) and Acid Rain Program (trading & emissions)

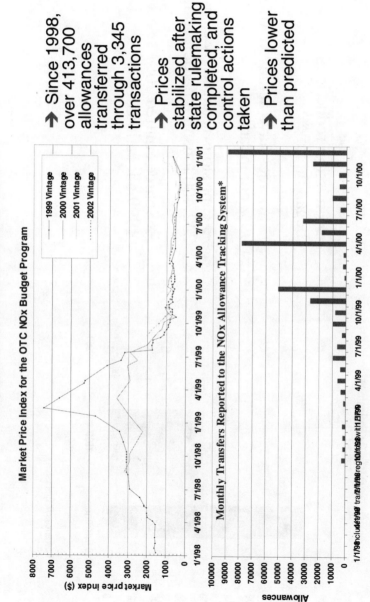

Figure 12: OTC NOx Allowance Market

Sources: Cantor Fitzgerald (MPI) and NOx Allowance Tracking System (NATS)

are several differences between the programs. First, rather than one set of rules for all participants, as is the case for the SO_2 program, the OTR program is implemented through separate rulemakings by each state. Although a model rule was developed, states deviated from the model in several ways. For example, some allocated allowances for four years while others allocated allowances one year at a time. This differentiated the allowance market and reduced fungibility.

Second, the rules were adopted less than one year before the beginning of the first compliance period (May 1, 1999) with some adopted only a few months before compliance was expected. Most rules were challenged in state courts with resolution extending into the compliance period. As rules were adopted and concern over the ability of sources to comply rose, so did allowance prices. Prices peaked in February and March after all rules had been adopted and then dropped after a Maryland court ruled in favor of industry petitions in that state to delay compliance. Emissions in Maryland were expected to be about 23,000 tons above available allowances, and sources had not taken actions to reduce their emissions, hoping for a favorable ruling. This contributed to a concern that demand for allowances would exceed supply.

Third, the OTR program allowed sources to earn allowances for taking actions in 1997 and 1998, prior to the first compliance period in 1999. However, the first of these early reduction credits were not given to EPA to put into the allowance market until May, 1999. By October, a total of 24,635 allowances were added to the market because of actions taken in 1997 and 1998. The withdrawal of Maryland sources' demand for 23,000 allowances coupled with the increase in supply of allowances throughout the compliance period and the knowledge of the actual emissions as the season progressed, helped to drive down allowance prices.

In addition to the variations in allowance allocation procedures across the various states, the OTR has a provision to limit the use of banked allowances. Known as "progressive flow control" this provision requires that after the current year's allowances are used to cover emissions, a portion of the previous years' unused (or banked) allowances (up to 10 percent of the region's current year's allocation) may be used to cover emissions on a one allowance for one ton basis. However, after those banked allowances are used, two banked allowances for every ton will be required. This is intended to discourage the excessive use of banked allowances (and subsequently lessen the chance that emissions will rise significantly during the summer ozone season). However, this causes allowances of different year vintages to be valued differently, further segmenting the allowance market into smaller pools of similarly valued products and further reducing fungibility and liquidity.

To varying degrees these factors may help to explain the lower volume and higher volatility of the NO_x market compared to the SO_2 market. Nonetheless, the NO_x allowance market settled down as the summer season progressed, and importantly, the environmental goal was achieved.

COMPARING POLICY OPTIONS

For many air pollution problems, command and control (or direct regulation) may be the best course. For example, where a specific facility can be identified as the source of a public health problem, limiting its emissions may be the simplest and most effective solution. Also, in the multi-industry transportation sector where fuel characteristics can have a direct impact on the effectiveness of engine technology, it may be best to directly specify fuel parameters, such as sulfur content, to permit engines to be designed in the most cost-effective way to reduce harmful emissions of NO_x, hydrocarbons, and carbon monoxide.

However, specificity of requirements may also inhibit innovation, in which case economic instruments such as taxes or tradeable permits may be preferred to encourage more efficient solutions. If properly designed, economic incentives can harness market forces to work toward environmental improvement. By internalizing pollution control costs, they can make pollution reduction in the interest of the firm and promote innovation.

Whether such instruments should be tradeable permits or taxes is a topic for other papers and research. However, setting the quantity of allowable emissions (and letting the price of allowances vary), as is the case with cap and trade programs, is more attractive to many environmental policy makers than setting the price (and letting emissions fluctuate), as is the case with environmental taxes. One may also want to consider the behavioral component of markets in choosing between these instruments. For those engaged in the competitive business world the "greed and fear" of the marketplace may be viewed as more conducive to creativity than the simple price signal offered by a tax. Some might argue that the prospect of making money (by freeing up allowances for sale) is more motivating than saving money (by minimizing taxes).

The tradeable permit instrument can be further subdivided into tradeable credits and tradeable allowances. Tradeable credits are based on traditional emissions rate regulation where credits are created on a project-by-project basis when the emissions rate is reduced. This approach is preferred by some companies because it provides a predictable plant operating parameter and allows flexible utilization of the facility. However, as with the price versus quantity debate, the emissions rate (and tradeable credit) approach provides less certainty regarding environmental impact than the emissions cap (and tradeable allowance) approach. As a consequence, where emissions grow, the government needs to lower emissions rates periodically simply to maintain environmental quality; this, in turn, undermines the purported predictability of the rate approach.

On the other hand, an emissions cap with tradeable allowances provides more environmental certainty and is consistent with the notion that natural resources -- air, land, and water -- are finite and that impacts to them must be limited to protect them. An emissions cap does not restrict economic growth, as some have charged. It simply requires that sources consider the emission implications of their business plans, and if they plan to increase production (and emissions), they must either reduce their emissions rate commensurately or purchase allowances from other sources sufficient to offset their increased emissions. This internalization of environmental consequences can probably be achieved at lower cost to sources than the iterative (and less predictable) government-imposed requirements intended to achieve the same effect. Furthermore, should the economy contract, this approach automatically allows some relaxation of emissions rates without increasing overall emissions or worsening the environment.

CONCLUSIONS

The benefits of an emissions cap and trade approach compared to the traditional command and control approach (even coupled with credit trading) can be summarized as follows:

- more certainty that a specific level of emissions will be achieved and maintained over time
- more regulatory certainty for sources
- more compliance flexibility and lower transaction costs for sources
- fewer administrative resources needed by industry and government

Since cost is often an obstacle to pollution reduction, it should also be noted that by driving down the cost of compliance, the flexible cap and trade approach actually makes further environmental improvement feasible.

Based on the experience of designing and implementing multi-state

SO_2 and NO_x cap and trade programs, there appear to be three keys to a successful program:

1. The Cap. The allowance cap (which needs to cover all major existing and new sources of an industrial sector) ensures achievement of the environmental goal and provides predictability for the tradeable permit market.

2. Accountability. To determine environmental compliance and to support the integrity of the tradable allowances, it is critical that emissions data be accurately and consistently measured and that all emissions be accounted for. It is also important that all emissions and allowance information be publicly accessible both to facilitate the market and to overcome public reservations regarding emissions trading. Finally, it is important that there be predictable and significant consequences for noncompliance.

3. Simplicity. To keep transaction and administrative costs low, facilitate active trading and innovation, and maximize cost savings, program rules must be simple and easily understood by all participants. Simplicity can best be achieved if the government focuses on setting goals and measuring results, and lets sources and the market figure out how to meet those goals. Command and control programs (even with credit trading) are more complex because they try to address all three -- often prescribing in great detail exactly how goals are to be met.

Although there is much rhetorical support for designing and implementing a successful emissions trading program, those involved (policymakers, legislators, regulators, affected sources, environmentalists, and would-be litigators) often find it difficult in practice to accept one or more of the above elements. However, as they are omitted or diminished, so too is the likelihood of success.

[Author's Note: The conclusions and opinions expressed are those of the author and do not necessarily reflect those of the U.S. Environmental Protection Agency.]

REFERENCES

Burtraw, Dallas, Alan J. Krupnick, Erin Mansur, David Austin and Deidre Farrell (1998). "Costs and Benefits of Reducing Air Pollutants Related to Acid Rain." *Contemporary Economic Policy* 16:379-400

Ellerman, A. Denny, Paul L. Joskow, Richard Schmalensee, Juan-Pablo Montero and Elizabeth M. Bailey (2000). *Markets for Clean Air: The U.S. Acid Rain Program.* Cambridge: Cambridge University Press

Ostro, Bart T., Lauraine G. Chestnut, David M. Mills and Ann M. Watkins (1999). "Estimating the Effects of Air Pollutants on the Population: Human Health Benefits of Sulfate Aerosol Reductions Under Title IV of the 1990 Clean Air Act Amendments," in: *Air Pollution and Health*, edited by S.T. Holgate, J.M. Samet, H.S. Koren, R.L. Maynard. Academic Press, 899-915; and updated in "Benefits Assessment of Multi-Pollutant Strategies" by Ann M. Watkins, presented at the Electric Utilities Environmental Conference, Tucson, Arizona, April 8, 2001

U.S. General Accounting Office (GAO) (1994). *Allowance Trading Offers an Opportunity to Reduce Emissions at Less Cost.* GAO/RCED-95-30, Washington, DC

U.S. Environmental Protection Agency (EPA)(1990). "Comparison of the Economic Impacts of the Acid Rain Provisions of the Senate Bill (S.1630) and the House Bill (S.1630)." Draft report prepared by ICF Resources Inc, Washington, DC, July

U.S. Environmental Protection Agency (EPA) (2001). www.epa.gov/airmarkets

GREEN TAX REFORMS IN OECD COUNTRIES: AN OVERVIEW

Jean-Philippe Barde
Head, National Policies Division
Environment Directorate, OECD

The last decade witnessed a large increase in the use of economic instruments to protect the environment in OECD countries, with a growing emphasis on tax instruments, in particular in the context of "green tax reforms". (Figure 1) This tendency is due to many factors such as the need to improve the effectiveness of policies based to a great extent on rigid and cumbersome regulations, the need to integrate environmental policies effectively with sectoral policies (such as energy, transport or agriculture), and, sometimes, the search for more tax revenues to finance the general government budget, as well as specific environmental funds or programmes (Barde 1992, 1997, 1999; OECD 1994, 1996a). In this context, fiscal instruments provide an ideal means of injecting appropriate signals into the market, of eliminating or reducing structural distortions (such as unsuitable energy and transport tariffs) and of internalizing externalities, while at the same time improving the efficiency of existing measures. If properly conceived and implemented, green tax reforms can contribute to a real structural adjustment of economies.

ENVIRONMENTAL TAXES AND GREEN TAX REFORM

Most countries need to introduce more flexibility and efficiency in their economic structures. This implies, inter alia, adjusting tax systems in order to reduce distortions, increase market flexibility and making environmental policies more effective. Most OECD countries have undertaken significant tax reforms since the end of the 1980s, chiefly in two ways: first by reducing tax rates in the higher income tax brackets (which fell on average by more than ten points between 1986 and 1997) and lowering corporate tax rates (down 10 points over the same period); secondly, by broadening the tax base, and thirdly, by giving a greater

Figure 1: The evolution of economic instruments

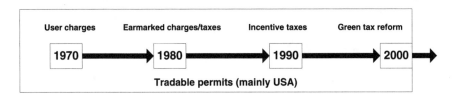

weight to general consumption taxes such as VAT. These tax reforms provide an excellent opportunity to introduce an environmental dimension in taxation, i.e. a "greening " of tax systems. This greening of taxation may consist of three complementary policies: eliminating tax distortions, restructuring existing taxes, and introducing new environmental taxes.

Eliminating tax distortions

Many fiscal measures can either directly or indirectly produce adverse effects for the environment. One such measure is direct subsidies.[1] (See Table 1). For example, subsidies to agriculture (estimated at 362 billion dollars a year in OECD countries in 1998, or 1.4% of GDP) are one of the causes of over-farming of land, excessive use of fertilizers and pesticides, soil degradation and other problems (OECD 1996a). Similarly, irrigation water is often charged below its real price, which leads to wastage. In the area of energy, subsidies to coal production, the most polluting fuel, still came to 7.7 billion dollars in 1997 in five OECD countries, which admittedly was lower than the 13.2 billion dollars for 1987. It is estimated that subsidies to industry amounted to 43.7 billion dollars in 1993; when subsidies encourage the use of certain raw materials and greater energy consumption, there can be negative fallout in terms of recycling and waste and lock in inefficient technologies.

A second category of distortion arises from specific tax provisions (tax rates variations or exemptions). For instance, coal, the most polluting fuel, is taxed in only five OECD countries and subject to many tax rebates. The transport sector, a major source of pollution and other harmful effects, is affected by many distortions: a case in point is the widespread under-taxing of diesel oil in many countries which contributed to a constant increase in the number of diesel vehicles, which are more polluting[2] and noisy, and to a sharp increase of road freight transport. In OECD countries, the consumption of diesel fuel for road transport grew from 15% of total consumption in 1970 to 32% in 1997 (OECD, 1999). Other types of distortionary measures include deductibility of commuting expenses from taxable income, company cars excluded from taxable benefit, and tax free aviation fuel (kerosene). It is clear that the "greening" of taxation should start with a systematic inventory and a correction of fiscal measures (subsidies and taxes) which are harmful for the environment.

Restructuring existing taxes

Many existing taxes could be changed so as to benefit the environment.

Table 1. Changes in support levels in some countries

Agriculture	1986-88 (average)	1991-93 (average)	1996-98 (average)	1997p	1998p	Remarks
Total transfers	326	394	349	336	362	US$ billion
	297	320	298	297	324	ECU billion
- Total transfers as % GDP	2.1	1.7	1.3	1.3	1.4	
- Percentage PSE[1]	41	39	33	32	37	as % of production value
Coal production	1987	1991	1993	1995	1997	Remarks
Total PSE in select countries	13.2	10.8	9	11	7.7	Germany, Japan, Spain, Turkey, UK (US$ billion)
Industry[2]	1989	1990	1991	1992	1993	Remarks
Reported net government expenditures	36.9	41.6	45.7	44.1	43.7	US$ billion

p - preliminary

(1) Producer subsidy equivalent - a measure of the value of the monetary transfers to producers resulting from policies in a given year, including transfers from both consumers and taxpayers. The percentage PSE is the gross total PSE expressed as a percentage of total farm receipts.

(2) The support to industry overlaps with other support estimates; e.g., to energy.

Sources: OECD (1999), Agricultural Policies in OECD Countries: Monitoring and Evaluation; IEA (1999), Energy Policies of IEA Countries; OECD (1998), Spotlight on Public Support to Industry.

It is a question of adjusting relative prices by increasing taxes on the most polluting products and activities. Since energy is one of the main sources both of pollution and of tax revenue, an "environmental" restructuring of prices and taxes is essential. The possibilities are to restructure existing energy taxes and/or to introduce new environmental taxes. For instance, in most OECD countries, taxes on fuel account for over 50% of the pump price. This leaves large scope for restructuring taxes on the basis of environmental parameters, such as carbon or sulphur content (see Figure 2), as the Nordic countries and the Netherlands have done. For instance, the introduction of a new CO_2 tax in Denmark, Norway and Sweden was accompanied by a decrease in existing energy taxes, in particular on industry.[3]

The environmental impact of such measures will depend both on the total tax burden on taxed fuels and on the availability of substitute products. Thus most OECD countries have introduced a tax differential between leaded and unleaded petrol. This has led to a marked fall in the proportion of leaded petrol and to its disappearance from the market in most OECD countries. All countries apply differentiated car sales taxes and/or annual car taxes according to engine capacity and/or vehicle weight (which can be a proxy of the environmental impact of the vehicle), but in several countries (e.g., Austria, Denmark, Germany, Nor-

Figure 2: Tax Rates on the Sulphur Content of Fuels in Selected OECD Countries

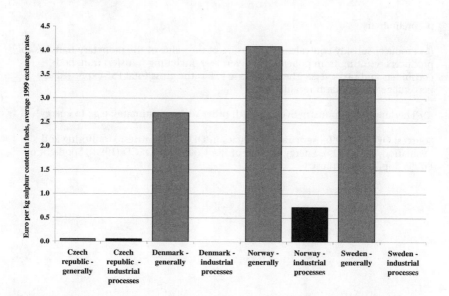

way) taxes have been adjusted to the specific emission characteristics of the vehicles. Denmark, Finland, Norway and Sweden apply differentiated taxes on unleaded gasoline, according to environmental criteria (e.g., in Sweden according to their sulphur, benzene and phosphorous content). Environment-related differentiation of diesel taxes is applied in Austria, Denmark, Finland, Norway, Sweden and the UK.[4] This has been leading to a gradual reduction in the use of the most polluting automotive fuels.

In fact, many studies show that while fuel taxes generally cover or more than cover infrastructure costs, they are still not enough to internalize the external costs of road transport (Table 2). According to the European Conference of Ministers of Transport (ECMT) estimates, in order to cover external costs, fuel taxes should on average be increased as follows: car petrol, +0.83 ECU; car diesel, +1.04 ECU; and truck diesel, +0.74 ECU (ECMT, 1998).

Introducing new environmental taxes

An obvious practice is to introduce new taxes whose prime purpose is to protect the environment. These may be taxes on emissions (for instance on atmospheric pollutants or water pollution) or taxes on products. The latter are more frequent. Since the early 1990s, many environmental taxes have been introduced on products ranging from packaging to fertilizers, pesticides, batteries, chemical substances (solvents), lubricants, tires, razors, disposable cameras and beverage containers (See for example Figure 3). The OECD database indicates 51 different taxes (other than energy-related taxes) in 11 countries (Table 3).[5]

Green tax reforms

Any "green" tax reform entails many aspects, ranging from the in-depth reform of existing taxation to the introduction of new taxes. This means that the objective pursued by the reforms may not only be environmental. Other benefits may be obtained in economic terms (greater efficiency by internalizing externalities and eliminating distortions), and possibly in terms of employment (lower unemployment thanks to a lowering of labour taxes financed by new environmental taxes - see below).

Since the early 1990s, several countries have introduced comprehensive green tax reforms; in most cases, in a context of a constant tax burden, in the sense that new environmental taxes offset reductions in existing taxes (tax shift). In fact, a constant tax burden is an essential condition for the acceptability of environmental taxes. Industry, in par-

Bringing Business On Board

Table 2: Revenues generated by road usage as a percentage of road-related expenditure, including and excluding external costs, in France, Japan and the United States in 1991

	France - urban areas	France - rural areas	Japan	United States
	(billion FF)	(billion FF)	(billion Yen)	(million US dollar)
Revenues	57	100.2	9 530	62 747
Expenditure	44.2	61.2	11 665	78 260
Balance	12.8	39	-2 135	-15 513
Revenues as percentage of expenditure	*127 %*	*164 %*	*82 %*	*80 %*
External costs[a]	56 to 92.7	33.8 to 48.2	2 742	117 800 to 371 700[b]
Balance – external costs	-43.2 to -79.9	- 9.2 to +5.2	-4 877	-356 187 to -102 287
Revenues as percentage of expenditure + external costs	*42 % to 57 %*	*92 % to 105 %*	*66 %*	*14 % to 32 %*

(a) In all three studies, external costs include costs related to the following factors:
France: local and regional pollution; greenhouse effects; congestion; accidents; noise.
Japan: pollution; greenhouse effects; accidents; noise; disappearance of natural areas.
United States: effects of air pollution on human health, materials and crops; climatic changes; congestion; accidents; noise; vibrations.
(b) These external cost estimates do not include non-taxable parking space for employees, which represents an estimated total cost of US$ 19 billion.

Source: OECD (1998), Part II, p.81.

ticular, is usually strongly opposed to environmental taxes on the grounds of a possible loss of competitiveness (see section entitled "Environmental Taxes and Competitiveness"). Similarly, consumers may fear that environmental taxes might lead to price increases; it is then essential to show clearly that other taxes are being reduced to ensure the political acceptability of green tax reforms. A few significant examples are presented below.

Finland was the first country to introduce a carbon tax in 1990, followed by a progressive greening of the tax system. While the carbon

Table 3: Non-energy / transport environment related taxes in OECD countries

AUSTRIA
Waste deposit levy
Belgium
Écotaxes

CANADA
Federal air conditioner tax
Manitoba -- Non deposit containers tax
Prince Edward's Island -- Tires Tax
Nova Scotia -- Tires Tax
Ontario -- Alcoholic Beverage Container Tax
Manitoba -- Tires tax
Alberta -- Tires tax
British Columbia -- Tires tax
New Brunswick -- Tires Tax
British Columbia -- Batteries tax

CZECH REPUBLIC
Waste deposit fee
Effluent charges on waste water
Air pollution charge

DENMARK
Duty on certain retail containers
Duty on waste water
Duty on disposable tableware
Duty on certain chlorinated solvents
Duty on electric bulbs
Duty on sealed NiCd-batteries
Duty on carrier bags made of paper, plastics, etc.
Duty on waste
Duty on CFC
Duty on pesticides

FINLAND
Surtax on alcoholic beverages
Oil waste levy
Soft drinks surtax
Oil damage levy
Tax on waste

HUNGARY
Noise abatement levy
Water pollution levy
Air pollution levy
Product charge on tires
Product charge on refrigerators and refrigerants
Product charge on packaging materials
Toxic waste levy

NETHERLANDS
Aviation noise tax
Tax on tap water
Levy on water pollution
Minerals accounting system
Tax on the pollution of surface waters

NORWAY
Basic tax on non-refillable beverage containers
Tax on Lubricating Oil
Tax on final treatment of waste
Tax on trichloroethane and tetrachloroethane
Product tax on beverage containers
Tax on pesticides

SWEDEN
Tax on waste

UNITED KINGDOM
The Landfill tax

Source: OECD Database (2000)

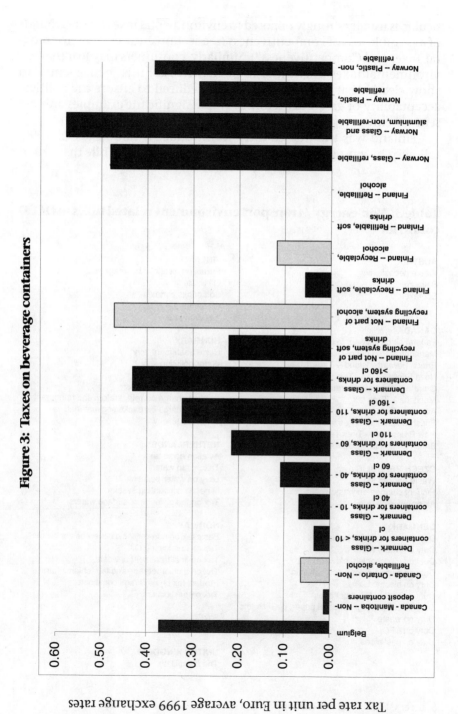

Figure 3: Taxes on beverage containers

Note to Figure 3:

Note: Denmark only sells beverages in glass containers. The Finnish tax — imposed (with the same rate) on alcohol beverages and soft drinks only — is based on per litre of beverage. To estimate a per unit tax, it was assumed that alcohol containers contain 0.7 litres and that containers for soft drinks contain 0.33 litres. Denmark and Norway exempt containers for liquid milk from their product taxes on beverage containers. Norway also exempts containers for lemonade. Denmark applies rebates for certain glass containers if their content meets certain requirements and the containers in question are recycled in glass production. Norway has one tax (0.1 EUR) per unit that applies to all non-refillable beverage containers, and one tax that depends on the type of material used and on the degree of recycling. Beverage containers that are part of a return system with return rates above 95% are completely exempt from this tax, while reduced rates apply for containers being part of any deposit-refund system with a return rate above 25%.

Source: *OECD/EU database on environmentally related taxes.*

---

tax started in 1990 at a fairly modest level of FIM 24.5 per ton of carbon, the rate has been steadily increased since, to reach FIM 374 in 1998. The greening of the tax system includes other measures such as the exemption of rail transports from the electricity tax (1998) and the implementation of a new waste landfill tax in 1996. A strong focus is put on the revenue neutral aspect as this increase in green taxes is compensated by a reduction of the tax wedge on labour (decreased income tax and social insurance contributions) with the explicit objective to reduce unemployment (the "double dividend" approach: see section entitled "The Effectiveness of Environmental Taxes").

Norway implemented a CO_2 tax on mineral oils in 1991 (NOK 0.46 per litre), which was then extended to coal and coke for energy purposes (NOK 0.46 per kilo), limestone and gas (with exemptions). The CO_2 taxes cover about 60% of total Norwegian CO_2 emissions (Norwegian Green Tax Commission 1996). In 1999, it was decided to extend the tax to some of the hitherto exempted sectors (supply fleet in the North Sea, domestic air transport and transportation of coastal goods) and to implement a tradable permit systems for the other exempted sectors (metals, industrial chemicals, cement, refinery products, domestic use of gas, fisheries); this tradable permit system is now investigated by a Government Commission. A sulphur tax is also being applied to almost all fossil fuels (NOK 17 per kg of SO_2 and a reduced rate of NOK 3 per kg for coal and coke). Due a favourable employment situation, less emphasis was placed on the double dividend; however part of the revenue of these taxes was applied to a reduction in income tax. A number of other environmental taxes are applied to various products, such as pesticides (see Table 3).

In Sweden, a major tax reform was introduced in 1991 in a strict revenue neutral context. It was based on a significant reduction in income tax, which was largely offset by a series of new environmental taxes, especially on carbon, sulphur and nitrogen oxides, by a restructuring of energy taxation (the general energy tax on oil was differentiated according to the environmental quality of the oil) and by a broadening of the VAT tax base. On the other hand, energy taxes on industry were significantly reduced. The net effect was a 6% redistribution of GDP, including about 1% related to environmental taxes. The rates of the CO_2 tax vary according to the type of fuel (Nordic Council of Ministers 1999). The sulphur tax (SEK 30 per kg) is imposed on peat, coal, petroleum, coke and other gaseous products. A tax differentiation is applied to three different categories of diesel oil according to their sulphur content. Other energy-related taxes with an environmental purpose are also applied (consumer and producer tax on electricity, tax on domestic air traffic, taxation of motor vehicles).

Denmark introduced a CO_2 tax on fuels in 1992 and has been engaging in a general reform of its tax system, since 1994 with a continuing evolution of energy-related taxes until 2002 (Larsen 1998). The main objectives of the reform are the reduction of marginal tax rates in all income brackets; the elimination of a series of loopholes in the tax law; and a gradual transfer of tax revenue from income and labour to pollution and scarce environmental resources (Danish Ministry of Finance 1995). One key aspect of the Danish tax reform was the introduction in 1995 of the "Energy Package" consisting mainly in an increase of the CO_2 tax and a tax on SO_2 emissions (DKK 10 per kg of SO_2). The revenue produced by these taxes is returned entirely to industry in the form of investment aids for energy saving and reduced employers' social security contributions. Other taxes on household and industrial waste, wastewater, pesticides and chlorinated solvents have also been put in place.

The Netherlands, through the 1988 "General Environmental Provision Act", introduced a "general fuel charge" which replaced five existing charges (on air pollution, traffic and industrial noise, chemical waste and lubricants). Between 1992 and 2000, a series of other taxes were introduced (on waste, groundwater, uranium and small energy users). The "energy regulating tax" (introduced in 1996) was levied on small, non-transport, energy consumers (households, small businesses, office blocks, etc.), with its revenue returned to households in the form of reduced social security contributions (Vermeend and Van der Vaart, 1998). The greening of the Dutch tax system is continuing in 2001.

After a "first wave" of green tax reforms in the early 1990s in the above countries, France, Germany, Italy, Switzerland and the UK have initiated a similar process since 1999.

In France, a restructuring of environmental taxes and charges was initiated in 1999. Like in the Netherlands, one objective is to streamline and simplify a set of existing earmarked emission charges. As from 1st January 2000, existing charges on air pollution, household waste, special industrial waste, lubricating oils and noise (hitherto levied by the ADEME, Agence de l'Environnement et de la Maîtrise de l'Energie), have been merged into a single "Taxe générale sur les activités polluantes" (General Tax on Polluting Activities - TGAP), levied by the Ministry of Finance. The revenue of the TGAP is be paid back to ADEME as an annual budget allocation. Taxes on pesticides, granulates and detergents were also introduced. A progressive reduction of the tax differential between gasoline and diesel fuel for automobiles also started in 1999. However, an extension of the TGAP with a new taxation of energy use by industry was rejected by the French Constitutional Court in late 2000.

Germany initiated a green tax reform in April 1999. The main goals are to stimulate energy savings (in the context of the German objective to reduce CO_2 emission by 25% by the year 2005, compared to 1990 levels), and to increase employment. The green tax reform comprises two main components: a new taxation on electricity and an increased taxation of mineral oil; both taxes will be regularly increased over the period 1999-2003. The increased tax burden on energy is compensated by a reduced tax wedge on labour (reduced social security contributions). As in most other countries, a number of special provisions and exemptions apply to different energy sources, in particular renewable, energy sources, co-generation power plants, and to the production sector.

In Italy, a green tax reform is being implemented over the period 1999-2005. The main components are a re-modulation of excises on mineral oil according to their carbon content and to their use, and the introduction of a consumption tax on coal, petrol-coke and natural bitumen used in combustion plants (as defined by EC Directive 88/609). The revenue of these new taxes will be applied to a reduction of the tax wedge on labour.

Switzerland introduced new environmental taxes on extra light heating oils (from 1 July 1998), and on volatile organic compounds (VOCs, from 1 January 1999). The revenue will be fully returned to households in the form of reduced compulsory sickness insurance premiums.

In the UK, a "climate change levy" on energy use by business was introduced by the government in April 2001. The revenue will be recycled back to industry through lower employers' National insurance contributions. Fuel duty excises were increased by 6% p.a. until 1999; this "road fuel duty escalator" was designed to reduce CO2 emissions and to take into account other environmental factors. The revenue of the "Landfill Tax", introduced in 1996, is also paid back to reduce employers' National Insurance Contributions; a similar approach will be taken for the proposed new tax on the extraction of mineral aggregates.

REVENUE FROM ENVIRONMENTAL TAXES

The revenue of environmentally related taxes

The OECD, EUROSTAT and IEA have developed a joint statistical framework for data on environmentally related taxes.[6] The revenues from (pollution-oriented) environmentally related taxes on average represents 2.5% of GDP and 7 % of total tax revenues. Despite clear differences from country to country, the revenues from these taxes are thus significant in all the 27 countries covered (Figure 4).

Practically all the revenues (90%) from environmentally related taxes arise from petrol, diesel fuel and motor vehicle taxes (Figure 5). Very few taxes are levied on heavy fuels used by industry. The proportion accounted for by other environmentally related taxes (such as pesticides, detergents, etc.) is negligible. Another feature is that industry is little affected, owing to numerous exemptions so that the bulk of the tax burden of energy-related taxes falls on households. Note, however, that the revenue of taxes is not an indication of their environmental effectiveness (indeed it should be the contrary), but it is an important information for the implementation of any tax reform (competitiveness and distributive implications, scope for reform, overall structure of the tax system, etc.)

The sustainability of revenue

From a fiscal point of view, a "good" tax is one that produces a given revenue with efficiency, stability and simplicity. In the case of environmentally related taxes, this configuration may turn out to be complex or even paradoxical. The tax rate must be sufficiently high to have an incentive effect.[7] However, the more the incentive works, the more pollution will diminish and therefore the less tax revenue will be collected. For instance, taxes on polluting fuel oils in Sweden have led to their virtual disappearance from the market. Again in Sweden, the revenue obtained from the sulphur tax has fallen rapidly owing to the environmental success of the tax: before the tax was introduced, annual revenue was estimated at SEK 0.5-0.7 billion; between 1991, when the tax

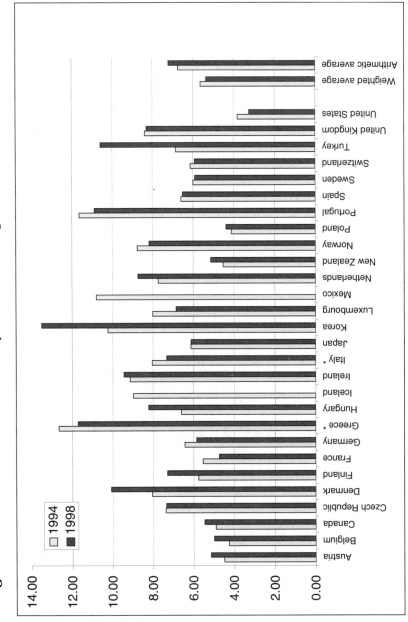

Figure 4: Revenue from environmentally-related taxes as percent of total tax revenue

Per cent of total tax revenue

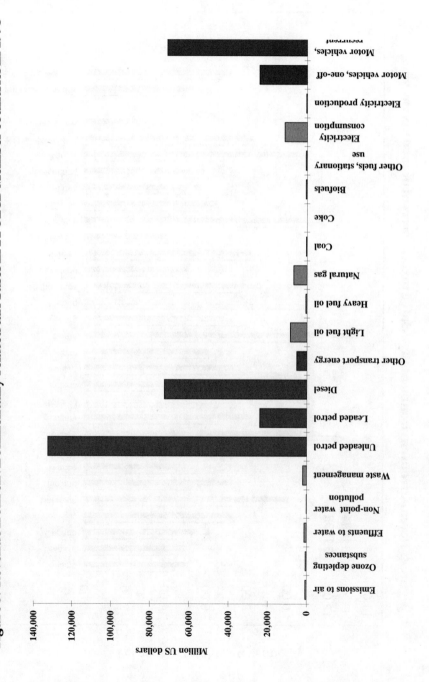

Figure 5: Revenue from environmental-related tax-bases in 21 OECD Member countries in 1995

was introduced, and 1997, revenue fell from SEK 0.3 to under 0.2 billion. For the same reason, leaded petrol has disappeared altogether in many OECD countries. In Denmark, the revenue from the tax on nickel-cadmium batteries decreased from DKK 35 million in 1996 to DKK 30 million in 1998 due to a reduction of the consumption of these batteries.

In other words, there is a contradiction, at least once rigidities and reaction times have been allowed for, between the environmental effectiveness of the tax and its fiscal effectiveness, leading to a potential conflict between the ministries of finance and the environment. In practice, however, the conflict between effectiveness and revenue is not so clear cut. In order to ensure that revenue is sustainable, there will be a tendency to tax products with low demand elasticity, such as energy products (see below). Moreover, when environmentally related taxes produce long-term or gradual effects, the fall in revenue is deferred or gradual, which allows for appropriate tax adjustments and smoothing of revenue in good time; an example is the UK "Road Fuel Duty Escalator" (discontinued in 2000). One last point is that the stability of the tax base is never guaranteed for any tax, as illustrated, for instance, by the fall in revenue from labour taxes and the difficulties affecting social security financing as a result of unemployment.

The use of revenues

How should environmentally related taxes revenues be used? This is a key question which has not only fiscal, but also environmental implications. The revenue of environmentally related taxes can be used in two ways.

The first way such tax revenue can be used consists in paying it in to the general government budget, in accordance with fiscal orthodoxy. The revenue can then be used to reduce public sector deficits, to increase public expenditure or, the tax burden remaining equal, to reduce other distortionary taxes (e.g., the "double dividend").

Secondly, the tax revenue can be earmarked to specific public expenditure or particular government agencies, a case in point being environmental expenditures. There are many examples in waste management and water management (through the financing of public equipment or the payment of de-pollution subsidies). In most cases, however, this category concerns charges rather than taxes; i.e. requited payments (see Box 1). The amounts involved are far from negligible: in France, over the period 1992-1996, water charges (effluent and abstraction charges) came to an annual average of 8 billion French francs (or 1.6 billion US dollars); in the Netherlands, revenue from water pollution charges came to 1.9 billion guilders (1.2 billion US dollars). Taxes may also be earmarked, as in the case where fuel taxes are allocated to road building. The OECD database shows a number of earmarking cases: 45 different taxes in 21 countries and 106 fees and charges in 28 countries (1997).

Earmarking entails serious drawbacks, however. Fixing the use of tax revenue in advance, without evaluating its economic or even environmental rationale beforehand, may lead to economic wastage. This may prevent an optimization of public expenditure. Spending then is less governed by Government priorities than by the revenue from the earmarked tax, as the revenue cannot be used for other purposes. In the case, for instance, of the considerable revenue generated by energy and transport taxes, allocation may prove dangerous and may introduce rigidities. Allocating taxes to road infrastructures may lead to over-investment in that sector. Programmes may also last longer than their optimal period as a result of habits, administrative slowness, situation returns or other "acquired rights". If the allocation of a certain proportion of public revenue creates a precedent, the public authorities may over time find themselves unable to redefine priorities.

Nevertheless, allocating revenues can be an attractive option. In particular, the political acceptability of taxes and charges might be enhanced thanks to transparency of use, clearly dedicated to the popular cause of environmental protection. Similarly, payers feel, rightly or wrongly, that the revenue from such taxes or charges is in some way returned to them in the form of subsidies or public investments.

Another option is "revenue recycling", when environmentally related taxation, particularly those taxes that impact on industry, are fully recycled back to industry by some mechanism. For example, the Swedish NOx charge is refunded back to industry in proportion to the polluters' energy production. In several countries, energy-related taxes are recycled back to industry as financial assistance for energy savings. Another form of use of tax revenue is the "tax shift", where new environment related taxes are compensated by reduction in other existing taxes in a revenue neutral context (see below).

TAX SHIFTS IN PRACTICE: IS THERE A "DOUBLE DIVIDEND"?

In most existing cases, green tax reforms are implemented within a context of revenue neutrality, usually by operating a "tax shift" substituting environmental taxes for existing distortionary taxes. According to Bovenberg and Mooij (1994), this concept of a "double dividend" may have three meanings: in one sense, the double dividend arises from greater economic efficiency due to the environmental tax, compared with direct controls (the static efficiency concept of taxes); in a second sense,

Box 1. Environmentally related taxes, fees and charges

A large number of environmental taxes and charges have been introduced in OECD countries with the explicit purpose of environmental protection. Examples are taxes on polluting emissions in the atmosphere and water, or on specific polluting products (sulphur, carbon, chemicals, lubricants, packaging, pesticides, fertilisers, etc.). But the environmental relevance of a tax comes primarily through its impact on relative consumer and producer prices of environmentally related goods and services (and by the relevant price elasticities), regardless of the purpose or name of the tax. For example, a tax on fuel oil introduced for purely fiscal reasons will have the same environmental impact as a fuel tax introduced to combat CO_2 emissions, as they will both lead to similar changes in relative prices. In the context of sustainable development, what matters is the extent to which these taxes have a bearing, positive or negative, on environmental protection. Therefore, in co-operation with the European Commission and IEA, the OECD has set up a comprehensive database* of "Environmentally Related Taxes", which includes all energy and transport related taxes that are of major relevance to environmental protection.

Taxes are defined as compulsory, unrequited payments to general government. Taxes are unrequited in the sense that benefits provided by government to taxpayers are not normally in proportion to their payments.

The OECD classification also uses the terms **fees and charges** (as opposed to taxes) and **levies** without providing precise definitions. In practice, these terms are used interchangeably to refer to compulsory requited payments to either general government or other bodies (e.g., environmental funds or water management board).

Source: OECD

* This database can be accessed at: http://www.oecd.org envpolicies/taxes/index.htm

the double dividend is related to the "ancillary benefits" resulting from the supplementary environmental improvements obtained for example by a carbon-energy tax beyond the targeted gains and objectives (e.g., through greater energy efficiency, less road transport congestion, less emissions of other air pollutants produced by fossil energy combustion); in the third sense, the double dividend relates to efficiency gains obtained with an environmental tax, which both internalizes external costs and replaces existing distortionary taxes. In this third case, the really burning question at present is whether this type of fiscal reform could extend to the drive against unemployment by financing a reduction in labour taxes (including employers' social security contributions) with new environmental taxes, especially on energy (CO2 tax).

This question of a double environment-employment dividend has generated prolific literature and lively controversy, which is still not over. According to Majocchi (1996 and 2000), key conditions for the realization of a double dividend are:

1. The initial structure of the tax system should be sub-optimal in order for a dividend to emerge from removing sub-optimal tax provisions.

2. The tax incidence is a crucial issue. If the burden of pollution taxes finally falls upon households through higher prices of the taxed commodities (which is a reasonable assumption), the reduction of the tax wedge on labour will be less effective and the employment effect reduced or cancelled. Since labour is a relative immobile factor of production, this ultimate tax incidence on labour is likely to occur.

3. The degree of substitutability between factors of production is important: if there is a possibility to use more labour instead of energy and capital, increased employment is more likely to occur.

4. The issue of the mobility of production factors is crucial. In the case of an energy tax, if labour is a better substitute for energy than capital, there will be a shift to more labour-intensive production techniques. If capital is relatively immobile internationally, the tax burden will be shifted to capital. If the capital is internationally mobile, it will move abroad to avoid the tax. In this case a high degree of international co-ordination is required.

5. The more effective is the environmental tax, the more rapidly the tax base will erode. Therefore, to maintain the same revenue flow, governments will have to increase other taxes or increase existing environmental taxes with two possible consequences: a further incidence on labour and a possible reduction of pollution beyond the optimal level. In this case, environmental taxes exacerbate tax distortions.

What happens in reality? A number of simulations have been done, using economic models. The results of many models converge to indicate that a carbon-energy tax would yield some but small double employment-environment dividend Majocchi (1996, 2000). The main conclusions are summarized in Box 2.

Yet, despite the many restrictive hypotheses for the realization of an environment-employment double dividend, most countries having implemented green tax reforms have in one way or another already bet on the double dividend effect, or are considering doing so (see section entitled "Green Tax Reforms" and Table 4). How effective these mechanisms really are, however, still remains to be seen. Carrying out *ex post* evaluations of these schemes is a major challenge for the future to shed more light on this double dividend issue.

THE EFFECTIVENESS OF ENVIRONMENTAL TAXES

While the theoretical advantages (especially the static and dynamic efficiency) of environmental taxes are well known, ex post data on environmental effectiveness are still relatively scarce. There are several reasons for this. In the first place, experience is often too recent to allow for a meaningful evaluation. Secondly, there is a shortage of data and practice when it comes to policy evaluation. The problem of evaluating environmental taxes is particularly complex insofar as they are generally applied simultaneously with other instruments (such as regulations), which makes it difficult to isolate the impact of a tax. However, a growing body of data becomes available, albeit still dispersed (see OECD 1997a and 2001).[8]

Price elasticities of demand

Most environmentally related taxes apply to the energy and transport sectors. The magnitude of the responses to environment related taxes can be measured in terms of elasticities. If, after the introduction of an environmentally related tax, the price of the taxed good increases by 10% and, as a result of the higher price, its consumption falls by 2%, the price elasticity in this particular case is 0.2. Therefore, as an important first step in evaluating behavioural responses to environmentally-related taxes, OECD has collected information on the own price elasticities of energy and transport related goods (OECD, 2000).

Available estimates for energy show that, in most cases, demand for energy is rather inelastic in the short term; estimates for short run elasticities range between -0.13 to -0.26. However, long run elasticities are significantly higher (-0.37 to -0.46). Nevertheless, a price elasticity significantly different from zero indicates that prices increases can substantially reduce the demand for energy. Similarly, the reduction of en-

Box 2. Main conclusions from existing studies on the double dividend

• In general, a tax shift from the relative abundant factor labour to the scarce factor environment leads to positive effects on employment (substitution effect) and negative effects on GDP (nominal income effect). Theoretical studies show that negative employment effects have to be expected if negative income effects of the tax dominate over the substitution effect due to the change in the relative factor input prices. However, simulation studies, based on traditional assumptions with regard to substitution elasticities, show a dominance of the substitution effect.

• Positive employment effects can be expected if the revenues are used for lowering taxes on labour in general and social security contributions of employers and employees in particular. Using the revenue for lump sum payments to households or for lowering VAT leads to less significant or negative employment effects.

• For most European countries, larger employment effects can be expected if the cut in social security contributions are targeted at the unskilled labour force.

• Positive effects on GDP can be expected if the revenues are used for a cut in capital taxes, (thus favouring investment), and gradually implemented.

• Both GDP and employment effects depend on the size of the tax reform. Generally, the results of the simulations show positive effects on GDP and employment when the energy tax is introduced stepwise and the energy price increase does not exceed 4-5% per year. Higher tax rates lead to negative effects on employment and GDP.

• The effects in the labour market are larger if unemployment is linked with wage rigidity: if the level of wages does not decrease with unemployment, lower social security contributions will reduce real labour costs and increased employment is likely to occur. In the case of a non-competitive market for goods, tax reductions will be captured by increased profits.

• Negative impacts on international competitiveness can be controlled effectively by introducing offsetting methods, such as border tax adjustments, sectoral recycling of the revenue or a rebate scheme for buffering the negative short-term effects on energy intensive industries.

Source: based on Majocchi, in OECD (2000).

Table 4: Double Dividend Packages

Country	Start year	Taxes raised on	Taxes cut	Magnitude
Sweden	1990	CO_2	PIT	2.4% of total tax revenue
		SO_2	Energy taxes on agriculture	
		Various	Continuous education	
Denmark	1994	Various *	PIT	Around 3% of GDP by 2002, or
		CO_2	SSC	over 6% of total tax revenue
		SO_2	Capital income	
Netherlands	1996	CO_2	CPT, PIT, SSC	0.3% of GDP in 1996, or around 0.5% of total tax revenue
United Kingdom	1996	Landfill	SSC	Around 0.1% of total tax revenues in 1999
Finland	1997	CO_2	PIT	0.3% of GDP as of March 1999, or
		Landfill	SSC	around 0.5% of total tax revenue
Norway	1999	CO_2	PIT	0.2% of total tax revenue in 1999
		SO_2		
		Diesel oil		
Germany	1999	Petroleum products	SSC	Around 1% of total tax revenue in 1999
Italy	1999	Petroleum products	SSC	Less than 0.1% of total tax revenue in 1999

Notes: * (gasoline, electricity, water, waste, cars). PIT is personal income tax, CPT is corporation tax, SSC is social security contributions.
Source: *Bosquet (2000).*

ergy prices in the last decade has led to an increase in energy demand. Therefore, environmental taxes could have a significant impact on reducing energy demand especially in the long run. Cross-price elasticities (e.g., between different fuels) should also be considered.

Studies on the price elasticities for gasoline show comparable, albeit less homogeneous results. While most estimates show low elasticities in the short run (-0.15 to -0.28), some estimates indicate significantly higher values (-0.51 to -1.07). Long-term elasticities are definitely higher (-0.23 to -1.05) (OECD, 2000). There are differences between countries and variances are mainly explained by the use of different estimation methods. This leaves policy makers with certainty about the fact that taxes will have some behavioural effect, but uncertainty about the magnitude of this effect. Furthermore this underlines the fact that "green-tax policies" must be implemented in a long-term perspective, avoiding steps back due to political pressure (e.g., when world oil prices increase), and with advanced planning and warning of the introduction and/or gradual increase of the taxes.

Examples of available estimates

As experience in environmental taxes grows, an increasing body, albeit still limited, of estimates becomes available. A few examples are presented below.

In Belgium, the tax differentiation between heavy fuels with a sulphur content below or above 1% induced a decrease in the use of the fuel with the higher sulphur content from 20% of the market in 1994 to less than 1% in 1998 (also due to a switch to natural gas). Taxes on non reused or recycled beverage containers, disposable cameras, batteries and diverse packaging, introduced in 1993, led industry to meet all recycling and reuse targets, thus avoiding paying the taxes.

In Denmark, the sulphur tax caused a reduction of emission of 34,000 tons between 1996 and 2000. The tax on non-hazardous waste has reduced the net delivered waste to municipal sites by 26% in the period 1987-1996, and waste to smaller fills and private waste sites by 39% (1990-1996). Industrial waste, however, increased by 8%. Recycling also increased considerably: +77% for paper and cardboard, +50% for glass (Andersen 1998). Ex ante, the CO_2 tax is expected to contribute to a 4% reduction in CO_2 emissions by 2005 compared to 1995.

In Finland, it is estimated that, in the absence of CO_2 taxation, carbon emissions would have been higher by 7% in 1998 if taxes had remained at the 1990 level (Finnish Economic Council, 2000).

In Norway, carbon dioxide taxes introduced in 1991 lowered CO_2 emissions of some stationary combustion plants by some 21%, whereas in other sectors the fall was less. It is estimated that CO_2 emissions produced by mobile household combustion devices fell by 2 to 3% as a consequence of the CO_2 tax (Larsen and Nesbakken 1997). It is also estimated that CO_2 emissions per unit of oil produced by the Norwegian oil sector fell by 1.5% due to measures taken by the industry in response to the CO_2 tax (ECON 1994).

The Swedish sulphur tax (introduced in 1991) led to a fall in the sulphur content of oil-based fuels of more than 50% beyond the legal standards. The sulphur content of light oils has now fallen below 0.076% (i.e. less than half the legal limit of 0.2%). The tax is estimated to have reduced emissions of sulphur dioxide by 80% compared to 1980 (Nordic Council of Ministers 1999). Also in Sweden, a tax differentiation was introduced in 1991 on diesel fuels in order to stimulate the use of less polluting fuel oils. From 1992 to 1996, the proportion of "clean" diesel sold in Sweden rose from 1 to 85%, which led to a reduction of more than 75% on average in the sulphur emissions of diesel-driven vehicles (Swedish Environmental Protection Agency 1997).

In the United States, about 3,400 local communities in 37 States apply taxes on household waste, which are calculated according to the volumes discharged. The result was a significant reduction in the volume of discarded waste and a significant increase in recycling (Anderson et al. 1997).

In most countries, the tax differentiation between leaded and unleaded petrol, combined with a series of measures such as regulations making it compulsory for service stations to offer unleaded petrol and introducing new emission standards for motor vehicles based on such requirements as catalytic converters, led to a heavy fall in consumption and in the share of leaded petrol, which is now withdrawn from sale in 12 OECD countries. The fiscal incentive greatly speeded up the process, despite slow penetration of new vehicles equipped with catalytic converters.

Not all taxes have been successful, however. The effects of taxes in Belgium (on disposable razors, etc.) were hardly noticeable. Similarly, the Swedish tax on pesticides was too low to produce incentive effects (Swedish Environmental Protection Agency 1997).

DISTRIBUTIONAL IMPLICATIONS OF ENVIRONMENTAL TAXES

Potential distributive effects

Are environmental taxes socially regressive? This question is increasingly being asked by stakeholders, in particular, households and the business community. The distributional effects of environmental taxes, especially those on energy, may be observed in three ways (Smith 1998):

1. There will be a direct distributional impact related to the structure of household energy expenditure (on heating and transport) for different income brackets. The bigger the proportion of low-income household expenditure devoted to energy, the more regressive will be the impact of the tax.

2. Indirect distributional effects will result from the taxation of production inputs. The more the processes are energy-intensive, the greater will be the incidence of a tax on the goods produced. Of course, the more the products fall into the prime necessity category, the more regressive the tax will be.

3. Lastly, the distributional impact will be related to the incidence of the tax. An energy tax may affect end consumers, but it may also affect energy producers or production factors (e.g., through a fall in wages or lower return on capital). At the same time, part of the tax may

be borne by energy consuming countries, and another part by energy exporting countries, according to the elasticities of supply and demand.

In so far as many environmental taxes apply to mass consumption products, such as motor-driven vehicles and energy, they can have a potentially substantial effect on lower-income households. The level of the tax also matters; relatively low environmental taxes on products such as detergents, fertilizers, batteries and pesticides, are likely to have a limited impact, while large-scale and fiscally heavier environmental taxes, such as those on energy can have more profound implications.

For example, an analysis of possible distributional effects of the carbon-energy tax in the United Kingdom, initially proposed by the European Commission, showed that the impact of this tax would be distinctly more marked on poorer households. While a tax of 10 dollars a barrel (e.g., \$88 per tonne of carbon) would reduce total household energy consumption by 6.5%, the reduction would be 10% for the poorest 20% of households (Pearson and Smith 1991). The figures vary considerably from country to country (Pearson 1992). To be environmentally effective, however, an environmental tax on energy should be much higher (\$200 to 300 per tonne of carbon, according to estimates).

Available evidence

Evidence on the distributive implications of environmental taxes remains scant. It indicates some, but limited regressivity, as can be expected from any indirect tax. But little systematic, in-depth ex ante or ex post analysis has been carried out.

In its 1997 report, the Swedish Green Tax Commission estimated that doubling the CO_2 tax (from a 1997 rate of 0.37 to 0.74 Kronor per kg of CO_2) would have a fairly marked regressive impact; in order to maintain the same consumption level, the lowest incomes would need to receive compensation of 1.24% of their consumption expenditure, and the highest revenues only 0.78%. In Denmark, the distributional impact of taxes on water, heating and electricity seems to be of particular concern. In the UK, the lowest income decile spend 5.6% of net household income on road fuel duty, three times more than the richest decile and more than twice as much as the average. Therefore the "road fuel duty escalator" could have regressive consequences. In Norway, environmental taxes are not expected to cause any significant regressivity; one issue is an income distribution effect between regions were public transportation is available (hence a possibility to switch to public transports when fuel taxes increase), vs. regions where it is not the case.

Policy options

Basically, three types of corrective measures can be envisaged: mitigation, compensation and tax shift.

(a) Mitigation is an ex ante measure consisting of a reduction of the rates of environmental taxes to alleviate the tax burden on specific segments of the population. This can take the form of reducing tax payment for low income groups or on specific mass consumption and indispensable commodities such as heating fuels or agricultural inputs. However, the outcome would be to weaken the desired environmental impact of the tax, not to speak of the administrative complexities. Nevertheless, a large number of special tax provisions are applied in OECD countries. The OECD-EC database indicates hundreds of provisions such as tax exemptions and reduced rates. Note that these provisions are introduced both on distributive and competitiveness grounds, to the benefit of both households and the business sectors, which makes the assessment of the strictly "social" benefit of these measures quite uncertain.

(b) Compensation measures are basically ex post and outside the realm of the taxes as such; i.e. do not affect their rate or structure. These are corrective measures, such as lump sum compensation calculated on the basis of average tax payments per household. In this case, compensation will have a progressive incidence on the assumption that the poorest households on average pay less tax than the richest households. Tax refunds are a typical compensation measure; for instance, the Swiss taxes on VOCs and light heating oil are refunded to households. In several countries, energy taxes are partly repaid to household and/or business in the form of subsidies for energy saving investments/expenditures.

(c) Tax shifts; e.g., the reduction of other taxes, such as labour and income taxes (see section entitled "The Effectiveness of Environmental Taxes") is a widespread form of compensation. It is assumed that the regressive impact of the new environmental tax will be compensated by the reduction of other taxes. The net distributional implication of this approach is not clear, however, considering that the poorest households pay the least income tax, unlike wealthy households, who will benefit most from any lowering of income tax. According to Smith (1998), this form of compensation may even prove to be strongly regressive.

To sum up, there is no simple or uniform answer to the problem of the distributional impact of environmental taxes. The distributive implications should be assessed more thoroughly, in particular, if the number and level of environmental taxes is due to increase in the future.

ENVIRONMENTAL TAXES AND COMPETITIVENESS

A stumbling block?

The key issue confronting countries which have implemented green tax reform is the possible loss of international competitiveness. Since the bulk of environment related taxes concern energy and transport taxes, there is an obvious risk that industry's competitiveness be hurt. This is why some industry sectors (in particular energy intensive industries) are strongly opposed to environmental taxes and tend to promote other instruments such as voluntary approaches. Furthermore, the greater the "visibility" of environmental taxes compared with other environmental policy instruments, the more outright the opposition will be, insofar as taxes are a direct levy which is additional to the costs of other anti-pollution measures. Another problem, which may turn into an explicit threat, is the "relocation" of activities to countries which are less fussy about environmental protection or to other "pollution havens".

It is important to note that the concept of "competitiveness" can be interpreted in different ways. For instance, one should differentiate between the competitiveness of individual companies and sectors of the economy and of the economy of a country.[9] Similarly, competitiveness may have a national or an international dimension.

Therefore, in a macroeconomic context, environmental taxes should rather reinforce the overall competitiveness of an economy, for at least two reasons:

1. From a general point of view, the tax is only a form of transfer between economic agents: there may be winners and losers, but overall the transfer is neutral.

2. An economically efficient tax should reduce and ideally minimize the total cost of combating pollution ("static efficiency" of taxes). Environmental taxes should therefore produce a competitive advantage, at least in the longer term, even if there may be some short-term adjustment costs.[10]

Confronted with the competitiveness issue, countries can adopt two strategies. First a wait-and-see attitude: who will go first? This is a situation of "prisoner's dilemma" where no one wants to start before the others. The other strategy is to introduce environmental taxes, but with special provisions to protect sectors subject international competition; this is a widespread policy: the OECD-EC database indicates a large number of tax exemptions, particularly for industry (see below).

A biased picture?

Currently available studies and data show no significant impact of environmental taxes on international trade. Jaffe et al. (1995) examined over 100 studies on the potential effect of environmental regulations (and therefore not only taxes) on the competitiveness of American industry. They concluded that: "Overall, there is relatively little evidence to support the hypothesis that environmental regulations have had a large adverse effect on competitiveness, however that elusive term is defined". This conclusion is based on the following arguments: (1) generally speaking, environmental protection costs are relatively modest and in any case too low to affect competitiveness; and (2) environmental constraints in OECD countries are comparable (which is not necessarily the case in other regions of the world); in most cases, whenever environmental constraints are less restrictive in a given country, outside investors tend to apply stricter standards than those of the host country.

Several other studies do converge. Adams (1997) concludes: "In general terms, the point of view whereby there is a conflict between competitiveness and environmental protection must be rejected." The OECD study on Economic Globalization and the Environment (OECD 1997b) reaches the same conclusion.

However, this does not mean that competitiveness is not an issue; on the contrary, the presently negligible impact on international competitiveness is the outcome of a series of mitigation measures specifically designed to prevent such impacts, indicating that competitiveness at the firm or sectoral levels is an overriding concern of green tax reforms.

Current mitigation practices

A review of current green tax policies in OECD countries shows clearly that a wide array of measures are implemented to prevent any negative impact on competitiveness; at least six different measures are applied.

1. *Reduced tax rates for certain sectors, products or inputs.* Most countries apply reduced tax rates to the production sector. For instance, Sweden initially gave industry a 75% rebate on the carbon tax (and total exemption in the case of the energy tax); this rebate was then reduced to 50% in July 1997. In Denmark, a 50% rebate on the CO_2 tax was granted to industry for the period 1993-1995. Both cases are interesting cases of "front runners" who were amongst the first set of countries to introduce CO_2 taxes. In Germany, electricity taxes are lower (20% of standard rate) for the production sector. A number of tax breaks are also granted on purely environmental grounds (e.g., renewable energies or clean processes); this nevertheless is likely to affect positively the competitiveness of the beneficiaries.

2. *Tax exemptions for specific activities, sectors or products.* There is a large number of tax exemptions related to environment related taxes; the OECD database indicates a total number of 800 exemptions for 170

recorded taxes in 21 countries. These data must be interpreted with caution: exemptions are introduced for a number of social, environmental and economic reasons, and only part of these exemptions can be construed as motivated by competitiveness concerns. If one looks at exemptions specifically targeted to industry, 26 cases are recorded in 9 countries. One approach is simply to exclude the main industries from the application of the tax: in the Netherlands the new regulatory tax on energy applies exclusively to households and small businesses. Generally speaking, the database on environmental taxes shows clearly that about 90% of the revenue of environmentally related taxes comes from taxes on automotive fuels and motor vehicles; industry is virtually exempt.

3. *Tax refunds for certain sectors or activities.* The OECD database records 19 cases of refunds applied to the business sector. Here again, it is difficult to ascertain whether refunds are specifically crafted to alleviate possible competitiveness effects: while a few refunds aim at "rewarding" environment-friendly practices or processes (e.g., use of chlorinated solvents in closed plants in Denmark), most other cases are designed to lighten the tax burden of industry under specific conditions.

4. *Recycling tax revenue.* This is a specific form of tax refund. In Denmark, for example, CO_2 and SO_2 taxes are fully redistributed to industry in the form of subsidies for energy saving investments and lower employers' social security contributions.

5. *Gradual phasing in of taxes.* This tool is used to soften the financial impact of the tax. For instance, the UK "Road Fuel Escalator" was designed to provide industry with clear and advanced signals enabling it to plan appropriate decisions.

6. *Tax conditionality.* These are provisions whereby a new tax will be applied only if industry does not achieve predefined objectives or commitments. For instance, in Switzerland, the CO_2 bill provides for a "subsidiary tax" on carbon if industry fails to attain emission abatement objectives (down 10% by 2010, compared with the 1990 level). In Denmark, concessions on the CO_2 tax are granted to industries having entered a negotiated agreement with the government for energy saving. Such combinations of voluntary agreements and "tax conditionality" are more and more common.

Concluding remarks

The rather reassuring view that environmental policies have negligible effects on international trade and competitiveness is only provisional: first, as mentioned earlier, heavy and export industries are generally totally or partially exempted from carbon and energy taxes. Furthermore, this view is based on fairly limited data and reflects a situation where these policies have perhaps not yet crossed a certain intensity threshold.

It is likely that environmental taxes will grow in number (more taxes) and in intensity (higher levels). The competitiveness issue will thus become more and more acute.

Therefore, an international co-ordination of policies is needed. The European Commission is striving to promote such co-ordination at the EU level. In 1997, for instance, the European Commission submitted a "Communication on environmental taxes and charges in the single market" and, also in 1997, a draft Directive on the taxation of all energy products, with minimum rates and a regular increase between 1998 and 2002; this draft Directive is, however, still being negotiated.

Therefore, the question of competitiveness will remain central to the debate on environmental taxes and the most advanced countries in this area will continue to proceed very carefully, in particular through specific tax provisions designed to mitigate the competitiveness impact, at the expense of environmental effectiveness. Some kind of co-ordination between OECD countries would avoid the "prisoner's dilemma" whereby countries hesitate to move forward in a significant way by fear of competitiveness loss.

ACCEPTANCE BUILDING

Environmental taxes face opposition from stakeholders for a variety of reasons, such as fear of competitiveness losses, reduced profits or possible income regressivity. For instance, the sharp increase in nominal oil prices in the year 2000 has exacerbated the opposition to energy taxes in Europe. Therefore acceptance building is a key component of the implementation strategy of environmental taxes. Three series of measures can contribute to a better acceptance.

First, the purpose of the tax must be clear from the outset; in particular, the fact that the objective is to reduce a specific pollution, rather than provide government revenue.

Second, the active involvement of stakeholders is crucial. Several countries have set up successfully "green tax commissions", where public and private stakeholders can meet and work together. For example, these commissions may include different government departments (e.g., finance and environment), representatives from the concerned economic sectors (agriculture, energy, transport, industry, etc.), environmental NGOs and technical experts. These green tax commissions provide public and technical legitimacy to the tax reform (Table 5). They usually have a mandate of several years, enabling them to achieve solid work and progressively build confidence and dialogue. When the tax reform is decided, these commissions may also have to monitor and assess the implementation.

Third, green tax reforms must be implemented gradually. In particular, the initial introduction of environmental taxes is often followed by a gradual increase in tax rates, a widening of the application of the tax and the progressive introduction of new taxes. For instance, in Finland, the rate of the CO_2 tax was raised from FIM 24.5 per ton of carbon in 1990 to FIM 374 in 1998; the tax was initially limited to heat and electricity production and later broadened to transport and heating fuels. In Norway, the CO_2 tax was initially limited to mineral oils and now applies to coal and gas, covering 60% of CO_2 emissions; the tax is now applied to hitherto exempted sectors (air and maritime transport). In Denmark, the CO_2 tax introduced in 1992 was followed by a multiannual "Energy Package" (1995-2002) comprising a progressive increase of the tax. The green tax reforms initiated in 1999 in France, Germany, Italy and the UK are gradually implemented over several years.

CONCLUSIONS

Environmental taxes are a potentially effective way of protecting the environment and at the same time enhancing economic efficiency. However, current green tax reforms remain relatively limited by a number of factors such as the fear of competitiveness losses. Key considerations for the implementation of green tax reforms are the following:
1. The prime objective of an environmental tax must be clearly to protect the environment.

Table 5: OECD Green Tax Reform Commissions

Country	Date of Introduction	Environmentally related taxes	Recycling revenues	Damaging subsidies	Other damaging effects of fiscal reform	Within the context of broader tax reform
Belgium*	1993	Yes	Yes	No	No/N/A	N/A
Denmark	1993	Yes	Yes	No	No	Yes
Italy						Yes
Japan	1994	Yes	Yes	Yes	No/N/A	N/A
Netherlands	1999/1995/	Yes	Yes	No/N/A	Yes	Yes
Norway	1994/1990	Yes	Yes	Yes	Yes	Yes
Sweden	1993	Yes	Yes	Yes	Yes	Yes

*The mandate of the Belgium commission is to evaluate and monitor implementation.

Source: *based on Schlegelmilch, K.,* Green Tax Commissions, *Environmental Policy Research Briefs, No. 4, The European Union, 1997.*

2. Environmental taxes are likely to work in the context of "policy mixes" where regulations, standards, voluntary agreements, tradable permits, etc. are combined. The right "mix" of policy instruments need to be carefully analyzed for each particular context.
3. Green tax reforms should preferably be implemented in the context of broader tax reforms providing an opportunity to reduce or eliminate tax distortions and "niches" and modernize taxation systems, hence achieving real structural adjustments of economies and greater economic efficiency.
4. Green tax reforms should be used to ensure an effective integration of the economic, social and environmental dimensions of sustainable development.
5. It is likely, in the light of the Kyoto Protocol on Climate Change, that environmental taxes will play an increasingly important role as a means of combating greenhouse gas emissions. But this will be, to a large extent, conditional upon internationally coordinated policies.
6. Internationally coordinated implementation of environmental taxes is a key condition for more widespread and more efficient environmental taxes and green tax reforms. This is a key challenge for the future.

REFERENCES

Adams, J. (1997) "Environmental Policy and Competitiveness in a Global Economy: Conceptual Issues and a Review of the Empirical Evidence", in OECD, *Globalisation and Environment: Preliminary Perspectives*, OECD, Paris.

Andersen, M.S. (1998) "Assessing the Effectiveness of Denmark's Waste Tax," *Environment*, May 1998.

Anderson, R.C., A.Q. Lohof and A. Carlin (1997) "The United States Experience with Economic Incentives in Pollution Control Policy," Environmental Law Institute and U.S. EPA, Washington DC.

Barde, J.-Ph. (1992) *Economie et politique de l'environnement*, Presses Universitaires de France, Paris.

Barde, J.-Ph. (1997) "Economic Instruments for Environmental Protection: Experience in OECD countries" in OECD (1997), *Applying market-based instruments to environmental policies in China and OECD countries*, OECD, Paris.

Barde, J.-Ph. (1999) "Environmental taxes in OECD Countries: An Overview", in OECD (1999), *Environmental Taxes: Recent Developments in China and OECD Countries*, OECD, Paris.

Barde, J.-Ph. and St. Smith (1997) "Do Economic Instruments Help the Environment?" *The OECD Observer*, No. 204, March.

Bosquet, B. (2000) "Environmental tax reform: does it work? A survey of the empirical evidence." *Journal of Ecological Economics*, 34, 19-32.

Bovenberg, L. and R. De Mooij (1994) "Environmental Levies and Distortionary Taxation", *American Economic Review*, Vol. 84, No. 4, September.

Braathen, N.A. (2000) "The OECD/EU Database on Environmentally-Related Taxes". Paper for the International Conference on the Use of Economic Incentives and Instruments in Environmental Policy, Vancouver, 11-13 December 2000.

Danish Ministry of Finance (1995) *Energy Taxes on Industry in Denmark.*

ECMT (1998) Efficient Transport for Europe, ECMT, Paris.

ECON (1994) report 326/94, Oslo.

Finnish Economic Council (2000) *Environmental and Energy Taxation in Finland - Preparing for the Kyoto Challenge* - Summary of the Working Group Report.

Jaffe, A., S.R. Peterson, P.R. Portney, and R.N. Stavins (1995) "Environmental Regulation and the Competitiveness of US Manufacturing: What Does the Evidence Tell Us?", *Journal of Economic Literature*, Vol. XXXIII, March.

Larsen, B.M. and R. Nesbakken (1997) "Norwegian Emissions of CO2 1987-1994. A Study of Some Effects of the CO2 Tax", *Environmental and Resource Economics*, vol.9 N° 3 April 1997.

Larsen, Hans (1998) "Energy Taxes, The Danish Model." Ministry of Taxation, Copenhagen.

Majocchi, A. (1996) "Green Fiscal Reform and Employment: a Survey", *Environmental and Resource Economics*, Vol. 8, No. 4, December.

Majocchi, A. (2000) "Greening Tax Mixes in OECD Countries: an Assessment", OECD, Paris.

Nordic Council of Ministers (1999) The Scope for Nordic Co-ordination of Economic Instruments in Environmental Policy, *TemaNord*, 1999-50.

OECD (1994), *Managing the Environment: the Role of Economic Instruments*, OECD, Paris.

OECD (1996a), *Subsidies and Environment: Exploring the Linkages*, OECD, Paris.

OECD (1996b), *Implementation Strategies for Environmental Taxes*, OECD, Paris.

OECD (1997a), *Environmental Taxes and Green Tax Reform*, OECD, Paris.

OECD (1997b), *Economic Globalisation and the Environment*, OECD, Paris.

OECD (1998), *Improving The Environment Through Reducing Subsidies*, Parts I and II, OECD, Paris.

OECD (1999), OECD *Environmental Data, Compendium 1999*, OECD, Paris.

OECD (2000), OECD, "Behavioural responses to environmentally-related taxes", unclassified document, OECD, Paris.

OECD (2001-forthcoming), *Environmentally-Related Taxation in OECD Countries: Issues and Strategies*, OECD, Paris.

Pearson, M. and St. Smith (1991) "The European Carbon Tax: an Assessment of the European Commission Proposal", Institute for Fiscal Studies, London.

Pearson, M. (1992) "Equity Issues and Carbon Taxes", in: *Climate Change: Designing a Practical Tax System*, OECD, Paris, 1992.

Smith, St. (1998) "Distributional Incidence of Environmental Taxes on Energy and Carbon: a Review of Policy Issues", presented at the colloquy of the Ministry of the Environment and Regional Planning, "Green Tax Reform and Economic Instruments for International Cooperation: the Post-Kyoto Context", Toulouse, 13 May 1998.

Swedish Environmental Protection Agency (1997) *Environmental Taxes in Sweden*, Stockholm.

Vermeend, Willem and Jacob Van der Vaart (1998) *Greening Taxes: The Dutch Model*, Kluwer, Deventer.

FOOTNOTES

1. For a detailed assessment on subsidies, see OECD (1998).

2. In particular for NOx and particulates emissions.

3. This restructuring of energy taxes was done with different modalities according to countries. For instance, in Norway, the decrease in energy taxes took place a few years after the introduction of the CO_2 tax.

4. Based on the OECD/EC database on environmentally related taxes.

5. Energy taxes can also be construed as product taxes (see Section "Structuring Existing Taxes").

6. See Braathen (2000). The data base is available on www.oecd.org/env/policies/taxes/index.htm.

7. Considering that we are in a "second best" universe, below the ideal of a "Pigovian" tax.

8. See also Barde and Smith (1997).

9. A country's competitiveness can be defined as "the degree to which it can, under free and fair market conditions, produce goods and services which meet the test of international markets, while simultaneously maintaining and expanding the real incomes of its people over the longer term." (OECD, 1992).

10. In any case, any environmental policy is bound to affect costs to some degree, for instance through pollution standards, technical standards or regulations. There is no need to single out an environmental tax in particular.

ACKNOWLEDGMENT

This paper is adapted from a presentation made at the Conference "Supporting a Sustainable Future: Making Dollars and Sense", organized by Environment Canada (Vancouver 11-13 December 2000). The views expressed in this text are the author's own and do not necessarily reflect those of the OECD. The author wishes to acknowledge the comments and contribution of his OECD colleague, Nils-Axel Braathen.

THE CHALLENGE OF SUSTAINABLE DEVELOPMENT IN MEXICO

Raul Pacheco-Vega
Department of Resource Management and Environmental Studies
University of British Columbia

Maria del Carmen Carmona-Lara
Instituto de Investigaciones Jurídicas
Universidad Nacional Autónoma de México
and
Obdulia Vega-Lopez
Universidad de Guanajuato
Guanajuato, Gto., Mexico

INTRODUCTION

Mexico is among the most developed of all the Latin American nations. With a total population of 95.9 million by mid-1998[1] and GNP per capita of $3,970 USD, it belongs to the upper-middle income range of Latin American countries. Mexico has re-structured its economy largely through trade liberalisation and reform, strong industrialisation, prudent fiscal and monetary policies and deregulation (Ros et al. 1996). Ever since the late 1940s and until the crisis of 1994, Mexico's growth performance was considered bold and impressive. Economic growth rates of close to 7% per year and increases in per-capita income of 3% during this period (Ros et al. 1996) led many to believe this growth would be sustainable. However, by 1982, Mexico was immersed in an economic crisis whose effects were felt strongly in several areas including the environment, the economy, and social welfare. These effects were very negative and contrasted sharply with the world-wide launch of the sustainable development movement (1987). Mexico had to deal, therefore, with two interrelated challenges to sustainable development: economic recovery and environmental degradation.

In this chapter, we address the challenges to sustainable development (SD) faced by Mexico. We begin by briefly outlining the history of SD, both world-wide and in Mexico, from the early stages of Stockholm (1972) to Agenda 21 (1992) and Rio+5 (1997). We then present a few selected indicators of sustainable development in Mexico. This set of indicators related to SD was developed specifically for Mexico and contains data from 1984 to 1999. We believe that these indicators may prove useful in designing sustainability strategies because they quantify environmental, social and political conditions related to sustainable development. However, their usefulness is somewhat limited because of the difficulty in comparing developing vis-à-vis developed countries. Each nation has unique issues and circumstances and therefore may not be compared without thoroughly analysing the implications of those indicators. Having said that, these SD indicators are nonetheless useful because they help to describe the correlation between the environment and development. There is promise that further research will help refine these measurements (Jing-zhu and Opschoor 1999).

There are several dimensions to the sustainability challenge: economic, social, political and institutional, among others. After reviewing Mexico's SD indicators, we then turn to a specific dimension: the legal and institutional framework. Analysing the legal framework has become a relevant issue in Mexico since the enactment of a constitutional right to sustainable development and an adequate environment. This is a major breakthrough in Mexican environmental and constitutional law because it enables a citizen to sue on a constitutional foundation for his right to an adequate environment. This may lead to stronger enforcement of environmental regulations and, therefore, in the long run to a more sustainable future.

We take the theoretical stance that SD is a multidimensional issue that cannot be addressed solely on the basis of economic, social or political issues, but rather as a whole. We must, however, state clearly that it is our belief that extreme poverty and social inequity play an important role that must be addressed by Mexican sustainability strategies. We conclude this chapter with a reflection that should prove fertile ground for further research, keeping in mind that SD is an idealistic goal (Pacheco-Vega 1997).

SUSTAINABILITY AND SUSTAINABLE DEVELOPMENT

While there are economic and physical limits to the supply of non-renewable resources, even so-called renewable resources face serious threats to their continued supply. The accelerated use of these resources generates environmental problems. Pollution renders streams and aquifers unusable. Irresponsible logging leads to erosion and loss of habitat for many species. In many regions of the world, air pollution has reached extremes not previously experienced. Our ecosystems have been stressed and that stress has taken its toll on human health as well. If human beings live in an adequate and healthy environment, it is more likely that they will remain healthy. Therefore, from the human perspective, it is in our best interest to take good care of our environment. Otherwise, there is a high possibility that our chances of long-term survival will surely be jeopardised. Thus, there is an increasing need for humans to learn how to manage the environment in which they are embedded. This situation has led many researchers in the world to increase their efforts to find solutions to both the inevitable exhaustion of natural resources and the need for adequate environmental management.

There exist profoundly divergent viewpoints in the environmental arena. At one end of the continuum, there is neoclassical economic theory. At the other end is the ultra-conservationist perspective. Neoclassical theories claim that technological improvements will, eventually, lead to a sustainable level of consumption. Resources that become scarce will be replaced through the operation of the market. These ideas have been subject to heated discussion.[2] Hardin (1968) in his seminal work "The Tragedy of the Commons" argues that over consumption of a common resource has no technical solution (that is, we humans tend to consume in excess whatever common resource to which we have access). Now considered a classic, Hardin's work argues for the specific assignment of property rights as a solution to this problem. However, it is not so important whether or not technical change will provide a way of living for humankind in the future. The most important issue is to ensure that future generations will have enough resources to sustain life.

It is relevant to explore the notion of what is sustainability and what is sustainable development. The beginning of the sustainable development movement may be traced as far back as 1972. The early works of the Club of Rome, published in *The Limits to Growth* in 1972,[3] advanced the notion of "zero growth. As Jacobs (1993:53) points out:

[M]any Greens have argued that it is economic growth which is the primary cause of environmental degradation; therefore the objective of policy should be 'no growth.'

Although it has been strongly criticised, the "zero growth" paradigm still remains one of the most powerful concepts in environmental protection. Many radical environmental activists champion this paradigm today and mobilise resources to advance this position, usually through lobbying (Yearly 1994). This concept has evolved enormously in the last 28 years, through the World Commission on Environment and Development's *Our Common Future* (1987), and Agenda 21[4] (the Rio Summit) in 1992, to Rio+5 in 1997.

Sustainable development is a concept that has a multitude of definitions and meanings. Many people, including politicians, have used and misused the concept. Today, everything "needs to be sustainable". There are talks about "sustainable economic growth", "sustainable agriculture", "sustainable livelihood", etc. For the purposes of this chapter, we adopt the definition of sustainable development stated in the Bruntland report (WCED 1987:8):

Humanity has the ability to make development sustainable – to ensure that it meets the needs of the present without compromising the ability of future generations to meet their own needs. The concept of sustainable development does imply limits – not absolute limits but limitations imposed by the present state of technology and social organization on environmental resources and by the ability of the biosphere to absorb the effect of human activities.

It is important to note that it was the Bruntland report that advanced the idea that the environment has a limited capacity to absorb the effect of human activity; that is, the idea that every ecosystem is able and capable of receiving a threshold level of stress without suffering disruption. This led to the misconception that there is a right to impose such stress on the environment. While it is true that some ecosystems may be able to endure several kinds of stress (such as pollution, immoderate exploitation of resources, etc.), it does not necessarily grant an implicit right to impose such damages on the environment.

Even with the above-mentioned flaws, *Our Common Future* was important because it stressed the concept of intergenerational equity. Future generations may depend on the limited amount of resources that current generations are expending (and wasting). Therefore, the notion of sustainable development implicitly speaks of the need to conserve and ensure a steady reserve of resources that may be available for future consumption.

Sustainable development in many senses is a utopian goal, something every nation and person should be striving for. It is a central goal and a guiding norm for environmental politics (Lafferty and Langhelle 1999) yet it has been talked about so much that it has become a blurry concept, with over 70 definitions (Kirby et al. 1995). Nevertheless, the normative idea of sustainable development contains three valuable notions:

(a) There is a limited amount of resources on Earth. Future generations may need to make use of those resources; therefore it is this generation's responsibility to ensure there will be enough resources available in the future.

(b) There is more than one dimension to the sustainability challenge – environmental, social, political, etc. Thus, it is necessary to understand all these dimensions to design development strategies that are sustainable.

(c) Development that is in harmony with environmental protection can be sustainable. As Lafferty and Langhelle assert (1999:2), the Bruntland report attempts "to reconcile two themes that have long been in an antagonistic relationship with each other, namely environment and development". To ensure that there will be development without detriment to the environment is a concept that is embedded within the whole theme of sustainability.

The next stage in the sustainable development saga came in 1992. The Earth Summit held in Rio de Janeiro that year convened hundreds of government officials from a number of countries (including Mexico, which vigorously participated and voiced its opinions). The Rio meeting produced an agreed-upon document that drafted national and international responses to environmental challenges: Agenda 21. This Agenda for the 21st century provided guidelines to implement sustainable development both at the international and national levels. Agenda 21 expresses in 27 principles general guidelines and objectives in relation to environmental and developmental problems. These principles tended to be expressed in a general matter and were non-binding (Moffatt 1996). Nonetheless, Agenda 21 provides a general framework within which every country that signed the agreement would work to ensure environmental protection and economic growth with a view to sustainability. As posed by Moffat (1996), a major achievement of Agenda 21 is the recognition of the complex links between economic growth and environmental conservation while recognising the importance of cultural values and people empowerment.

With respect to how Agenda 21 is being implemented, each country that signed and agreed to it has developed its own implementation strategy and drafted national plans (local Agenda 21) to make sustainable development operational. There have been follow-up actions and meetings -- such as Rio+5 in 1997 -- that have been aimed at evaluating the effectiveness and depth of implementation by each country of the principles of Agenda 21.

The emergence of international organisations and an increased mobilisation of resources to promote sustainability, as well as creation of national sustainability programs is not an accident. It is the result of the realisation that environmental issues do not recognise national frontiers or local boundaries. Environmental problems such as the greenhouse effect, international loss of habitat, etc., do not remain within a sole national jurisdiction. Therefore, efforts directed towards a sustainable future must come from every nation. All countries have a stake in the environment. It could also be said that the environment is at stake as well. As part of Agenda 21, the Mexican environmental authorities have committed resources and efforts that are geared towards achieving sustainable development, and already have achieved some progress.

INDICATORS OF SUSTAINABLE DEVELOPMENT

Although it still remains a blurry concept, sustainable development must be measured somehow. Indicators are designed for this purpose. They are a set of figures that provides information on how sustainable our society is becoming. The reason for developing indicators is mostly pragmatic. There is a need to have relevant data that can be used for environmental management purposes. Both scientists and government decision-makers need to have guidelines that can indicate the progress of environmental management. At a micro level, these indicators are aimed at providing information on individual betterment projects. At a macro-level, they prove useful markers that government officials can follow. They also help design target sustainable development strategies.

A number of international organisations such as UNEP, UNCSD and OECD have been involved in the process of designing these indicators. The Organisation for Economic Cooperation and Development (OECD), for example, has developed a core set of environmental indicators which are:

> A commonly agreed upon set of indicators for OECD countries and for international use, published regularly. It covers issues that reflect the major environmental concerns in OECD countries. The publication incorporates major indicators derived from sectoral sets as well as from environmental accounting.

> One framework to calculate sustainability indicators is the methodological sheet of the United Nations Commission on Sustainable Development (UNCSD), which focuses on sustainability through four dimensions: social, economic, environmental and institutional. The basic theoretical model that was used to evaluate these indicators is based upon the pressure-state-response framework (PSR) (INEGI/INE 2000). Originally designed by Statistics Canada in 1979, PSR was adapted into a Driving Force-State-Response (DSR) framework by the UNCSD. In the DSR framework, the term "pressure" has been replaced by that of "driving force" in order to "accommodate more accurately the addition of social, economic and institutional indicators" (UNCSD 2000:2).

These sustainability indicators were developed in part as a response to Chapter 40 of Agenda 21, which obliges countries to calculate indicators to monitor their progress.

Sustainable development indicators serve a number of purposes:[5] (a) to keep track of environmental progress; (b) to ensure integration of environmental concerns into sectoral policies; (c) to ensure integration of environmental concerns into economic policies; and (d) to measure environmental performance and to help determine whether countries are on track towards sustainable development. These indicators are not static and may change over time. New indicators may be included, for example, as a result of new international legal agreements or as national-level experience is gained.

Lawrence (1998) offers a typology of sustainability indicators that proves valuable. He categorises indicators of sustainable development in three main divisions: (1) distinct, (2) comparative, and (3) directional.

Distinct indicators have no normative content. They are simply measurements with no evaluative action intended. There is no determination whether the number is good or bad. Lawrence indicates that these indicators do not prompt people to act and do something about the indicator's value.

Comparative Indicators are intended (as their name implies) to be compared across countries, states, provinces, or industrial sectors. This comparison would allow progress to be made. Knowing what is the value of a specific indicator may prompt another country, sector or individual to take actions towards improving its own position or value.

Directional Indicators are focused upon action. These indicators measure progress in relation to standards/benchmarks, and are intended to provide guidance or direction towards a specific goal. These indicators measure progress in implementing strategies. As such, actions are measured against specific benchmarks.

Projects where directional indicators are being used to monitor progress often use distinct indicators as standards and/or benchmarks (Lawrence 1998). By determining what is to be achieved (distinct indicator), it is easier to design alternative routes to get it done (directional indicators).

There is no 'right' set of sustainable development indicators. However, Lawrence's typology sheds some light on the appropriate design of sustainability indicators. Distinct indicators are located at the beginning of a continuum of action. As the emphasis on action increases, distinct indicators become comparative and then directional.

The OECD developed a set of distinct and comparative indicators that were published in 2000.[6] A selection of these environmental data for Canada, Mexico and the United States is presented in the Appendix. These data suggest that Mexico is in the best position of all three NAFTA countries with respect to some of these indicators. It has the lowest use of forest resources, the lowest level of municipal emissions and the lowest level of emission of sulphur oxides. However, it is also the country that has the lowest percentage of protected areas, and also the country with the lowest percentage of the population with wastewater treatment.

The intent of the above commentary is to show that sometimes indicators may be deceiving. Comparing two developed countries

(Canada and the U.S.) with a developing country (Mexico) on the sole basis of selected environmental indicators does not provide a clear and realistic picture of the situation. All three countries could be working towards improving their environmental indicators and still be far from achieving sustainable development. Nevertheless, these indicators prove valuable because:

(a) They provide a relatively accurate snapshot of the environmental situation of a country. While this snapshot may not be compared directly with that of other countries, it can help in understanding whether the country under analysis is doing better or worse in relation to sustainability.

(b) They are generally accepted world-wide. This international agreement is very important because environmental problems do not recognise frontiers and, therefore, co-ordinated cross-national efforts towards global sustainability must be intensified. If all countries measure environmental data according to a common framework, the above-mentioned efforts may be better co-ordinated.

(c) They provide benchmarks on a nation-by-nation basis that proves useful in the design of national environmental strategies. While sometimes environmental indicators may not facilitate cross-national comparisons, at the very least they provide national guidelines for each country. For example, if Mexico wants to design a national forest policy, it may use these environmental data to calculate annual targets and objectives.

THE CHALLENGE OF SUSTAINABLE DEVELOPMENT IN MEXICO

Mexico's attempts to come to grips with its environmental and social problems have revealed a paradox. While it is one of the strongest countries in Latin America and has proven capable of sustaining economic growth in a steady fashion, it also has tremendous poverty. And for Mexican people living in poverty, issues of sustainability are of much less concern than issues of economic survival. Yet a very important dimension of sustainability is economic development and social welfare. In a country where extreme poverty is prevalent in at least 11% of the total population, issues of sustainability will ultimately have a disproportionately negative impact on this group of people.

At the government level, there is an undertaking to promote sustainable development. Several factors have contributed to placing environmental issues on the Mexican political agenda (Mumme et al. 1988; Stern 1993; Carmona-Lara 1996; Mumme 1998; Vega-Lopez 1999). The fact that Mexico is undertaking comprehensive, nation-wide efforts to achieve sustainable development, despite the fact that it is a developing nation (and therefore, less likely to be able to implement SD policies and objectives) remains intriguing (Stern 1993).

The increased emphasis that the Mexican government has put on sustainability and sustainable development may be explained in several ways. Four factors we deem relevant in this increased attention by Mexico to environmental issues are: (a) international pressures and commitments to sustainable development (Agenda 21, Rio+5, OECD); (b) NAFTA and other trade agreements, as well as side agreements (i.e. NAFTA's Commission on Environmental Co-operation); (c) increased public awareness of the need to protect the environment; and (d) the rise of ENGOs in Mexico and cross-national movements of foreign ENGOs that are concerned with Mexican environmental issues.

(a) International pressures and commitments to sustainable development

Mexico was one of the many countries that participated in the Rio Summit of 1992. Under Chapter 28 of the Rio document, all local governments were supposed to submit a report on Local Agenda 21 (LA21) by 1997. LA21 is the transfer of Agenda 21 to the local level. It entails developing a nation-wide strategy to move toward sustainable development. Therefore, Mexico has found it relevant to pay more attention to environmental issues and design better environmental policies that aim at sustainability. Not only Agenda 21 exerted an influence on Mexican environmental policy; with the entrance of Mexico to the OECD in 1994, addressing relevant environmental issues became of utmost importance (Stern, 1993).

(b) NAFTA and other trade agreements, as well as side agreements

NAFTA deserves particular attention when analysing sustainable development issues because it links trade with environmental concepts. While some authors praise NAFTA for its efficiency in dealing with environmental issues (Griffith 1993), others criticise the validity of claims that NAFTA is effectively helping the environment (Marchak 1998). Mumme (1993) argues that NAFTA should have the ability to influence all three countries' environmental agendas, yet still is in its developmental stages. Whether NAFTA will play a decisive role in Mexico's goal of achieving sustainable development is still unknown and provides fertile ground for further research[7] (Johnson and Beaulieu 1996).

(c) Increased public awareness and realisation of environmental challenges

Both in highly populated urban centres and rural communities in Mexico, there has been an increase in expectations that environmental quality should be improved. Nevertheless, poverty stands in the way of these efforts at the local level. Public participation in environmental policy-making in Mexico is still very much in its infancy, yet it might prove a powerful force in shaping SD strategies. A recent example is the closure of and penalties imposed on Minera Peñoles, S.A. de C.V. in 1999 due to citizen complaints of lead poisoning in small children[8]. Citizen-initiated complaints gave rise to a legal suit that forced the Procuraduría Federal de Protección al Ambiente (PROFEPA, Federal Attorney for Environmental Protection) to close the plant.[9]

(d) The surge of national ENGOs and movement of international ENGOs to Mexico

Until recently, environmental non-government organisations (ENGOs) did not attract much attention. A few groups such as the Mexican Branch of the Group of Rome and The Grupo de los Cien (led by poet and environmental activist Homero Aridjis) had been operating for a few years. However, one of the most important mobilisations of ENGOs in recent years has been related to the Silva Reservoir.

In the latter months of 1994 and the beginning of 1995, the massive death of approximately 30,000 to 40,000 birds in the Silva Reservoir[10] led an ENGO, Fundacion Ecologica Guanajuato AC, to file a complaint with the Guanajuato State Office of PROFEPA. This complaint was aimed at punishing "whoever was responsible" for these deaths. More than anything, the ENGO tried to hold responsible a number of leather tanneries for this massive annihilation. These tanneries discharged their wastewater directly to a reservoir that was interconnected with the Silva reservoir. Not satisfied with the results of a report issued in June 1995 by PROFEPA (a report that exonerated the tanneries), three other ENGOs filed a citizen-complaint with the CEC in order to force Mexican environmental agencies to delve more deeply into this issue. It took the intervention of CEC and two additional years spent in research to placate these ENGOs.

The example described above shows that ENGOs are gaining more political power and may soon be a force to be reckoned with in Mexico. Not only are national ENGOs gaining strength, but also international ENGOs are crossing frontiers and becoming involved in Mexican environmental issues. This burgeoning non-governmental environmental movement may have a major influence on Mexican environmental policy towards sustainability.

The sustainability challenge is not only the responsibility of government agencies. All Mexican citizens are partly responsible. Mexico faces a tough challenge in its effort to make sustainable development operational. Although considered by the World Bank a "less-indebted upper middle income country", Mexico is still a developing nation. As a result, a large number of people are unable to access resources to satisfy their basic needs. If we are to follow Maslow's hierarchy of needs,[11] it seems less likely that the common Mexican will have sustainable development in the back of his/her mind because the concept of SD does not belong to the basic levels in the hierarchy which include food, shelter and clothing. This leads us to believe that if there were a way to operationalize SD in Mexico in such a way that ordinary people would embrace these principles, implementation of sustainability strategies would be much easier.

THE FUTURE

It is important to remark that a developing country faces a tougher challenge in achieving sustainability because there is a gap in access to economic resources. Mumme (1998) suggests that in the 1980s Mexico's quest for accelerated industrialisation increased the seriousness of the country's environmental problems. In addition to rapid industrialisation, increased poverty and inadequate/irresponsible resource management have contributed to Mexico's decline in environmental quality.

Several factors compound the already acute environmental problem in Mexico, including poverty, lack of education, non-equitable distribution of welfare, etc. As an example, in 1984, 11.4 % of the total households in Mexico were on the line of extreme poverty.[12] In 1992, this percentage had increased to 11.8%. The poverty percentage is just 1% lower than the composite average of Latin American & Caribbean countries. In 1998, 10% of the total population was illiterate and 26% lived below the national poverty line. These alarming indicators coupled with poor performance in other development indexes show that poverty is only one of several important factors that hinder the appropriate implementation of sustainable development in Mexico. On the long road to sustainability, Mexico will have to face not only poverty and overpopulation in large urban centres, but also increased environmental damage. It will take a few years before sustainable development strategies can be properly implemented.

INDICATORS OF SUSTAINABLE DEVELOPMENT IN MEXICO

Mexico participated in a pilot project started by the OECD to generate a set of indicators that would contribute to understanding the dimensions of the sustainability challenge. These indicators are also designed to provide a sound basis for decision-making at all policy levels and contribute to implementing sustainability goals at the national level. The published results of this ambitious project (the first of its kind in Mexico) was made available to the general public as well as experts and policy makers in June 2000.[13] The responsibility for compiling these indicators was shared by the Instituto Nacional de Estadística, Geografía e Informática (INEGI) (National Institute of Geography, Statistics and Information Technology) and the Instituto Nacional de Ecología (National Institute of Ecology).

It is hard to evaluate how much progress a country has made in implementing Agenda 21 both in qualitative and quantitative terms. However, these indicators aim to provide a broad (although only quantitative) view of how Mexico and other countries have been able to cope with the challenge of sustainable development and what are the strategies that are being following to achieve this goal.

To date, Mexico has calculated 113 out of 134 sustainability indicators required in the UNCSD methodological sheet. Of the remainder, 6 indicators are being developed and 15 have not been worked upon because they are not a national information priority (INEGI/INE 2000). To evaluate the progress that Mexico has achieved in terms of sustainability indicators, a number of statistics are presented in the book edited by INEGI and INE. However, we argue that in order for those indicators to be most useful, it is necessary that they be incorporated into national development strategies. It does not make much sense to calculate a sustainability indicator just for the sake of gathering data. These data must be readily translated into guidelines, programs and actions towards sustainable development.

Nevertheless, in going through the exercise of developing and calculating all these 113 indicators, Mexican environmental authorities have learned a few lessons:

- inter-agency co-operation should be increased to make information available within a reasonable time frame;
- increasing attention must be paid to environmental information systems that are required components of an international framework of co-operation (such as the National Registry of Release and Transfer of Contaminants);

- voluntary agreements and self-regulation as environmental policy instruments must be encouraged;
- implementation of economic (market-based) policy instruments should be promoted; and
- sustainable development cannot be achieved without paying attention to poverty, overpopulation, industrial development and economic growth. Sustainability is multidimensional and, as such, attention must be paid equally to all dimensions (social, political, economic and environmental).

Sustainable development must occur within an institutional and legal framework that encourages economic growth consistent with environmental protection. Mexican environmental laws are starting to be recognised as one of the strongest and best formulated bodies of law. In 1999, the Mexican Constitution was reformed. This reform led to the establishment of a right to sustainable development.

THE CHALLENGE OF SUSTAINABLE DEVELOPMENT GIVEN THE MODIFICATIONS TO THE MEXICAN CONSTITUTION

In Mexico, the right to an adequate environment has just recently been included as a foundational principle published in the 4th article of the Constitution. This inclusion occurred on June 28, 1999, when the reform to the 25th article was also published in the Official Newspaper of the Federation. This reform announces the right to sustainable development in Mexico and represents a breakthrough in Mexican environmental law.

Both concepts (the right to a sustainable development and the right to an adequate environment) have been subject to heated philosophical debates, mainly because there is little agreement among different scientists about the meaning of sustainable development. Now that these concepts have been inserted into the Constitution, they become debatable in courts of law. This is already occurring in Spain, Colombia, Peru and Bolivia. These countries have environmental laws where these terms are defined so that they can be further advanced through legal mechanisms.

From the Mexican environmental law perspective, environment is defined by the General Law of Ecological Equilibrium and Environmental Protection in its Article 3, Section I as:

...the set of natural and artificial or human-created elements that allow for existence and development of human beings and living organisms that interact in a specific space and time (SEMARNAP 1997).

The General Law in Article 3, Section XI, defines sustainable development as:

> A process that is measurable through environmental, social and economic criteria and indicators, whereby this process tends to enhance the quality of life and productivity of people. This process is founded in appropriate measures of preservation of ecological equilibrium, environmental protection and natural resource protection, in such manner that they do not compromise the satisfaction of necessities of future generations (SEMARNAP 1997).

SUSTAINABLE DEVELOPMENT IN THE MEXICAN CONSTITUTION AS A NATIONAL DEVELOPMENT POLICY

The need to have sustainable development as a basis for policy arises from the erroneous assumption that economic values are the sole and irreplaceable engine of human activity. While it is true that often these values are a moving force, this is not always the case. Depending on the time and place, other motives can be more compelling than pure economic considerations; including human survival, health, dignity, philanthropy, patriotism and religion.

Sustainable development as a government policy demands, in addition, a better knowledge of the interactions between economic and biophysical systems. This knowledge can prove a good foundation for public and private decisions that are efficient and consistent with long-term ecological and social viability criteria. Environmental costs that are incurred in every productive process must be valued and considered. The systematic valuation of environmental goods and services will help build better indicators of social welfare and quality of life.

In the case of Mexico, the policy of sustainable development is now included in the text of Article 25 of the Mexican Constitution that states in the first paragraph:[14]

> It is the State duty to regulate national development in order to ensure that it is well-rounded and sustainable, in such a way that it strengthens the Nation's sovereignty and its democratic regime, and through the encouragement of economic growth and employment and a more just distribution of income and wealth, allows for the best exercise of freedom and dignity of

individuals, groups and social classes, whose security are protected by this Constitution.

National development that stems from this reform should be sustainable because there is an expressed obligation by the State. The government is responsible for guaranteeing that this will be the type of development that will take place in Mexico, and it should not only strengthen national sovereignty but also promote economic growth, employment and a more equitable distribution of income and wealth.

From the text of the Mexican Constitution written in 1917, it is possible to infer the linkage of national development policy and conservation values. In the original text there was no reference to environmental issues as they are conceived nowadays. However, the text stated that:

> The Nation will have at all times the right to impose on private property any modality that the public interest dictates, as well *as the right to regulate, in light of the social benefit, the exploitation of natural resources that are subject to appropriation*, in order to create an equitable distribution of the public wealth; *take care of its conservation*, and achieve balanced development of the country and the betterment of living conditions of the urban and rural population.[15]

Therefore, the original version of the Constitution established the principle that national development must be sustainable. The combination of a national policy of sustainable development with the imposition of usage restrictions on private property with a view to resource conservation is a solid constitutional foundation that allows us to view this policy as a guiding principle of development.

It is useful to clarify what is defined in Mexico as national sustainable development. Under Article #25 of the Mexican Constitution, the main actor in this policy is the State which is in charge of planning, leading, guiding and implementing national economic activity. As such, the State is in charge of regulating and fostering all activities that the public interest requires.

In order to achieve national economic development, all sectors (public, social and private) must harmonize their economic activities. The public sector will be exclusively in charge of all strategic areas that are noted in Article #28, fourth paragraph of the Constitution and, as such, the federal government remains in full ownership and control of any entities or institutions that are established. The Federal government is able to participate in activities that are aimed at fostering and organizing all those areas that are a priority for development. The government can participate in these activities alone or jointly with the private sector within the Mexican legal framework.

It is important to note that in 1982, when it was reformed, Article #25 created an important tool to achieve environmental objectives. The Article reads as follows:

> Subject to criteria of social equity and productivity, all enterprises of both social and private sectors of the economy will be fostered and supported. These enterprises will be pursuant to any *modalities* that the public interest dictates and to the use of productive resources for the general benefit, *ensuring their conservation and environmental protection.*[16]

Article #26 of the Constitution indicates that the State will organise a democratic planning system for national development that can provide soundness, dynamism, equity and continuity to economic growth so that the Nation can be independent and democratic in all realms: political, social and cultural. One of the key principles relates to the conservation of all natural resources that might be available for use. This also emphasises sustainable development as national development policy as well as environmental principles for industrial activity. This leads us to believe that the ultimate objectives of the Mexican National Development Plan are now sustainability and the application of environmental and natural resource protection policies.

Article #26 also indicates that environmental planning must be democratic. This means that the demands of society will be reflected through democratic participation of all relevant actors and sectors in order to incorporate them into development programs and plans (with a view to sustainability). Thus, there will be a national (sustainable) development plan that will lead (as required by law) all Federal Public Administration efforts and programs.

The Mexican law enables the Executive to establish participation procedures for popular consultation in the national system of democratic planning. The Executive is responsible for designing appropriate criteria for formulation, implementation, control and evaluation of the above-mentioned programs and plans. This legal framework also determines which institutions are responsible for spearheading the planning process. Thus the Federal Executive is able to co-ordinate all actions through intra- and intergovernmental agreements with the private sector and all state governments.

Two main laws emanate from these constitutional articles: the Planning Law and the General Law for Ecological Equilibrium and

Environmental Protection[17] (LGEEPA). The Planning Law contains all foundational concepts to formulate and implement the National Democratic Planning System. The LGEEPA establishes Mexican environmental policy within an environmental planning system.

The main institutions of both laws presuppose the participation of every government level and every citizen through a consensus-based decision-making process. The Federal Government designs the National Development Plan (which is now, by definition, sustainable).

Environmental policy instruments defined by the LGEEPA include:

- Environmental planning (Art. 17 and 18)
- Ecological Land Use[18] (Art 19, 19bis, 20, 20bis, 20bis 1 to 7)
- Economic Instruments (Art. 21, 22 and 22b)
- Environmental Regulation of Human Settlements (Art. 23 to 27)
- Environmental Impact Assessment (Art. 28 to 35, 35bis, 35bis 1 to 3)
- Official Mexican Environmental Standards (Art. 36, 37 and 37bis)
- Self-regulation and Environmental Audits (Art. 38, 38bis, 38bis 1 and 2)
- Ecological Education and Research (Art. 39, 40 and 41)
- Information and Enforcement (Art. 42 and 43)

The Mexican Environmental Law indicates that environmental policies shall be incorporated into the national development planning process. Along the same line, land use shall conform to environmental regulations. This Law also permits the federal government to make full use of its powers to regulate, promote, restrict, prohibit, orient and induce any actions of the private sector so that these actions comply with environmental policy guidelines established by the National Development Plan and adjunct programs.

The Federal Government is responsible for promoting the participation of all interest groups in designing programs devoted to environmental protection and preservation of ecological equilibrium, as per environmental legal guidelines.

It should be noted that the reform to the Mexican Constitution that took place in 1999 in its Article #25 (the right to sustainable development) is an important step towards an innovative legal framework in Mexico. However, the legal obligation of every Mexican citizen to protect his/her environment was already embedded in the text of Article # 27. This article establishes a policy that resources should be protected while being used. This policy also indicates that the distribution of public wealth should be equitable in order to achieve sustainable development in Mexico.

Mexico will be facing new challenges in the near future. These challenges will have a strong impact on the way societies organise and protect their foundational values. One of these challenges will be how to effectively enforce the right to sustainable development, and how to design effective environmental policy instruments that ensure that every Mexican citizen can enjoy an adequate environment. It is quite a big challenge in a country with so many contrasts and inequities. However, as Barbara Ward said once, we have the duty of hope.

CONCLUSIONS

Mexico is in the process of moving towards sustainable development. Progress achieved so far is, however, still waiting to be evaluated. The Rio Declaration on Environment and Development (Agenda 21) requested, as part of the commitments of Mexico to the international community, that Mexico initiate the process of implementing Local Agenda 21 (LA21).

The Secretaría de Medio Ambiente, Recursos Naturales y Pesca (SEMARNAP, Secretariat of Environment, Natural Resources and Fisheries) led by biologist Julia Carabias, has committed many resources to the implementation of LA21, and has achieved a number of goals, including:[19]

- An increase in Natural Protected Areas to 15.8 million hectares.
- Approval of the General Law for Wildlife, which is meant to protect natural processes in ecosystems, reduce the probability of extinction of species and encourage recovery of endangered species.
- Implementation of Regional Sustainable Development Programs, and creation of 30 Regional Sustainable Development Councils.
- An increase in drinking water supply from 71.0 million inhabitants in 1994 to 74.0 million in 1999 (according to preliminary data).
- International adoption of the Code of Behaviour for Responsible Fishing. This is an international accord that was led and initiated by Mexico.
- Creation of new direct regulatory instruments such as the unique operation licence.

Even though the task is challenging, there is a reasonable hope that sustainable development can be implemented in Mexico. It will take a strong commitment not only by government agencies, but also by the Mexican society at large. While the government plays an important role in drafting, designing and implementing environmental policies towards sustainability, it will be a shared responsibility with the civil society.

This chapter has outlined part of the challenges that Mexico is facing with regard to sustainable development. Poverty and overpopulation play an important role. An adequate regulatory environment is also mandatory for sustainable development to be properly implemented. It is important that Mexico starts taking steps in this direction, and this effort seems to be underway.

FOOTNOTES

1. World Bank (2000). Obtained from the World Bank's web page - http://www.worldbank.org
2. An excellent and thorough discussion on the clash of neo-classical and non-neo-classical paradigms can be found in Hansen (1998).
3. 1972 was a very important year not only because of *The Limits to Growth* but more importantly, because of the United Nations Stockholm Conference on the Human Environment which was held in the same year. Talks about environmental issues were formalised in this Conference, and these provided fertile ground for further discussions in the late 1980s.
4. Agenda 21 is a document signed by all nations attending the Earth Summit in 1992, held at Rio de Janeiro. It outlines an "agenda for the 21st century" (hence the name) that should lead to sustainability.
5. OECD (2000) http://www.oecd.org/env/indicators/index.htm
6. http://www.oecd.org
7. For a detailed account of arguments for and against NAFTA and its environmental effects, see Johnson and Beaulieu (1996), especially Chapter 2. The Commission on Environmental Cooperation (CEC) has put special emphasis on the relationship between trade and environment and has fostered research programs and generously supported grants for research projects that focus on this issue.
8. http://www.infosel.com/noticias/Nota/20000512/100509.htm
9. http://www.profepa.gob.mx/dcs/PefEB-2000.html
10. A reservoir located in central Mexico, in the State of Guanajuato, close to San Francisco del Rincon.
11. Maslow (1968) has suggested that there is a hierarchy of human needs. At the basic level are the physiological needs of water, air, food and shelter. Higher material needs include safety and security. Social needs such as self esteem and sense of community are also included. For more on the hierarchy of needs, see Maslow (1968).
12. Extreme poverty is defined as "households whose total income is insufficient to purchase or pay the cost of a basic sub-basket, therefore the household cannot purchase enough food to provide adequate quan-

tities of protein and calories to all members of the household" (INEGI/INE 2000).

13. The report, *Indicadores de Desarrollo Sustentable en México* (Indicators of Sustainable Development in Mexico) was published in mid-June 2000. The authors would like to thank INEGI and INE for making this information available to us while writing this chapter.

14. This is the best available direct translation (translation by Raul Pacheco-Vega).

15. Free translation by Raul Pacheco-Vega. Emphases added by the authors.

16. Free translation by Raul Pacheco-Vega. Emphases added by the authors.

17. LGEEPA = Ley General del Equilibrio Ecologico y la Proteccion al Ambiente (General Law for Ecological Equilibrium and Environmental Protection).

18. The original text uses the word "Ordenamiento" which in Spanish describes (roughly) the spatial distribution of resources for land-use planning.

19. Data obtained from http://www.semarnap.gob.mx/gestion/avances/logros_semarnap.htm. It should be noted that SEMARNAP is a very young agency, having been created in 1994. As of December 1, 2000, SEMARNAP became SEMARNAT (Secretaria de Medio Ambiente y Recursos Naturales -- Secretariat of Environment and Natural Resources) and it is headed by Victor Lichtinger, former Executive Director of the North American Commission for Environmental Cooperation (NACEC). For a detailed account of how the environmental agencies in Mexico have evolved in the last decades, see Mumme (1998).

APPENDIX: Comparative Environmental Data from Mexico, Canada and the United States (all data 1997 or late 1990s)

INDICATOR	CANADA	MEXICO	USA
General Data			
National Population (1000s)	30,287	98,224	267,735
Population Density (Inhabitants/km^2)	3.0	50.2	28.6
Total Area (1000 km^2)	9,971	1,958	9,364
GDP (billion US$)	637	609	7,350
Structure of GDP (Sectoral contribution to GDP in %)			
Agriculture *(includes hunting, forestry and fishing)*	2.2	5.6	1.7
Industry *(ISIC groups 2 to 5)*	27.2	26.1	26.2
Services *(includes import duties)*	70.6	68.3	72.0
Land Use			
Arable and permanent crop land (%)	4.5	14.3	19.5
Permanent grassland(%)	2.9	41.7	26.5
Forest and other wooded land (%)	45.3	33.4	32.6
Total land area (km^2)	9,215,430	1,908,690	9,159,120
Air Pollution			
Total emissions (1000 tonnes)			
SOx	2,691	2,162	18,481
NOx	2,011	1,526	21,394
CO	10,144	2,314	70,655
Particulates	1,736	396	3,393
VOCs	2,668	485	16,653
Per capita emissions (kg/cap)			
SOx	88.9	23.2	69.0
NOx	67.1	16.4	79.9
CO	334.9	25.4	263.9
Particulates	57.9	4.3	12.7
VOCs	88.1	5.3	62.2
Emissions per unit of GDP			
SOx	4.4	3.9	2.6
NOx	3.4	2.8	3.0
CO	16.4	4.4	10.0
Particulates	2.9	0.7	0.5
VOCs	4.3	0.9	2.4
CO_2 emissions from energy use (million tonnes)	477	346	5470
CO_2 emissions by source (million tonnes)			
Transport	149	100.7	1658.4
Bunkers	1.7	2.5	74.1
Energy transformation	159.7	135.4	2504.1
Industry	92.4	69.5	627.1
Other	96.3	33.1	639.3
Water Pollution/Sewerage/Sewerage Treatment			
Population connected to public sewerage (% total population)	91.0	64.6	-
To a public treatment plant	78.0	21.8	70.8
To any other treatment	1.0	-	-
Population connected to public wastewater treatment plants			
Primary treatment	19.0	2.6	-
Secondary treatment	26.0	19.2	-
Tertiary treatment	33.0	-	-

INDICATOR	CANADA	MEXICO	USA
Protected Areas and Forestry Issues			
Total size of protected areas (km^2)	953,103	159,759	1,988,444
Percentage of national territory	9.6	8.2	21.2
Per 1000 inhabitants (ha/cap)	3146.9	162.6	742.7
Forest depletion and growth			
Harvest (1000 m^3)	202,050	5,875	521,516
Natural losses (1000 m^3)	181,957	-	175,277
Annual growth (1000 m^3)	459,439	34,747	866,855
Intensity of use (harvest/annual growth)	0.44	0.17	0.60
State of Wildlife			
Mammals			
Species known (number)	193	491	466
Threatened (% percentage)	19.2	33.2	10.5
Birds			
Species known (number)	426	1054	1090
Threatened (% percentage)	10.8	16.9	7.2
Fish			
Species known (number)	1021	2122	2640
Threatened (% percentage)	6.4	5.7	2.4
Reptiles			
Species known (number)	42	704	368
Threatened (% percentage)	33.0	18.0	7.1
Amphibians			
Species known (number)	42	290	222
Threatened (% percentage)	21.4	16.9	3.6
Invertebrates			
Species known (number)	34552	29495	-
Threatened (% percentage)	-	0.1	-
Solid Waste Management			
Generation of municipal waste (1000 tonnes)	14,740	29,272	190,204
(of which household waste is)	6,050	23,418	108,416
Generation of municipal waste per capita (kg/capita)	490	300	720
(of which household waste is)	200	240	410
Composition of municipal waste (%)			
Paper and paperboard	28.0	14.0	38.0
Food and garden waste, etc.	34.0	52.0	24.0
Plastics	11.0	4.0	9.0
Glass	7.0	6.0	6.0
Metals	8.0	3.0	8.0
Textiles and others	13.0	20.0	15.0
Collection and disposal of municipal waste (1000 tonnes)			
Total amount	20,598	29,272	190,204
Population served by municipal waste services (%)	99.0	77.0	100.0
Composting	576	-	10,270
Incineration	1,030	-	32,741
Landfill	19,568	29,272	105,453
Recycling	5,404	219	41,740
Waste recycling rates (% of apparent consumption)			
Paper and cardboard (1992)	33	2.0	33
Glass (1992)	17	4.0	22
Hazardous Waste Management			
Production and movement of hazardous waste (1000 tonnes)			
Production [Canada: 1991]	5,896	12,700	172,732
Imports	251	224	-
Exports	487	10	-

INDICATOR	CANADA	MEXICO	USA
Waste Treatment and Disposal Installations			
Non-hazardous waste			
Landfill sites (total number)	501	97	6840
Incineration plants (total number)	28	-	148
Treatment plants (total number)	-	-	7230
Hazardous waste			
Landfill sites (total number)	14	4	68
Incineration plants (total number)	22	10	162
Treatment plants (total number)	38	29	-
Nuclear waste:Spent fuel arisings (tonnes of HM)	1340	42	2100
Cropland (square km)	411,800	273,000	1,790,000
Apparent Consumption of Fertilisers (1000 tonnes)			
Nitrogenous	1,708	1,194	11,163
Phosphate	705	259	4,195
Commercial fertilisers (NPK)	2,753	1,603	20,205
Ratio of Fertilisers to Cropland (t/km^2)			
Nitrogenous	4.15	4.37	6.24
Phosphate	1.71	0.95	2.34
Commercial fertilisers (NPK)	6.69	5.87	11.29
Consumption of Pesticides (tonnes active ingredients)			
Total pesticides	29,206	36,000	367,863
Insecticides	3,426	-	77,564
Fungicides	3,780	-	72,121
Herbicides	21,910	-	218,178
Other pesticides	90	-	-
Ratio of Pesticides to Cropland (kg active ingredients/km^2)			
Total pesticides	70.92	131.87	205.51
Insecticides	8.32	-	43.33
Fungicides	9.18	-	40.29
Herbicides	53.21	-	121.89
Other pesticides	0.22	-	-
Pollution Abatement and Control Expenditure			
Invested by the public sector (US$/cap)	149	18	177
Invested by public & private sector (US$/cap)	248	52	422
Public R&D Expenditure for Environmental Protection			
Million USD at 1991 price levels and PPP	96.6	12.9	497.2
As % of total R&D budget appropriations	4.4	0.8	0.8
Revenues from Environmentally Related Taxes			
Total (tax bases)	-	3284	74811
% of GDP	1.8	1.1	1.0
% of total tax revenue	5.0	7.2	3.7

Source: OECD, *Environmental Data Compendium, 1999.*

REFERENCES

Carmona-Lara, M. d. C. (1996). La Politica Ecologica en Mexico. *Facultad de Ciencias Politicas y Sociales*. Mexico DF, Universidad Nacional Autonoma de Mexico: 381.

Commoner, B. (1972). *The Closing Circle; Nature, Man and Technology*. New York, NY, Knopf.

Griffith, K. A. (1993). "NAFTA, Sustainable Development, and the Environment: Mexico's Approach." *Journal of Environment and Development* 2(1): 193-203.

Hardin, G. (1968). "The Tragedy of the Commons." *Science* 162: 1243-1248.

Hansen, S. (1998). "Economic Initiatives and Sustainable Development: An Assessment of Possibilities and Limitations." In: *Towards Sustainable Development. On the Goals of Development - and the Conditions of Sustainability*. W. M. Lafferty and O. Langhelle. Houndmills, UK, MacMillan Press Ltd.: 173-192.

INEGI/INE (2000). *Indicadores de Desarrollo Sustentable en Mexico*. México DF, INEGI - INE.

Jacobs, M. (1993). *The Green Economy. Environment, Sustainable Development and the Politics of the Future*. Vancouver, BC, UBC Press.

Jing-zhu, Z. and J. B. Opschoor (1999). "Indicator System and Evaluation Framework for Sustainable Development." *Journal of Environmental Sciences* 11(4): 492-497.

Johnson, P. M. and A. Beaulieu (1996). *The Environment and NAFTA. Understanding and Implementing the New Continental Law*. Washington, DC, Island Press.

Kirby, J. et al., Eds. (1995). *The EarthScan Reader in Sustainable Development*. London, UK, EarthScan Publications.

Kiss, A. C. and D. Shelton (1994). *Manual of European Environmental Law*. Cambridge, Grotius Publications Ltd.

Lafferty, W. M. and O. Langhelle (1999). "Sustainable Development as Concept and Norm." In: *Towards Sustainable Development. On the Goals of Development - and the Conditions of Sustainability*. W. M. Lafferty and O. Langhelle. Houndmills, UK, MacMillan Press LTD: 1-29.

Lawrence, G. (1998). "Getting the Future that You Want: The Role of Sustainability Indicators." In: *Community and Sustainable Development. Participation in the Future*. D. Warburton. London, UK, EarthScan Publishers: 68-80.

Marchak, M. P. (1998). "Environment and Resource Protection: Does NAFTA Make a Difference?" *Organization and Environment* 11(2): 133-154.

Maslow, A. (1968) *Towards a Psychology of Being*. New Jersey: Princeton

University Press.

Moffatt, I. (1996). *Sustainable Development. Principles, Analysis and Policies.* New York NY, The Parthenon Publishing Group.

Mumme, S. P. (1993). "Environmentalists, NAFTA and North American Environmental Management." *Journal of Environment and Development* 2(1): 205-219.

Mumme, S. P. (1998). "Environmental Policy and Politics in Mexico." In: *Ecological Policy and Politics in Developing Countries. Economic Growth, Democracy, and Environment.* U. Desai. Albany NY, State University of New York: 183-203.

Mumme, S. P. et al. (1988). "Political Development and Environmental Policy in Mexico." *Latin American Research Review* 23(1): 7-34.

OECD (1999) *OECD Environmental Data Compendium.* Paris.

Pacheco-Vega, H. R. (1997). *Tecnología y Desarrollo Sustentable.* XII Encuentro Nacional de Curtiduría, León, Mexico, FMQTC.

Rodgers, W. L. (1994). *Environmental Law.* St. Paul MN, West Publishing Co.

Ros, J. et al. (1996). "Prospects for Growth and the Environment in Mexico in the 1990s." *World Development* 24(2): 307-324.

SEMARNAP (1997). *Ley General del Equilibrio Ecológico y la Protección al Ambiente (y disposiciones complementarias).* México DF, Editorial Porrúa.

Stern, M. A. (1993). "Mexican Environmental Policy Revisited." *Journal of Environment and Development* 2(2): 185-196.

UNCSD (2000). *From Theory to Practice: Indicators of Sustainable Development,* United Nations Commission on Sustainable Development. 2000.

Vega-Lopez, O. (1999). "Análisis Comparativo de Políticas Públicas para el Desarrollo Sustentable de la Industria Minera: Un Estudio de Contraste Binacional México-Canadá." Departamento de Ciencias Juridicas y Politicas. Leon, Mexico, Universidad Iberoamericana: 135.

WCED (1987). *Our Common Future.* Oxford UK, Oxford University Press.

World Bank (2000). World Bank Indicators.

Yearly, S. (1994). "Standing in For Nature. The Practicalities of Environmental Organizations' Use of Science." In: *Environmentalism: The View from Anthropology.* K. Milton. London, Routledge.

ACKNOWLEDGEMENT

The authors would like to thank Carlos Blanco, Anthony Brunetti, Alicia Hayman, Les M. Lavkulich, Evan Fraser and the editor of the volume for valuable criticisms and suggestions. Pacheco-Vega gratefully acknowledges the National Council of Science and Technology in Mexico (CONACyT) for Ph.D. scholarship (1999-2002). All errors remain the responsibility of the authors.

National Round Table
on the Environment
and the Economy

Table ronde nationale
sur l'environnement
et l'économie

The National Round Table on the Environment and the Economy (NRTEE) is pleased to co-sponsor this special issue of the *Journal of Business Administration and Policy Analysis,* as a further contribution to the greater understanding of the concept of sustainable development and its practical applications. This publication is based on a series of meetings held during a conference in Ottawa on sustainable development and business school education sponsored by the NRTEE.

Mandate

The National Round Table on the Environment and the Economy (NRTEE) is an independent advisory body that provides decision makers, opinion leaders and the Canadian public with advice and recommendations for promoting sustainable development.

Our members are distinguished Canadians appointed by the Prime Minister of Canada. They represent a broad range of sectors, including business, labour, academia, environmental organizations and First Nations.

The NRTEE at work

Working with stakeholders across Canada, the NRTEE identifies key issues with both environmental and economic implications, examines these implications and suggests how to balance economic prosperity with environmental preservation.

Progressing in sensitive areas is a challenge for stakeholders. The NRTEE has adopted a round table format that helps overcome entrenched differences by:
- Analysing environmental and economic facts and trends.
- Asking key stakeholders for their input.
- Assimilating research and consultation to clarify the debate.
- Pinpointing the consequences of action and inaction, and making recommendations.

Publications

The NRTEE offers a wide range of publications such as the "State of the Debate Series", various Reports and Book series. A list of publications and order form are available on request. Also, a visit to the NRTEE's new Virtual Library at **www.nrtee-trnee.ca/library** will allow access to over 150 NRTEE documents and publications that are organized in 15 easy-to-search categories including: natural resources, community awareness, atmospheric issues, greening government policy and health.

National Round Table on the Environment and the Economy

Canada Building, 344 Slater Street, Suite 200, Ottawa, Ontario, Canada K1R 7Y3
Tel.: (613) 992-7189 • Fax: (613) 992-7385 • E-mail: admin@nrtee-trnee.ca
Web: http://www.nrtee-trnee.ca